SHADOW LIFE

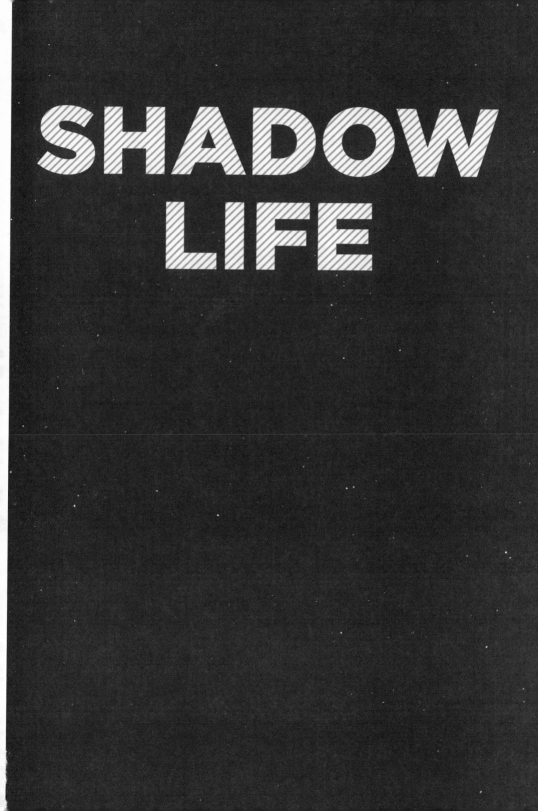

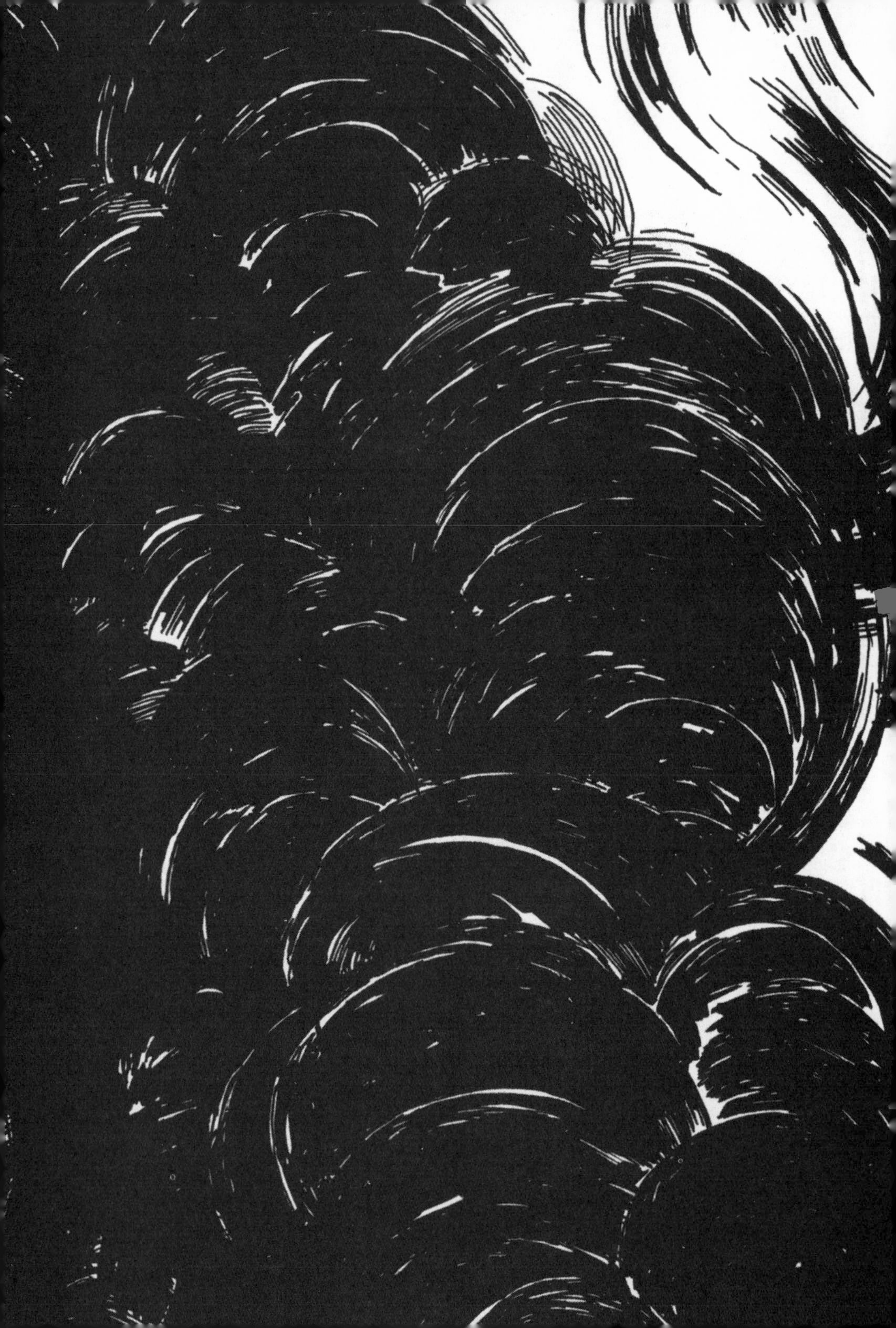

SHADOW LIFE

HIROMI GOTO **x** ANN XU

:01
First Second
New York

For Dana Putnam, my koibito.
—Hiromi Goto

Prologue

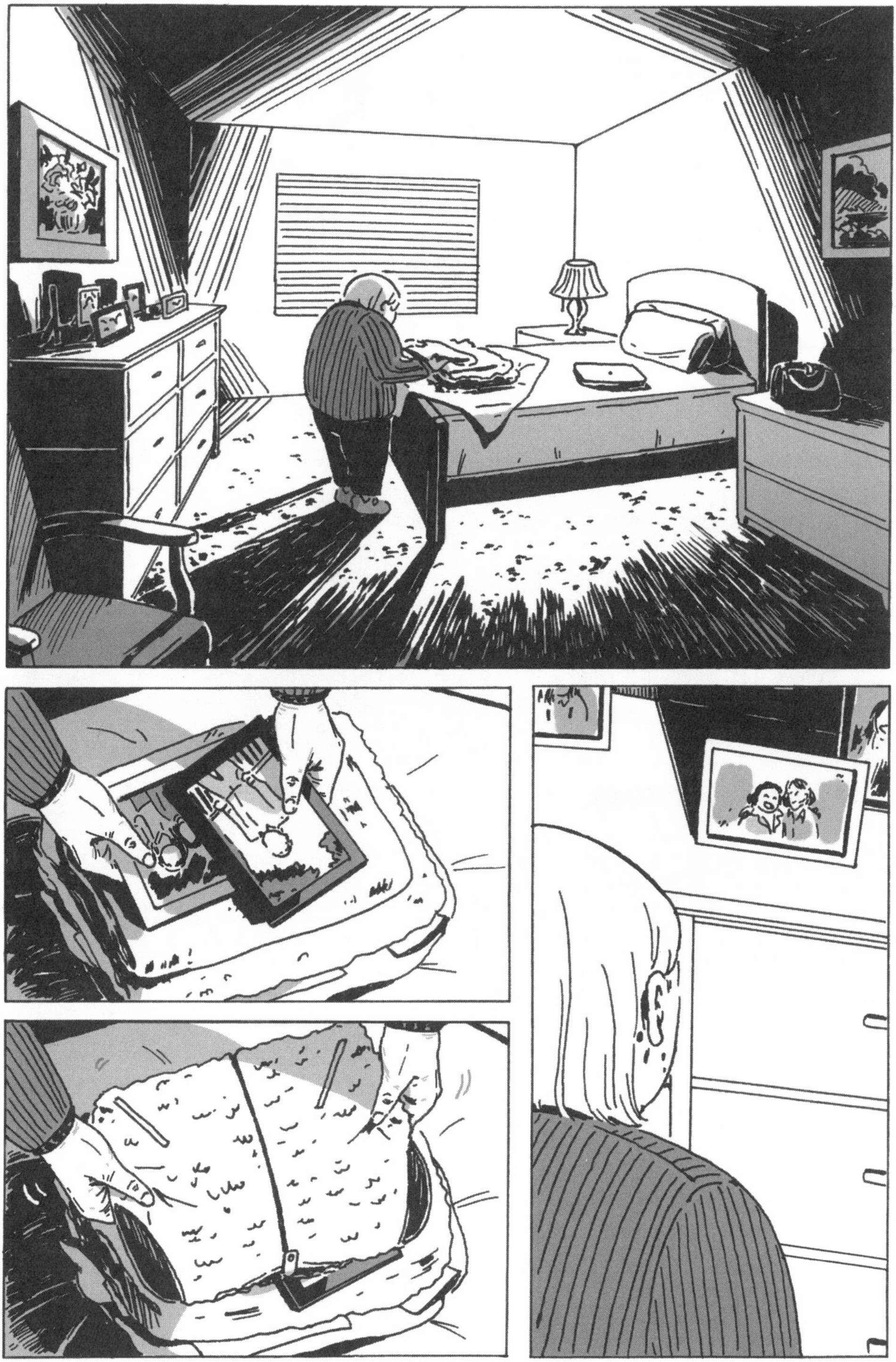

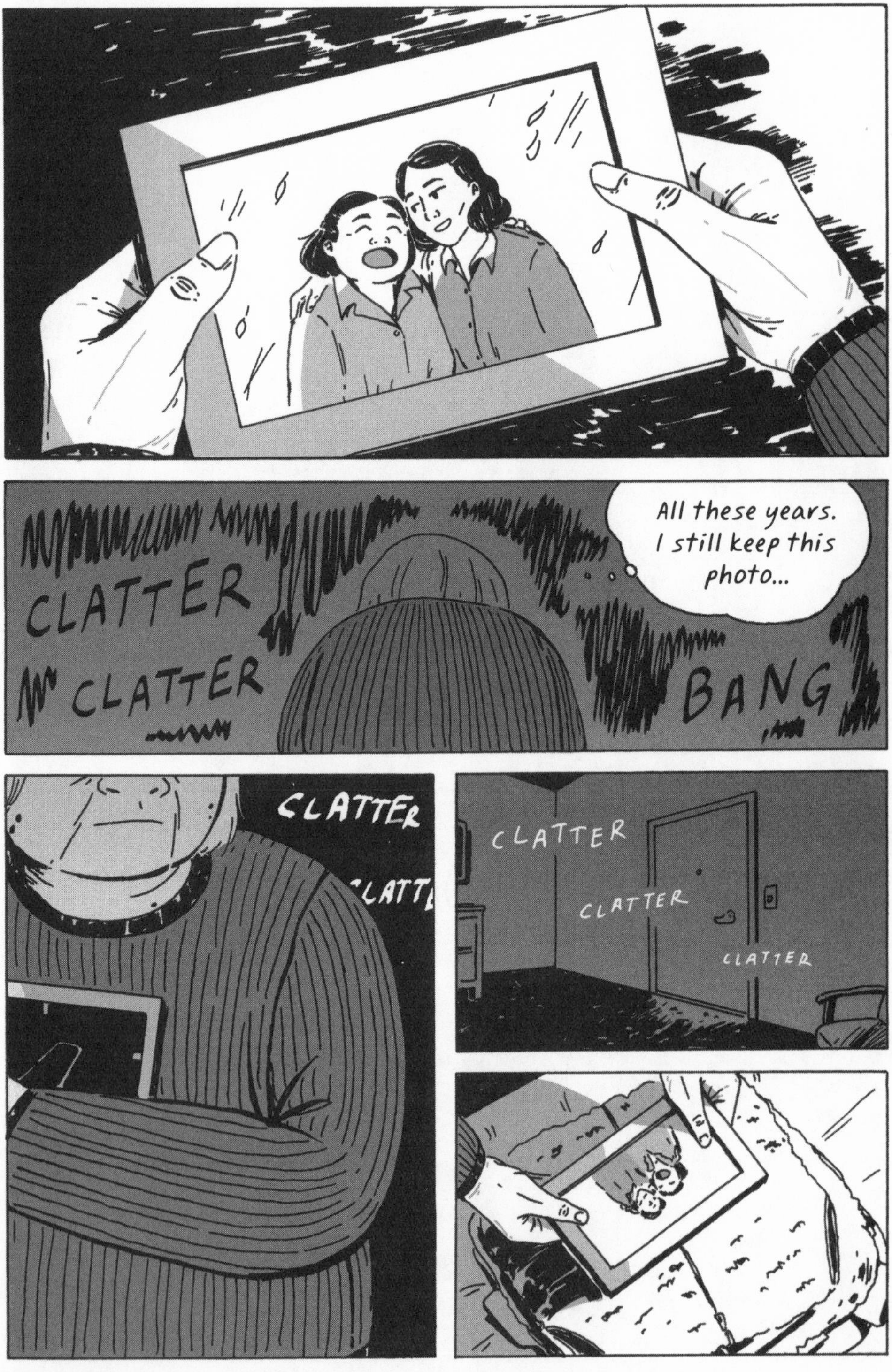
CLATTER
CLATTER
All these years. I still keep this photo...
BANG
CLATTER
CLATTE
CLATTER
CLATTER
CLATTER

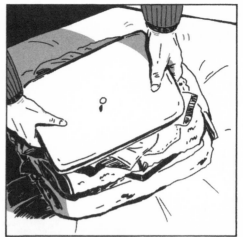

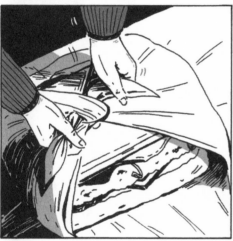

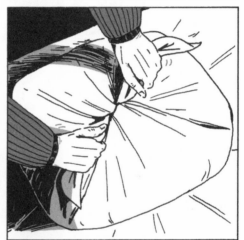

It's a relief to leave unnecessary things.

SIGH

But do the necessary things have to be so heavy?

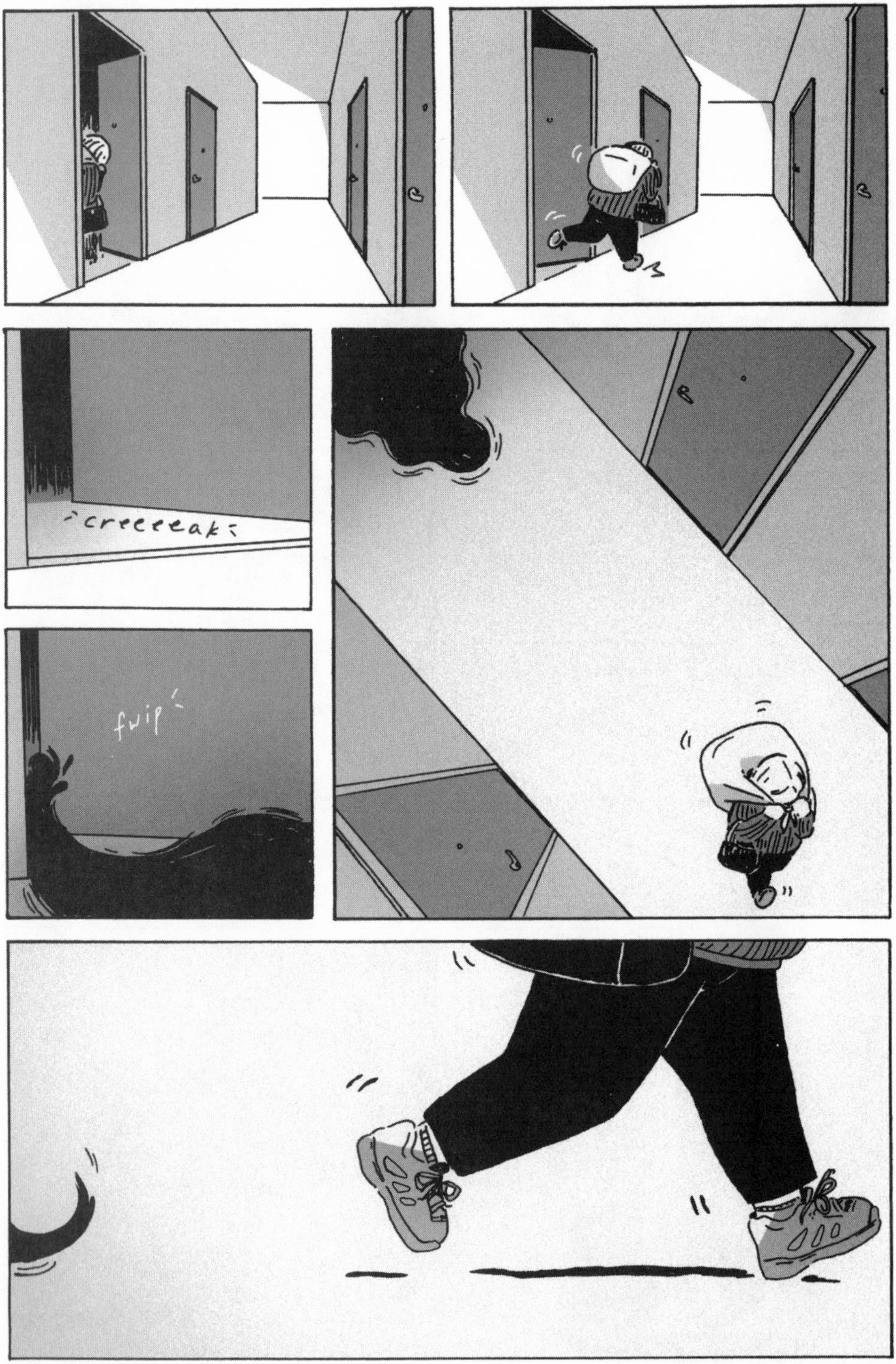
creeeeak
fwip

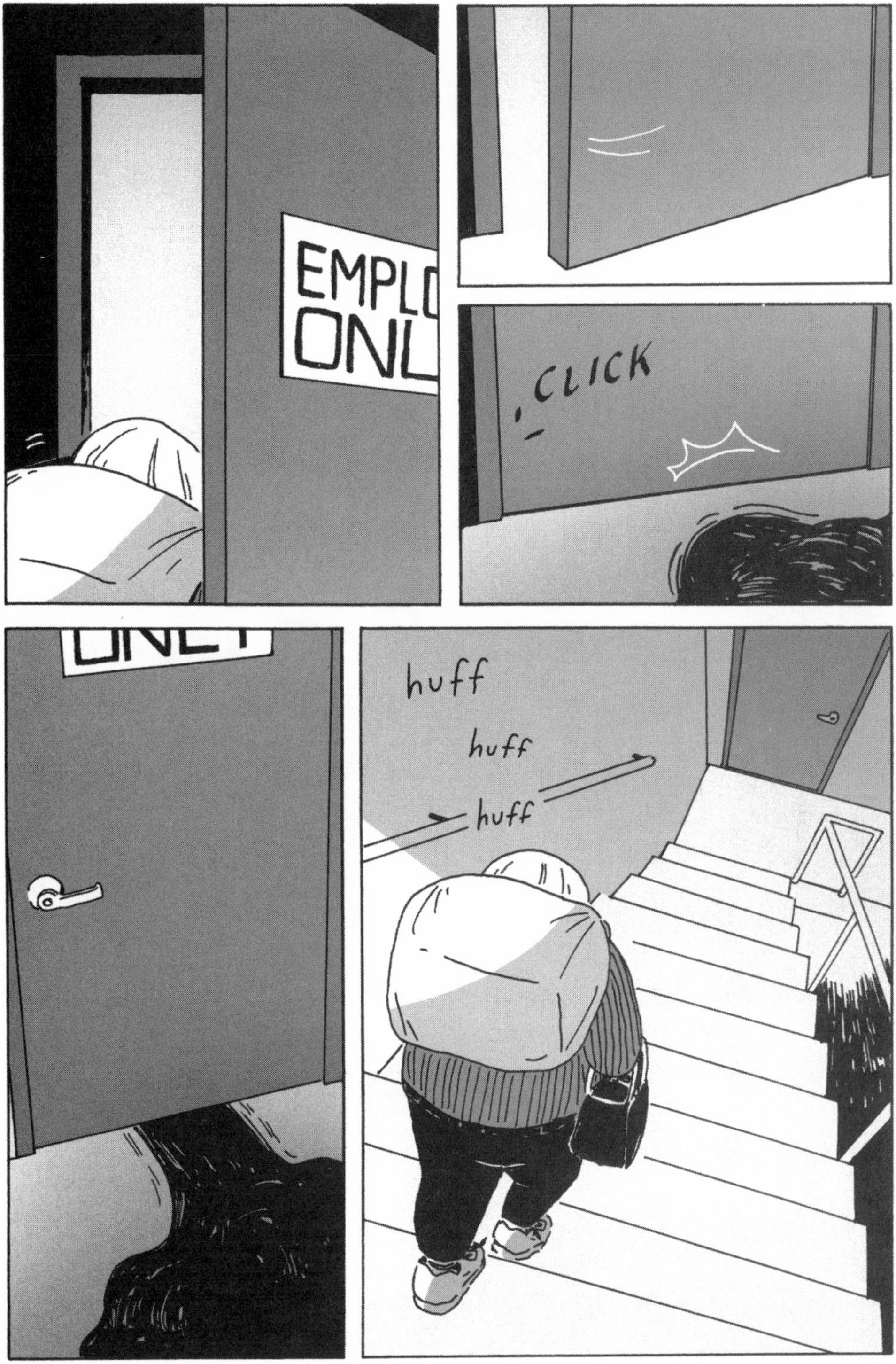
EMPLO
ONL
CLICK
huff
huff
huff

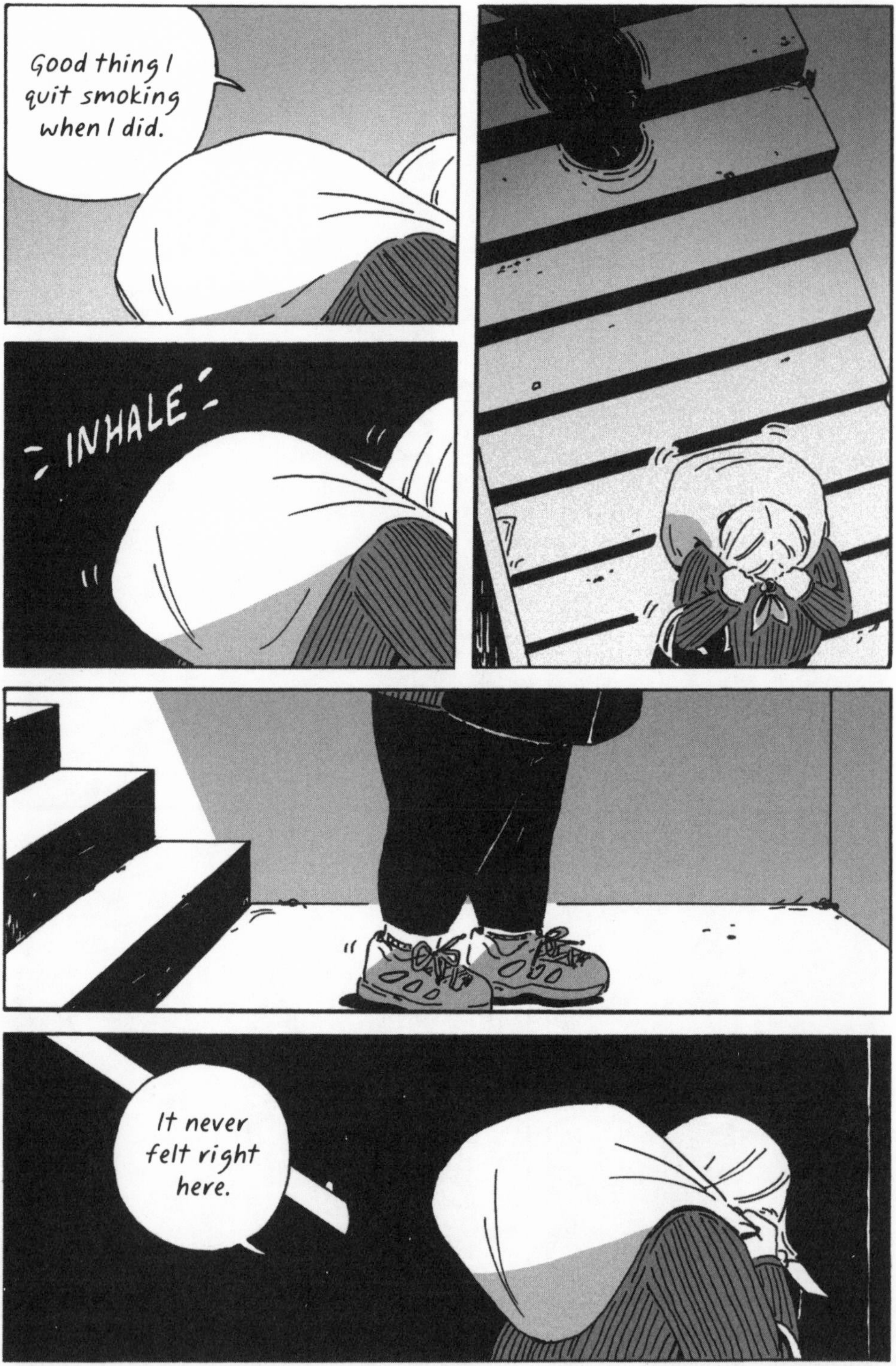
Good thing I quit smoking when I did.
INHALE
It never felt right here.

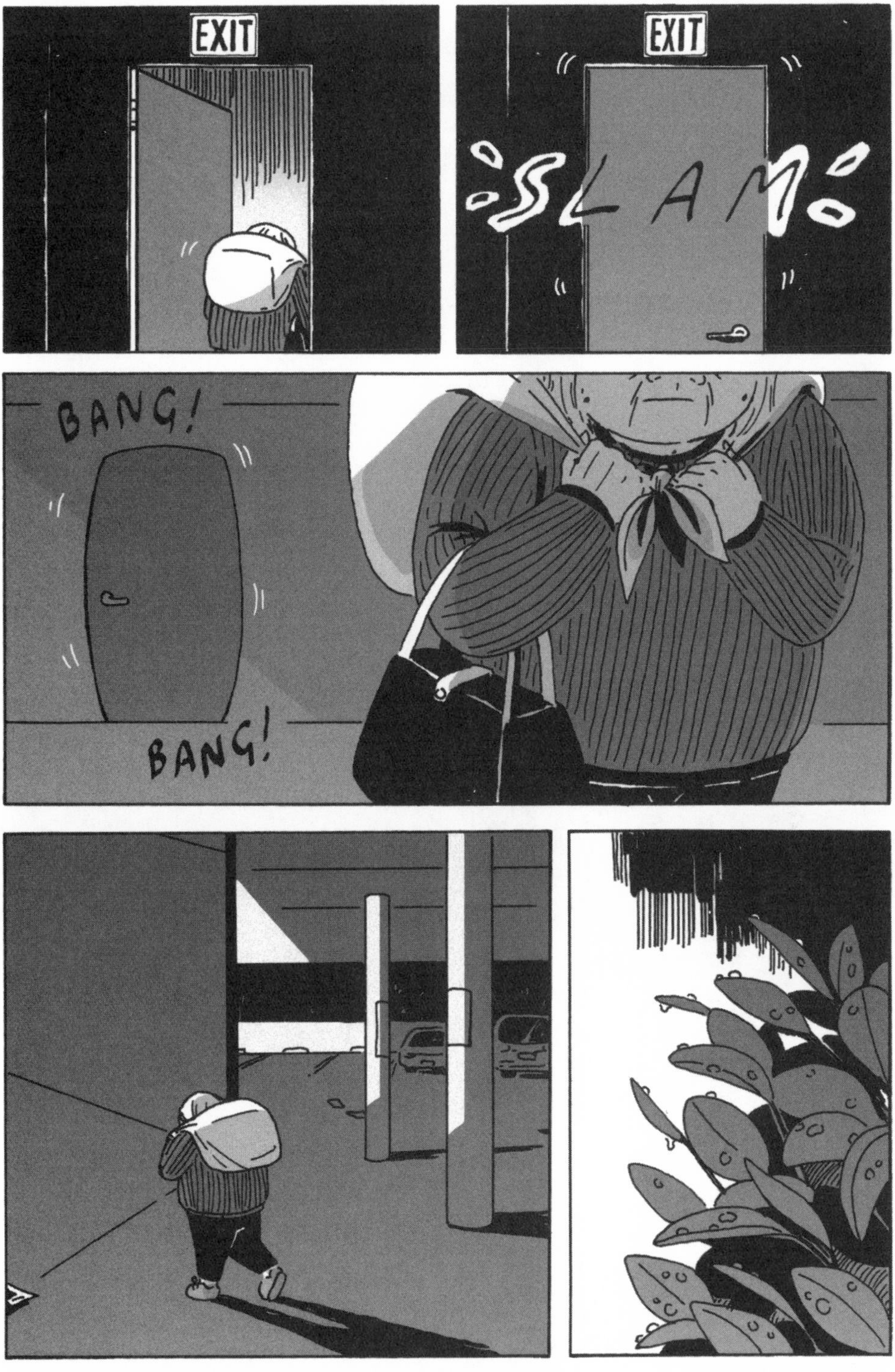
EXIT
EXIT
SLAM
BANG!
BANG!

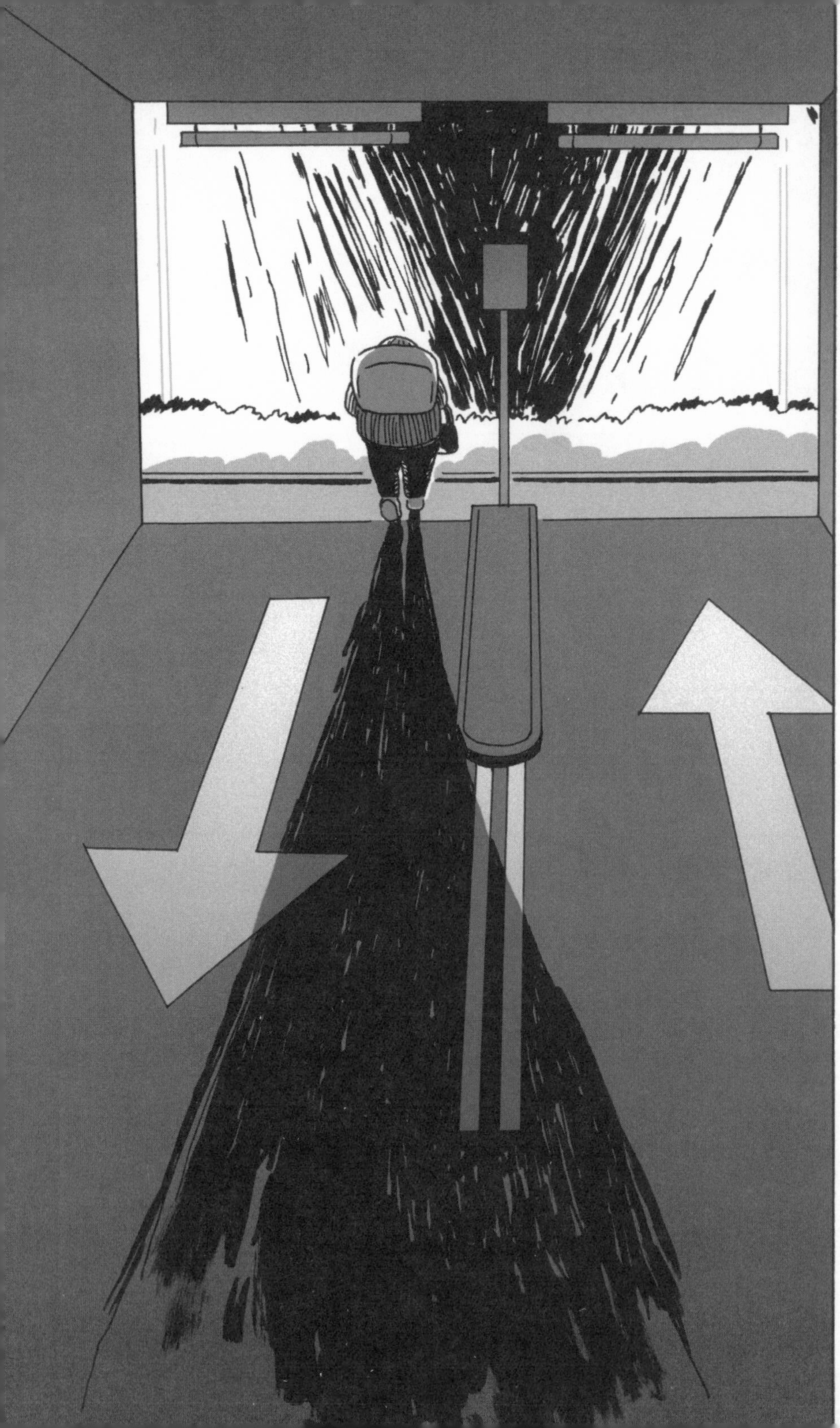

Chapter One

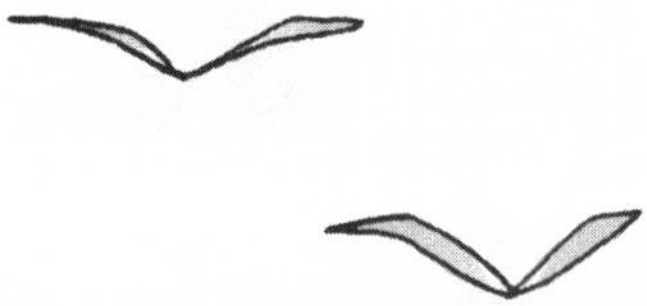

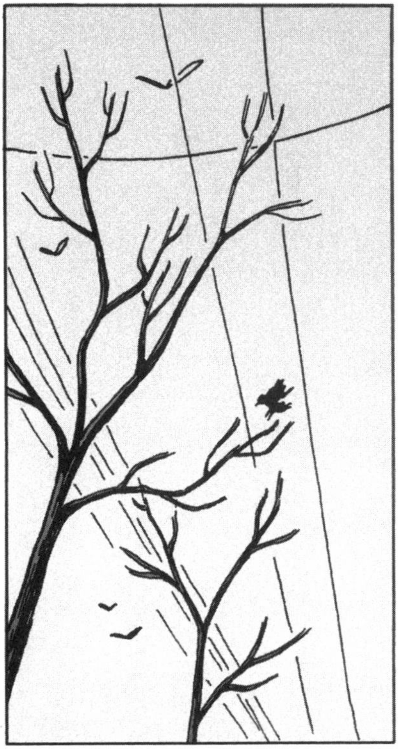

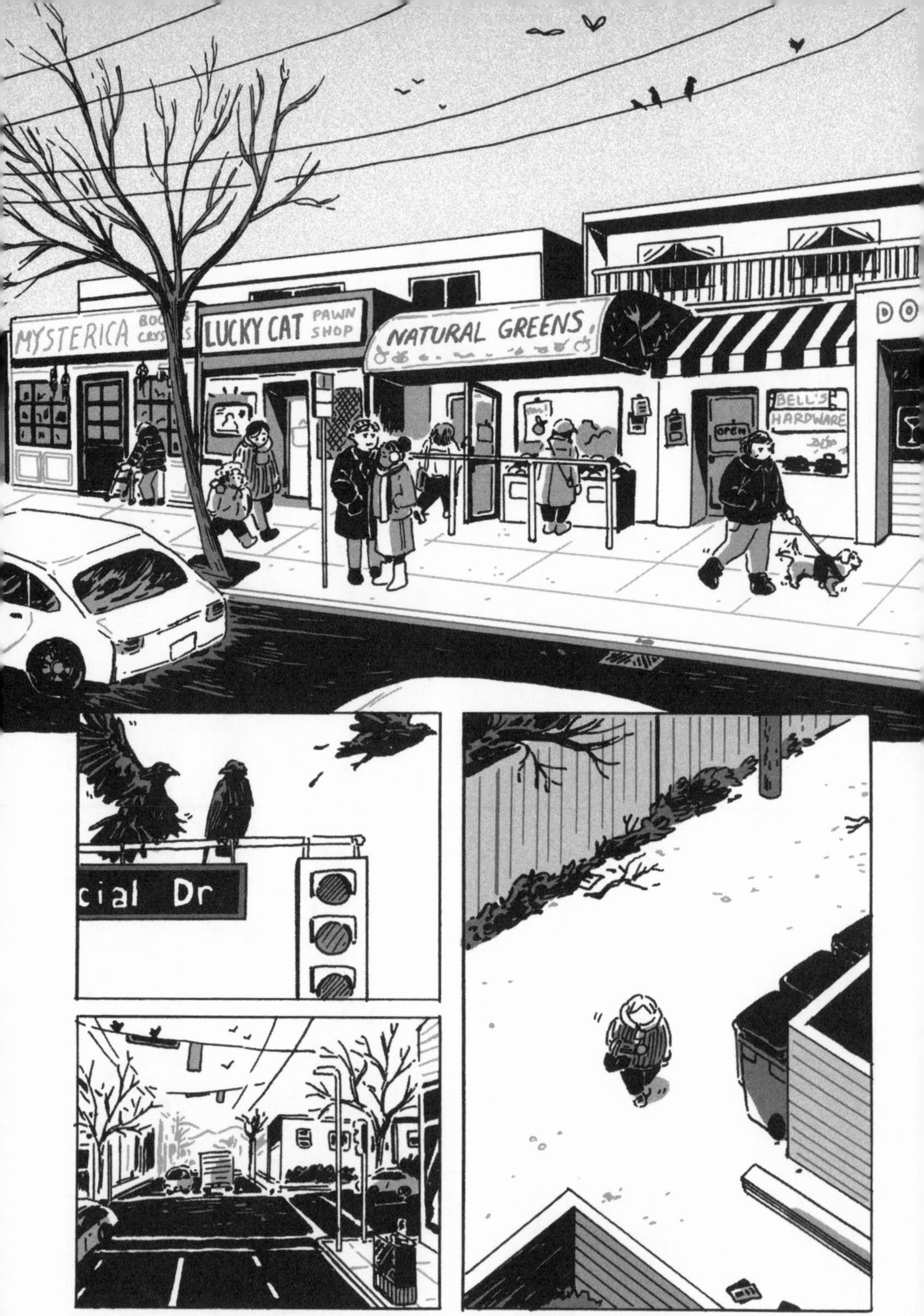
MYSTERICA
LUCKY CAT
PAWN SHOP
NATURAL GREENS
OPEN
BELL'S HARDWARE
cial Dr

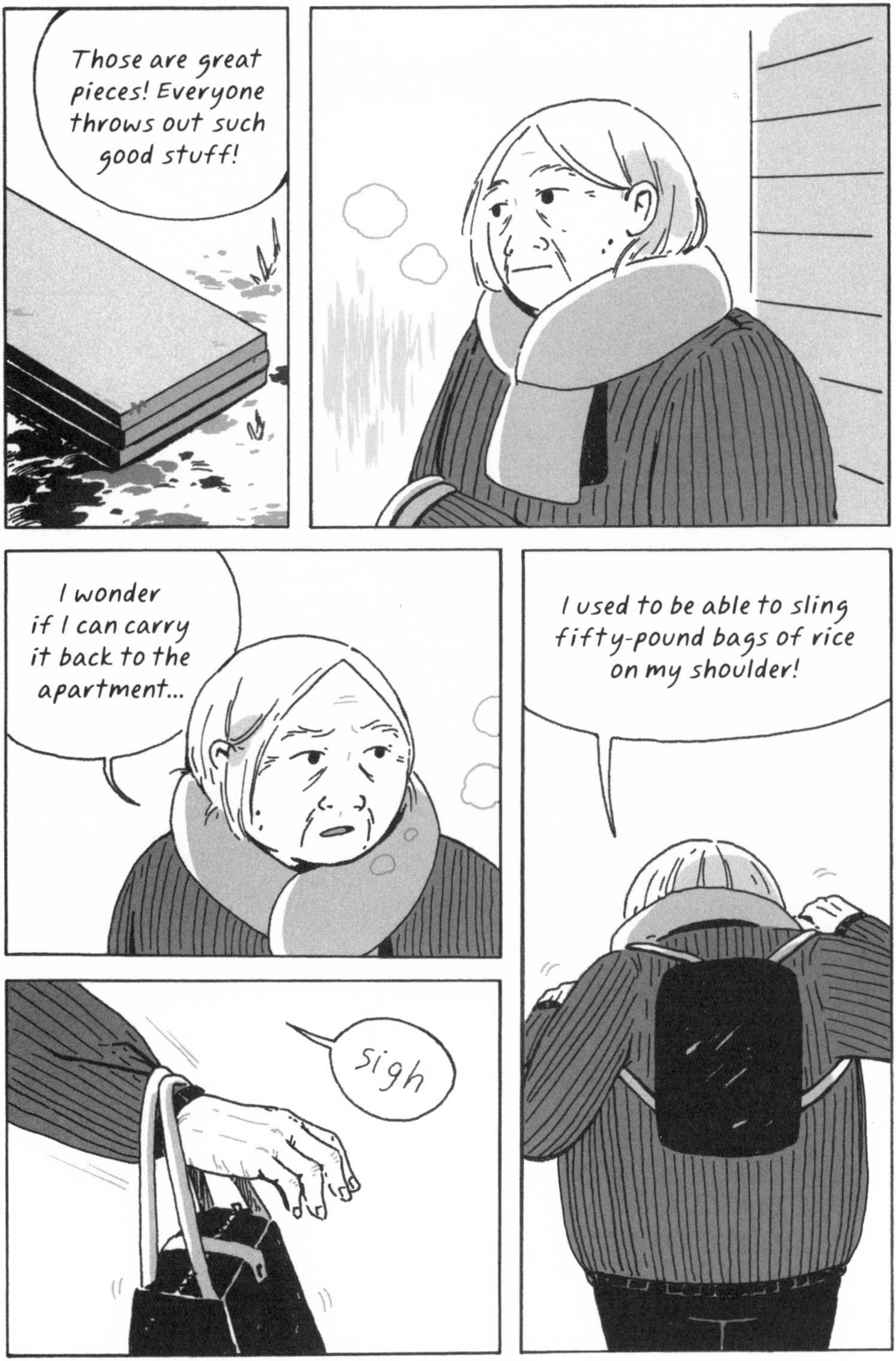
Those are great pieces! Everyone throws out such good stuff!
I wonder if I can carry it back to the apartment...
I used to be able to sling fifty-pound bags of rice on my shoulder!
sigh

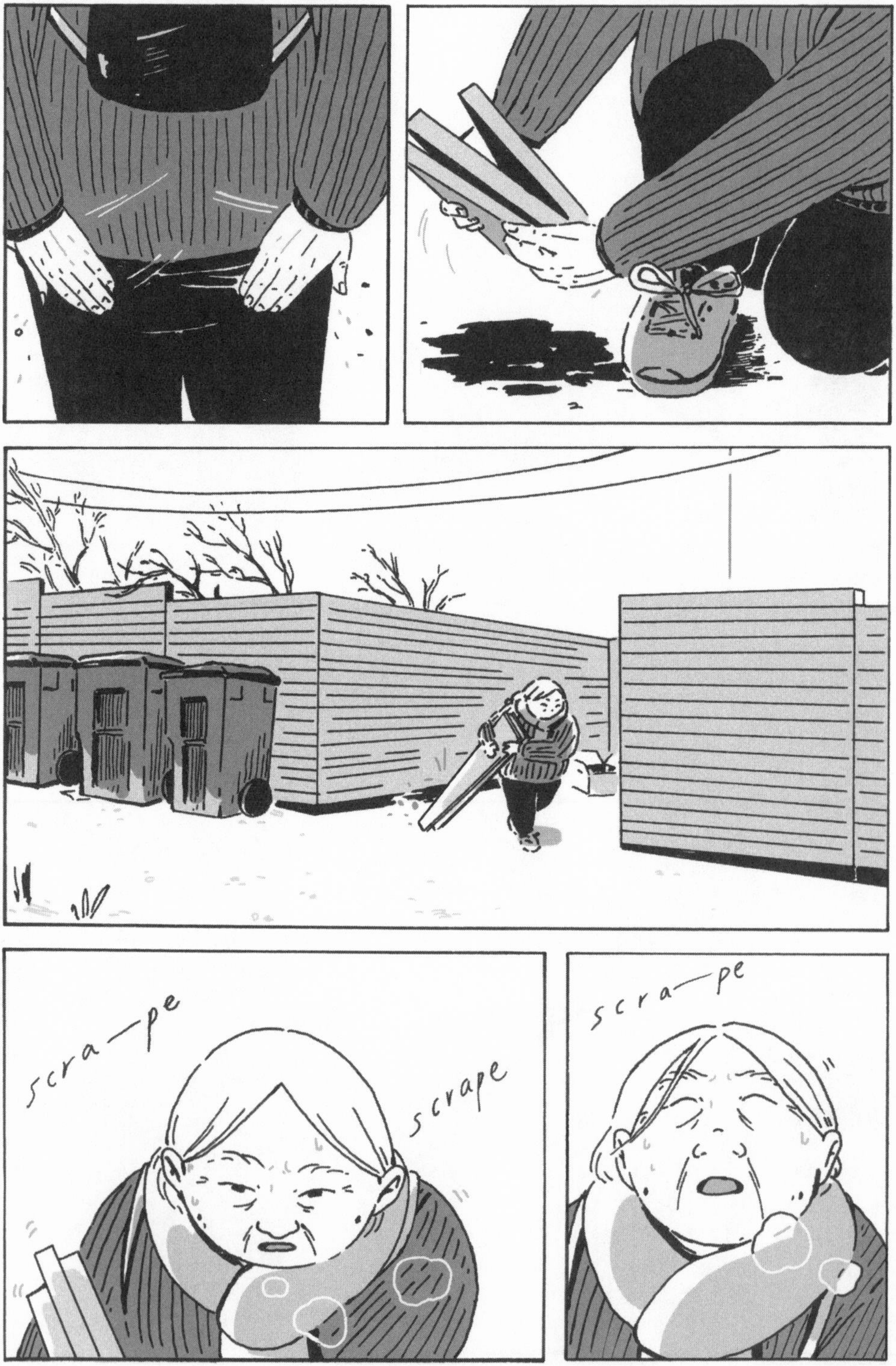
scra—pe
scrape
scra—pe

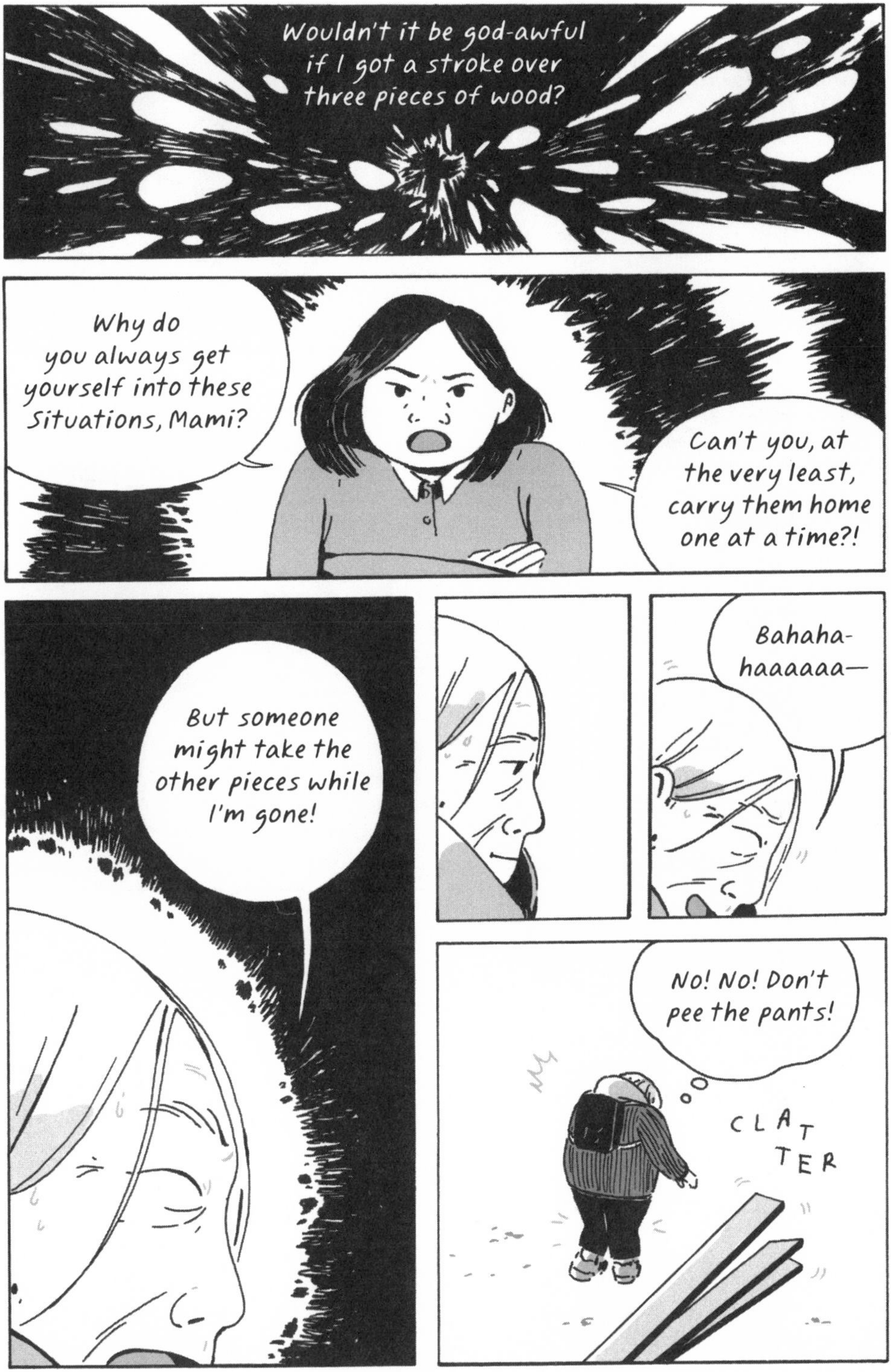
Wouldn't it be god-awful if I got a stroke over three pieces of wood?
Why do you always get yourself into these Situations, Mami?
Can't you, at the very least, carry them home one at a time?!
But someone might take the other pieces while I'm gone!
Bahaha-haaaaaa—
No! No! Don't pee the pants!
CLATTER

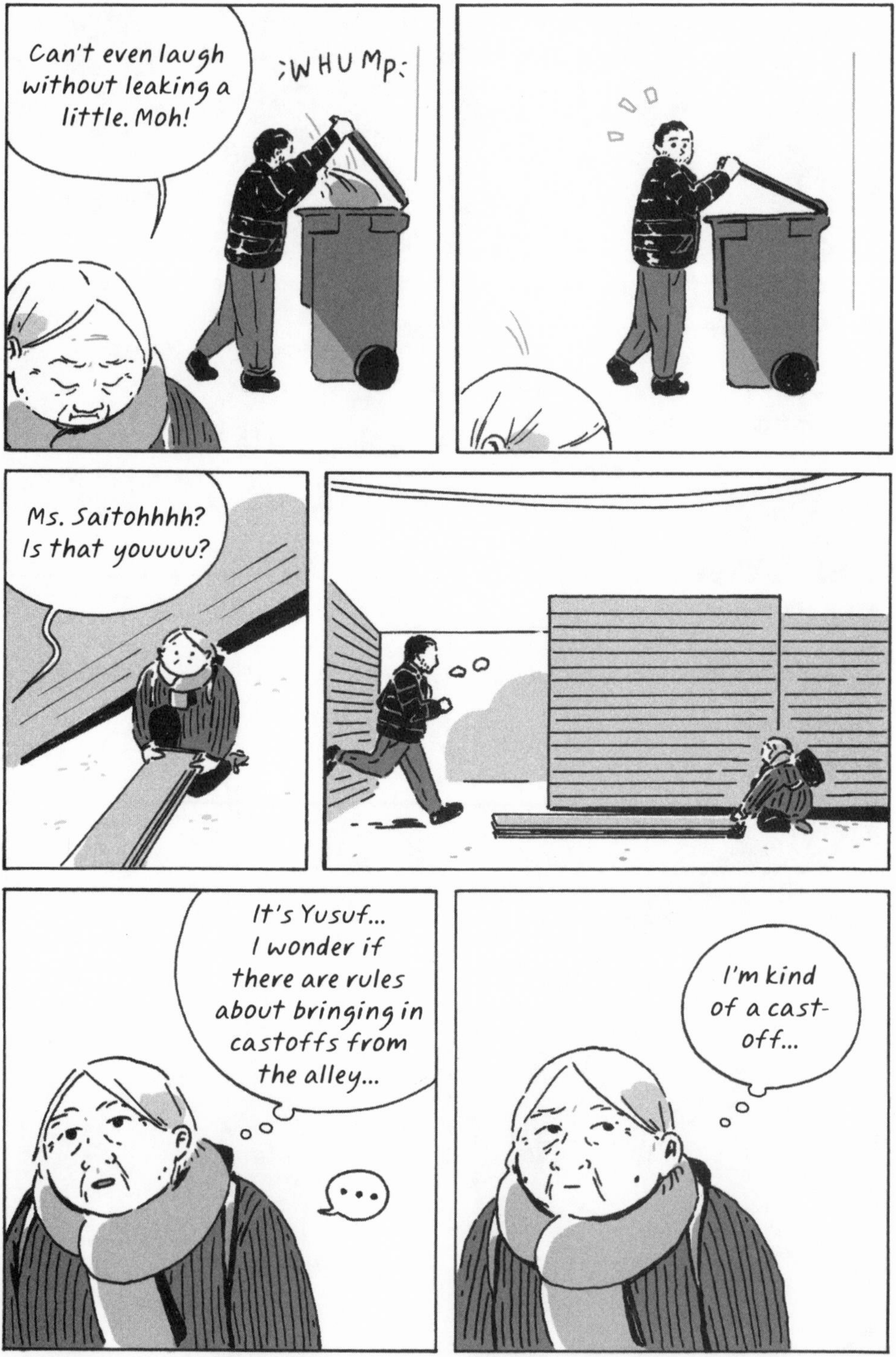
Can't even laugh without leaking a little. Moh!
WHUMp
Ms. Saitohhhh? Is that youuuu?
It's Yusuf... I wonder if there are rules about bringing in castoffs from the alley...
...
I'm kind of a cast-off...

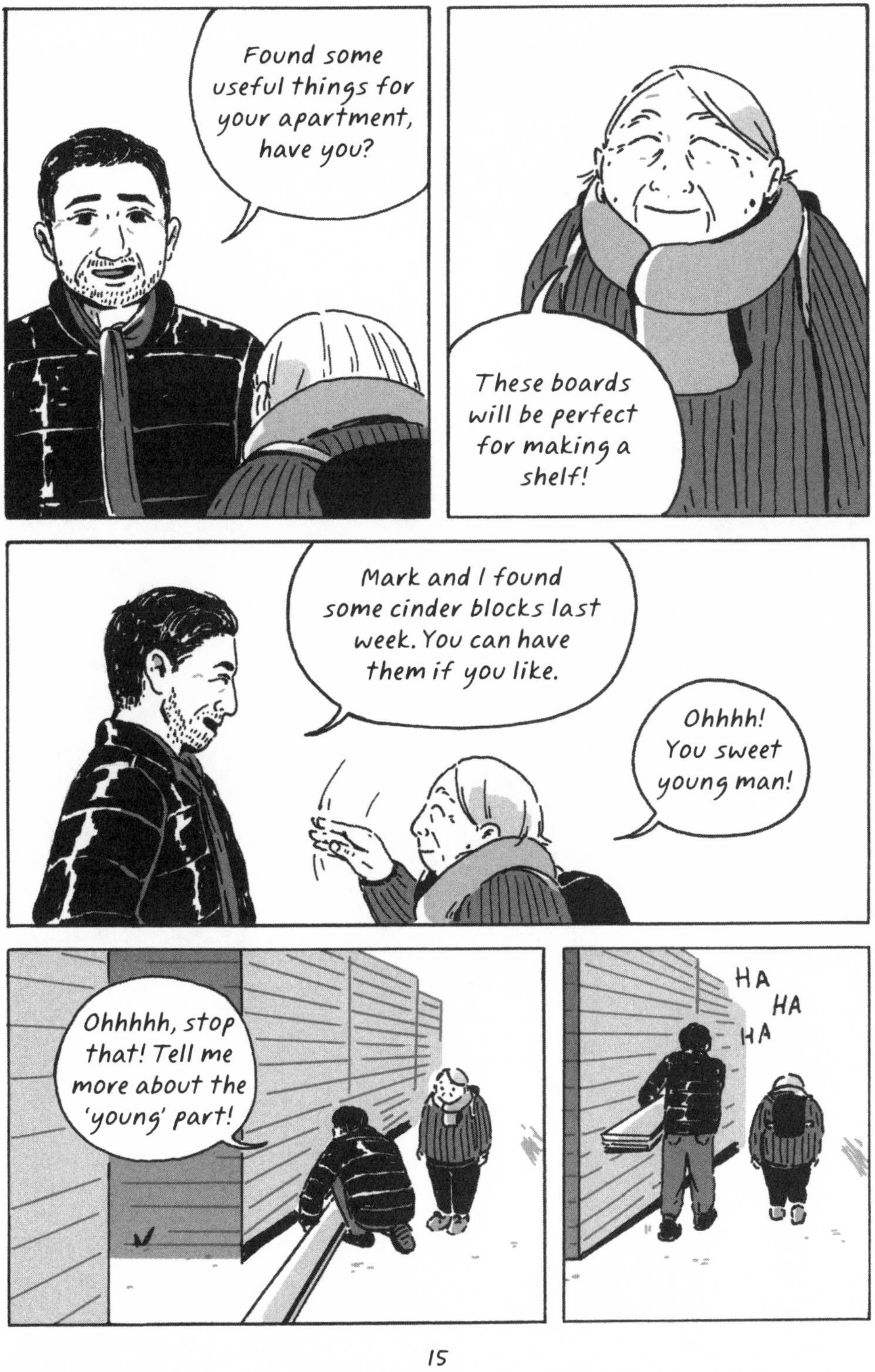
Found some useful things for your apartment, have you?
These boards will be perfect for making a shelf!
Mark and I found some cinder blocks last week. You can have them if you like.
Ohhhh! You sweet young man!
Ohhhhh, stop that! Tell me more about the 'young' part!
HA HA HA

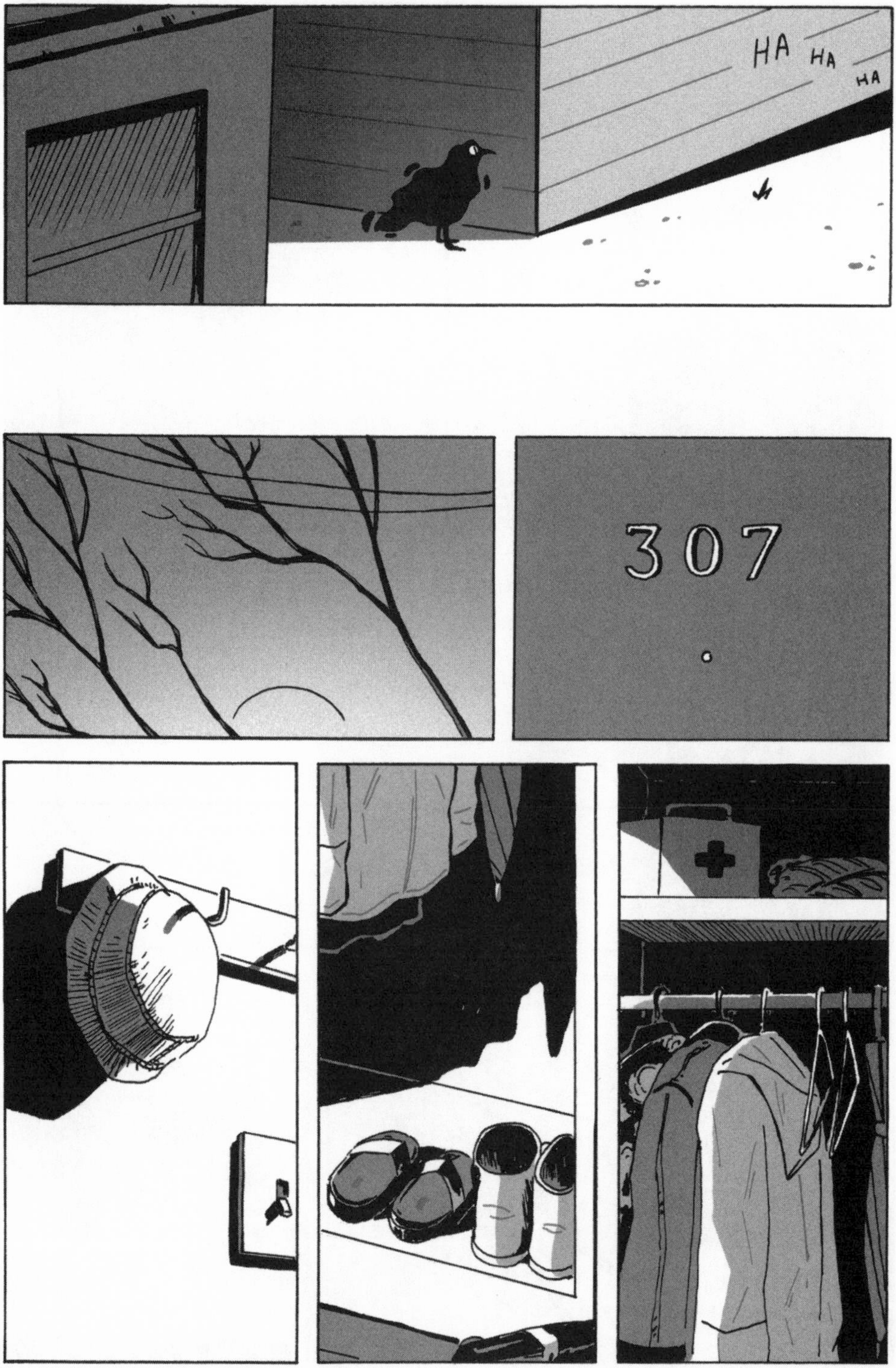
HA HA HA
307

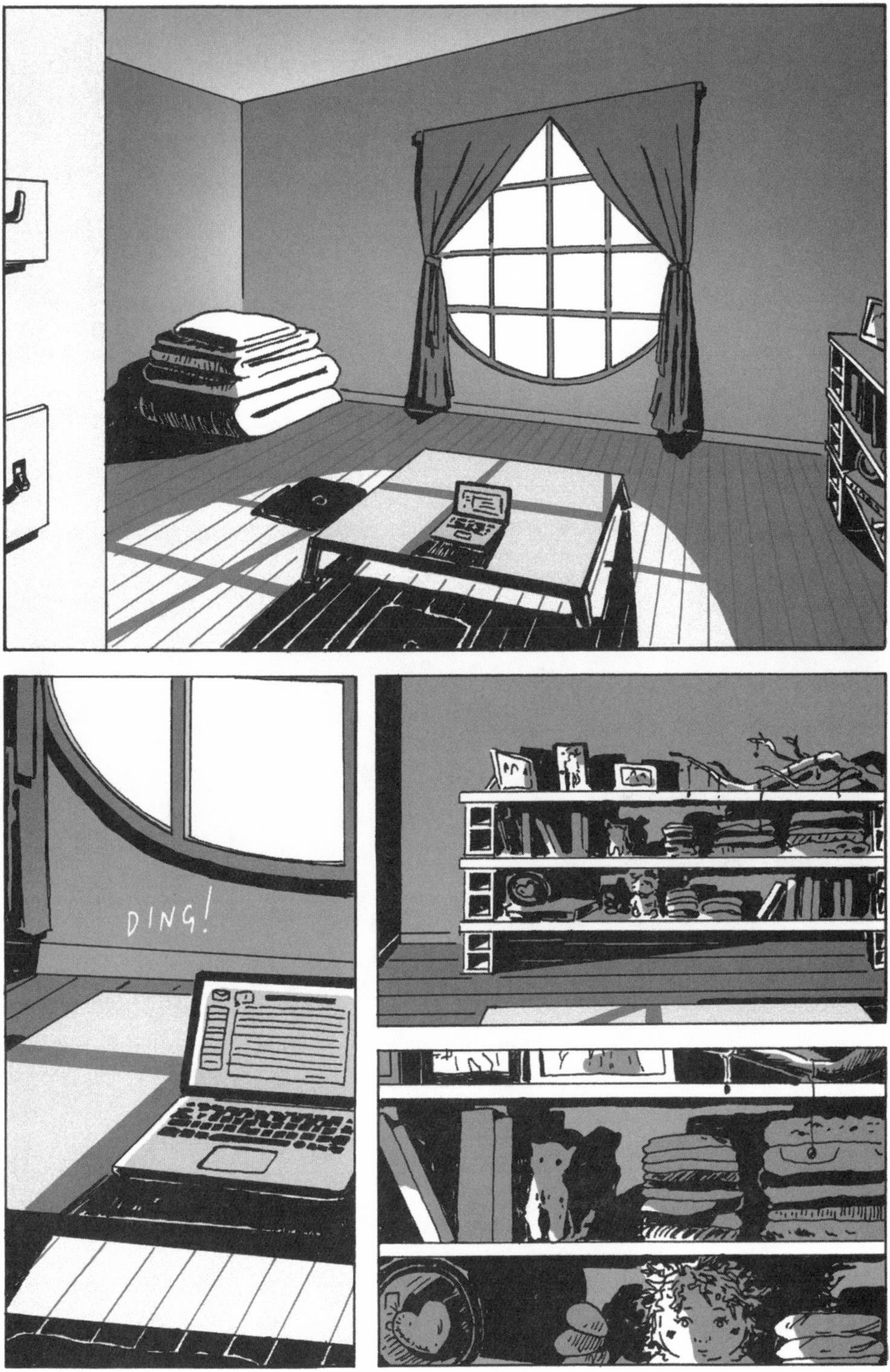
DING!

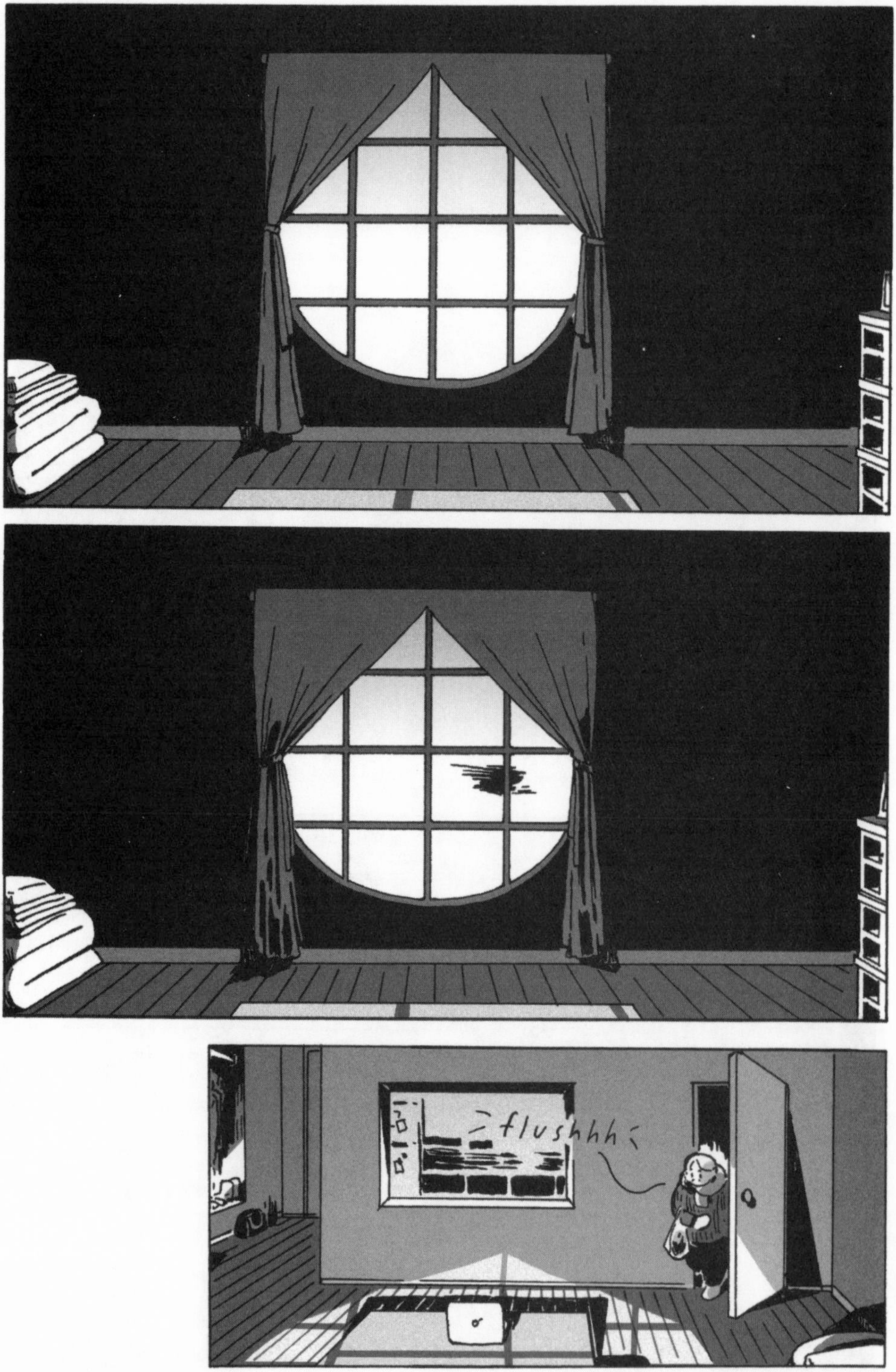
flushhh

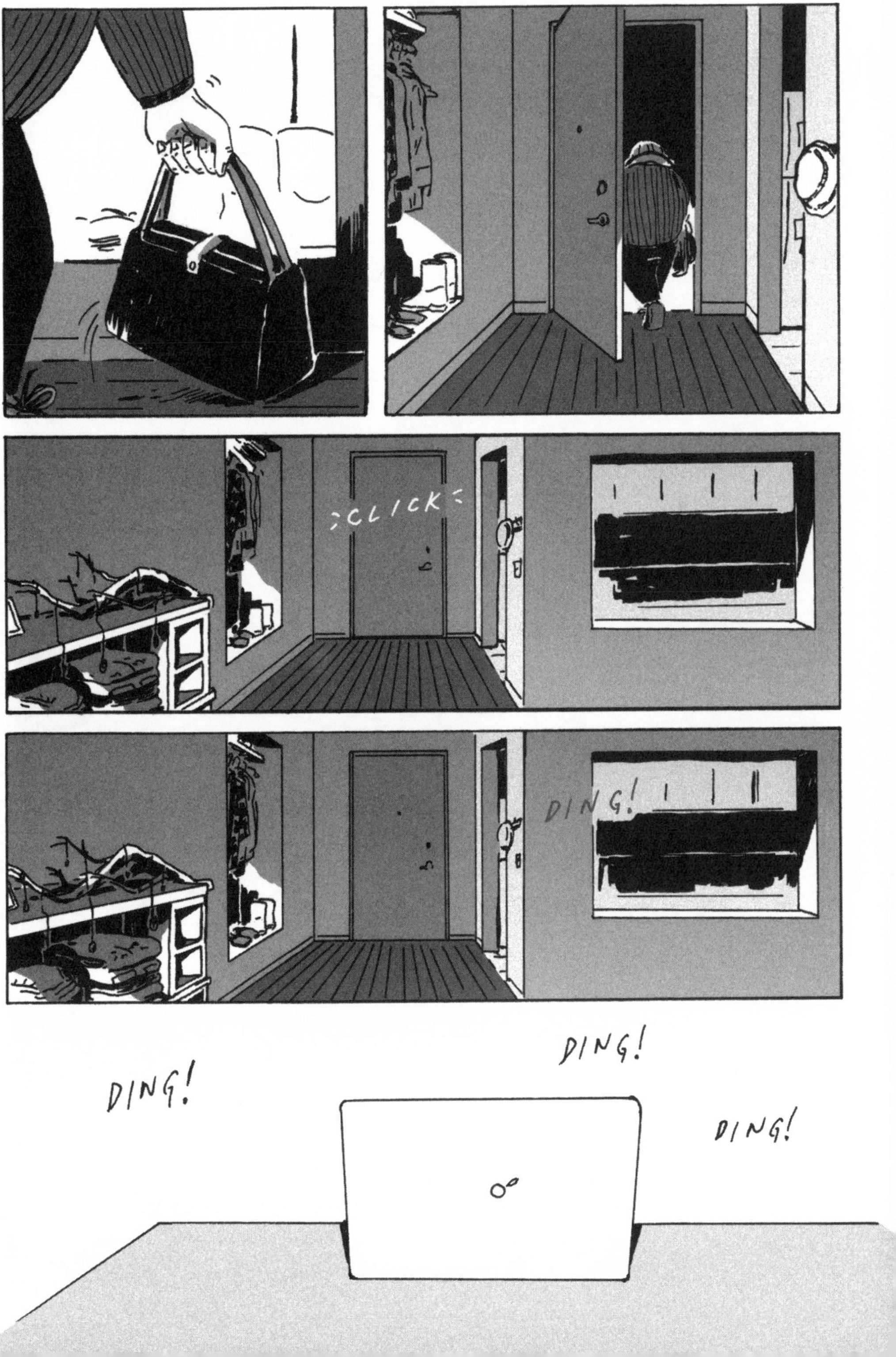
CLICK
DING!
DING!
DING!
DING!

Chapter Two

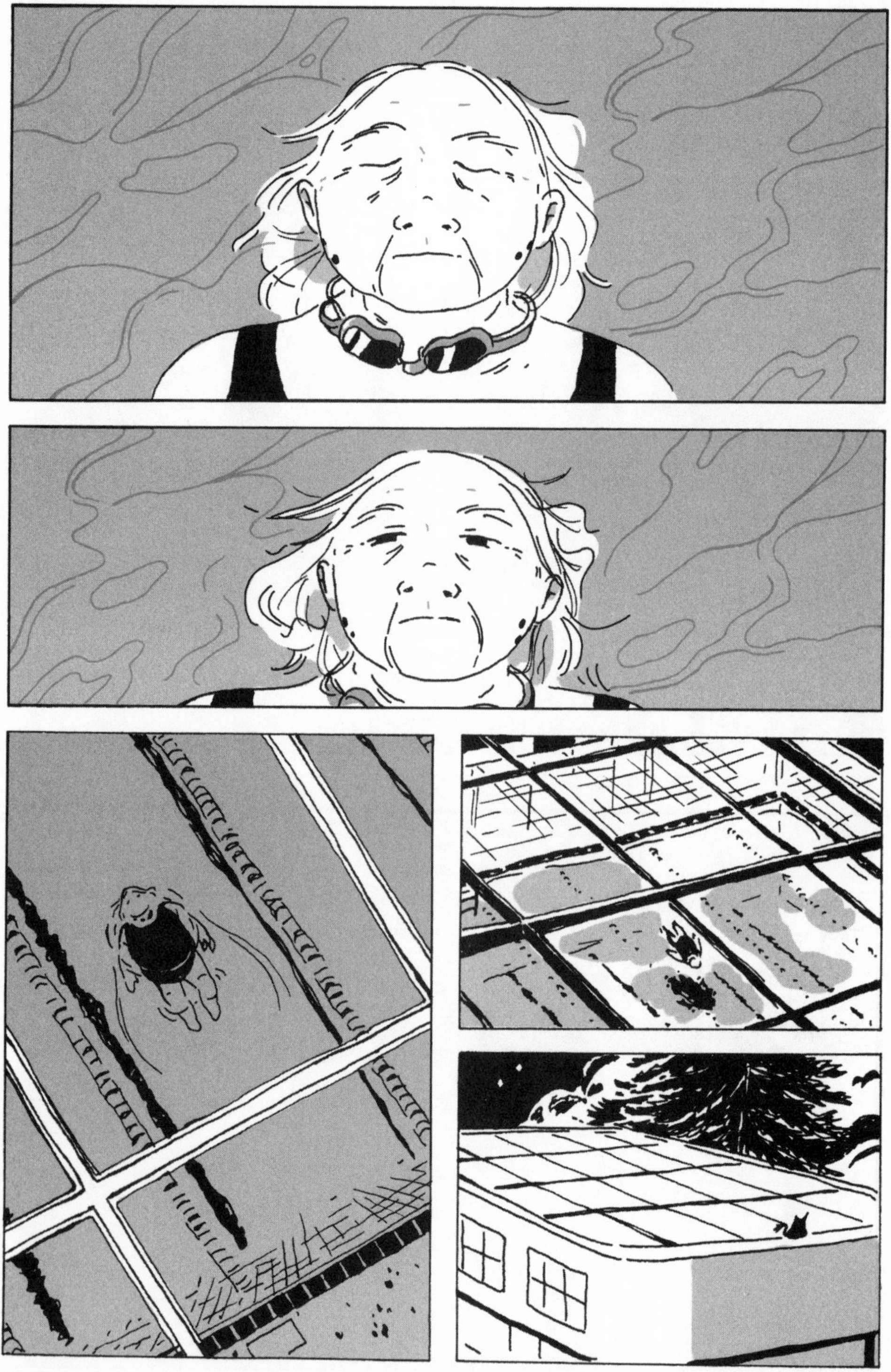

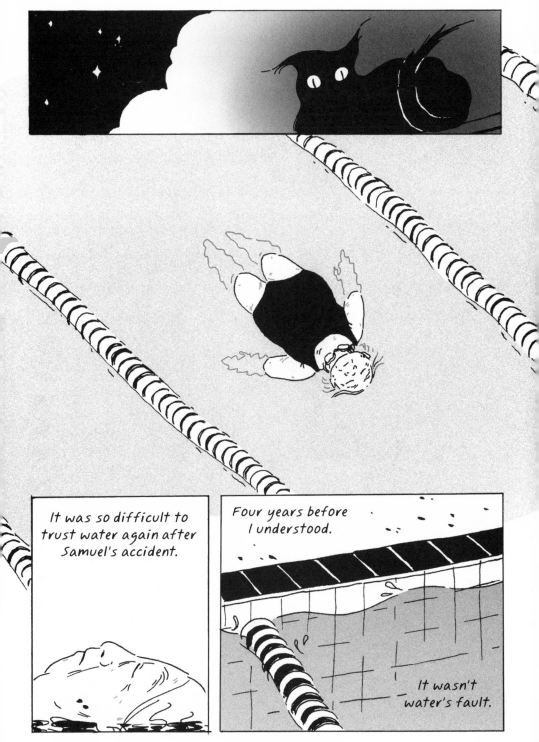

It was so difficult to trust water again after Samuel's accident.

Four years before I understood.

It wasn't water's fault.

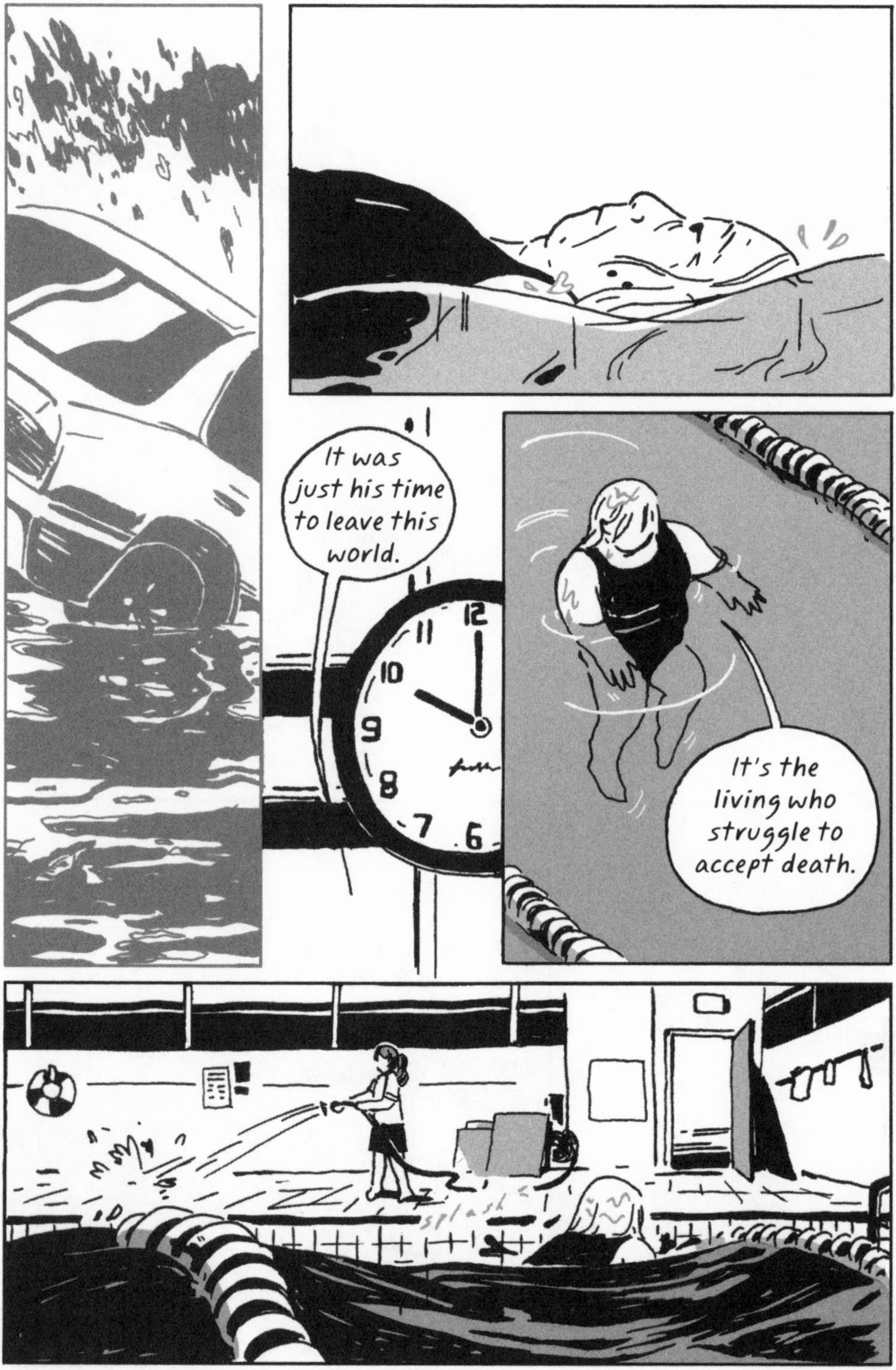
It was just his time to leave this world.
It's the living who struggle to accept death.
splash

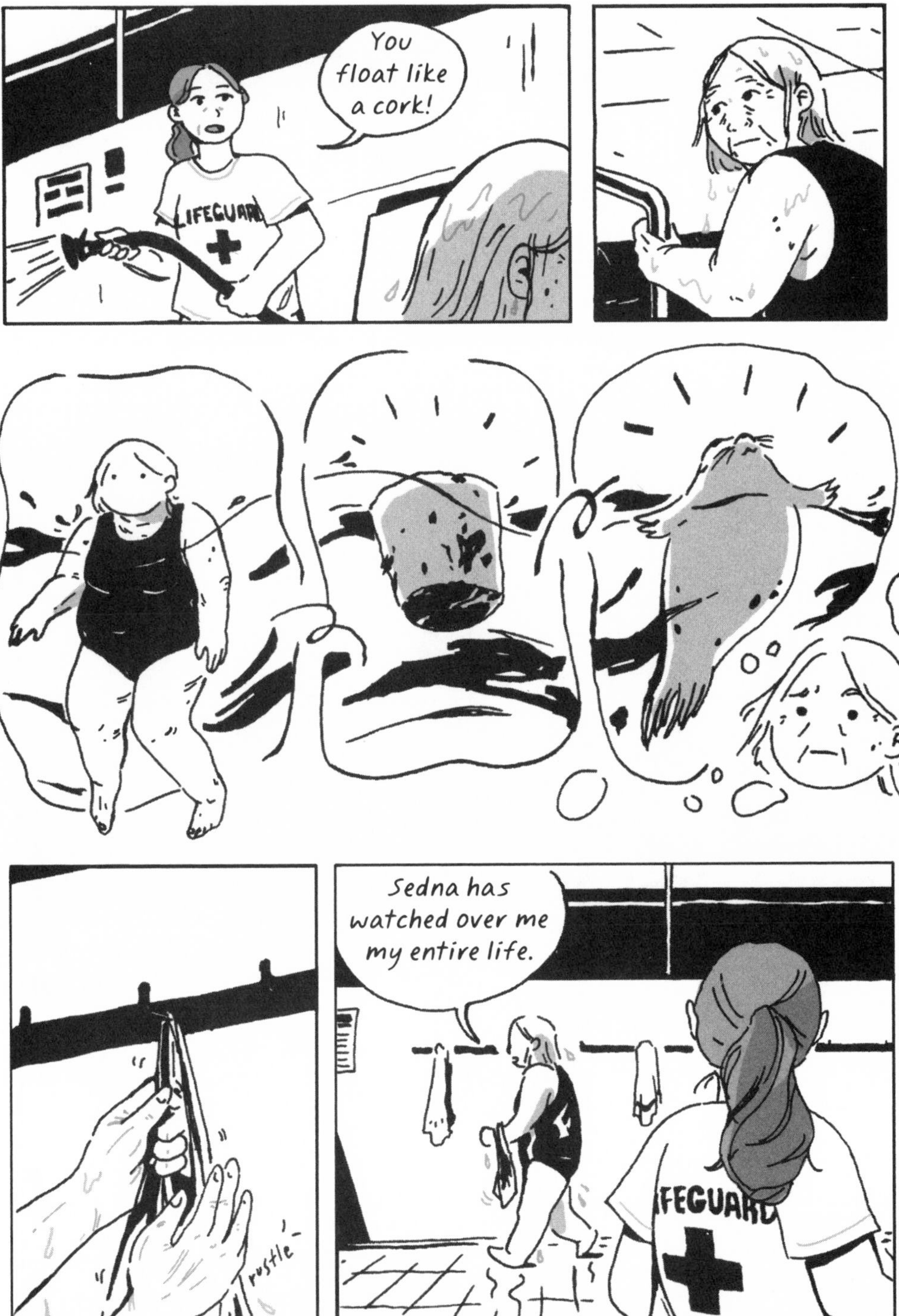
You float like a cork!
LIFEGUARD
Sedna has watched over me my entire life.
rustle
LIFEGUARD

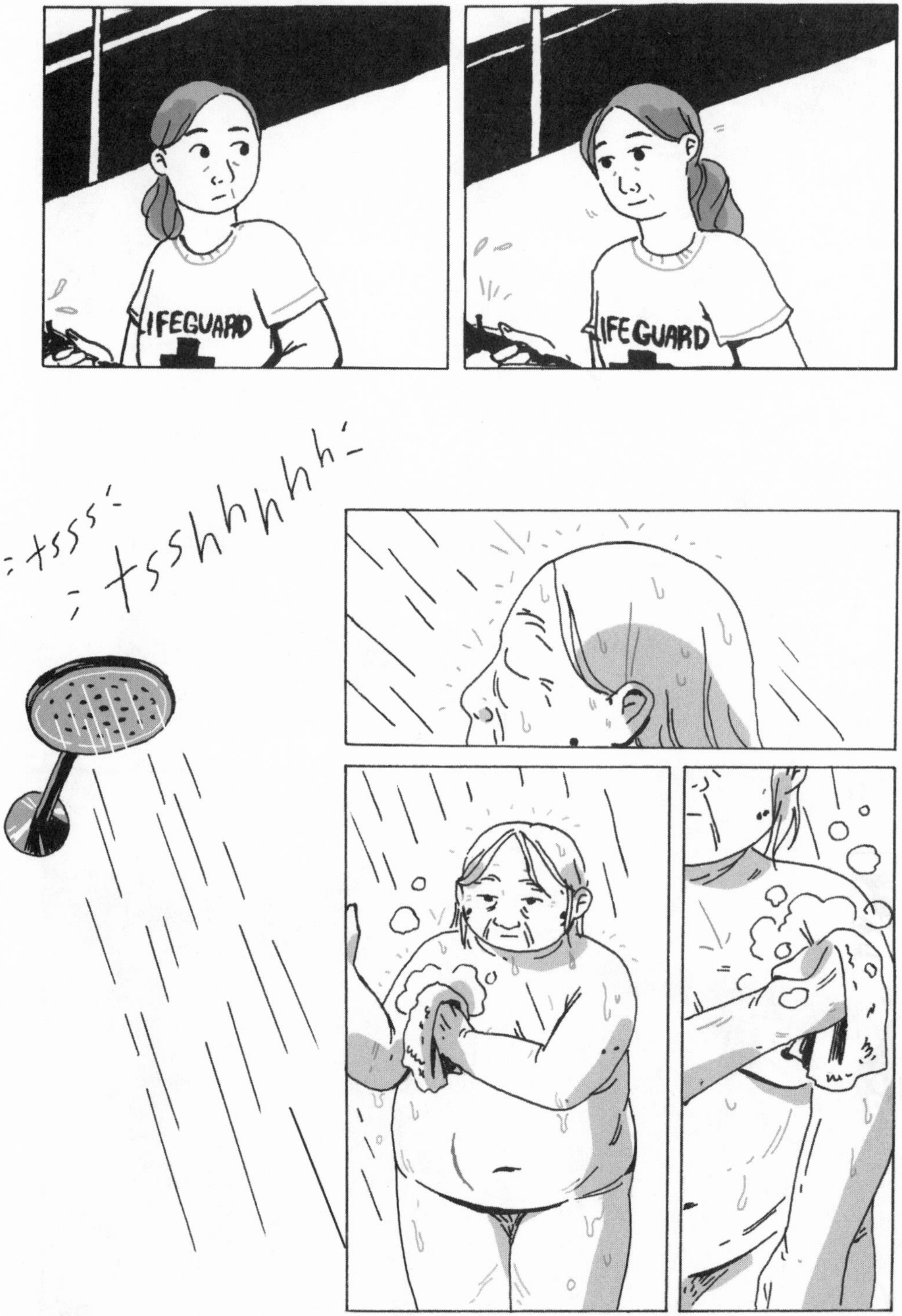
LIFEGUARD
LIFEGUARD
tsss
tsshhhhh

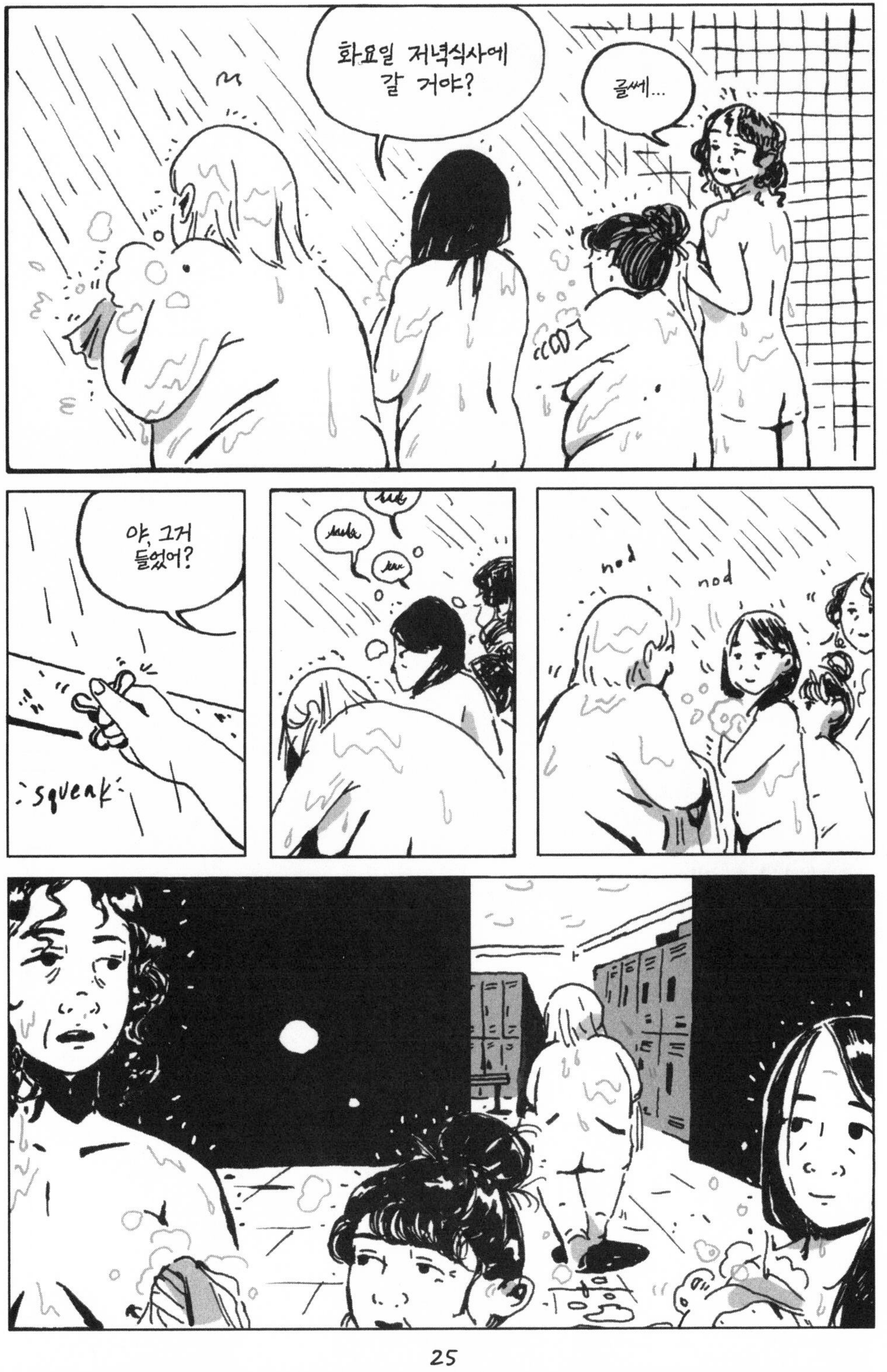
화요일 저녁식사에
갈 거야?
글쎄...
야, 그거
들었어?
squeak
nod
nod

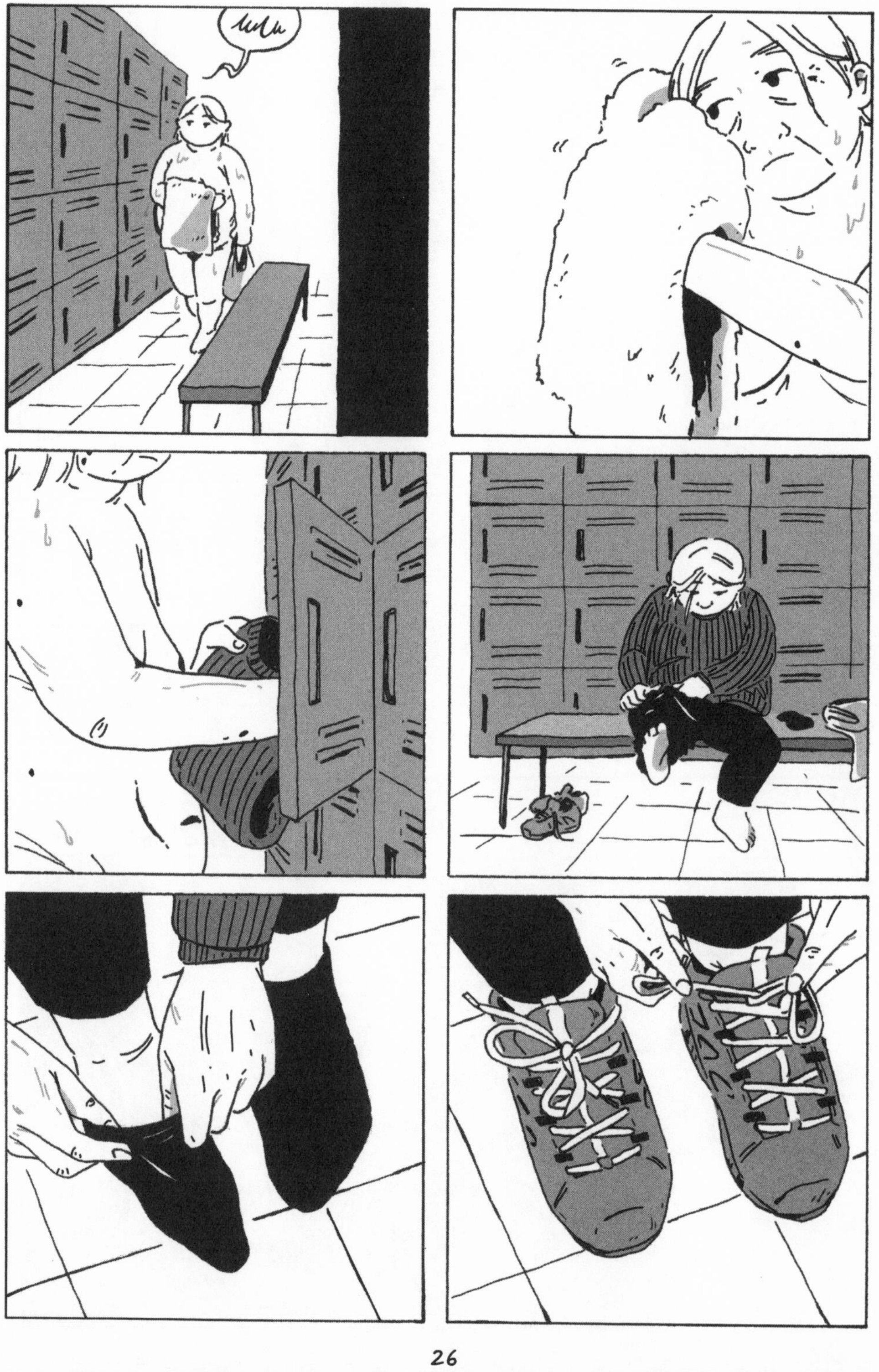

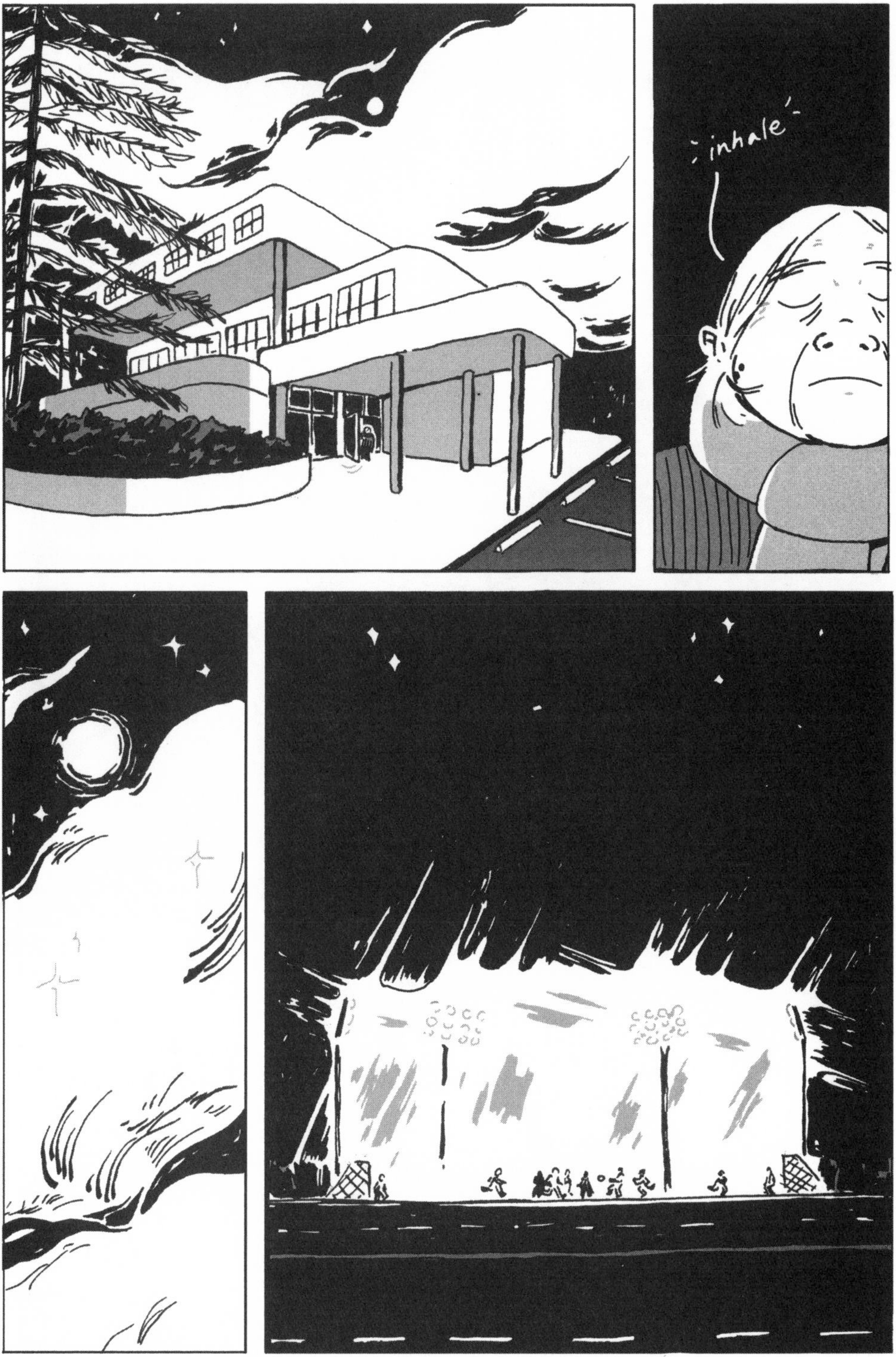
inhale

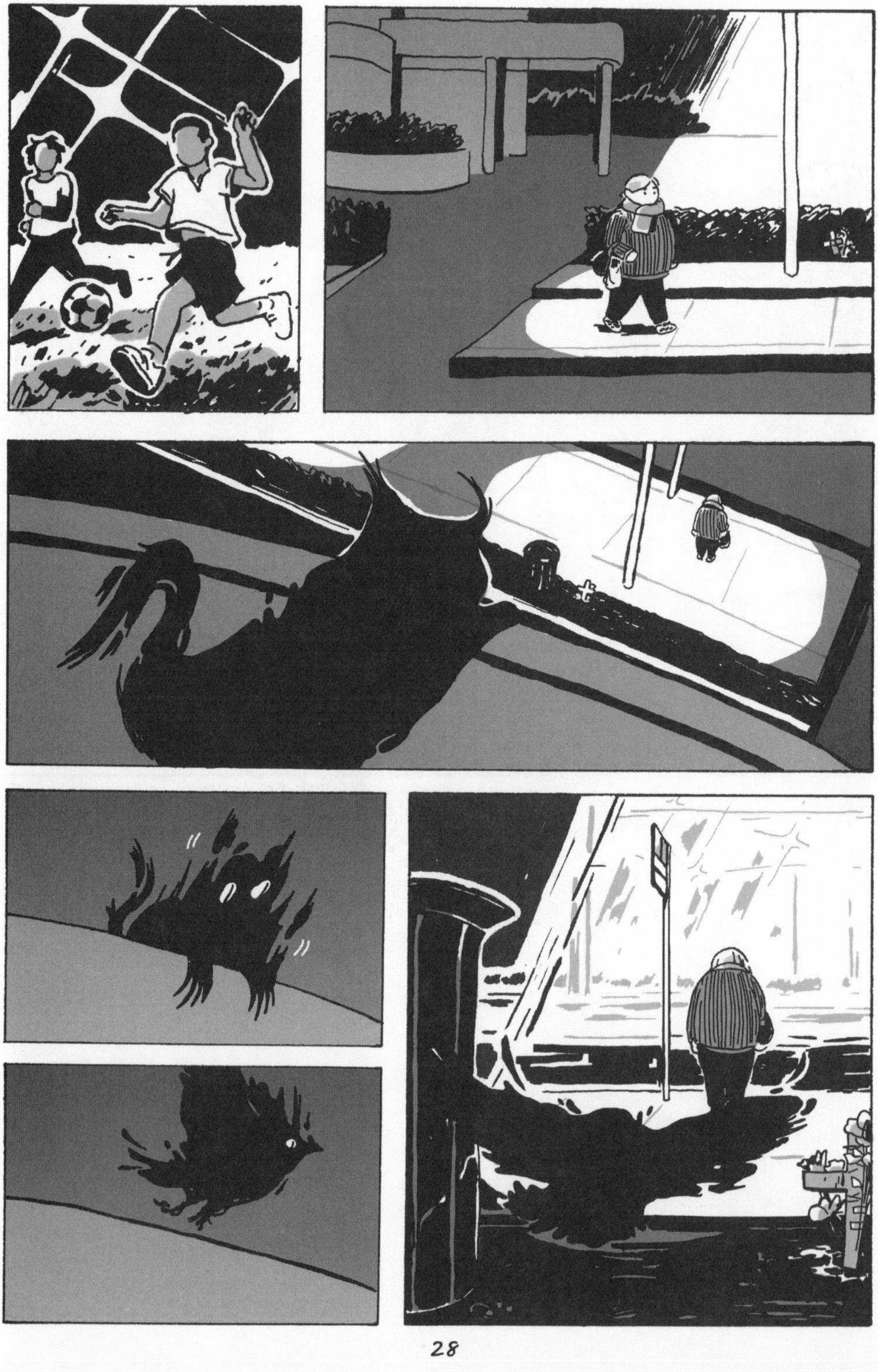

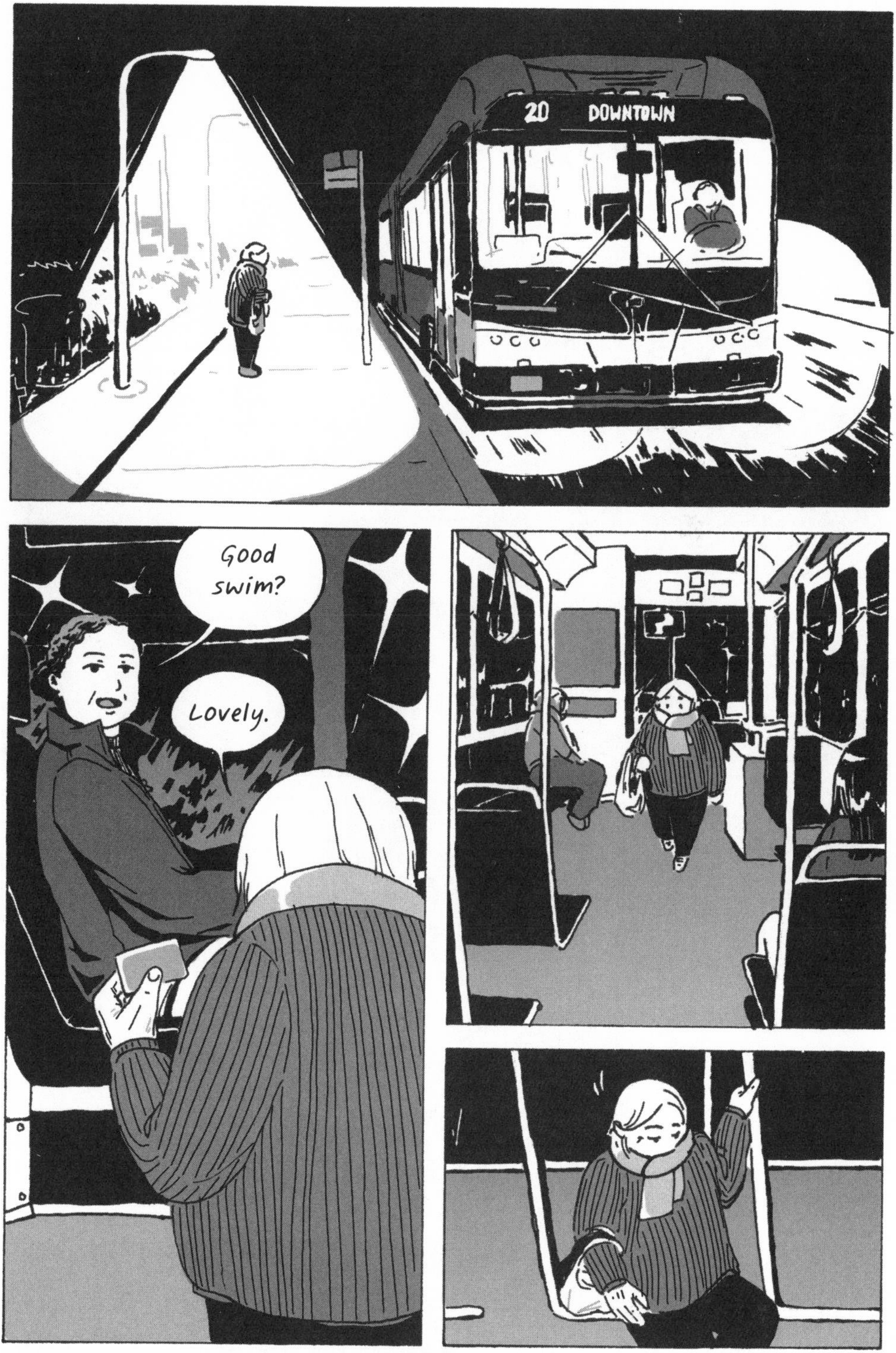
20 DOWNTOWN
Good swim?
Lovely.

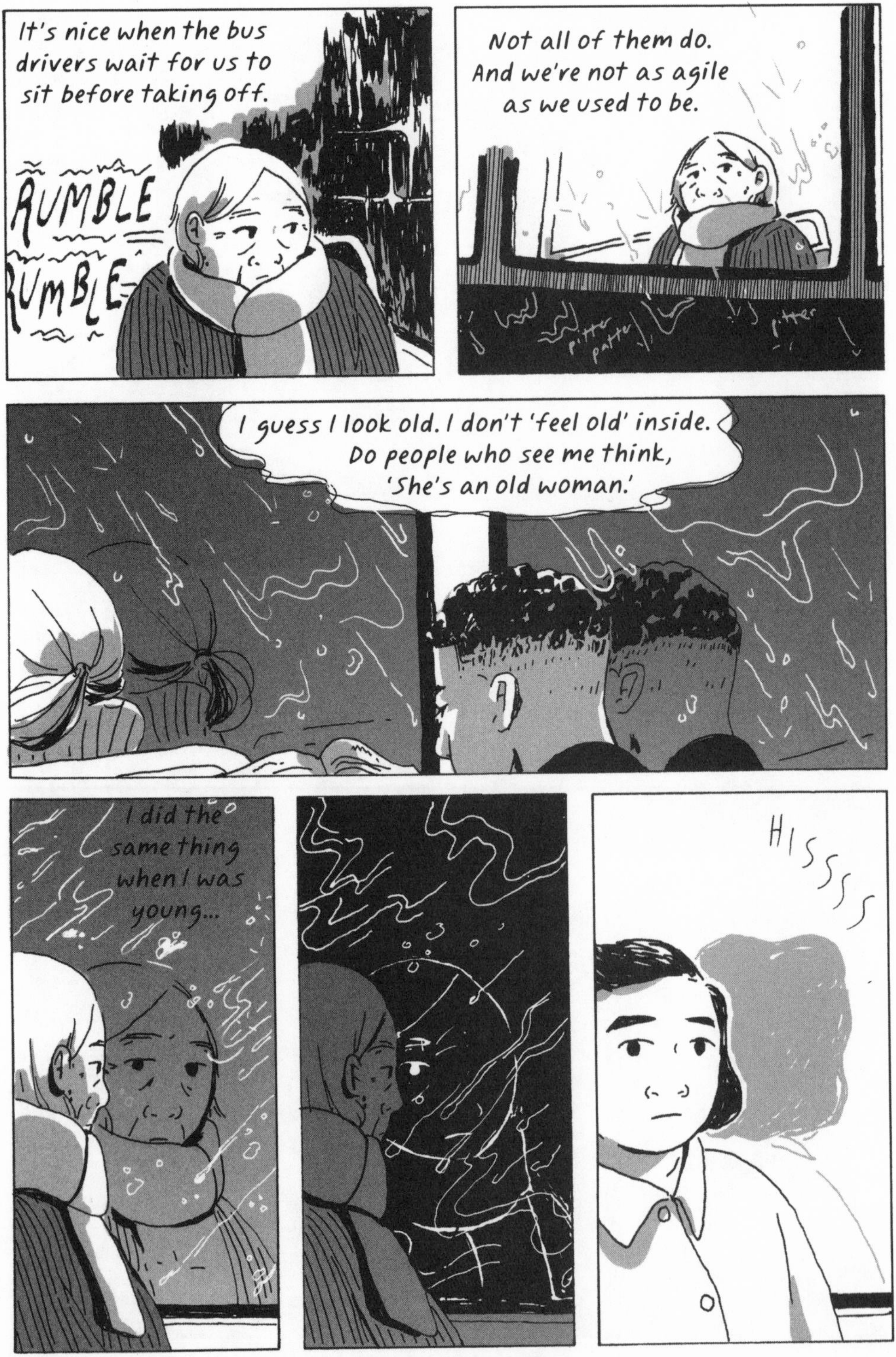
It's nice when the bus drivers wait for us to sit before taking off.
RUMBLE RUMBLE
Not all of them do. And we're not as agile as we used to be.
pitter patter pitter
I guess I look old. I don't 'feel old' inside. Do people who see me think, 'She's an old woman.'
I did the same thing when I was young...
HISSSSS

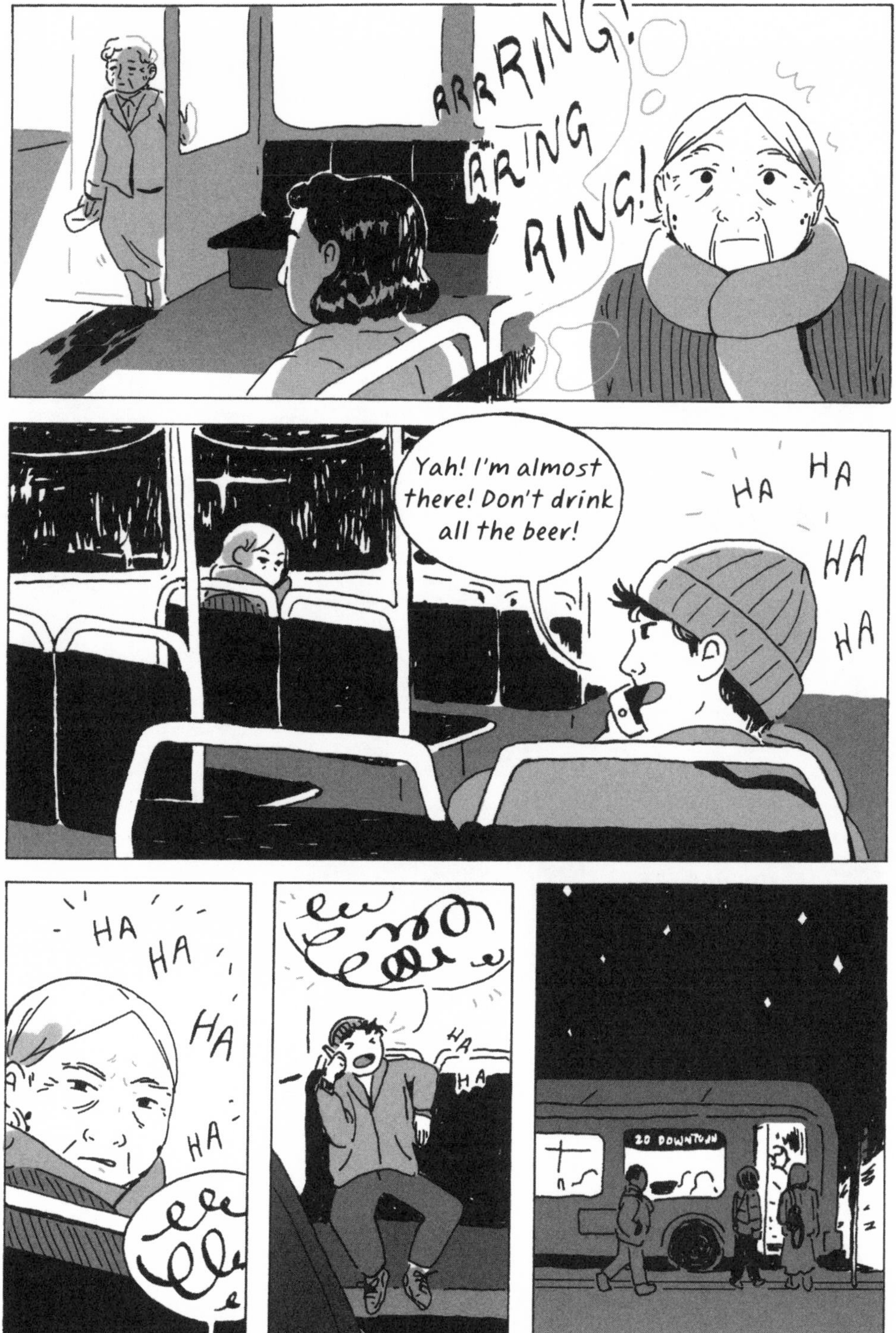
ARRRING!
ARRING
RING!
Yah! I'm almost there! Don't drink all the beer!
HA HA HA HA
HA HA HA HA
HA HA
20 DOWNTOWN

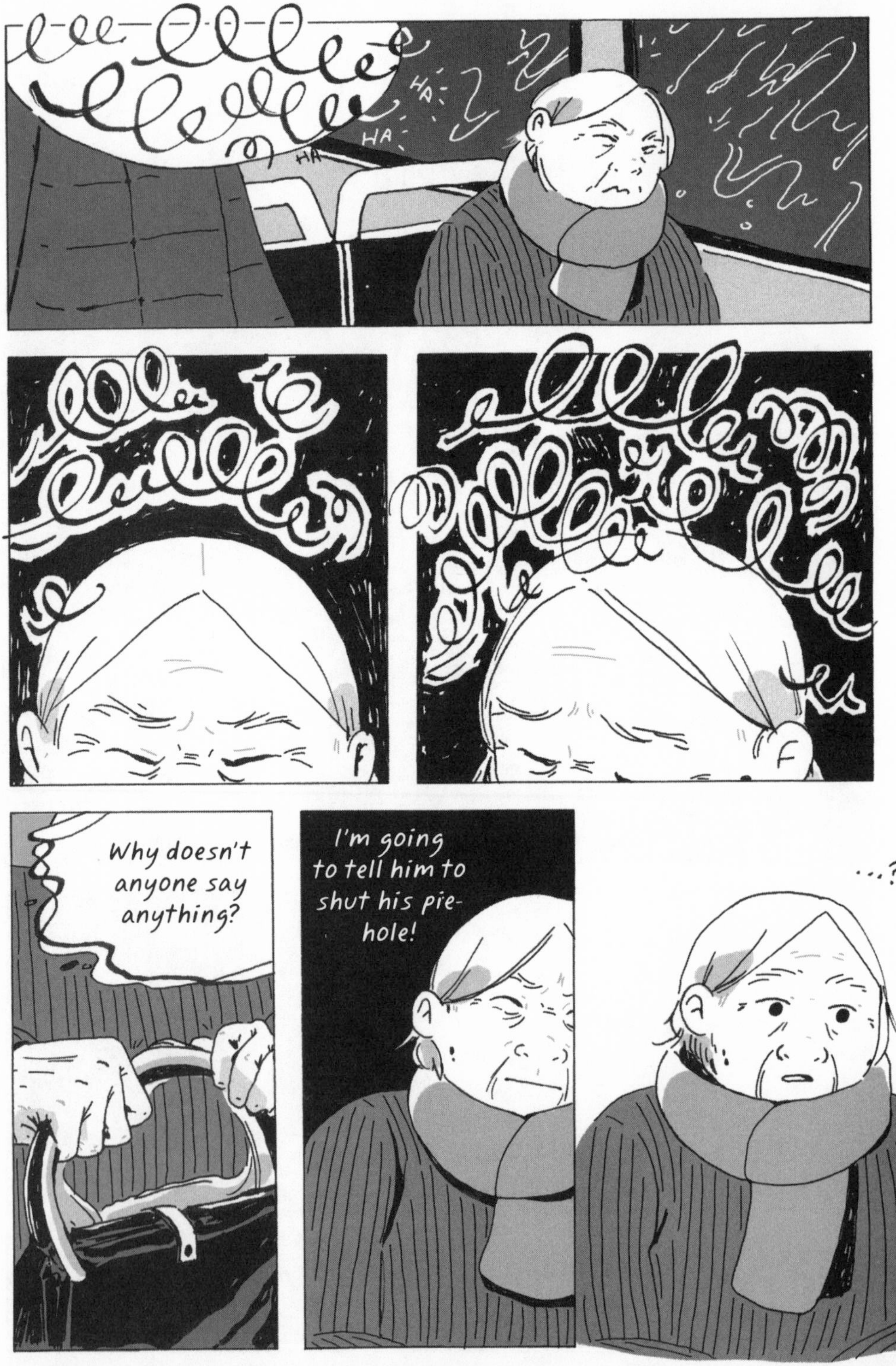
HA
HA
HA
Why doesn't anyone say anything?
I'm going to tell him to shut his pie-hole!
...?

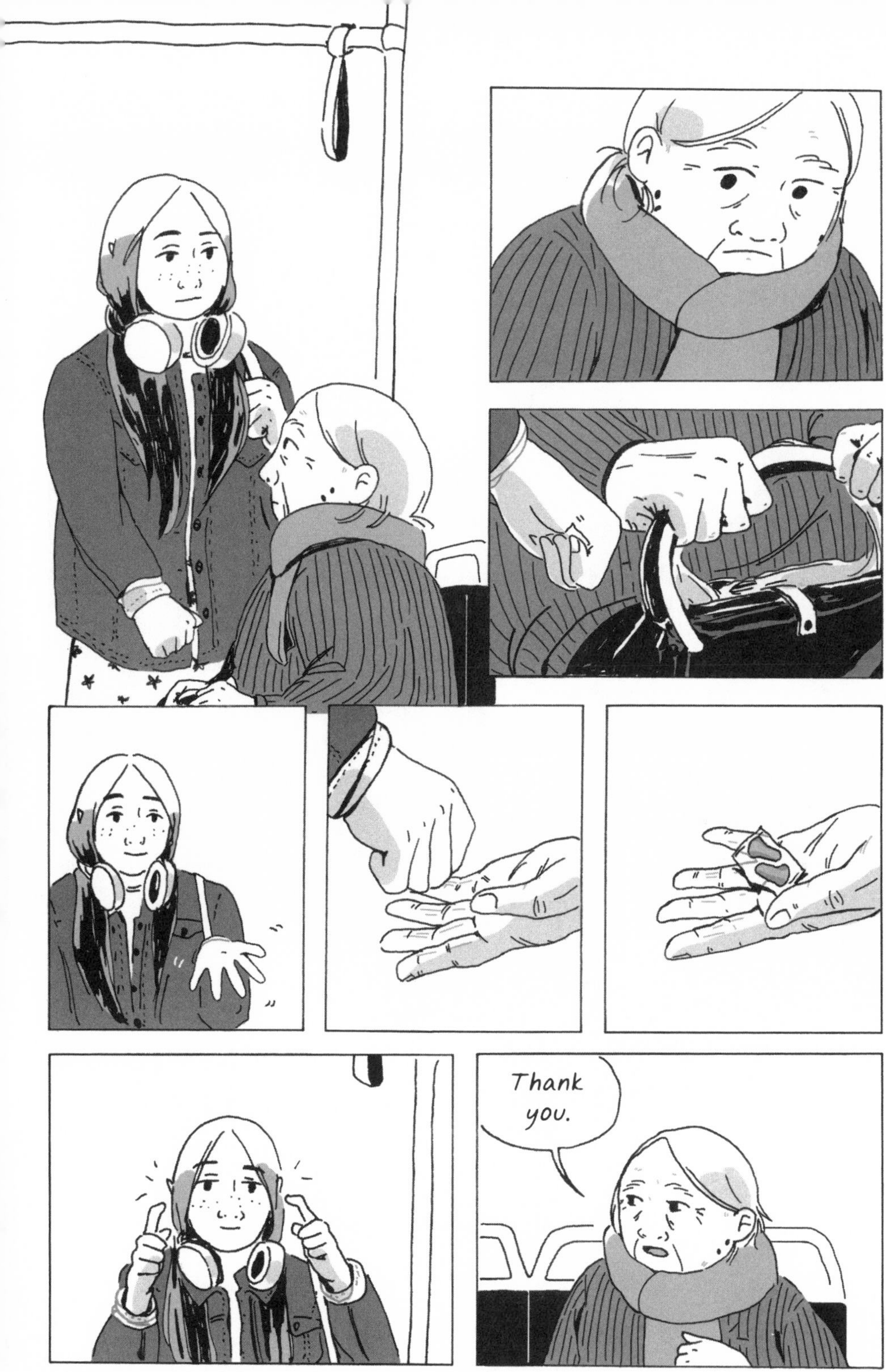
Thank you.

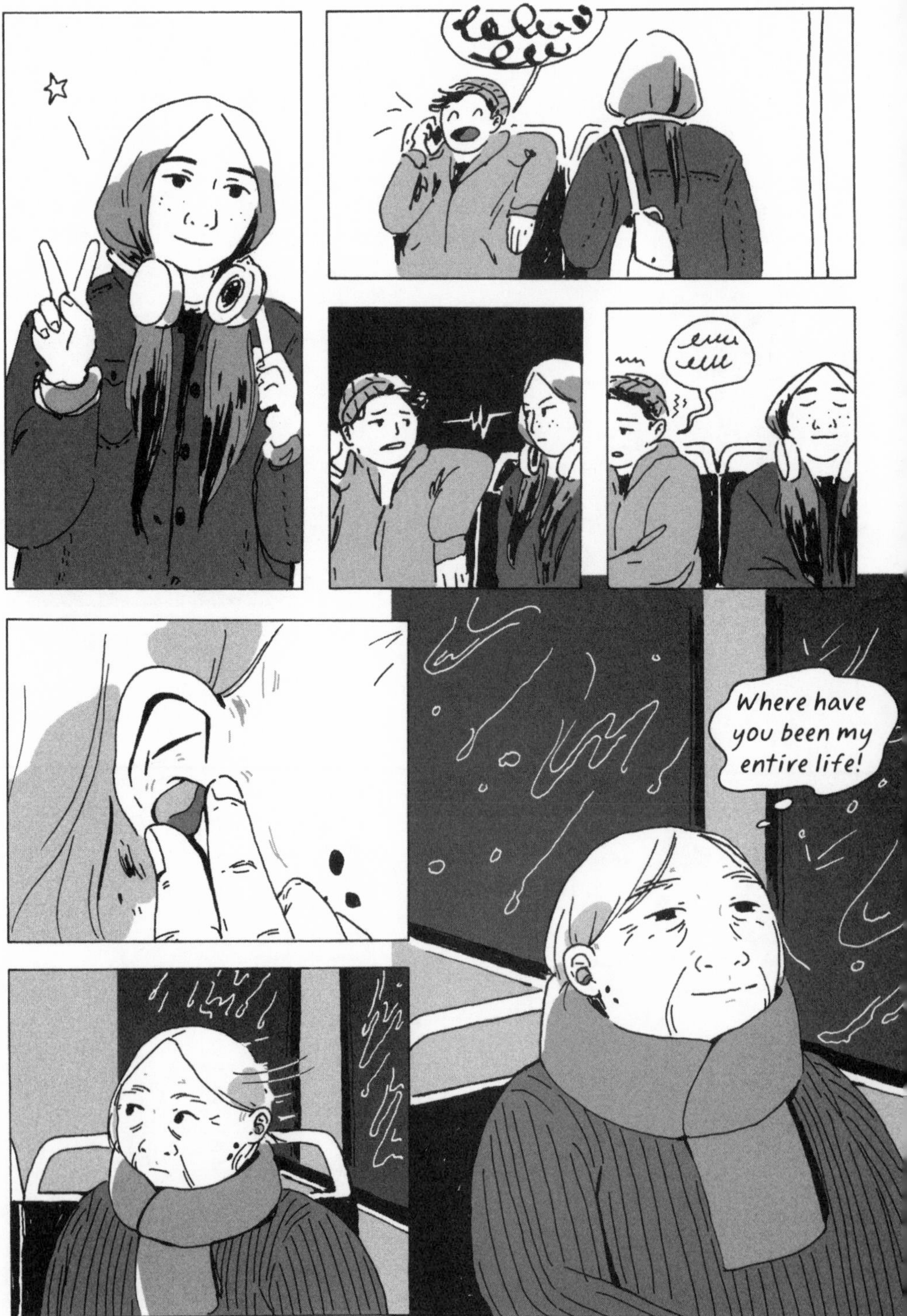
Where have you been my entire life!

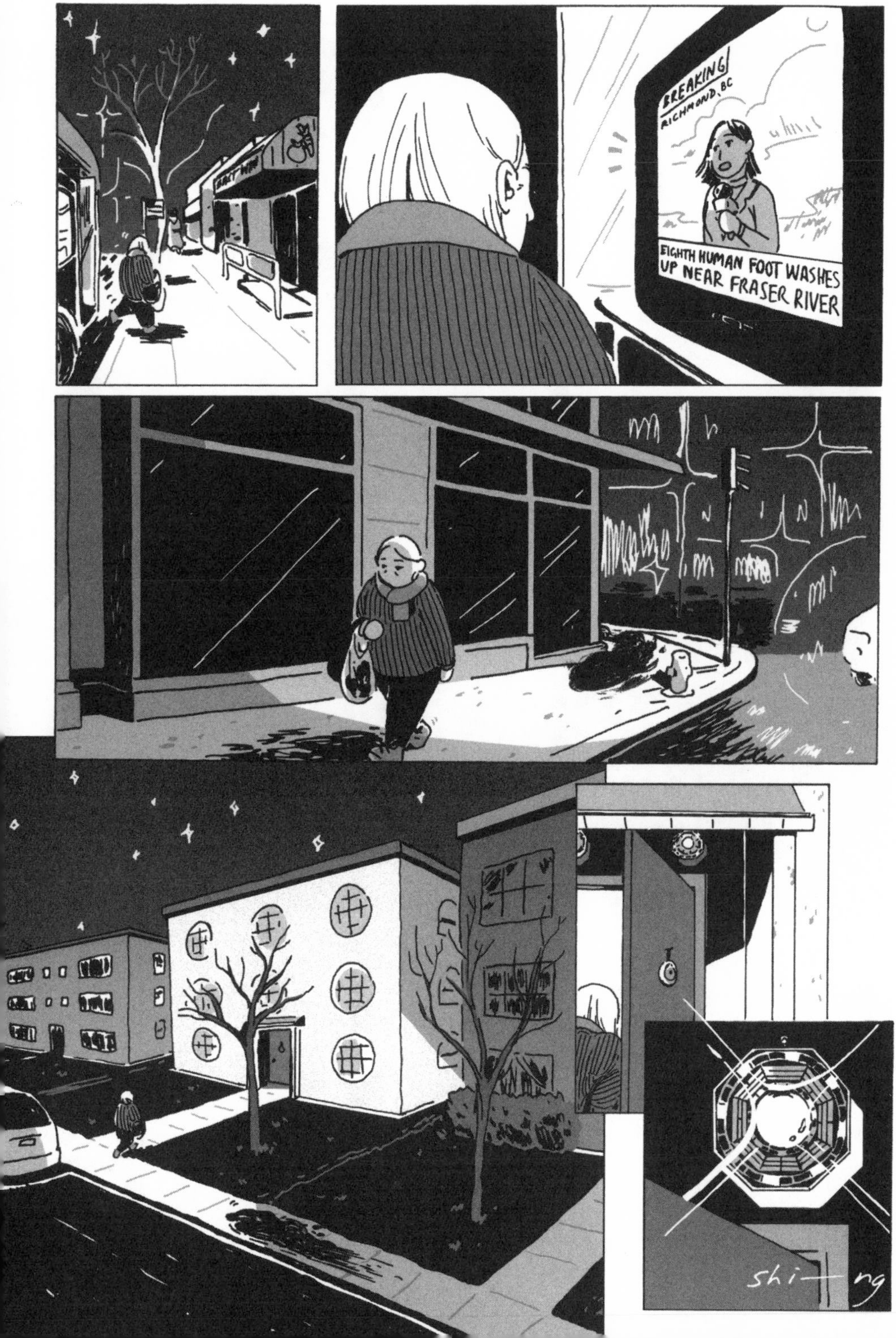
BREAKING
RICHMOND, BC
EIGHTH HUMAN FOOT WASHES UP NEAR FRASER RIVER
shi—ng

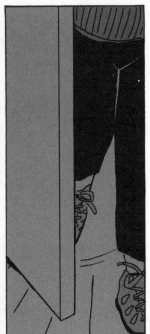

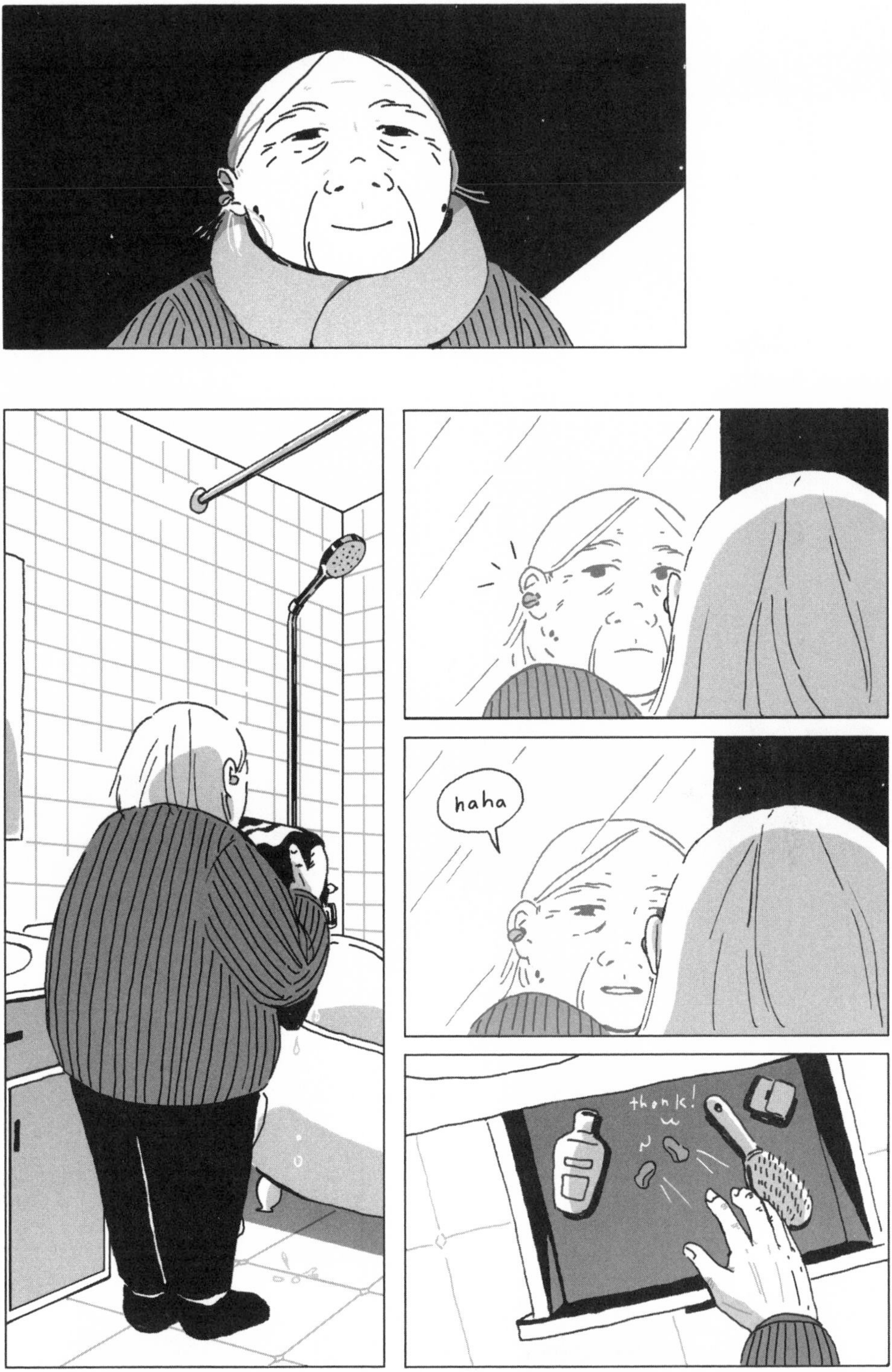
haha
thonk!

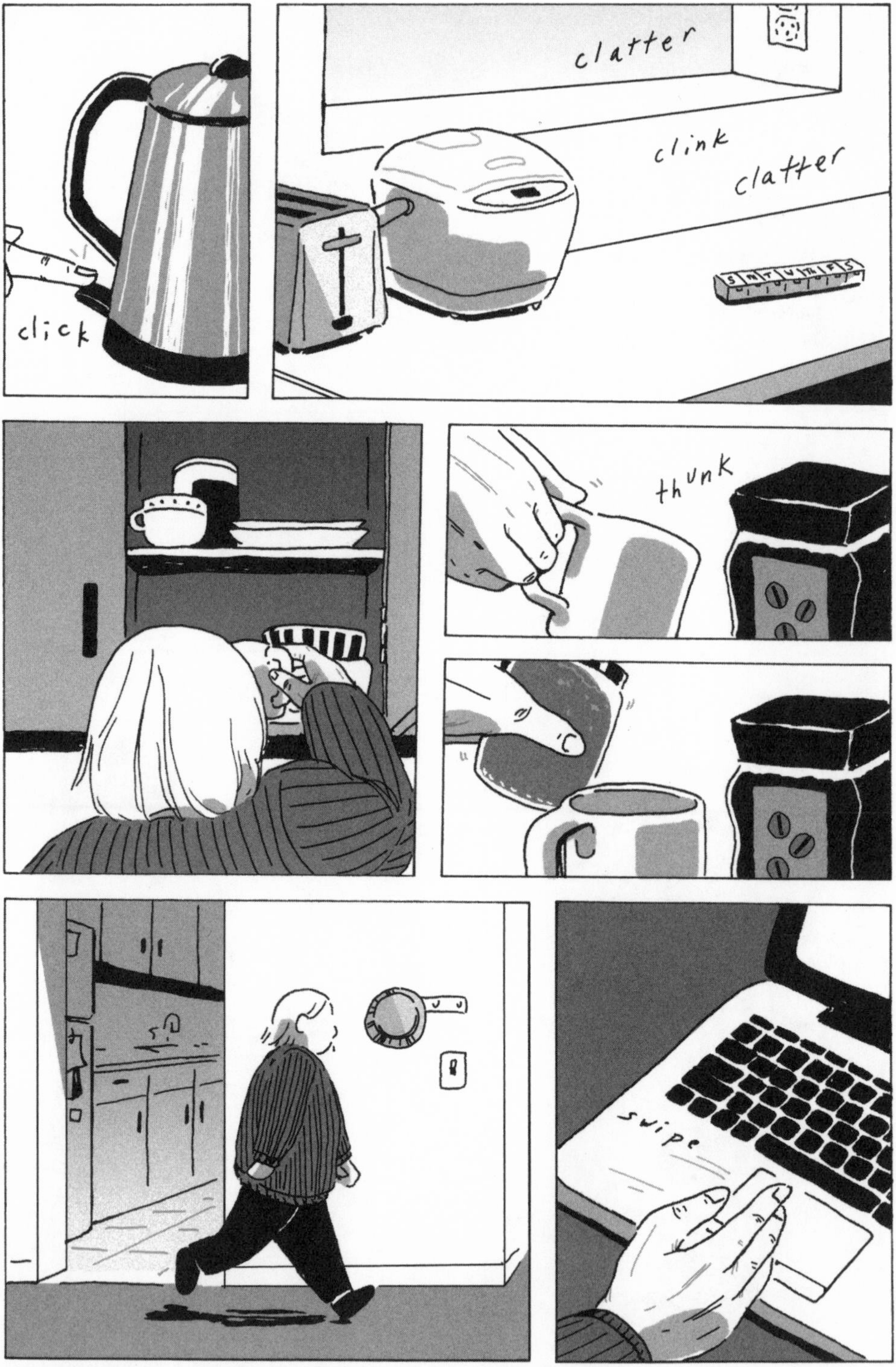
click
clatter
clink
clatter
thunk
swipe

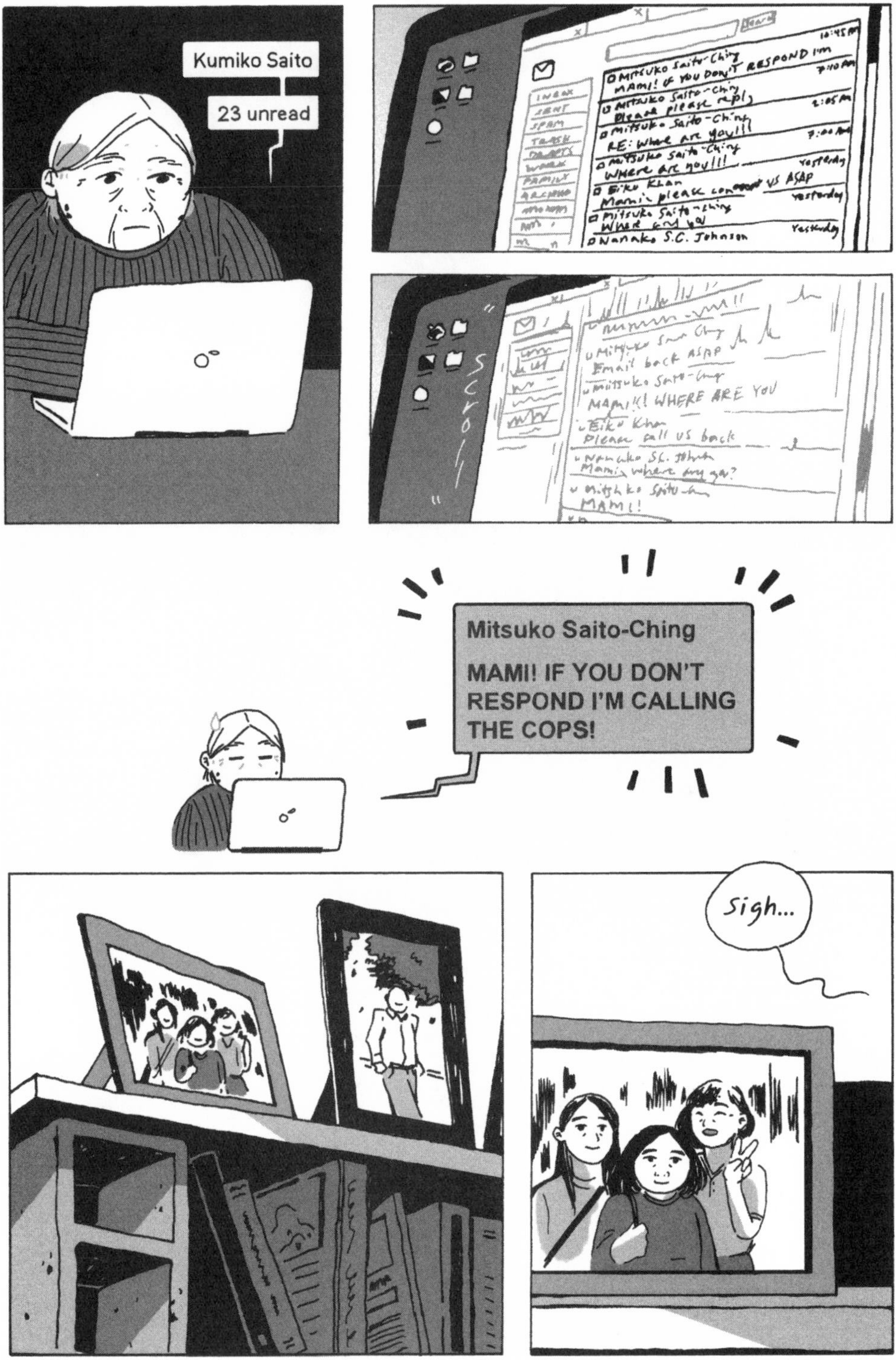

Kumiko Saito
23 unread
Mitsuko Saito-Ching
MAMI! IF YOU DON'T RESPOND I'm
Please please reply
RE: Where are you!!!
Where are you!!!
Eiko Khan
Nanako S.C. Johnson
Email back ASAP
MAMI!! WHERE ARE YOU
Please call us back
Mitsuko Saito-Ching
MAMI! IF YOU DON'T RESPOND I'M CALLING THE COPS!
Sigh...

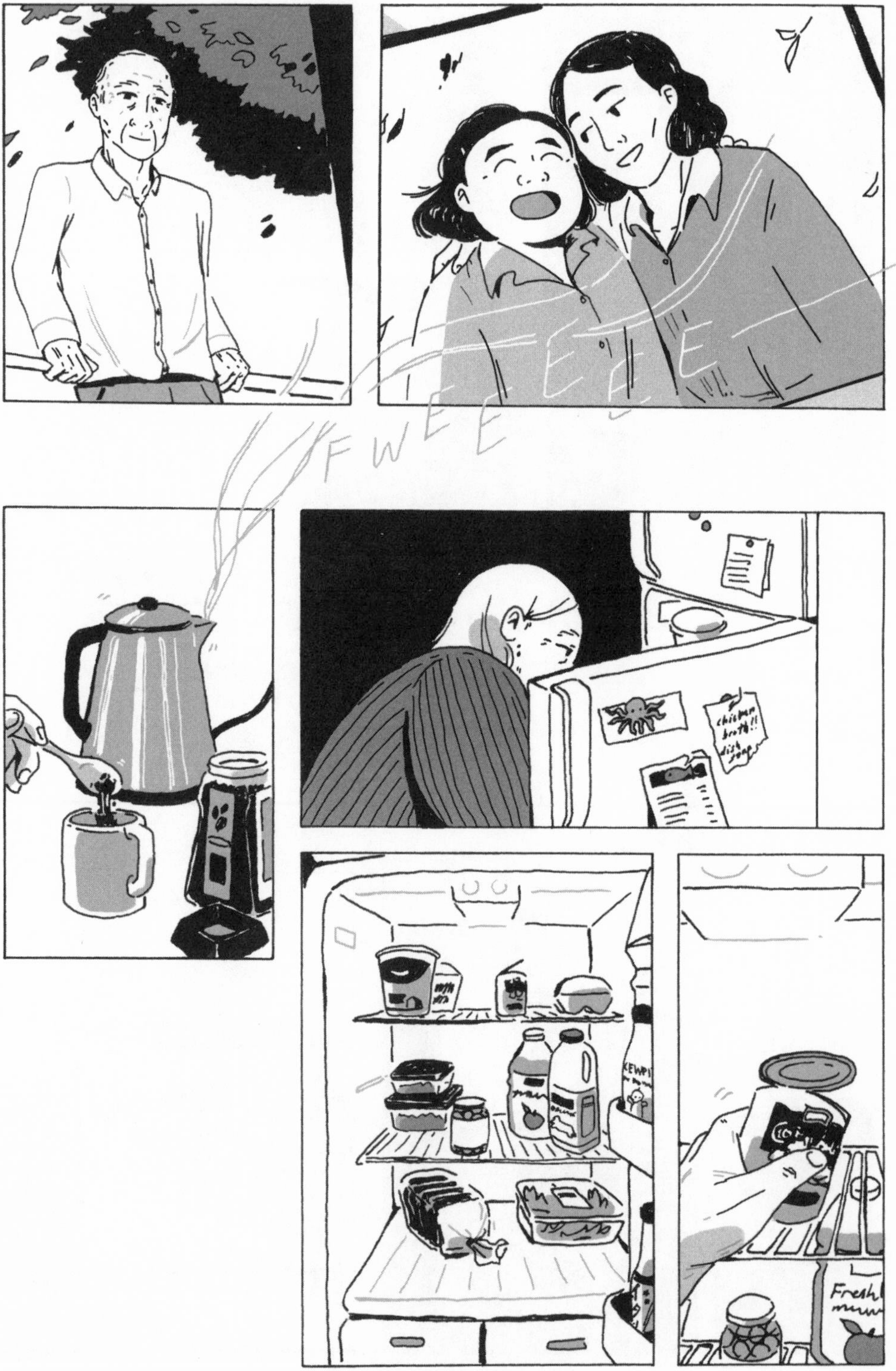
FWEEEEE
chicken broth!!
dish soap
KEWPIE
Fresh

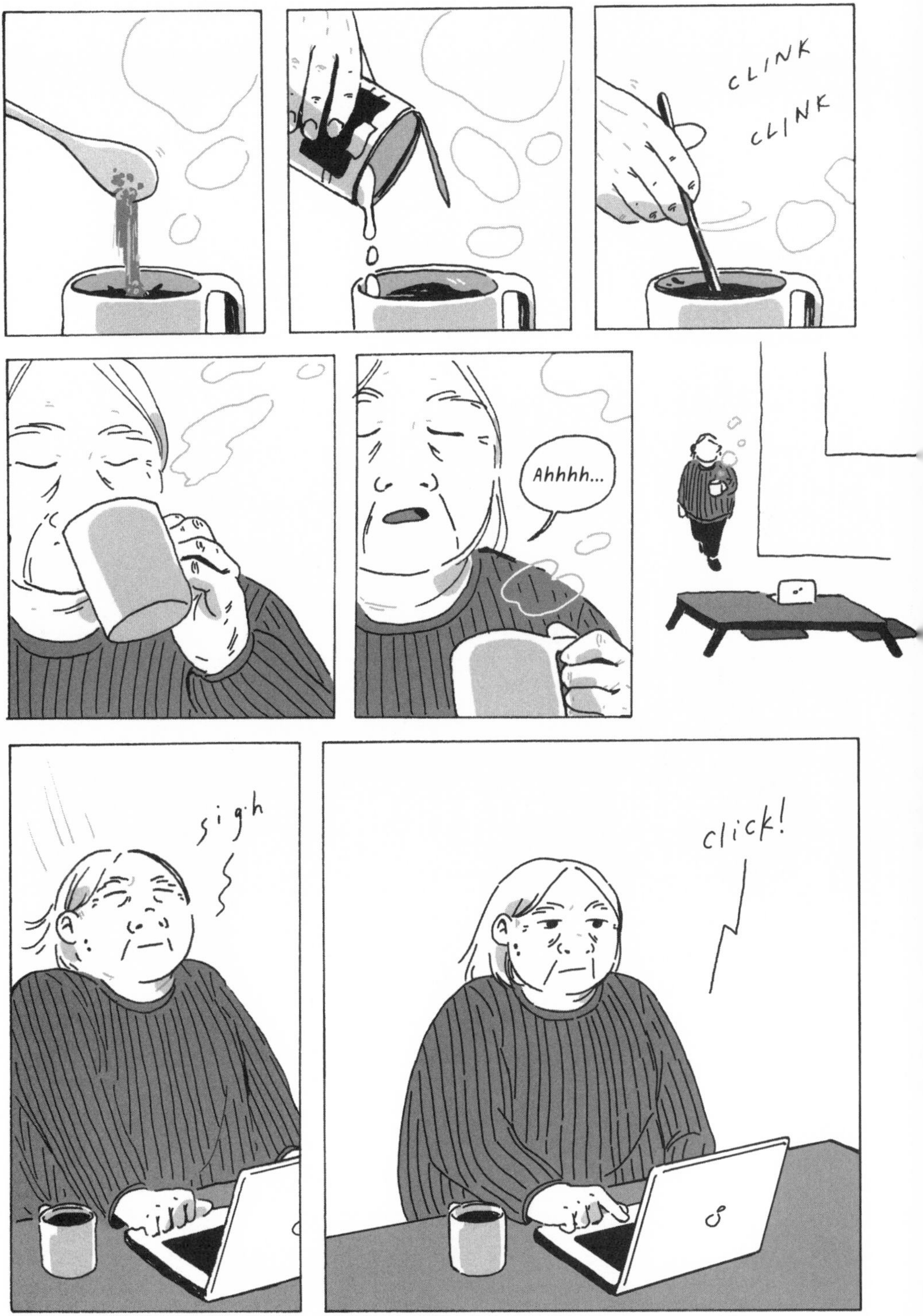
CLINK
CLINK
Ahhhh...
sigh
click!

MAMI, DO YOU REALIZE HOW WORRIED EVERYONE IS? YOUR BEHAVIOR DEMONSTRATES EXACTLY WHY WE WERE ALL OPPOSED TO YOUR IDEA OF FINDING YOUR OWN PLACE! MY GOD! IT IS IRRESPONSIBLE OF YOU NOT TO COMMUNICATE. THAT SHORT LETTER YOU WROTE WAS NOT ENOUGH INFO! YOU'LL CONTACT US AFTER YOU'RE 'SETTLED'? IT'S BEEN TWO WEEKS!!! WHAT IF YOU'VE HAD A MEDICAL EMERGENCY? DO YOU KNOW HOW THAT WOULD AFFECT ME? I WOULD FEEL SO GUILTY IF ANYTHING HAPPENED TO YOU! YOU ARE SO STUBBORN! HOW COULD YOU LEAVE ALL OF YOUR THINGS JUST LIKE THAT? WHAT WERE YOU THINKING? IF YOU ARE ILL, I REFUSE TO VISIT YOU IN THE HOSPITAL! TURN YOUR CELL PHONE BACK ON! YOU BETTER RESPOND BY MIDNIGHT OR I'M CALLING THE COPS! GOT IT, MA??? YOU'RE IN BIG TROUBLE!

MITSU!!!!

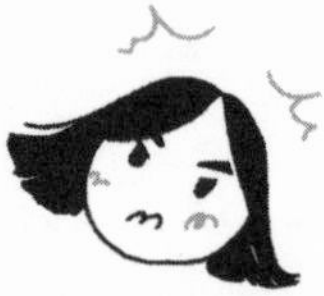

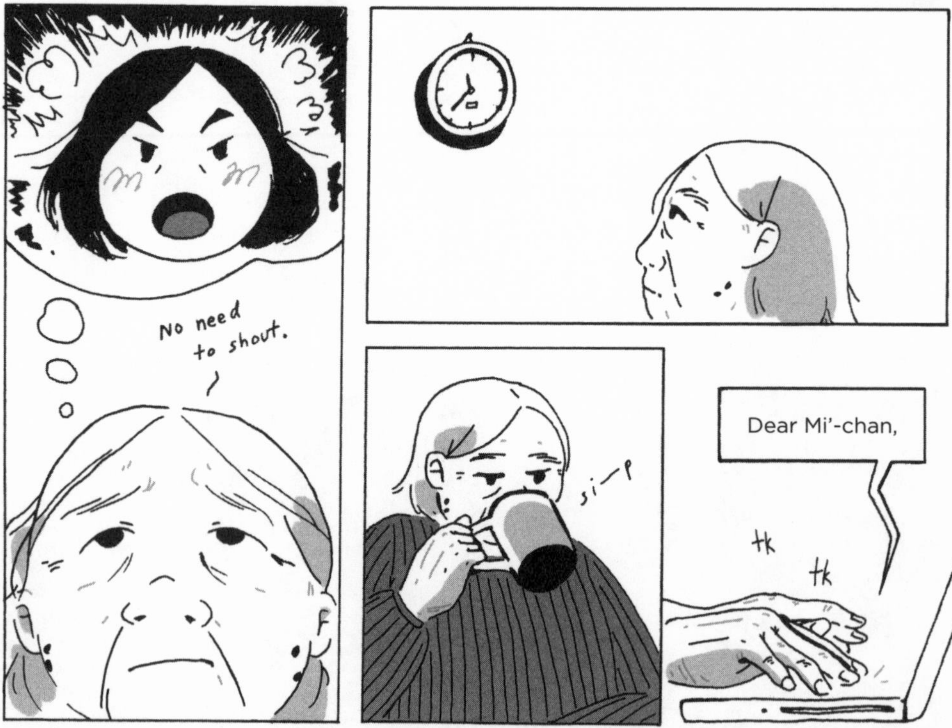
No need to shout.
si—p
Dear Mi'-chan,
tk
tk

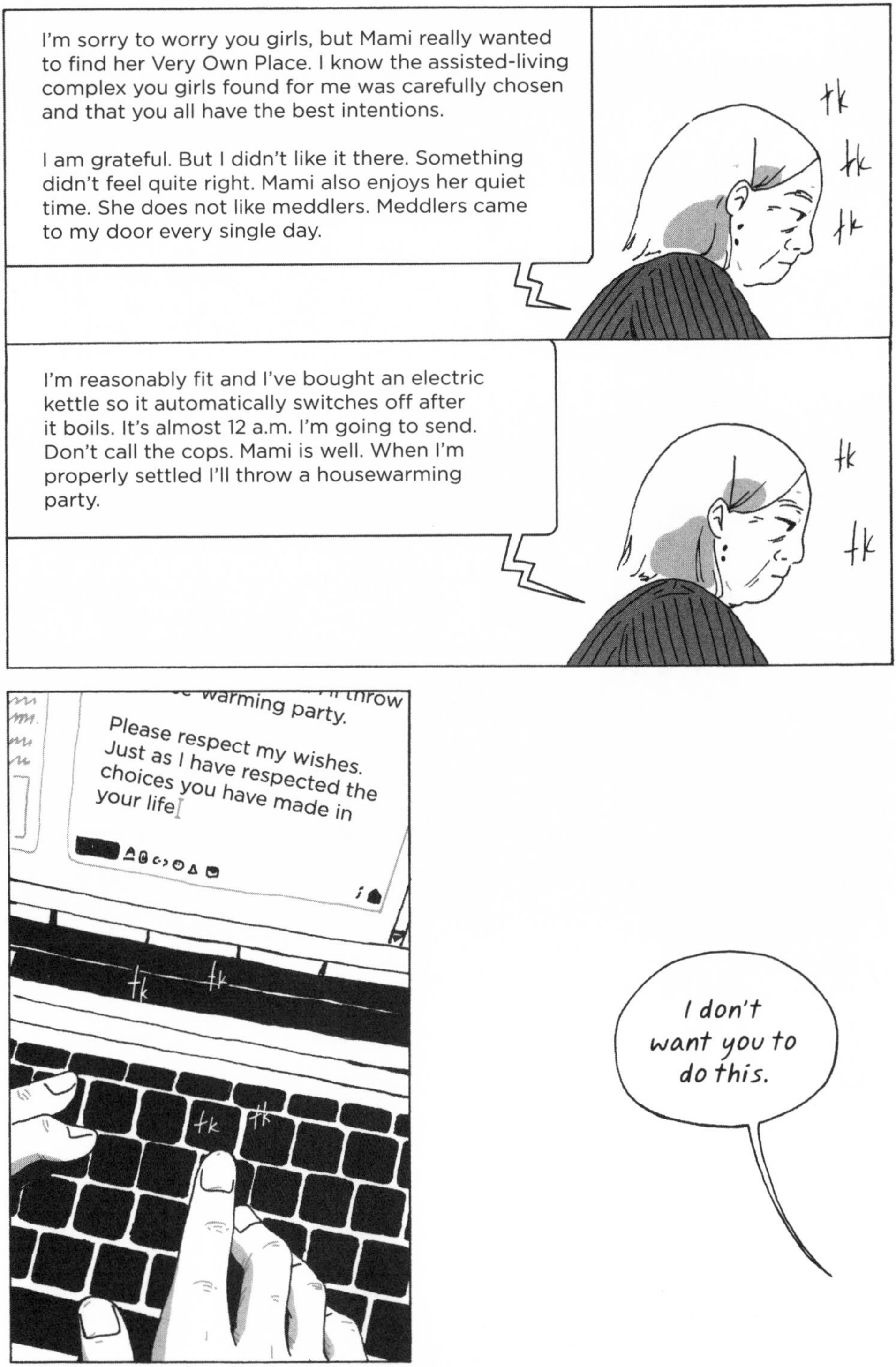
I'm sorry to worry you girls, but Mami really wanted to find her Very Own Place. I know the assisted-living complex you girls found for me was carefully chosen and that you all have the best intentions.
I am grateful. But I didn't like it there. Something didn't feel quite right. Mami also enjoys her quiet time. She does not like meddlers. Meddlers came to my door every single day.
tk
tk
tk
I'm reasonably fit and I've bought an electric kettle so it automatically switches off after it boils. It's almost 12 a.m. I'm going to send. Don't call the cops. Mami is well. When I'm properly settled I'll throw a housewarming party.
tk
tk
warming party.
Please respect my wishes. Just as I have respected the choices you have made in your life
tk
tk
tk
tk
I don't want you to do this.

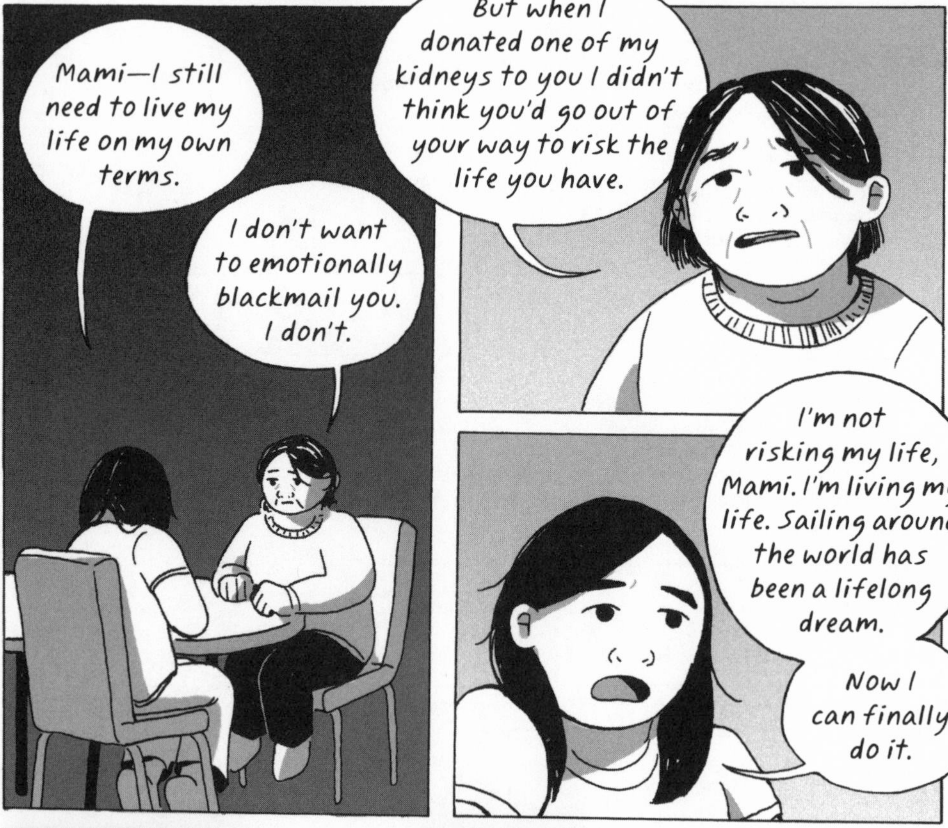

Mami—I still need to live my life on my own terms.
I don't want to emotionally blackmail you. I don't.
But when I donated one of my kidneys to you I didn't think you'd go out of your way to risk the life you have.
I'm not risking my life, Mami. I'm living my life. Sailing around the world has been a lifelong dream.
Now I can finally do it.

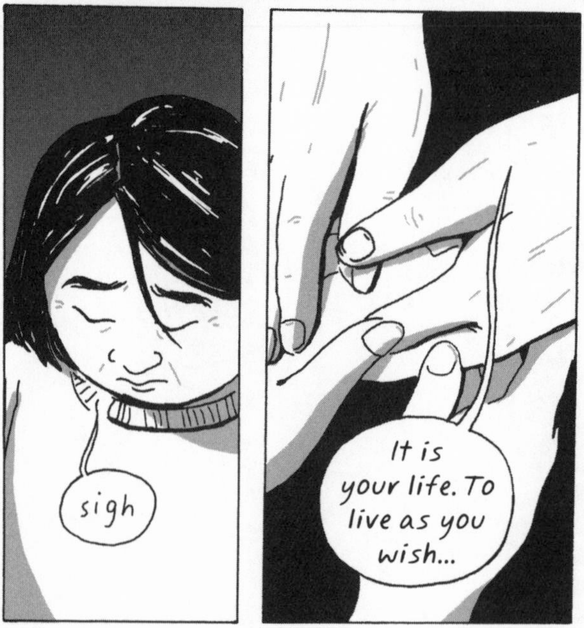

sigh
It is your life. To live as you wish...

Love,
Mami

PS: Don't write to me in all caps again or I'm cutting you out of my will.

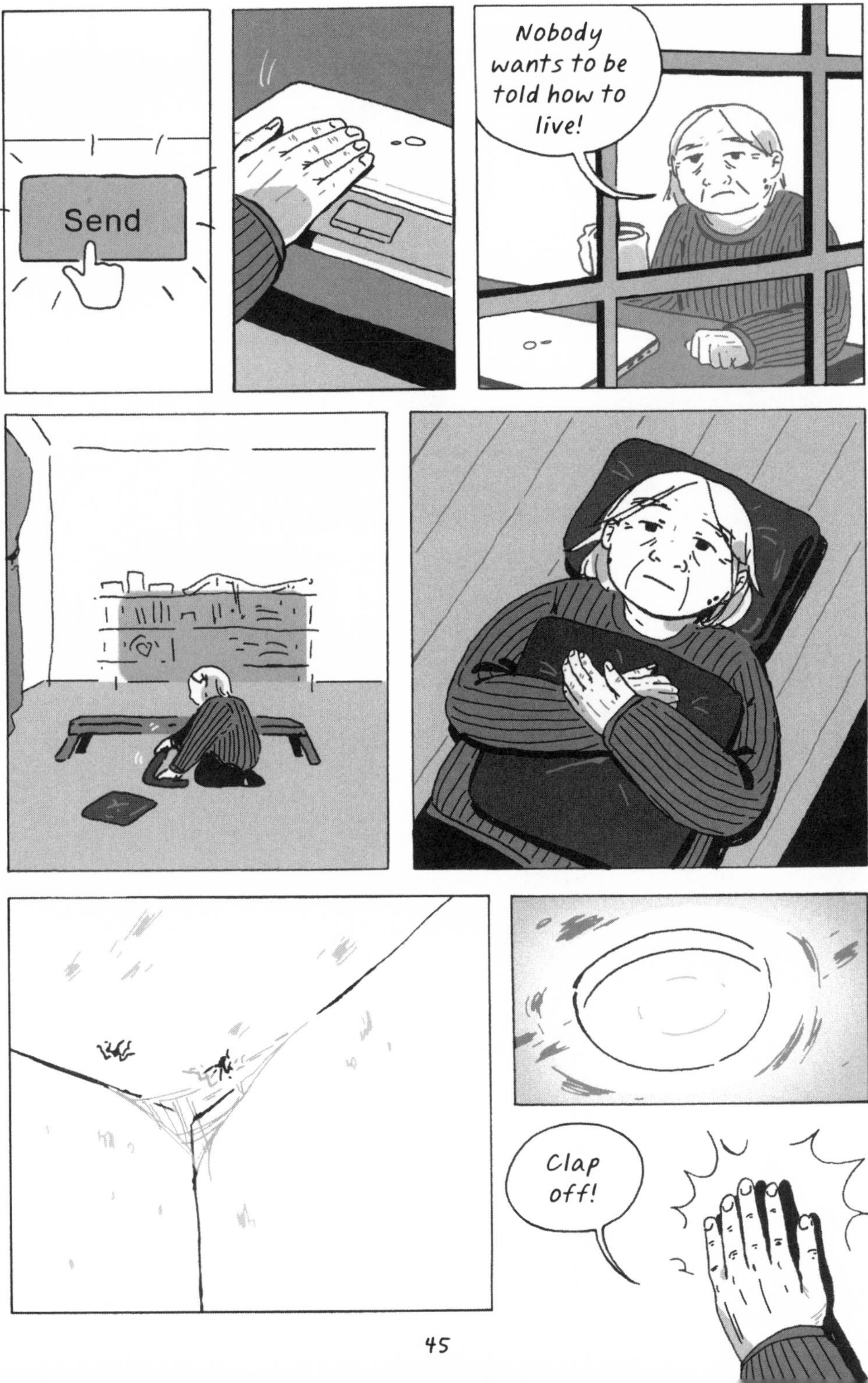
Send
Nobody wants to be told how to live!
Clap off!

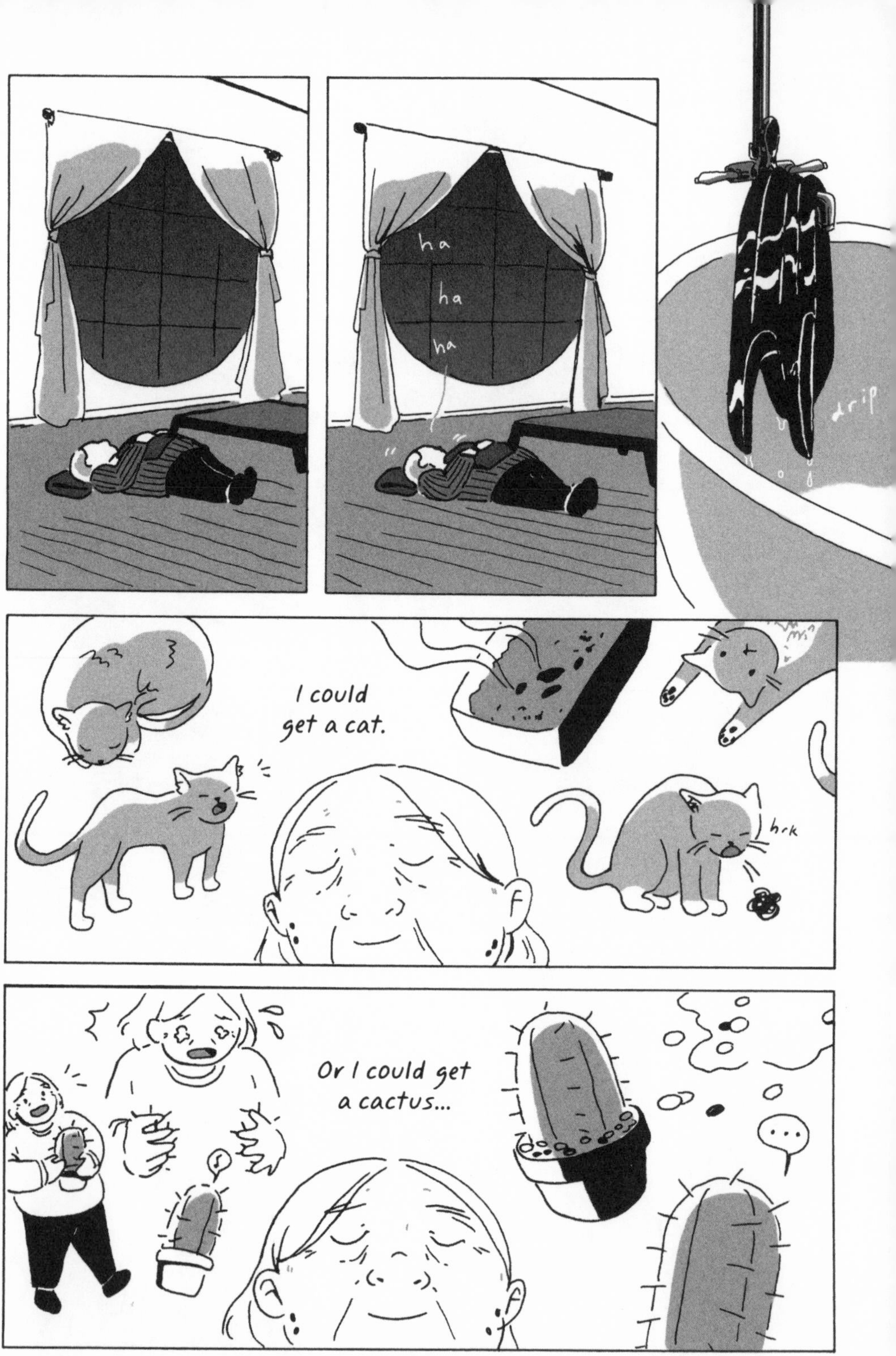
ha
ha
ha
drip
I could get a cat.
hrk
Or I could get a cactus...
...

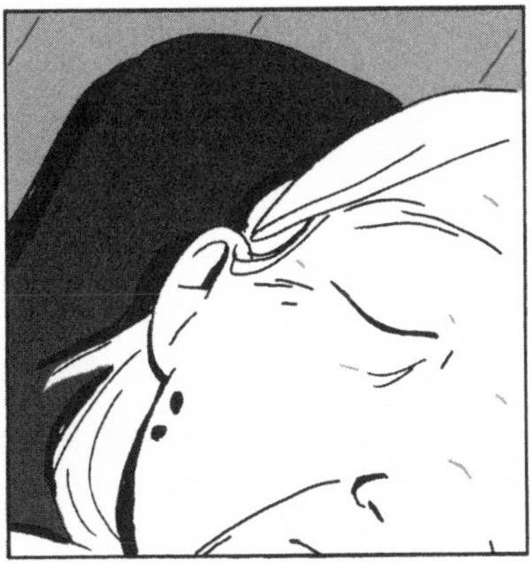
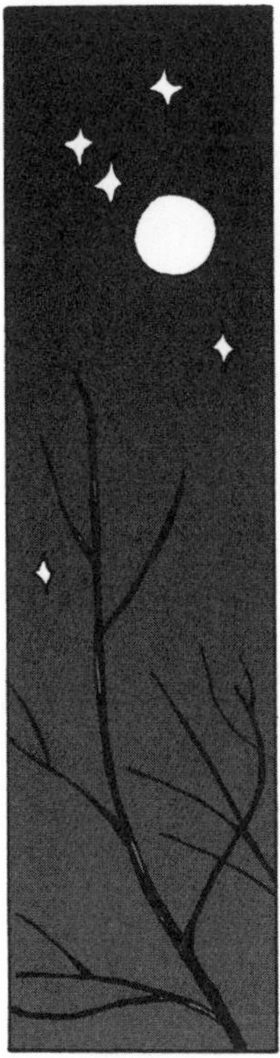
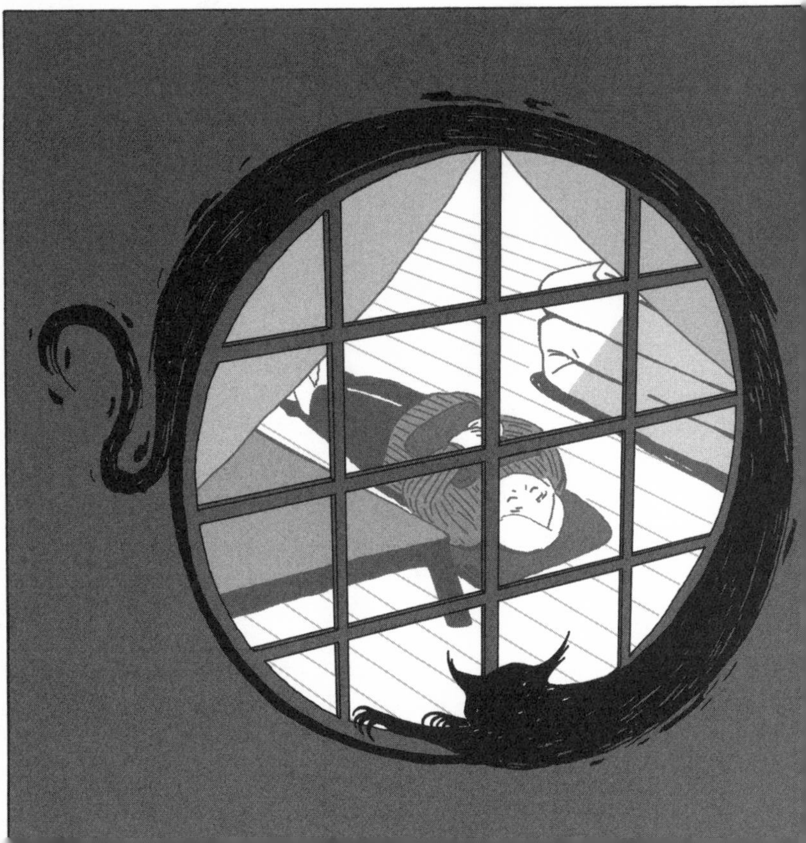

Chapter Three

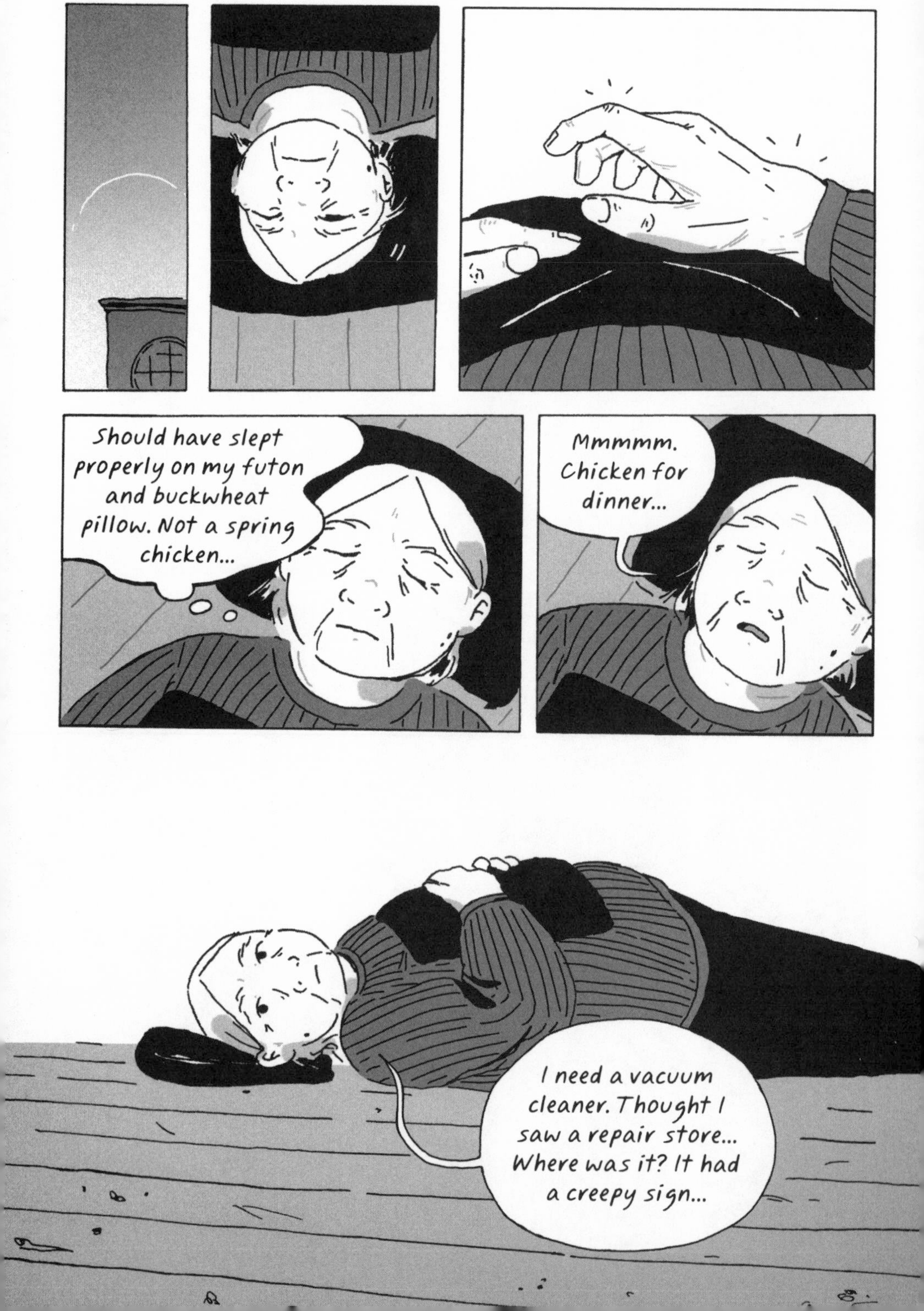
Should have slept properly on my futon and buckwheat pillow. Not a spring chicken...
Mmmmm. Chicken for dinner...
I need a vacuum cleaner. Thought I saw a repair store... Where was it? It had a creepy sign...

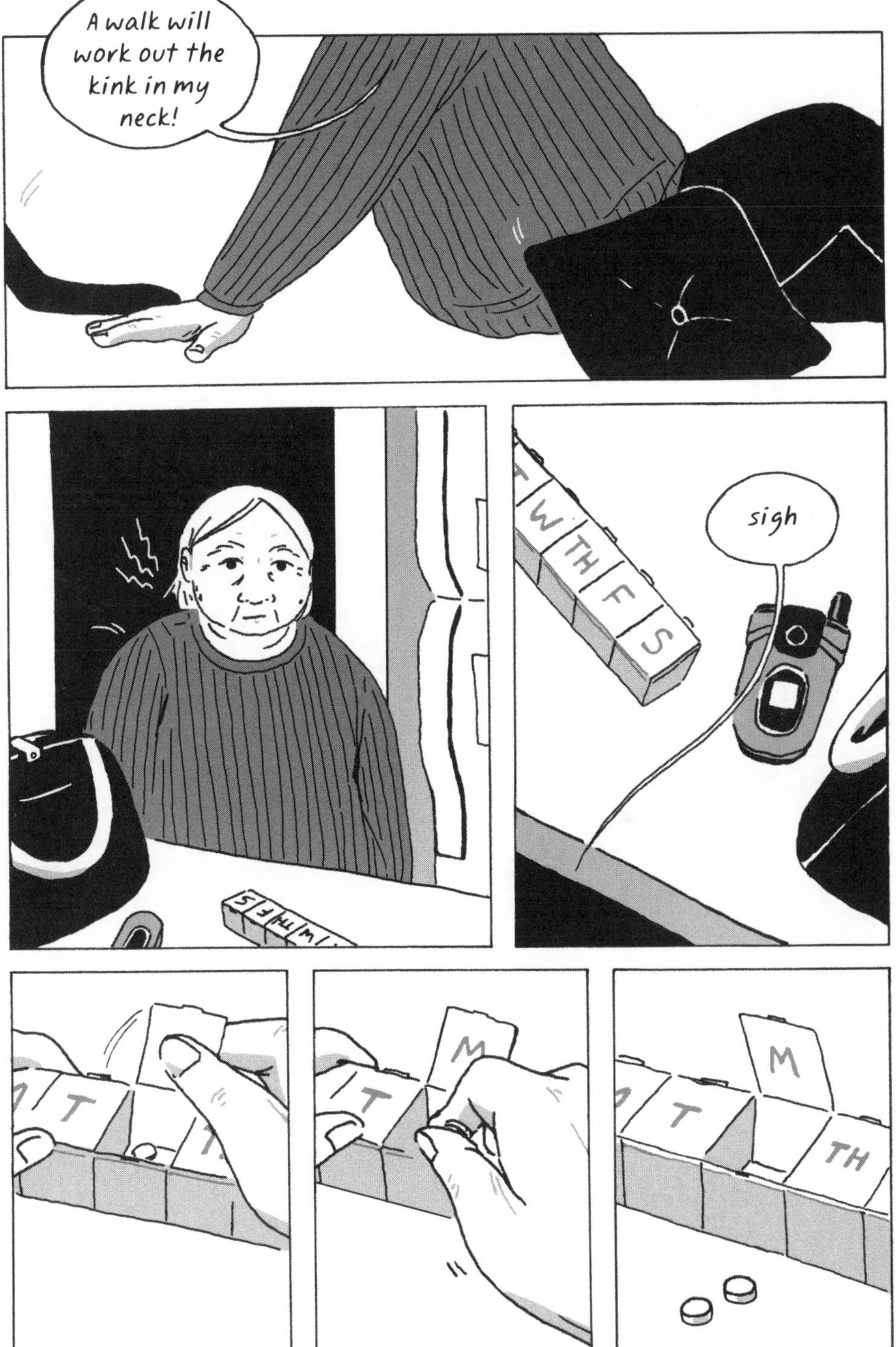
A walk will work out the kink in my neck!
sigh

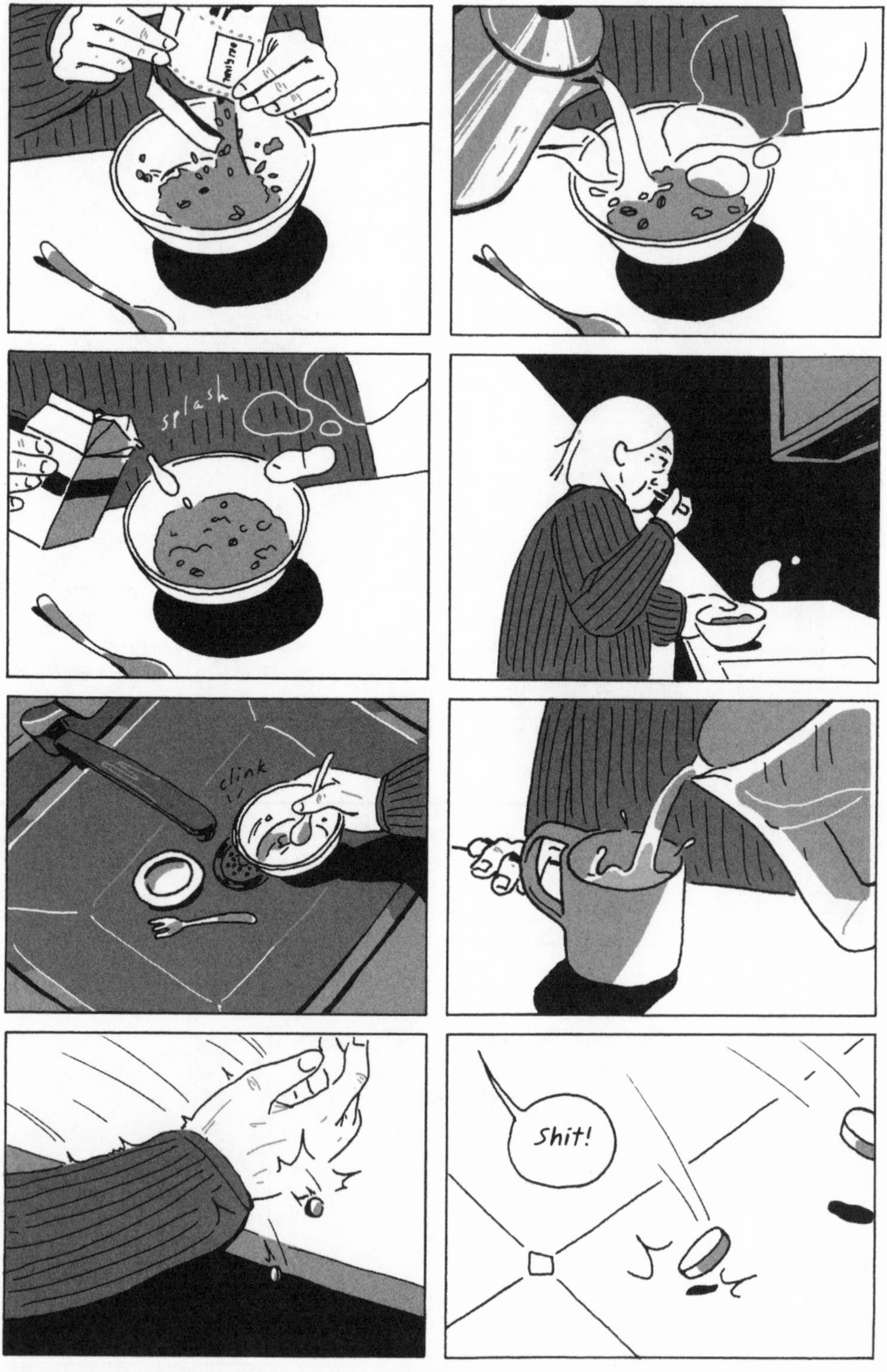
splash
clink
Shit!

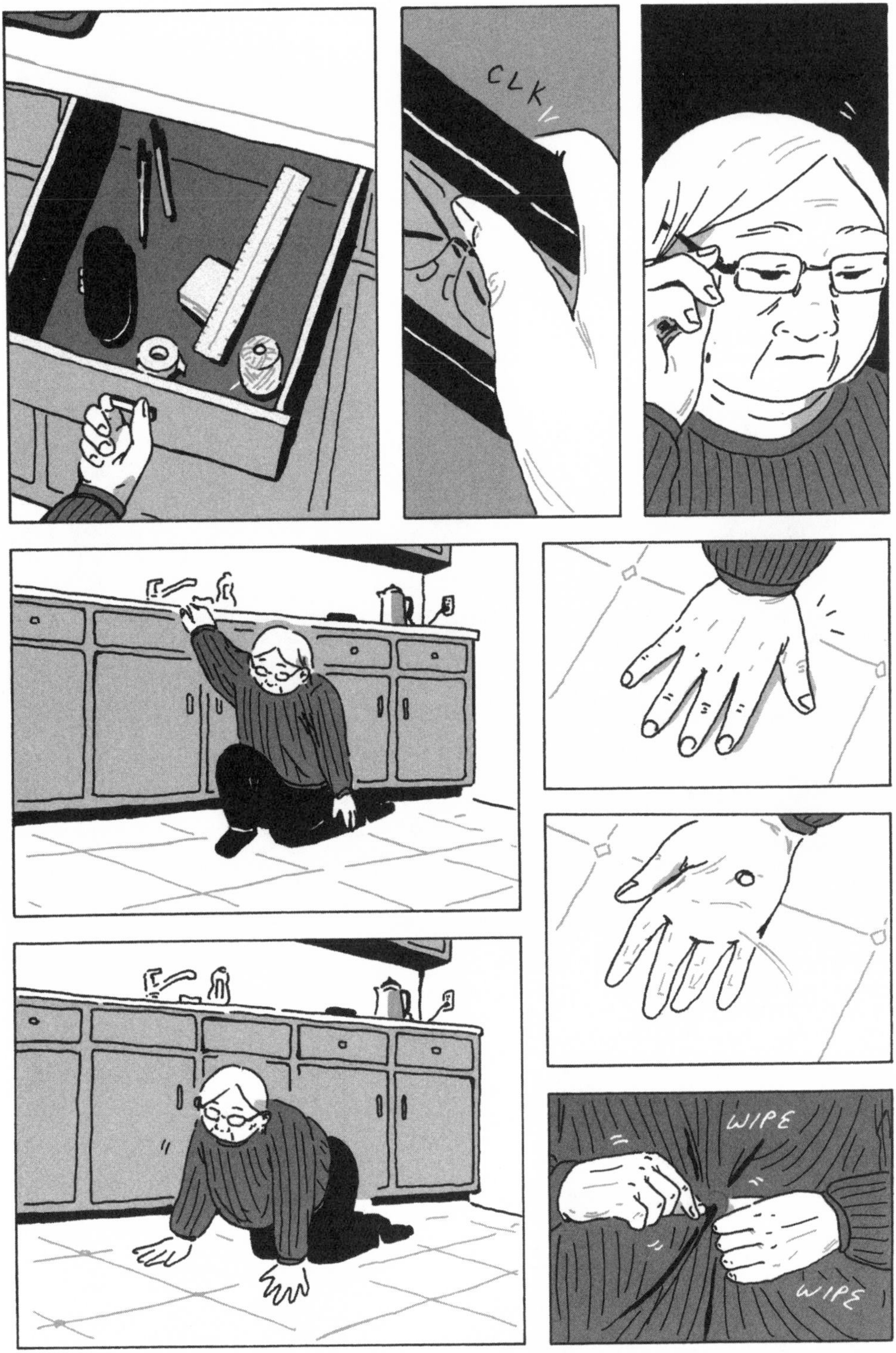
CLK
WIPE
WIPE

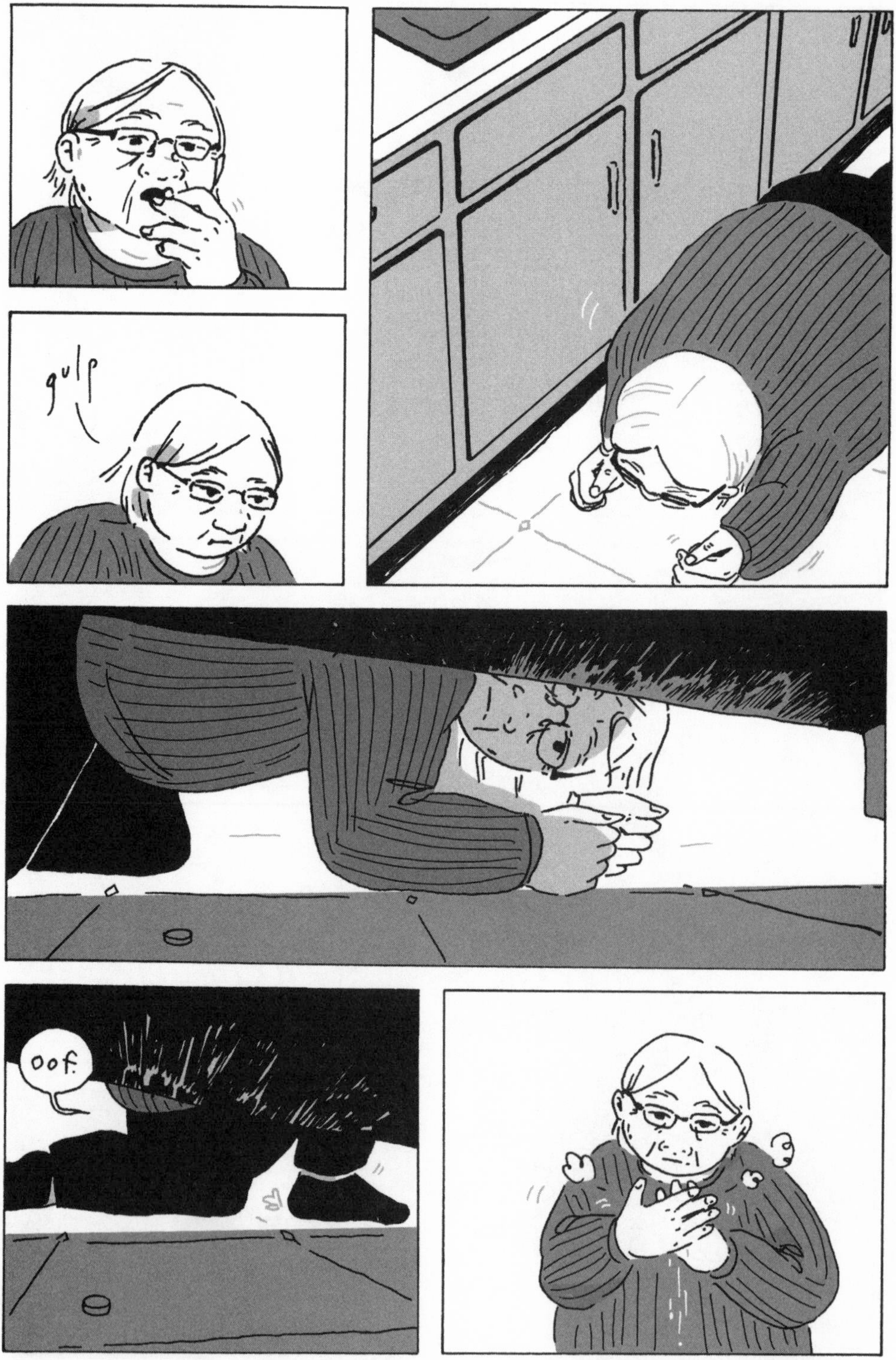
gulp
oof.

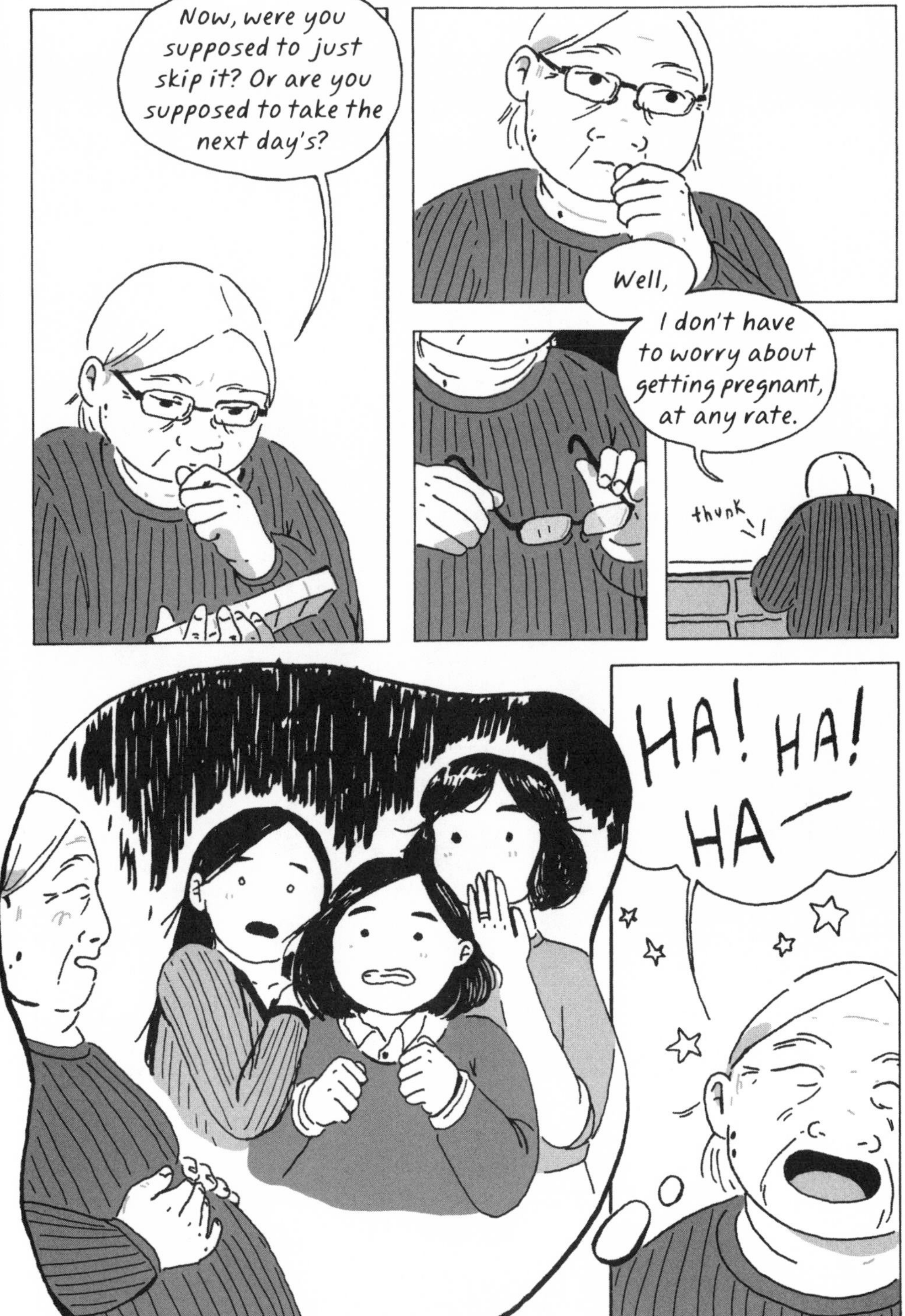
Now, were you supposed to just skip it? Or are you supposed to take the next day's?
Well,
I don't have to worry about getting pregnant, at any rate.
thunk
HA! HA! HA—

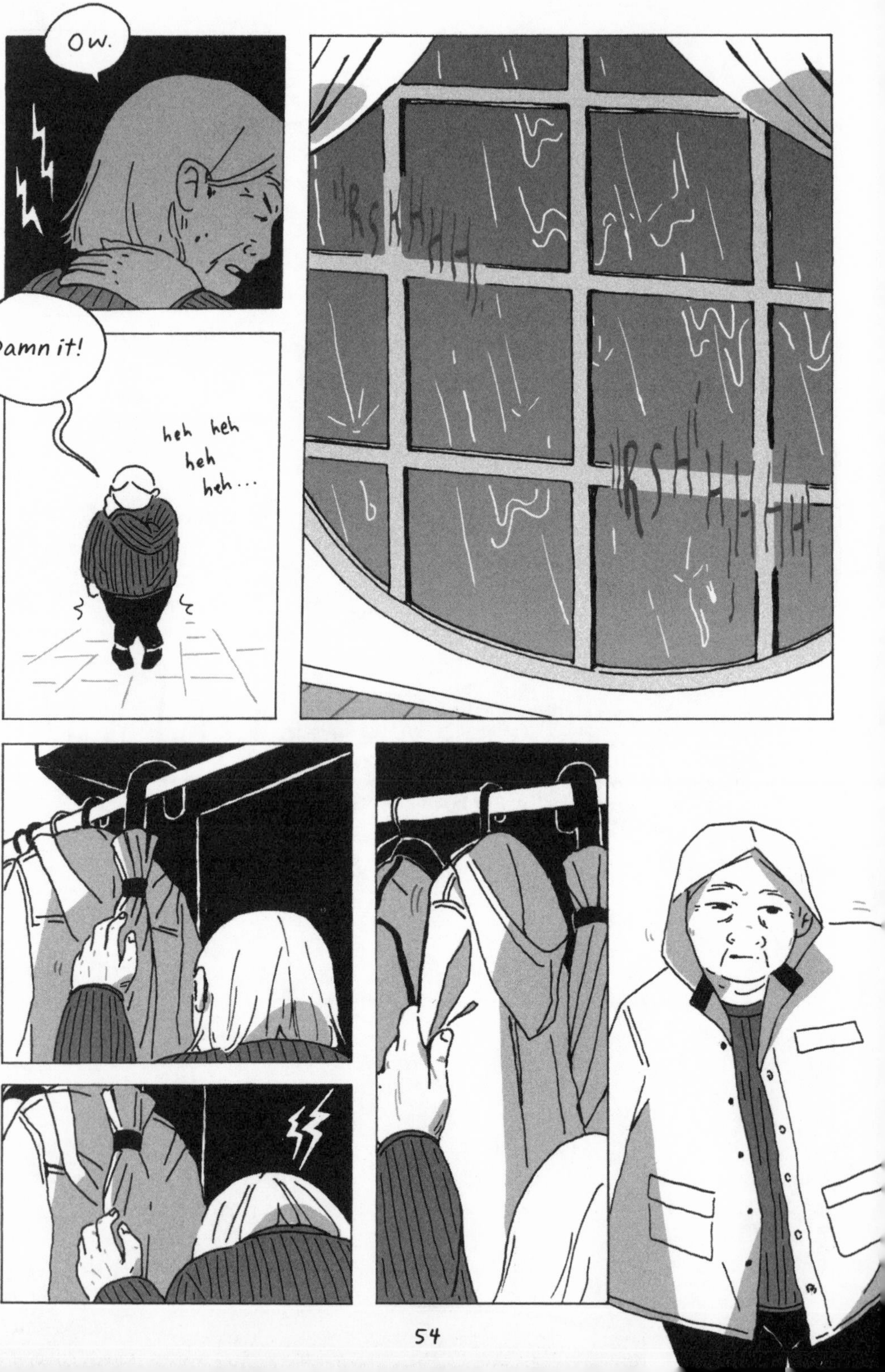
Ow.
Damn it!
heh heh
heh
heh...
RSHHHH
RSHHHHH

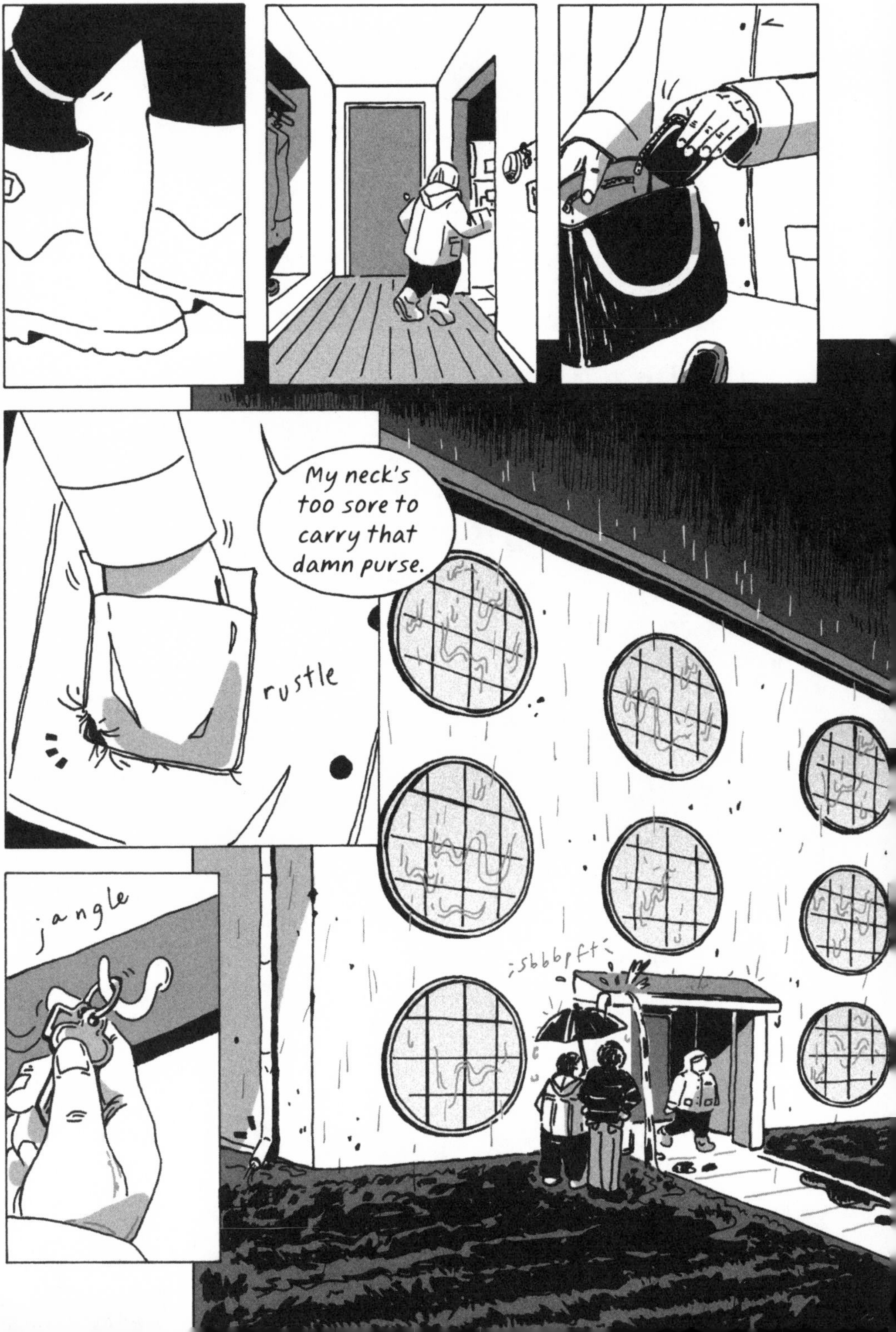
My neck's too sore to carry that damn purse.
rustle
jangle
¡sbbbpft!

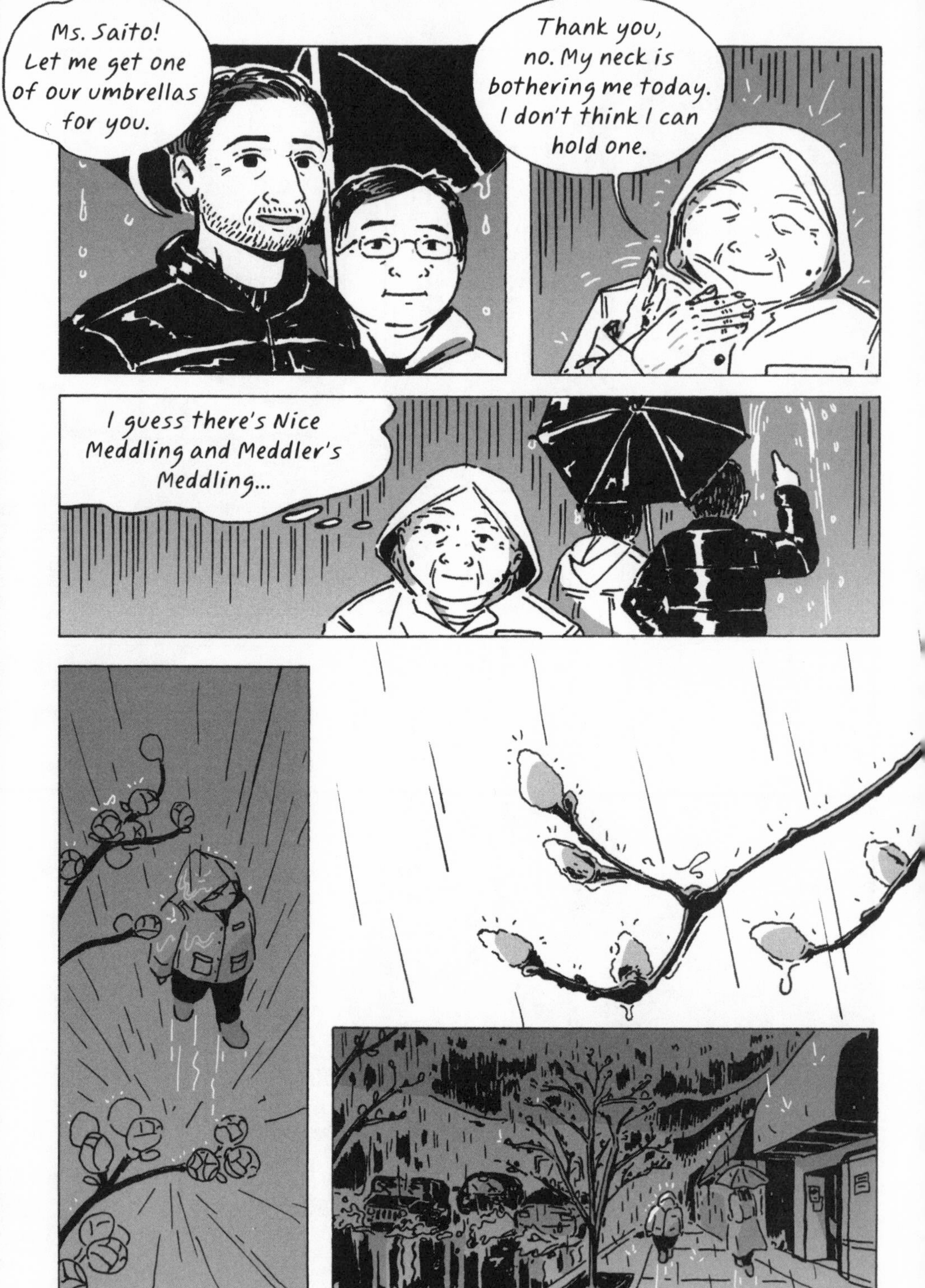
Ms. Saito! Let me get one of our umbrellas for you.
Thank you, no. My neck is bothering me today. I don't think I can hold one.
I guess there's Nice Meddling and Meddler's Meddling...

CANADA
2 DOLLARS

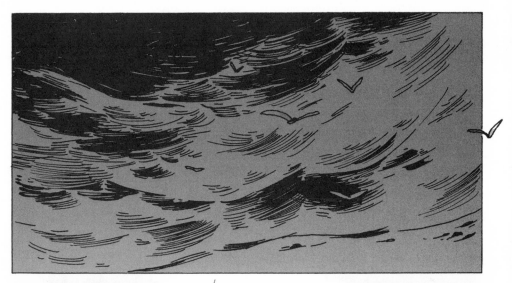

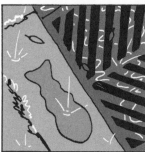

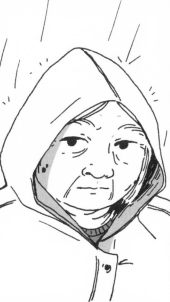

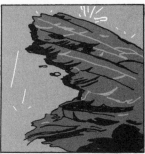

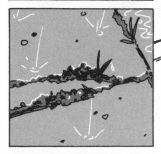

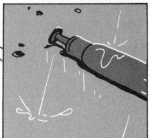

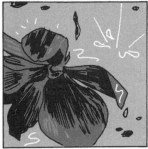

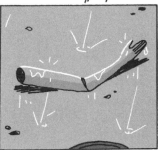

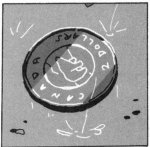

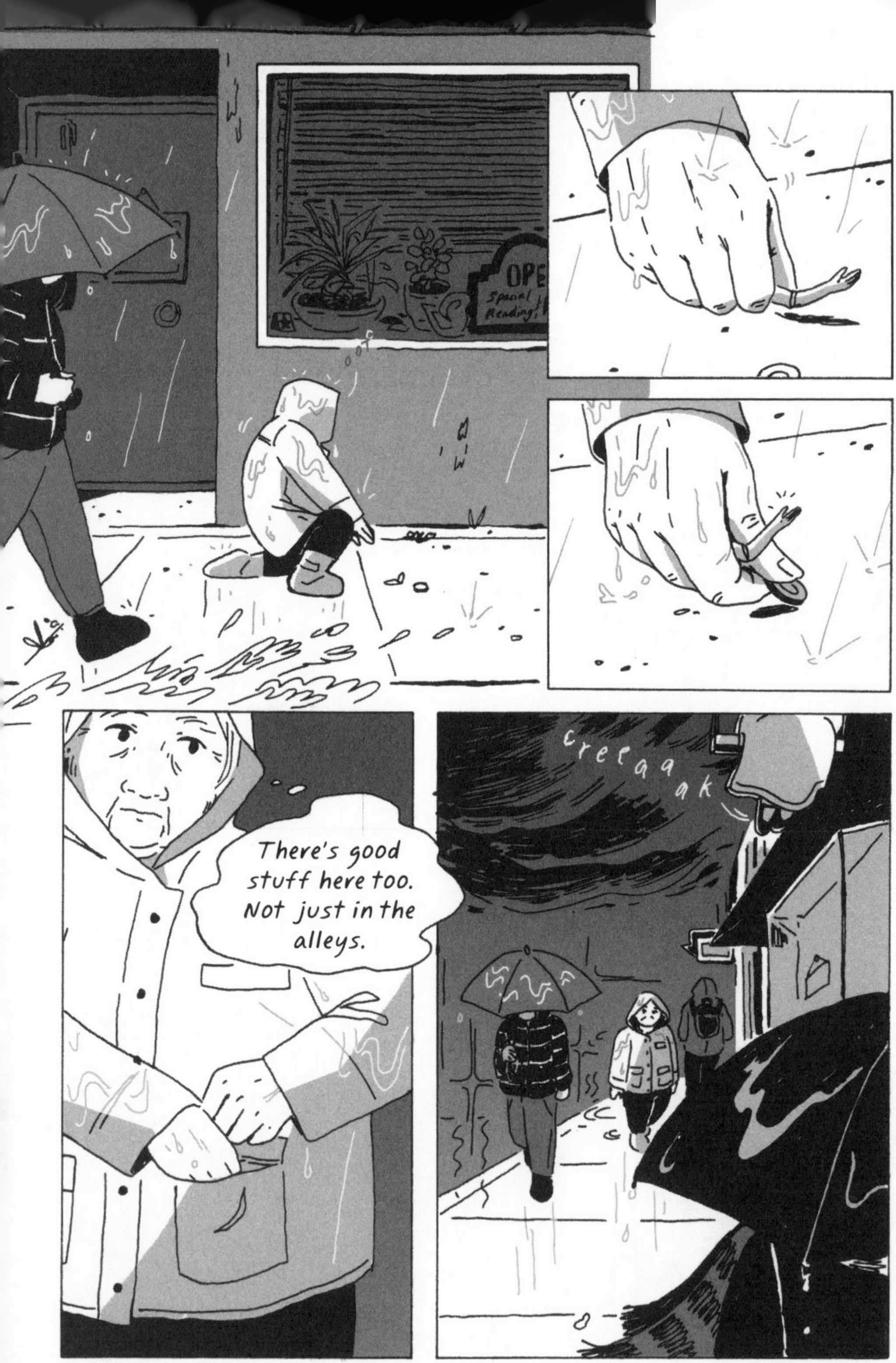
OPE
Special Reading
There's good stuff here too. Not just in the alleys.
creeaaak

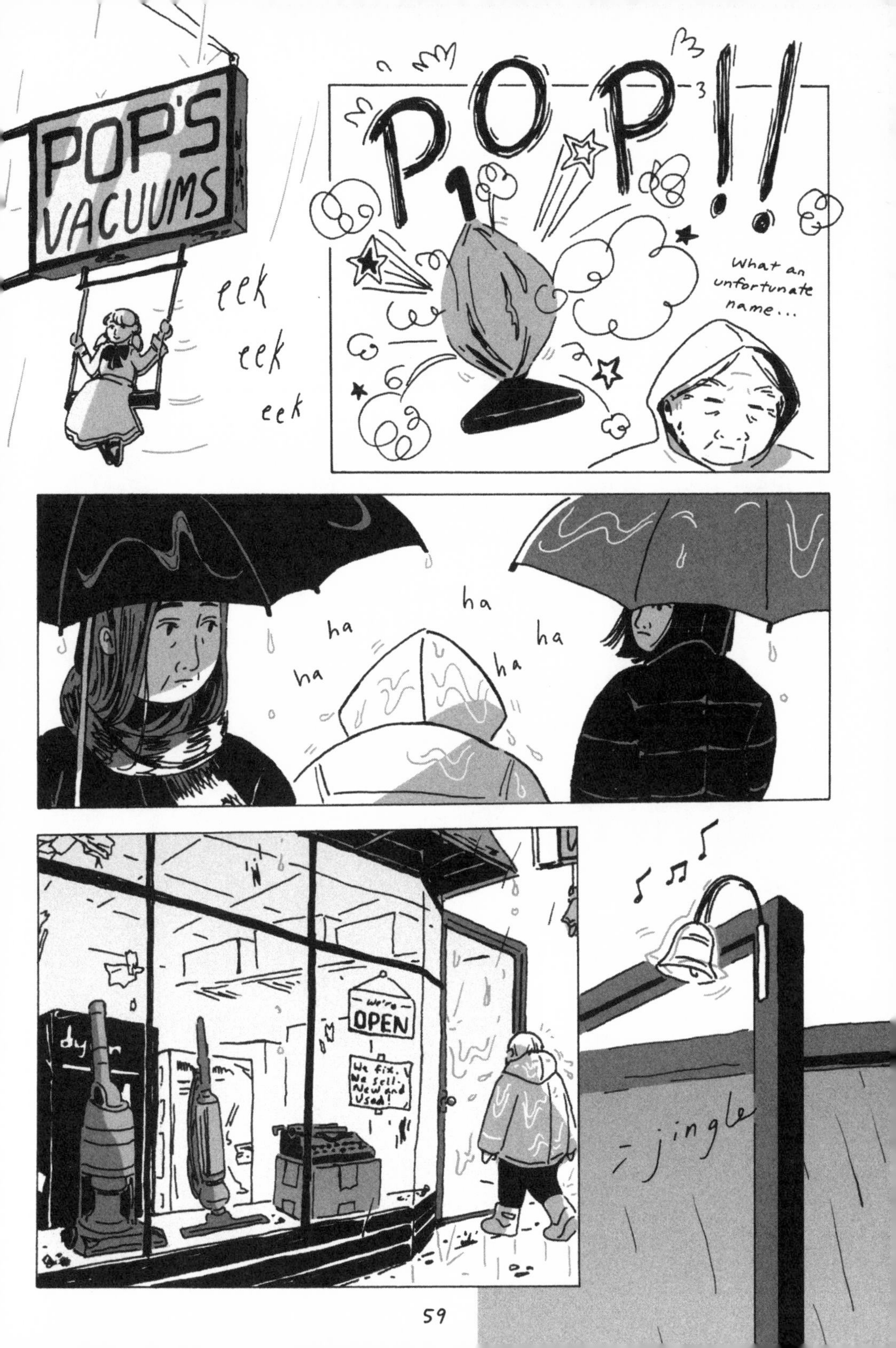
POP'S VACUUMS
eek
eek
eek
POP!!
What an unfortunate name...
ha
ha
ha
ha
ha
We're OPEN
We fix. We sell. New and Used!
jingle

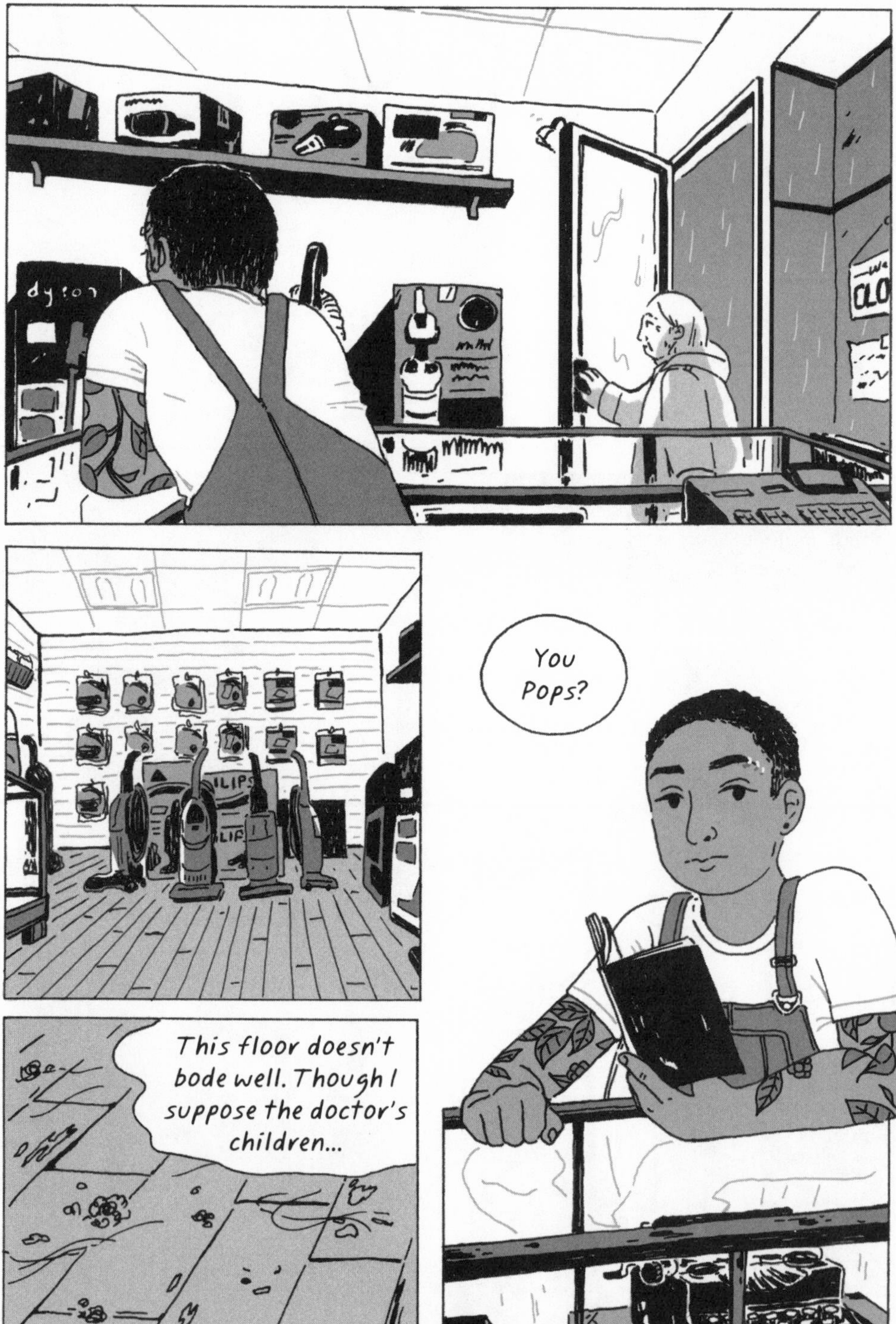
dyson
You
Pops?
This floor doesn't
bode well. Though I
suppose the doctor's
children...

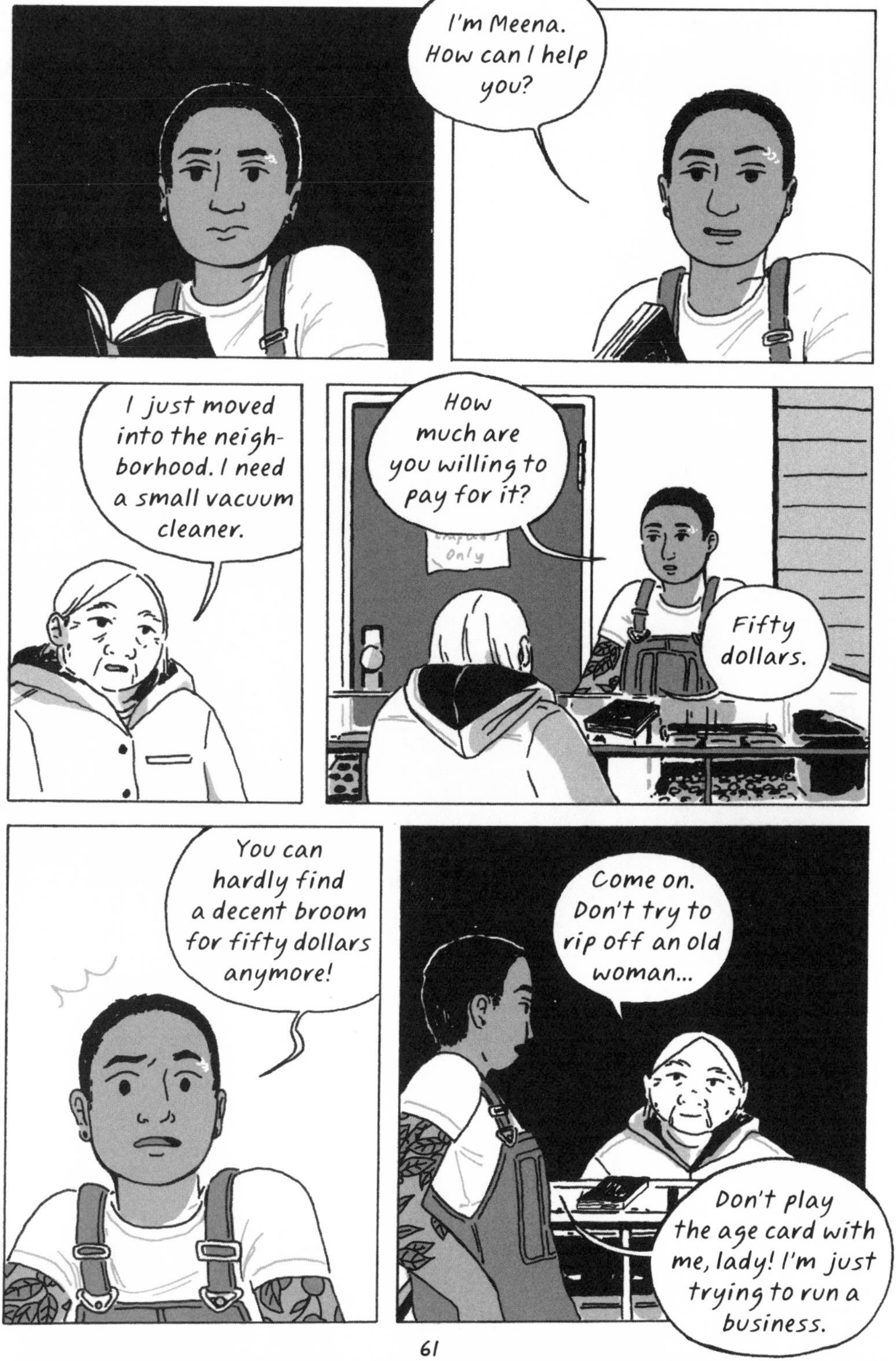
I'm Meena. How can I help you?
I just moved into the neighborhood. I need a small vacuum cleaner.
How much are you willing to pay for it?
Fifty dollars.
You can hardly find a decent broom for fifty dollars anymore!
Come on. Don't try to rip off an old woman...
Don't play the age card with me, lady! I'm just trying to run a business.

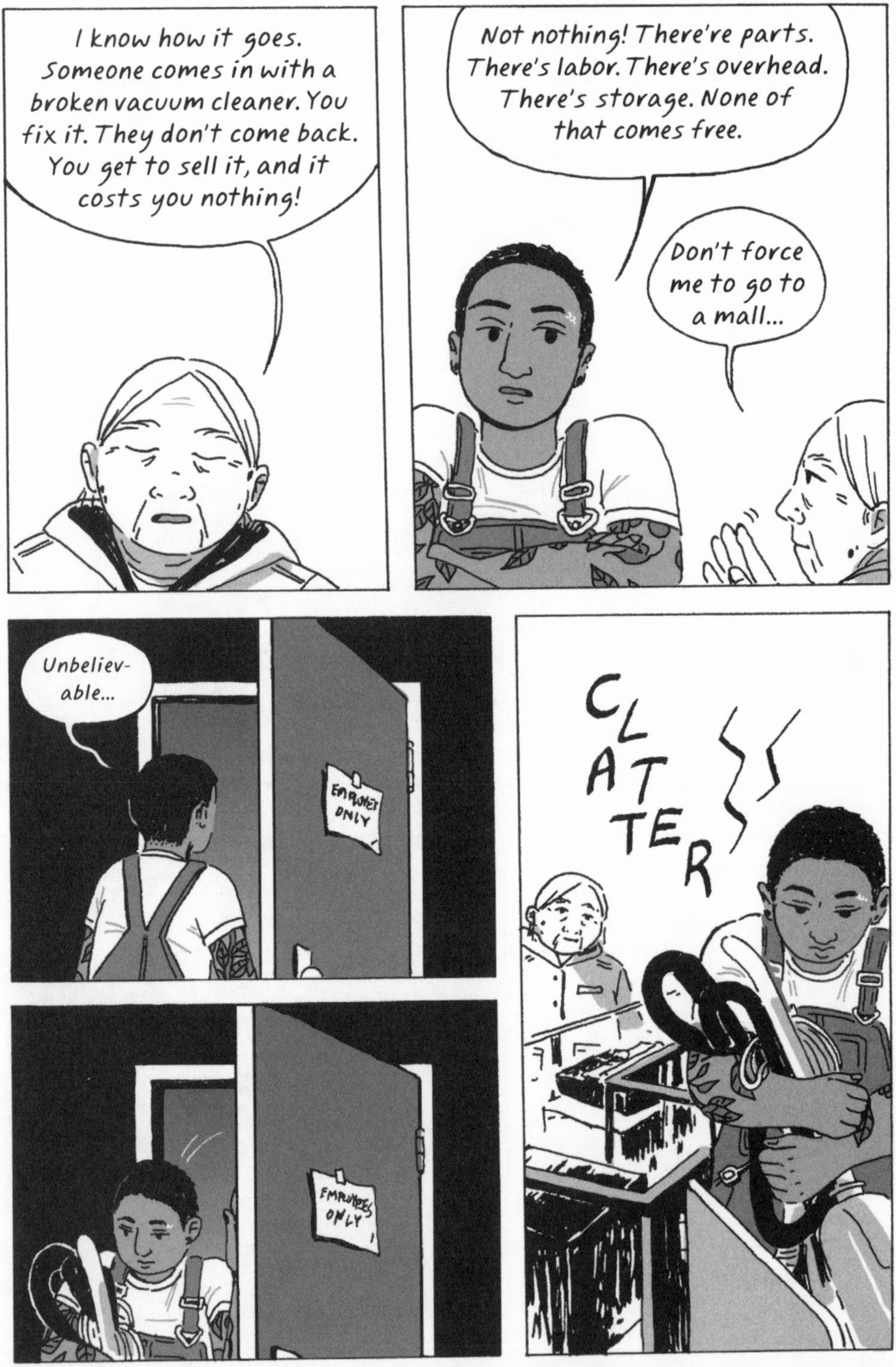
I know how it goes. Someone comes in with a broken vacuum cleaner. You fix it. They don't come back. You get to sell it, and it costs you nothing!
Not nothing! There're parts. There's labor. There's overhead. There's storage. None of that comes free.
Don't force me to go to a mall...
Unbeliev-able...
EMPLOYEES ONLY
EMPLOYEES ONLY
CLATTER

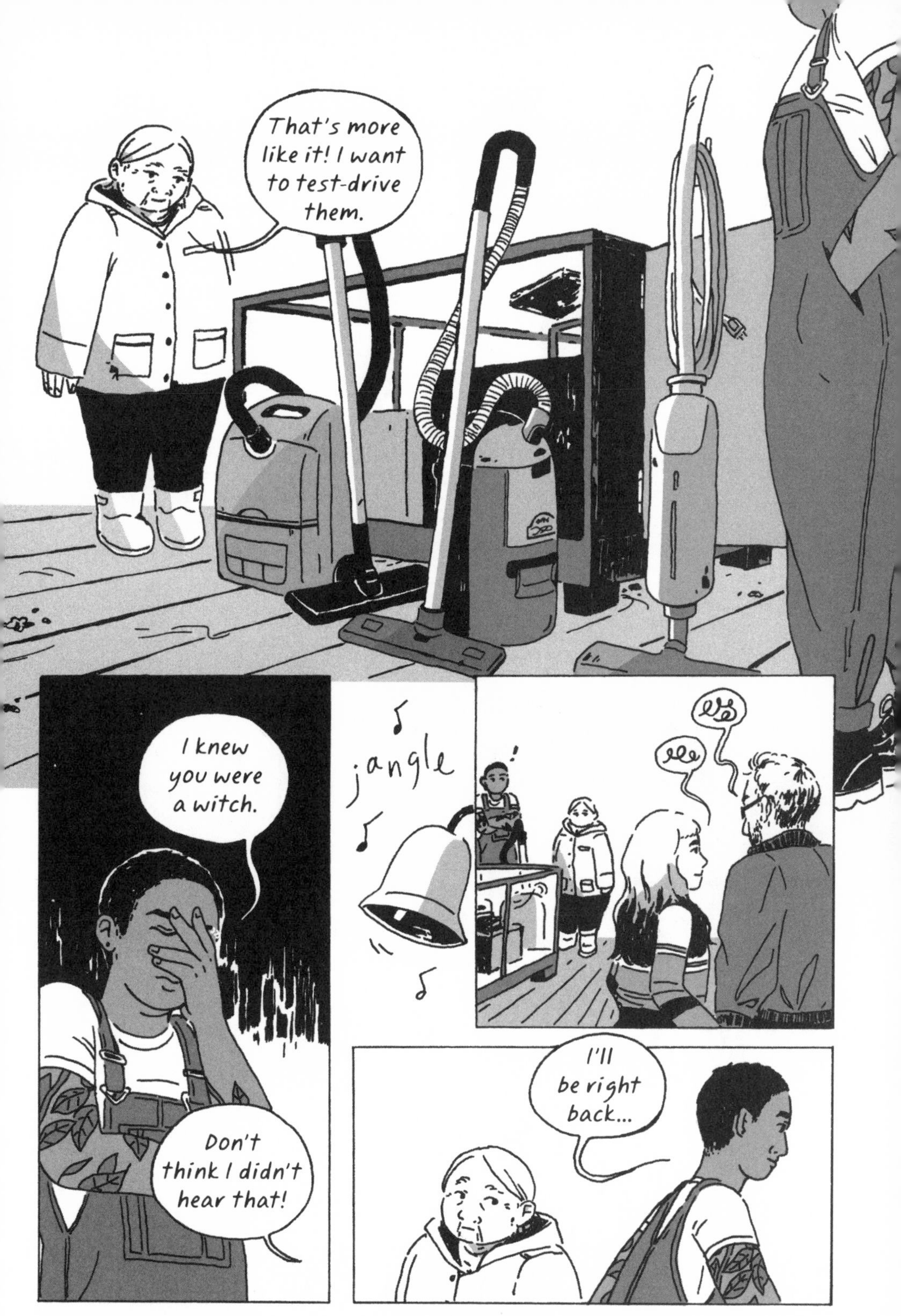

That's more like it! I want to test-drive them.
I knew you were a witch.
Don't think I didn't hear that!
jangle
I'll be right back...

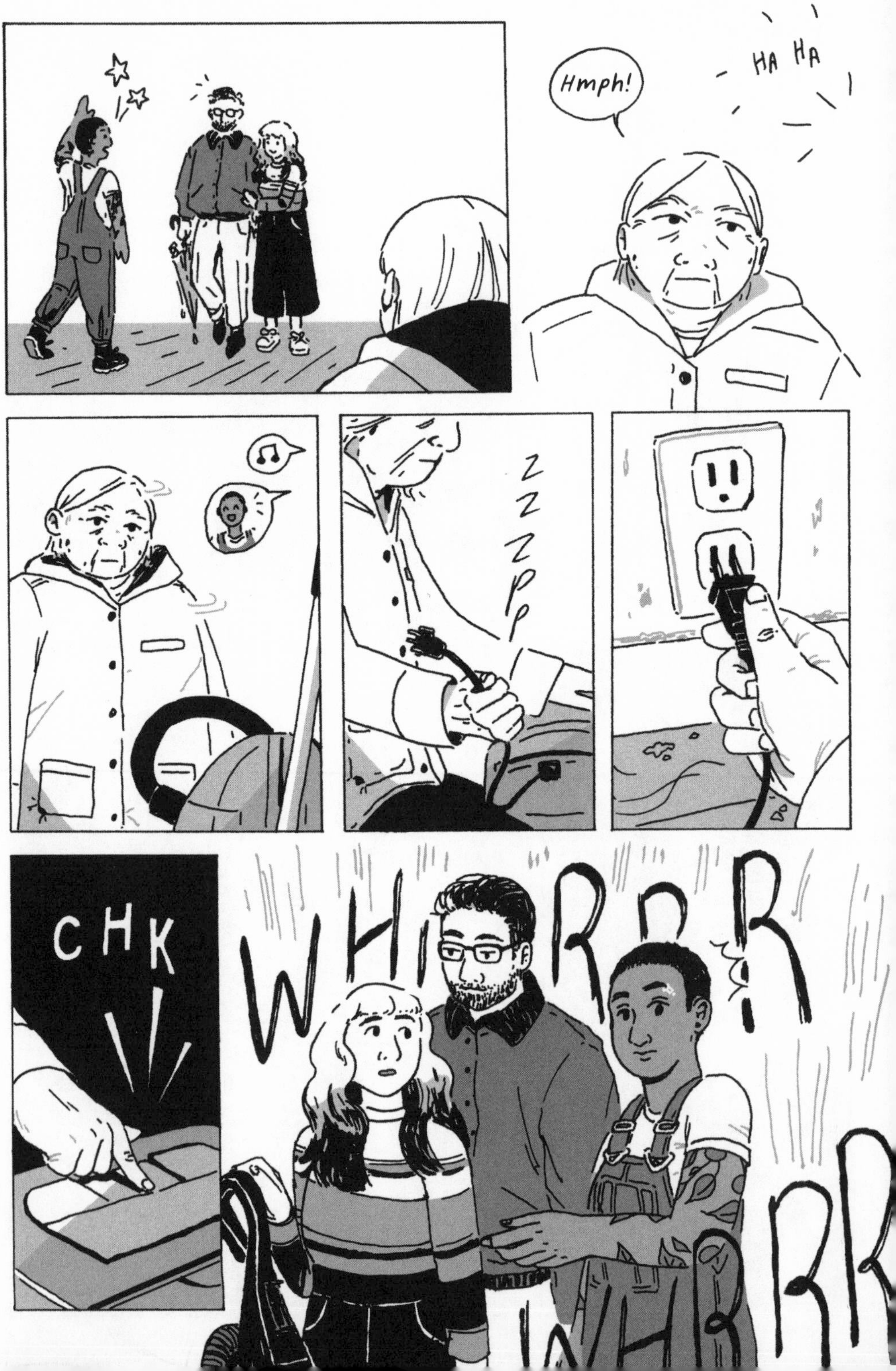

Hmph!
HA HA
CHK
WHIRRR
WHRRR

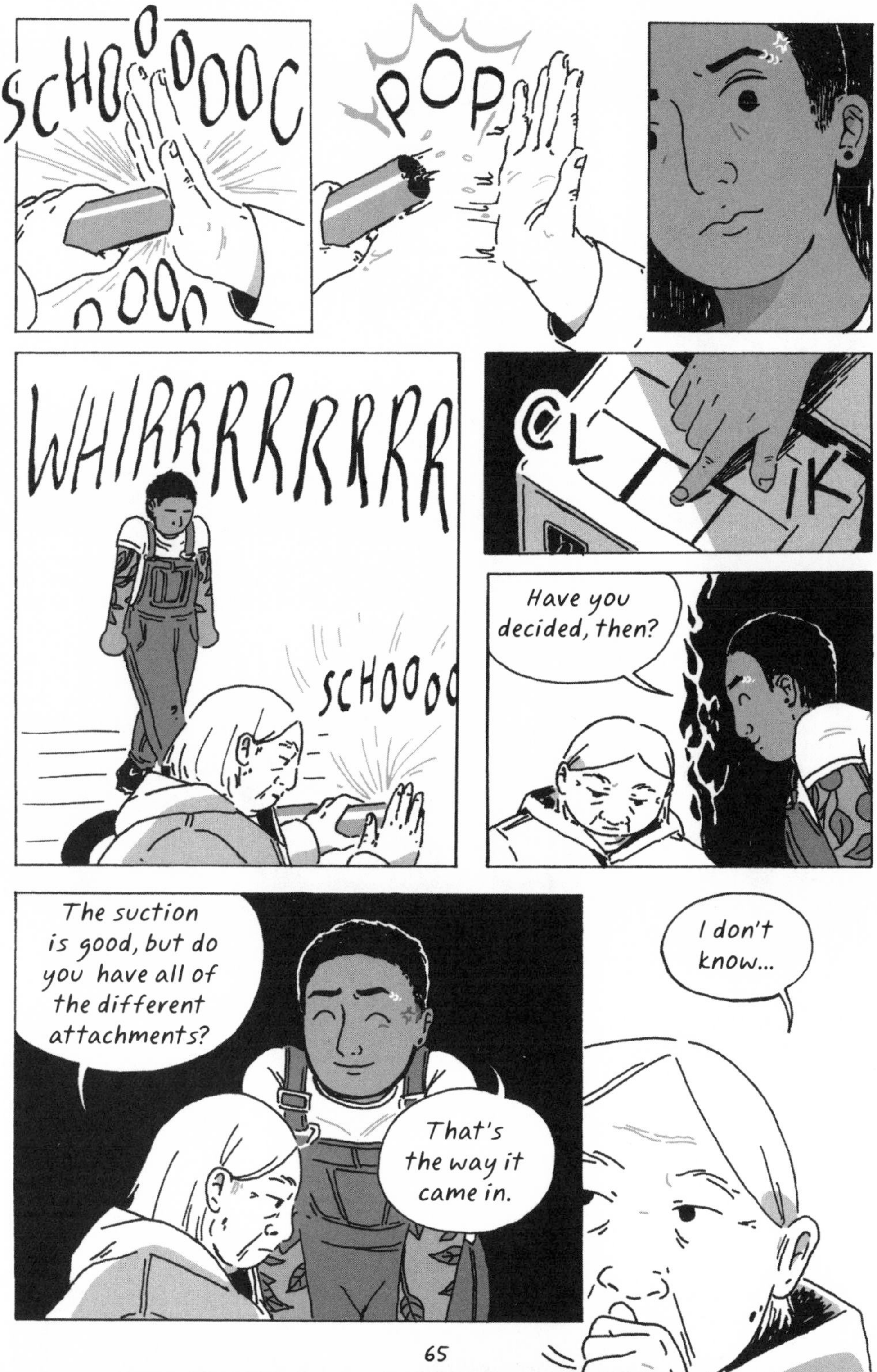
SCHOOOOOOC
POP
WHIRRRRRRRR
SCHOOOO
CLIK
Have you decided, then?
The suction is good, but do you have all of the different attachments?
I don't know...
That's the way it came in.

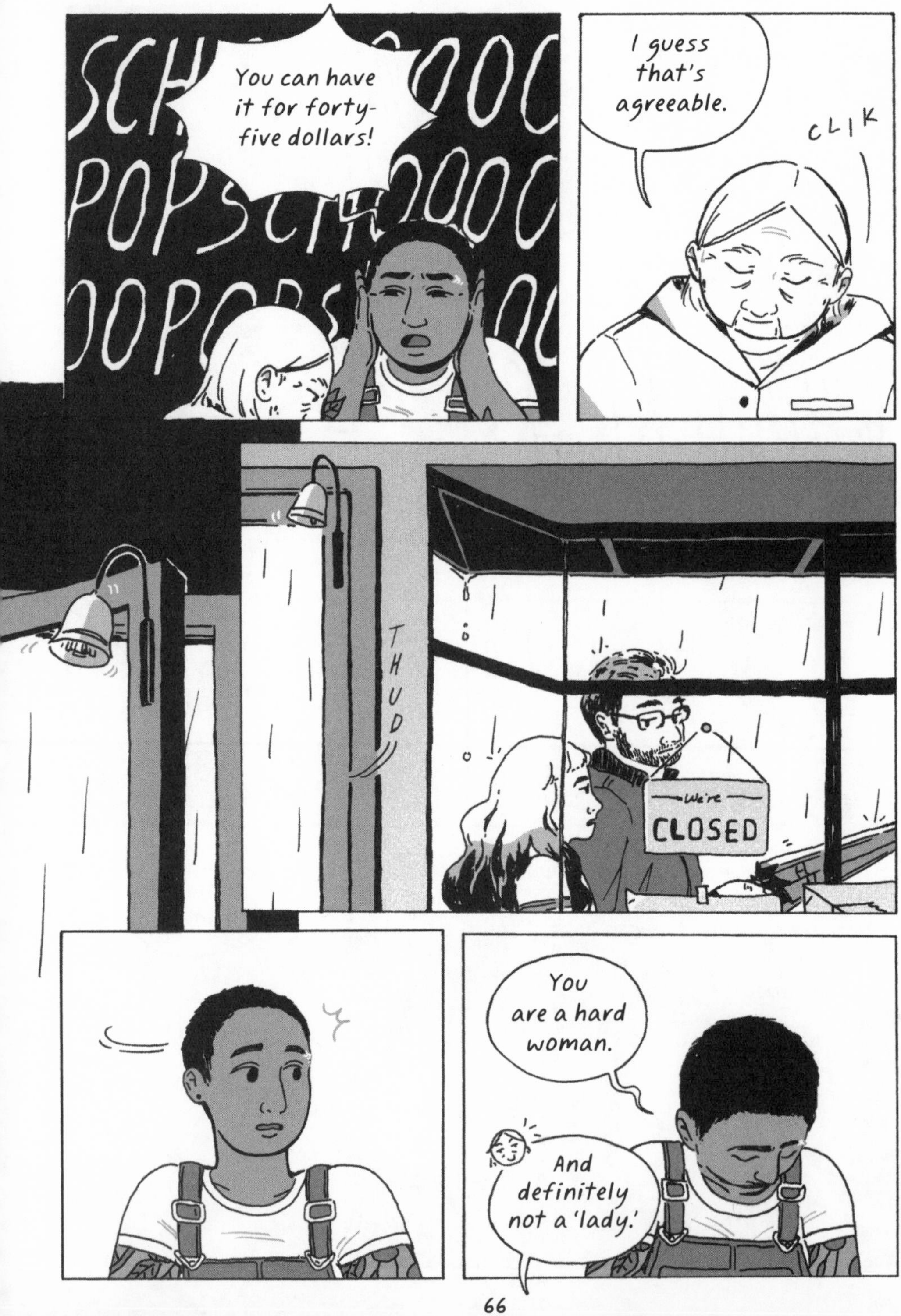
SCH
POP SCH
OOPOP
You can have it for forty-five dollars!
I guess that's agreeable.
CLIK
THUD
We're CLOSED
You are a hard woman.
And definitely not a 'lady.'

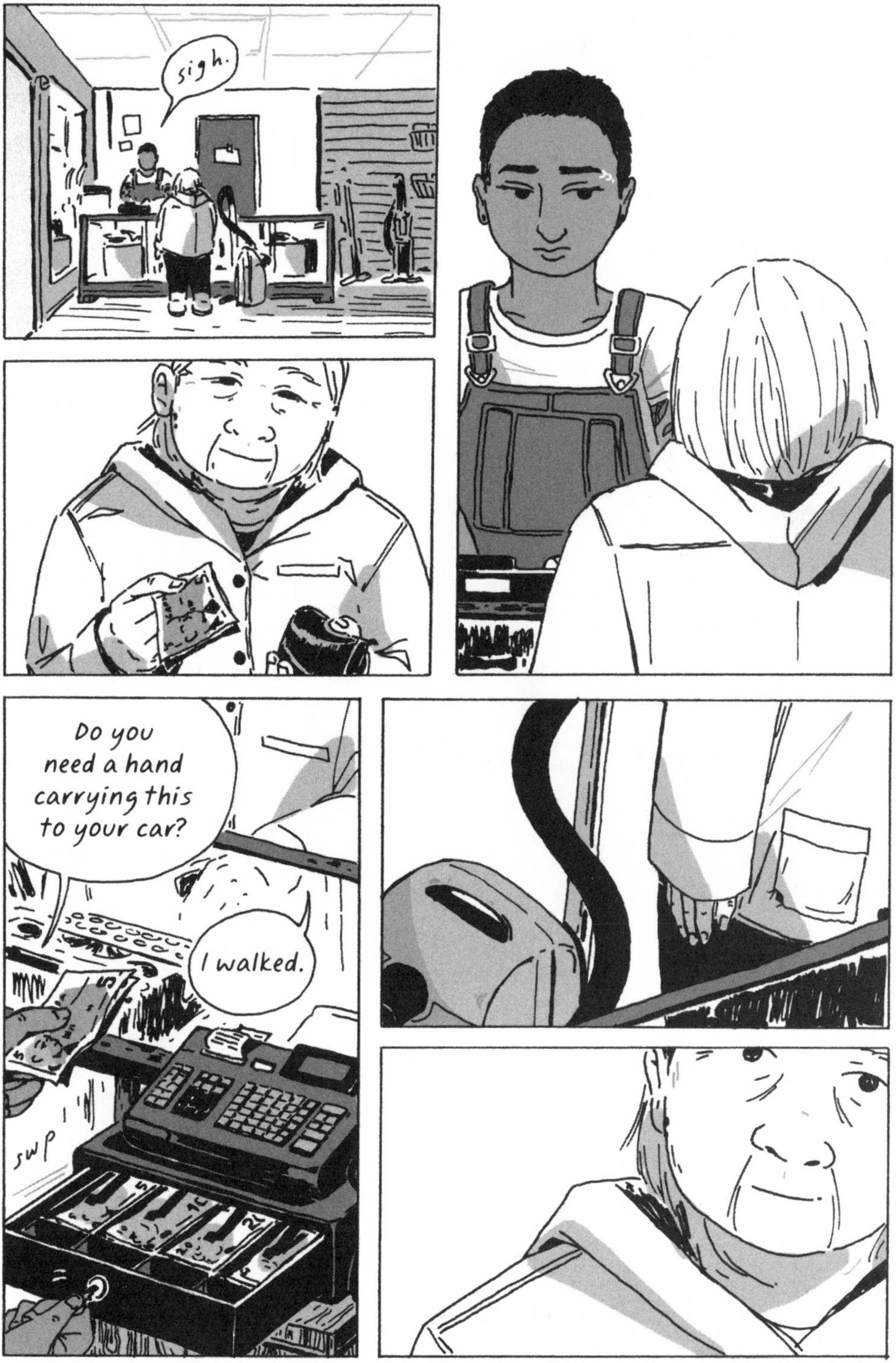
sigh.
Do you need a hand carrying this to your car?
I walked.
swp

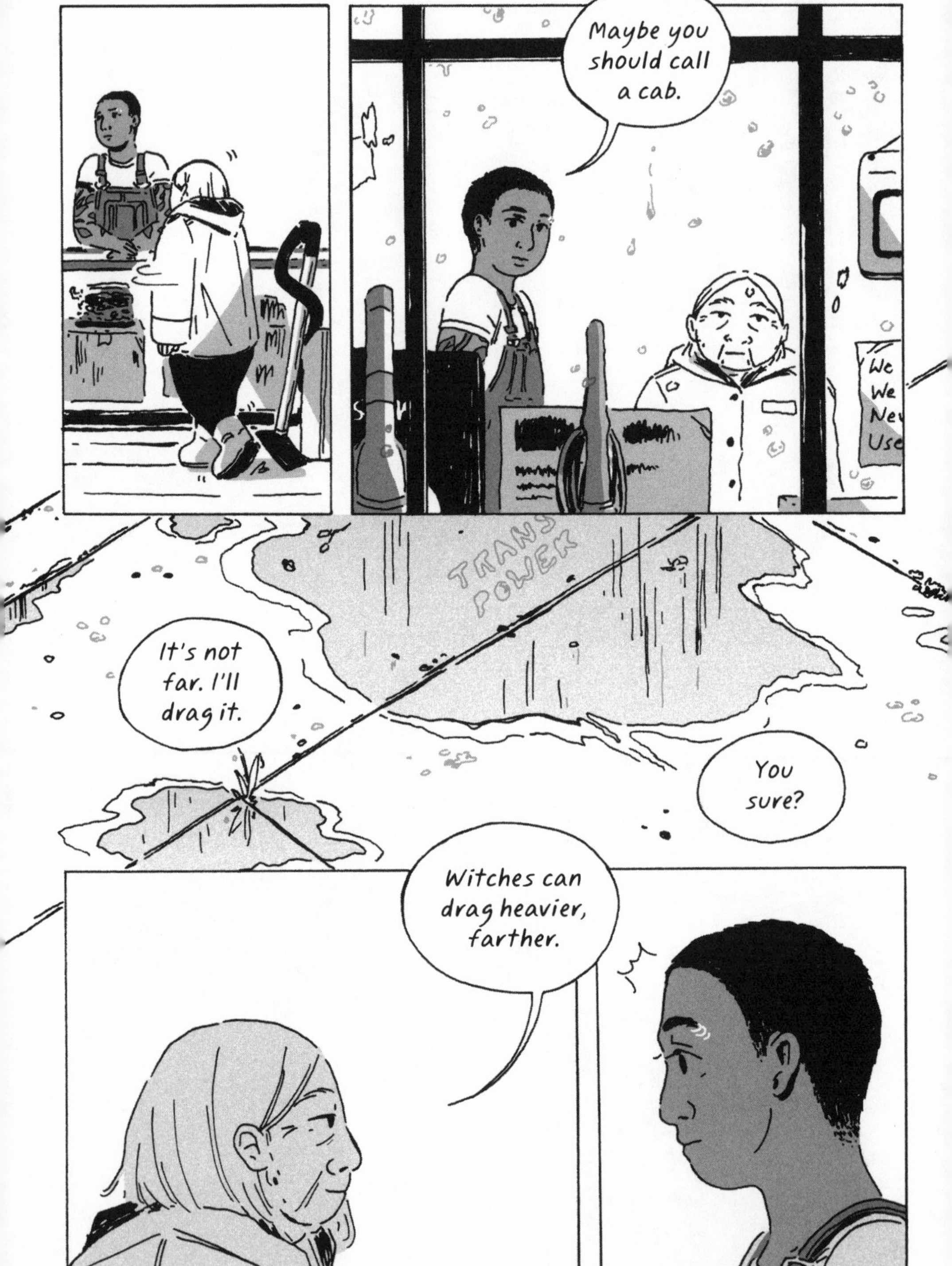
Maybe you should call a cab.
We
We
Ne
Use
TRANS POWER
It's not far. I'll drag it.
You sure?
Witches can drag heavier, farther.

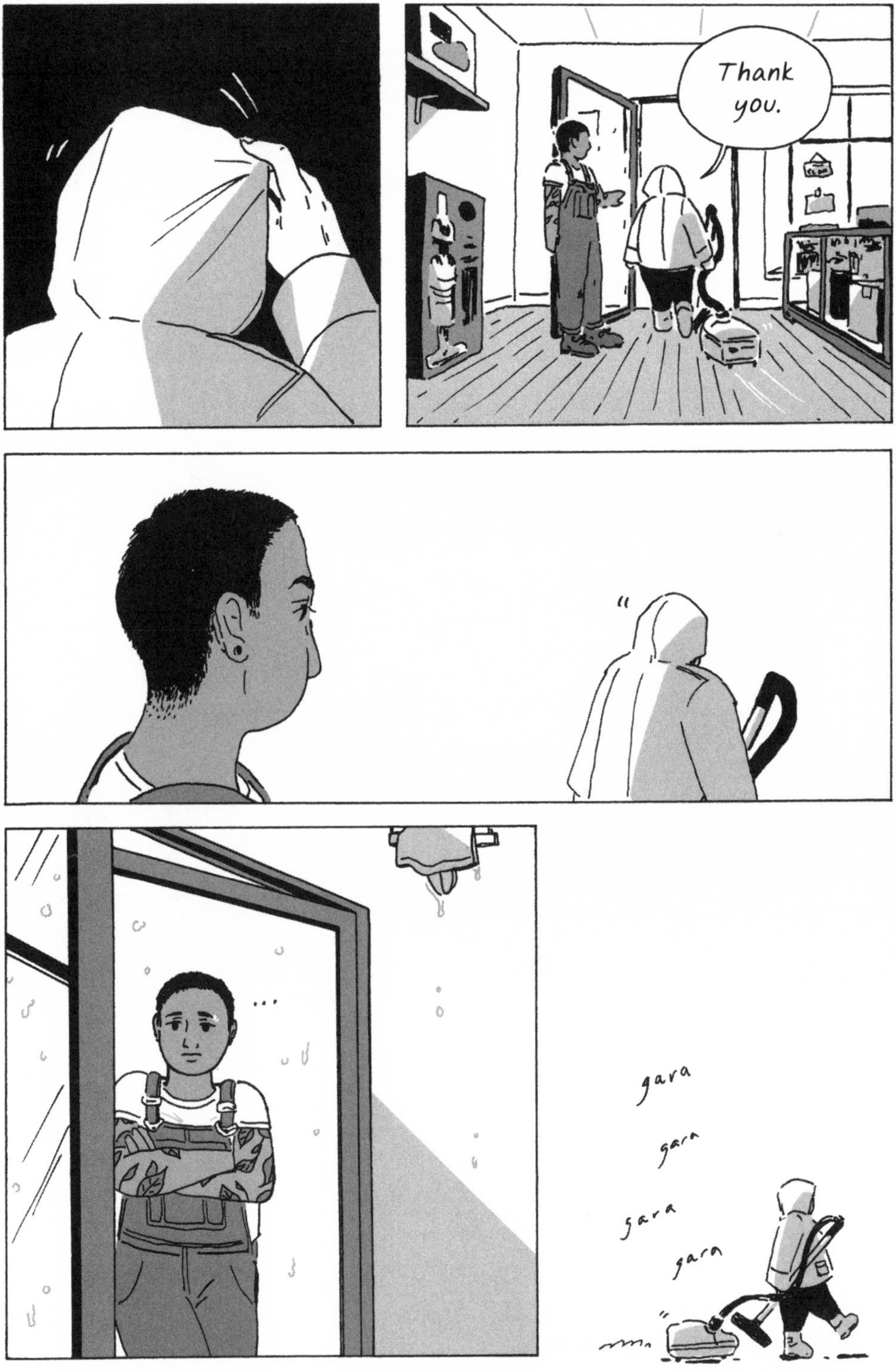
Thank you.
...
gara
gara
gara
gara

Chapter Four

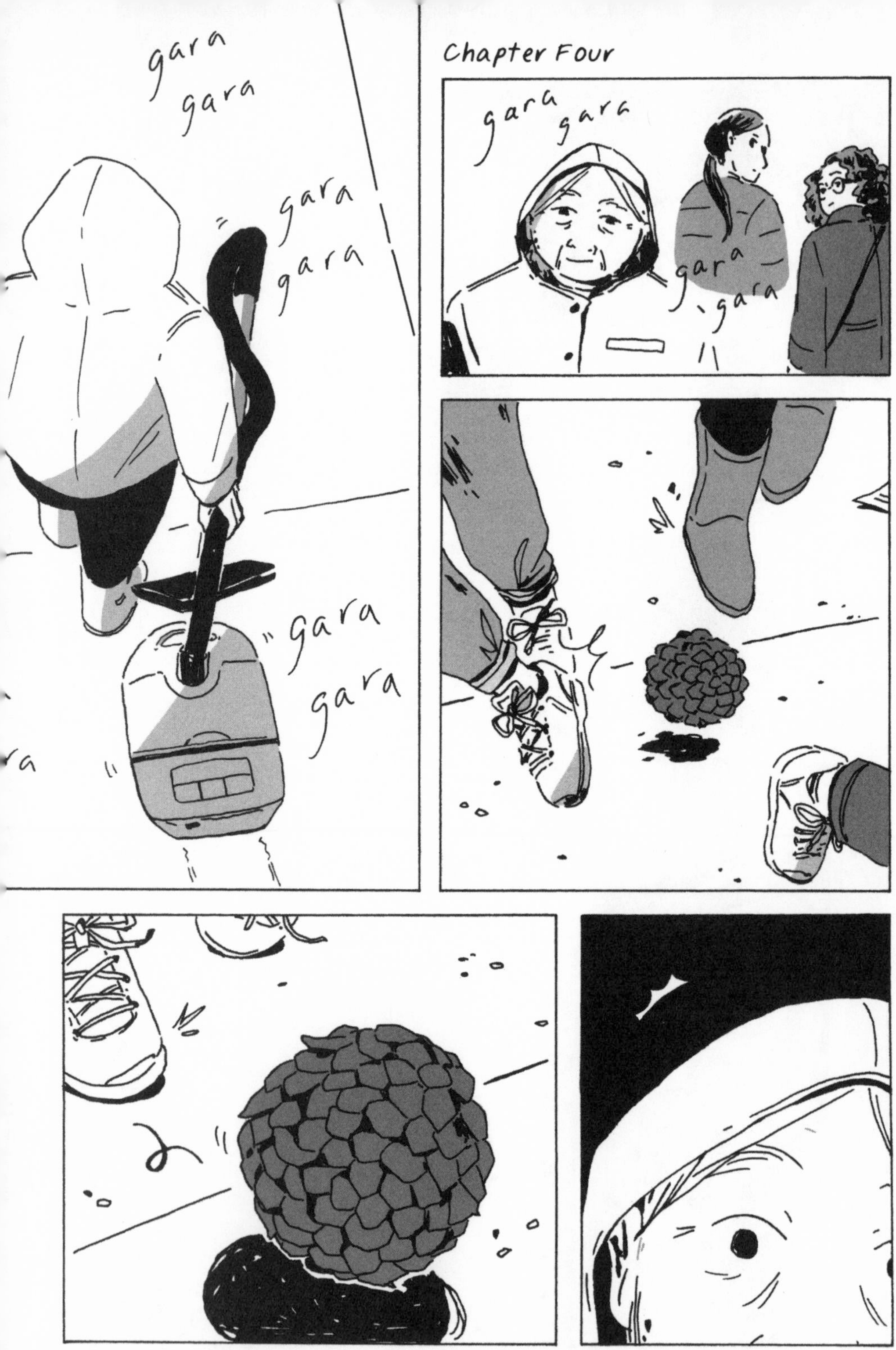
gara
gara
gara
gara
gara
gara
gara
gara
gara
gara

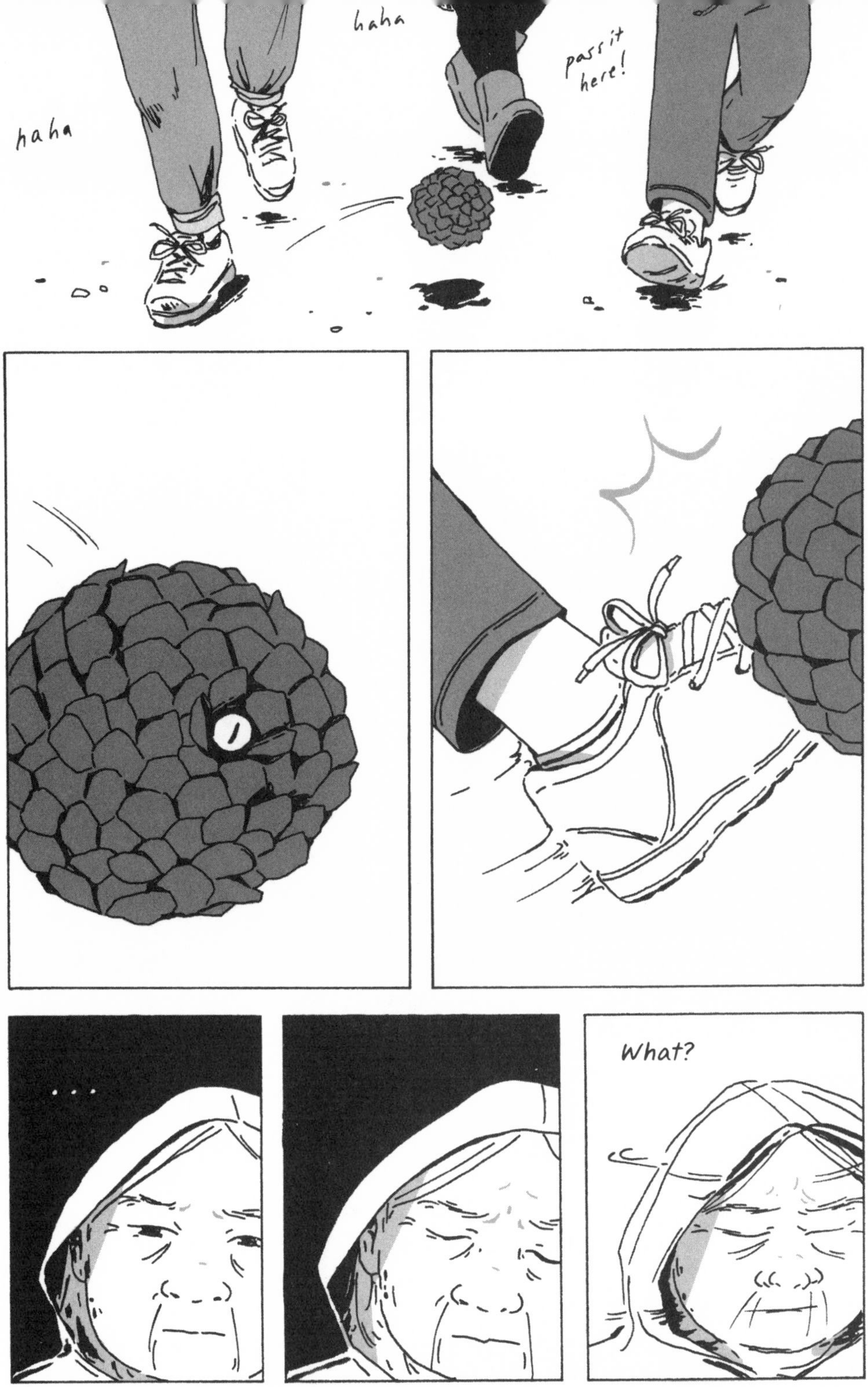
haha
haha
pass it here!
. . .
What?

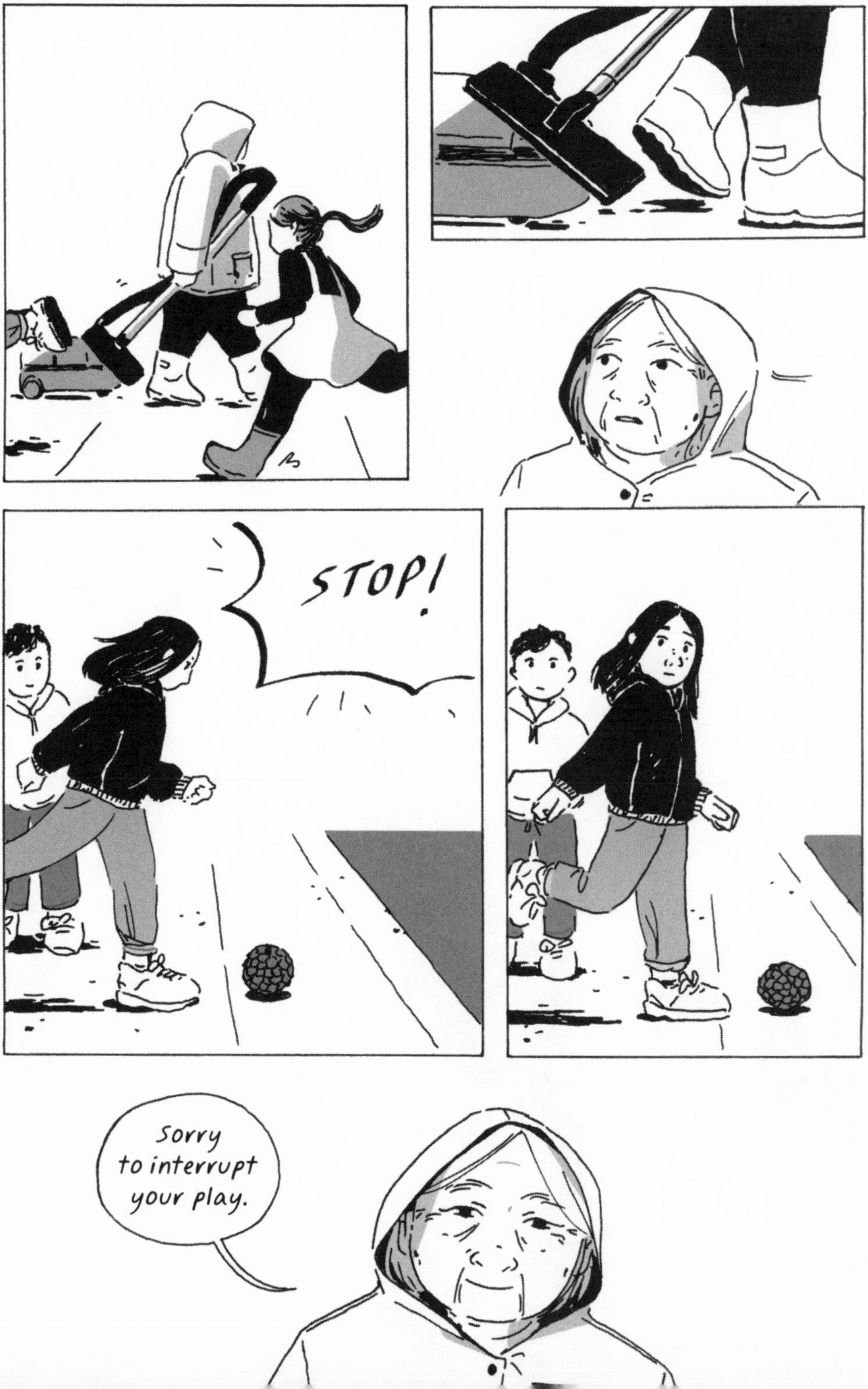
STOP!
Sorry to interrupt your play.

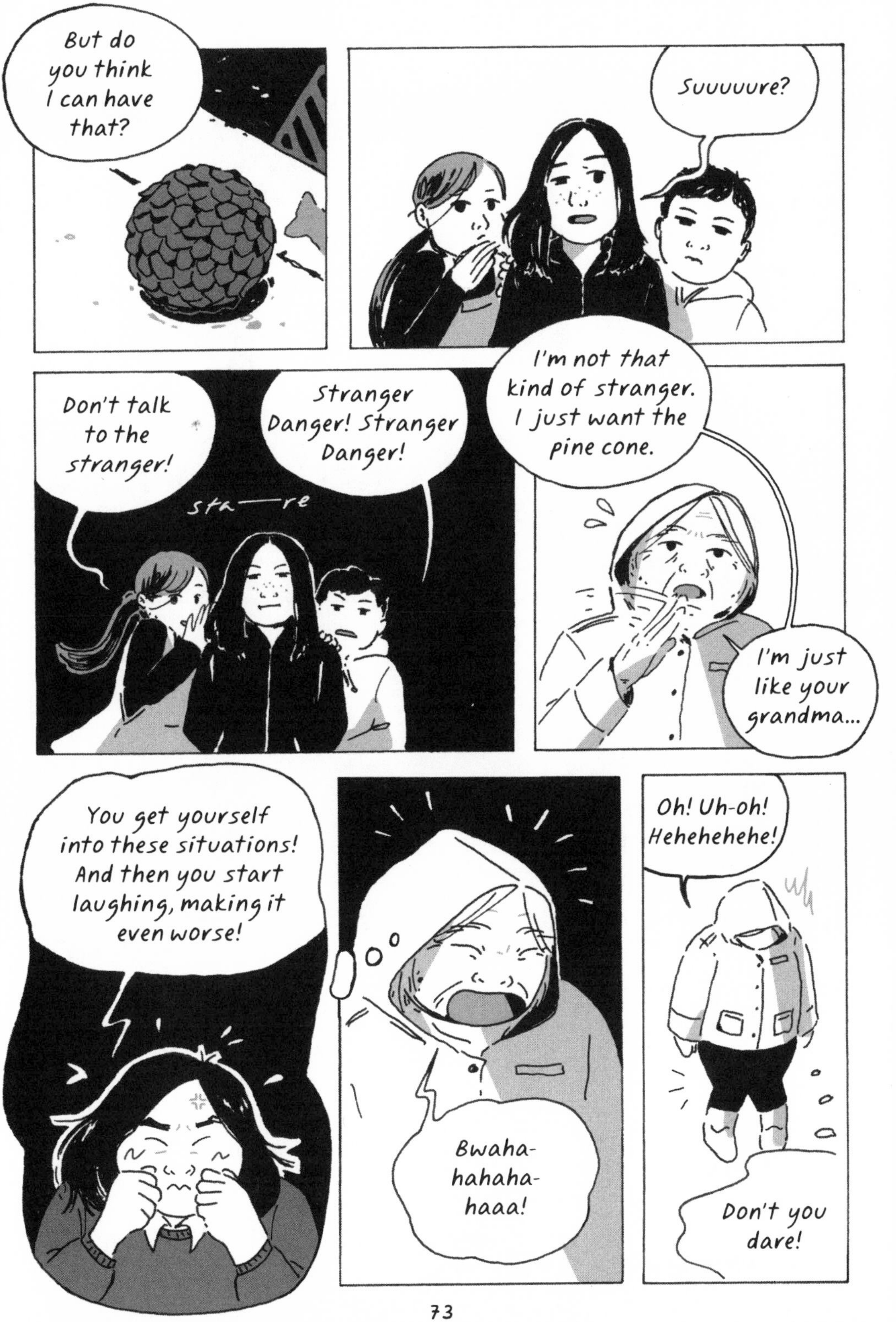
But do you think I can have that?
Suuuuure?
Don't talk to the stranger!
Stranger Danger! Stranger Danger!
sta—re
I'm not that kind of stranger. I just want the pine cone.
I'm just like your grandma...
You get yourself into these situations! And then you start laughing, making it even worse!
Bwaha-hahaha-haaa!
Oh! Uh-oh! Hehehehehe!
Don't you dare!

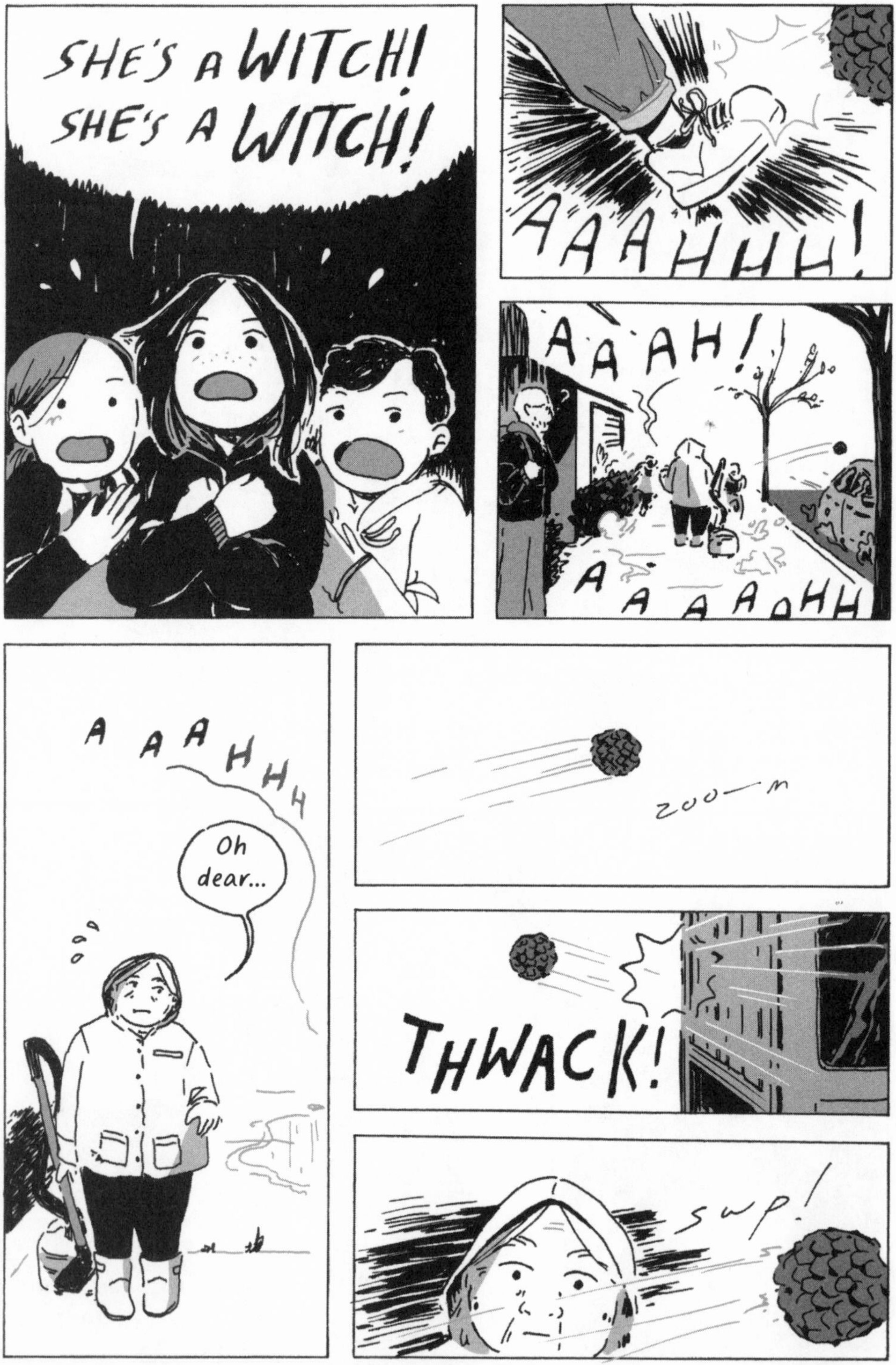
SHE'S A WITCH! SHE'S A WITCH!
AAAHHH!
AAAH!
AAAAAHH
AAAHHH
Oh dear...
ZOO—M
THWACK!
swp!

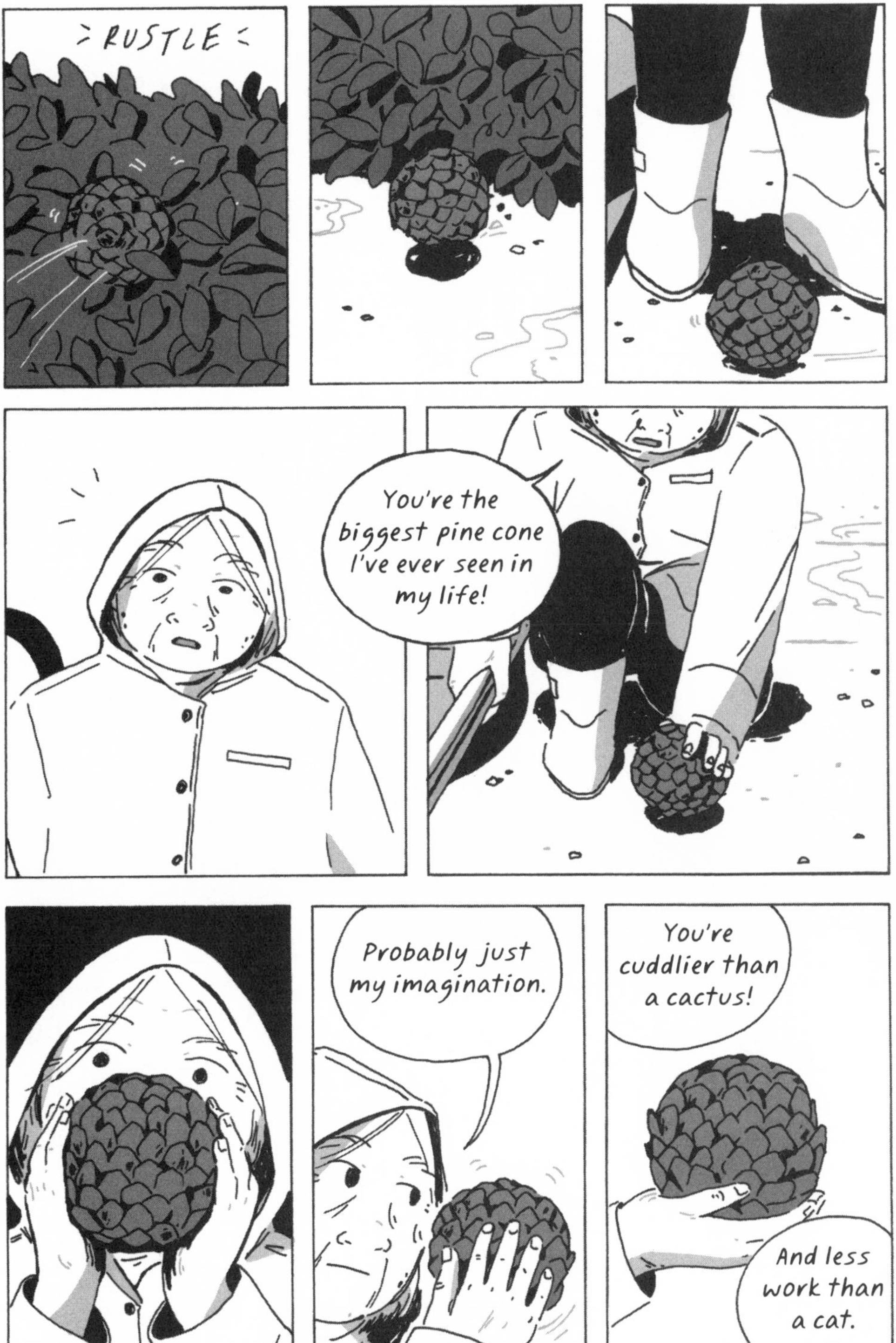
RUSTLE
You're the biggest pine cone I've ever seen in my life!
Probably just my imagination.
You're cuddlier than a cactus!
And less work than a cat.

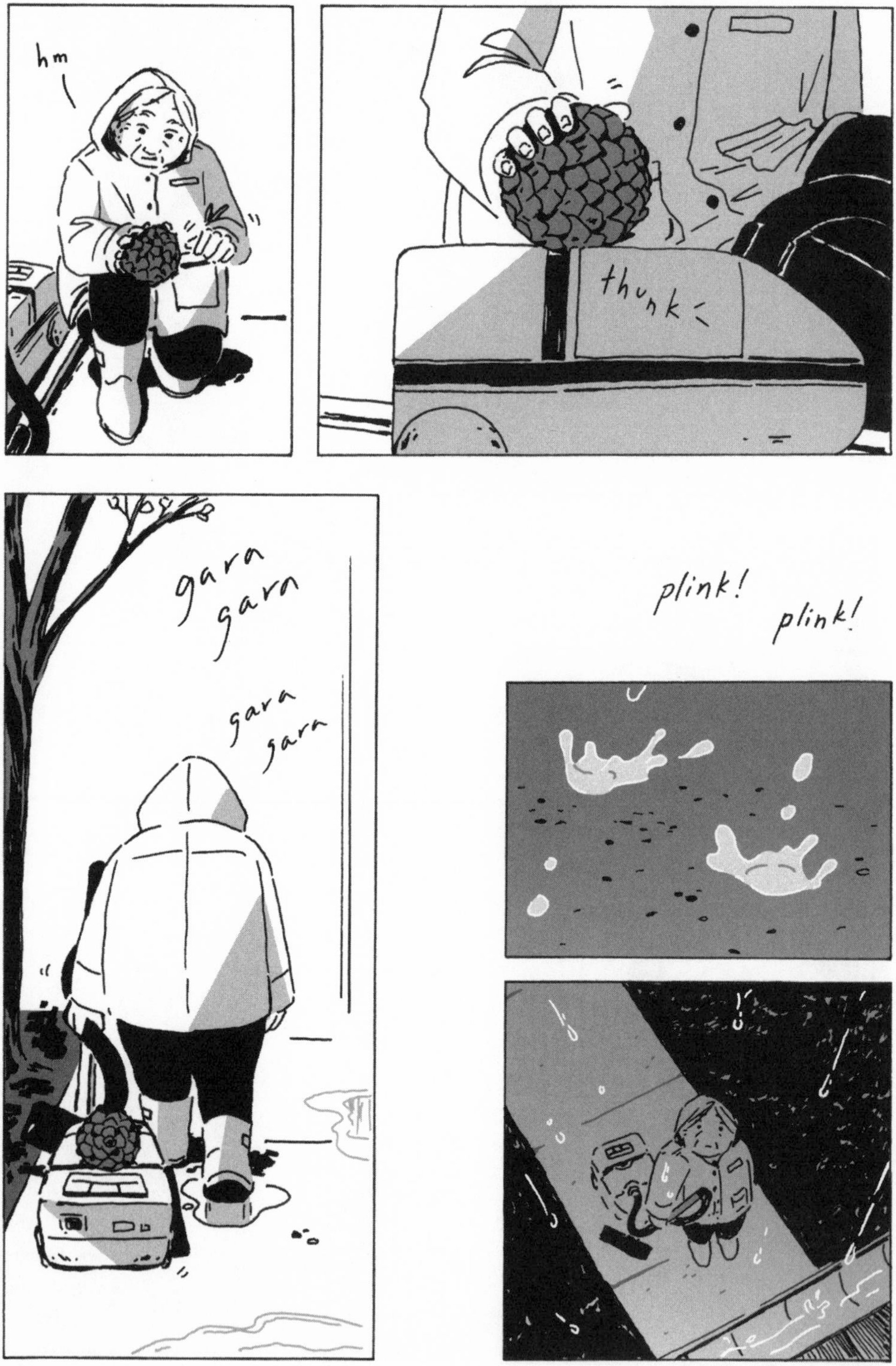
hm
thunk
gara
gara
gara
gara
plink!
plink!

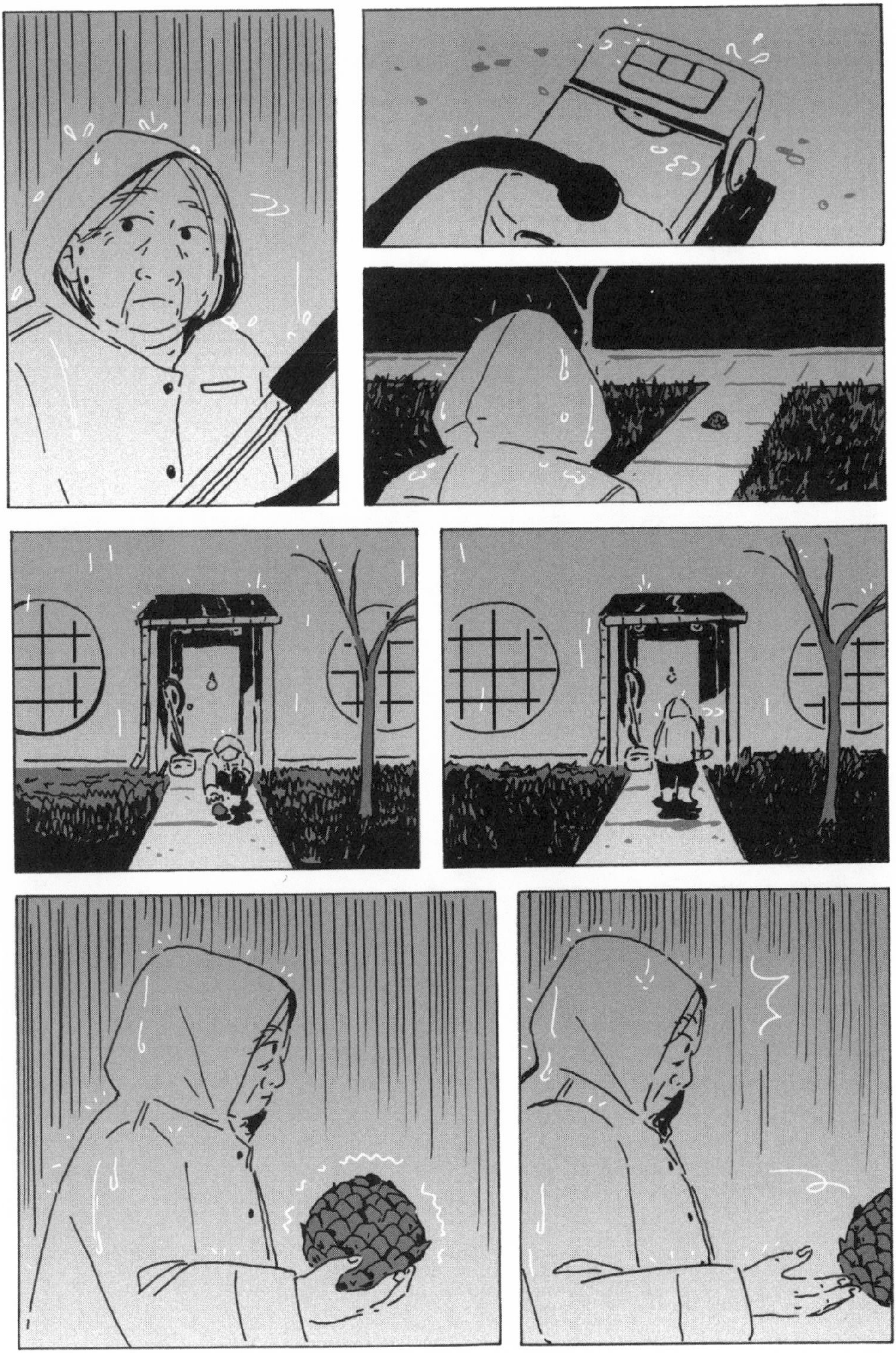

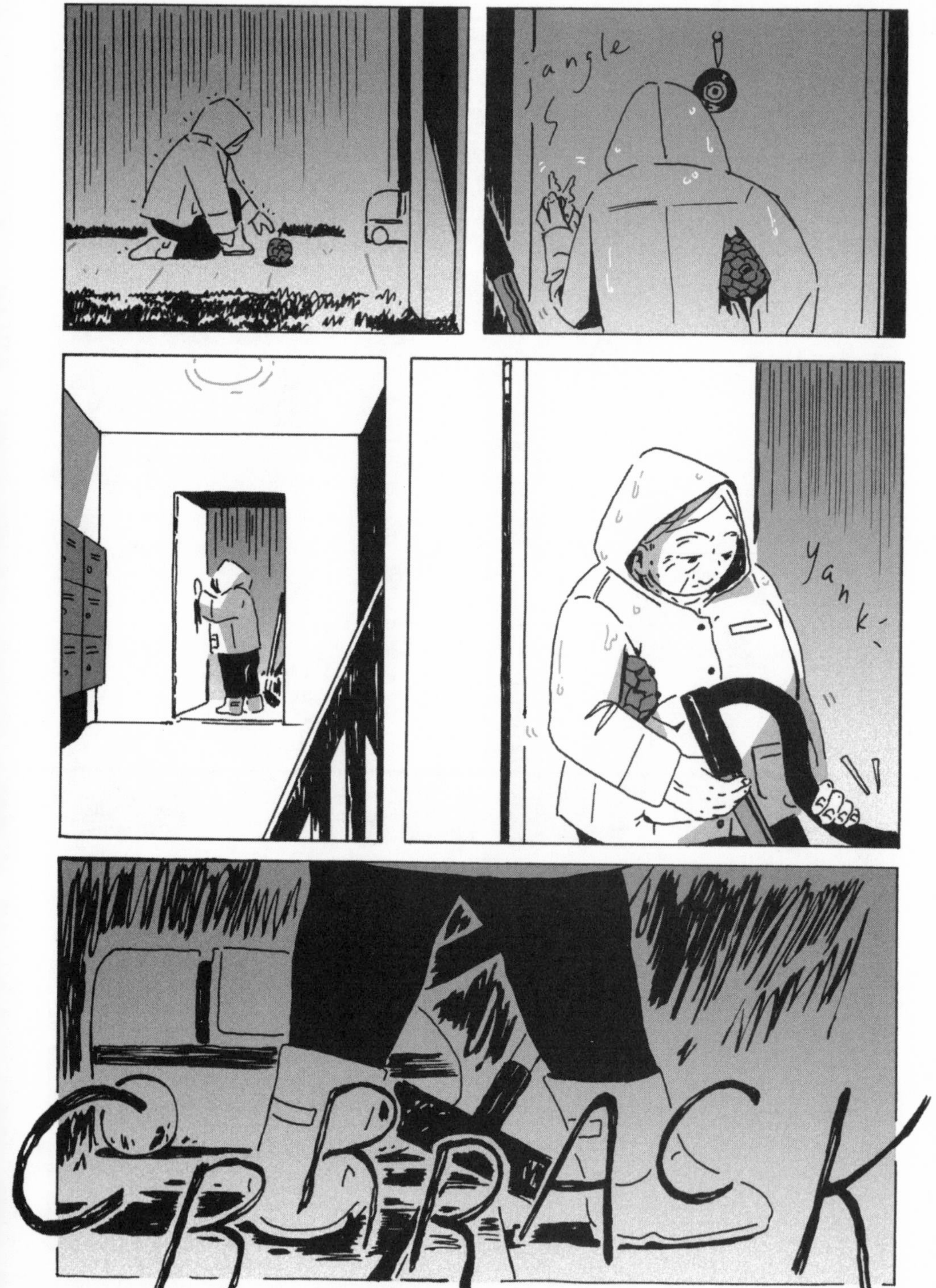
jangle
yank
CRRACK

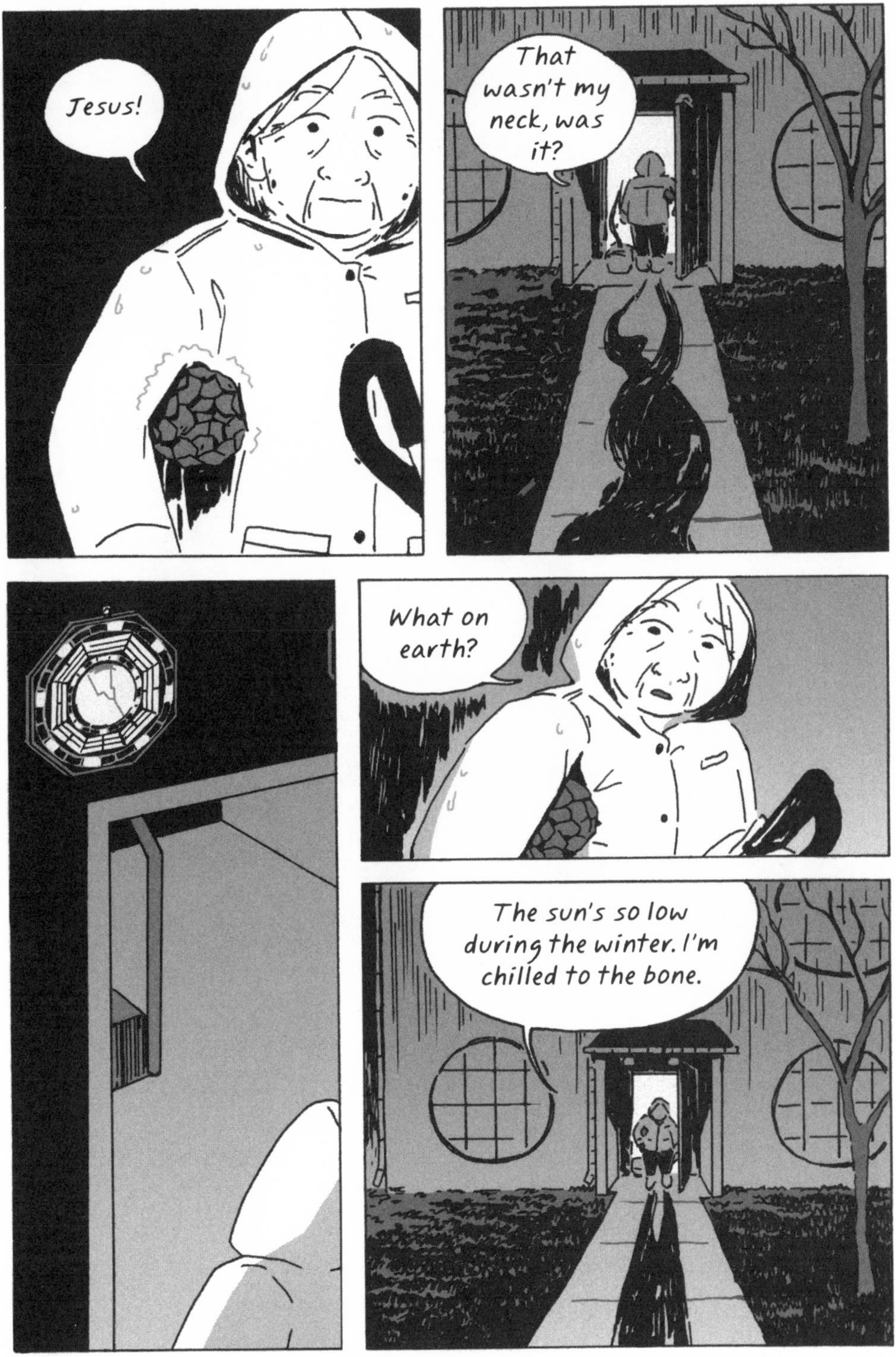
Jesus!
That wasn't my neck, was it?
What on earth?
The sun's so low during the winter. I'm chilled to the bone.

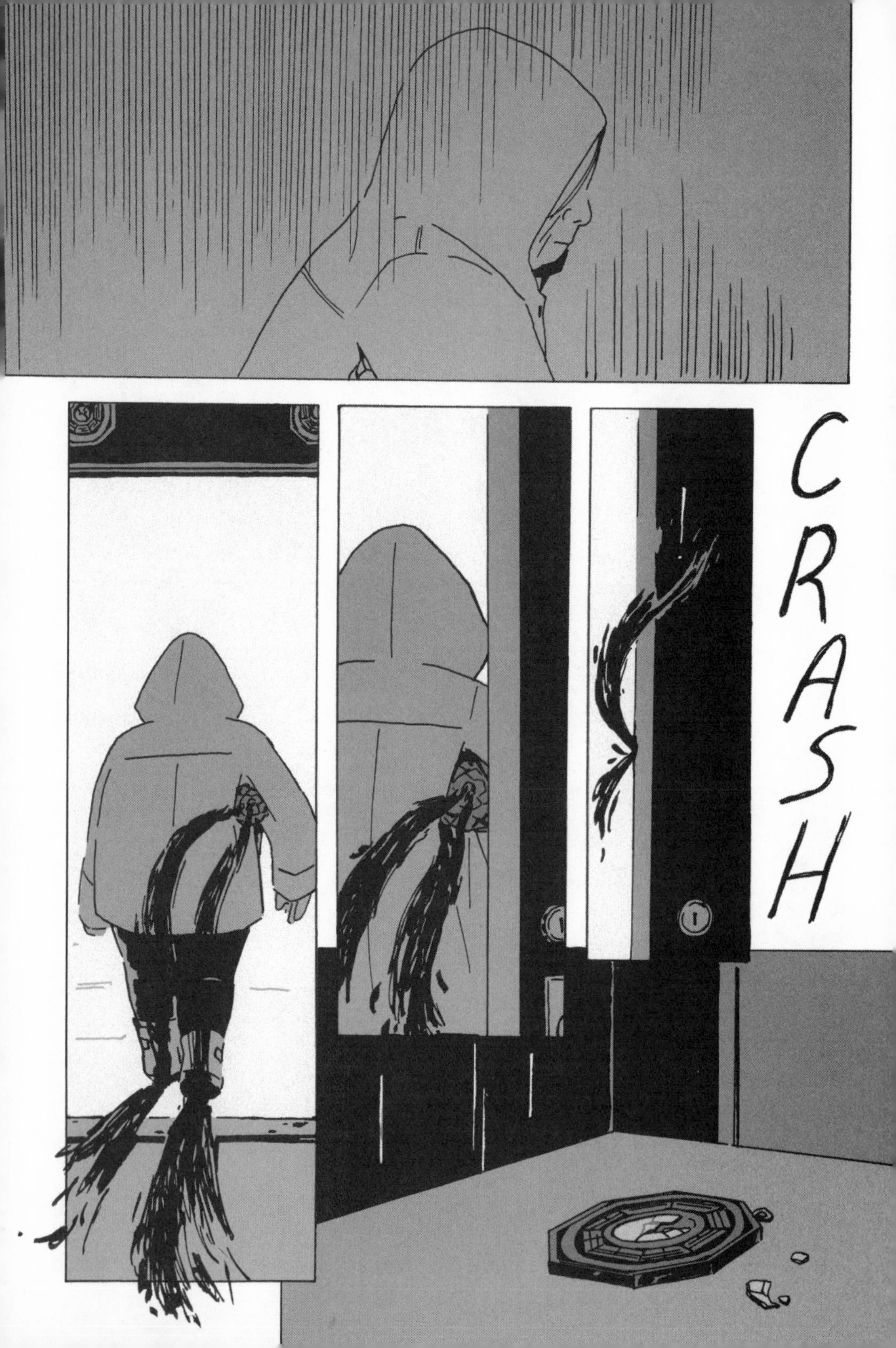
CRASH

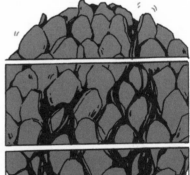

CRACK!

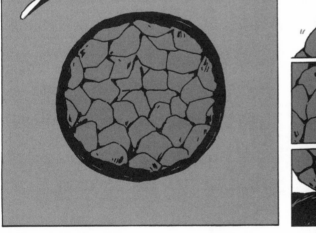

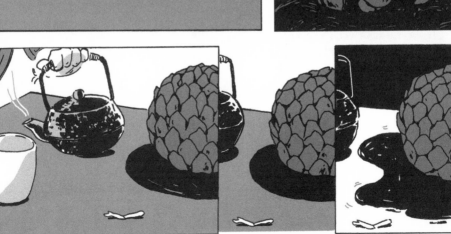

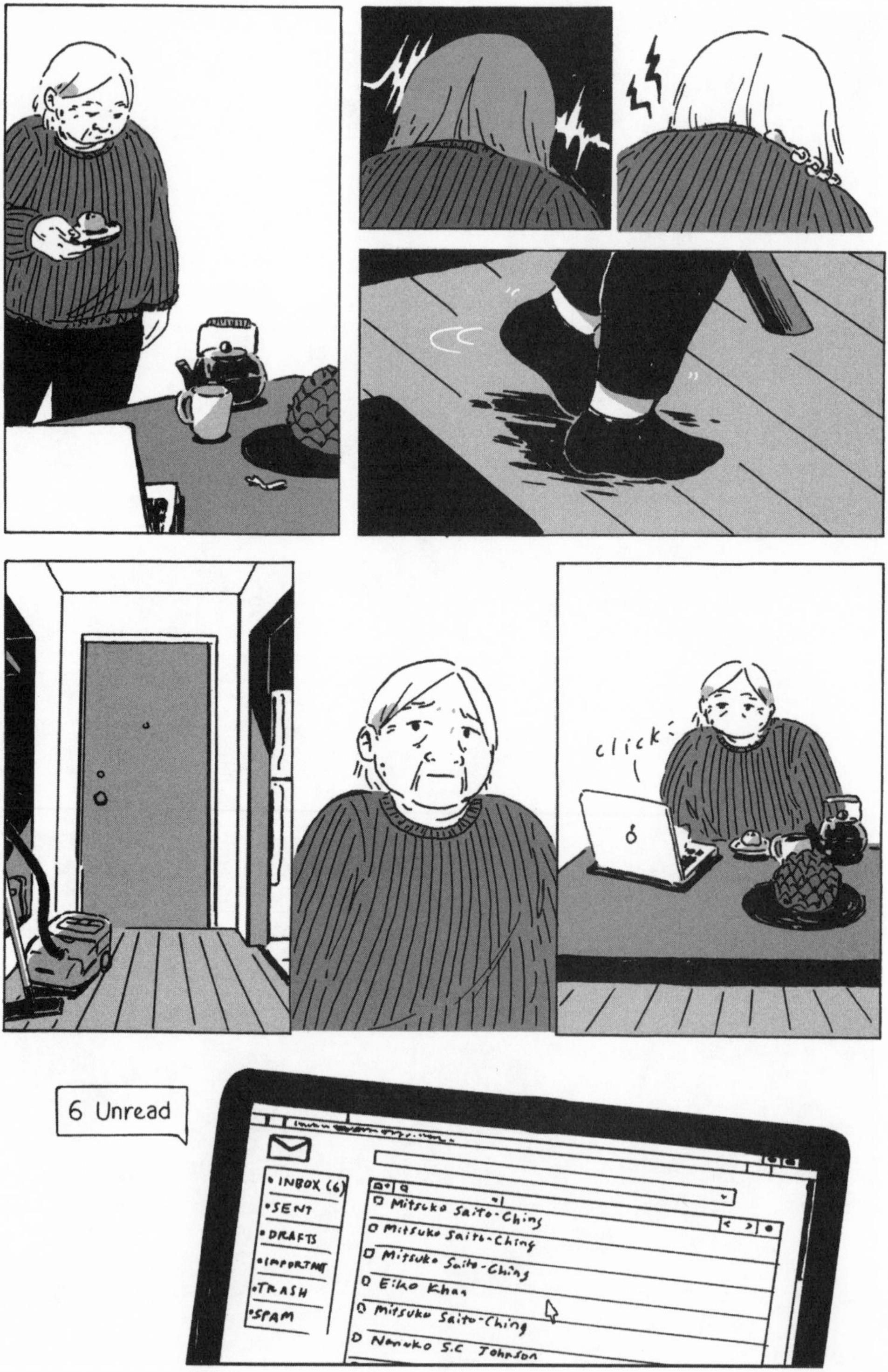
click
6 Unread
INBOX (6)
SENT
DRAFTS
IMPORTANT
TRASH
SPAM
Mitsuko Saito-Ching
Mitsuko Saito-Ching
Mitsuko Saito-Ching
Eiko Khan
Mitsuko Saito-Ching
Nanako S.C Johnson

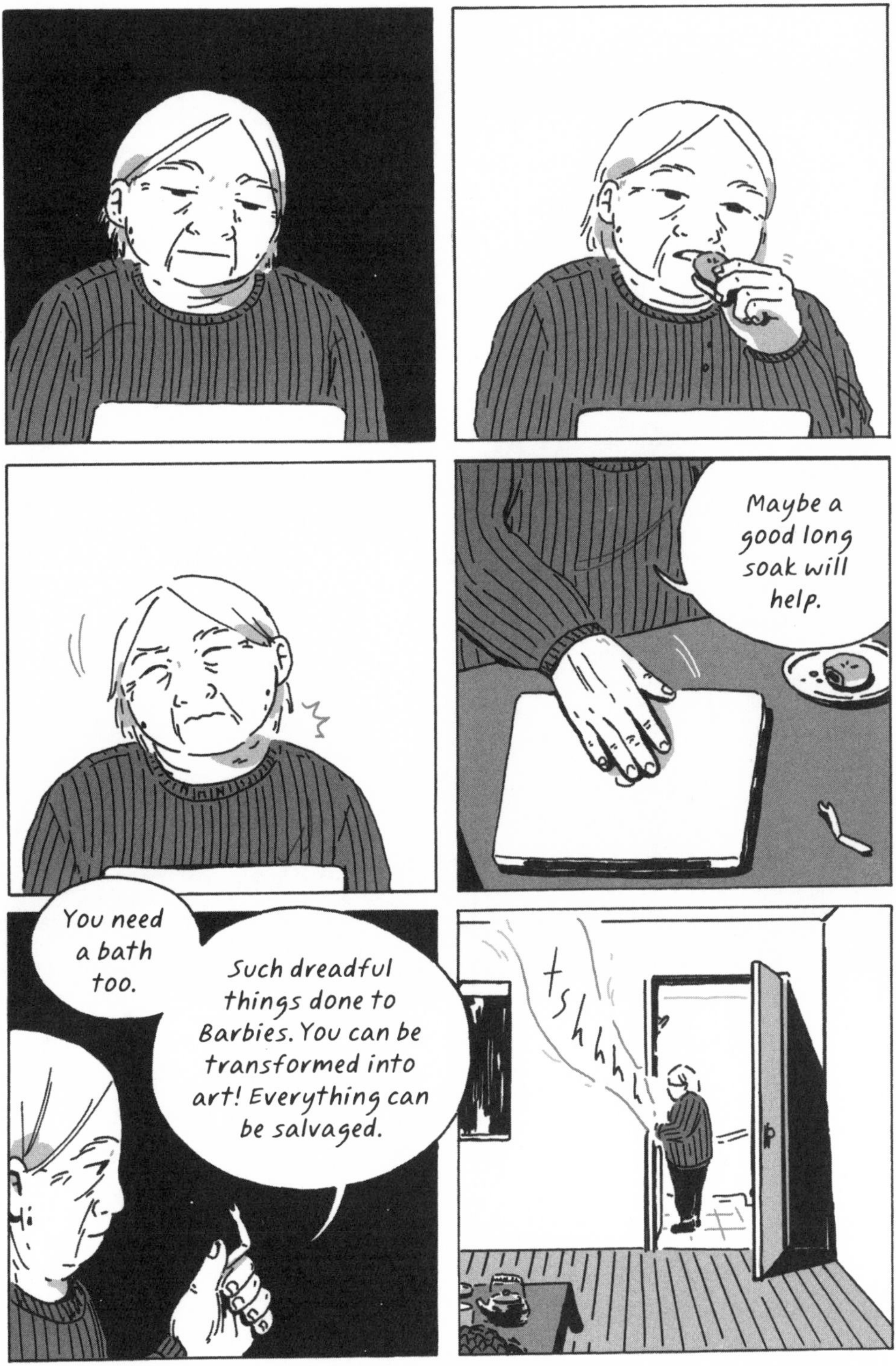
Maybe a good long soak will help.
You need a bath too.
Such dreadful things done to Barbies. You can be transformed into art! Everything can be salvaged.
tshhhh

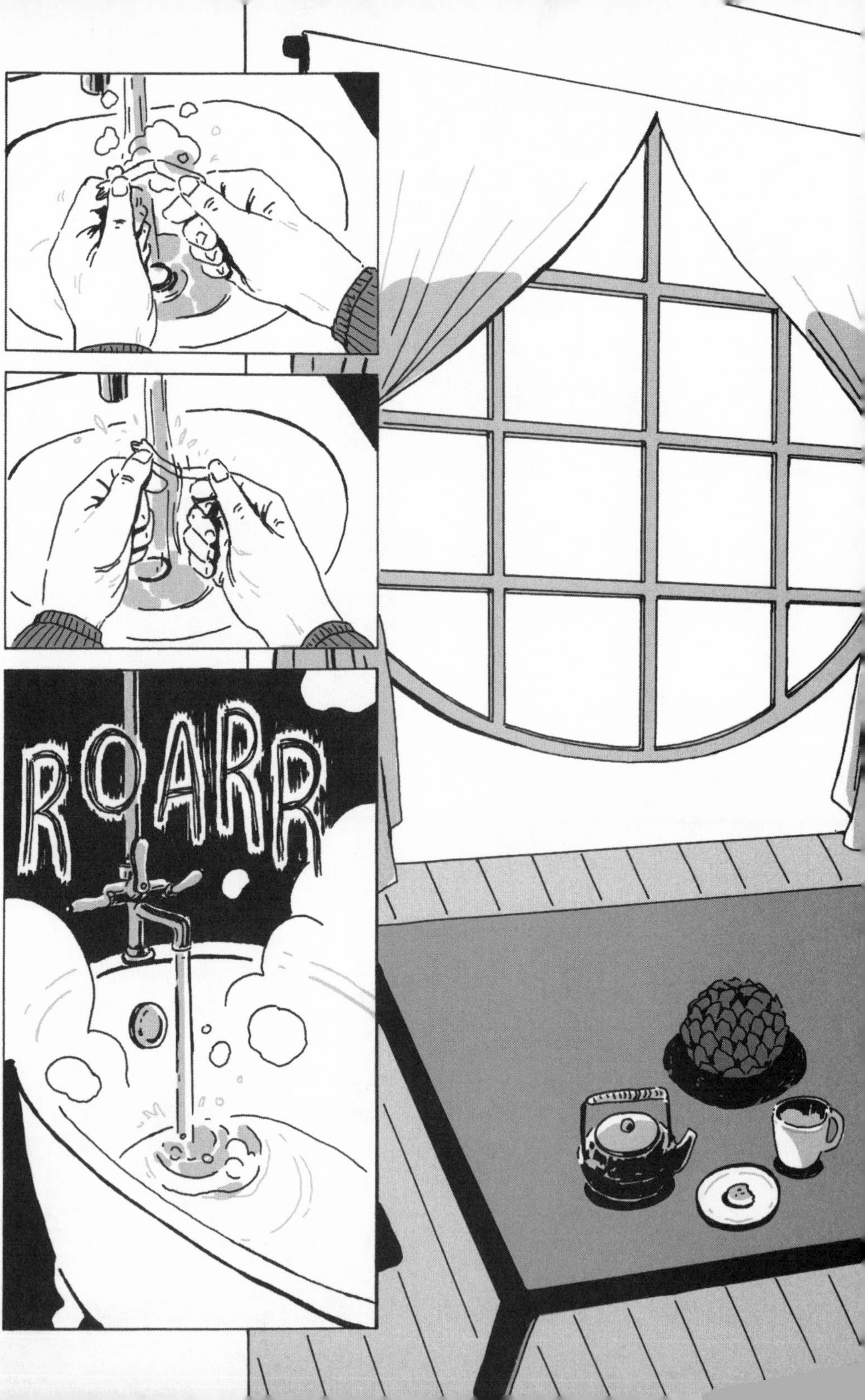
ROARR

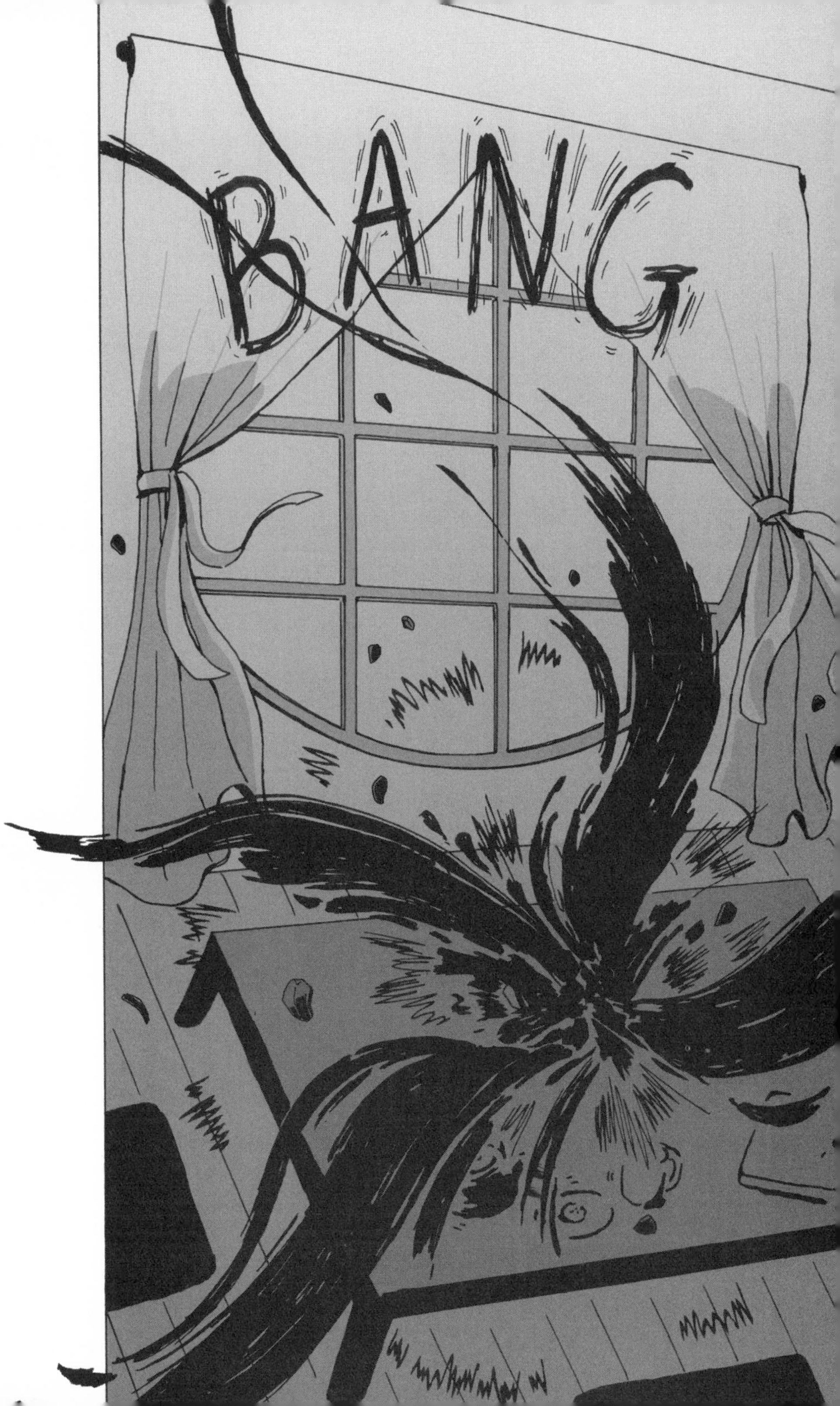
BANG

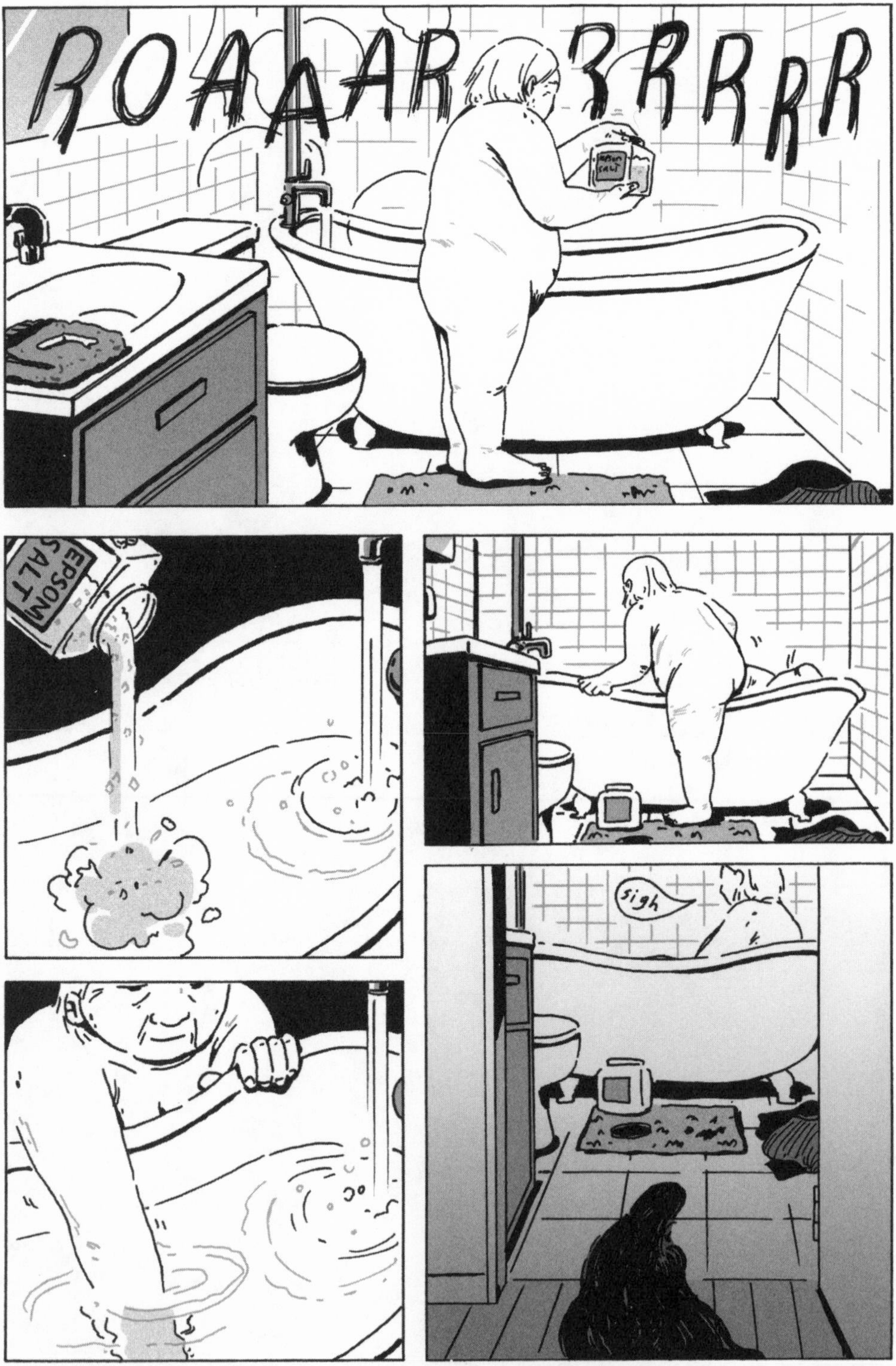
ROAAARRRRRR
EPSOM SALT
EPSOM SALT
sigh

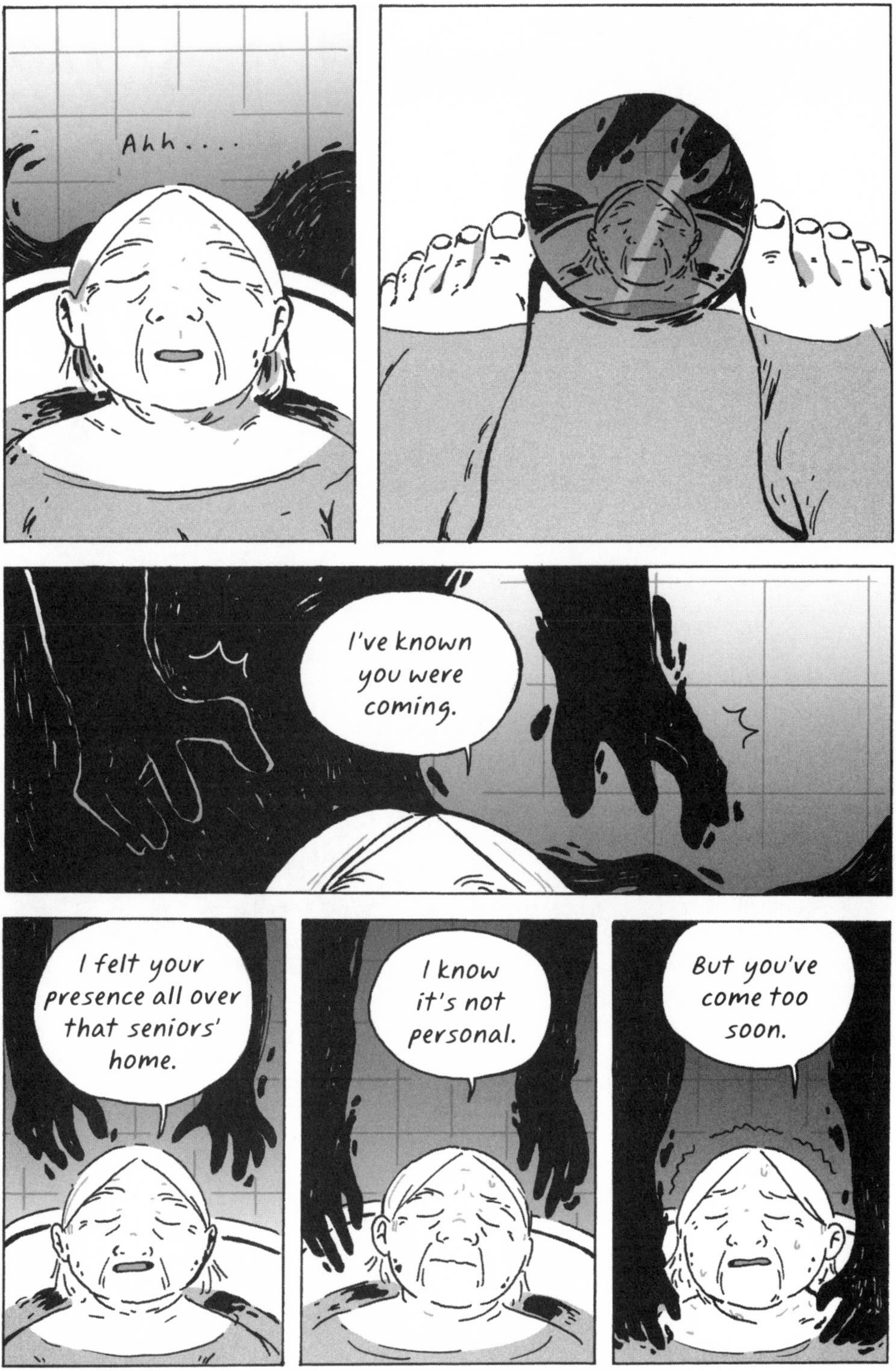
Ahh....
I've known you were coming.
I felt your presence all over that seniors' home.
I know it's not personal.
But you've come too soon.

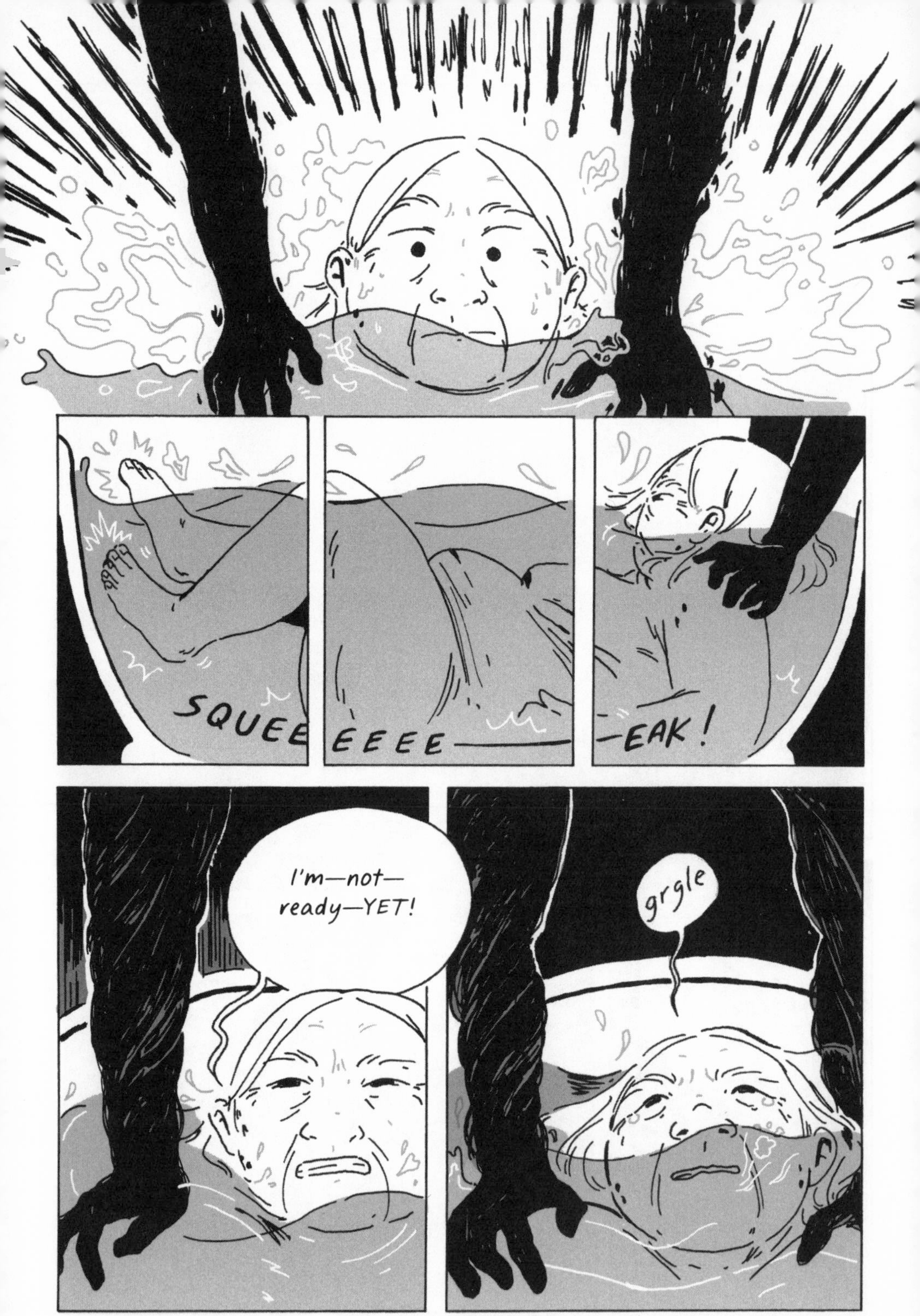
SQUEE
EEEE
—EAK!
I'm—not—ready—YET!
grgle

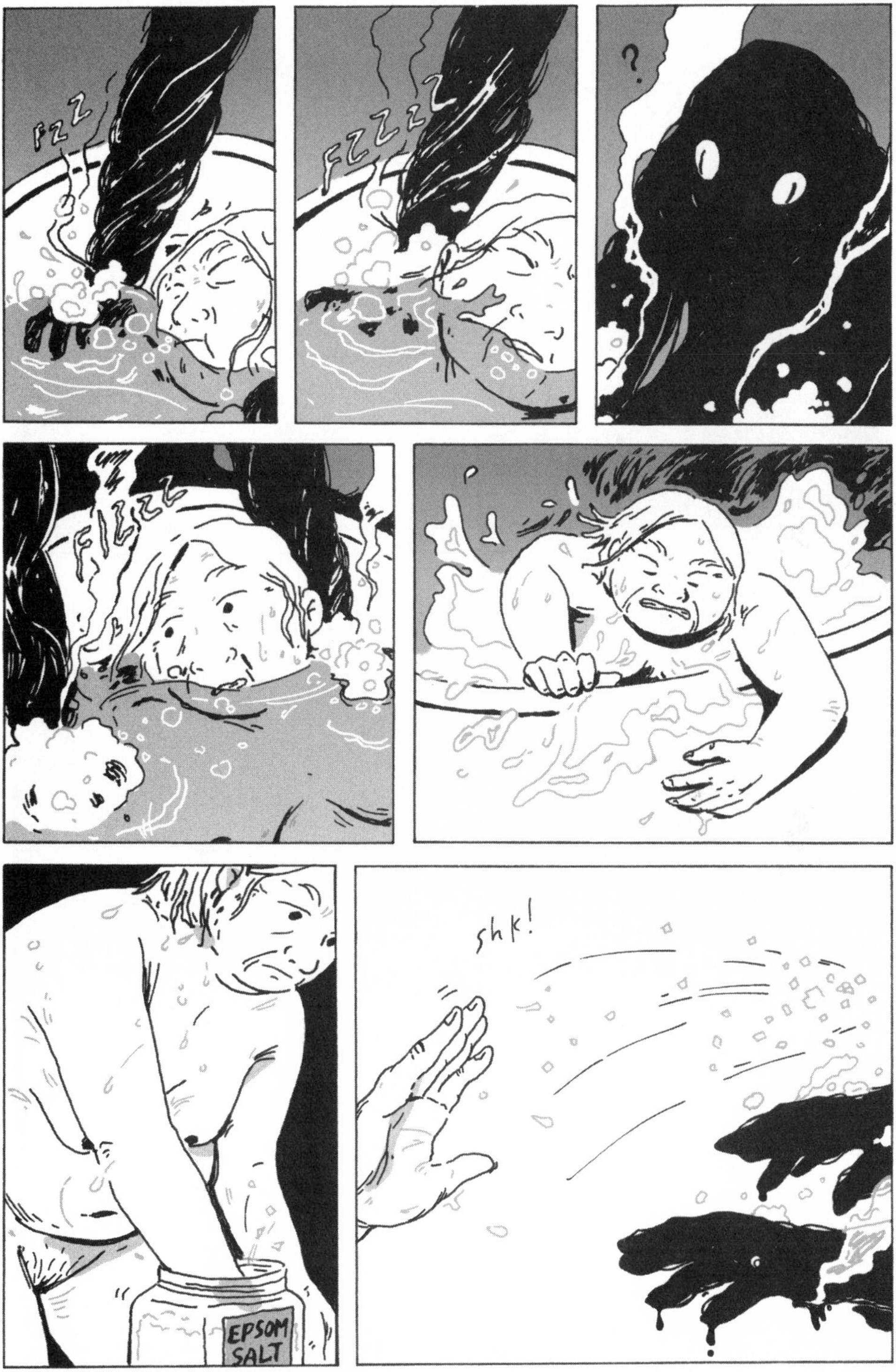
fzZ
FZZzZ
?
FIZZZ
shk!
EPSOM SALT

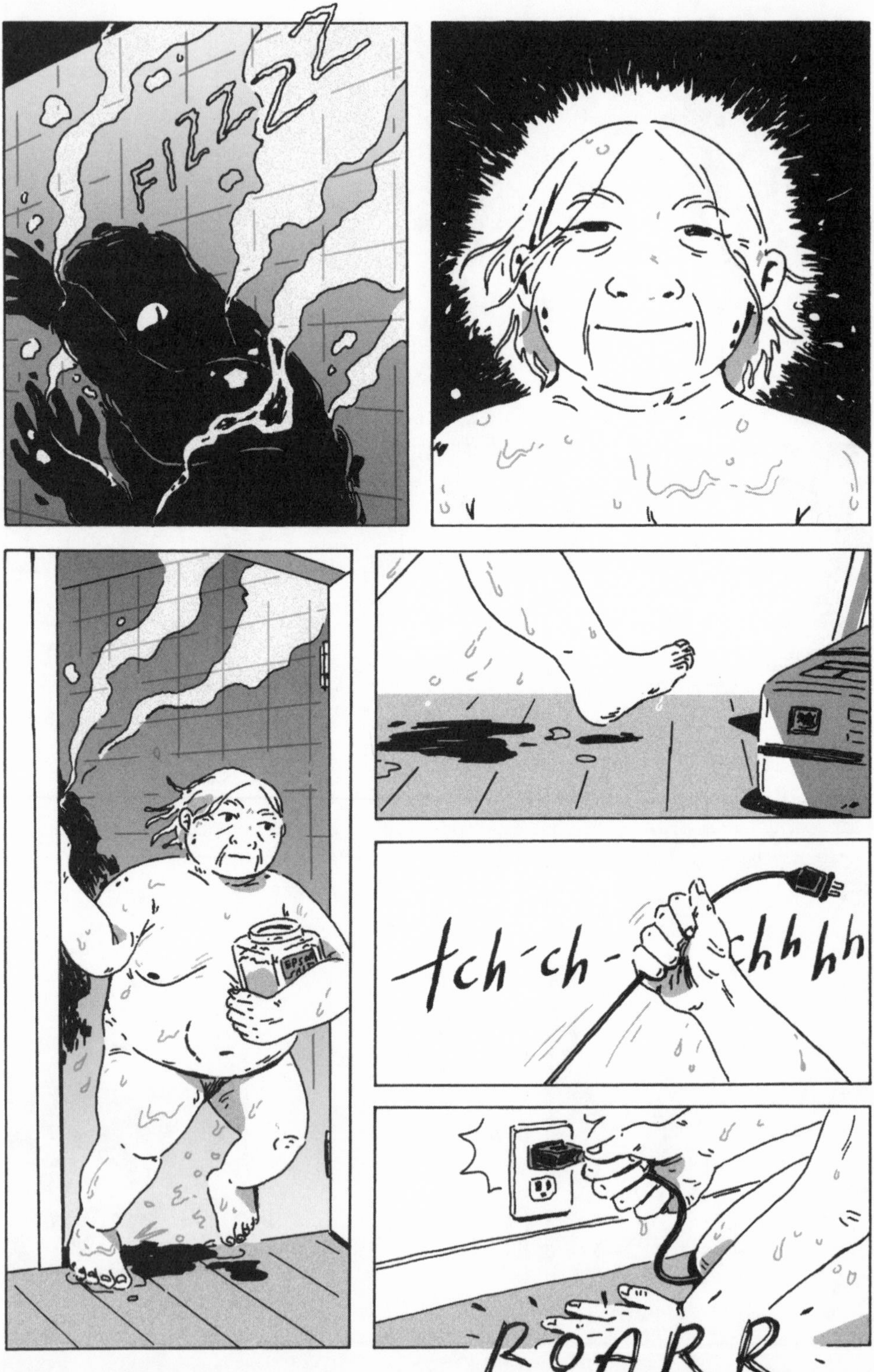
FIZZZZ
tch-ch-chhhhh
ROARR

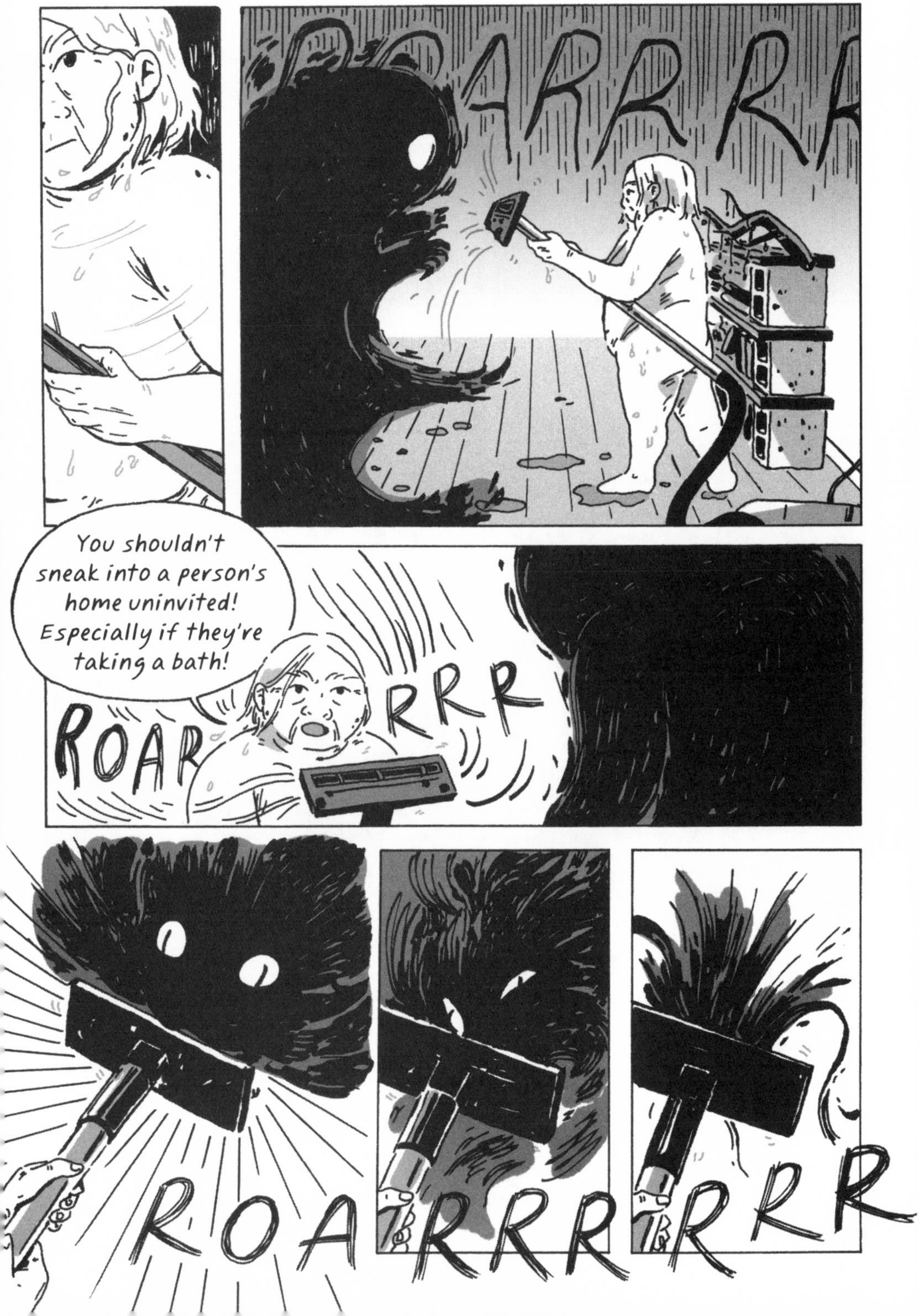
ROARRRRR
You shouldn't sneak into a person's home uninvited! Especially if they're taking a bath!
ROARRRR
ROARRRRRRR

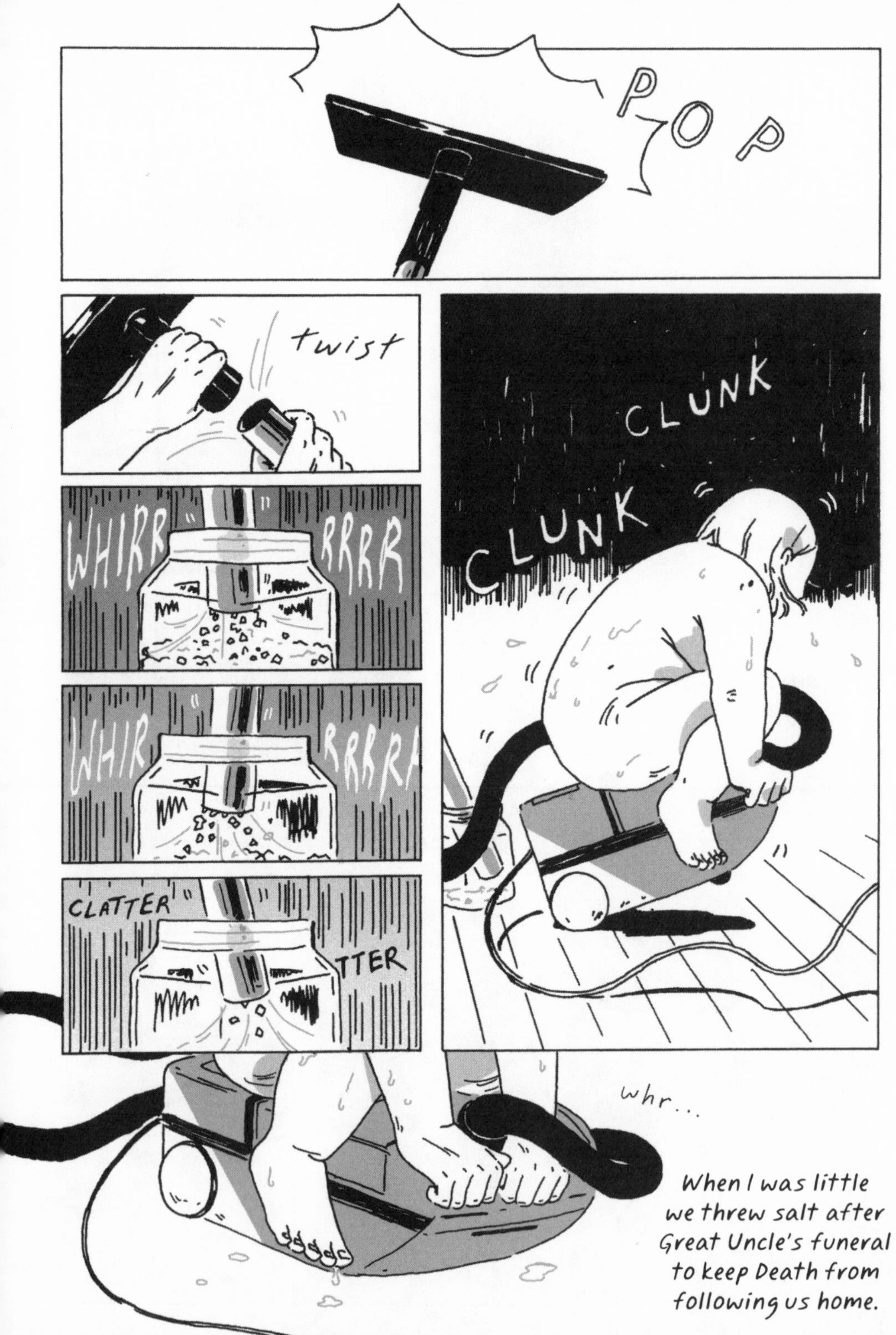
POP
twist
CLUNK
CLUNK
WHIRR
RRRR
WHIR
RRRRA
CLATTER
TTER
whr...
When I was little we threw salt after Great Uncle's funeral to keep Death from following us home.

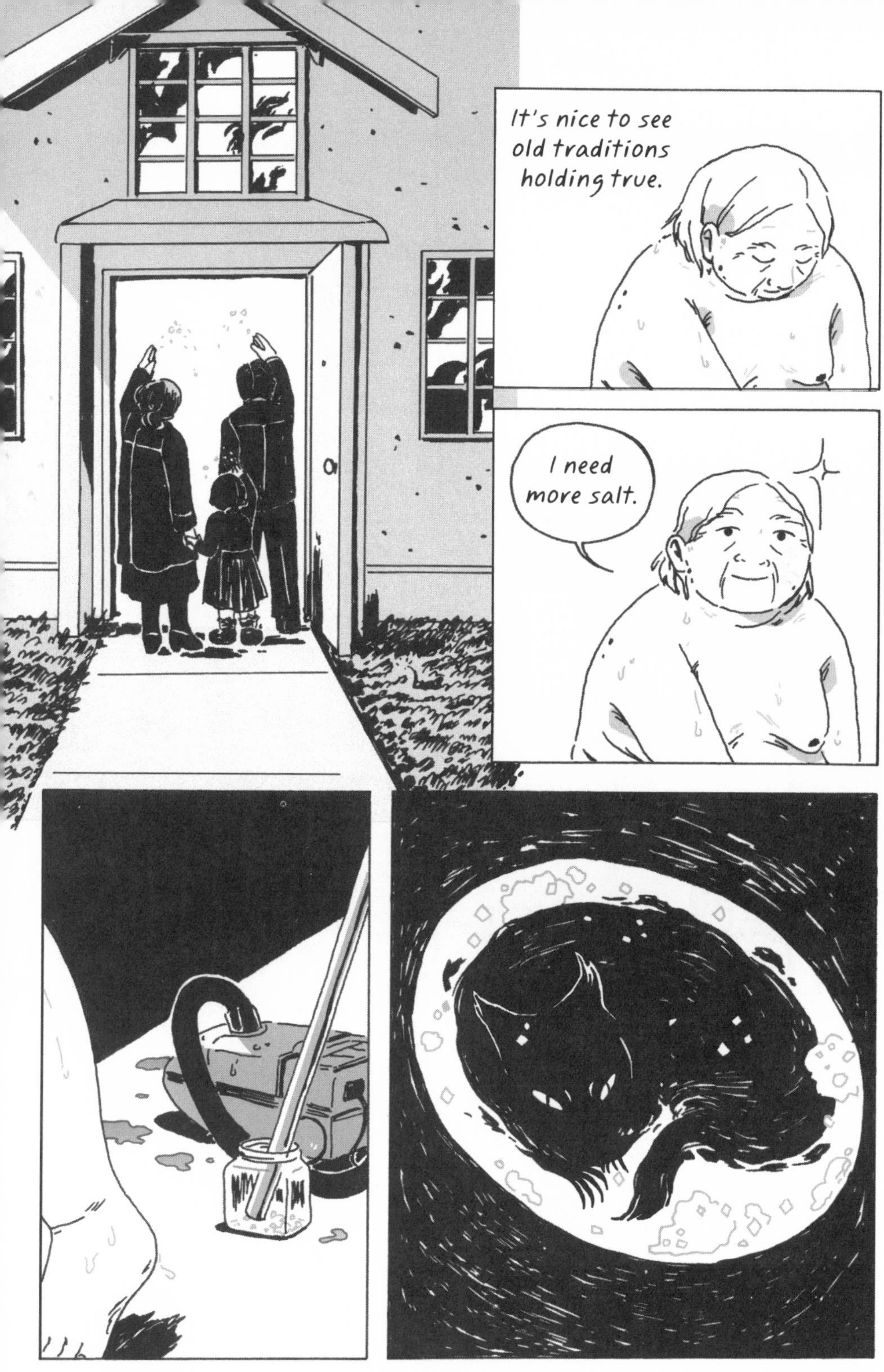
It's nice to see old traditions holding true.
I need more salt.

Chapter Five

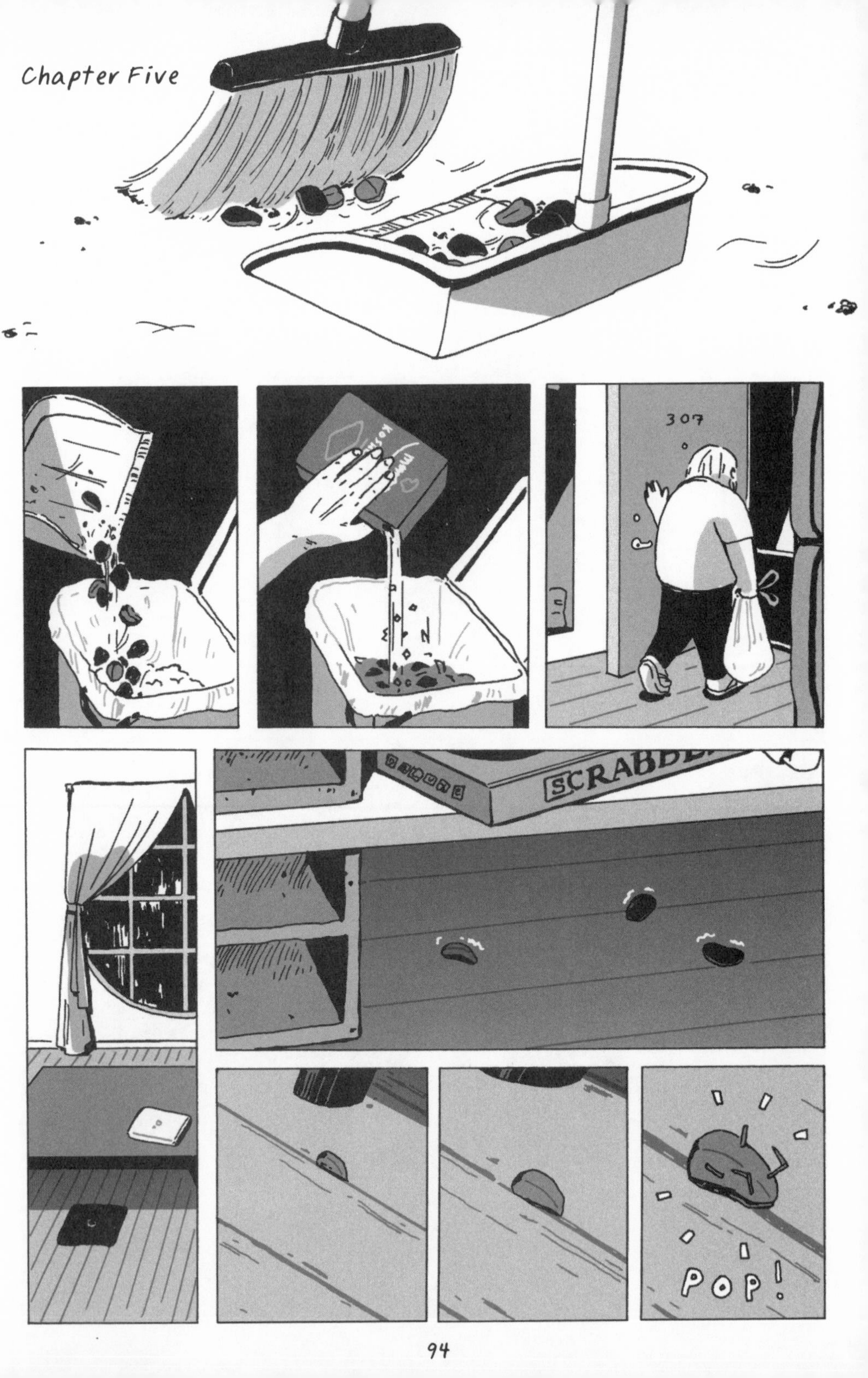
307
SCRABB
POP!

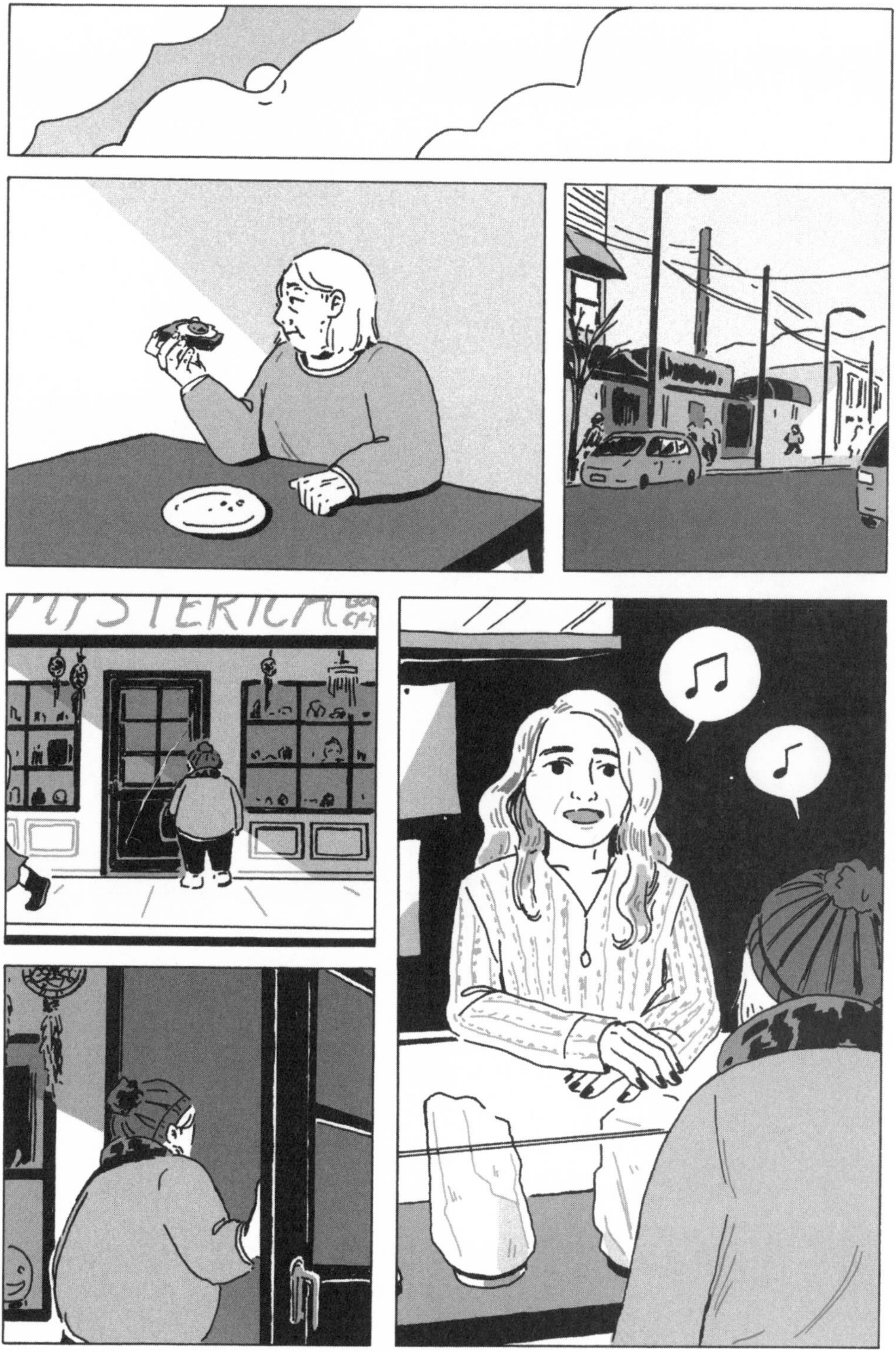
MYSTERICA

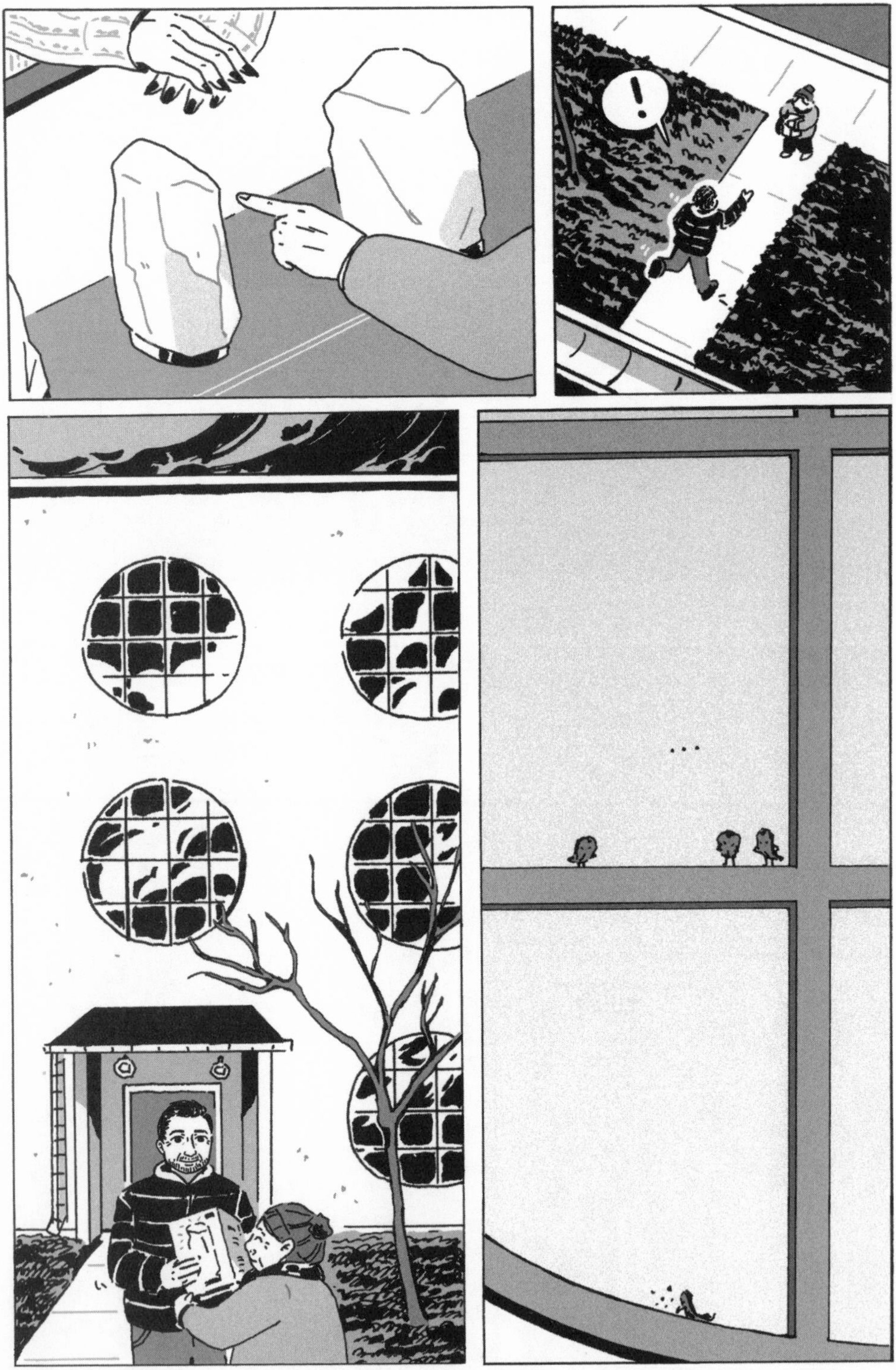
!
...

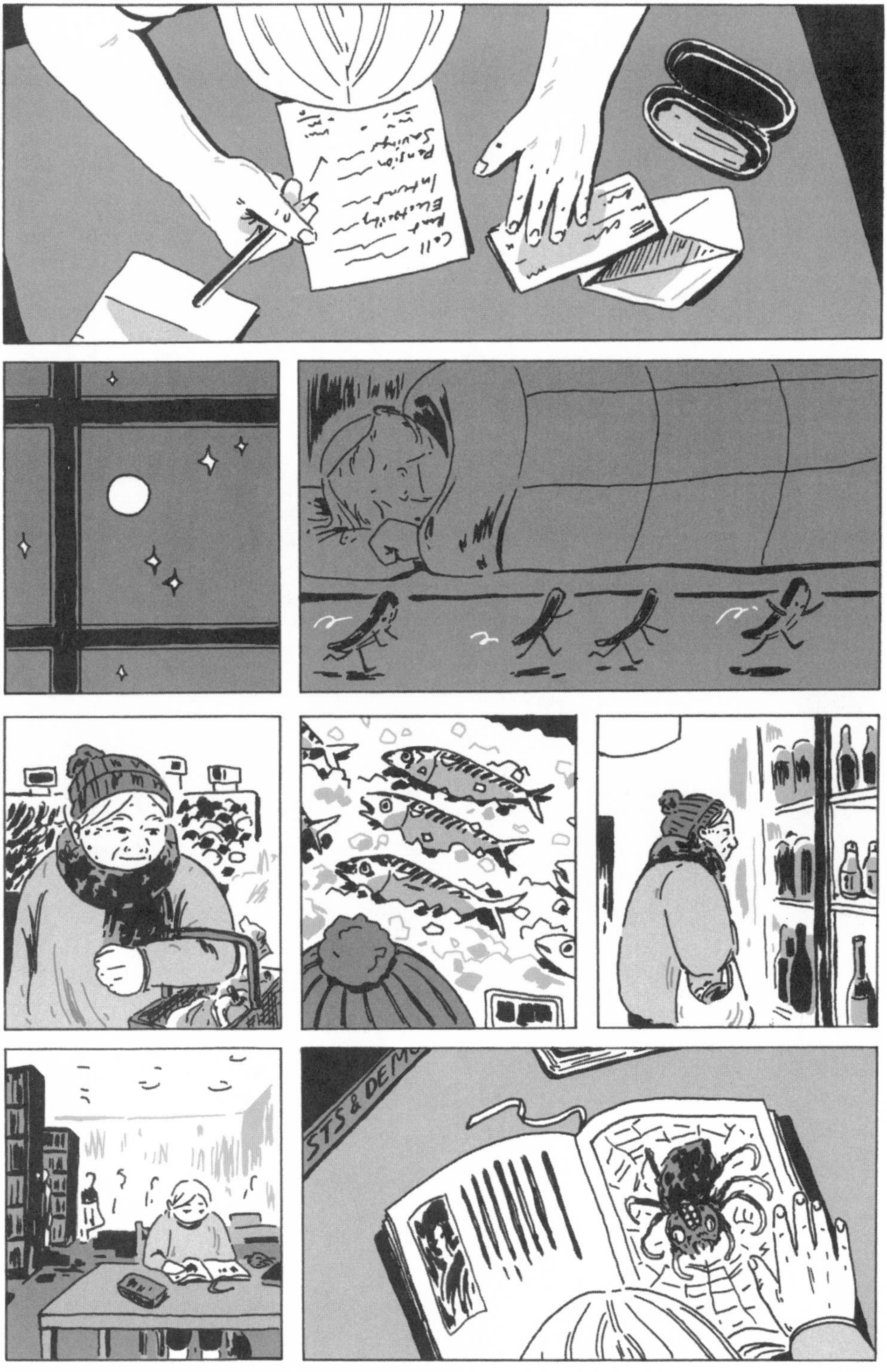
Call
Rent
Electricity
Internet
Pension
Savings

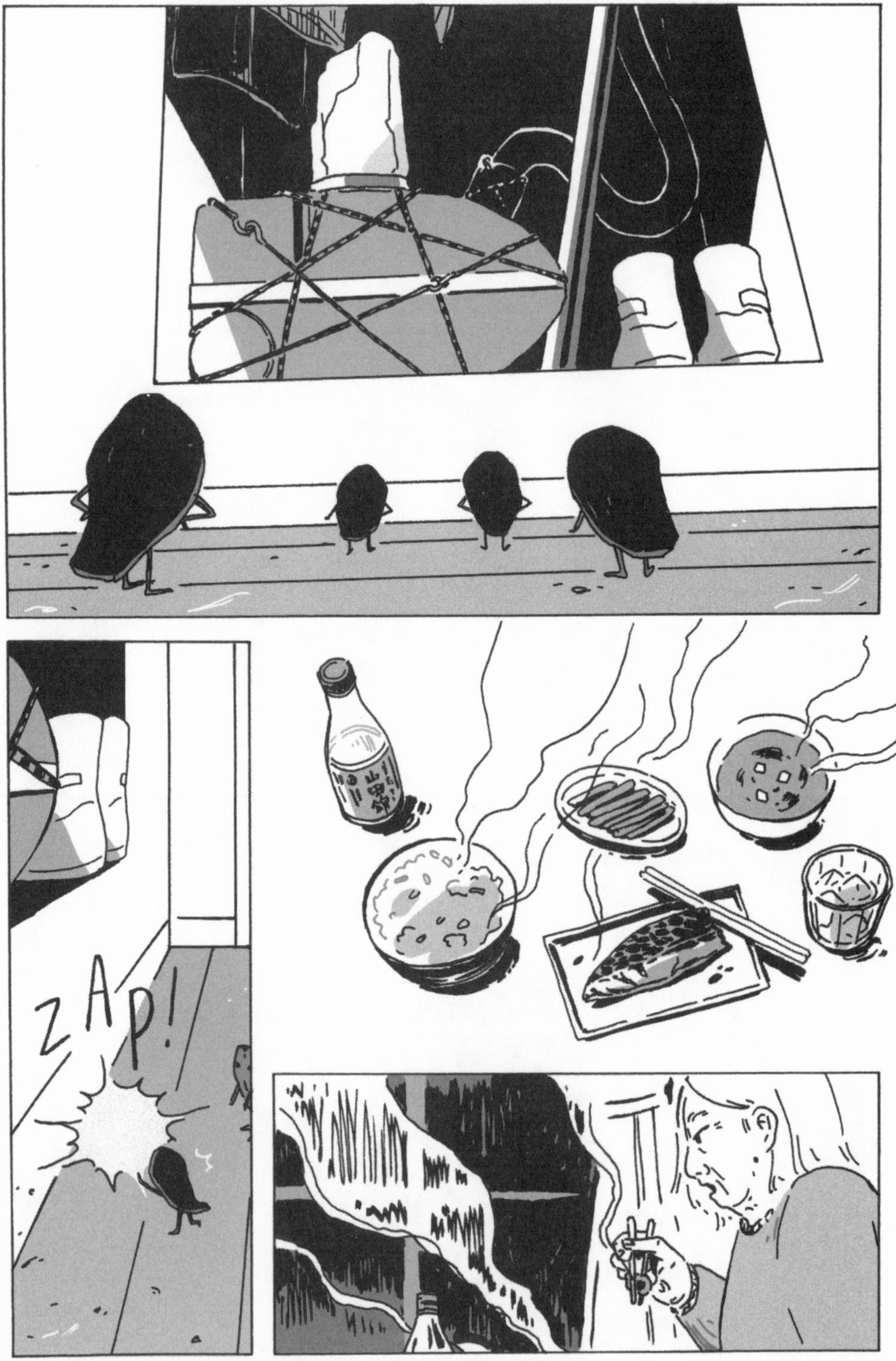
ZAP!

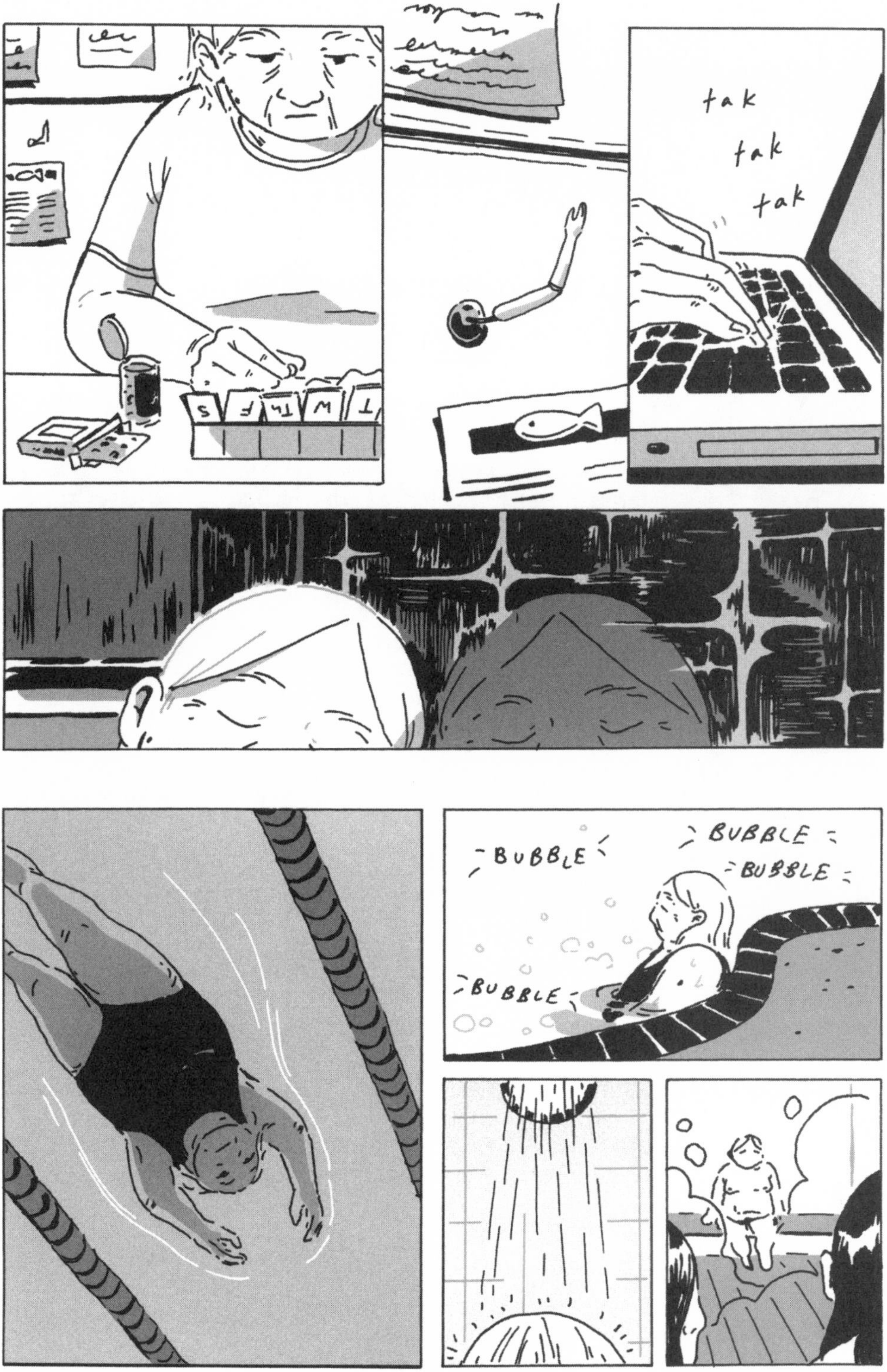
tak
tak
tak
BUBBLE
BUBBLE
BUBBLE
BUBBLE

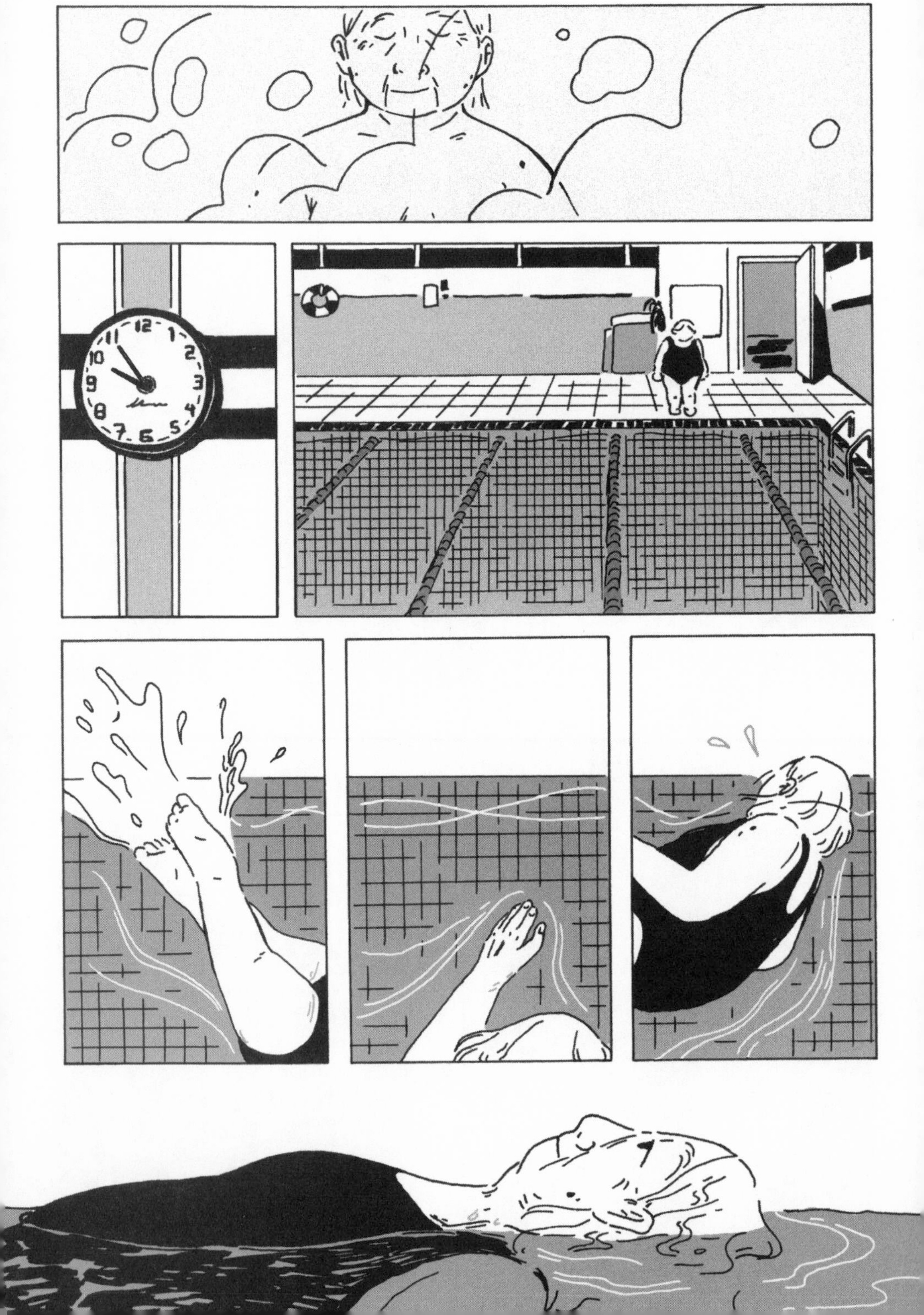

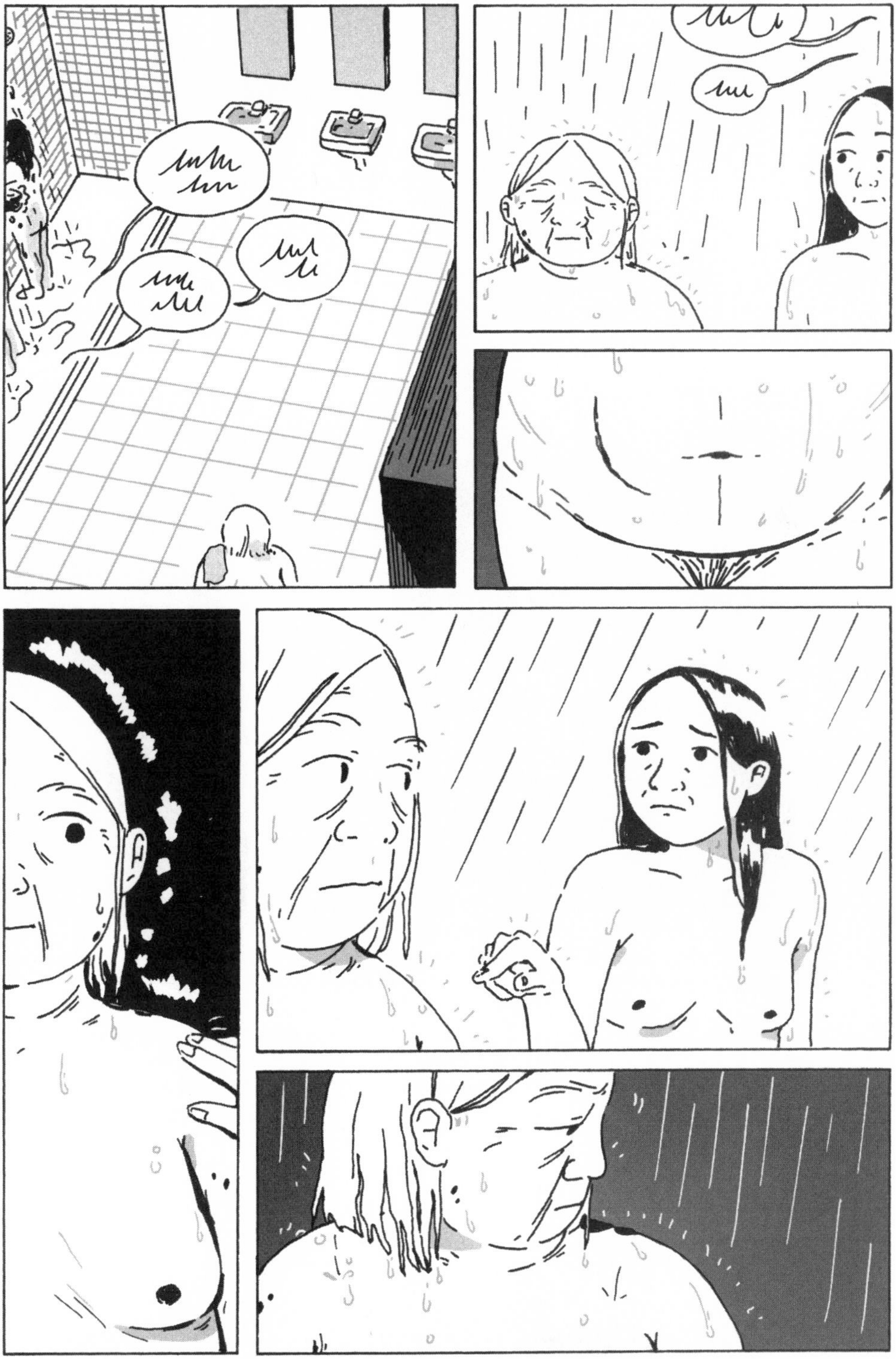

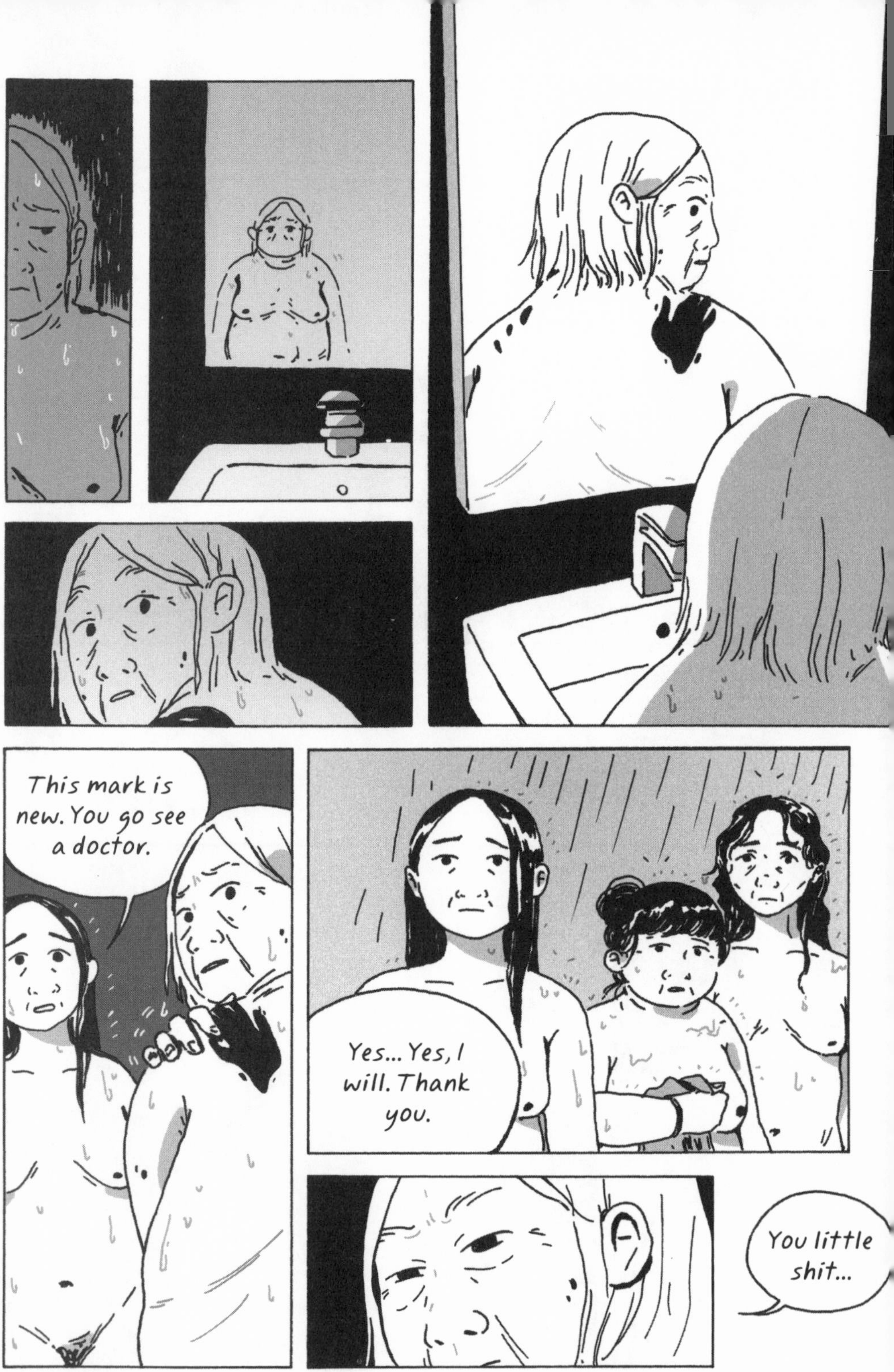
This mark is new. You go see a doctor.
Yes... Yes, I will. Thank you.
You little shit...

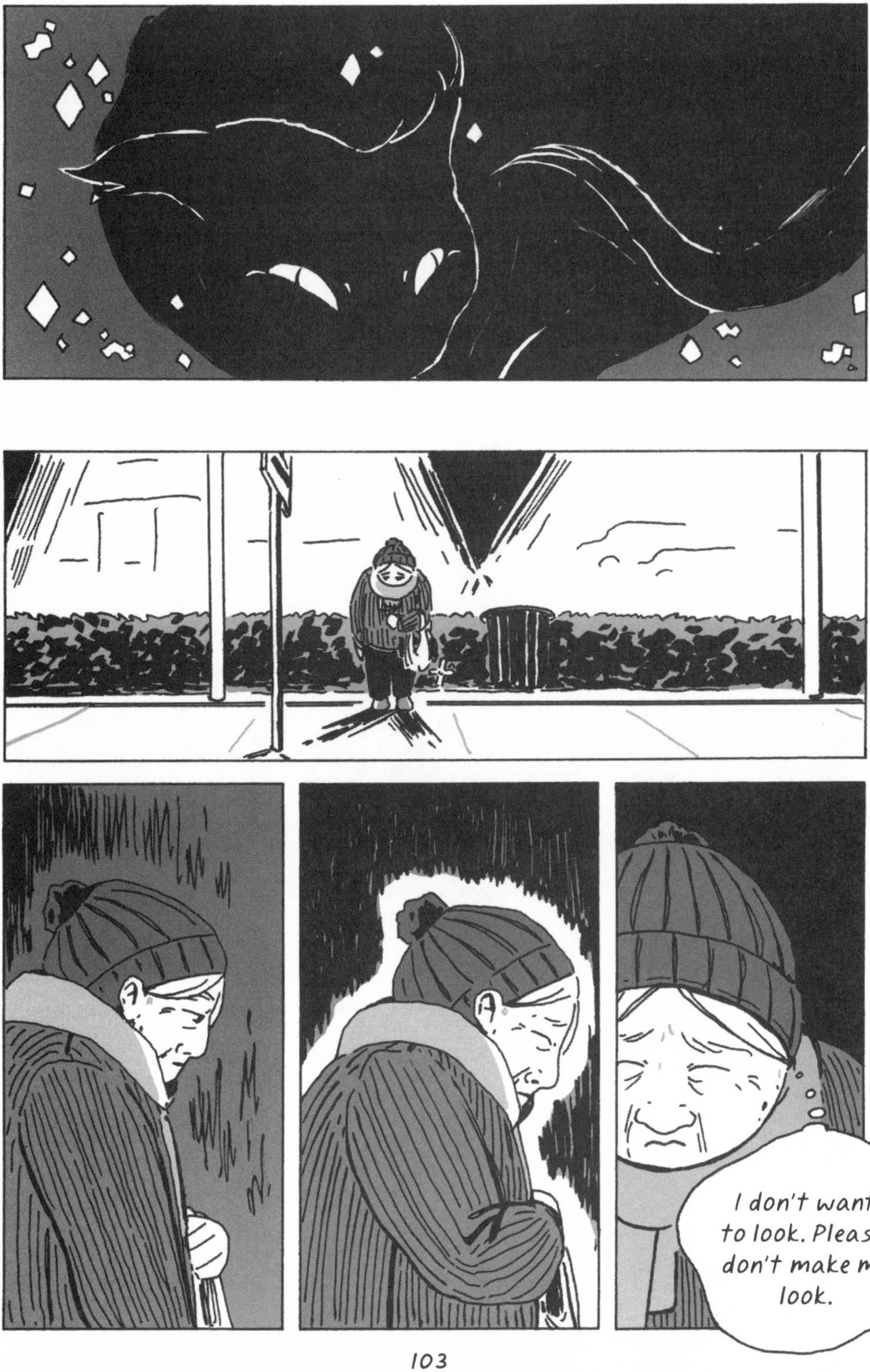
I don't want to look. Please, don't make me look.

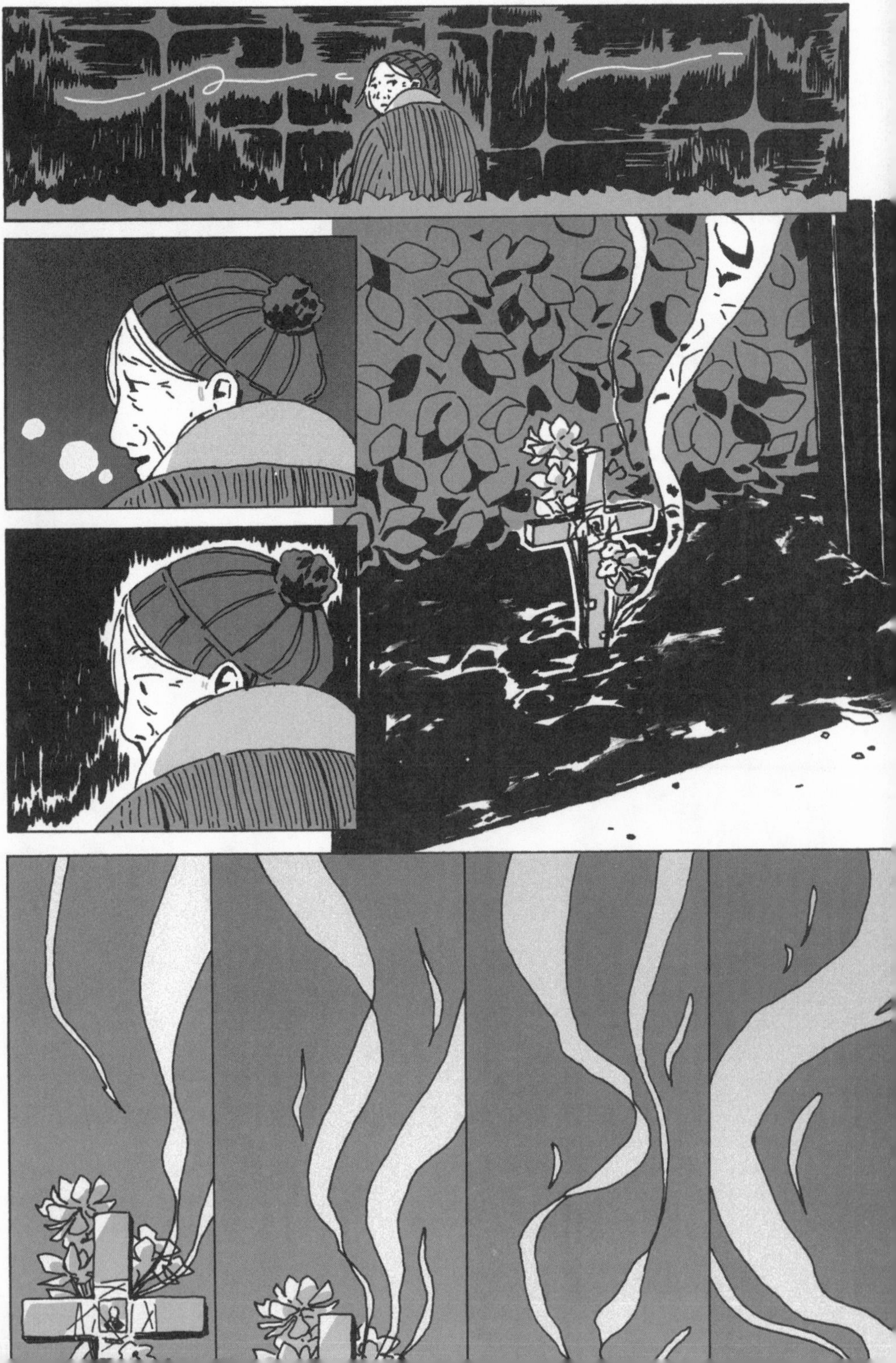

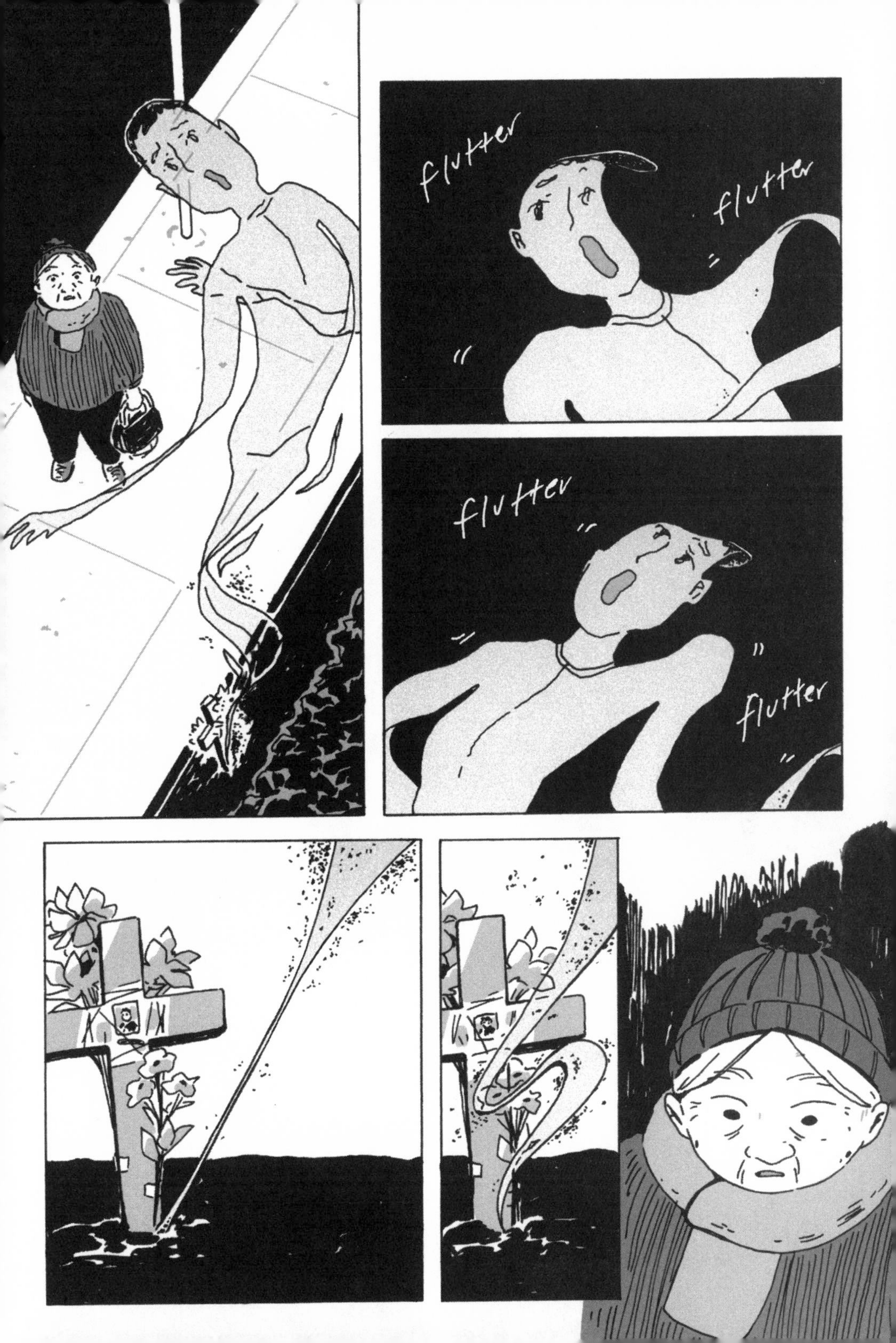
flutter
flutter
flutter
flutter

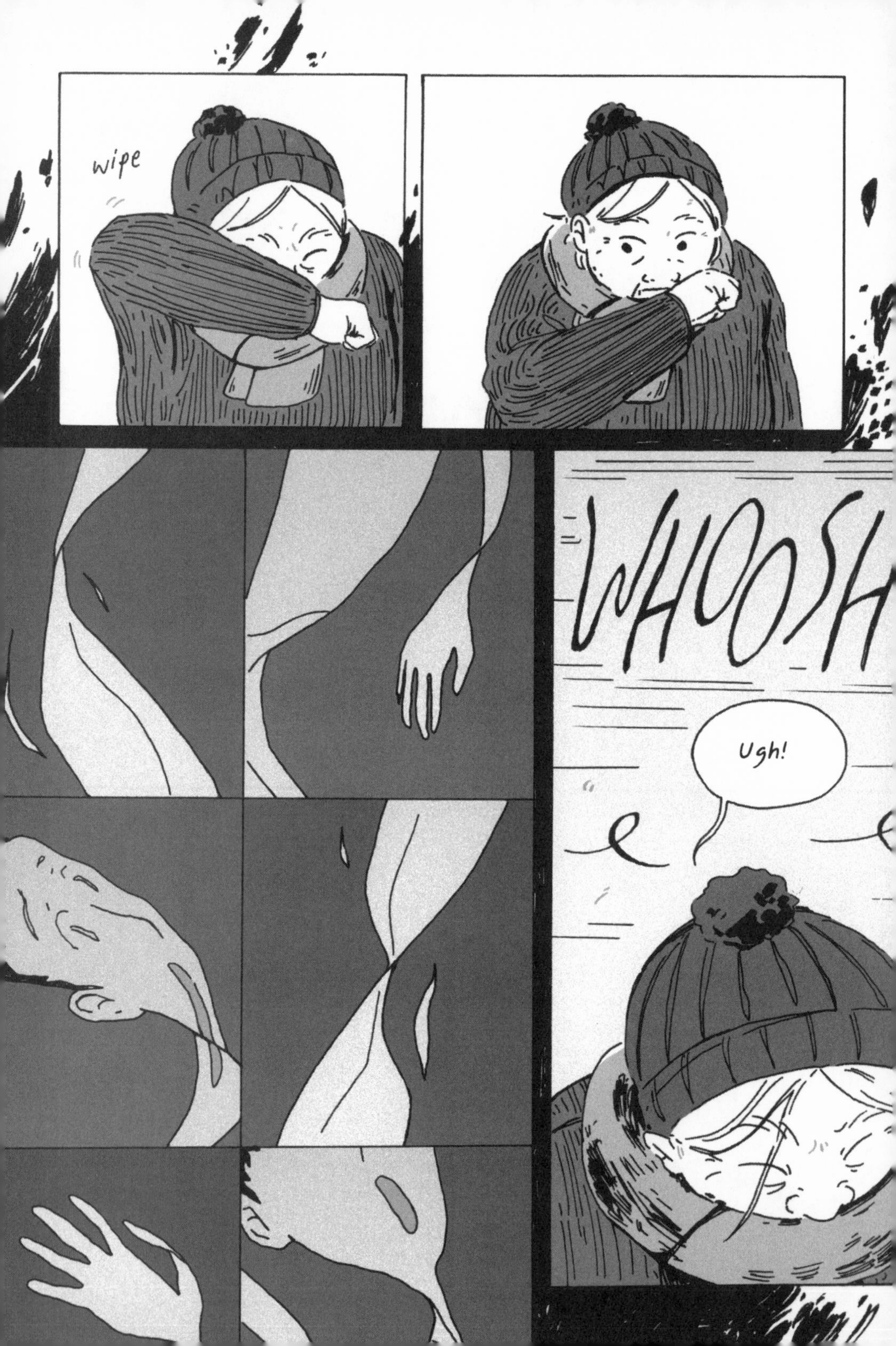
wipe
WHOOSH
Ugh!

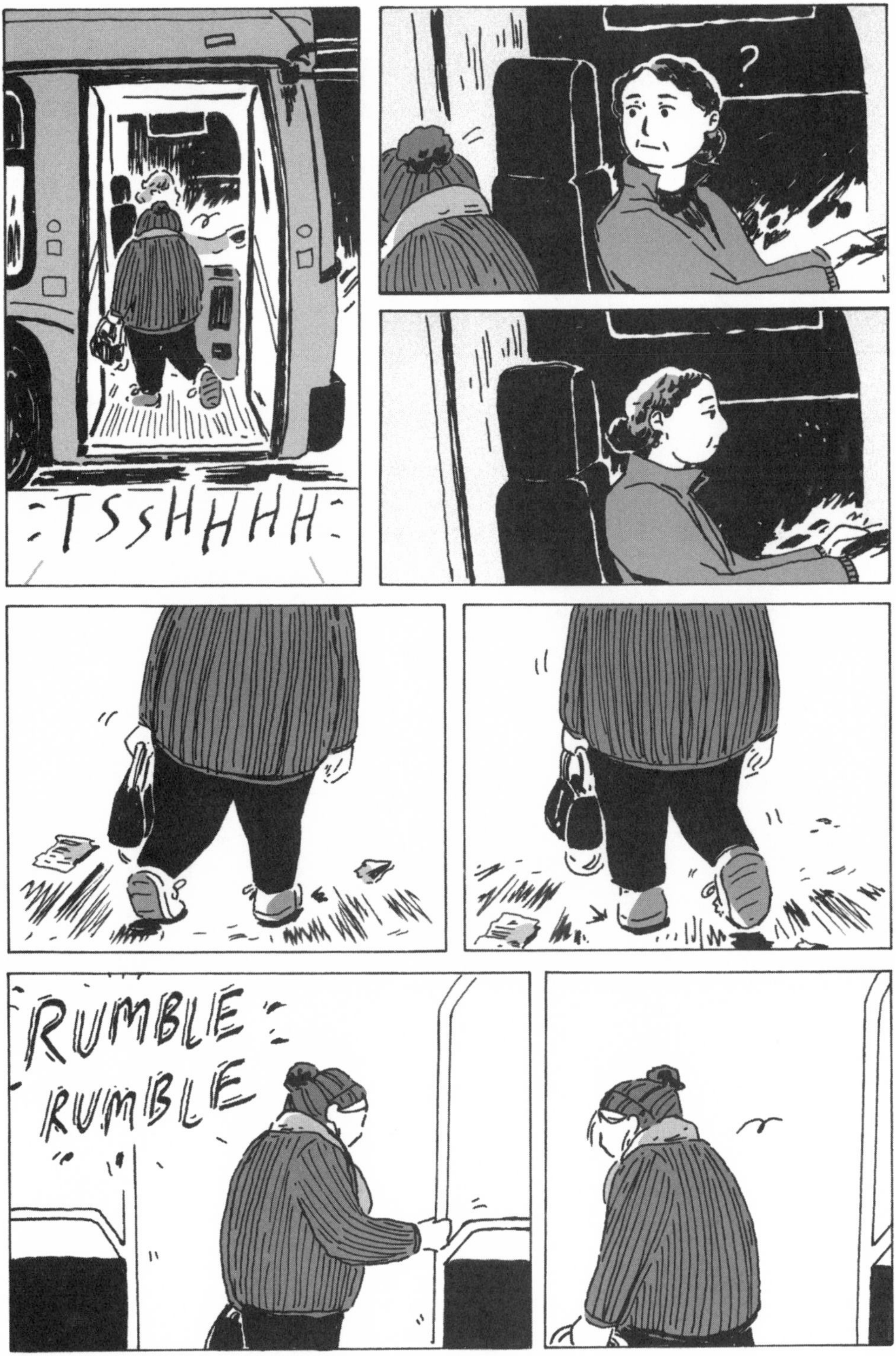
TSsHHHH
?
RUMBLE
RUMBLE

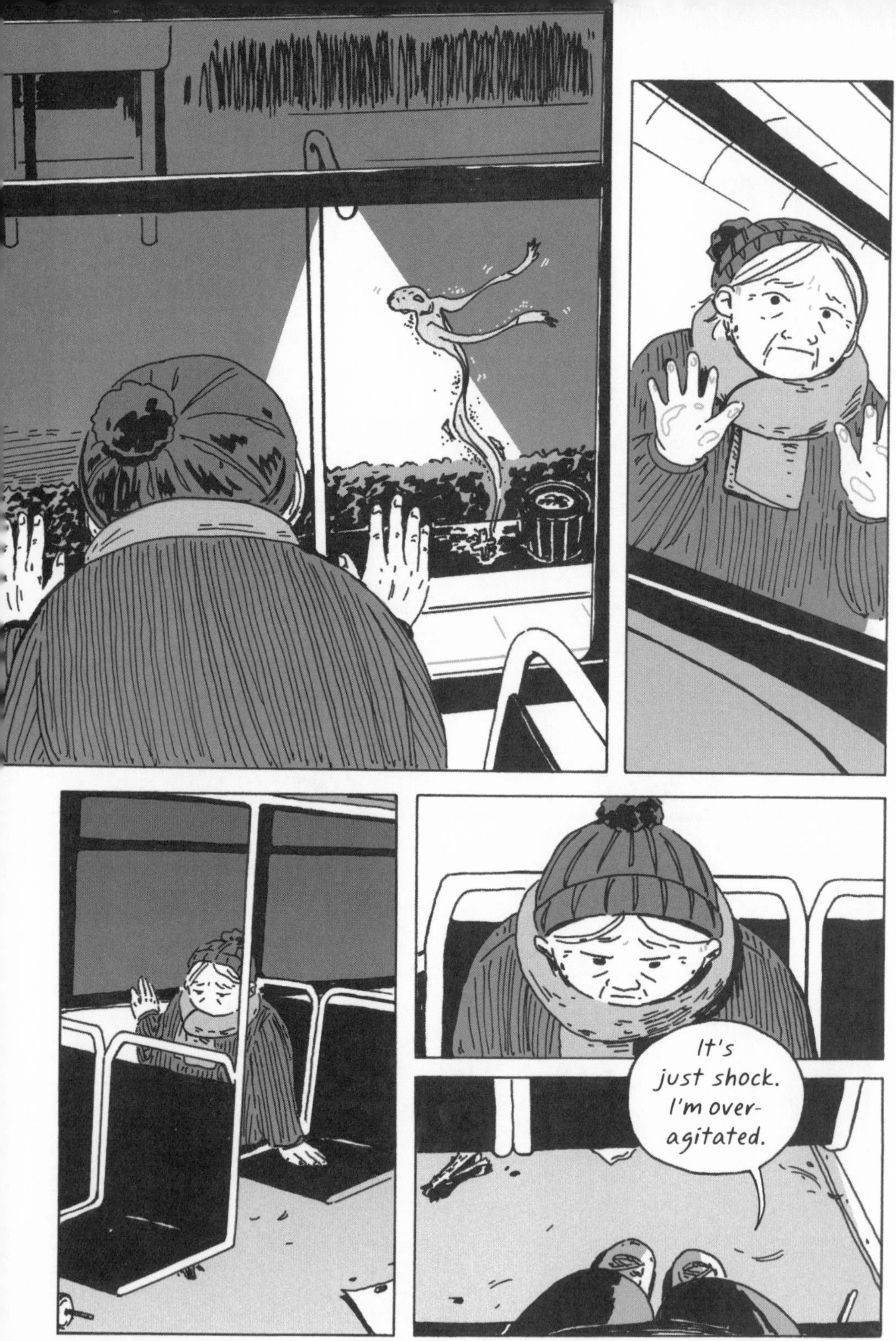
It's just shock. I'm over-agitated.

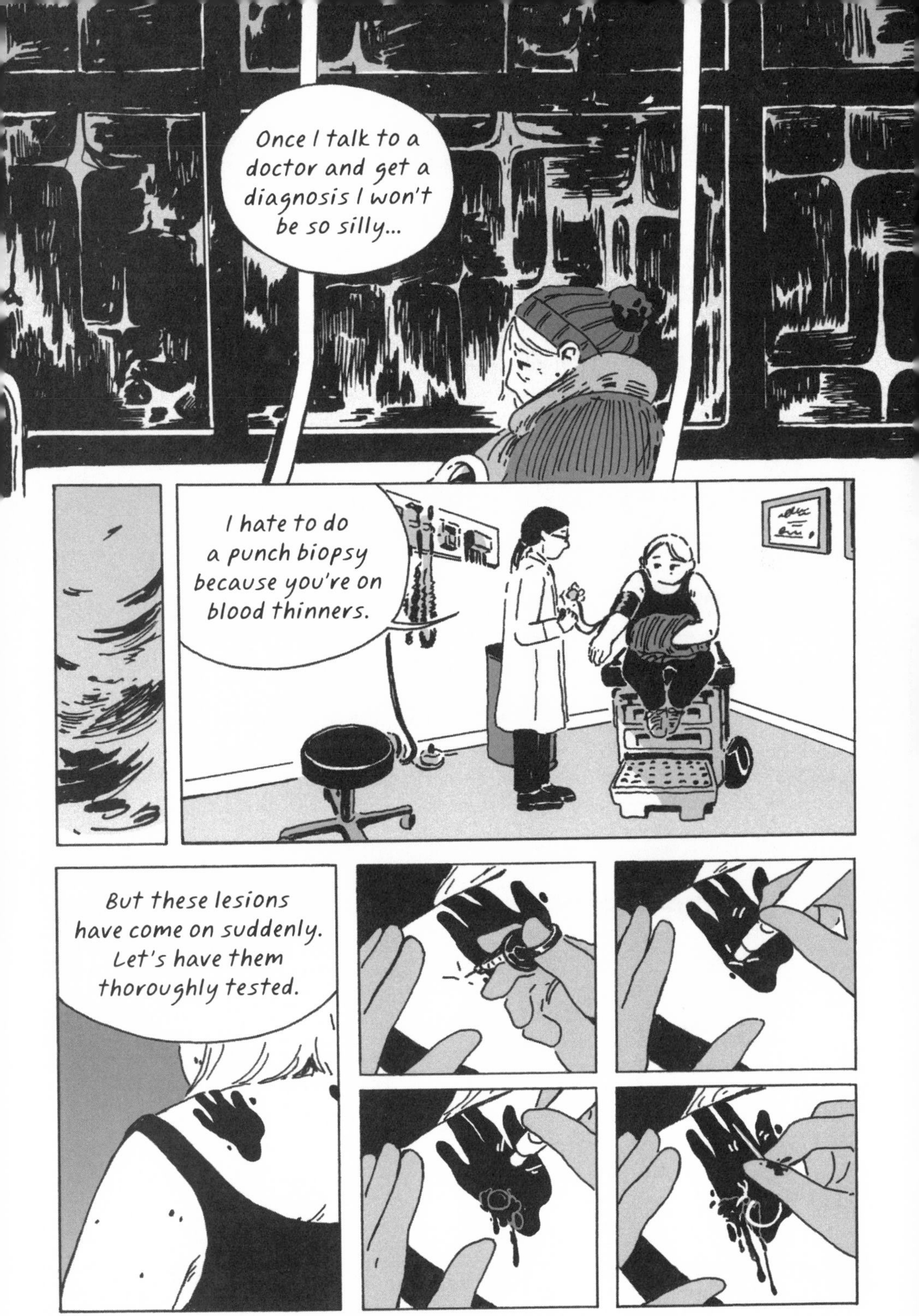
Once I talk to a doctor and get a diagnosis I won't be so silly...
I hate to do a punch biopsy because you're on blood thinners.
But these lesions have come on suddenly. Let's have them thoroughly tested.

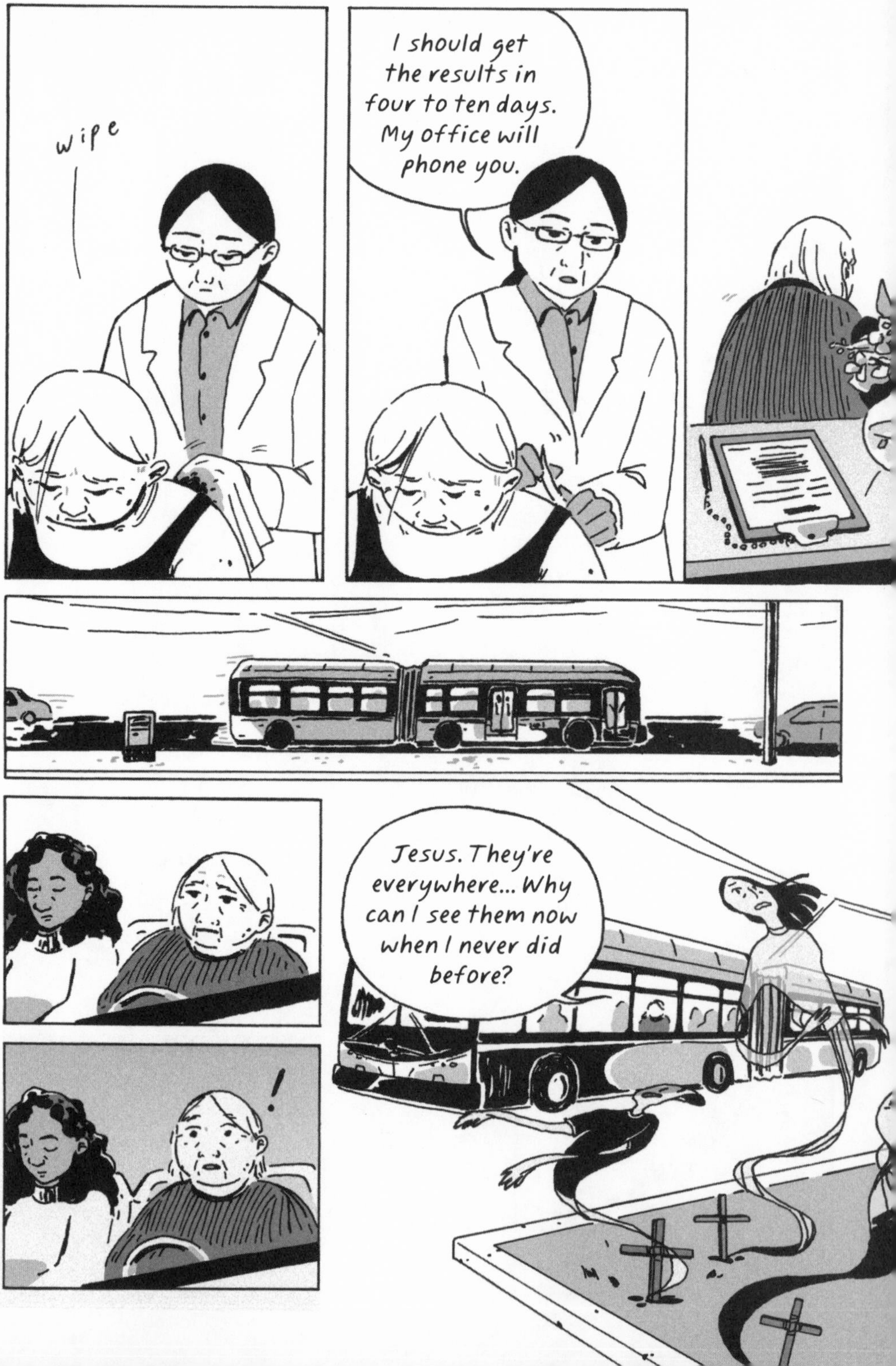
wipe
I should get the results in four to ten days. My office will phone you.
Jesus. They're everywhere... Why can I see them now when I never did before?
!

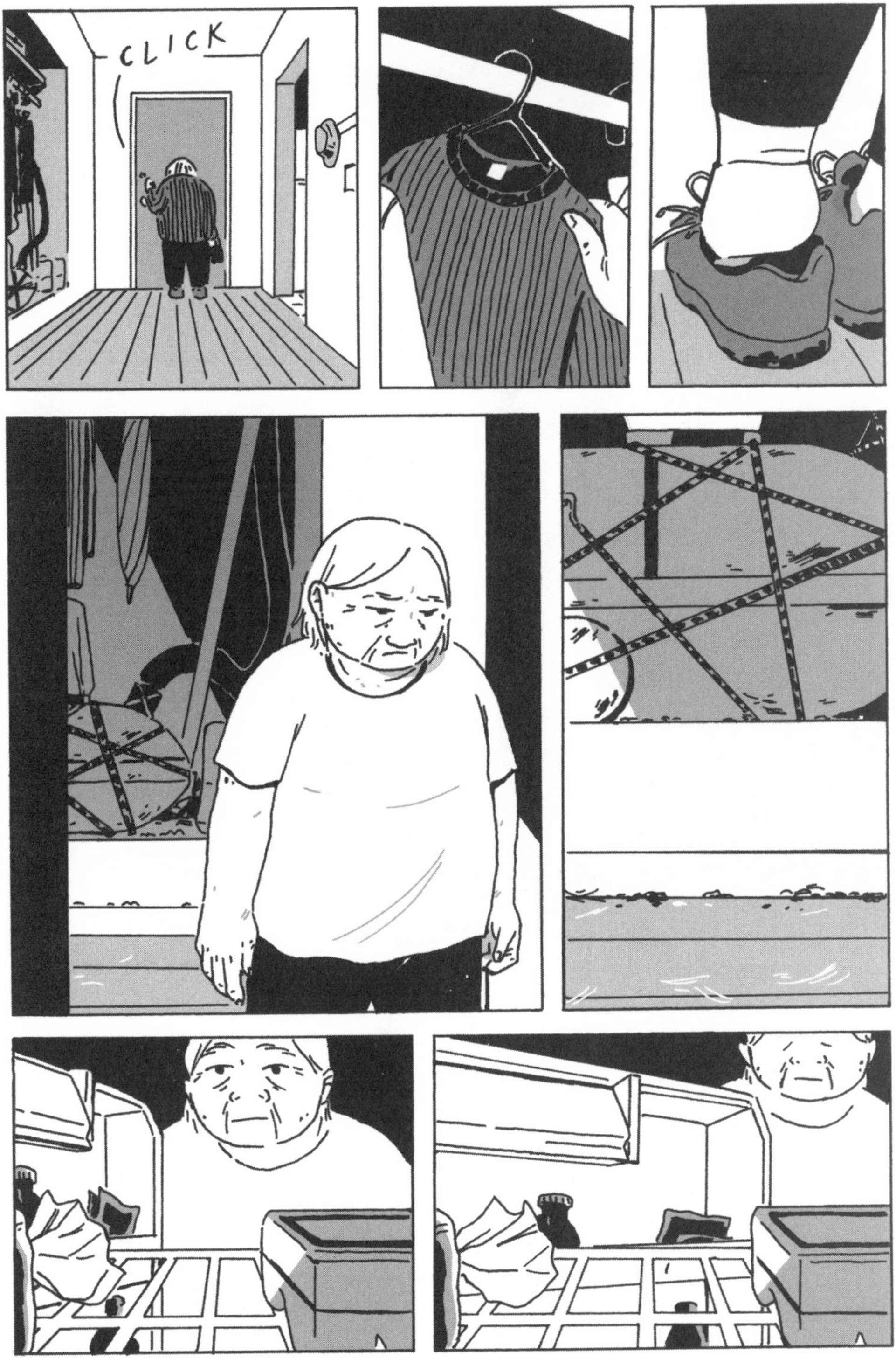
CLICK

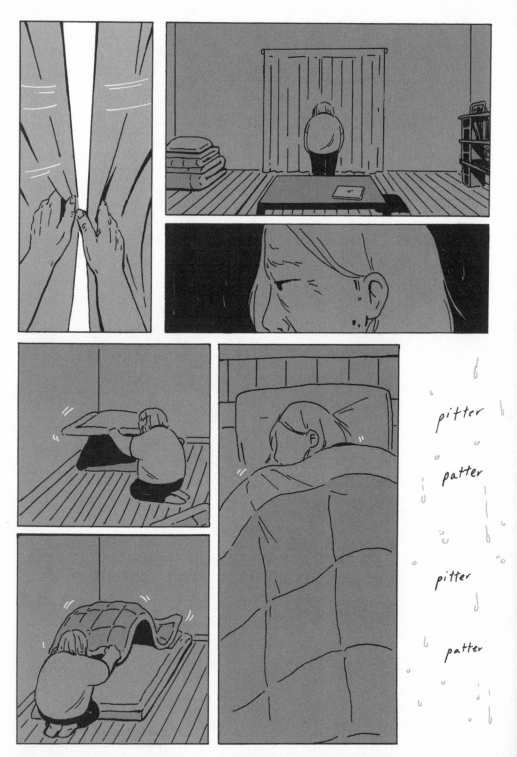

pitter

patter

pitter

patter

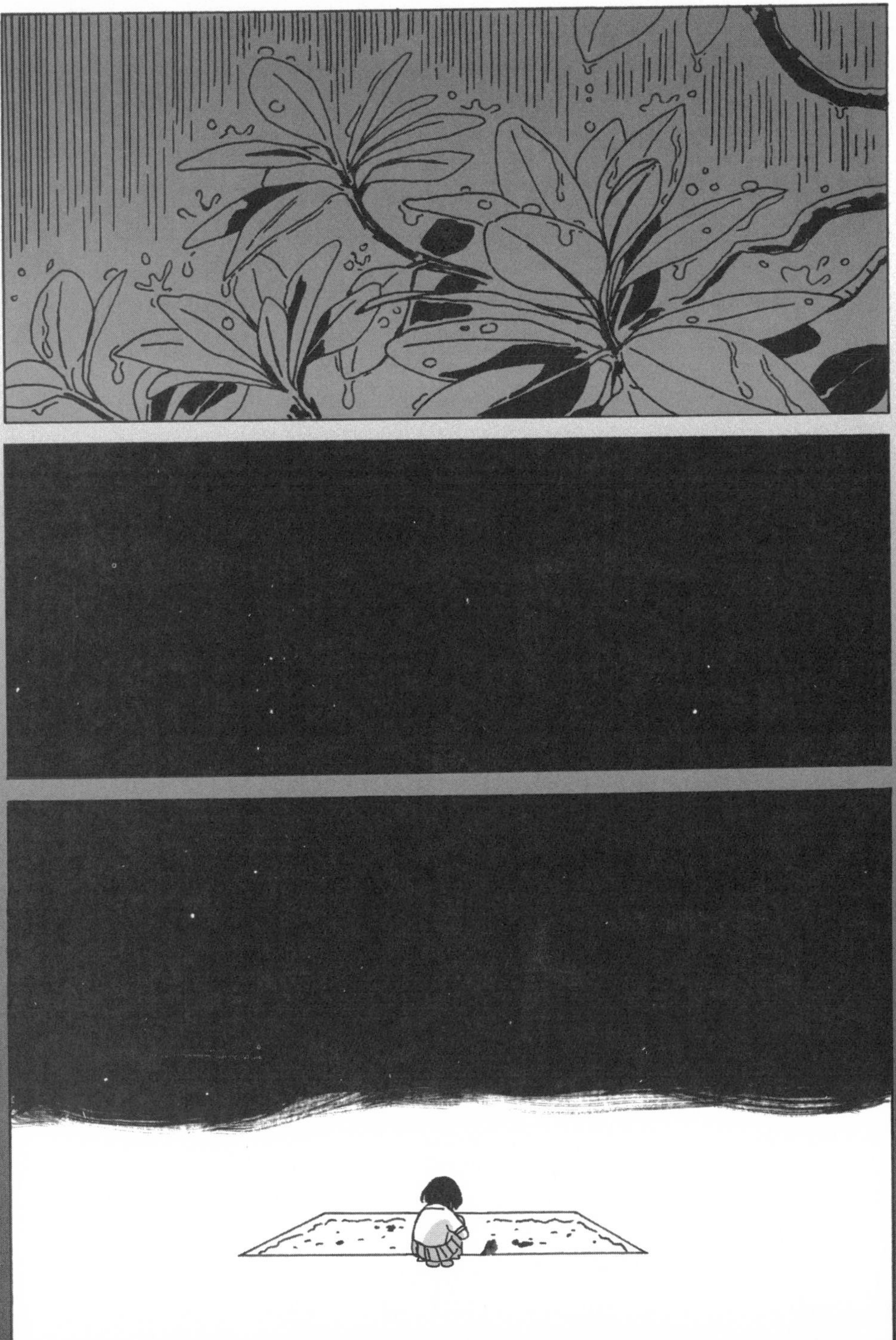

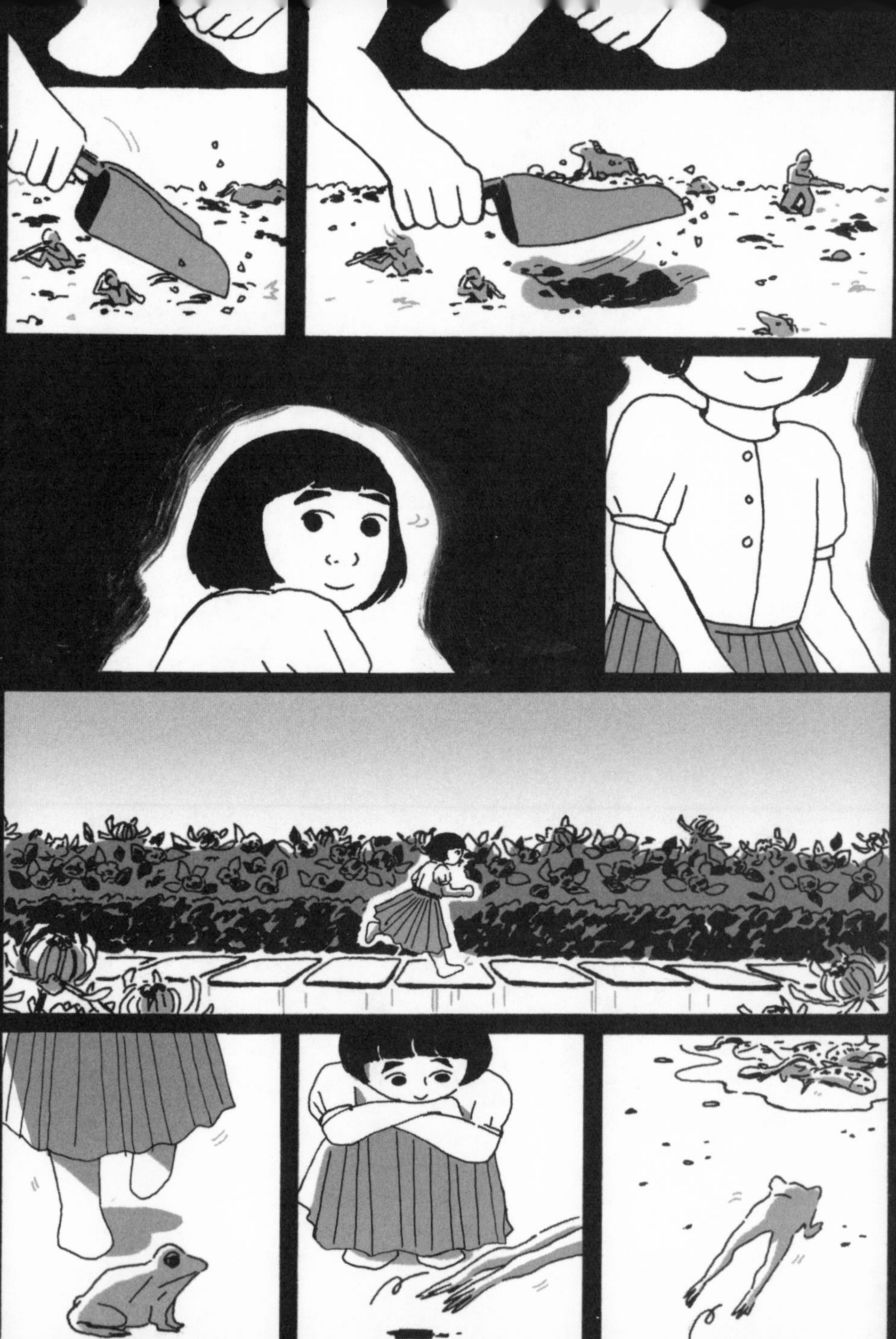

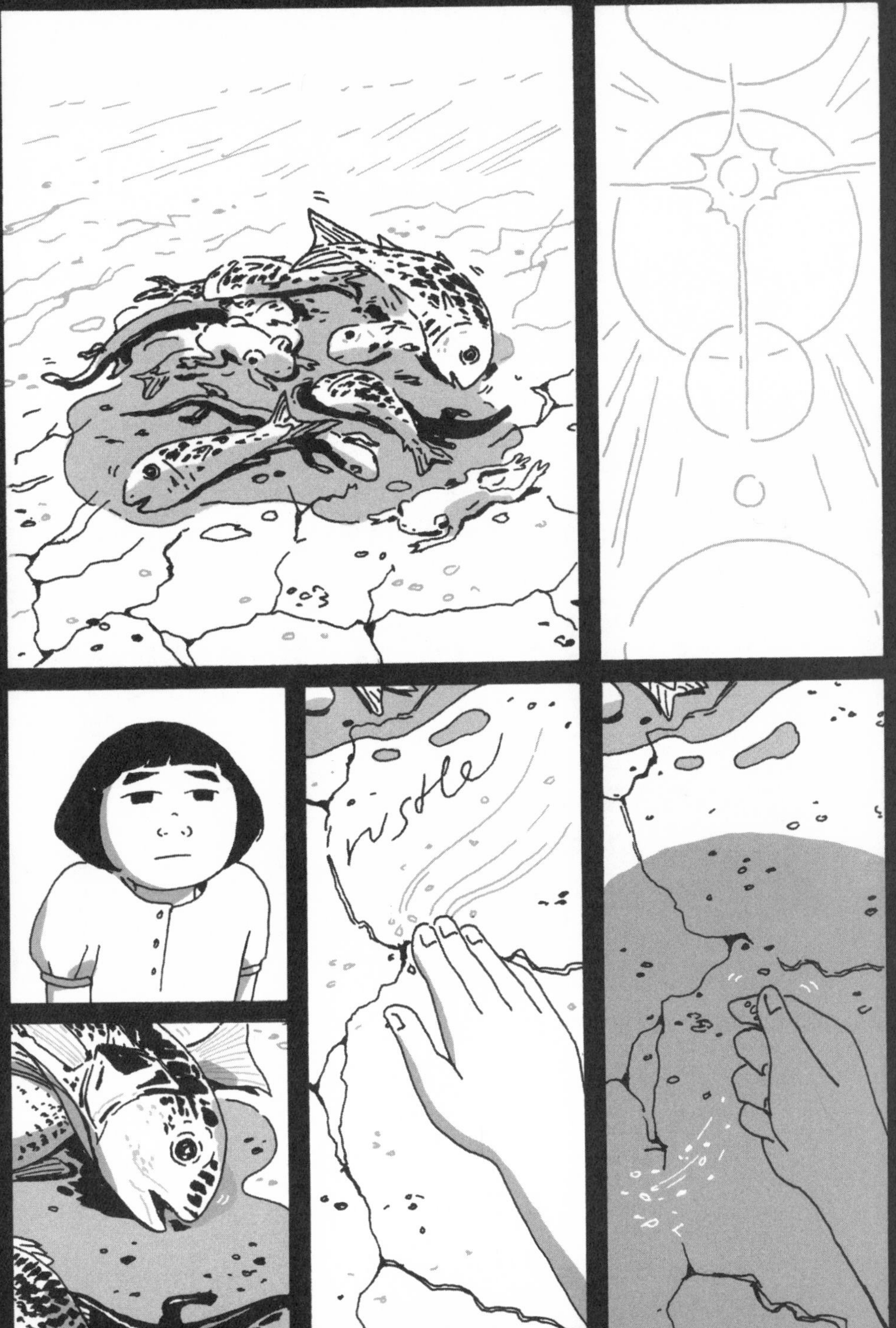
rustle

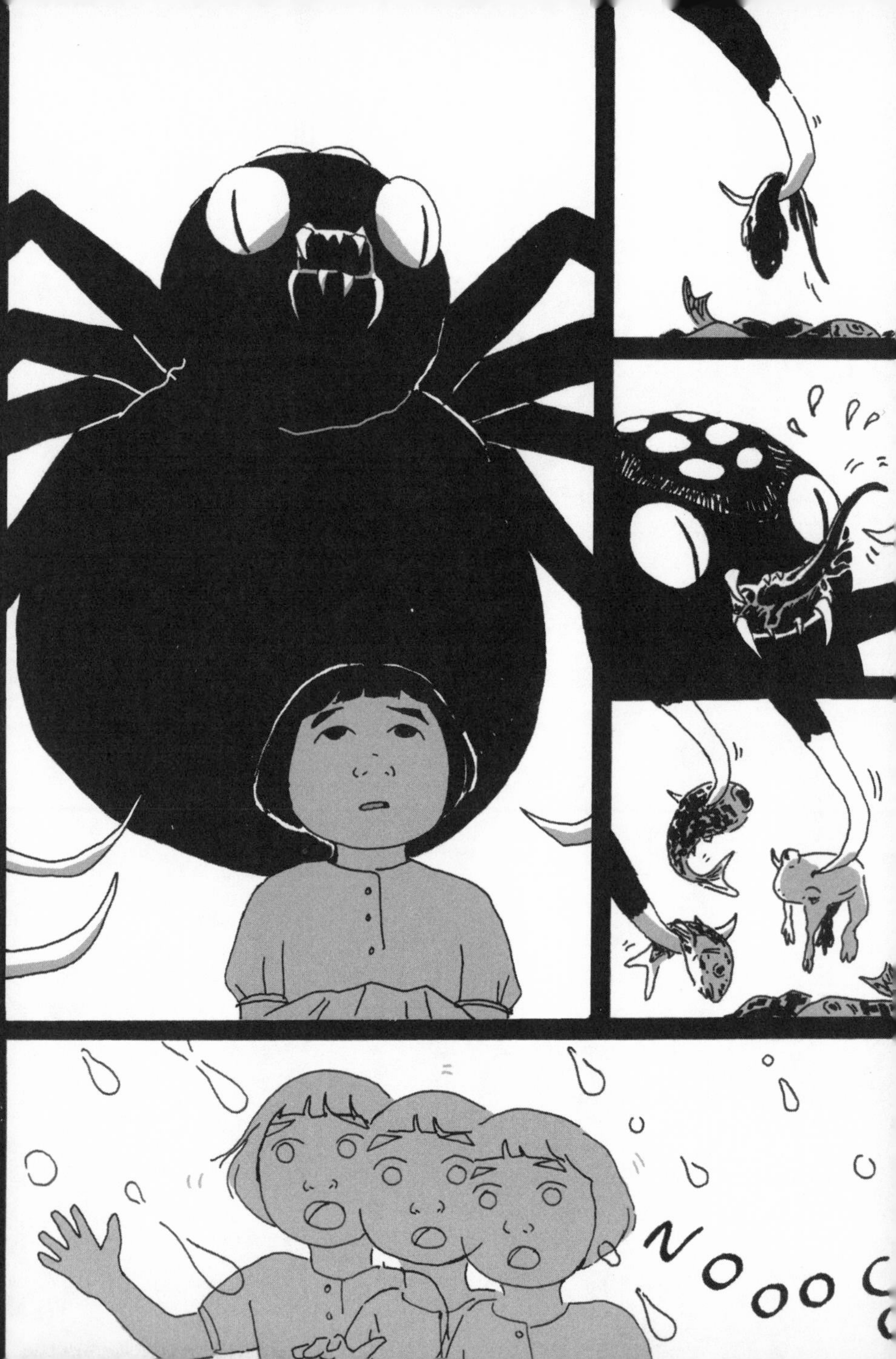
NOOO

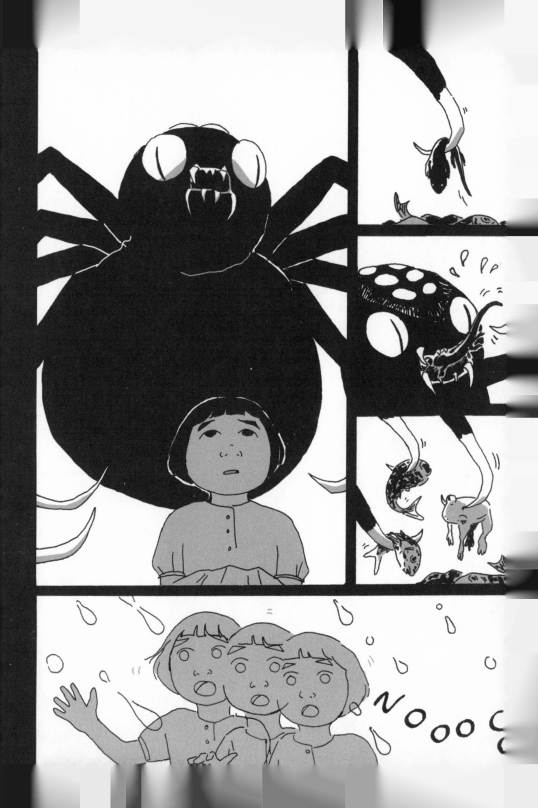

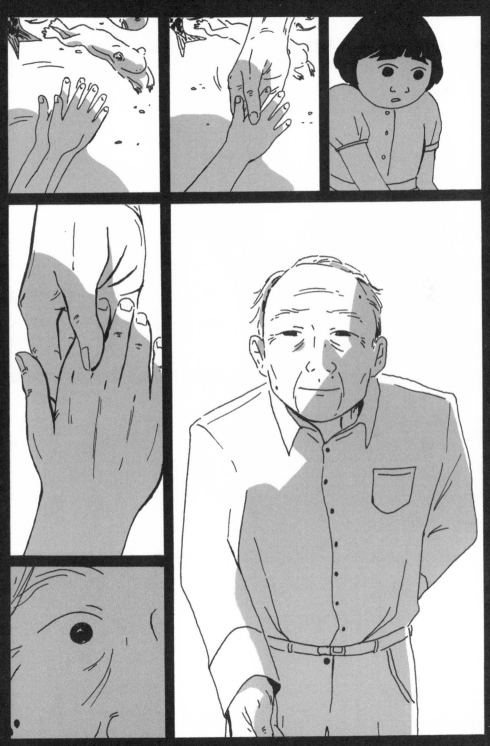

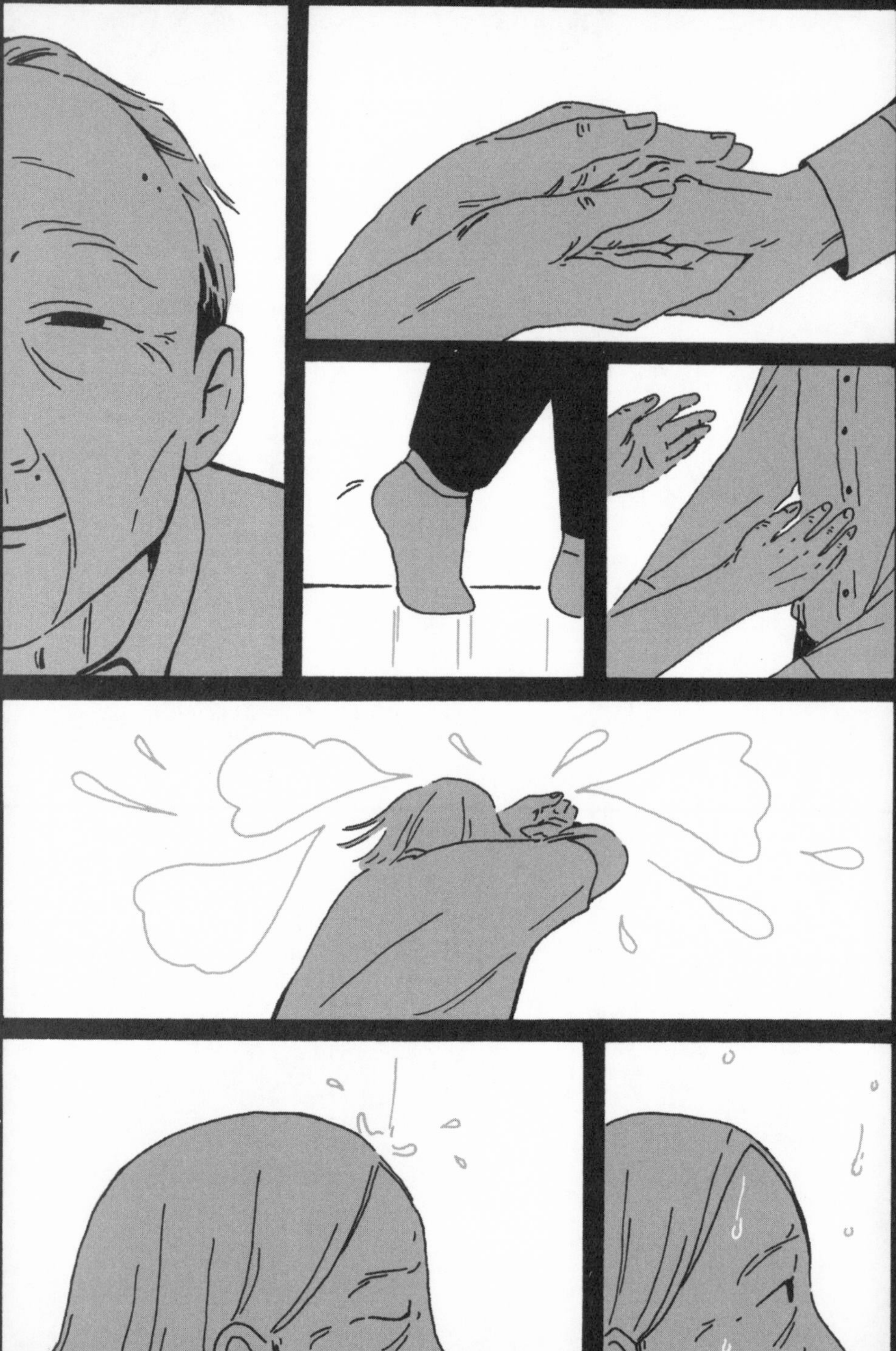

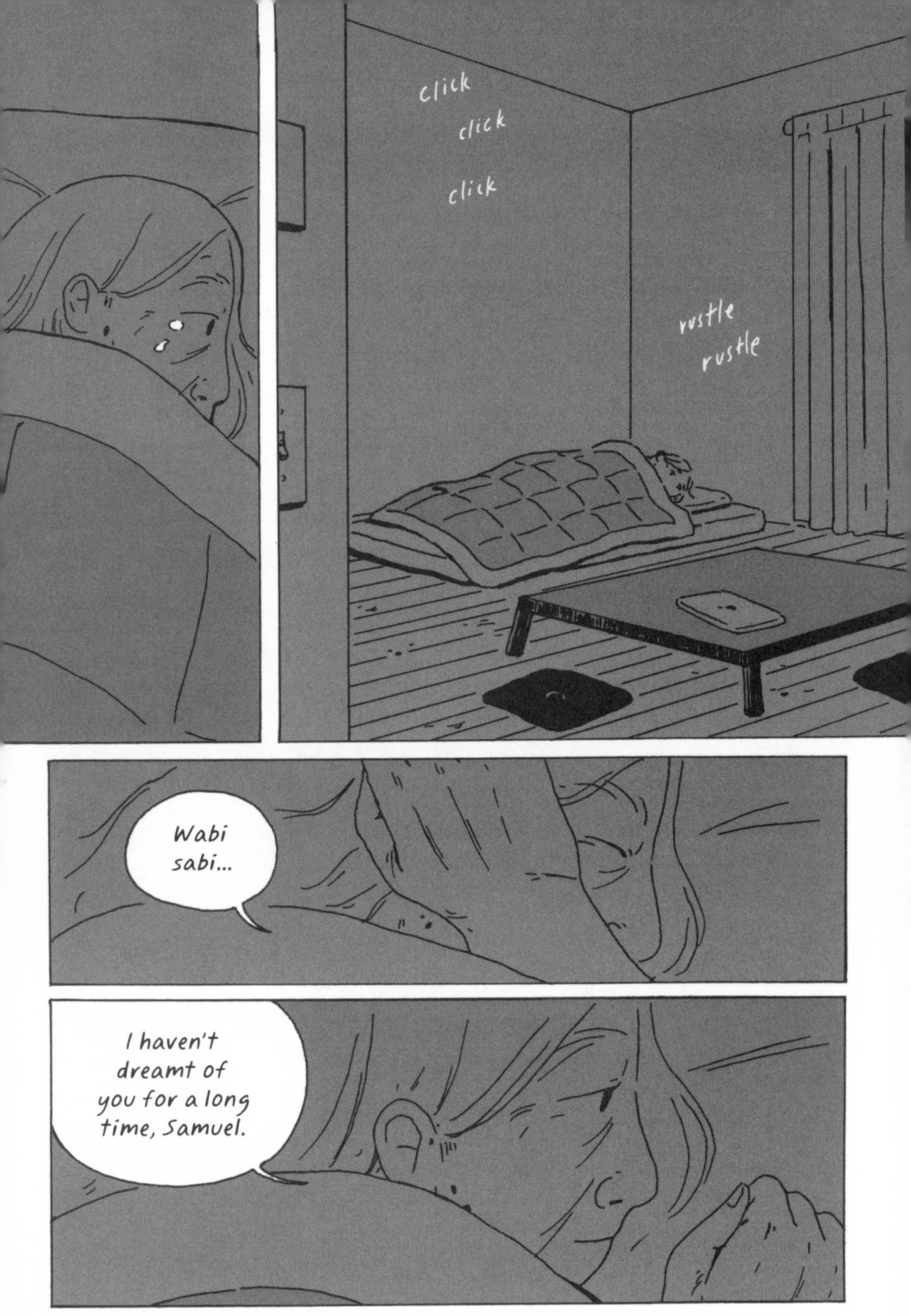
click
click
click
rustle
rustle
Wabi sabi...
I haven't dreamt of you for a long time, Samuel.

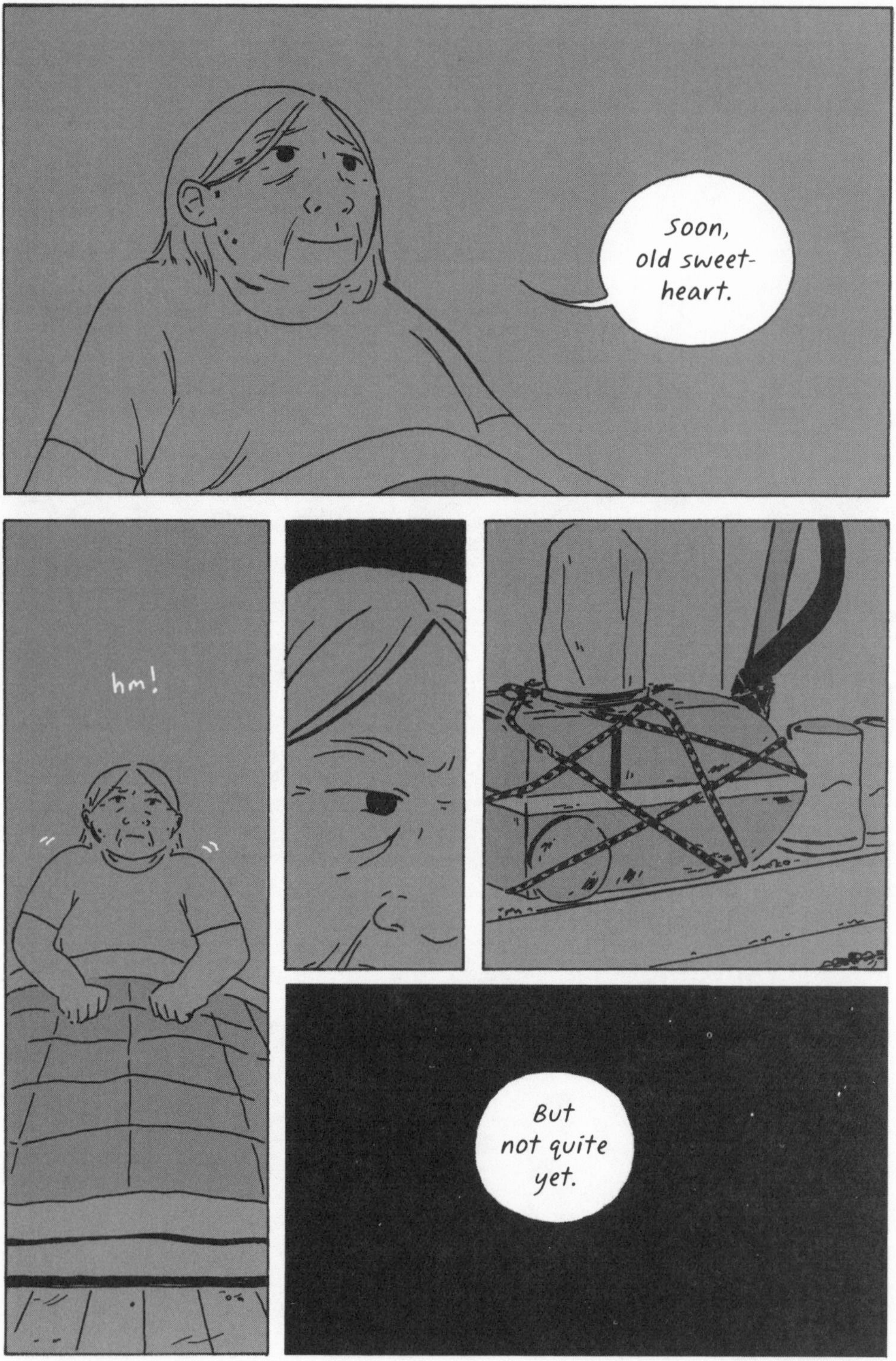
Soon, old sweet-heart.
hm!
But not quite yet.

Chapter Six

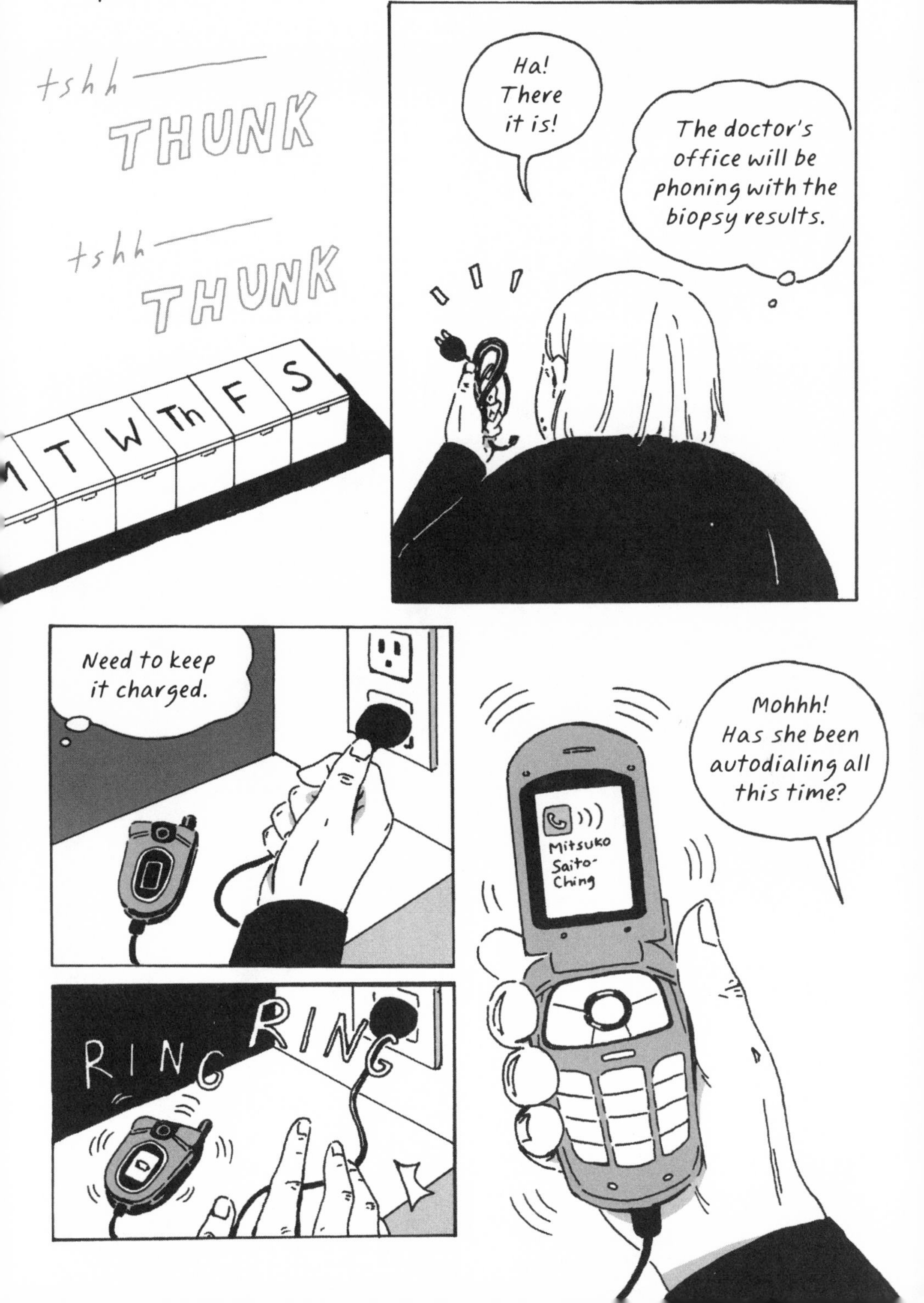
tshh
THUNK
tshh
THUNK
M T W Th F S
Ha! There it is!
The doctor's office will be phoning with the biopsy results.
Need to keep it charged.
RING RING
Mitsuko Saito-Ching
Mohhh! Has she been autodialing all this time?

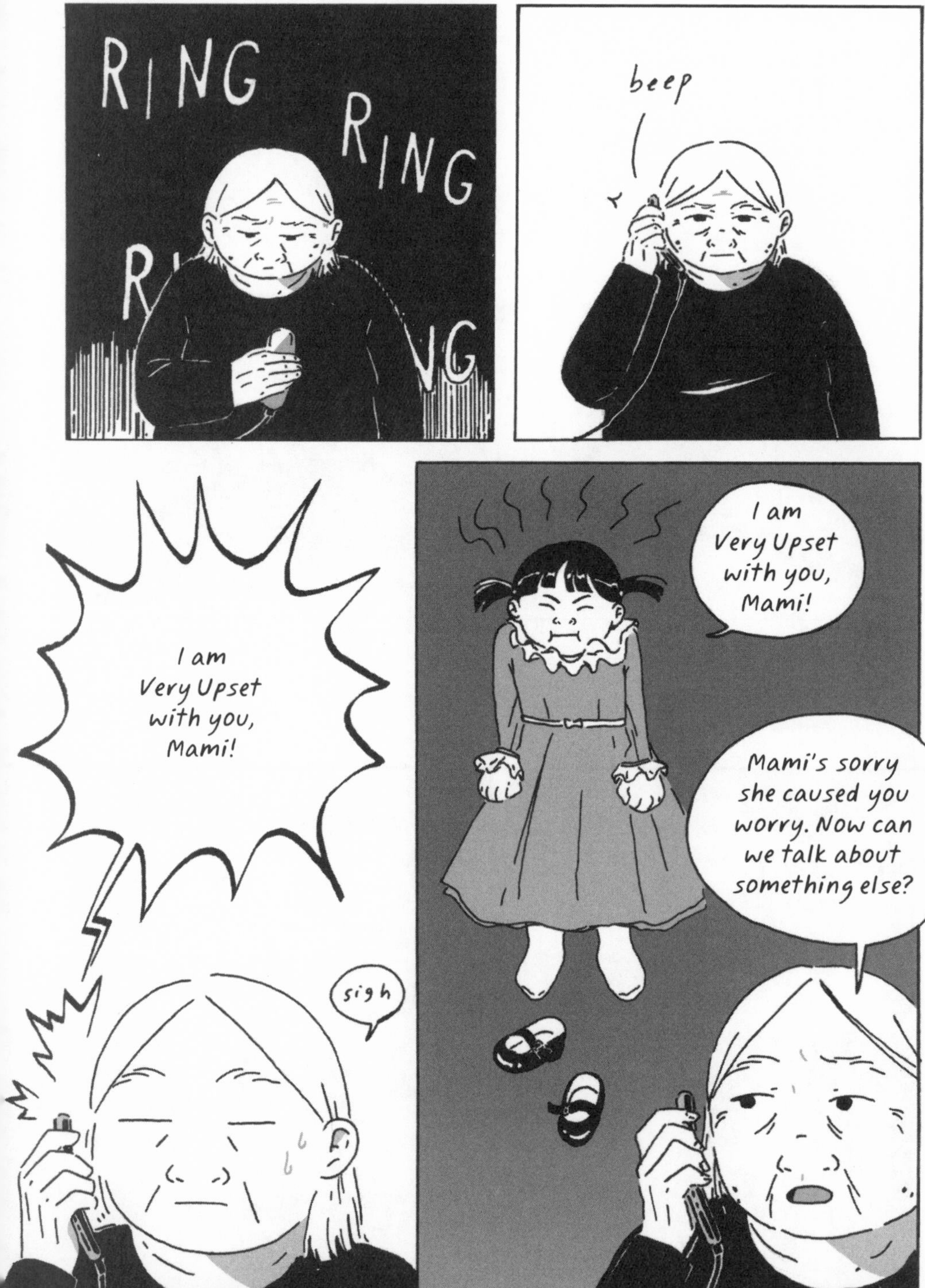
RING
RING
RING
beep
I am Very Upset with you, Mami!
sigh
I am Very Upset with you, Mami!
Mami's sorry she caused you worry. Now can we talk about something else?

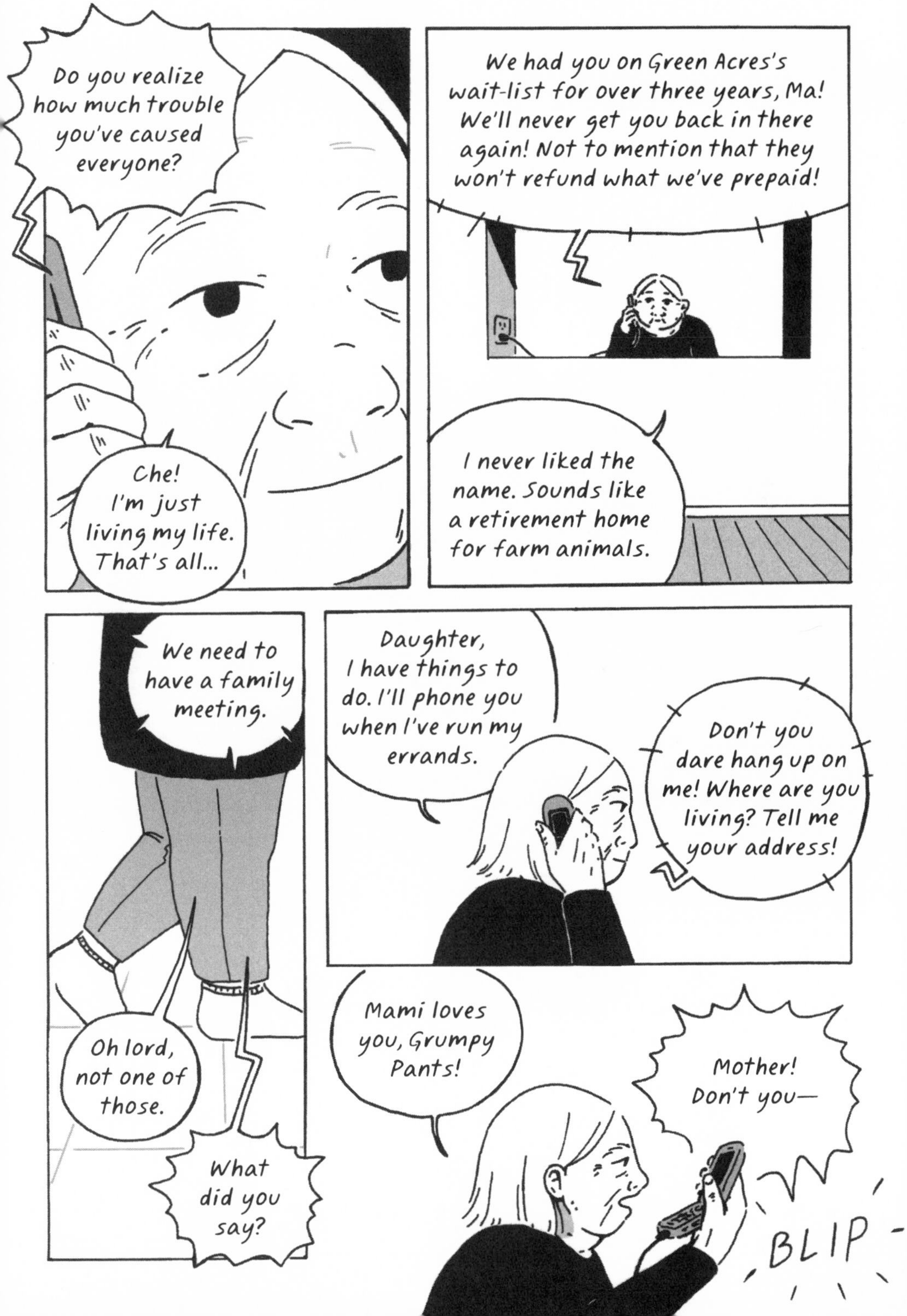
Do you realize how much trouble you've caused everyone?
Che! I'm just living my life. That's all...
We had you on Green Acres's wait-list for over three years, Ma! We'll never get you back in there again! Not to mention that they won't refund what we've prepaid!
I never liked the name. Sounds like a retirement home for farm animals.
We need to have a family meeting.
Oh lord, not one of those.
What did you say?
Daughter, I have things to do. I'll phone you when I've run my errands.
Don't you dare hang up on me! Where are you living? Tell me your address!
Mami loves you, Grumpy Pants!
Mother! Don't you—
BLIP

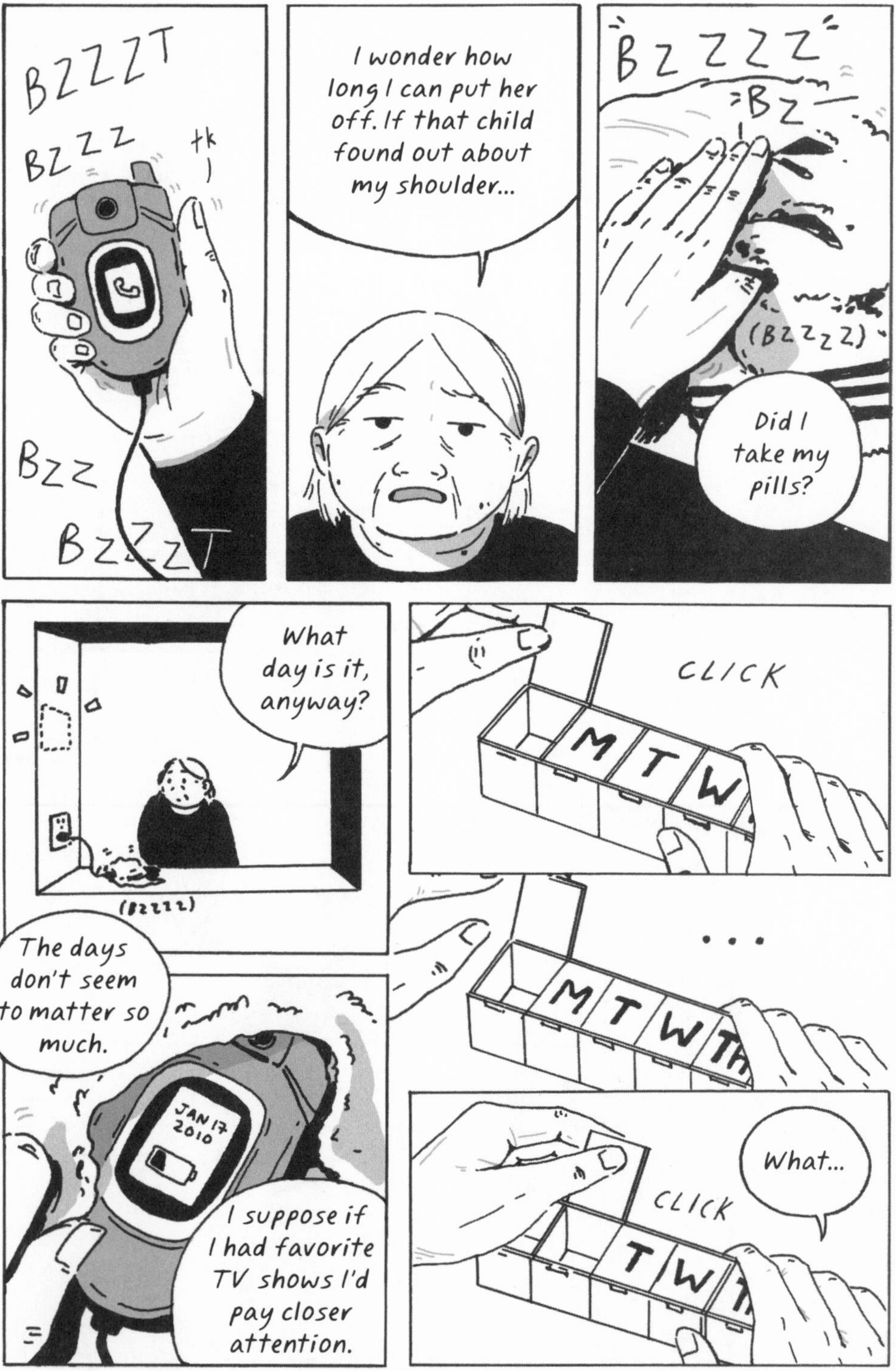
BZZZT
BZZZ
tk
BZZ
BZZZT
I wonder how long I can put her off. If that child found out about my shoulder...
BZZZZ
BZ
(BZZZZ)
Did I take my pills?
What day is it, anyway?
(BZZZZ)
CLICK
M T W
...
M T W Th
The days don't seem to matter so much.
JAN 17 2010
I suppose if I had favorite TV shows I'd pay closer attention.
What...
CLICK
T W

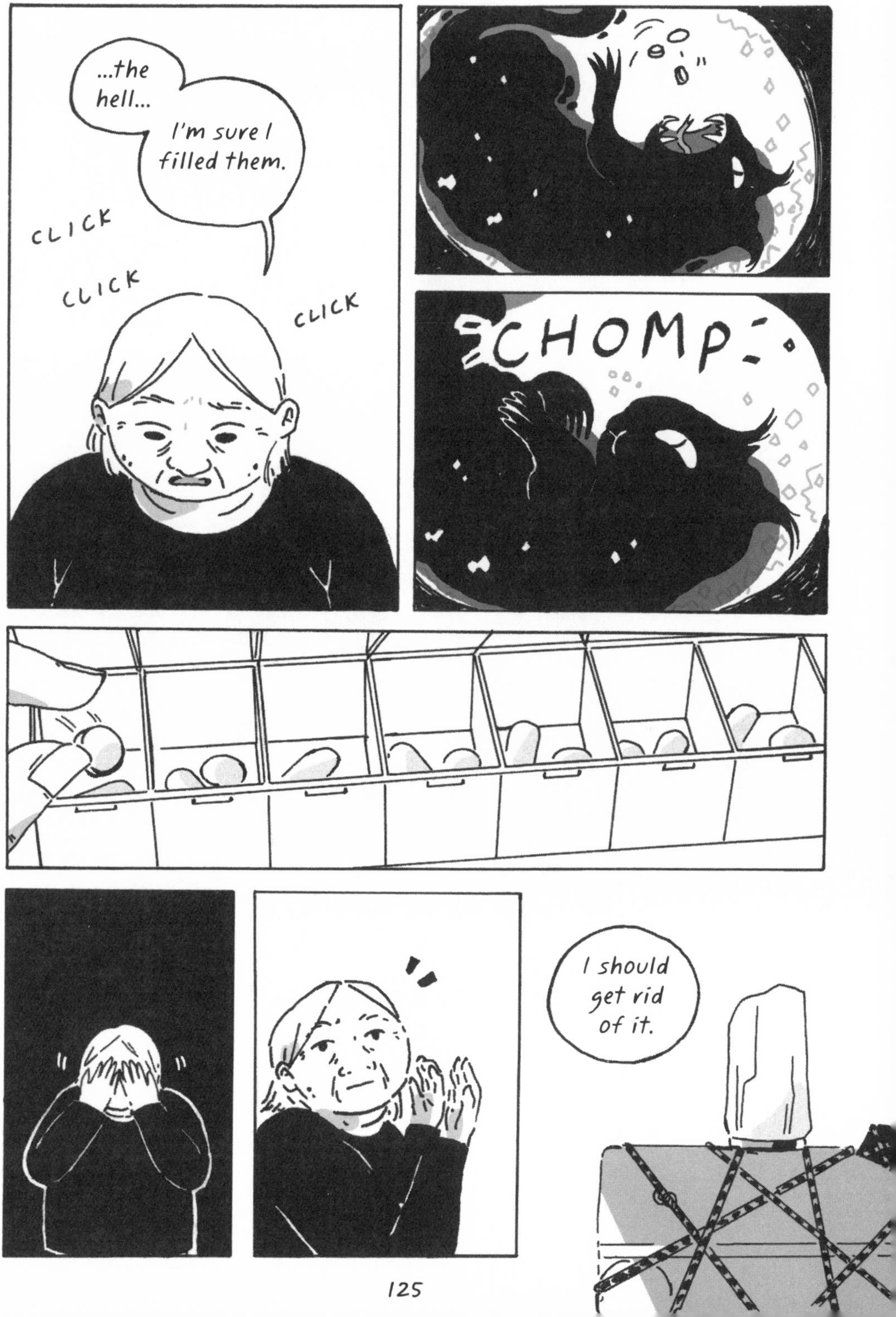
...the hell...
I'm sure I filled them.
CLICK
CLICK
CLICK
CHOMP
I should get rid of it.

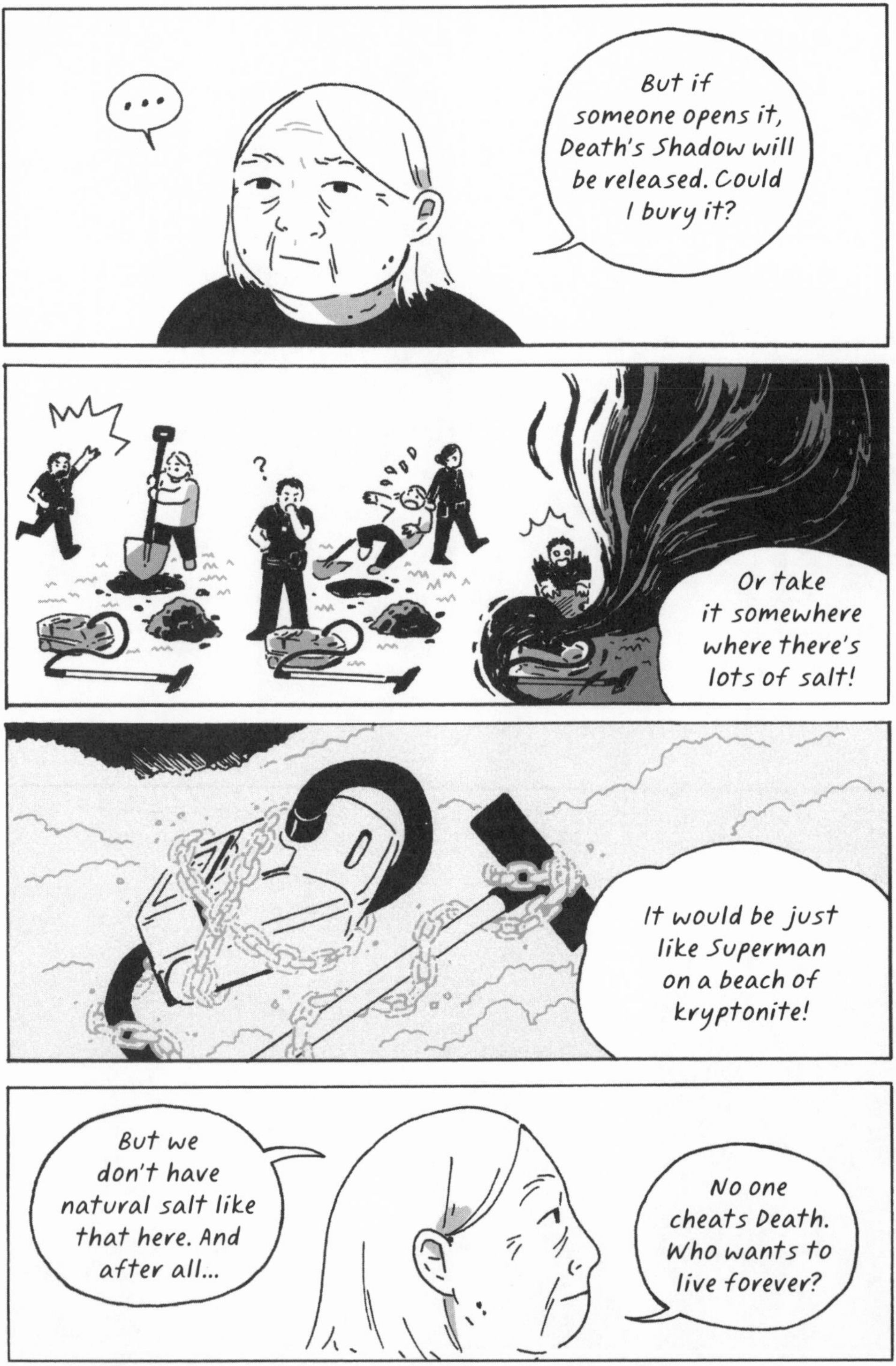

...
But if someone opens it, Death's Shadow will be released. Could I bury it?
Or take it somewhere where there's lots of salt!
It would be just like Superman on a beach of kryptonite!
But we don't have natural salt like that here. And after all...
No one cheats Death. Who wants to live forever?

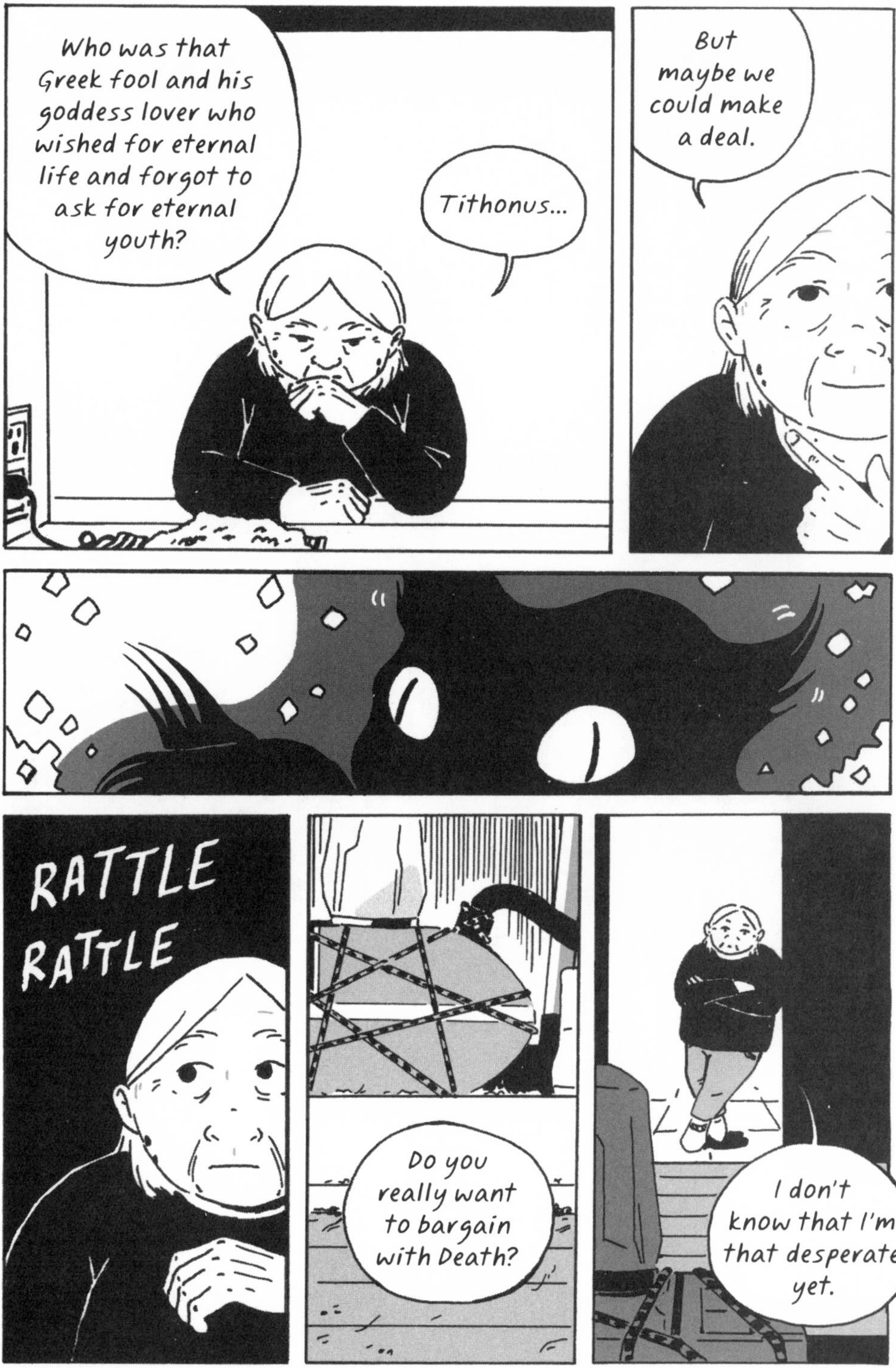

Who was that Greek fool and his goddess lover who wished for eternal life and forgot to ask for eternal youth?
Tithonus...
But maybe we could make a deal.
RATTLE RATTLE
Do you really want to bargain with Death?
I don't know that I'm that desperate yet.

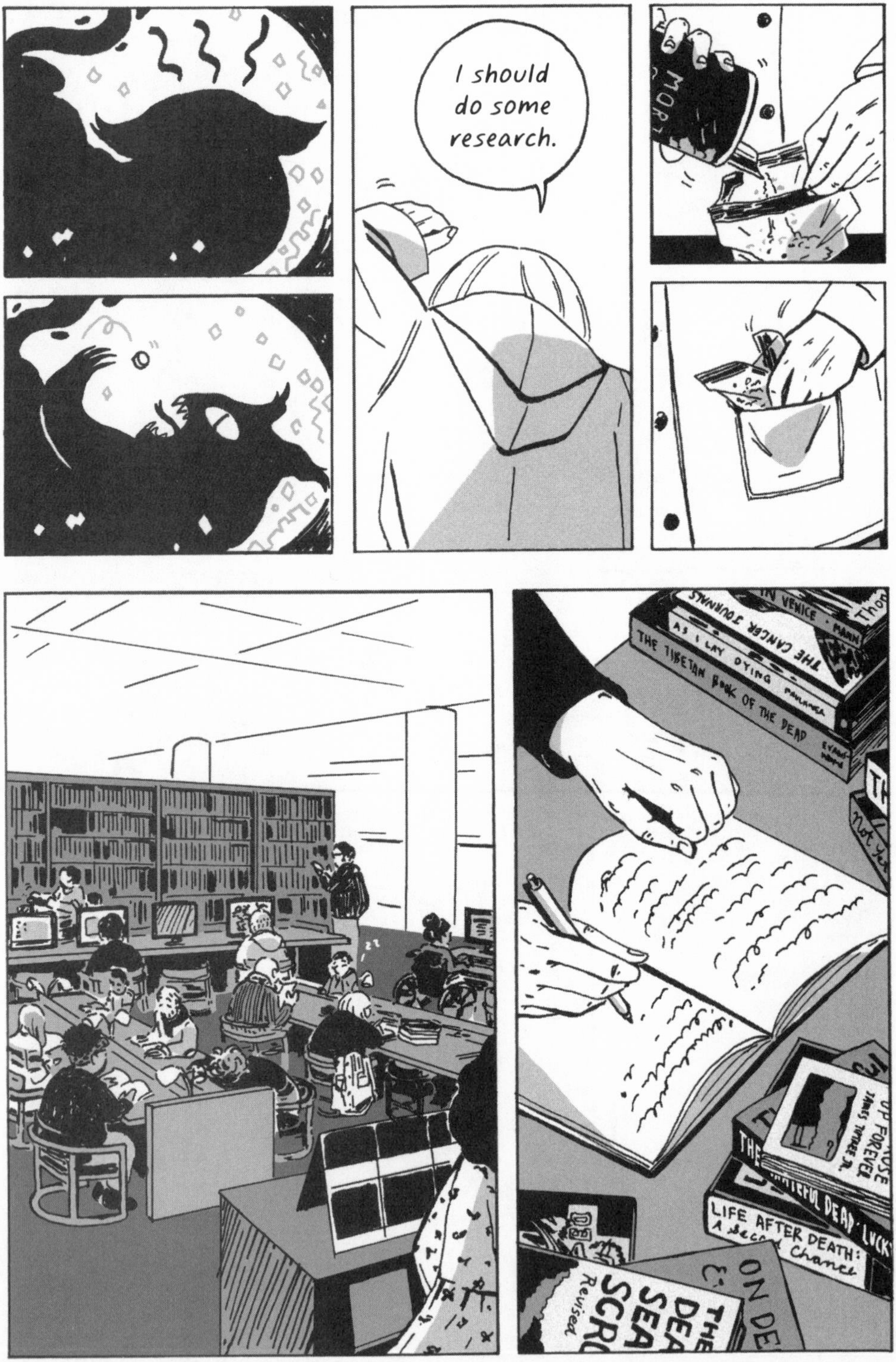
I should do some research.
IN VENICE
MANN
THE CANCER JOURNALS
AS I LAY DYING
THE TIBETAN BOOK OF THE DEAD
JAMES TIPTREE JR.
LIFE AFTER DEATH: A Second Chance
Revised

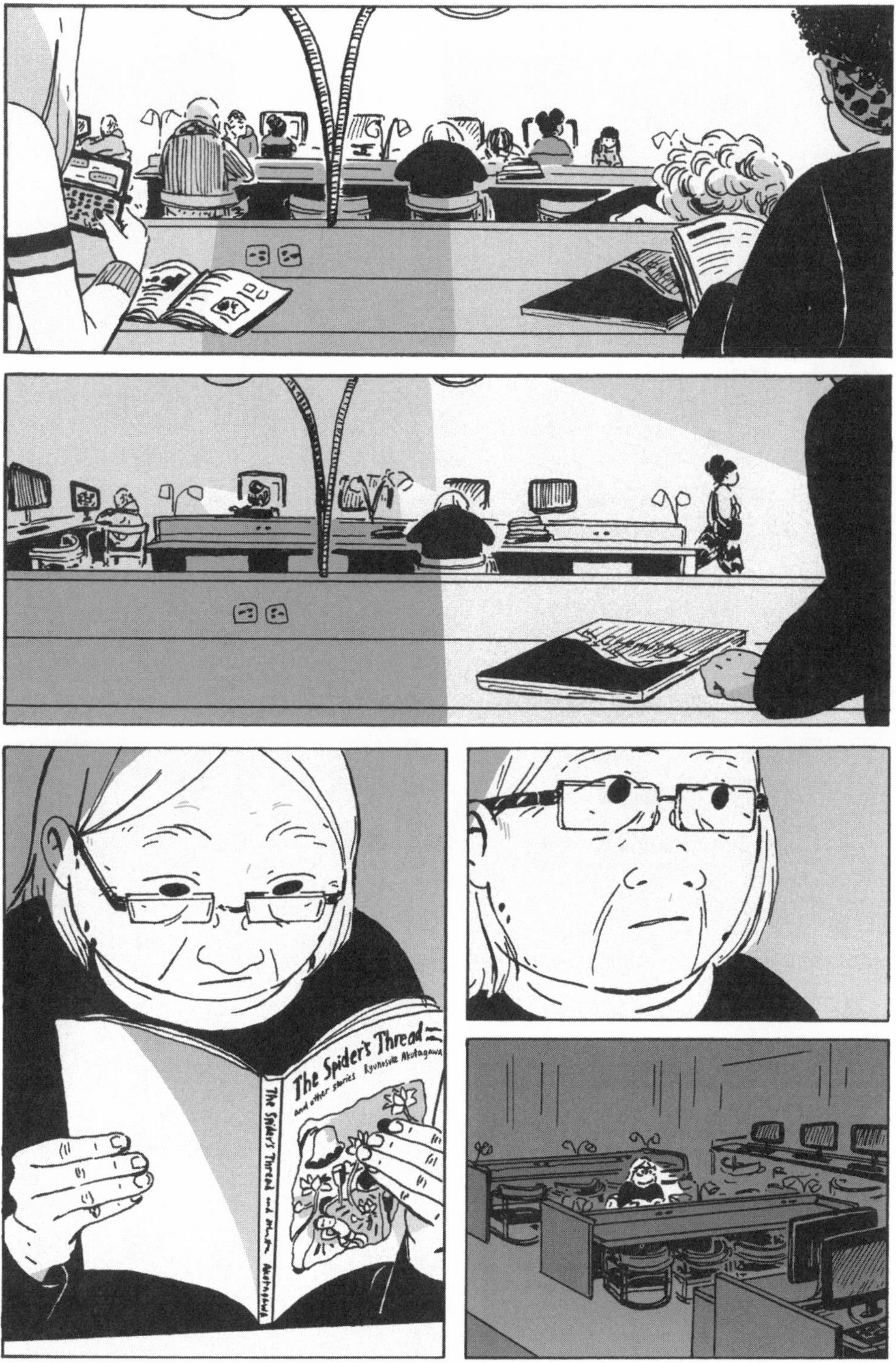
The Spider's Thread
and other stories
Ryunosuke Akutagawa
The Spider's Thread

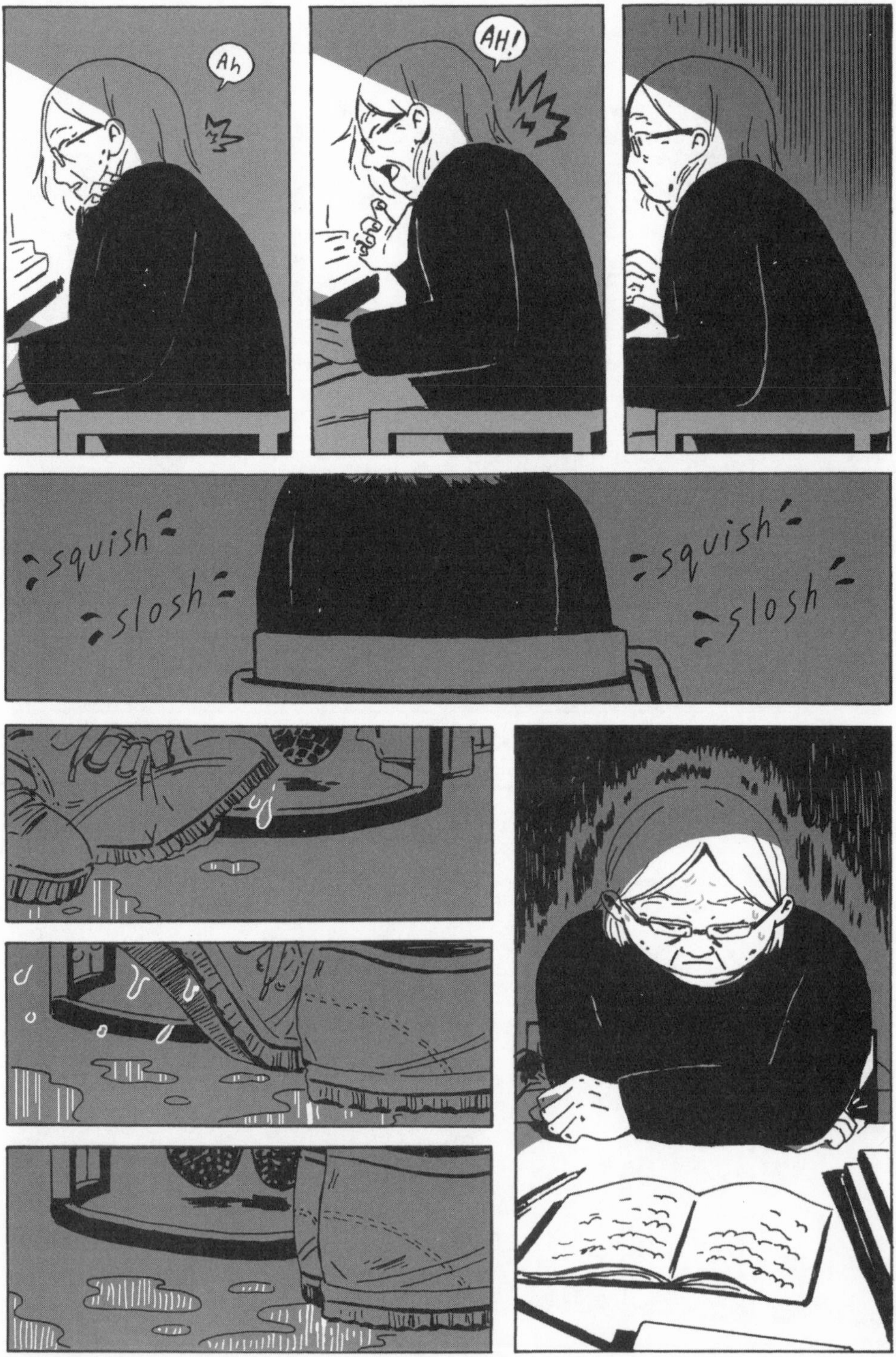
Ah
AH!
squish
slosh
squish
slosh

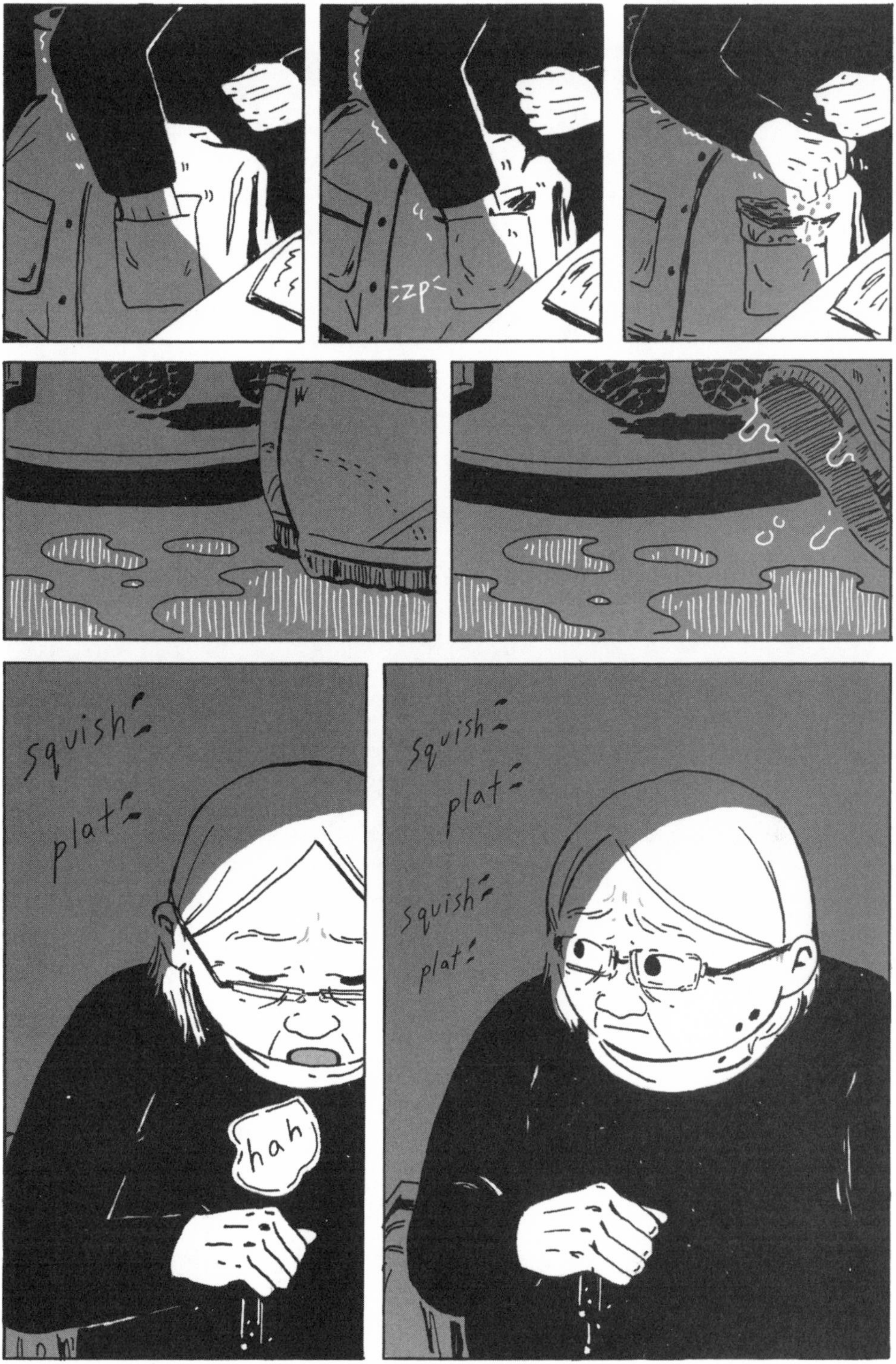
zp
squish
plat
hah
squish
plat
squish
plat

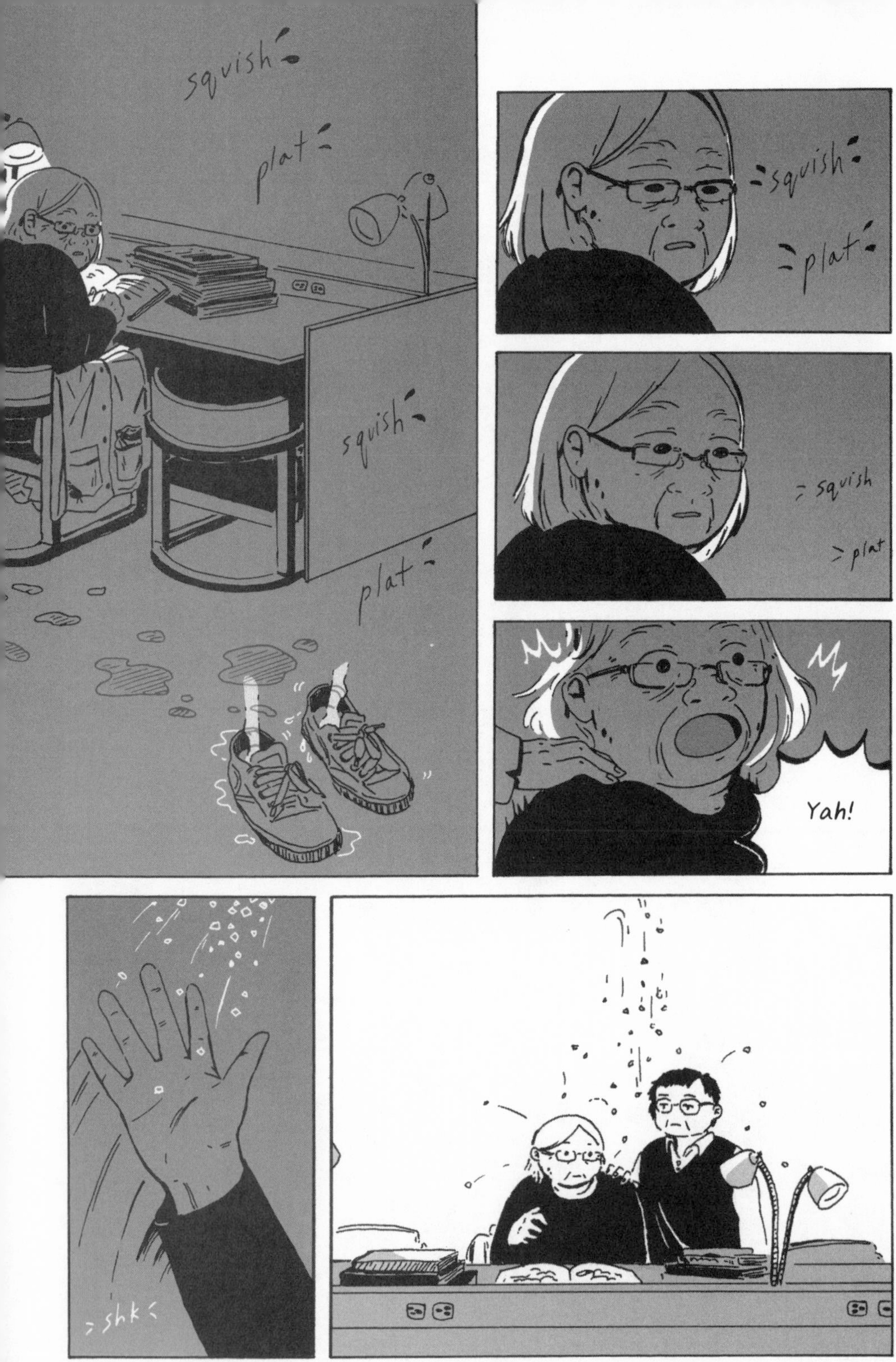
squish
plat
squish
plat
squish
plat
squish
plat
Yah!
shk

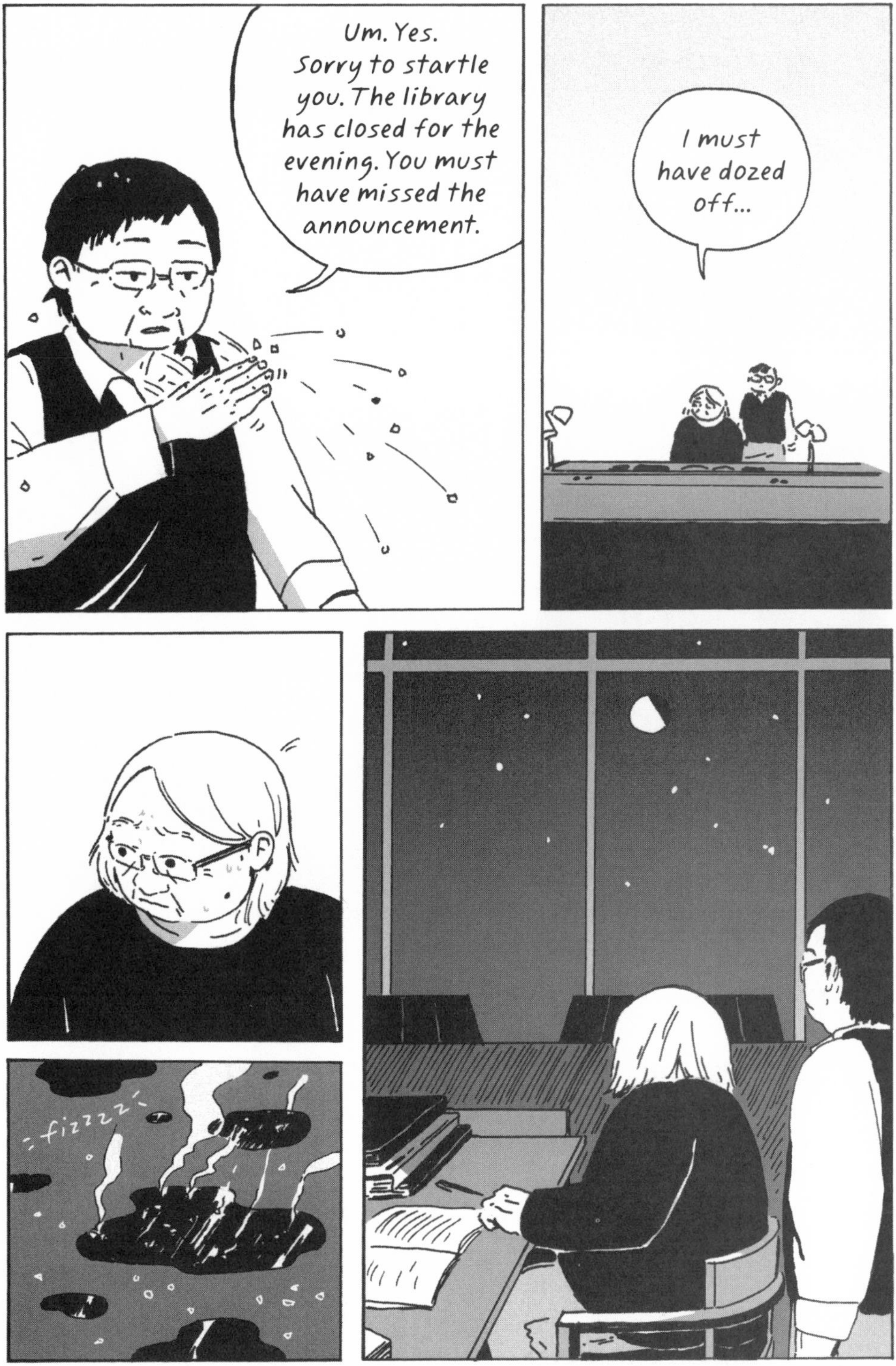
Um. Yes. Sorry to startle you. The library has closed for the evening. You must have missed the announcement.
I must have dozed off...
fizzzz

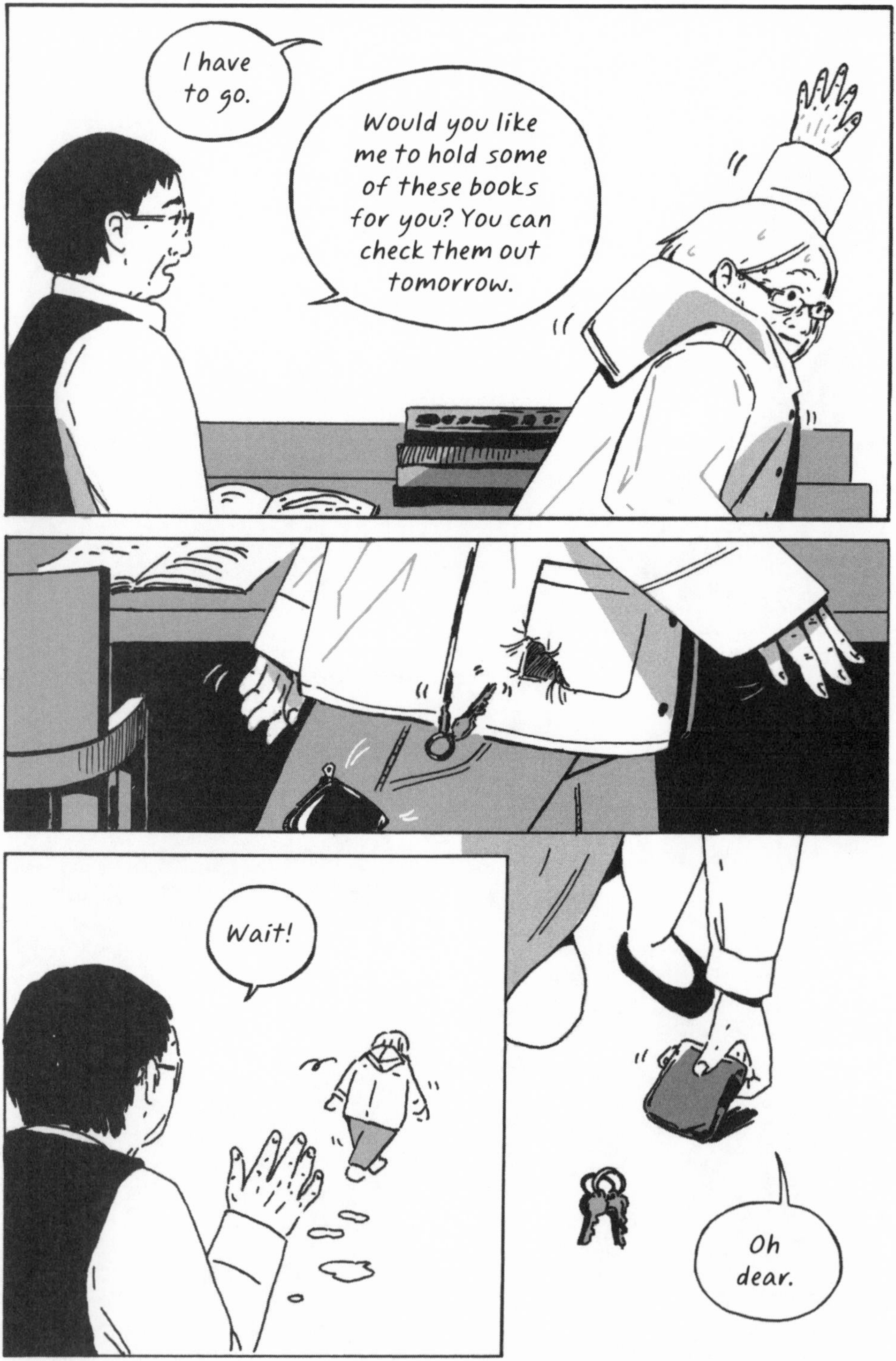
I have to go.
Would you like me to hold some of these books for you? You can check them out tomorrow.
Wait!
Oh dear.

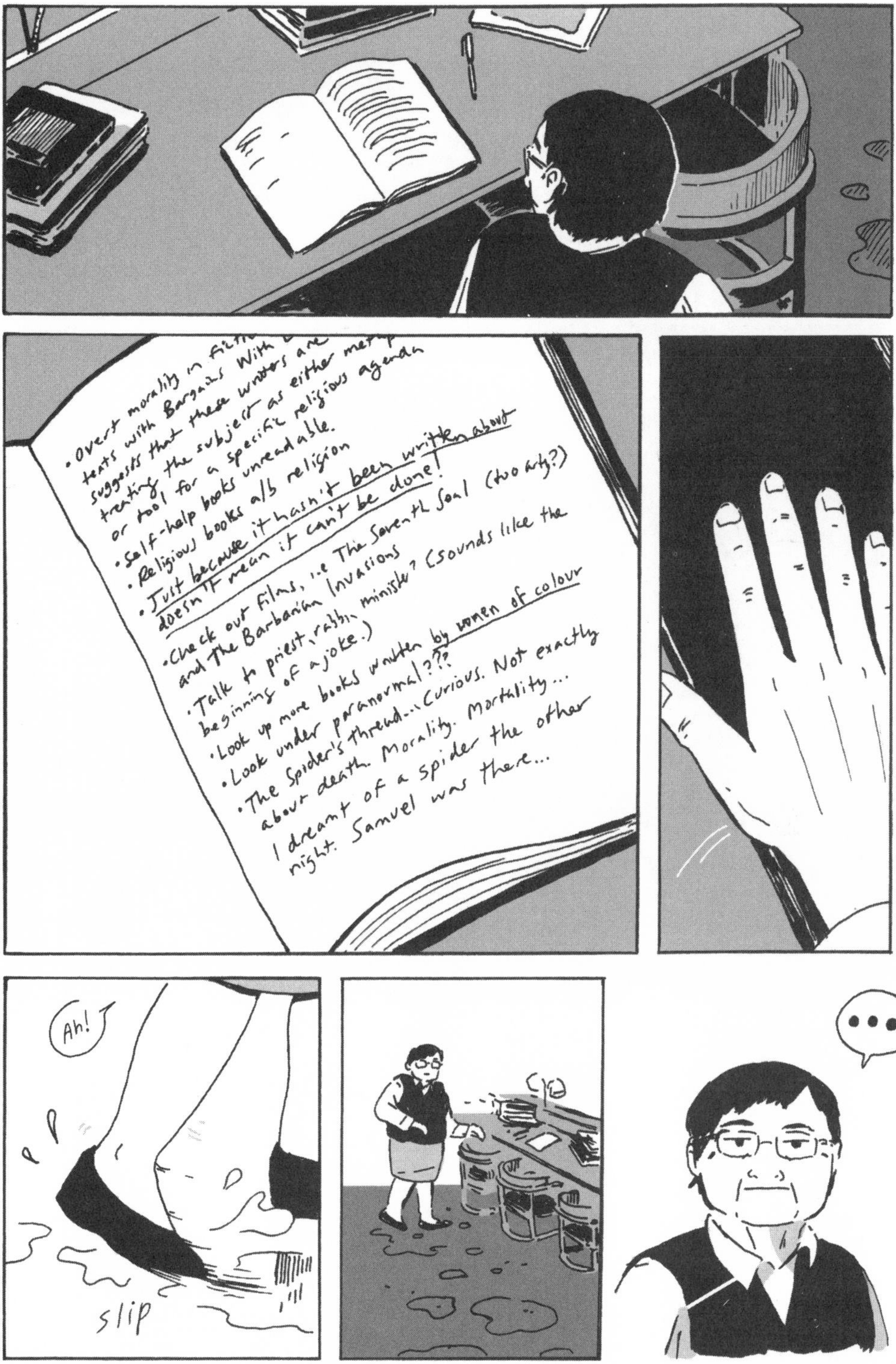

• Overt morality in
texts with Bargains With
suggests that these writers are
treating the subject as either
or tool for a specific religious agenda
Self-help books unreadable.
• Religious books a/b religion
• Just because it hasn't been written about
doesn't mean it can't be done!
• Check out films, i.e The Seventh Seal (too arty?)
and The Barbarian Invasions
• Talk to priest, rabbi, minister? (Sounds like the
beginning of a joke.)
• Look up more books written by women of colour
• Look under paranormal???
• The Spider's thread... Curious. Not exactly
about death. Morality. Mortality...
I dreamt of a spider the other
night. Samuel was there...
Ah!
slip

Chapter Seven

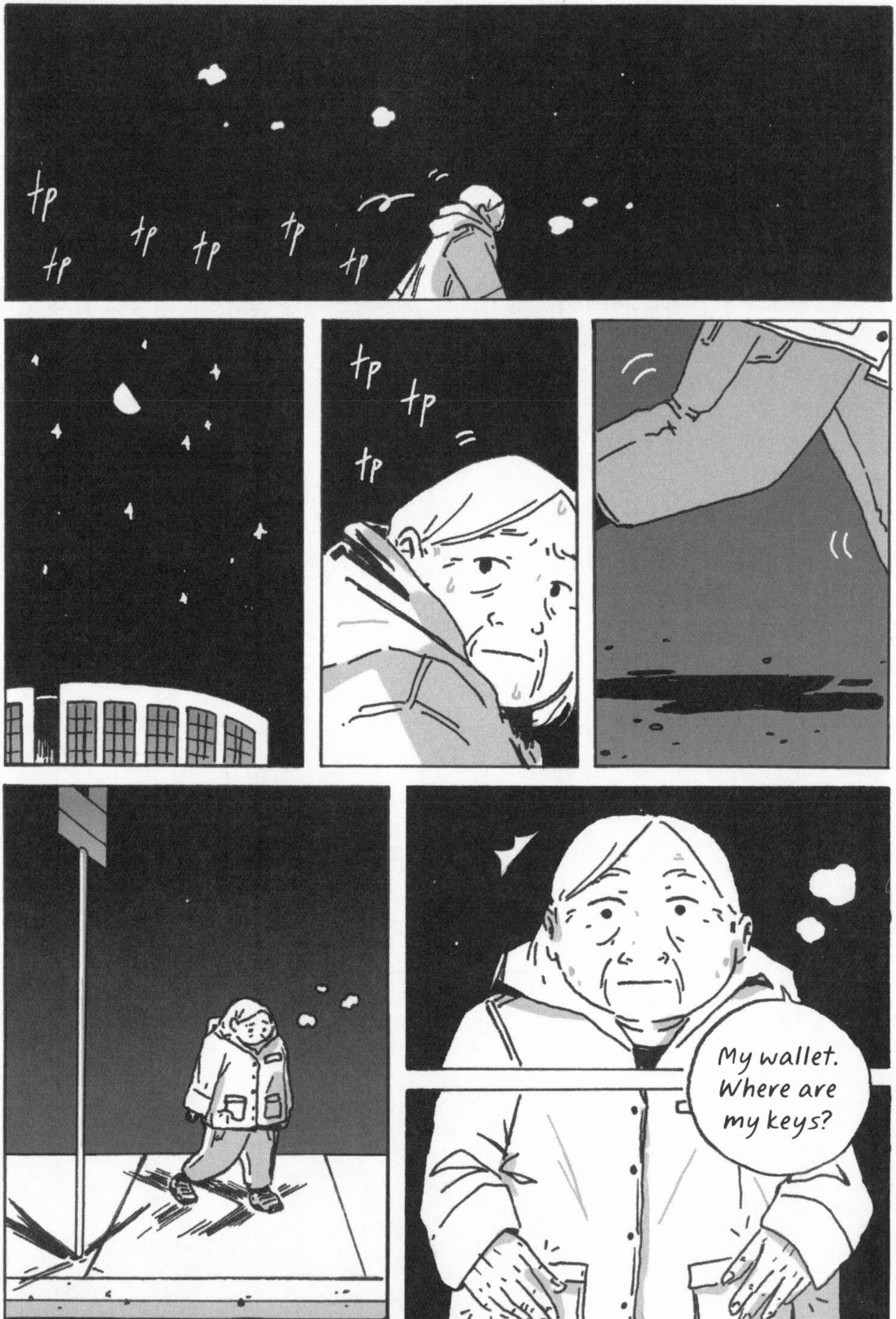
tp
tp
tp
tp
tp
tp
tp
tp
tp
My wallet. Where are my keys?

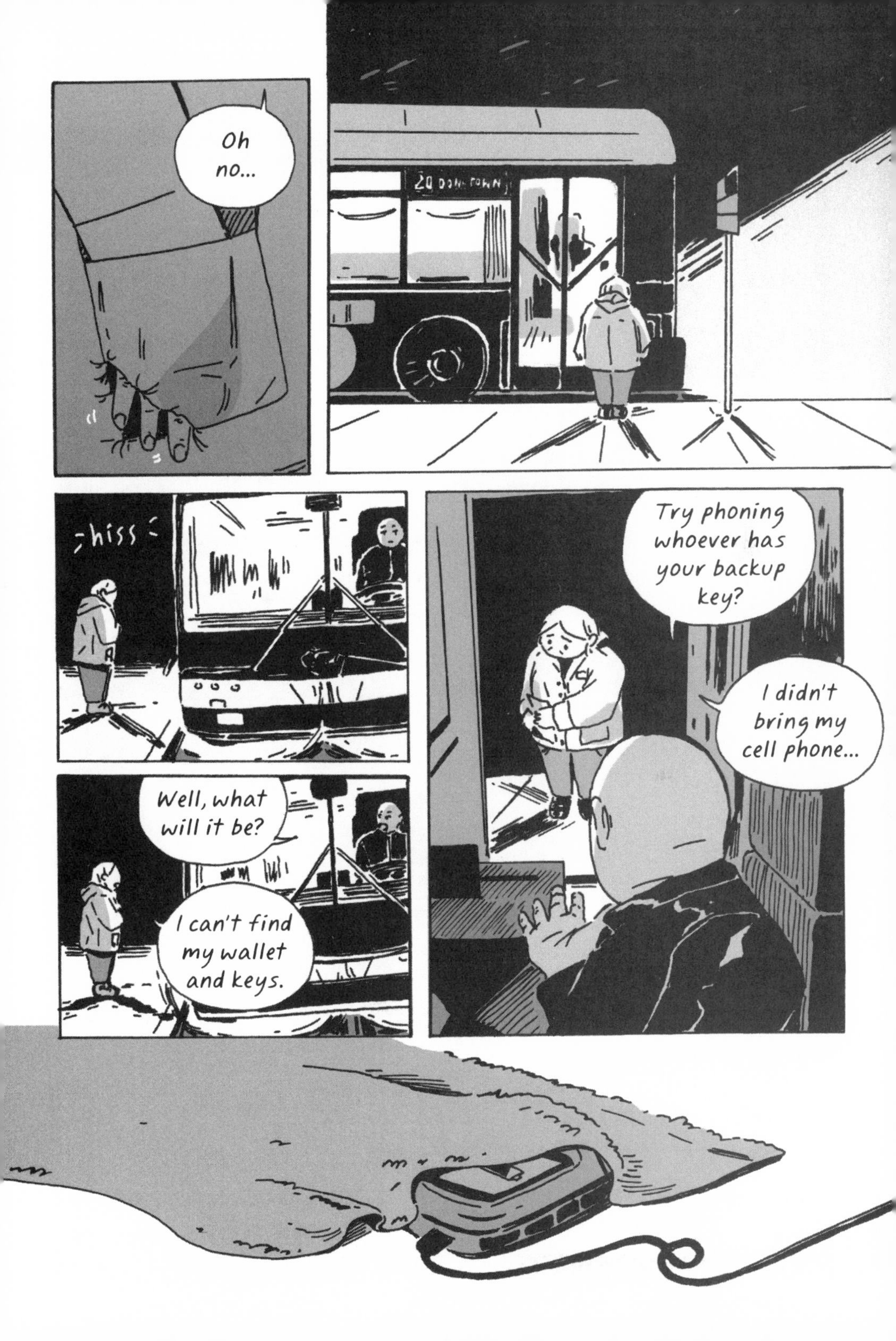
Oh no...
20 DOWNTOWN
hiss
Try phoning whoever has your backup key?
I didn't bring my cell phone...
Well, what will it be?
I can't find my wallet and keys.

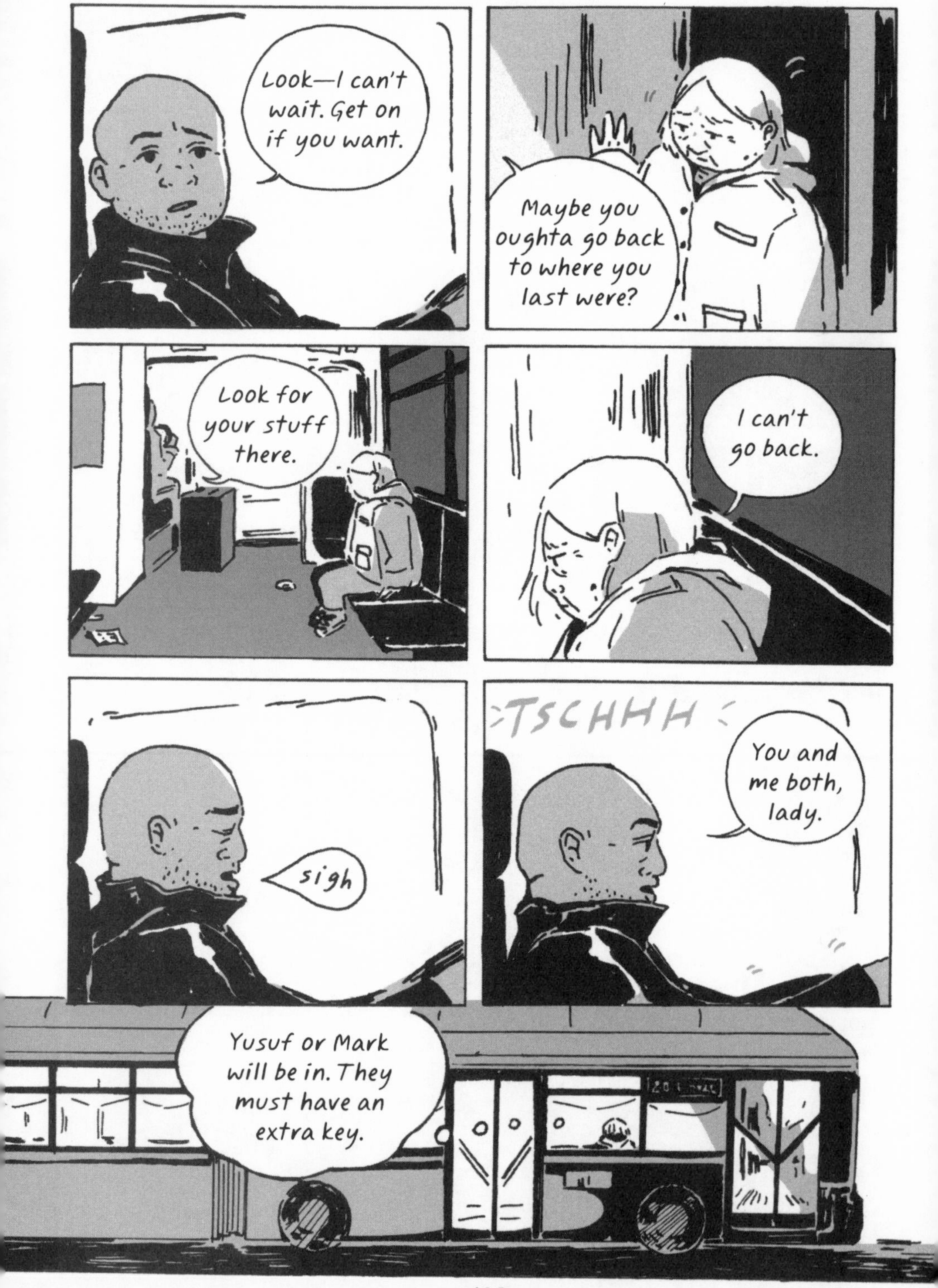
Look—I can't wait. Get on if you want.
Maybe you oughta go back to where you last were?
Look for your stuff there.
I can't go back.
sigh
TSCHHH
You and me both, lady.
Yusuf or Mark will be in. They must have an extra key.

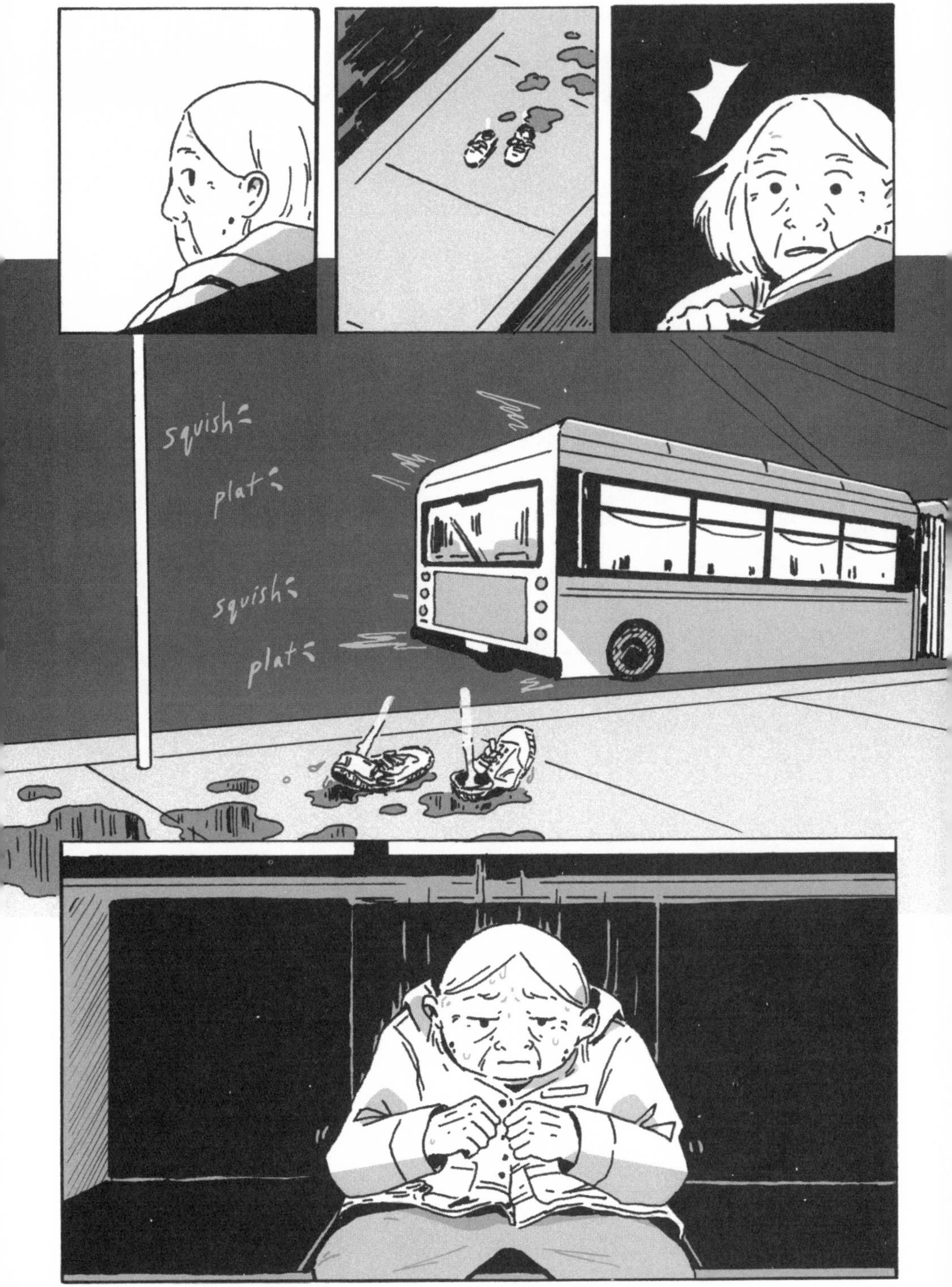
squish
plat
squish
plat

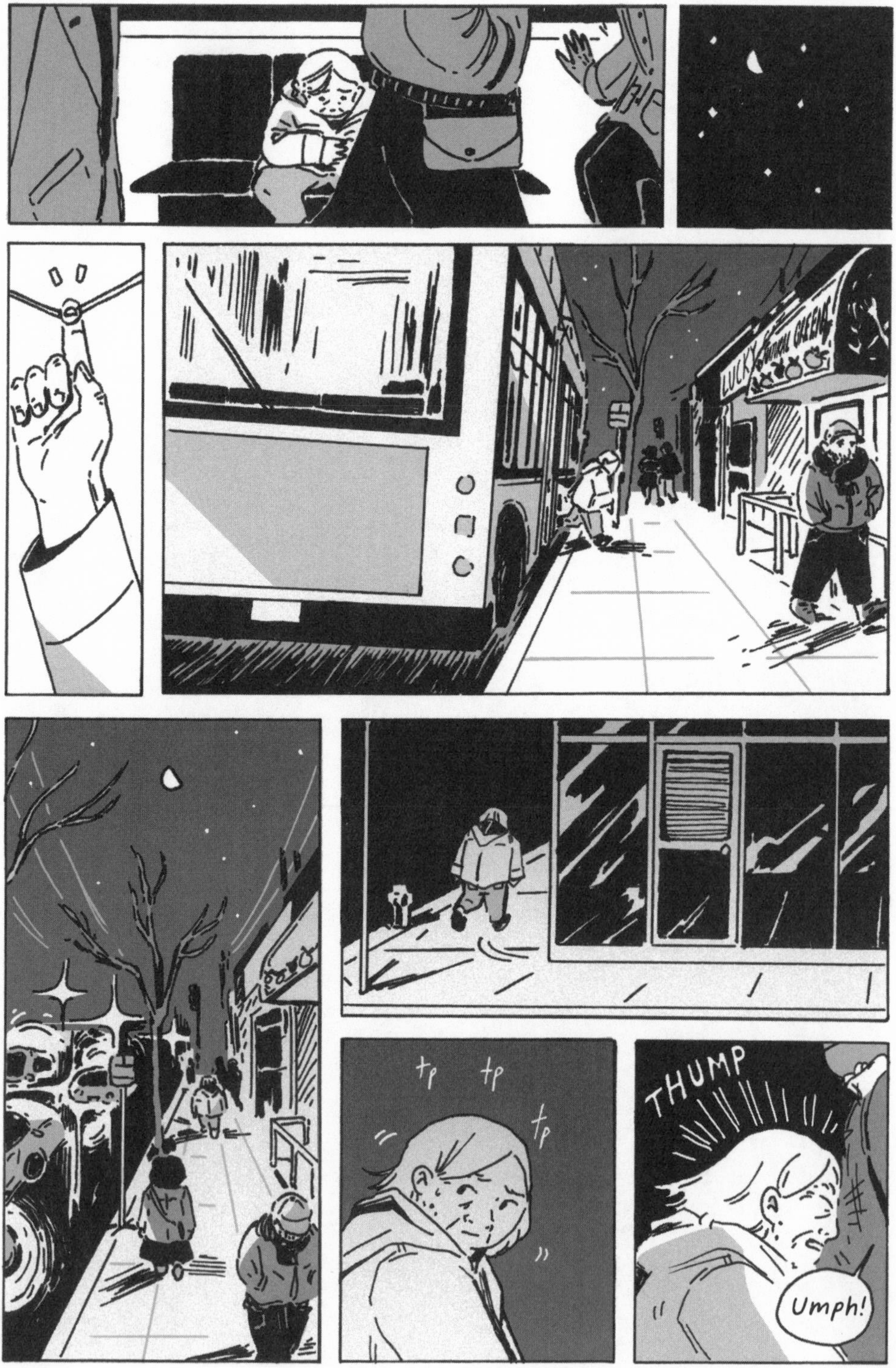
LUCKY
tp
tp
tp
THUMP
Umph!

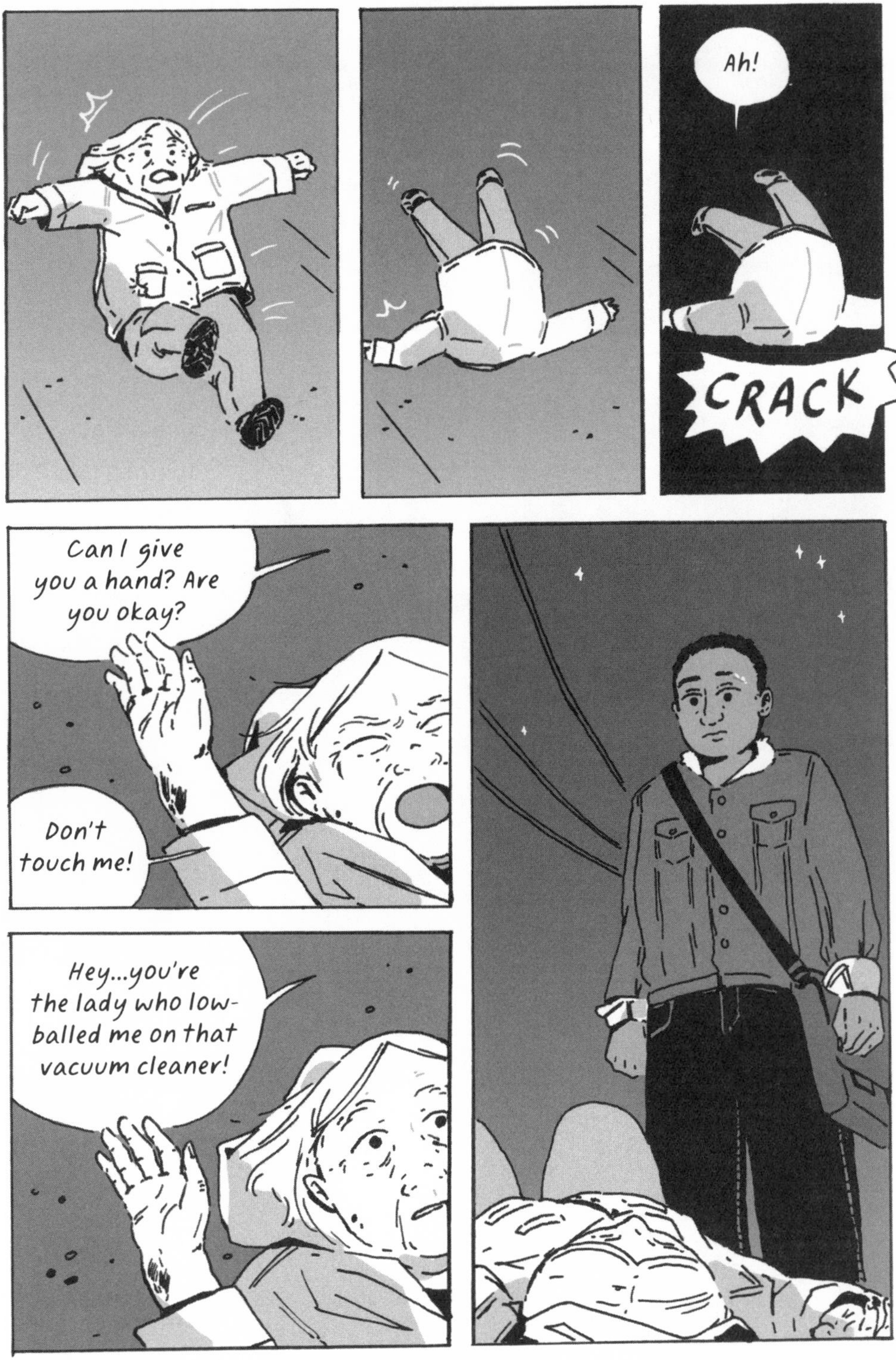
Ah!
CRACK
Can I give you a hand? Are you okay?
Don't touch me!
Hey...you're the lady who low-balled me on that vacuum cleaner!

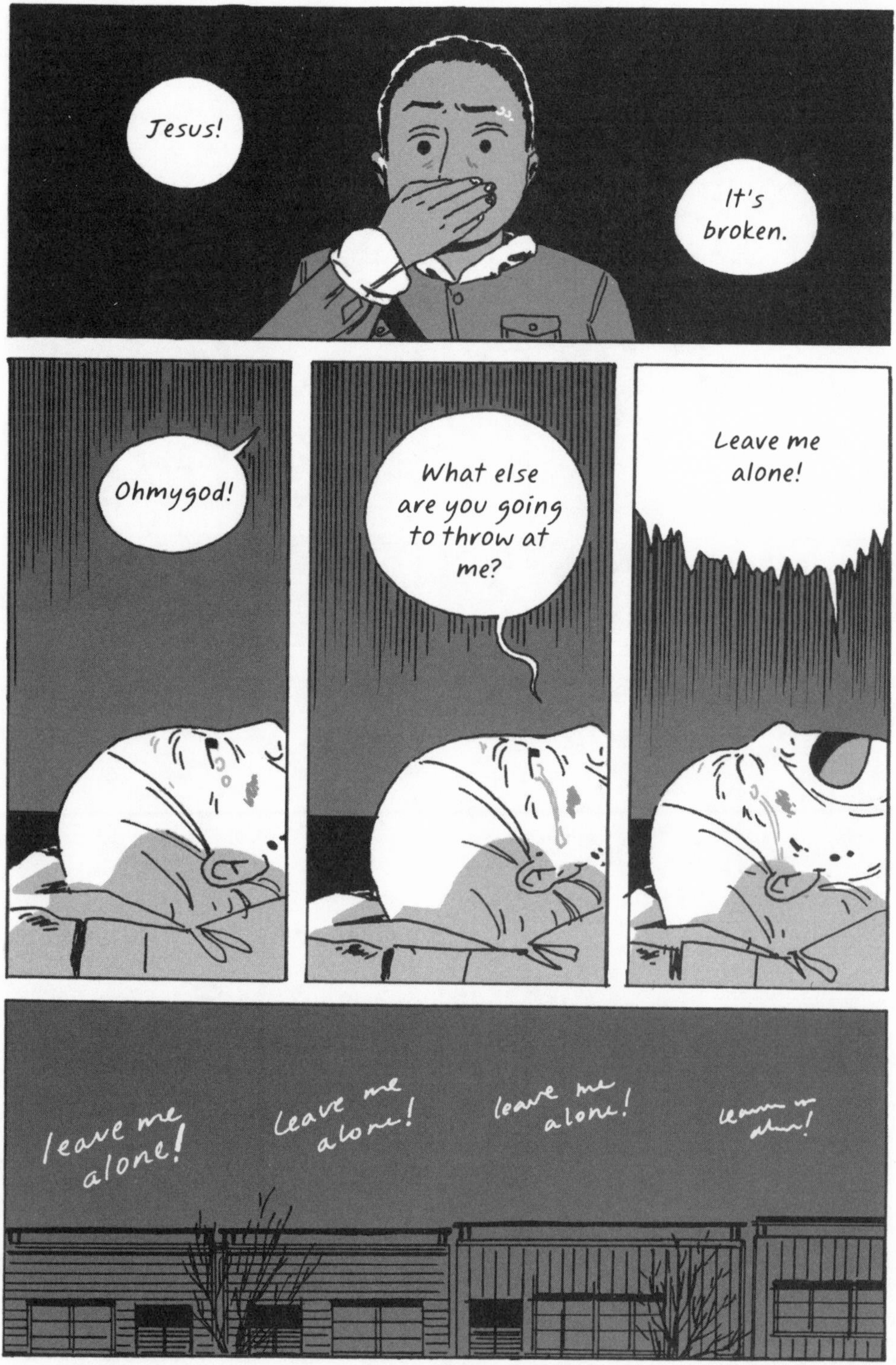
Jesus!
It's broken.
Ohmygod!
What else are you going to throw at me?
Leave me alone!
leave me alone!
Leave me alone!
leave me alone!

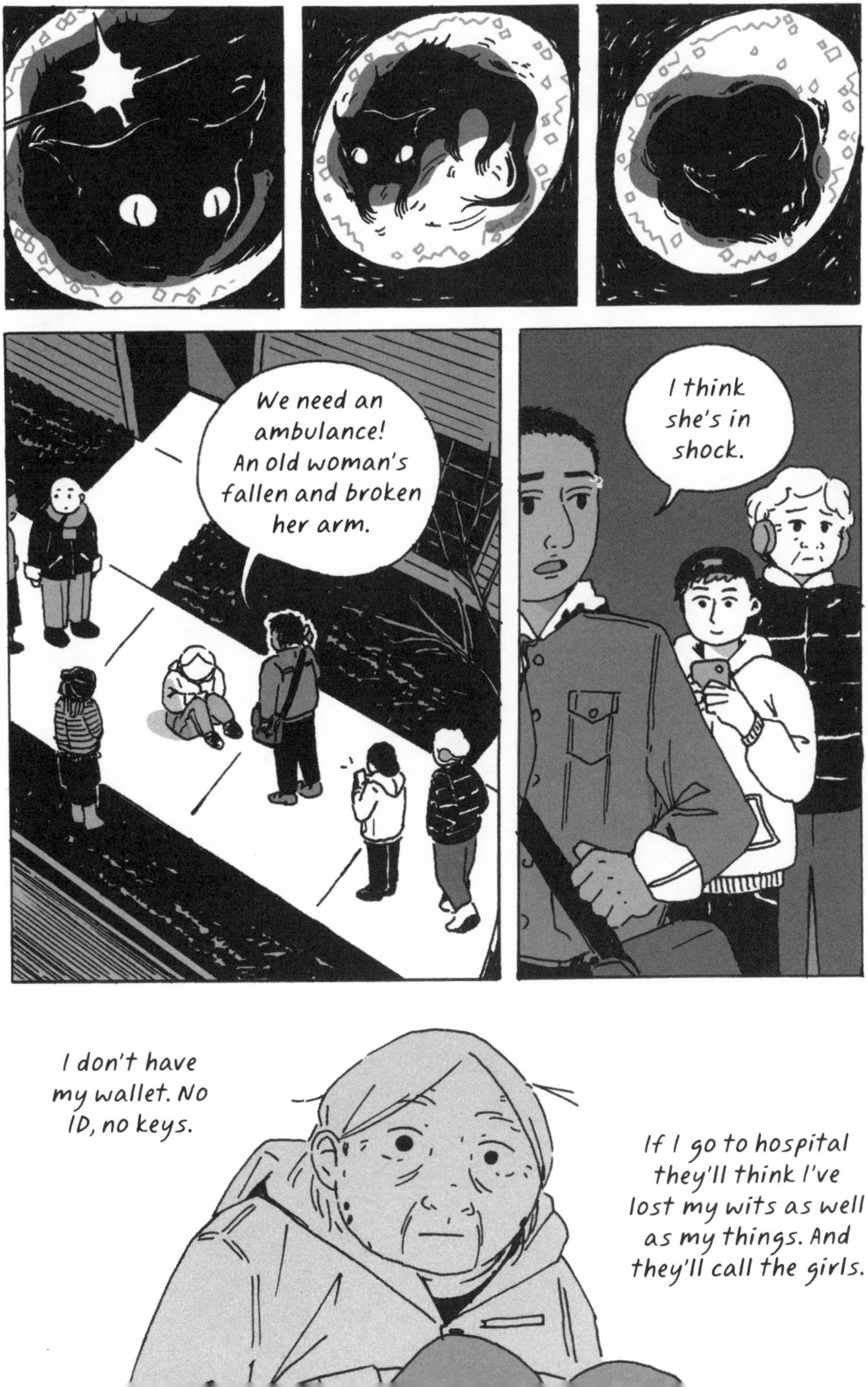
We need an ambulance! An old woman's fallen and broken her arm.
I think she's in shock.
I don't have my wallet. No ID, no keys.
If I go to hospital they'll think I've lost my wits as well as my things. And they'll call the girls.

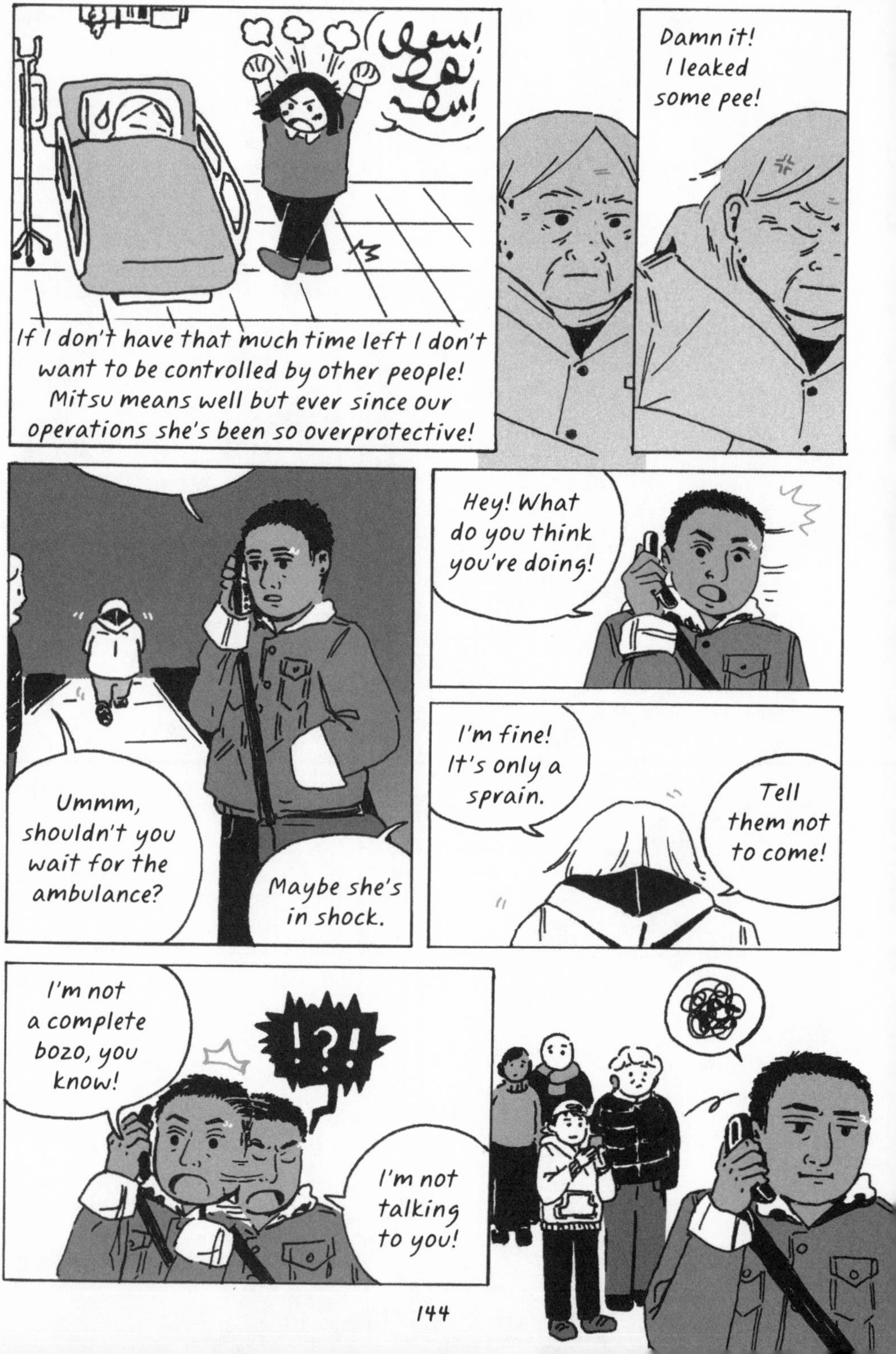
Damn it! I leaked some pee!
If I don't have that much time left I don't want to be controlled by other people! Mitsu means well but ever since our operations she's been so overprotective!
Ummm, shouldn't you wait for the ambulance?
Maybe she's in shock.
Hey! What do you think you're doing!
I'm fine! It's only a sprain.
Tell them not to come!
I'm not a complete bozo, you know!
!?!
I'm not talking to you!

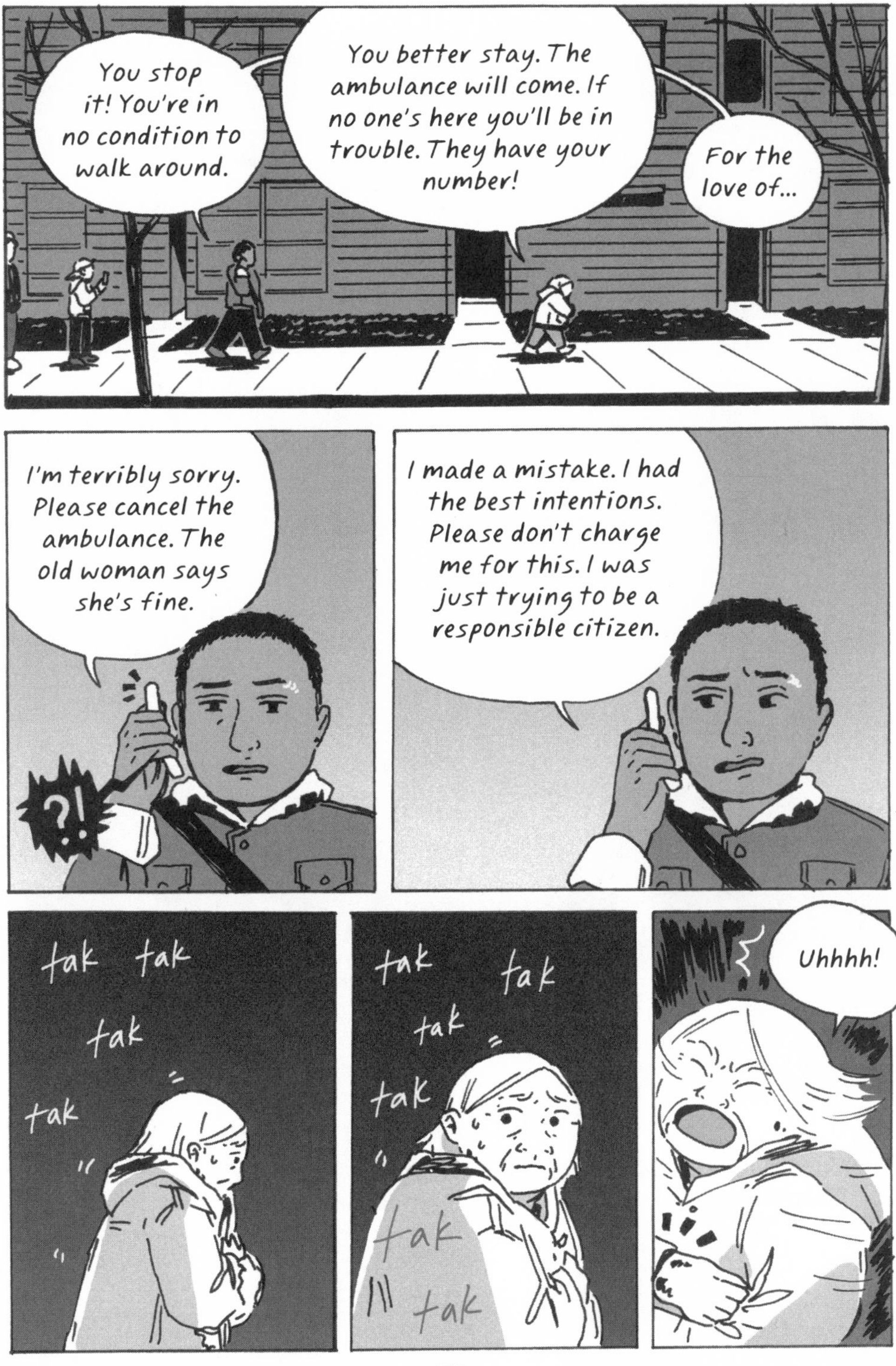
You stop it! You're in no condition to walk around.
You better stay. The ambulance will come. If no one's here you'll be in trouble. They have your number!
For the love of...
I'm terribly sorry. Please cancel the ambulance. The old woman says she's fine.
?!
I made a mistake. I had the best intentions. Please don't charge me for this. I was just trying to be a responsible citizen.
tak tak
tak
tak
tak
tak
tak
tak
tak
tak
Uhhhh!

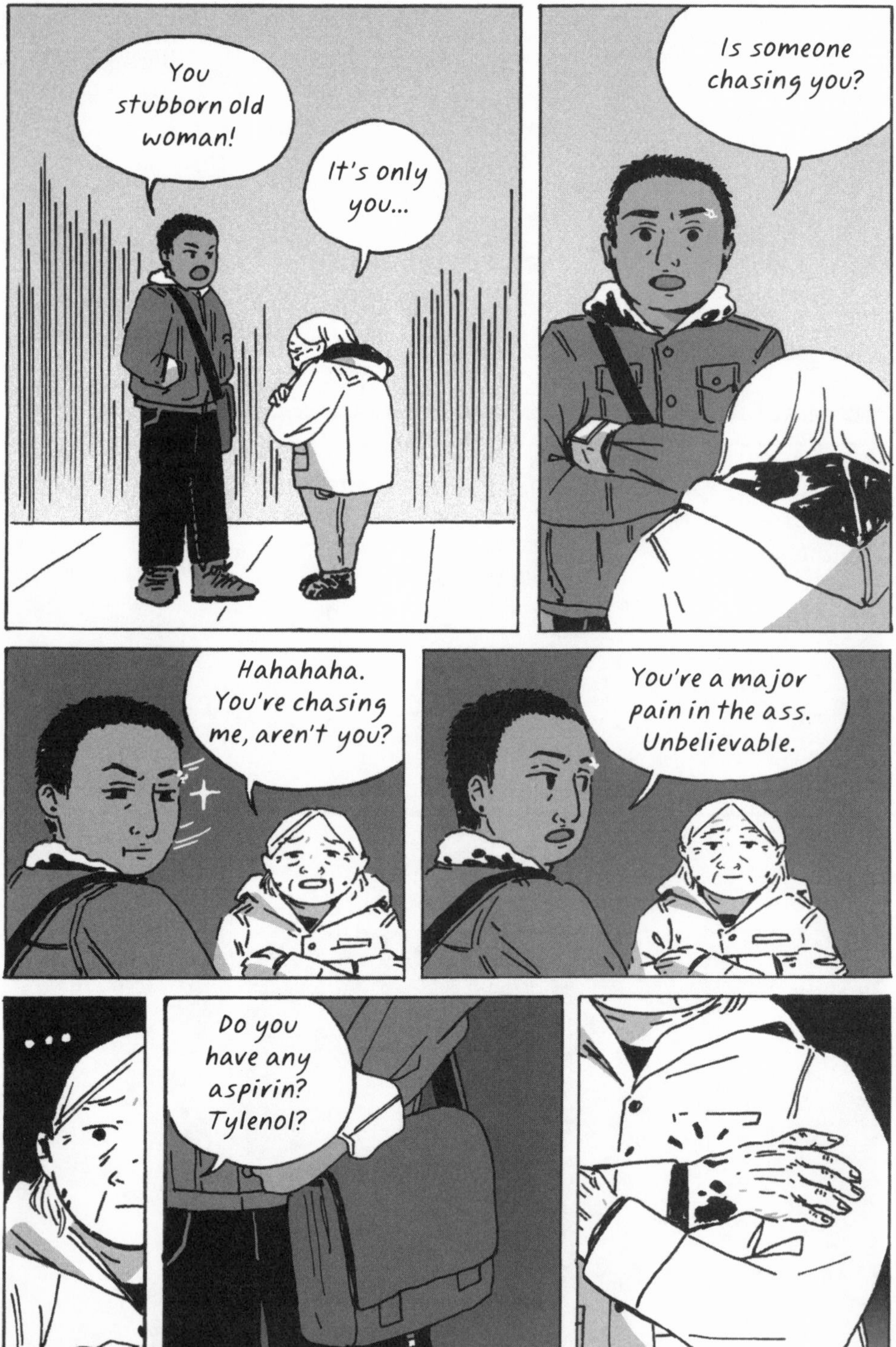
You stubborn old woman!
It's only you...
Is someone chasing you?
Hahahaha. You're chasing me, aren't you?
You're a major pain in the ass. Unbelievable.
...
Do you have any aspirin? Tylenol?

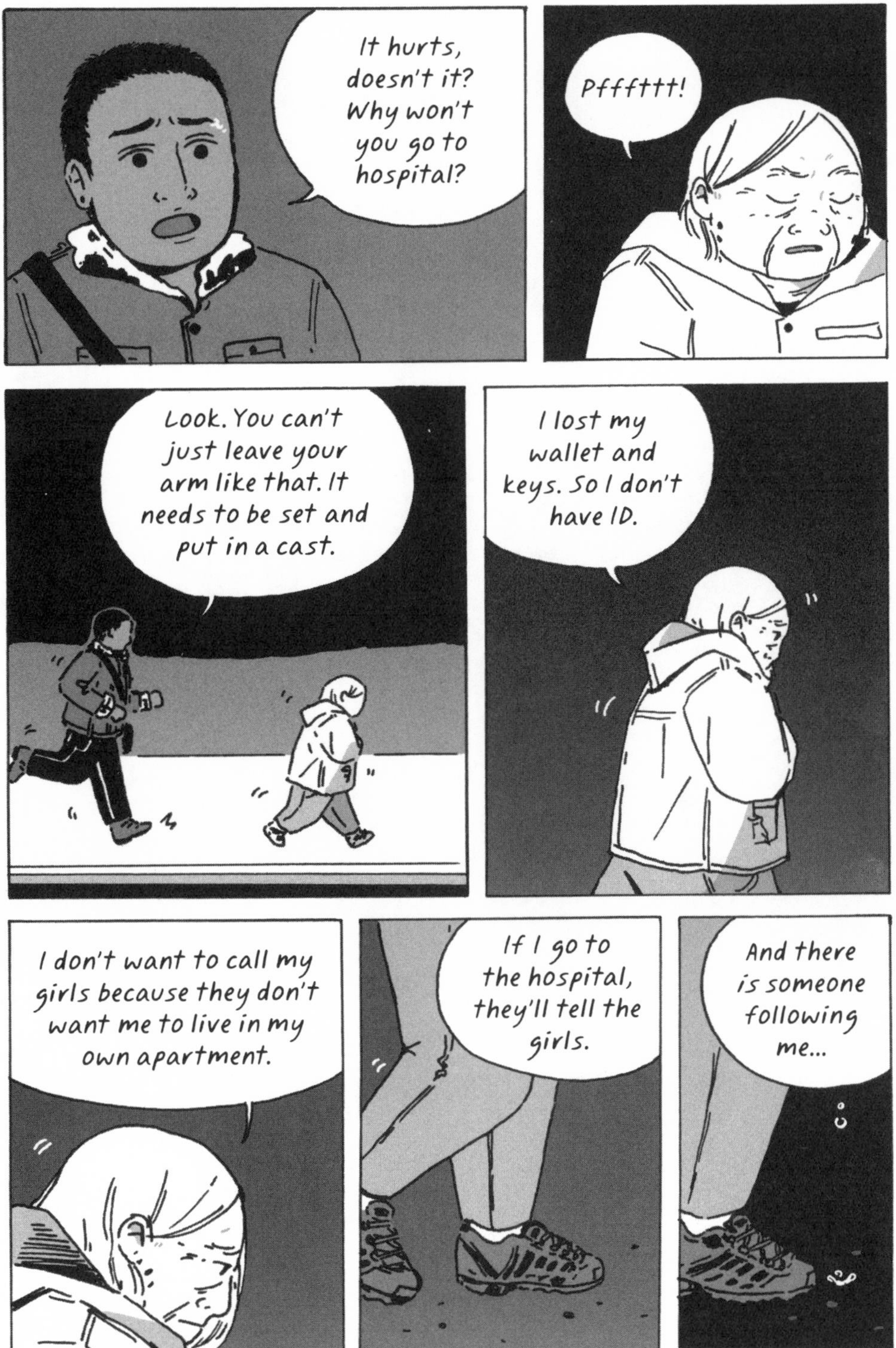
It hurts, doesn't it? Why won't you go to hospital?
Pffffttt!
Look. You can't just leave your arm like that. It needs to be set and put in a cast.
I lost my wallet and keys. So I don't have ID.
I don't want to call my girls because they don't want me to live in my own apartment.
If I go to the hospital, they'll tell the girls.
And there is someone following me...

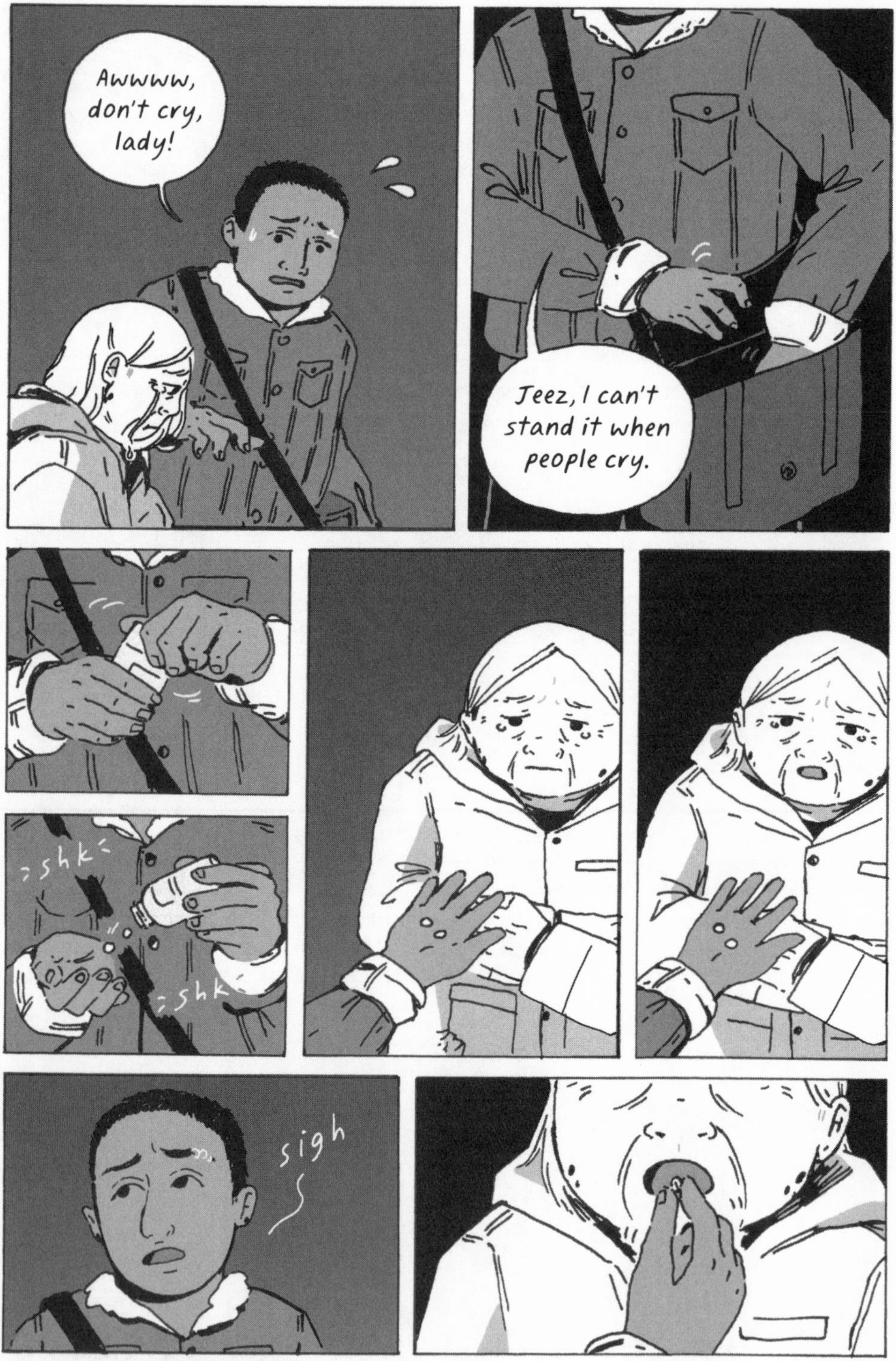
Awwww, don't cry, lady!
Jeez, I can't stand it when people cry.
shk
shk
sigh

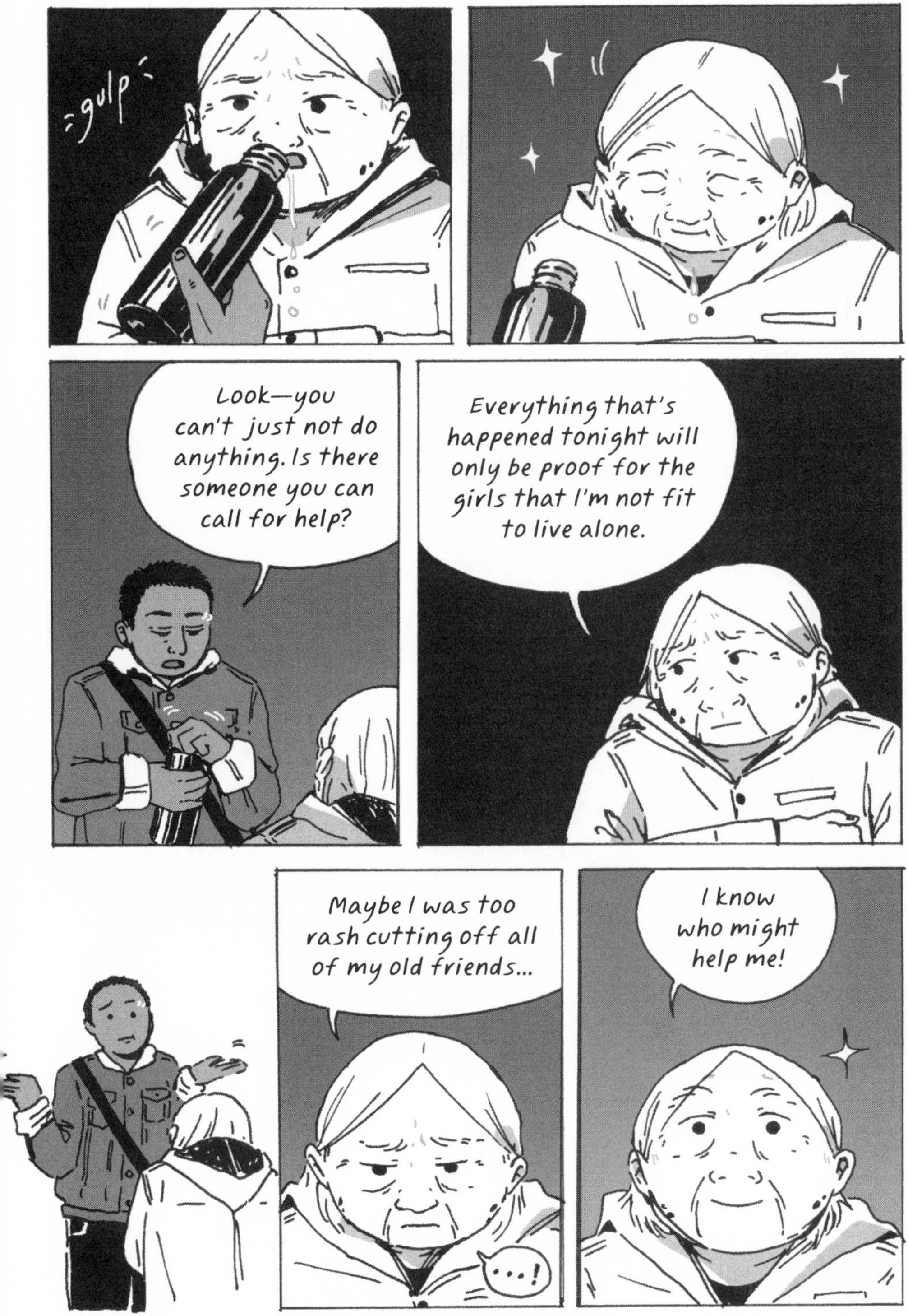
gulp
Look—you can't just not do anything. Is there someone you can call for help?
Everything that's happened tonight will only be proof for the girls that I'm not fit to live alone.
Maybe I was too rash cutting off all of my old friends...
...!
I know who might help me!

Chapter Eight

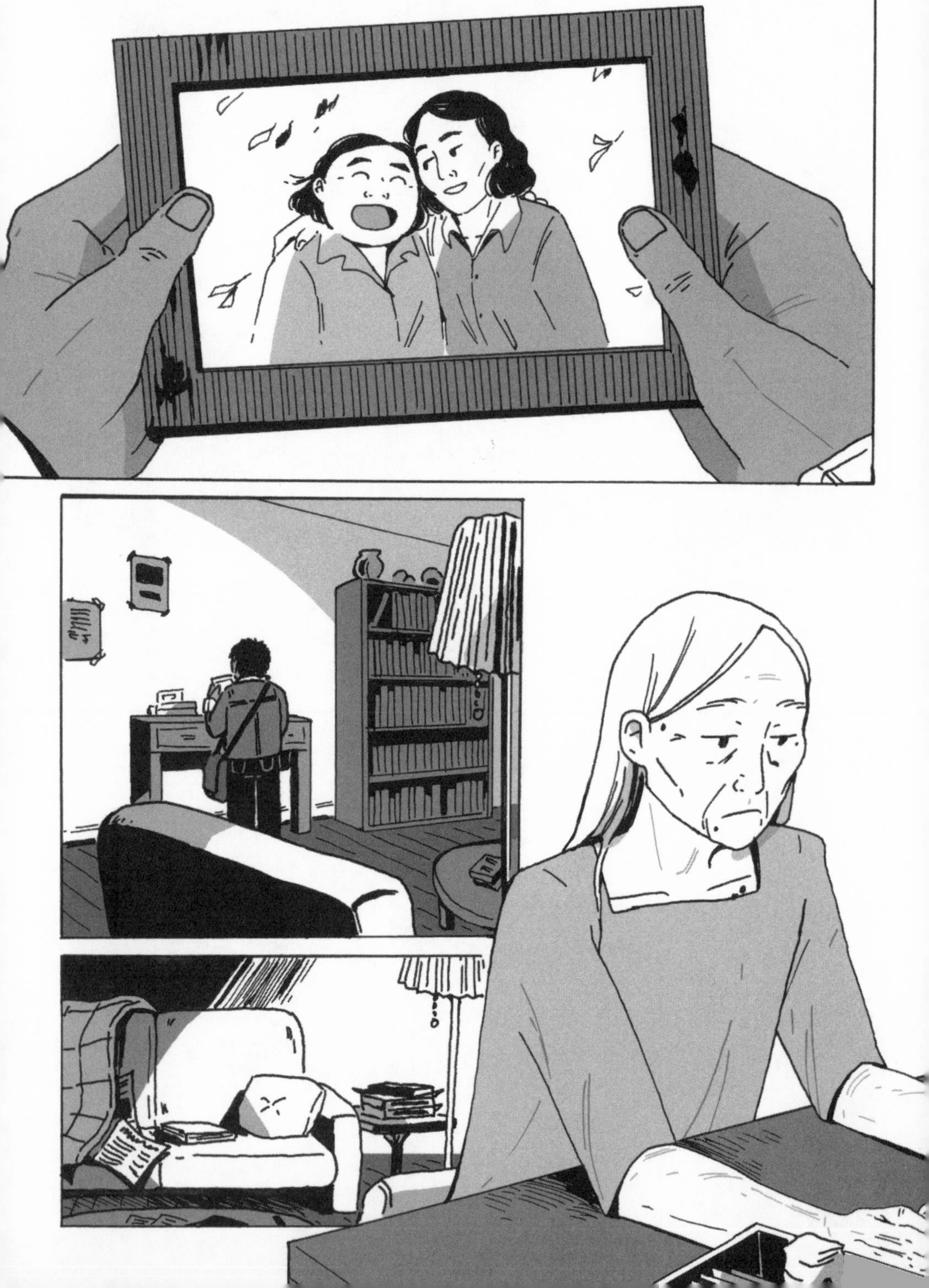

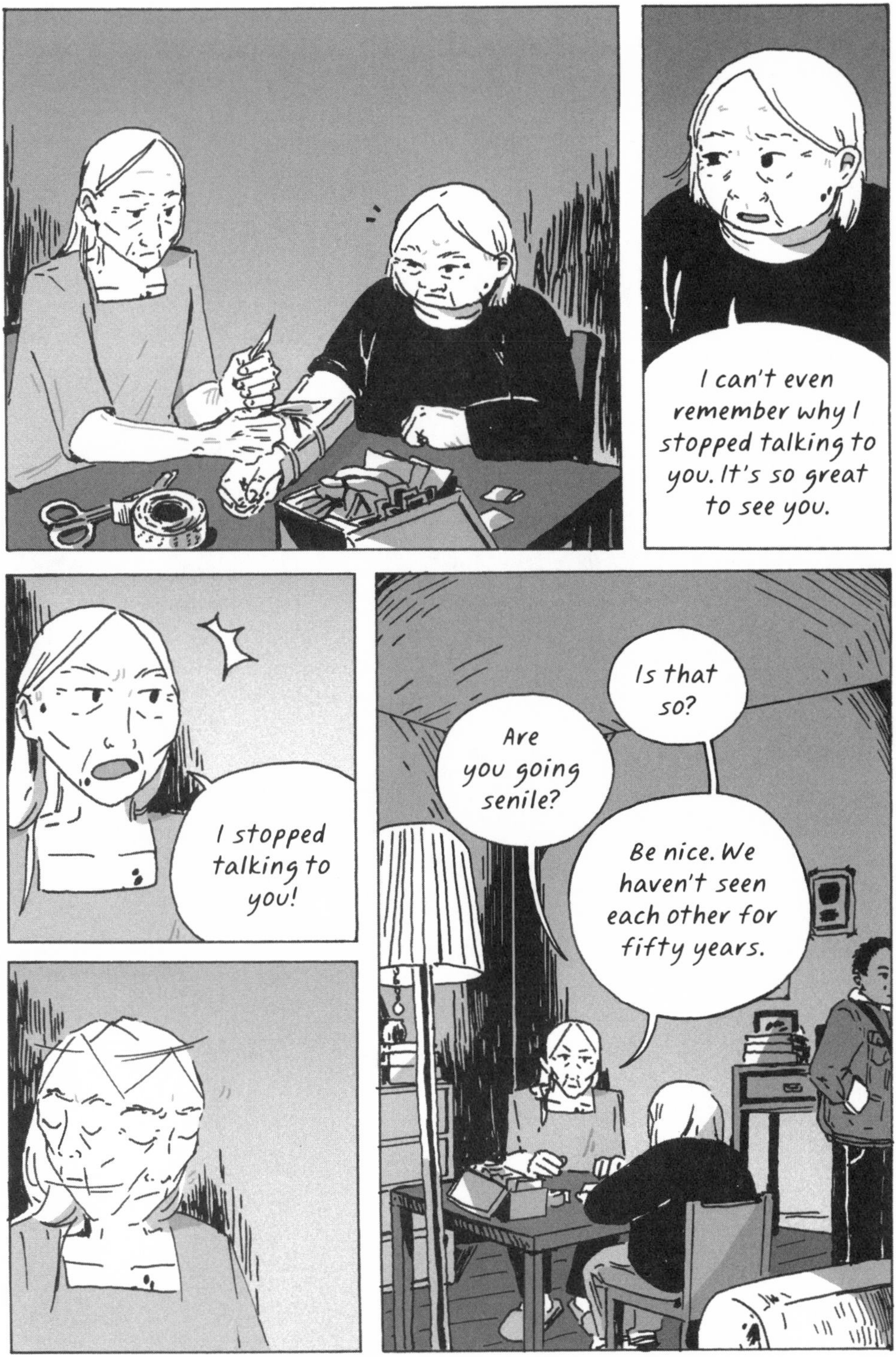
I can't even remember why I stopped talking to you. It's so great to see you.
I stopped talking to you!
Is that so?
Are you going senile?
Be nice. We haven't seen each other for fifty years.

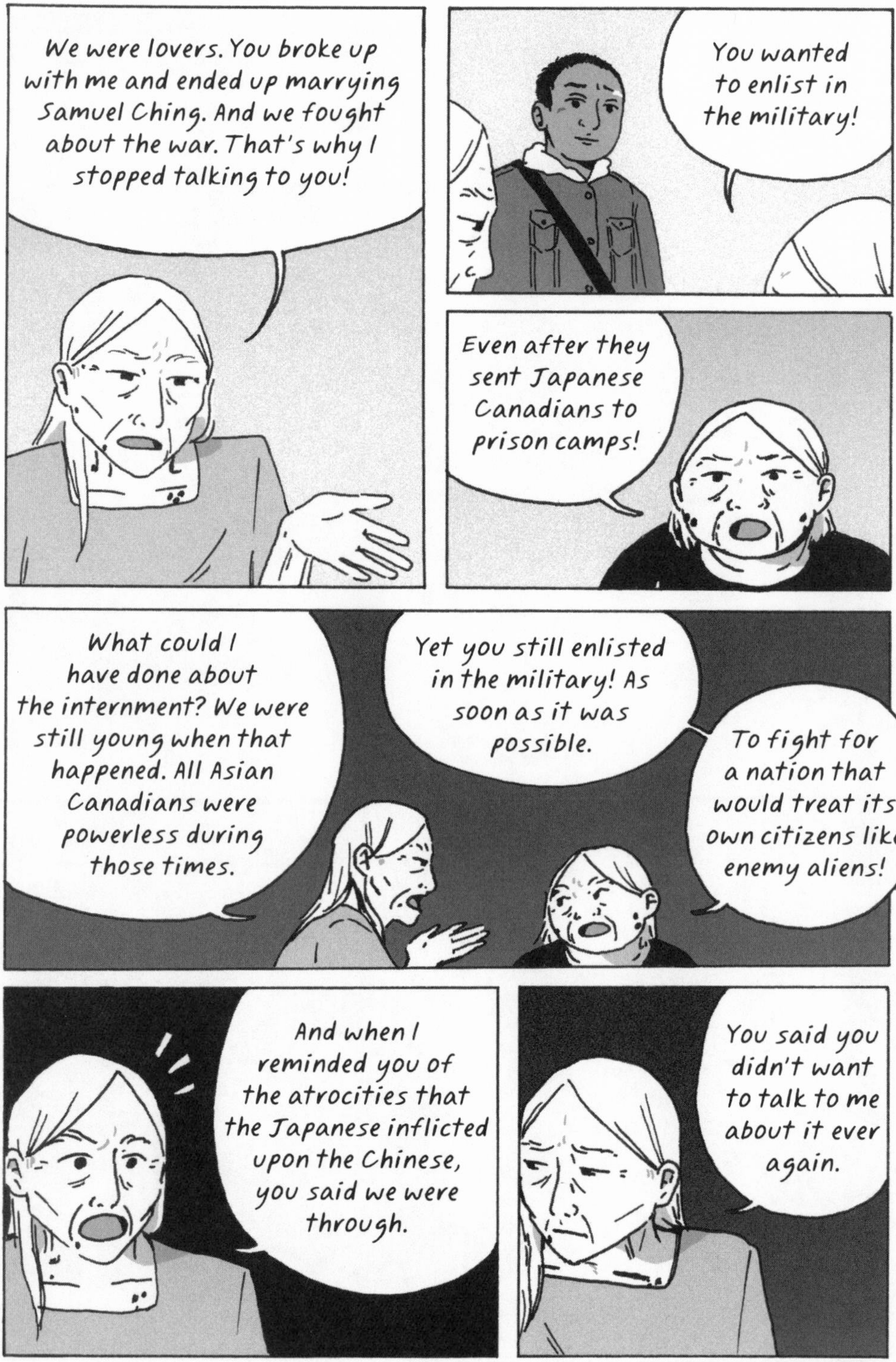
We were lovers. You broke up with me and ended up marrying Samuel Ching. And we fought about the war. That's why I stopped talking to you!
You wanted to enlist in the military!
Even after they sent Japanese Canadians to prison camps!
What could I have done about the internment? We were still young when that happened. All Asian Canadians were powerless during those times.
Yet you still enlisted in the military! As soon as it was possible.
To fight for a nation that would treat its own citizens like enemy aliens!
And when I reminded you of the atrocities that the Japanese inflicted upon the Chinese, you said we were through.
You said you didn't want to talk to me about it ever again.

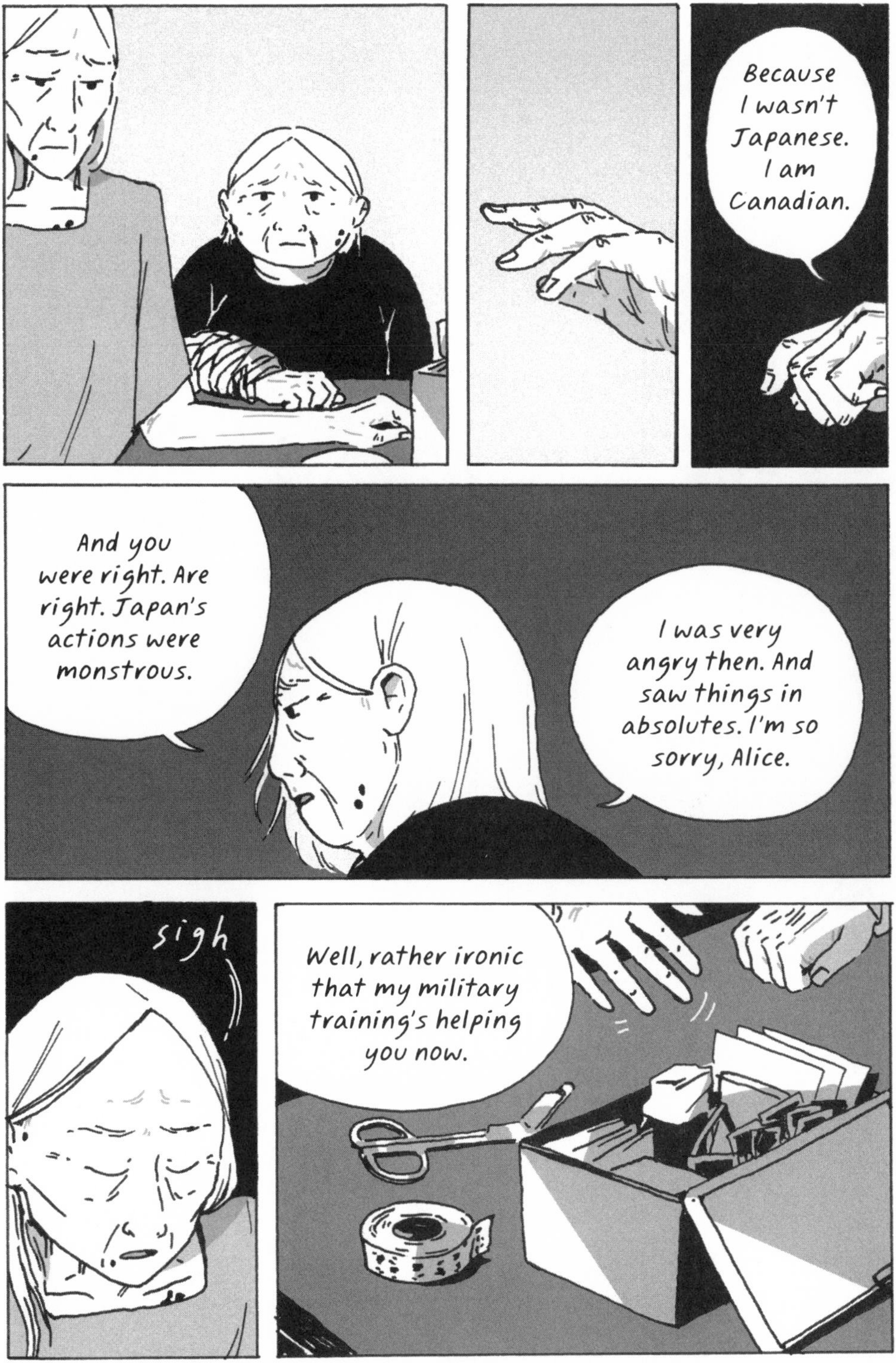
Because I wasn't Japanese. I am Canadian.
And you were right. Are right. Japan's actions were monstrous.
I was very angry then. And saw things in absolutes. I'm so sorry, Alice.
sigh
Well, rather ironic that my military training's helping you now.

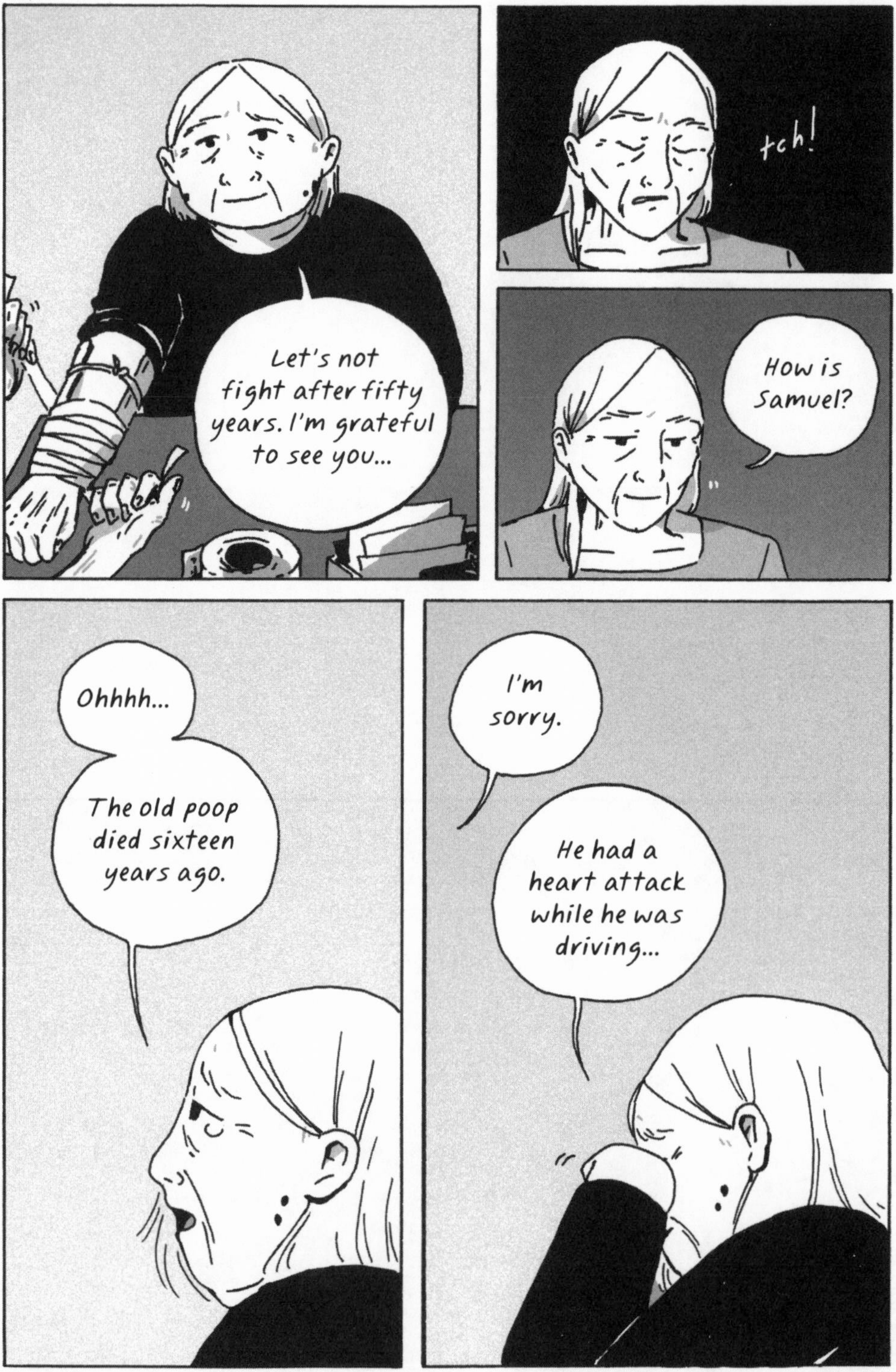
Let's not fight after fifty years. I'm grateful to see you...
tch!
How is Samuel?
Ohhhh...
The old poop died sixteen years ago.
I'm sorry.
He had a heart attack while he was driving...

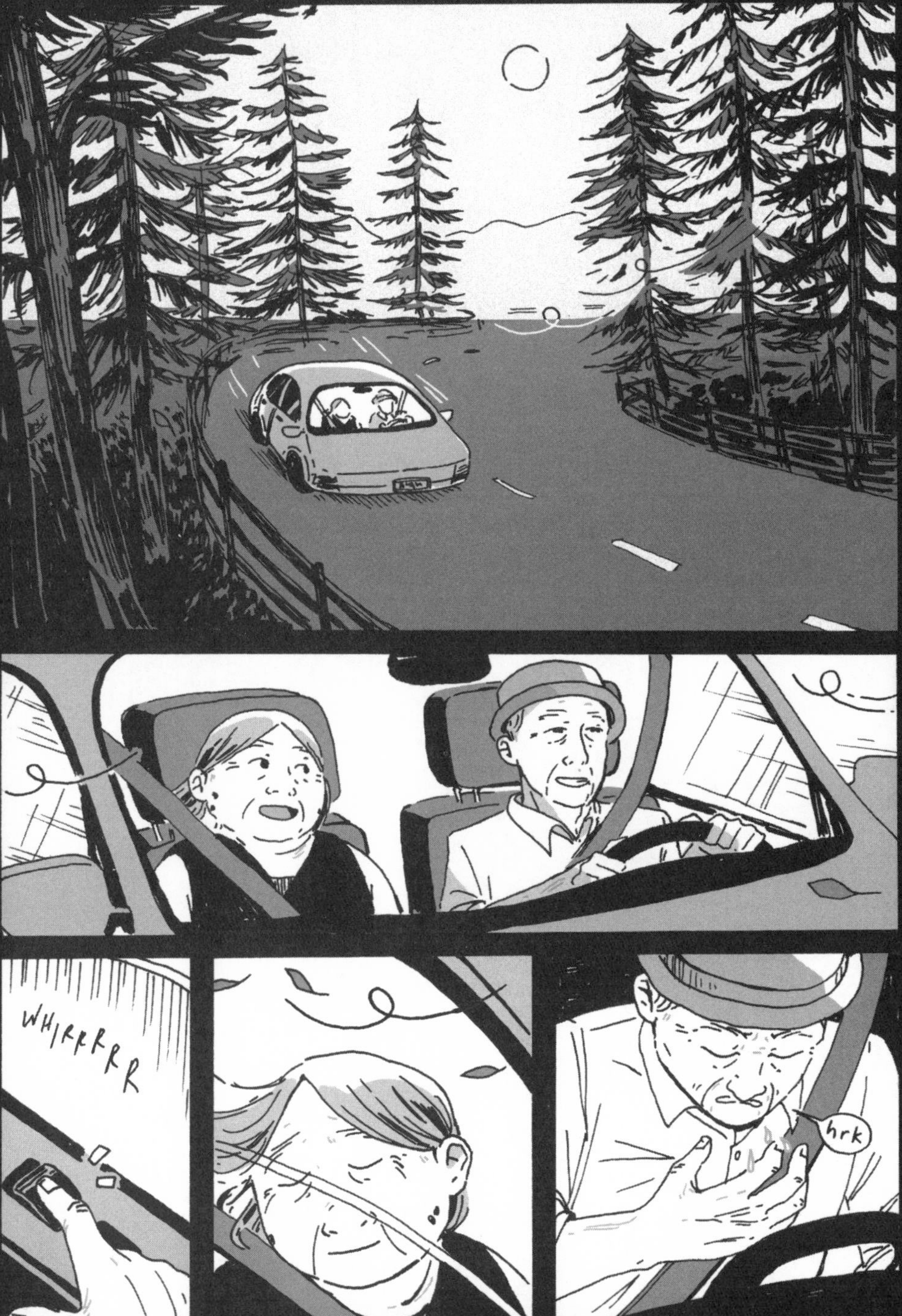
WHIRRRRR
hrk

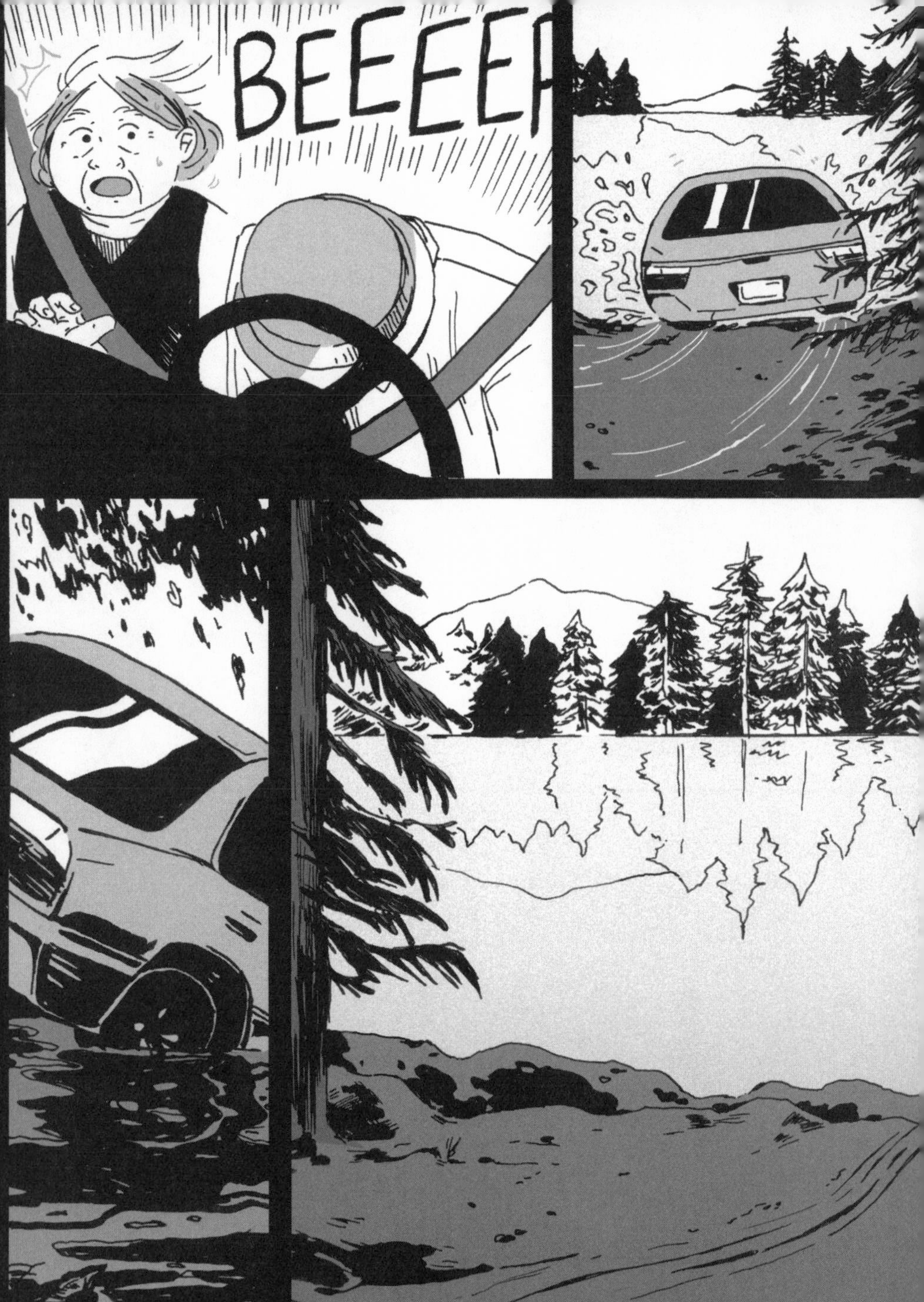
BEEEEP

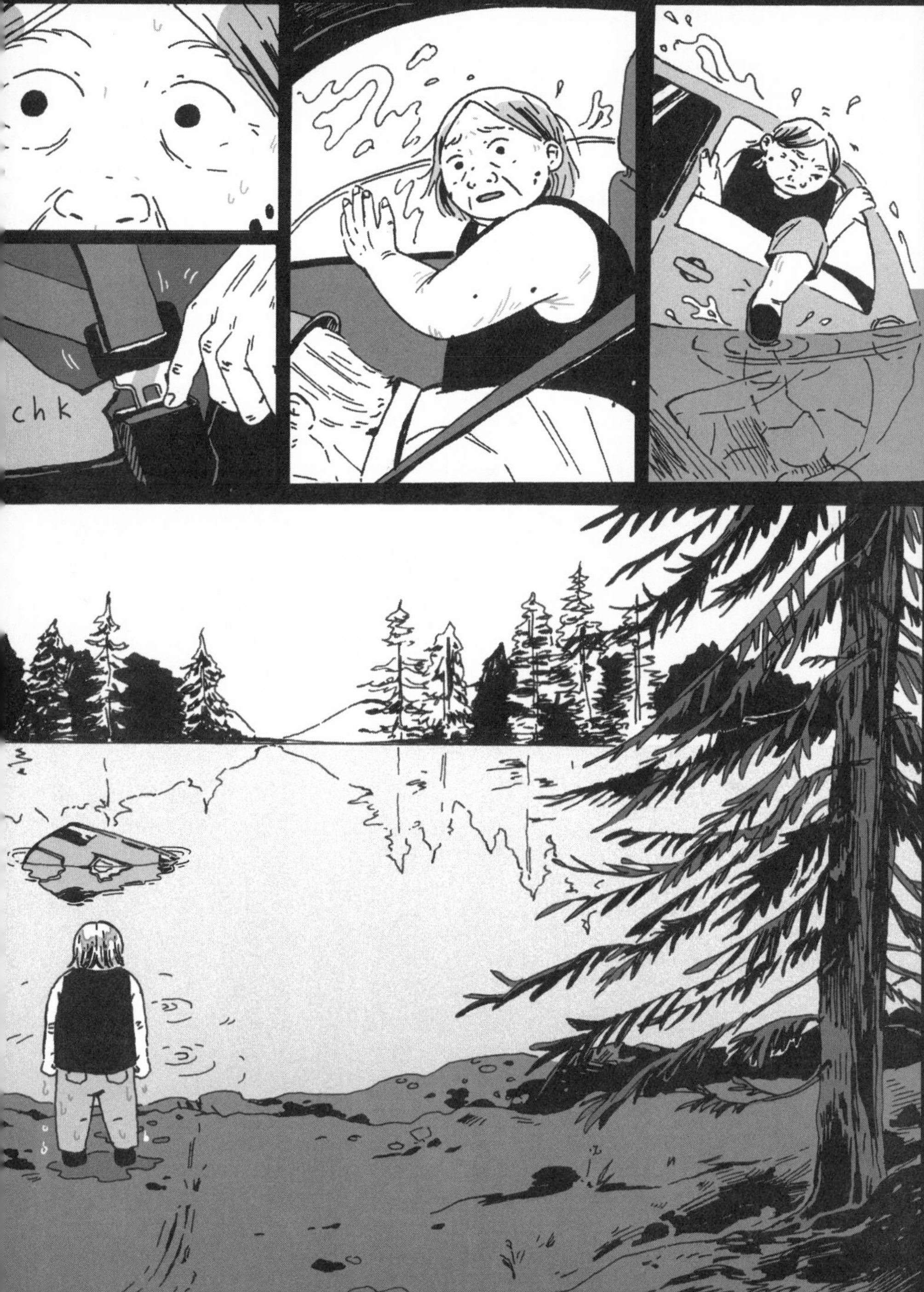
chk

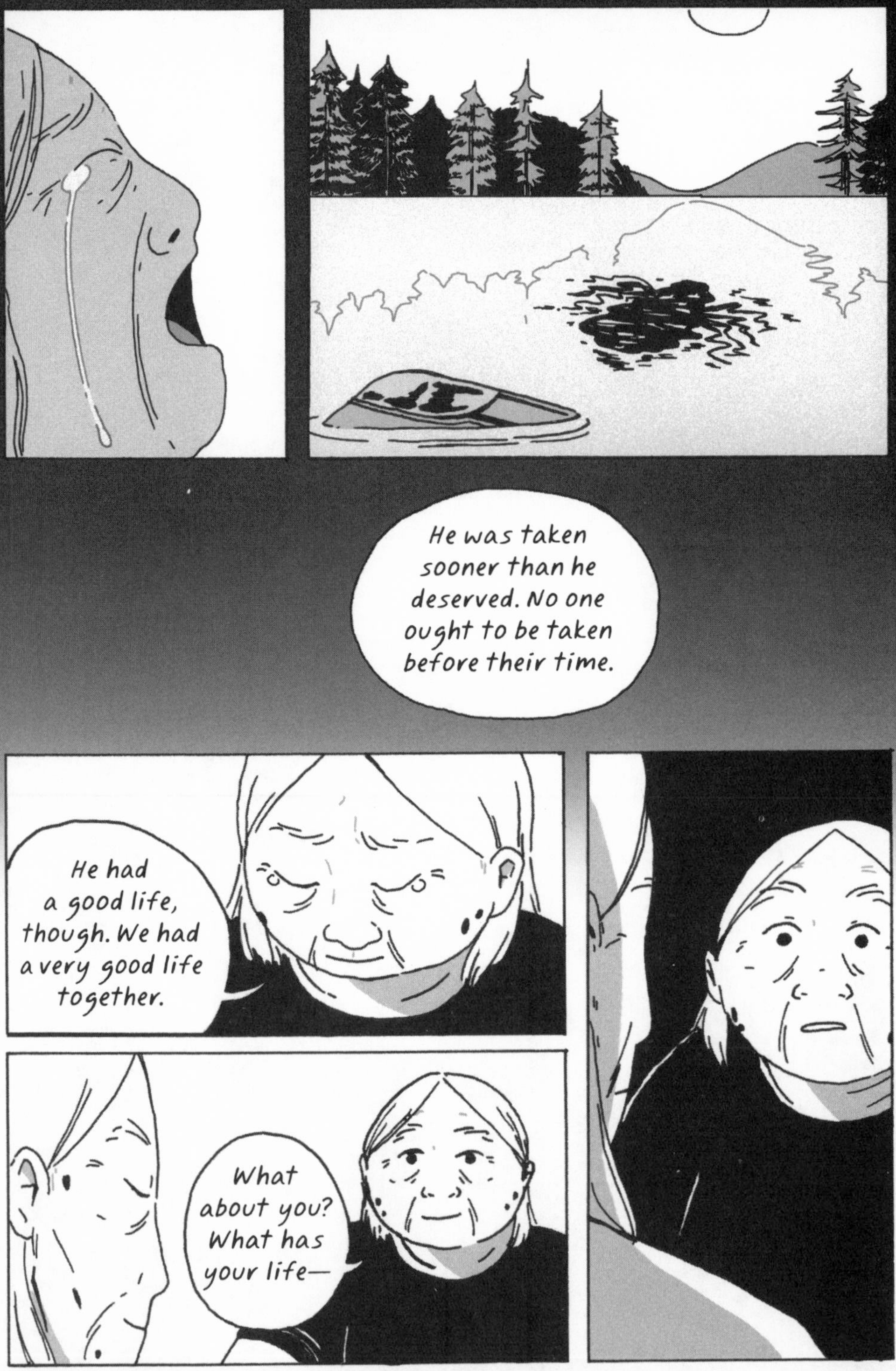
He was taken sooner than he deserved. No one ought to be taken before their time.
He had a good life, though. We had a very good life together.
What about you? What has your life—

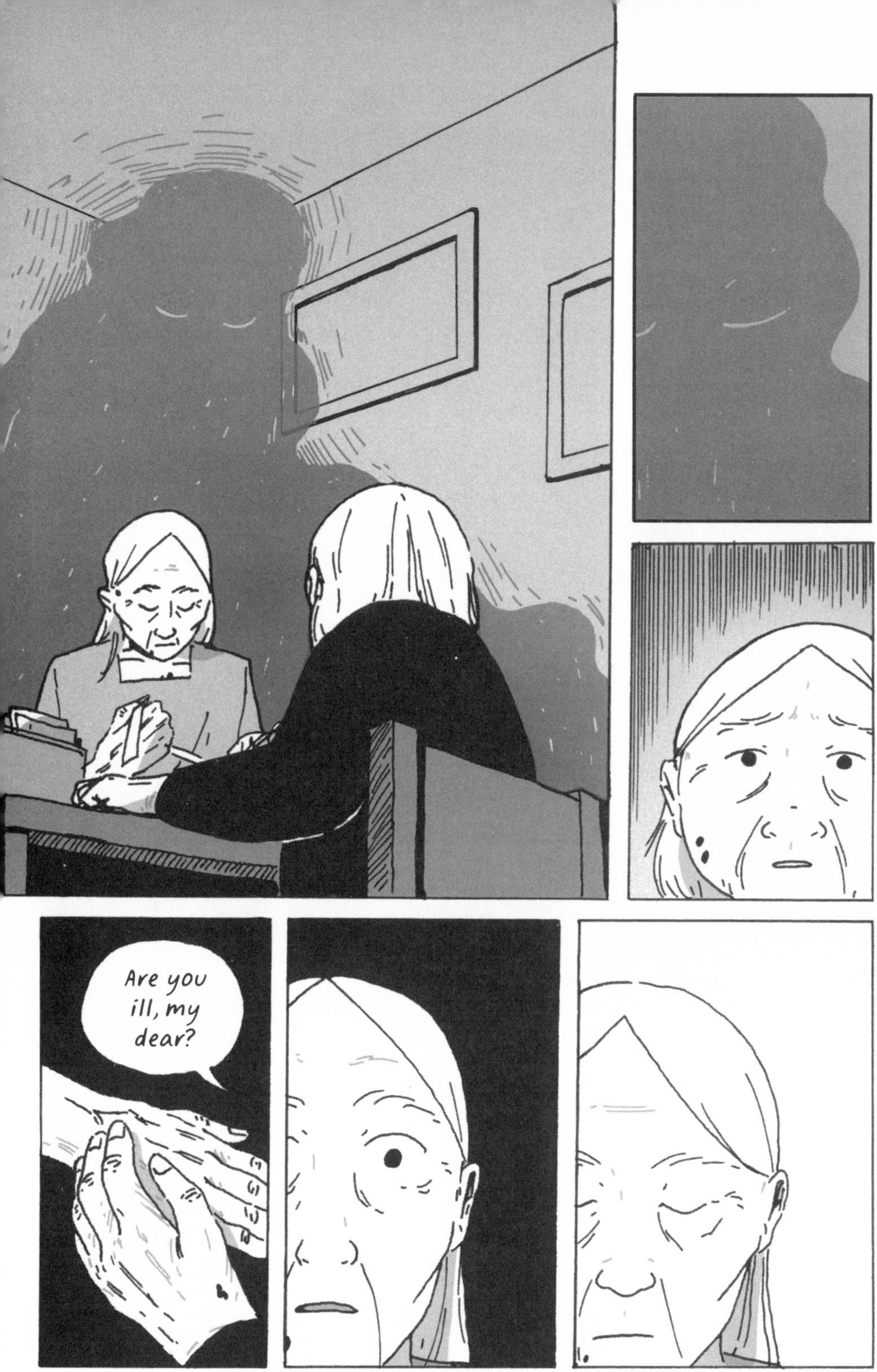
Are you ill, my dear?

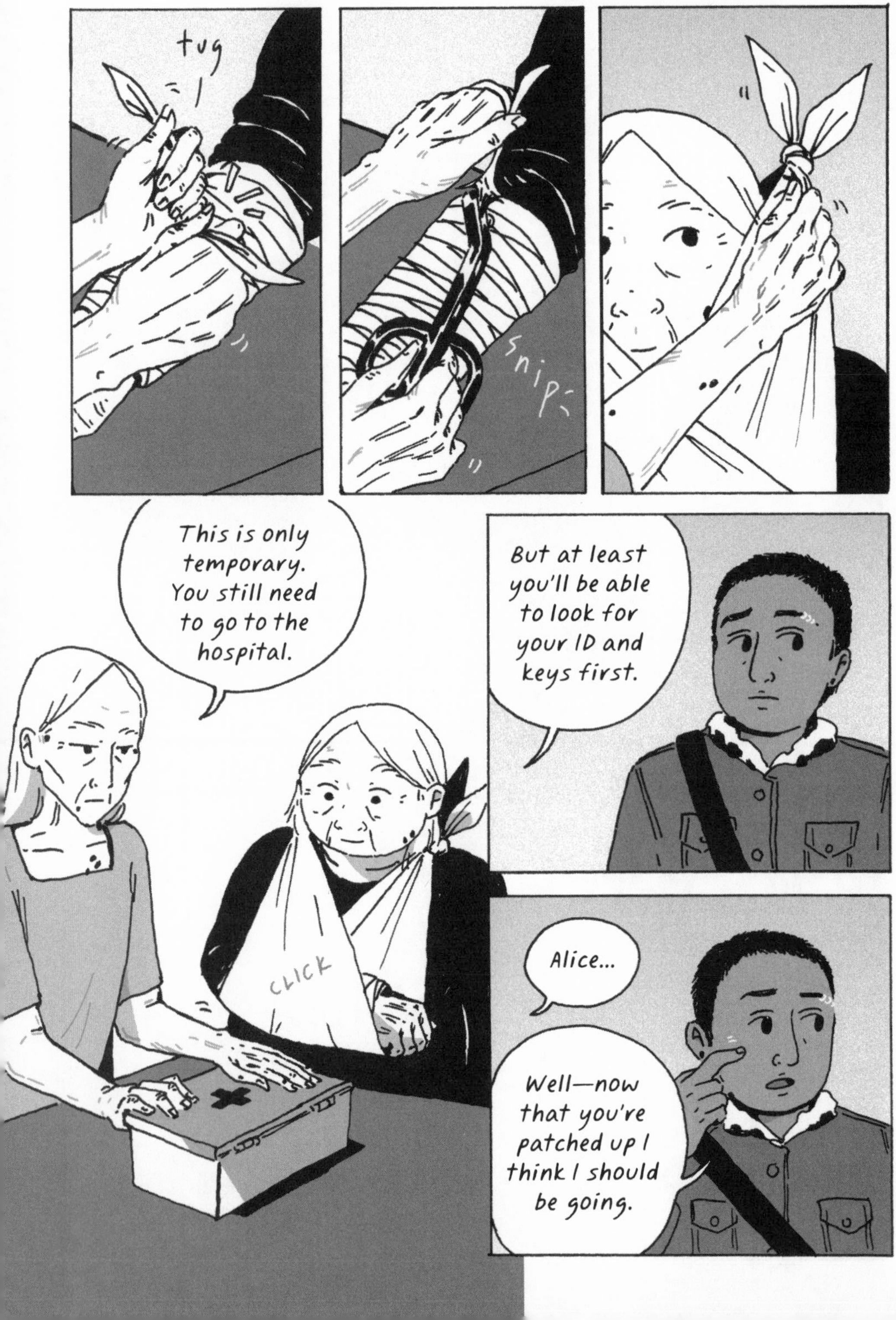
tug
snip
This is only temporary. You still need to go to the hospital.
But at least you'll be able to look for your ID and keys first.
CLICK
Alice...
Well—now that you're patched up I think I should be going.

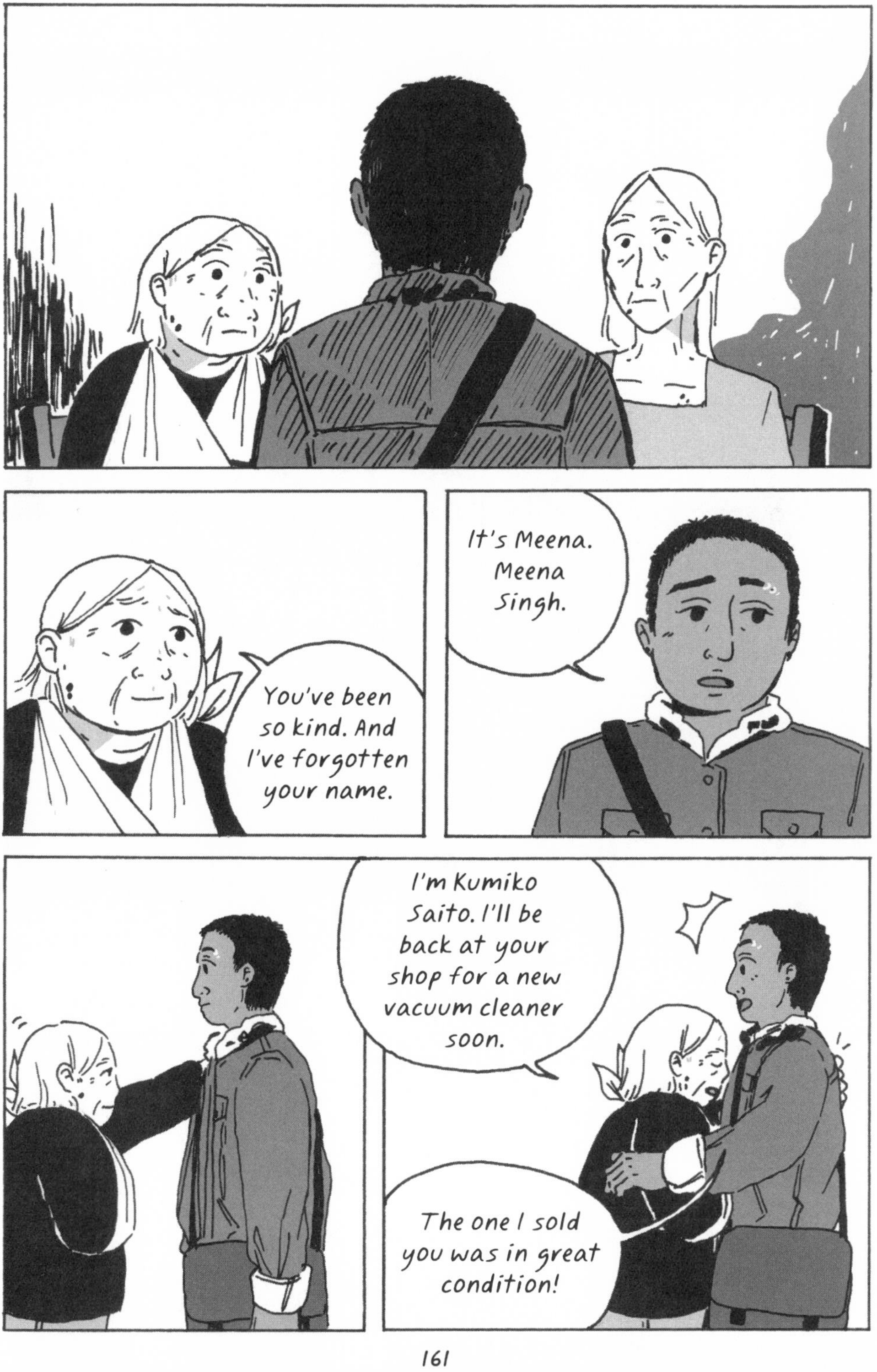
You've been so kind. And I've forgotten your name.
It's Meena. Meena Singh.
I'm Kumiko Saito. I'll be back at your shop for a new vacuum cleaner soon.
The one I sold you was in great condition!

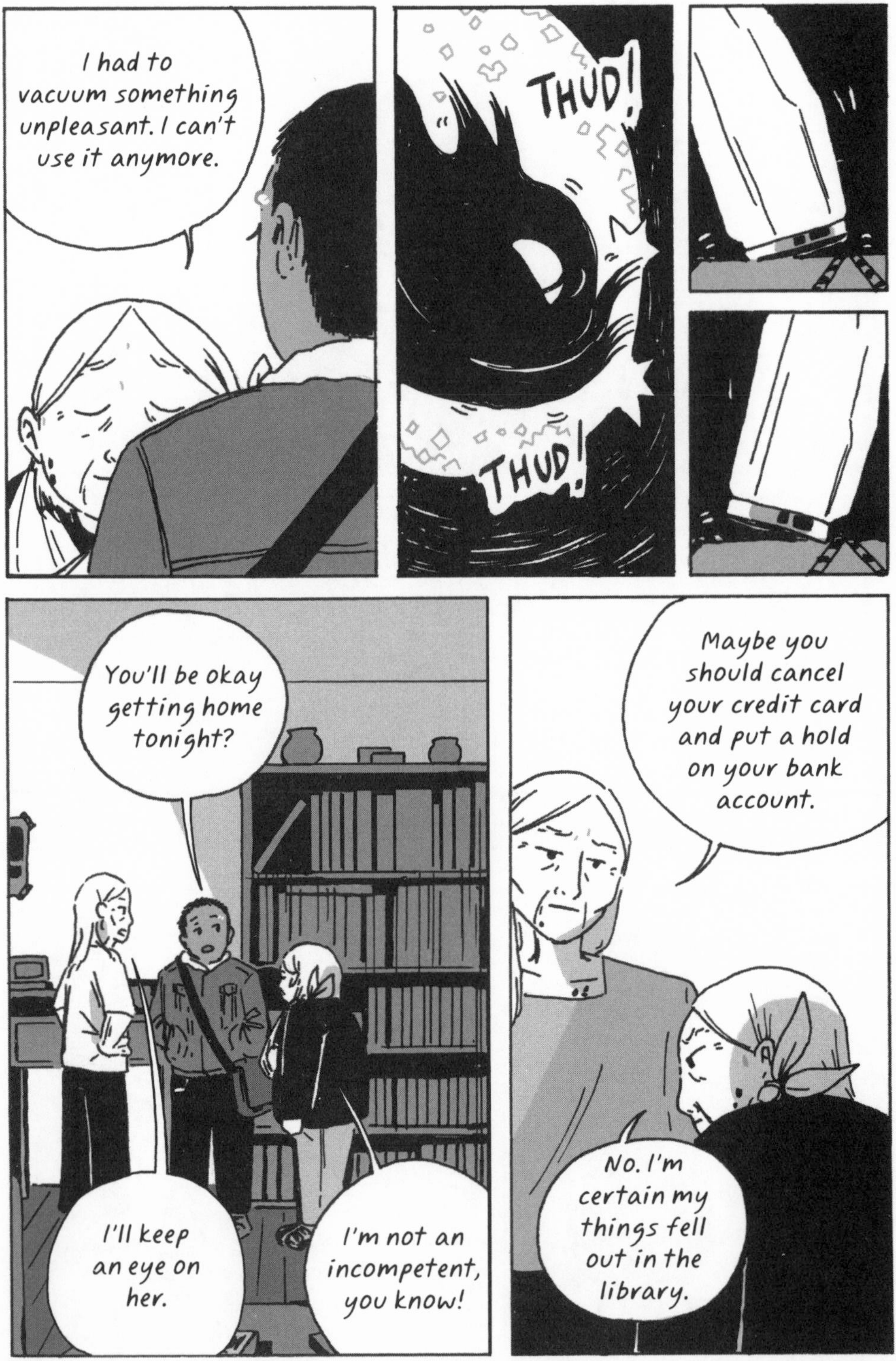
I had to vacuum something unpleasant. I can't use it anymore.
THUD!
THUD!
You'll be okay getting home tonight?
I'll keep an eye on her.
I'm not an incompetent, you know!
Maybe you should cancel your credit card and put a hold on your bank account.
No. I'm certain my things fell out in the library.

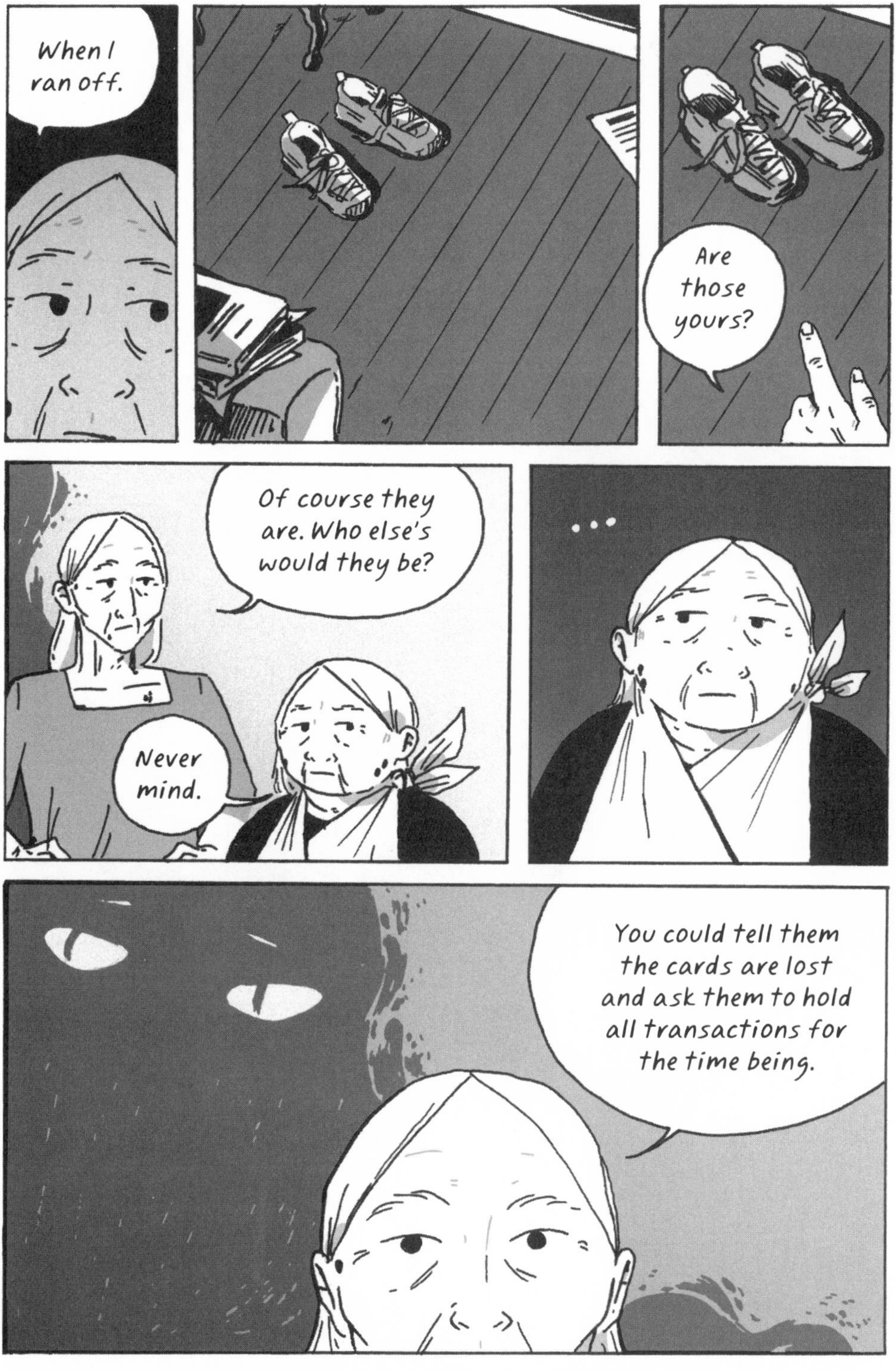
When I ran off.
Are those yours?
Of course they are. Who else's would they be?
Never mind.
...
You could tell them the cards are lost and ask them to hold all transactions for the time being.

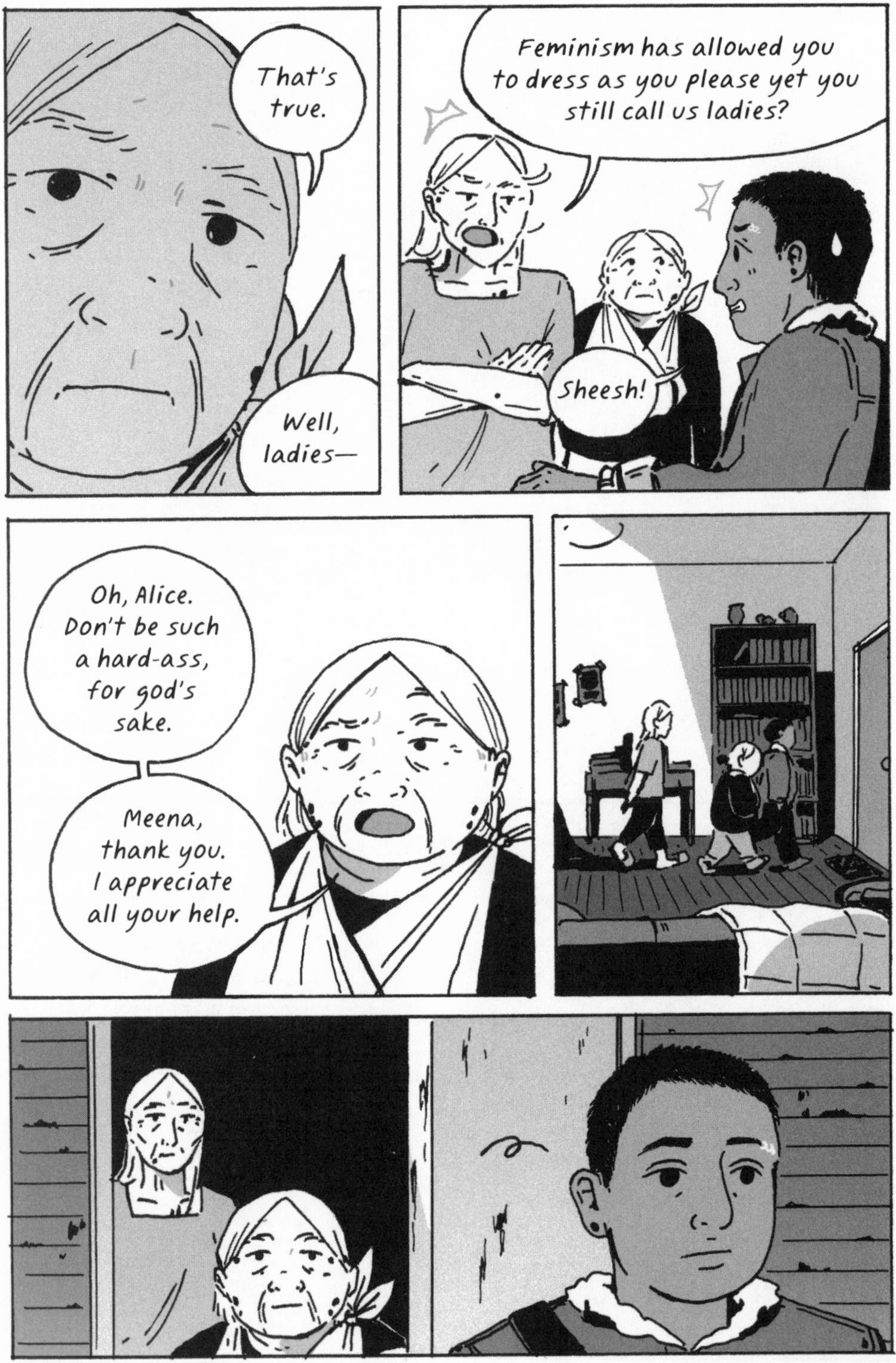
That's true.
Well, ladies—
Feminism has allowed you to dress as you please yet you still call us ladies?
Sheesh!
Oh, Alice. Don't be such a hard-ass, for god's sake.
Meena, thank you. I appreciate all your help.

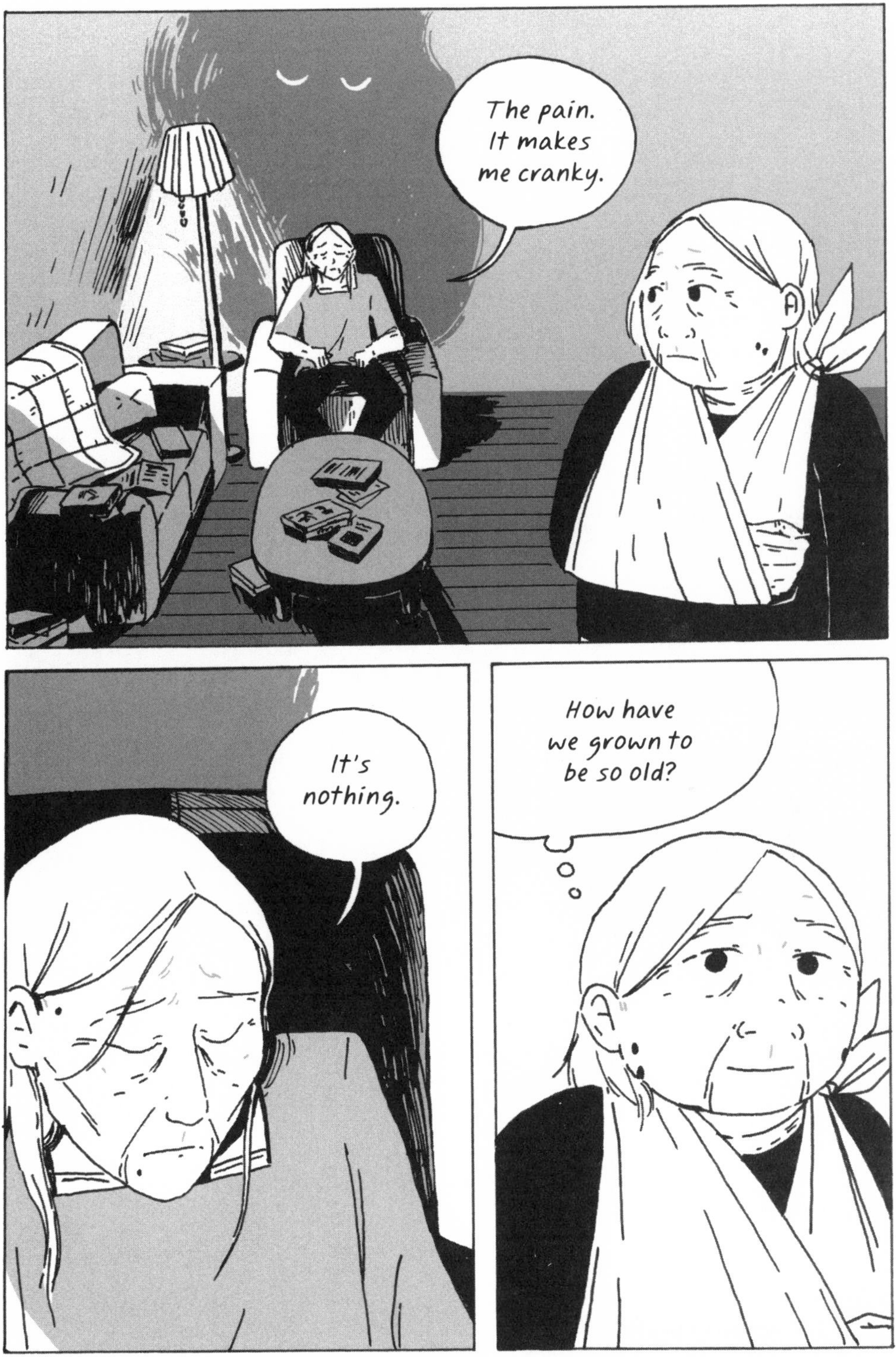
The pain. It makes me cranky.
It's nothing.
How have we grown to be so old?

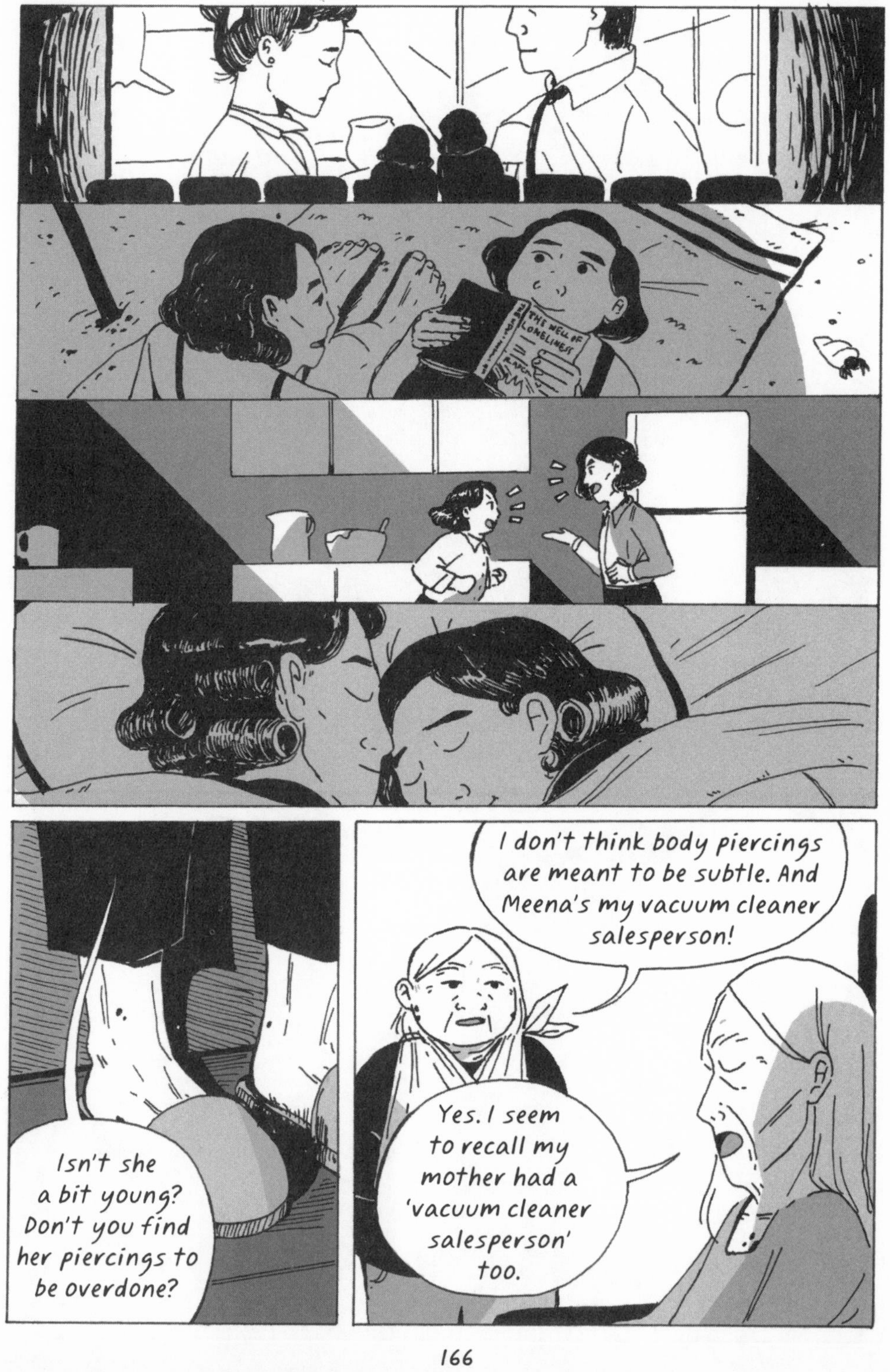
THE WELL OF LONELINESS
Isn't she a bit young? Don't you find her piercings to be overdone?
I don't think body piercings are meant to be subtle. And Meena's my vacuum cleaner salesperson!
Yes. I seem to recall my mother had a 'vacuum cleaner salesperson' too.

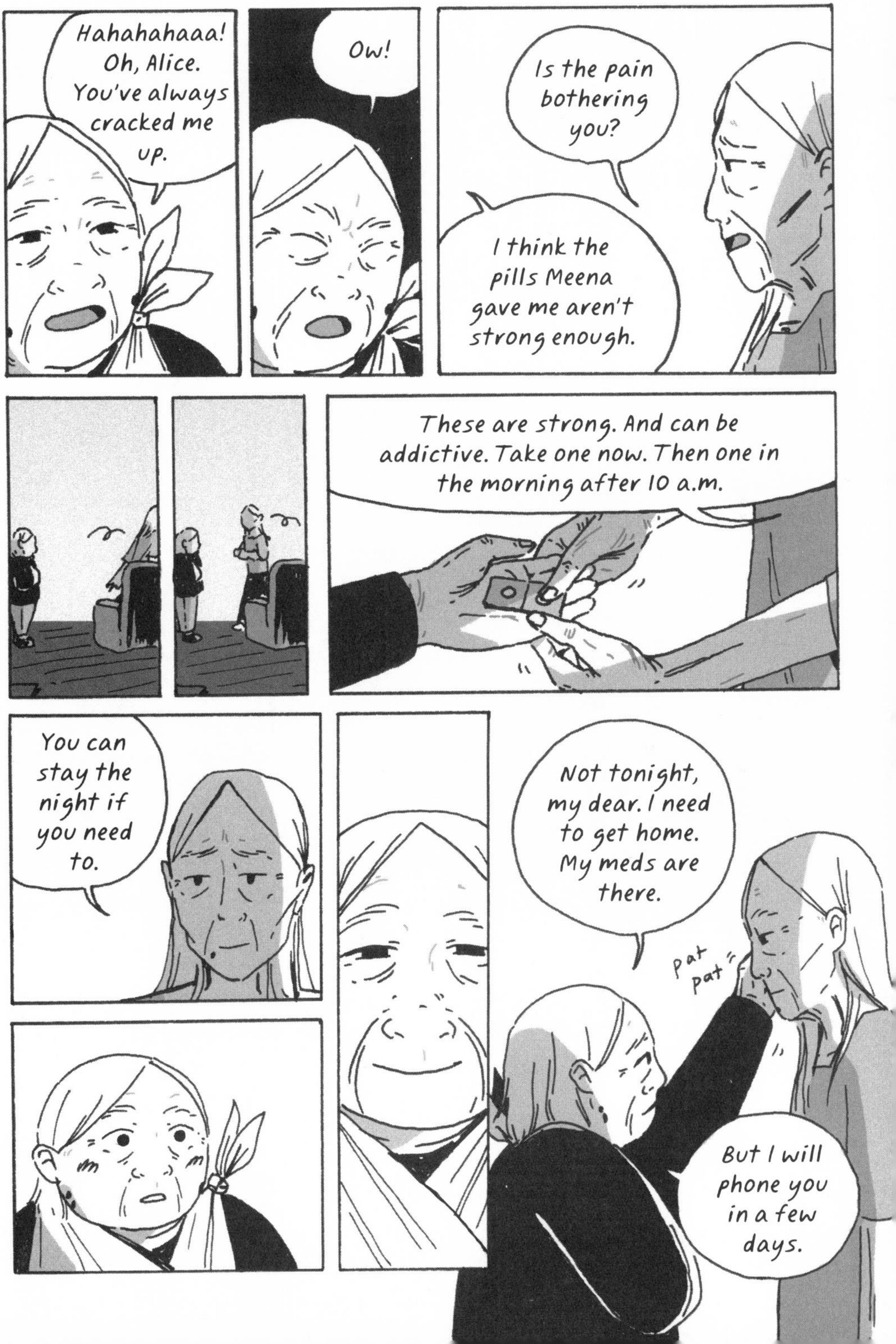
Hahahahaaa! Oh, Alice. You've always cracked me up.
Ow!
Is the pain bothering you?
I think the pills Meena gave me aren't strong enough.
These are strong. And can be addictive. Take one now. Then one in the morning after 10 a.m.
You can stay the night if you need to.
Not tonight, my dear. I need to get home. My meds are there.
pat pat
But I will phone you in a few days.

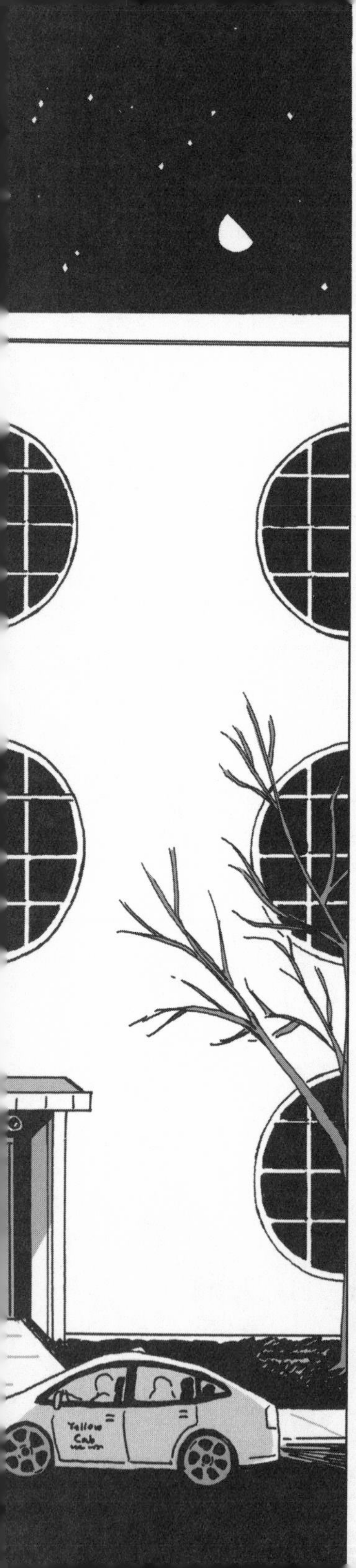
Yellow Cab

Chapter Nine

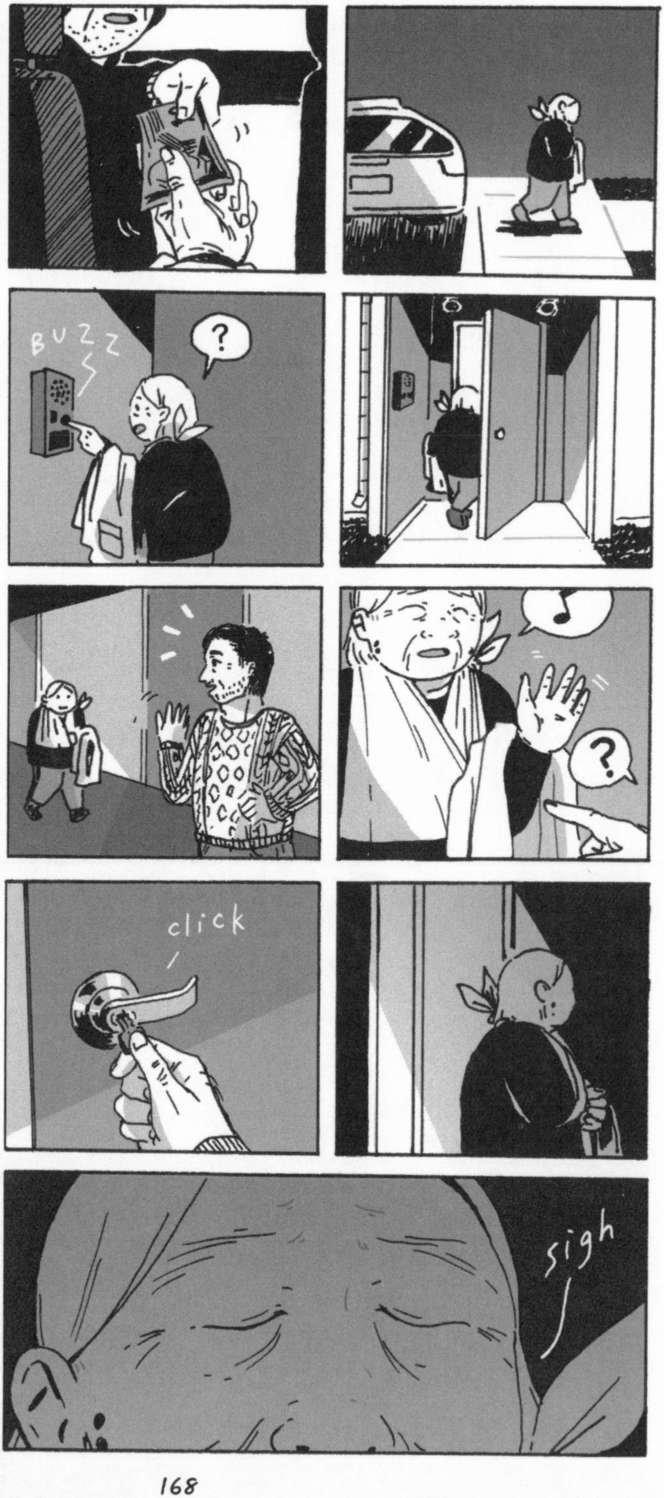
BUZZ
?
♪
?
click
sigh

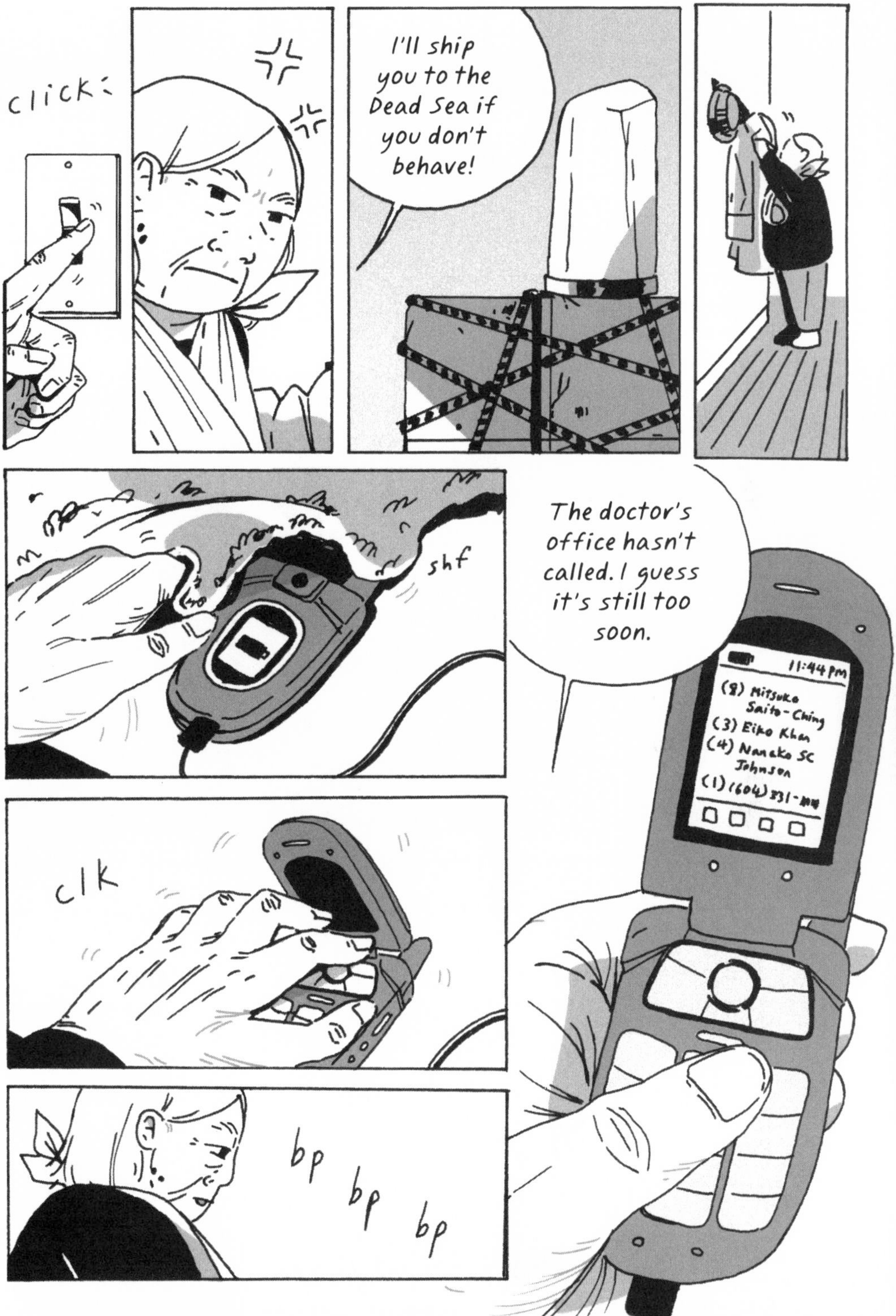
click
I'll ship you to the Dead Sea if you don't behave!
shf
The doctor's office hasn't called. I guess it's still too soon.
11:44 PM
(8) Mitsuko Saito-Ching
(3) Eiko Khan
(4) Nanako SC Johnson
(1) (604) 331-
clk
bp
bp
bp

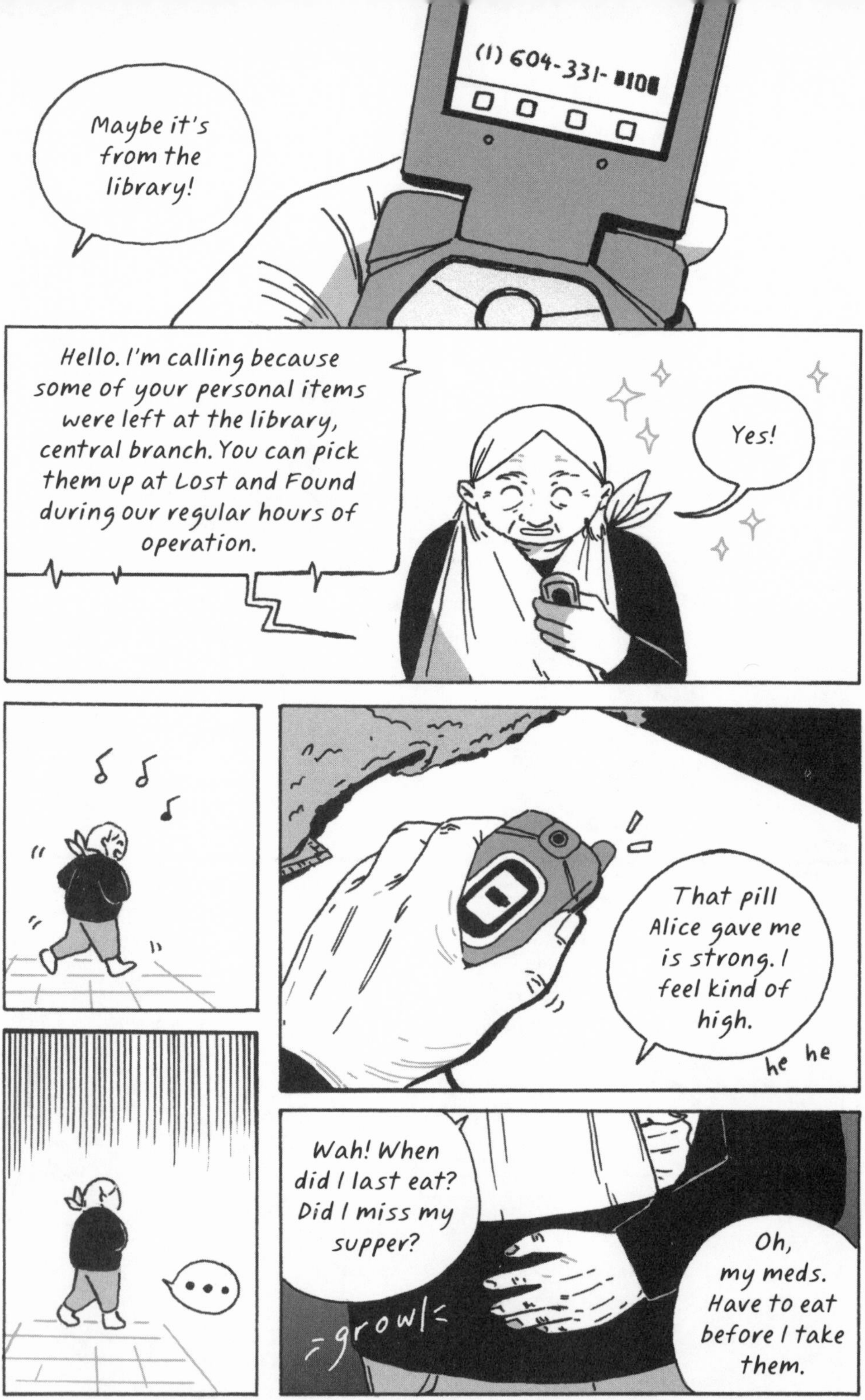
(1) 604-331-[redacted]108
Maybe it's from the library!
Hello. I'm calling because some of your personal items were left at the library, central branch. You can pick them up at Lost and Found during our regular hours of operation.
Yes!
That pill Alice gave me is strong. I feel kind of high.
he he
...
Wah! When did I last eat? Did I miss my supper?
Oh, my meds. Have to eat before I take them.
growl

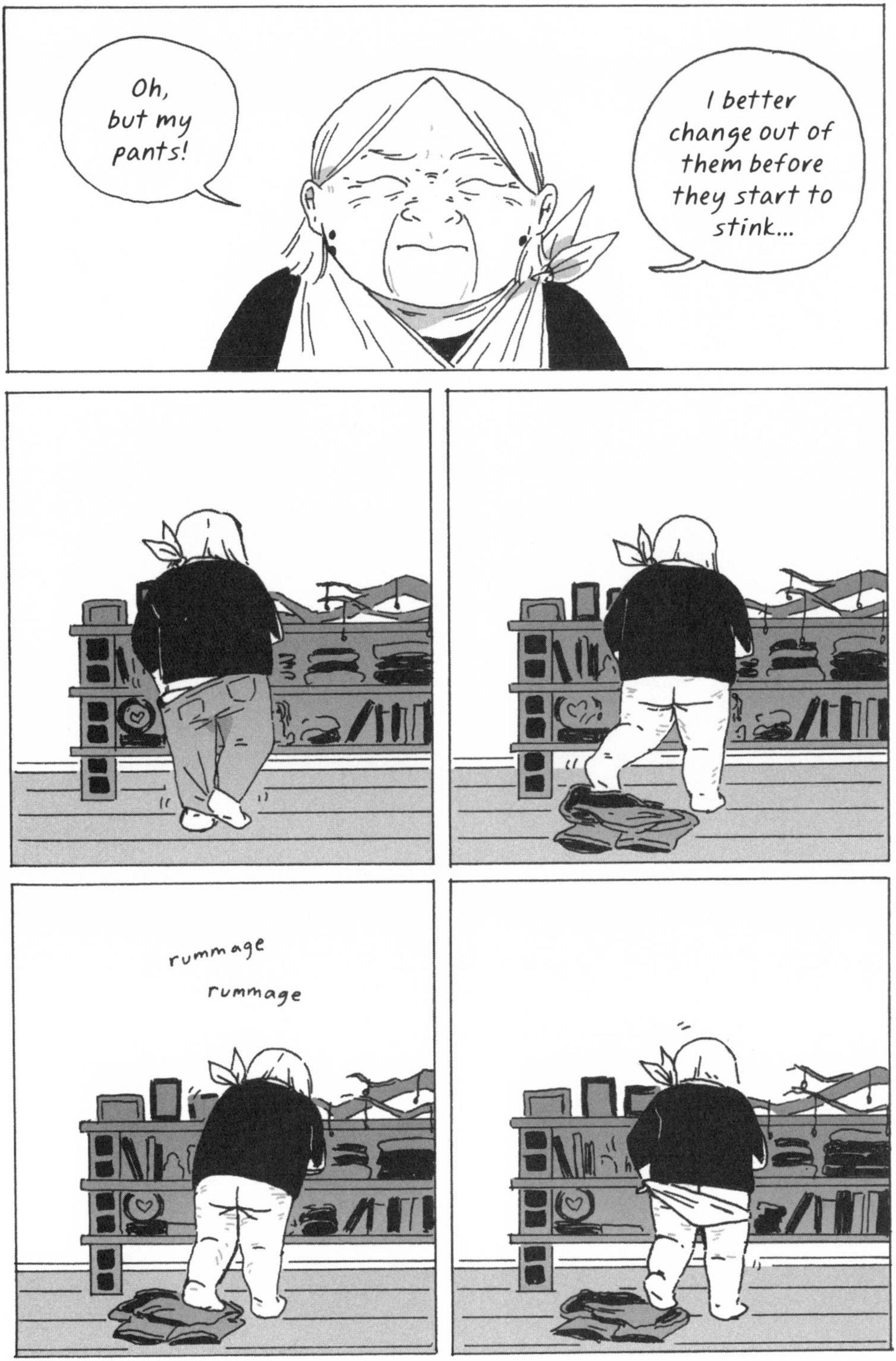
Oh, but my pants!
I better change out of them before they start to stink...
rummage
rummage

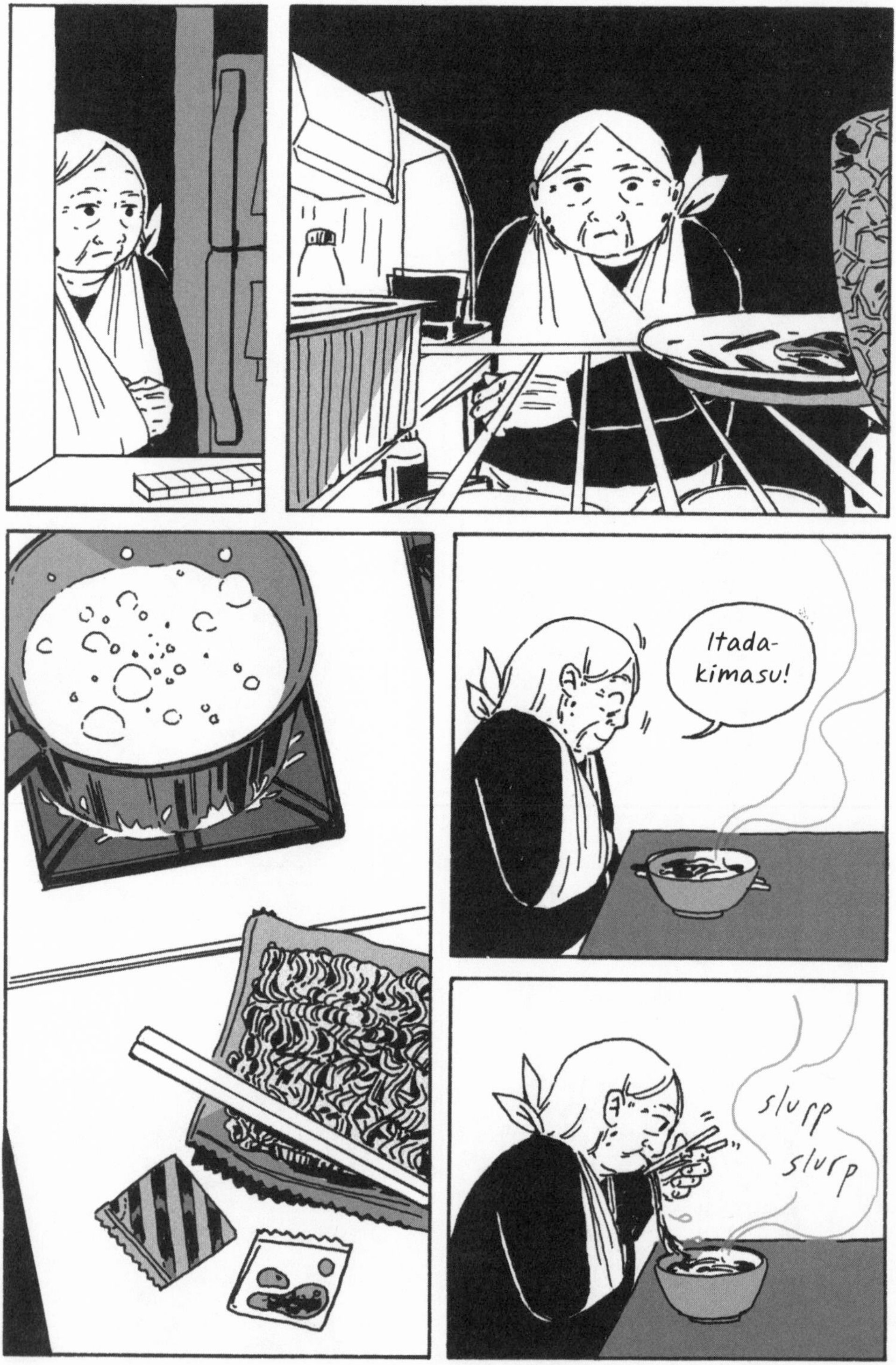
Itada-
kimasu!
slurp
slurp

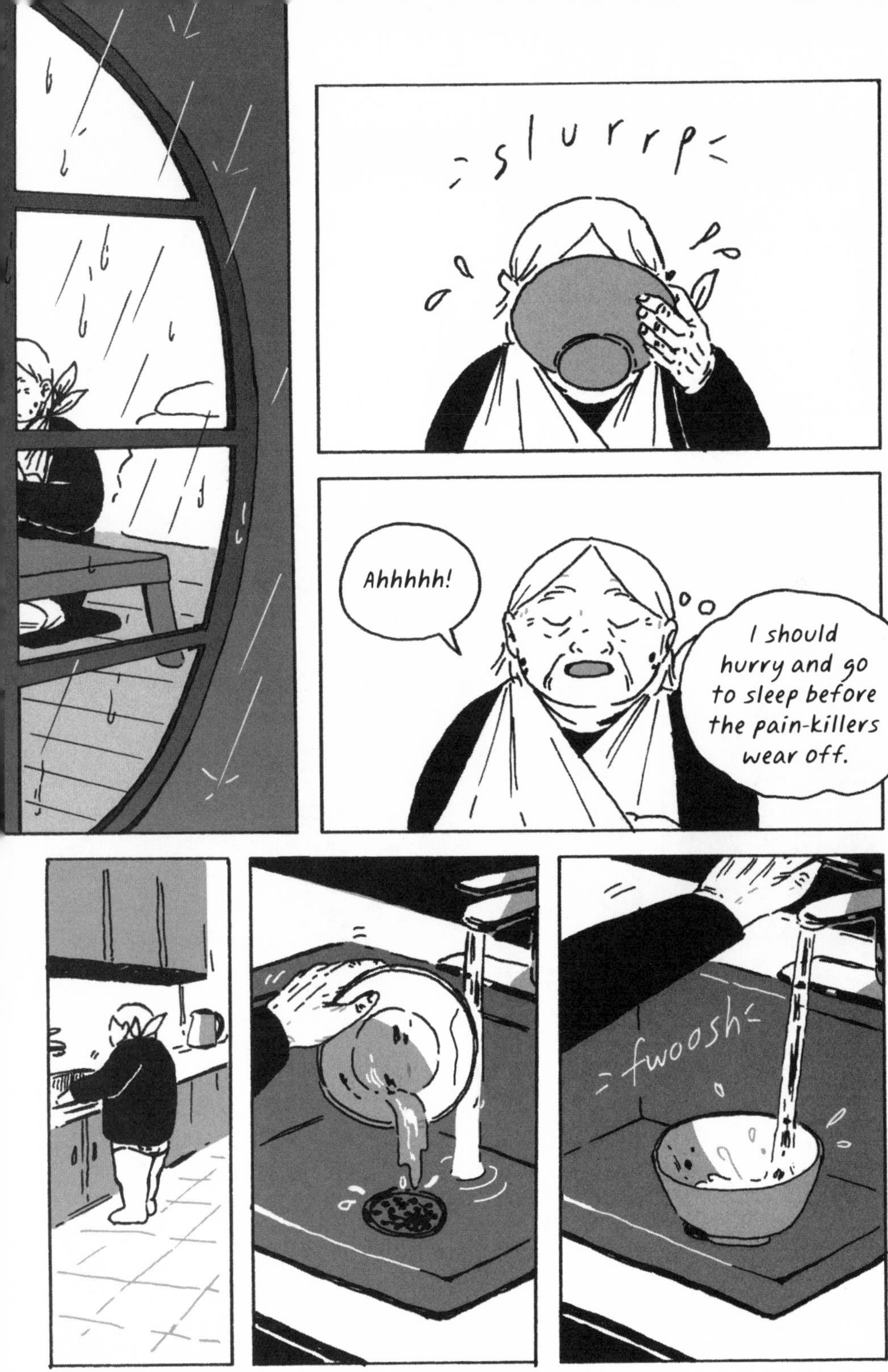
slurrp
Ahhhhh!
I should hurry and go to sleep before the pain-killers wear off.
fwoosh

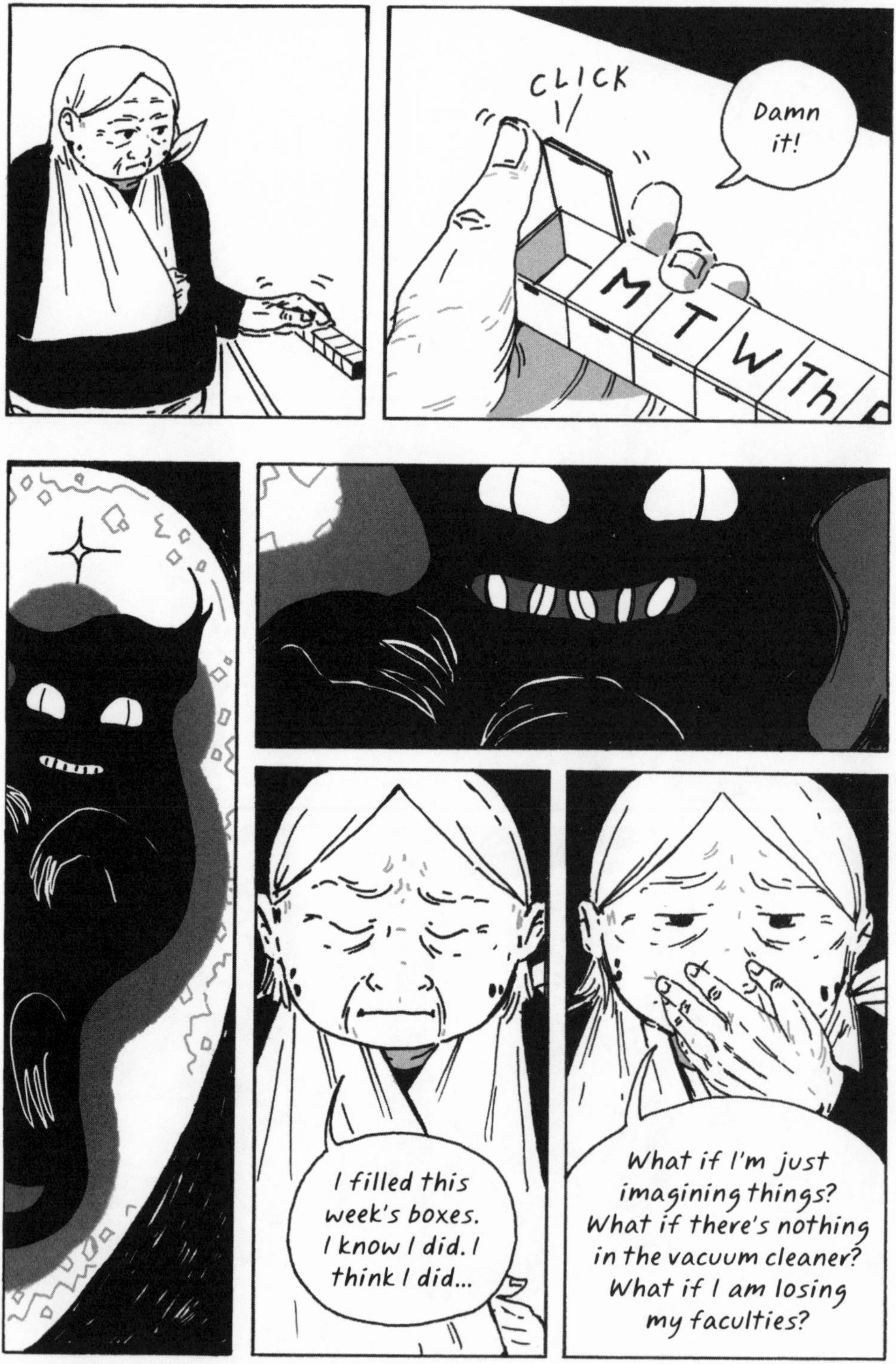
CLICK
Damn it!
I filled this week's boxes. I know I did. I think I did...
What if I'm just imagining things? What if there's nothing in the vacuum cleaner? What if I am losing my faculties?

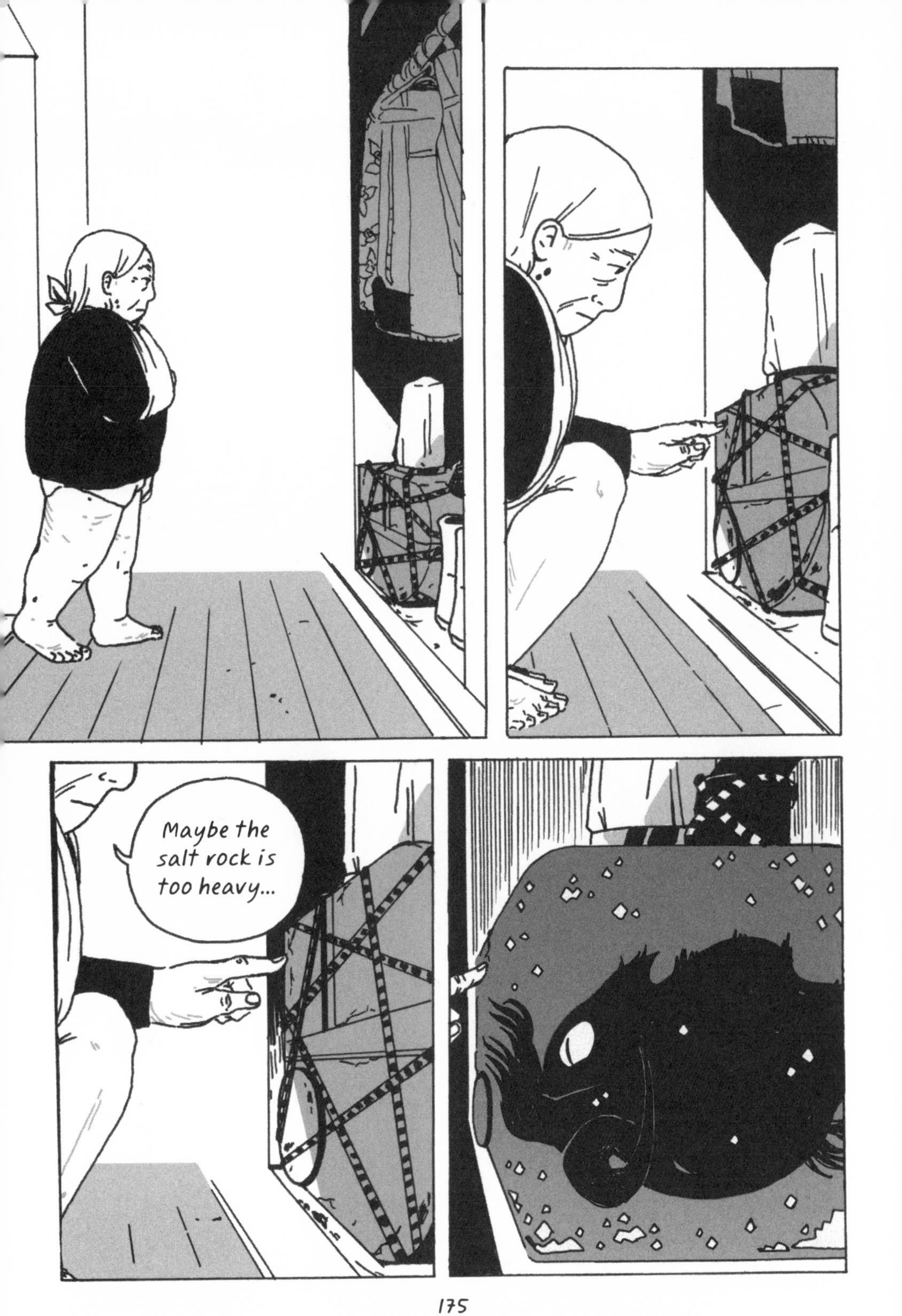
Maybe the salt rock is too heavy...

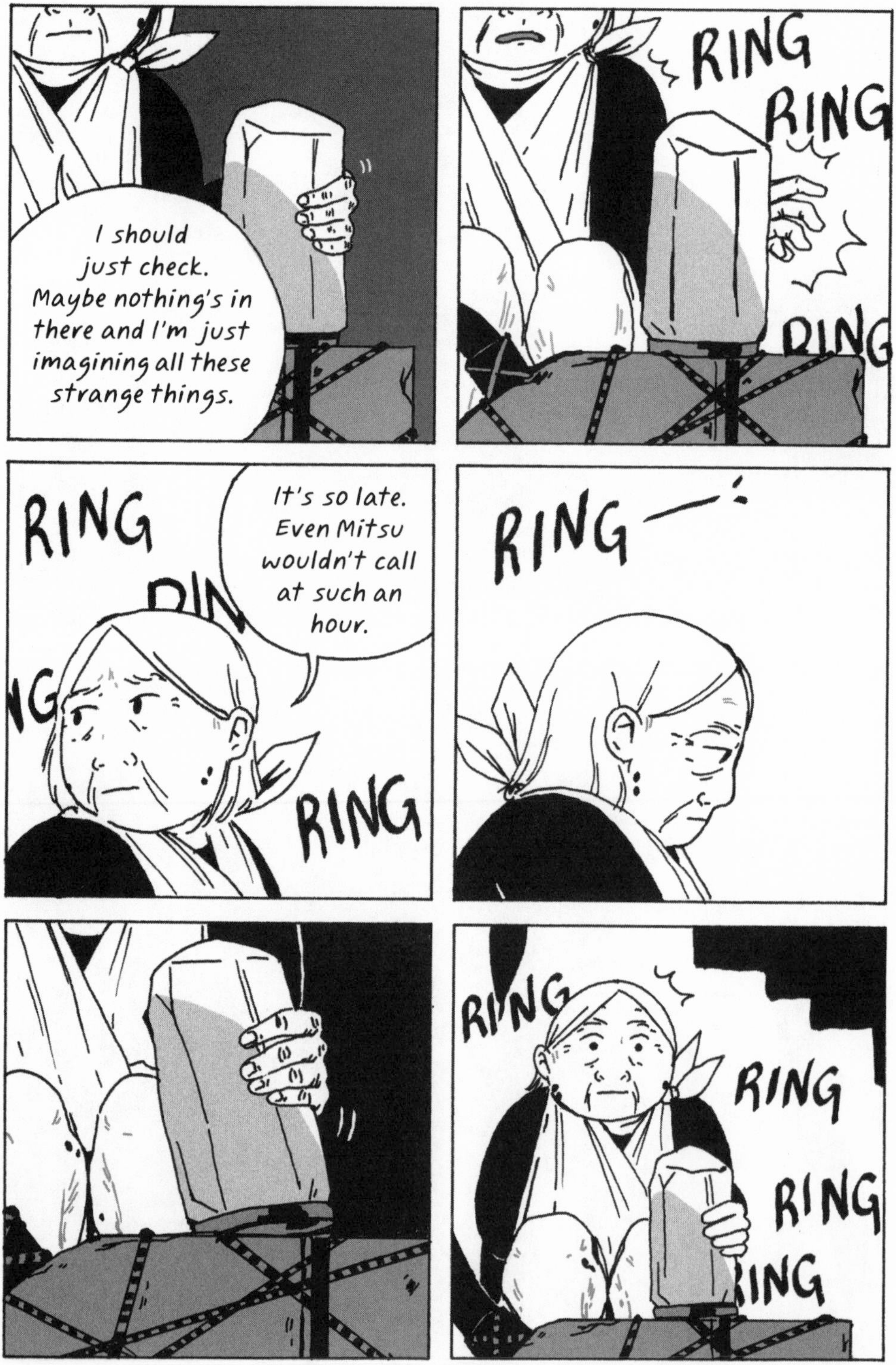
I should just check. Maybe nothing's in there and I'm just imagining all these strange things.
RING
RING
RING
RING
It's so late. Even Mitsu wouldn't call at such an hour.
RING
RING
RING
RING
RING
RING

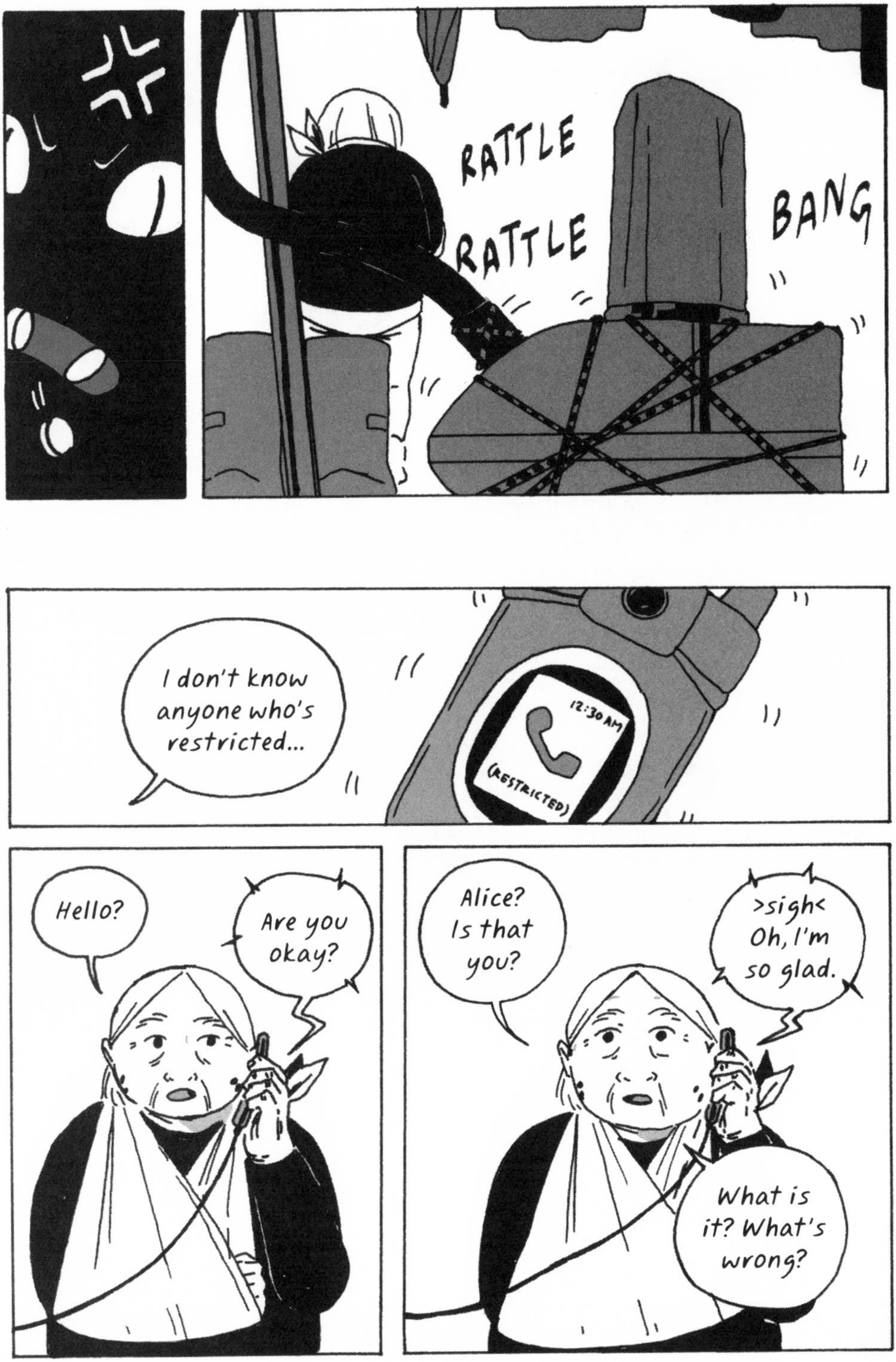
RATTLE
RATTLE
BANG
I don't know anyone who's restricted...
12:30 AM
(RESTRICTED)
Hello?
Are you okay?
Alice? Is that you?
>sigh< Oh, I'm so glad.
What is it? What's wrong?

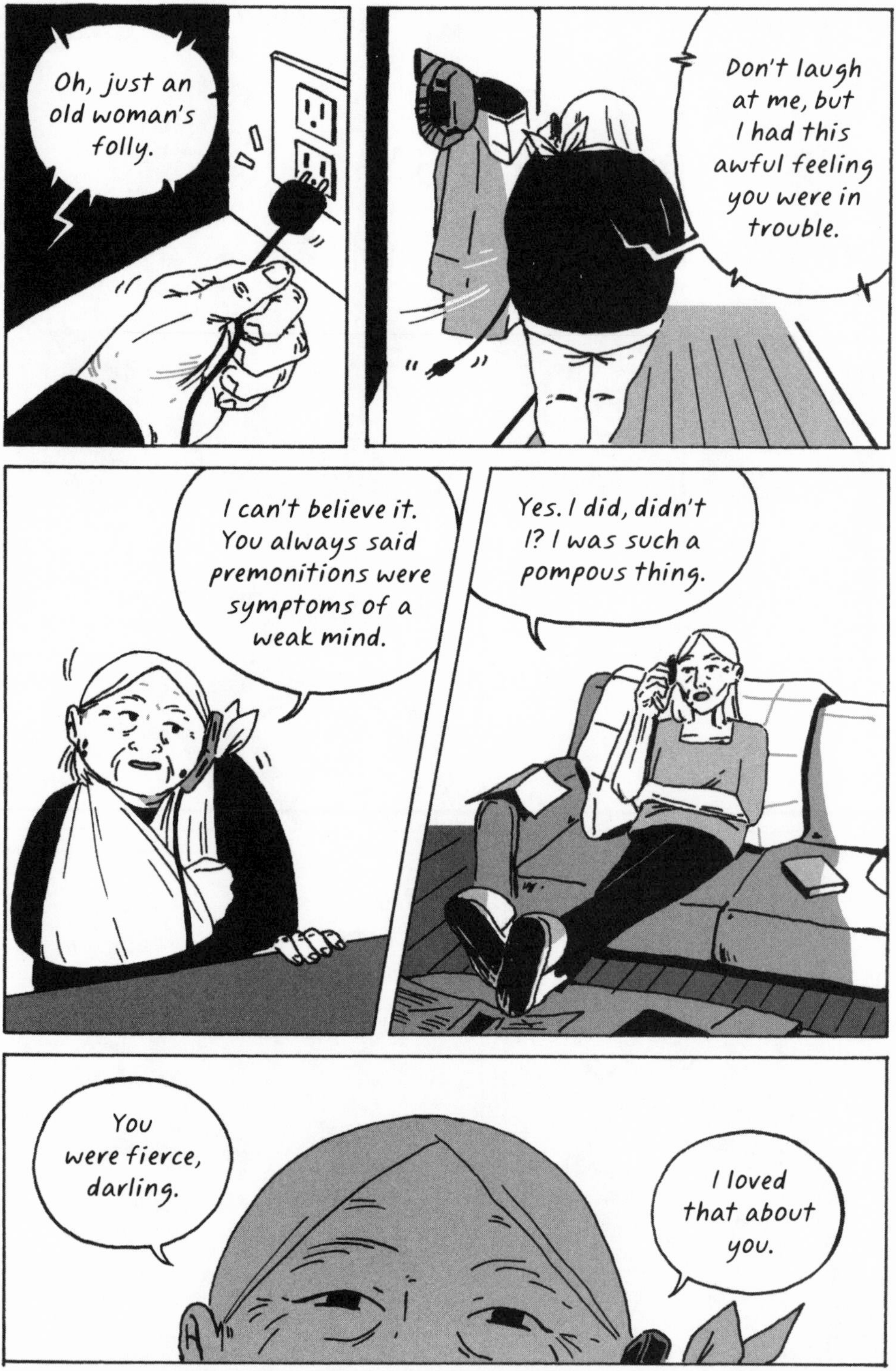
Oh, just an old woman's folly.
Don't laugh at me, but I had this awful feeling you were in trouble.
I can't believe it. You always said premonitions were symptoms of a weak mind.
Yes. I did, didn't I? I was such a pompous thing.
You were fierce, darling.
I loved that about you.

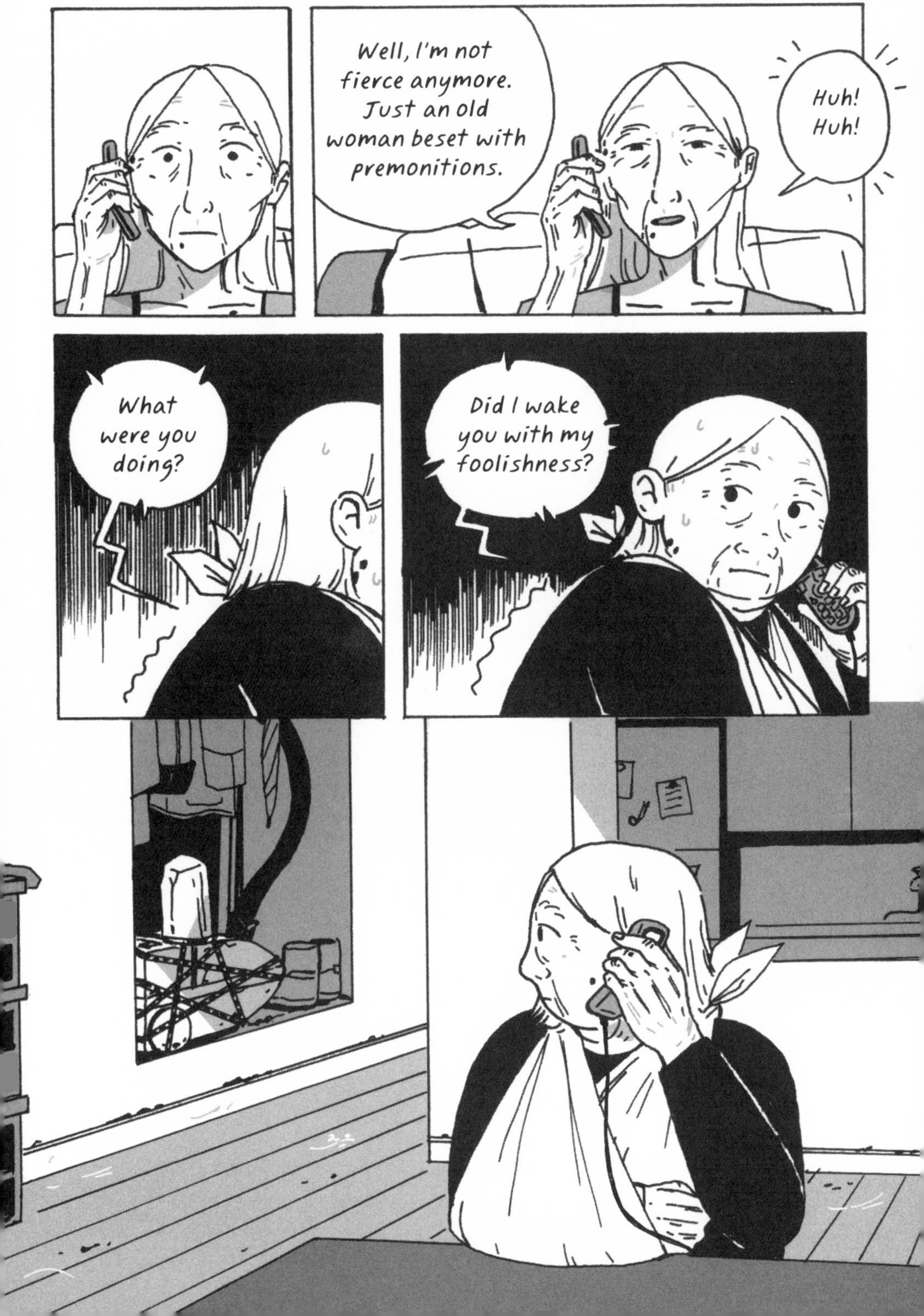
Well, I'm not fierce anymore. Just an old woman beset with premonitions.
Huh! Huh!
What were you doing?
Did I wake you with my foolishness?

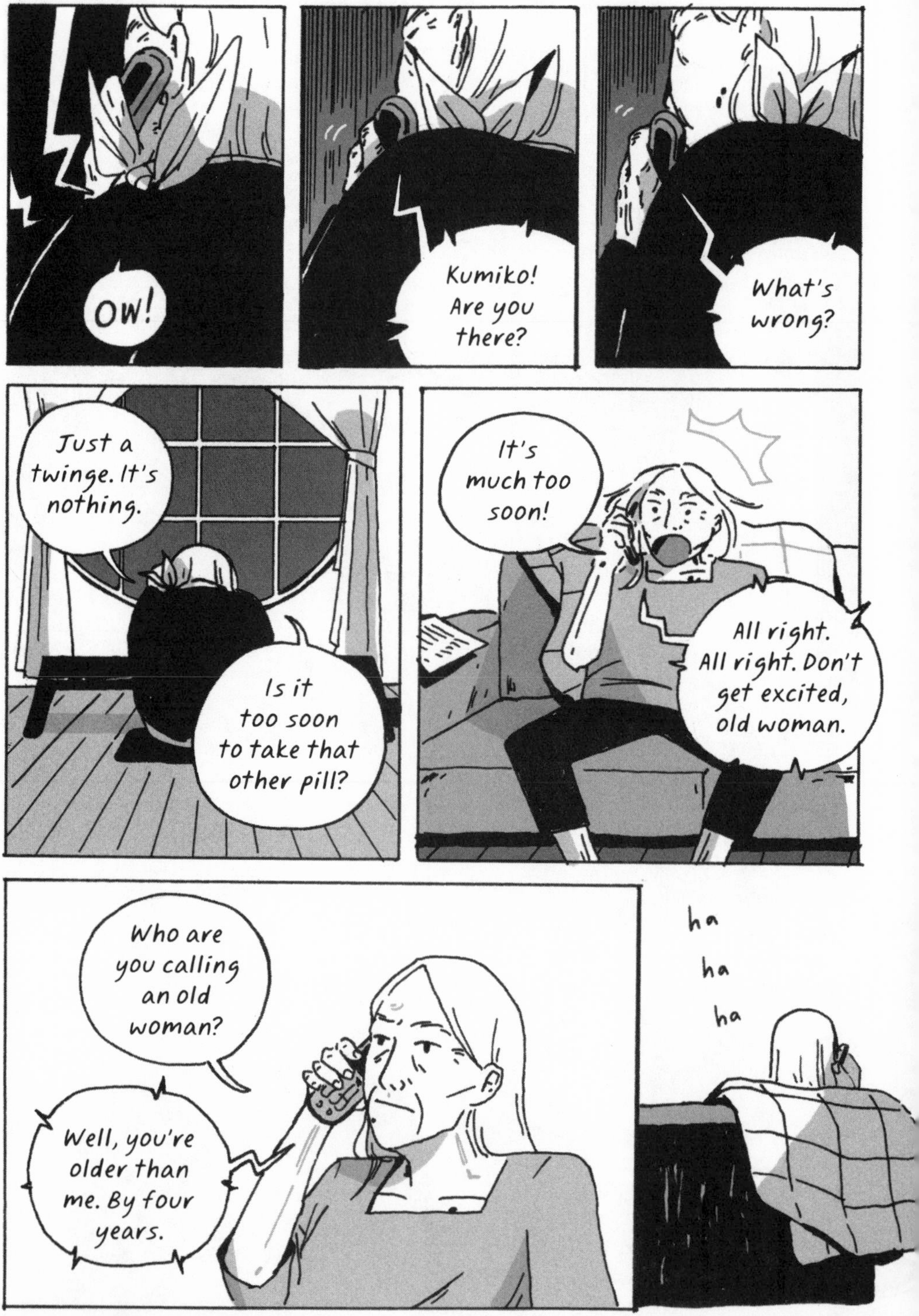
OW!
Kumiko! Are you there?
What's wrong?
Just a twinge. It's nothing.
Is it too soon to take that other pill?
It's much too soon!
All right. All right. Don't get excited, old woman.
Who are you calling an old woman?
Well, you're older than me. By four years.
ha
ha
ha

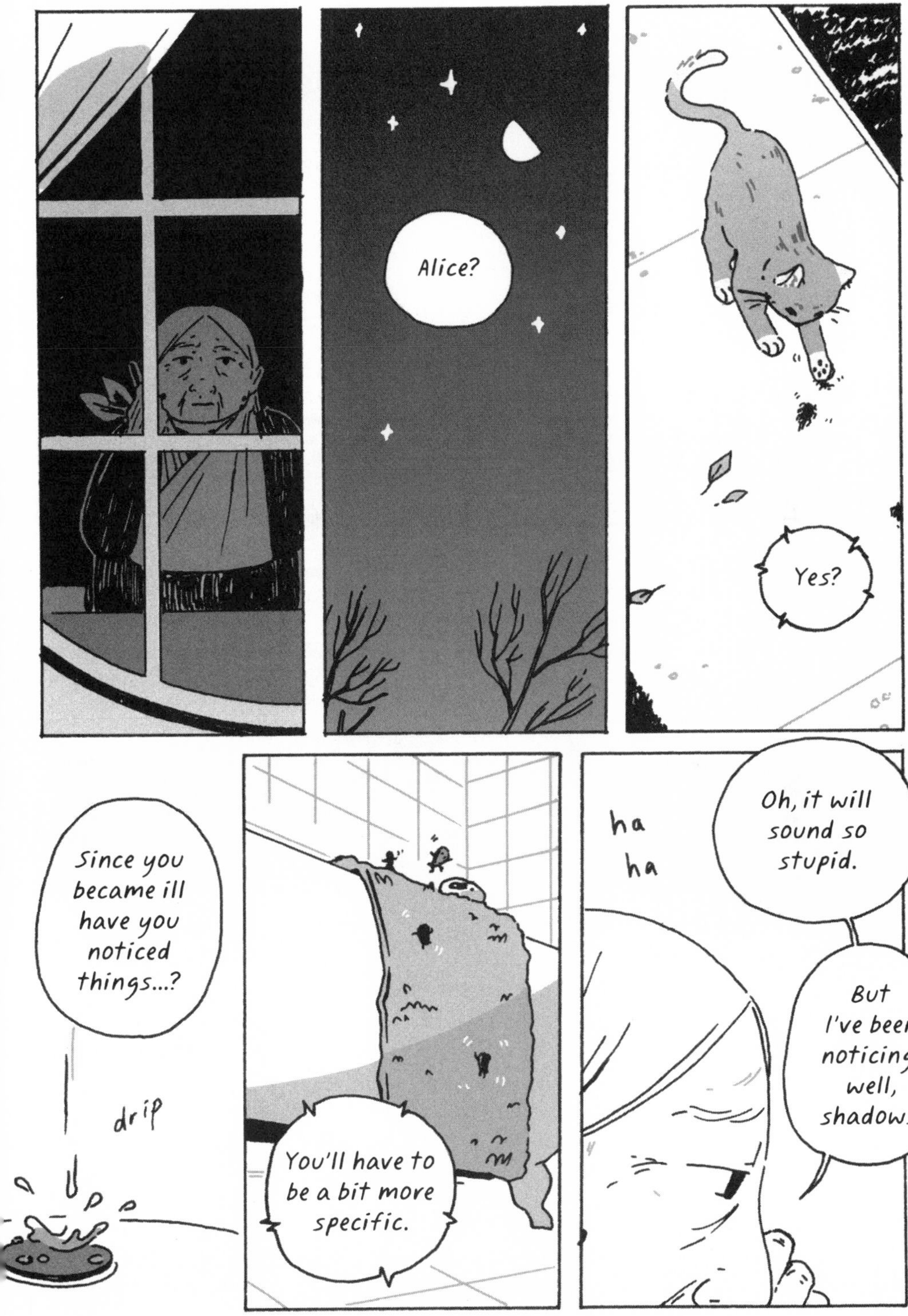
Alice?
Yes?
Since you became ill have you noticed things...?
drip
You'll have to be a bit more specific.
ha ha
Oh, it will sound so stupid.
But I've been noticing, well, shadows.

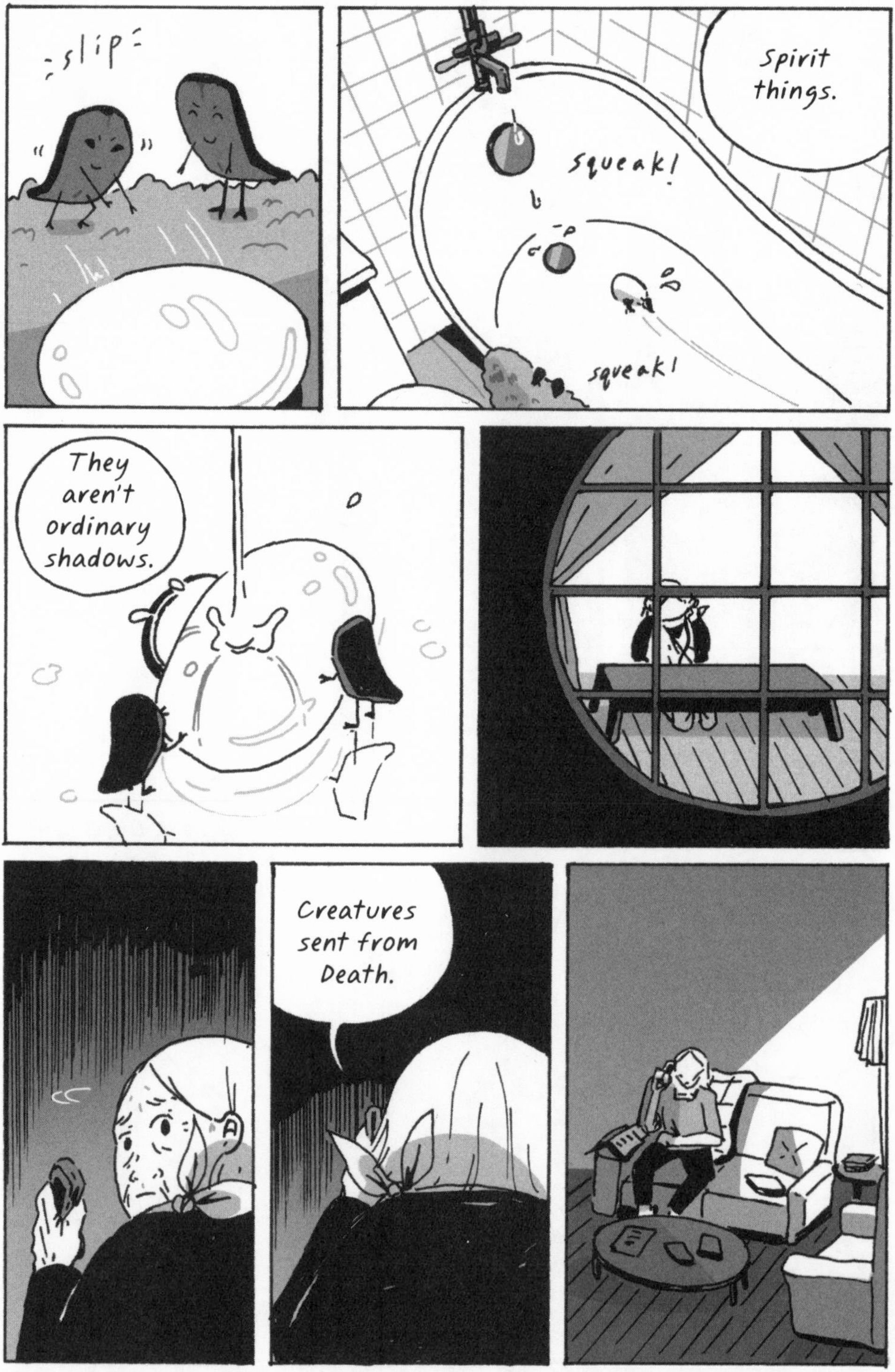
slip
Spirit things.
squeak!
squeak!
They aren't ordinary shadows.
Creatures sent from Death.

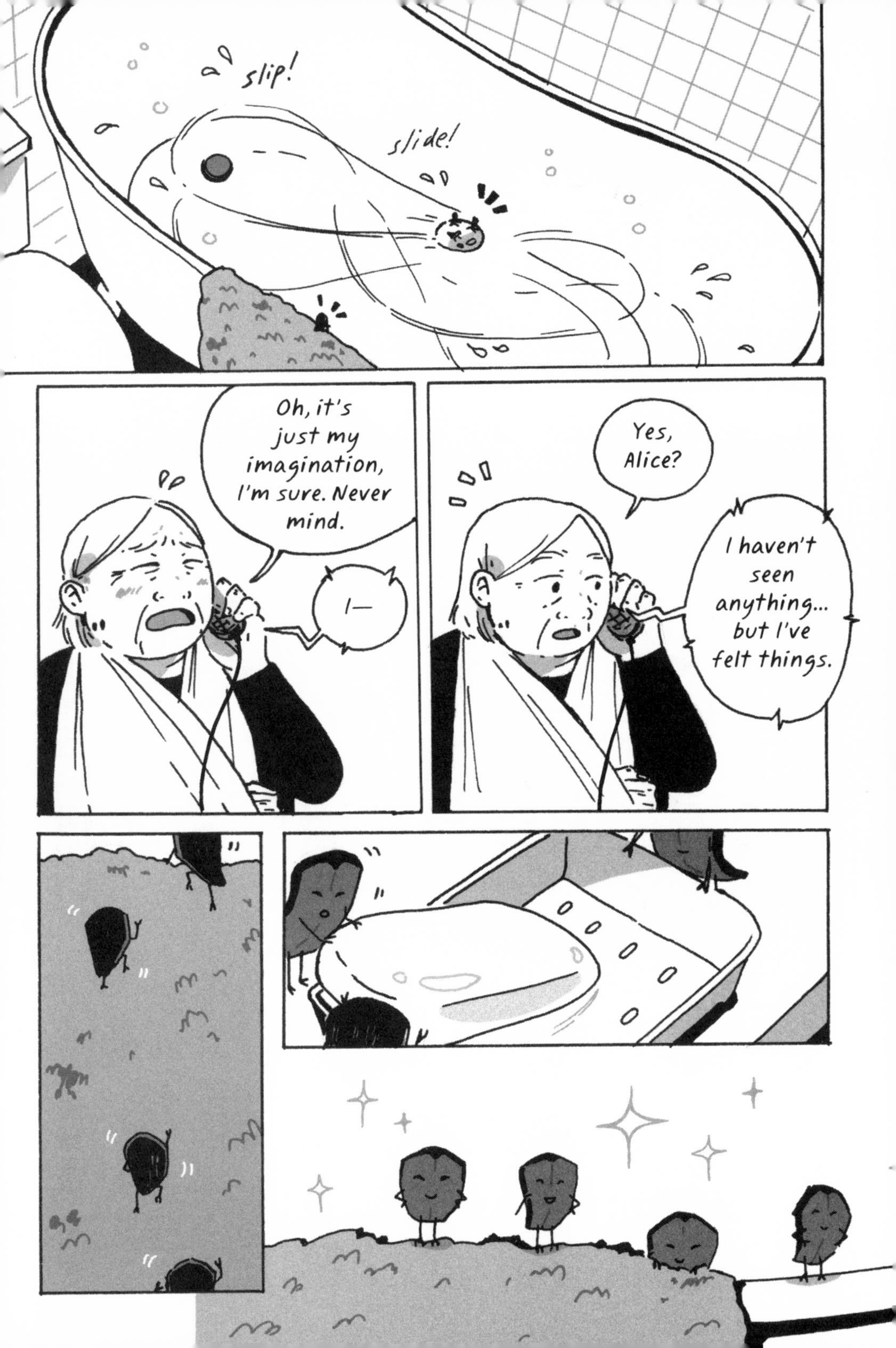
slip!
slide!
Oh, it's just my imagination, I'm sure. Never mind.
I—
Yes, Alice?
I haven't seen anything... but I've felt things.

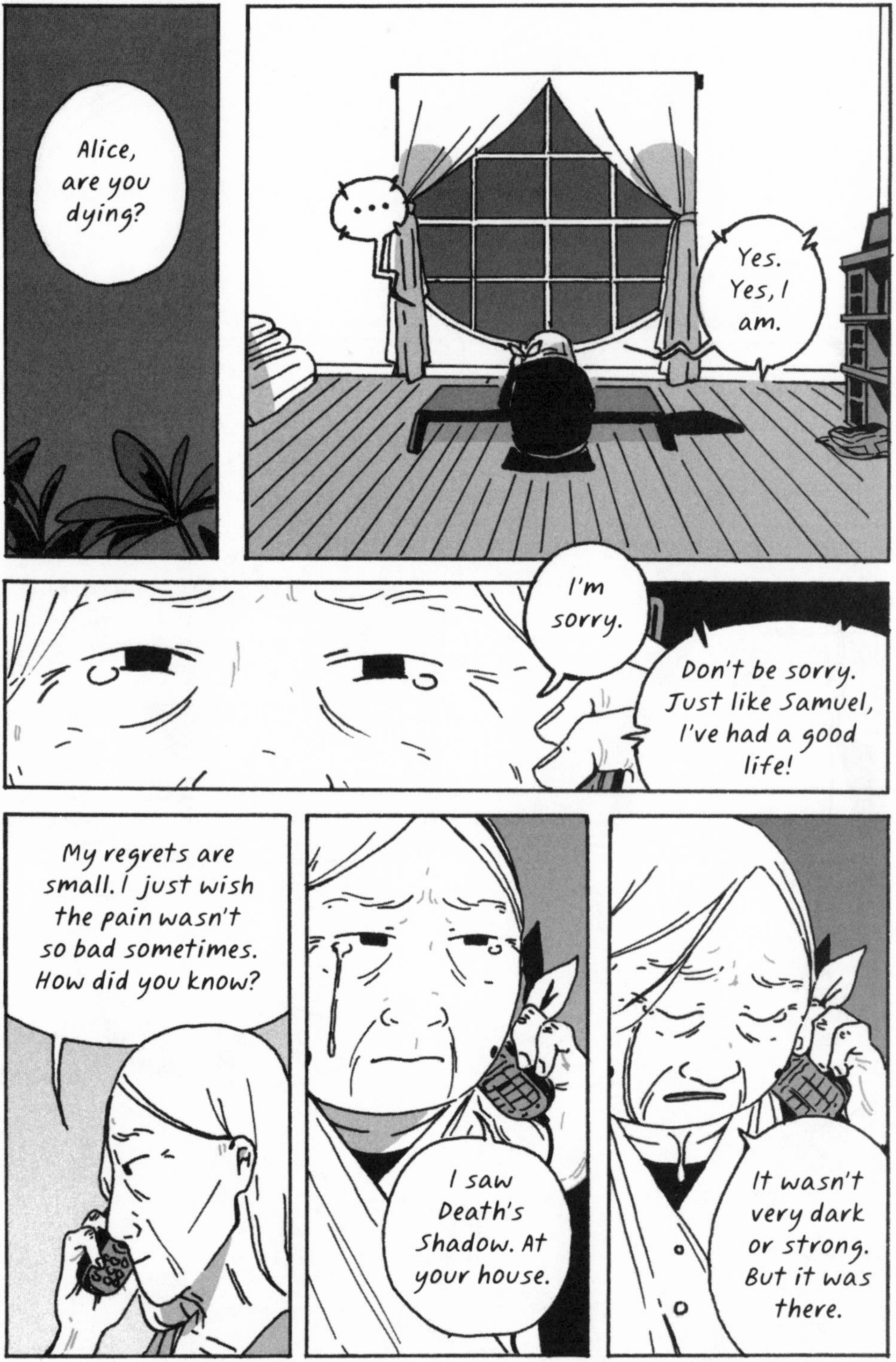

Alice, are you dying?
...
Yes. Yes, I am.
I'm sorry.
Don't be sorry. Just like Samuel, I've had a good life!
My regrets are small. I just wish the pain wasn't so bad sometimes. How did you know?
I saw Death's Shadow. At your house.
It wasn't very dark or strong. But it was there.

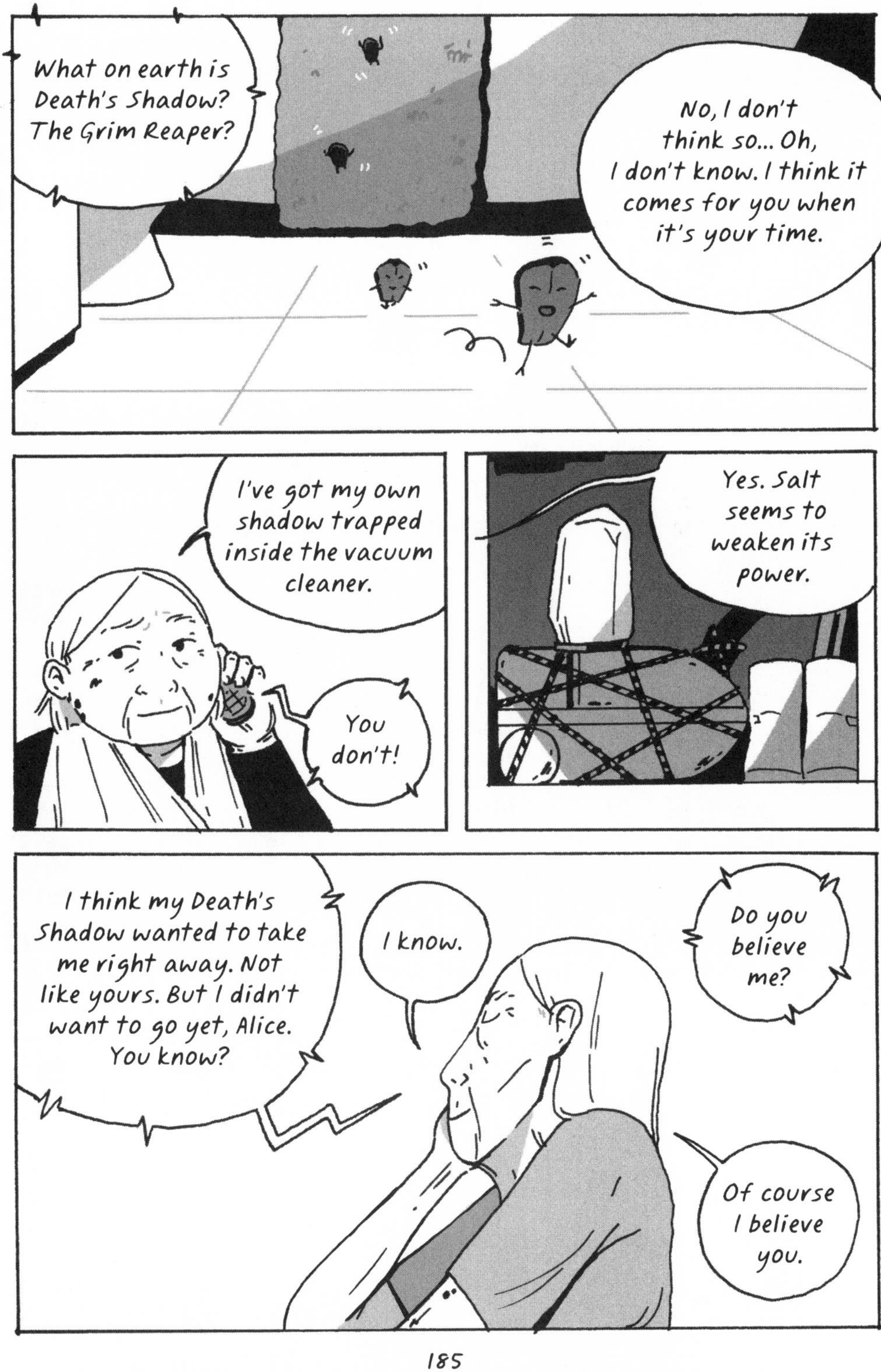
What on earth is Death's Shadow? The Grim Reaper?
No, I don't think so... Oh, I don't know. I think it comes for you when it's your time.
I've got my own shadow trapped inside the vacuum cleaner.
You don't!
Yes. Salt seems to weaken its power.
I think my Death's Shadow wanted to take me right away. Not like yours. But I didn't want to go yet, Alice. You know?
I know.
Do you believe me?
Of course I believe you.

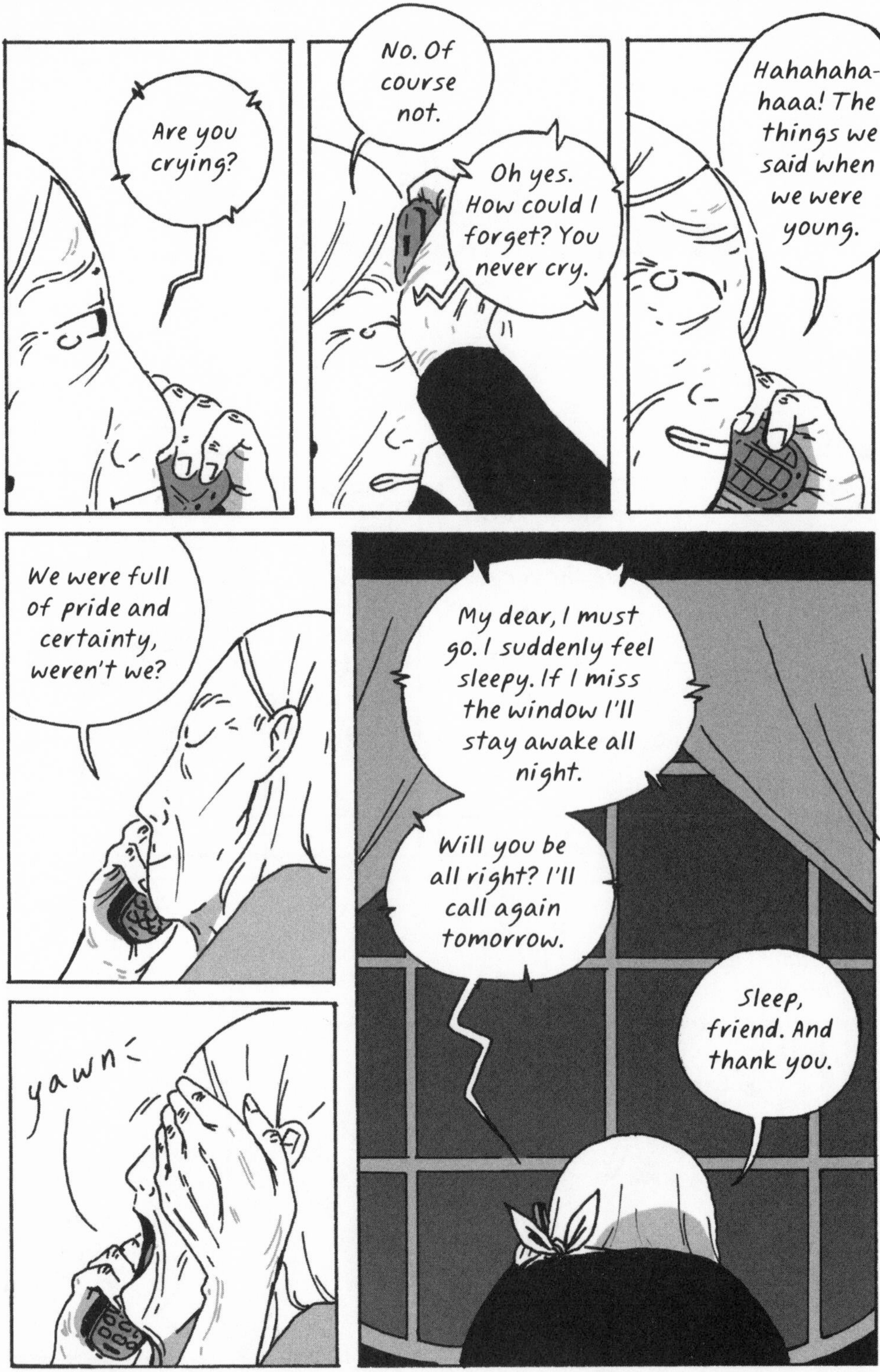

Are you crying?
No. Of course not.
Oh yes. How could I forget? You never cry.
Hahahaha-haaa! The things we said when we were young.
We were full of pride and certainty, weren't we?
yawn
My dear, I must go. I suddenly feel sleepy. If I miss the window I'll stay awake all night.
Will you be all right? I'll call again tomorrow.
Sleep, friend. And thank you.

Chapter Ten

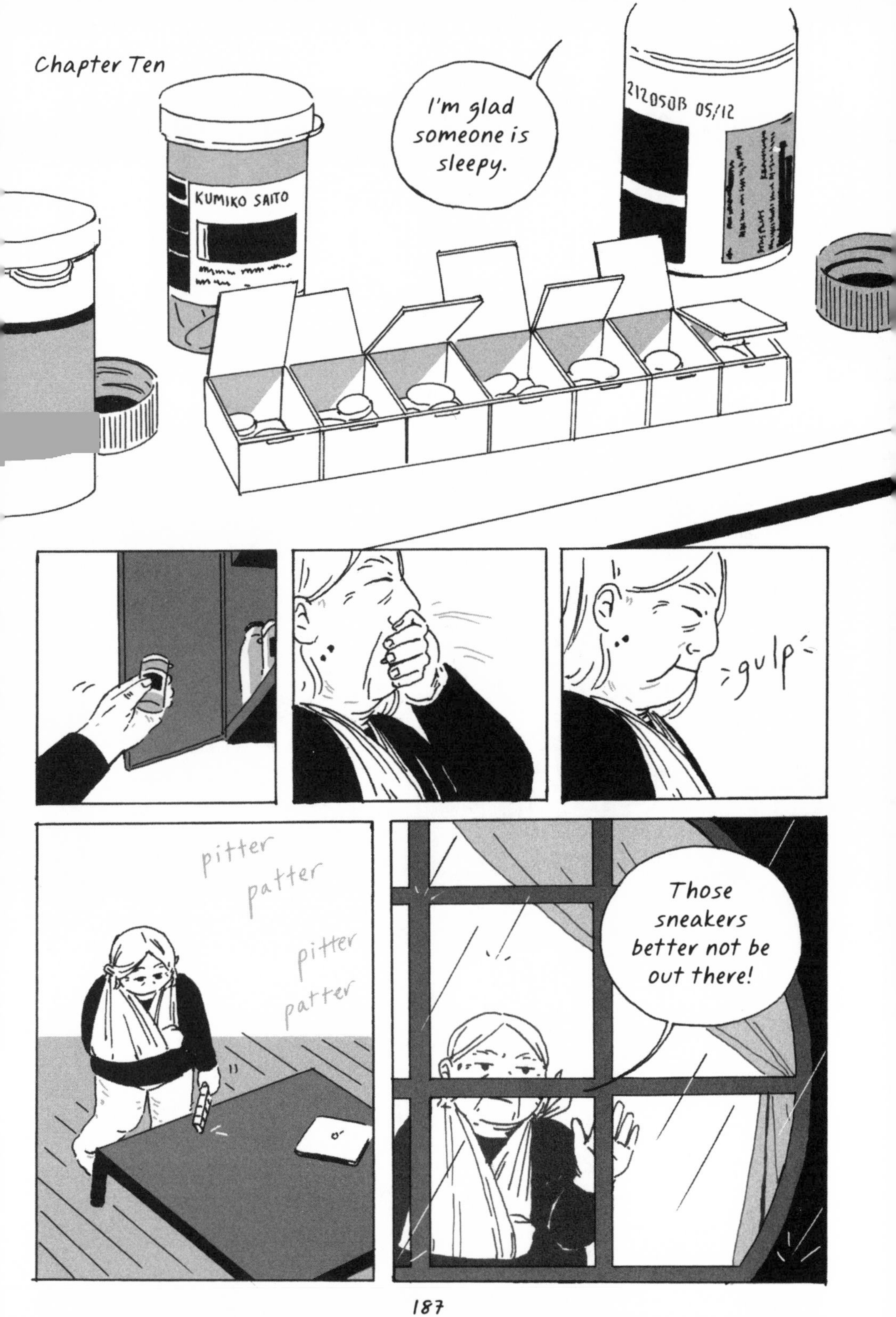

KUMIKO SAITO
I'm glad someone is sleepy.
gulp
pitter patter
pitter patter
Those sneakers better not be out there!

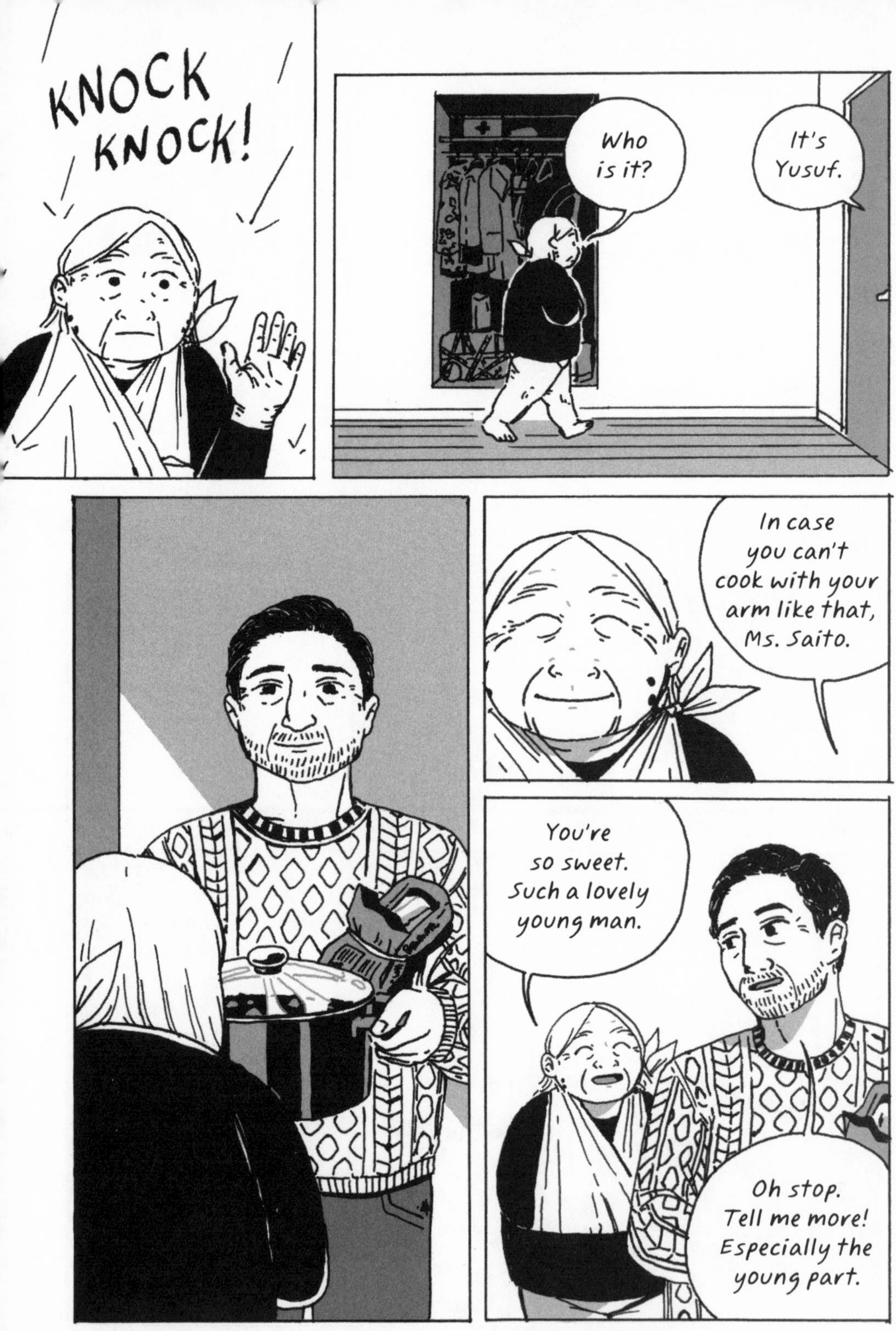
KNOCK KNOCK!
Who is it?
It's Yusuf.
In case you can't cook with your arm like that, Ms. Saito.
You're so sweet. Such a lovely young man.
Oh stop. Tell me more! Especially the young part.

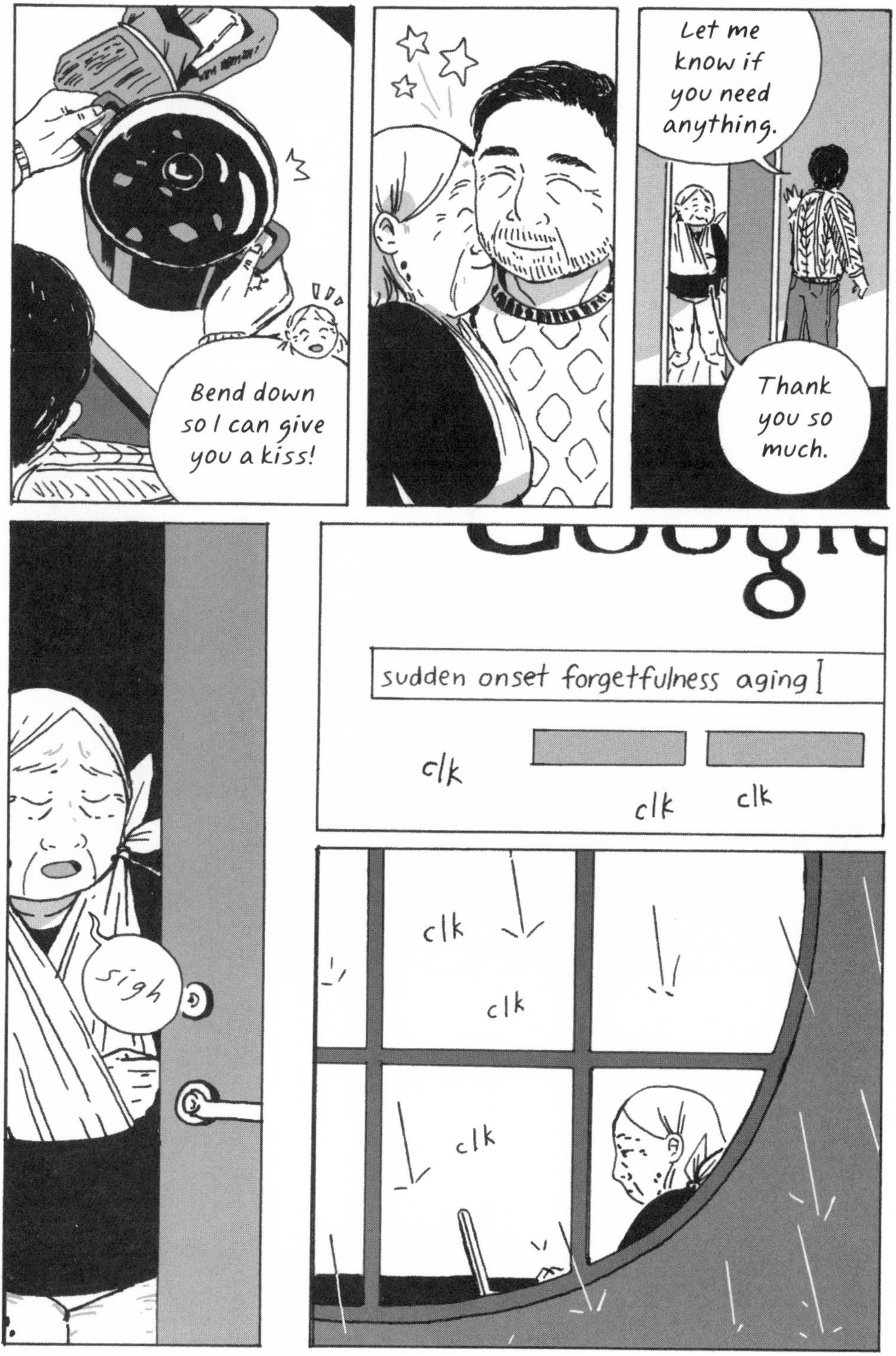
Bend down so I can give you a kiss!
Let me know if you need anything.
Thank you so much.
sigh
sudden onset forgetfulness aging
clk
clk
clk
clk
clk
clk

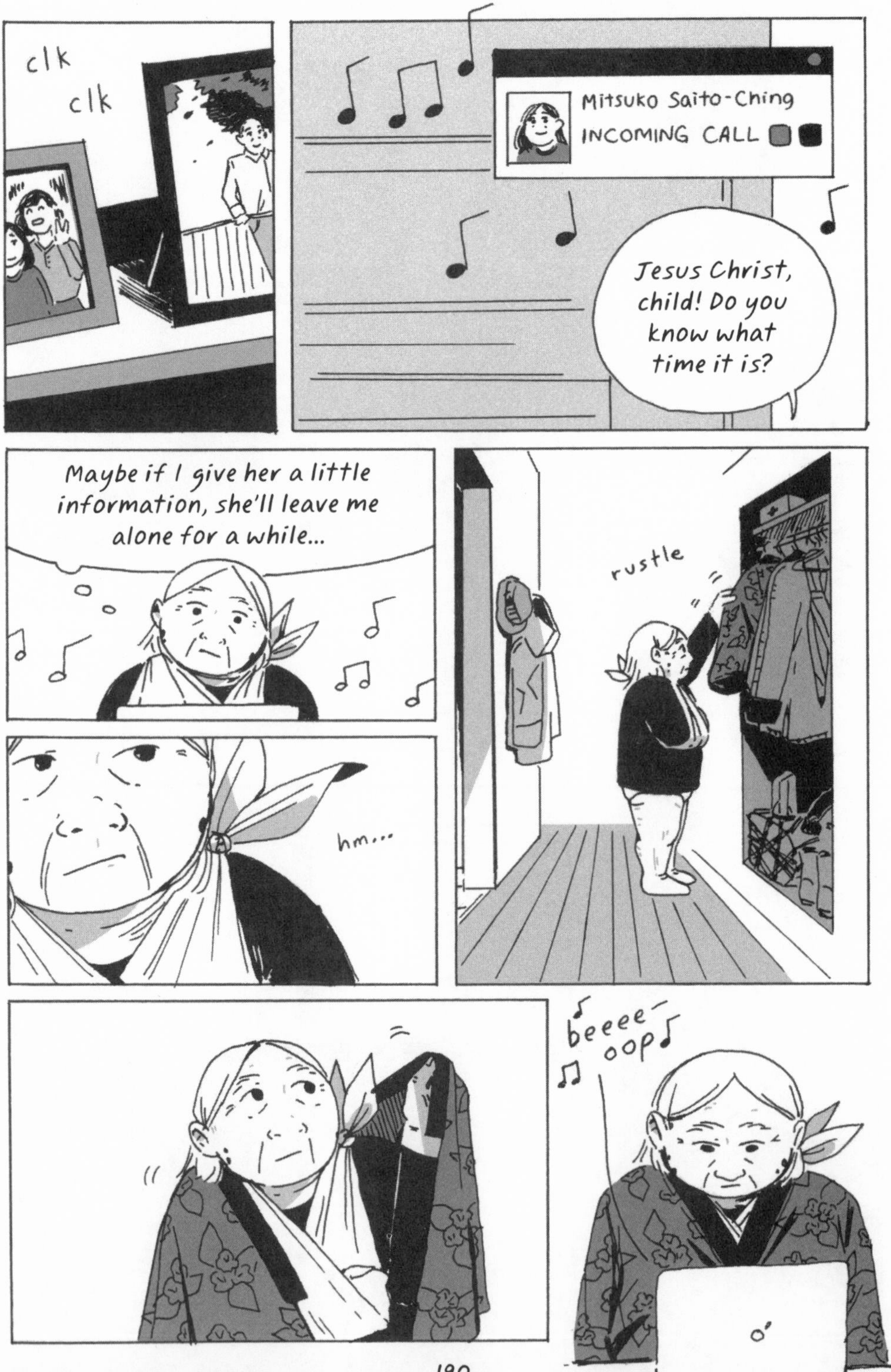
clk
clk
Mitsuko Saito-Ching
INCOMING CALL
Jesus Christ, child! Do you know what time it is?
Maybe if I give her a little information, she'll leave me alone for a while...
rustle
hm...
beeee-oop

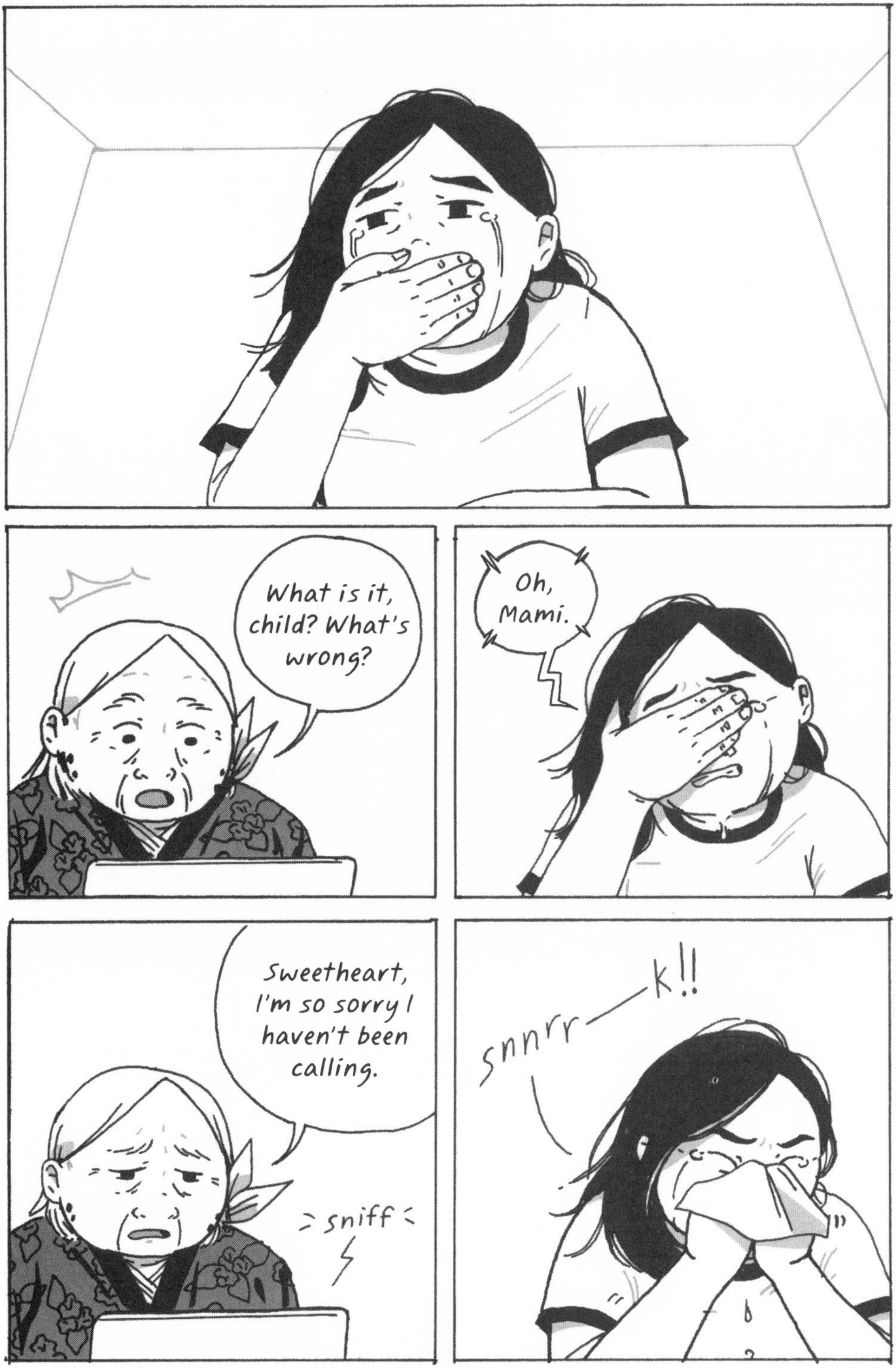
What is it, child? What's wrong?
Oh, Mami.
Sweetheart, I'm so sorry I haven't been calling.
sniff
snnrr—k!!

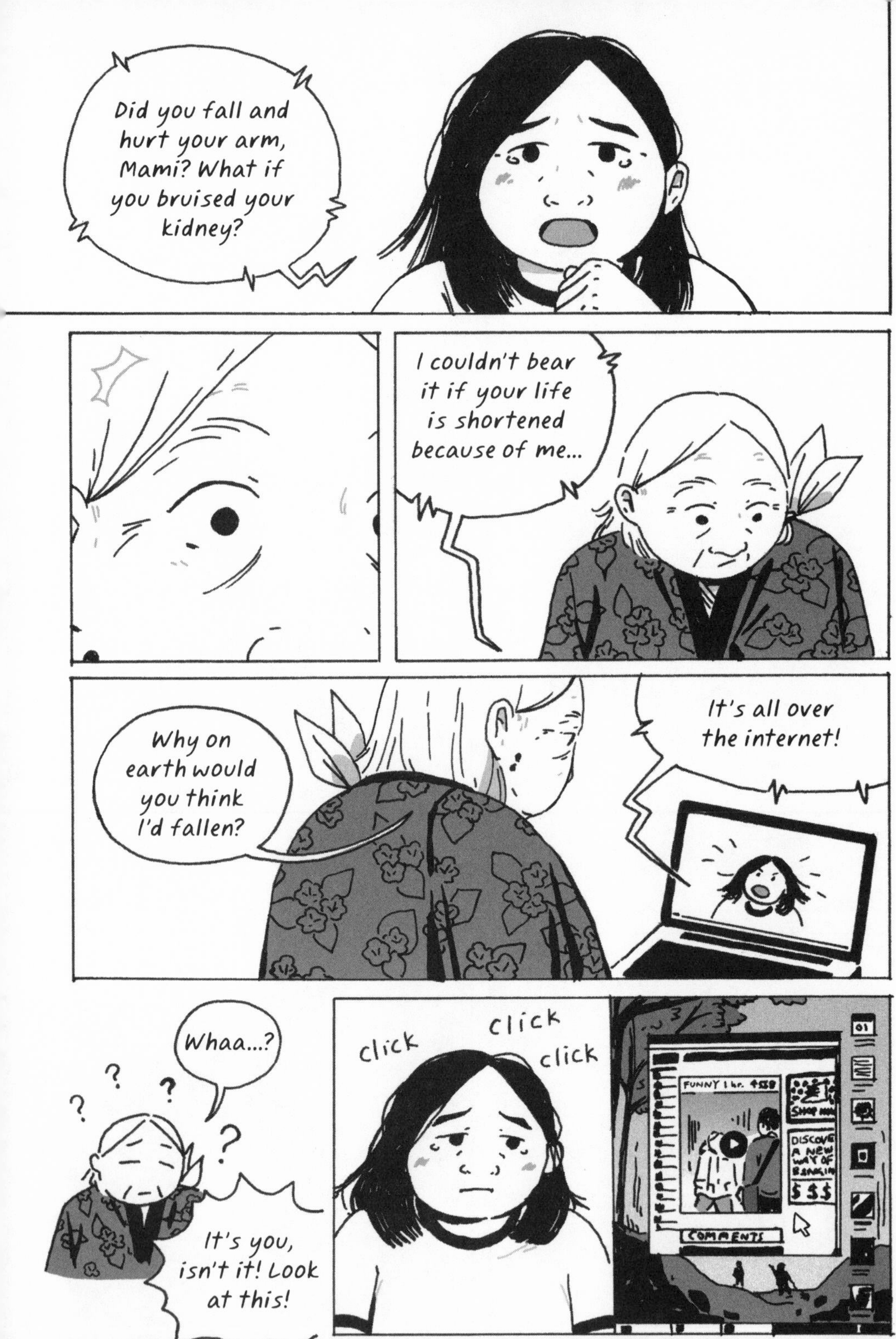
Did you fall and hurt your arm, Mami? What if you bruised your kidney?
I couldn't bear it if your life is shortened because of me...
Why on earth would you think I'd fallen?
It's all over the internet!
Whaa...?
?
?
?
?
It's you, isn't it! Look at this!
click
click
click
COMMENTS

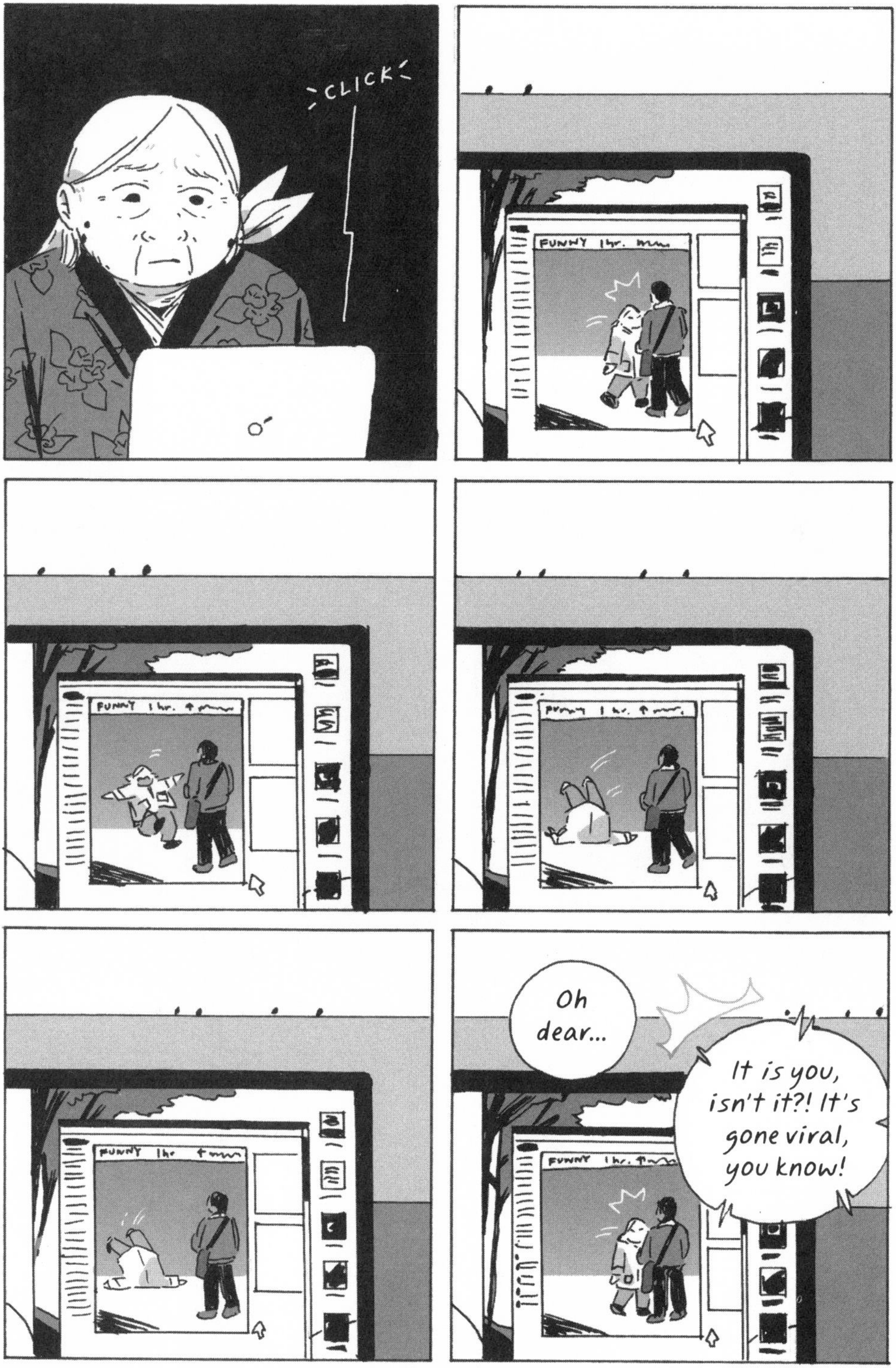
CLICK
Oh dear...
It is you, isn't it?! It's gone viral, you know!

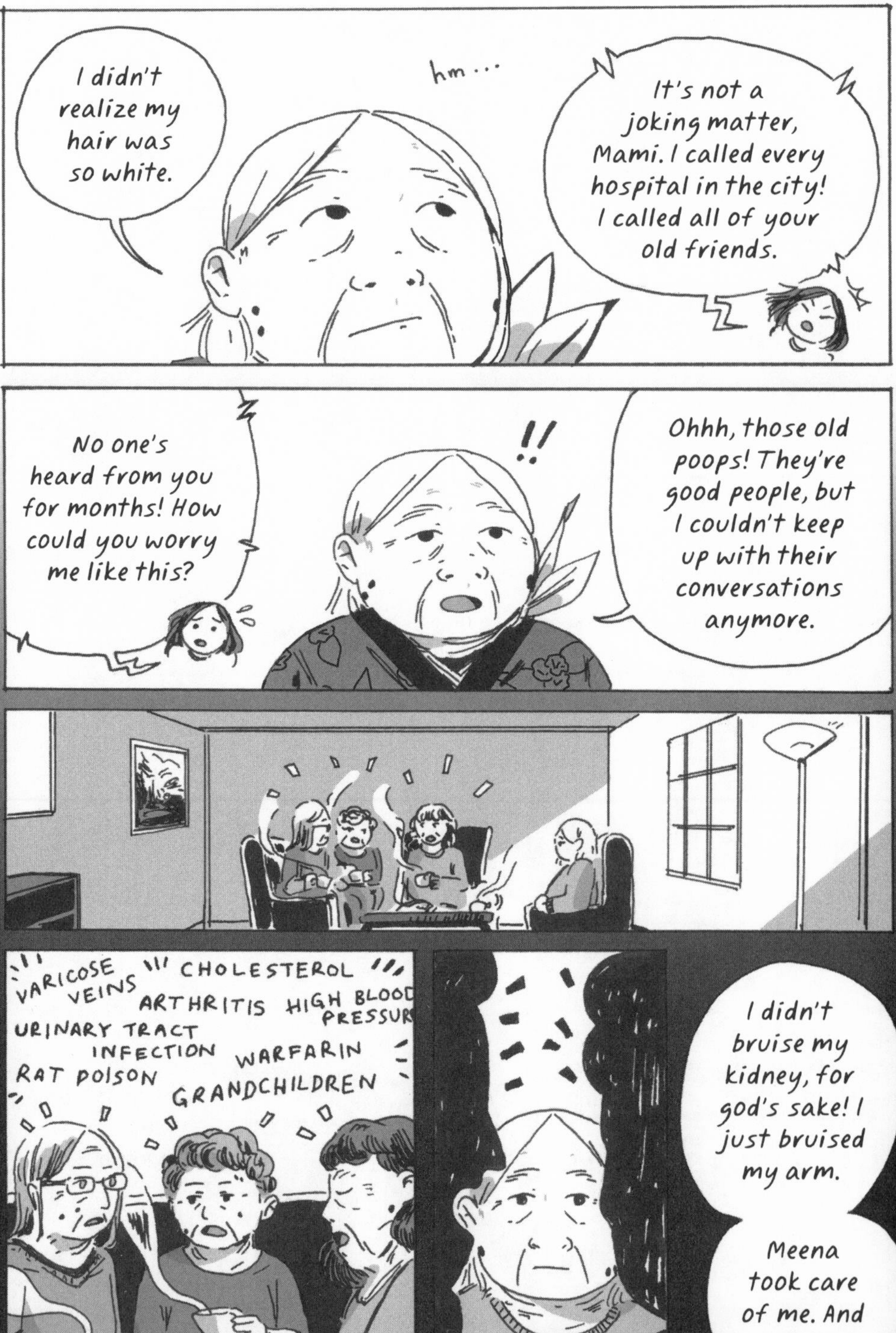
I didn't realize my hair was so white.
hm...
It's not a joking matter, Mami. I called every hospital in the city! I called all of your old friends.
No one's heard from you for months! How could you worry me like this?
!!
Ohhh, those old poops! They're good people, but I couldn't keep up with their conversations anymore.
VARICOSE VEINS CHOLESTEROL ARTHRITIS HIGH BLOOD PRESSUR URINARY TRACT INFECTION WARFARIN RAT POISON GRANDCHILDREN
I didn't bruise my kidney, for god's sake! I just bruised my arm.
Meena took care of me. And Alice.

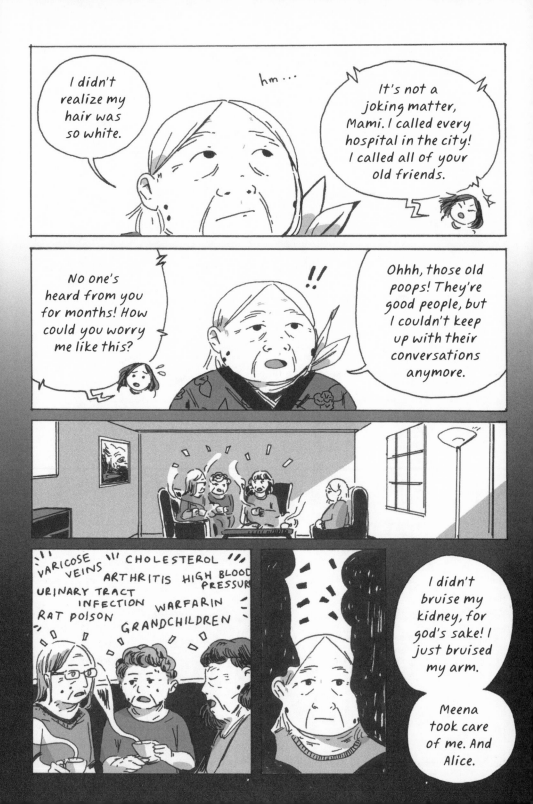

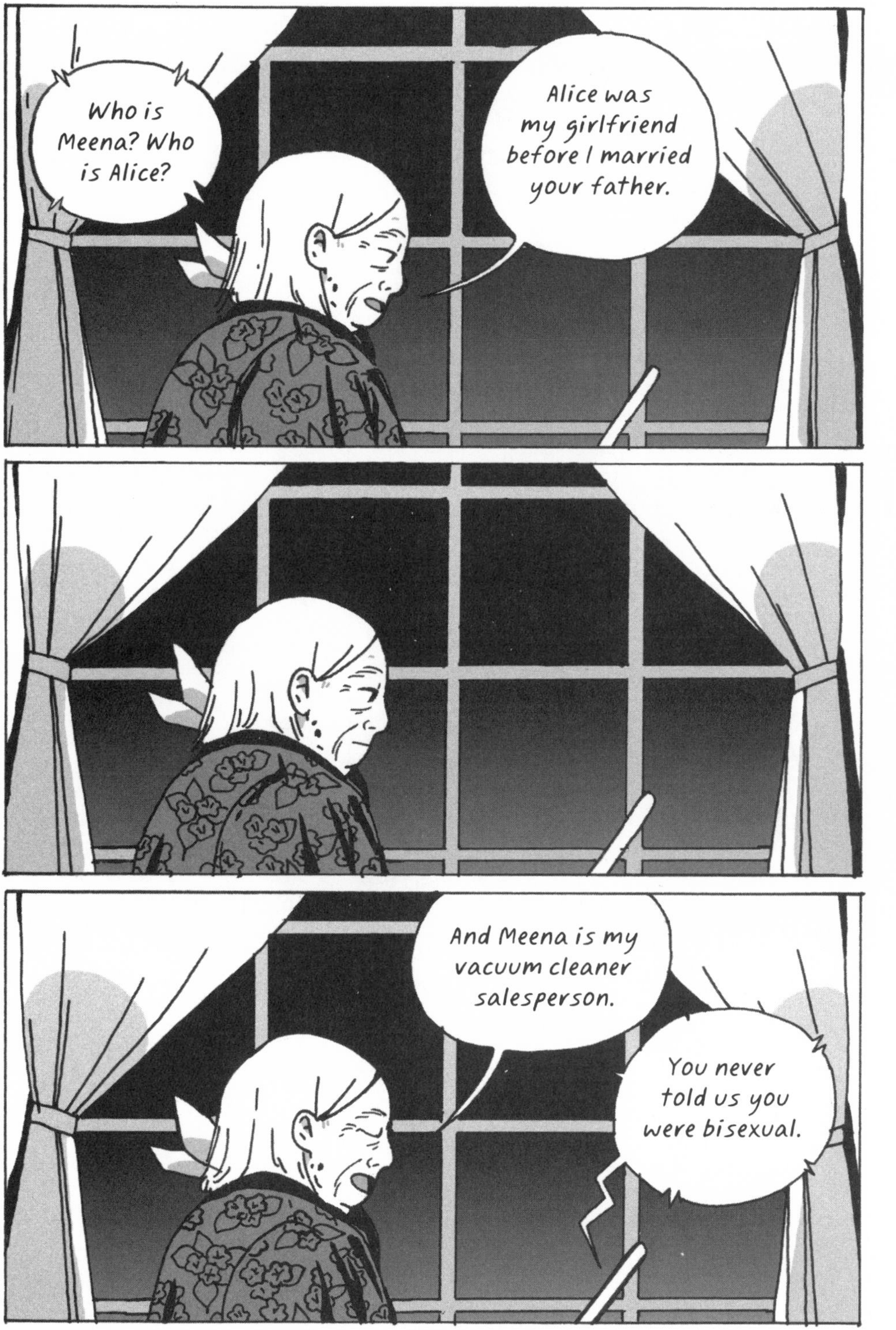
Who is Meena? Who is Alice?
Alice was my girlfriend before I married your father.
And Meena is my vacuum cleaner salesperson.
You never told us you were bisexual.

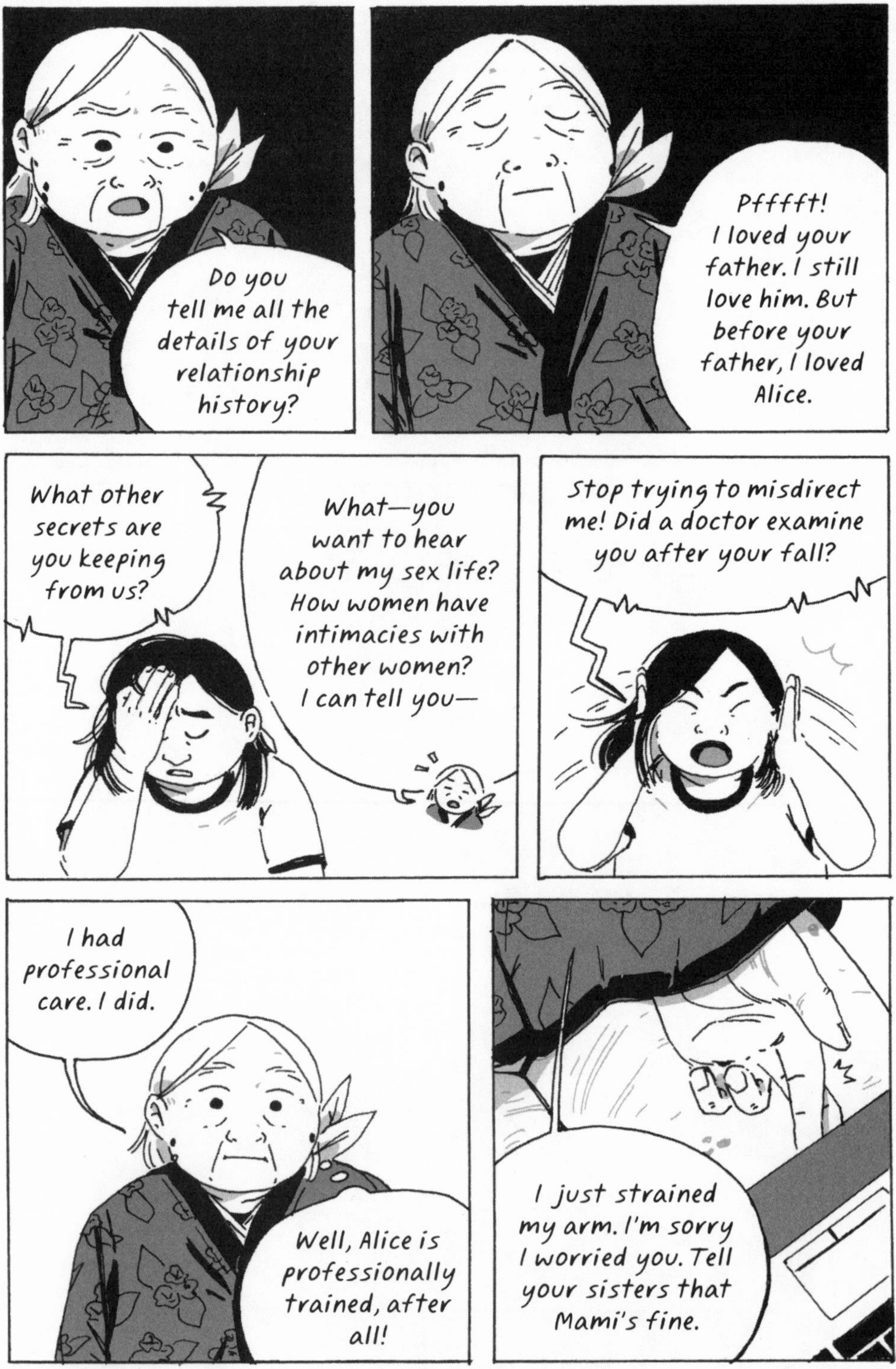
Do you tell me all the details of your relationship history?
Pfffft! I loved your father. I still love him. But before your father, I loved Alice.
What other secrets are you keeping from us?
What—you want to hear about my sex life? How women have intimacies with other women? I can tell you—
Stop trying to misdirect me! Did a doctor examine you after your fall?
I had professional care. I did.
Well, Alice is professionally trained, after all!
I just strained my arm. I'm sorry I worried you. Tell your sisters that Mami's fine.

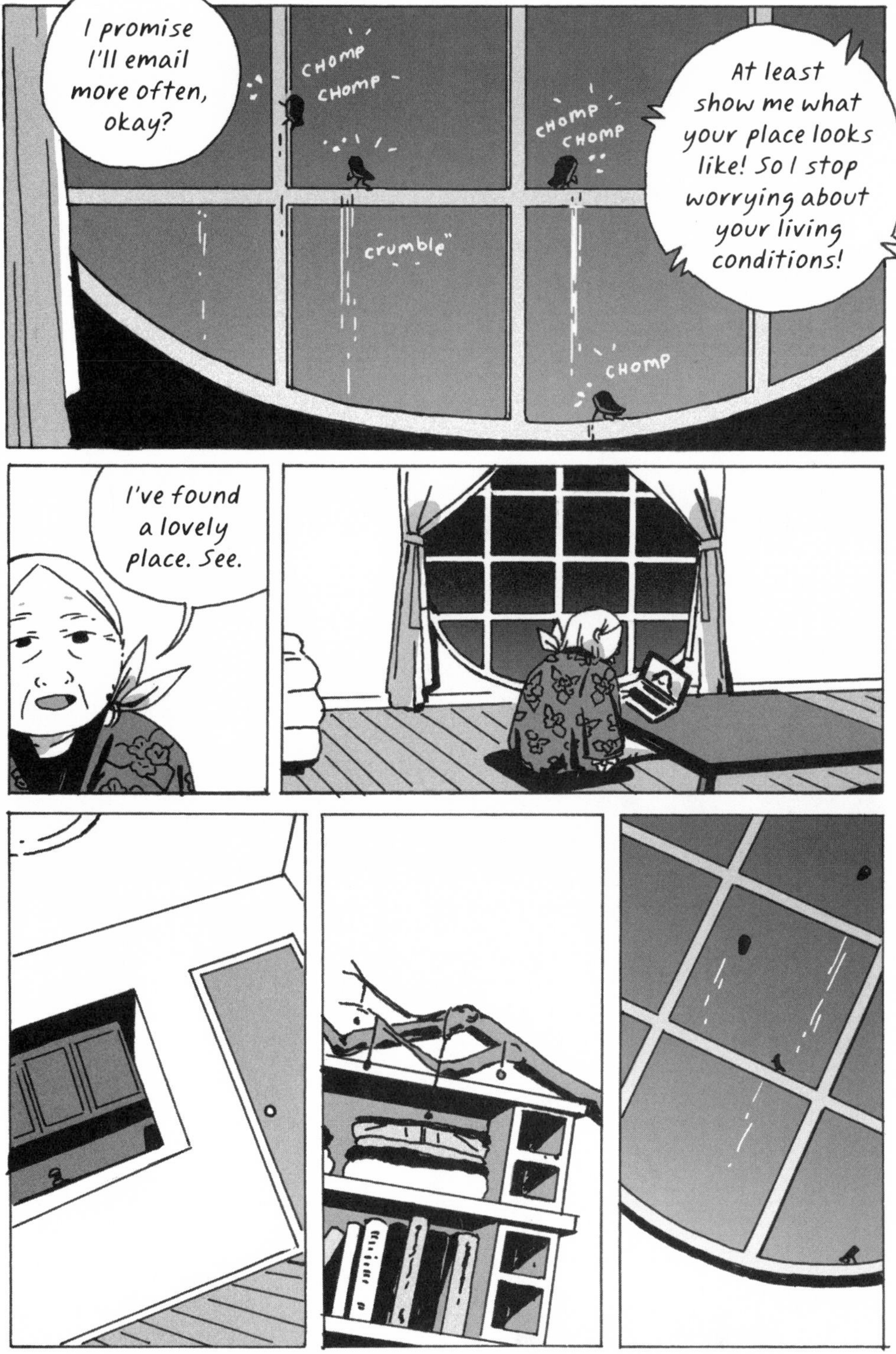
I promise I'll email more often, okay?
CHOMP CHOMP
CHOMP CHOMP
crumble
CHOMP
At least show me what your place looks like! So I stop worrying about your living conditions!
I've found a lovely place. See.

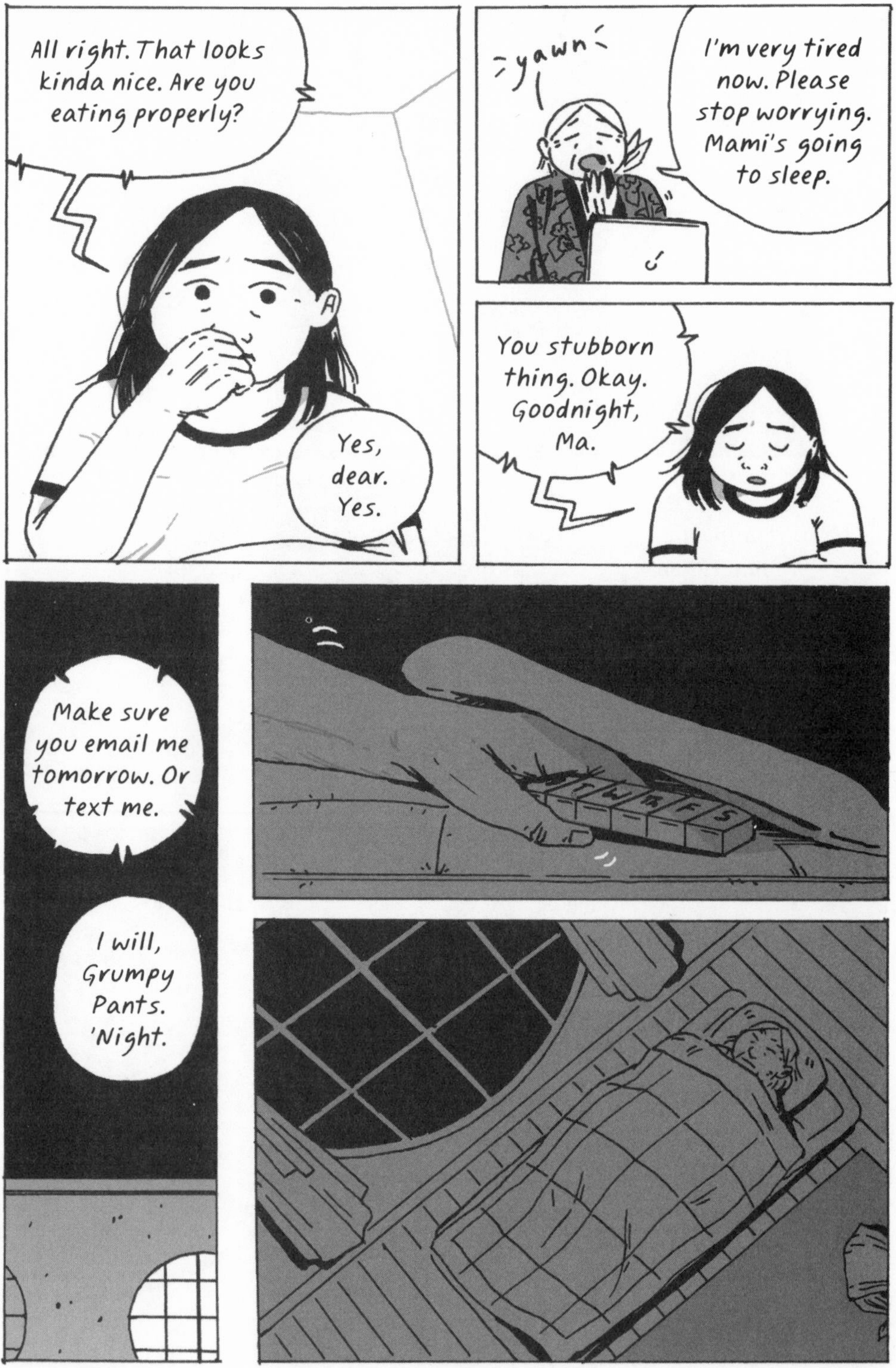
All right. That looks kinda nice. Are you eating properly?
Yes, dear. Yes.
yawn
I'm very tired now. Please stop worrying. Mami's going to sleep.
You stubborn thing. Okay. Goodnight, Ma.
Make sure you email me tomorrow. Or text me.
I will, Grumpy Pants. 'Night.

Chapter Eleven

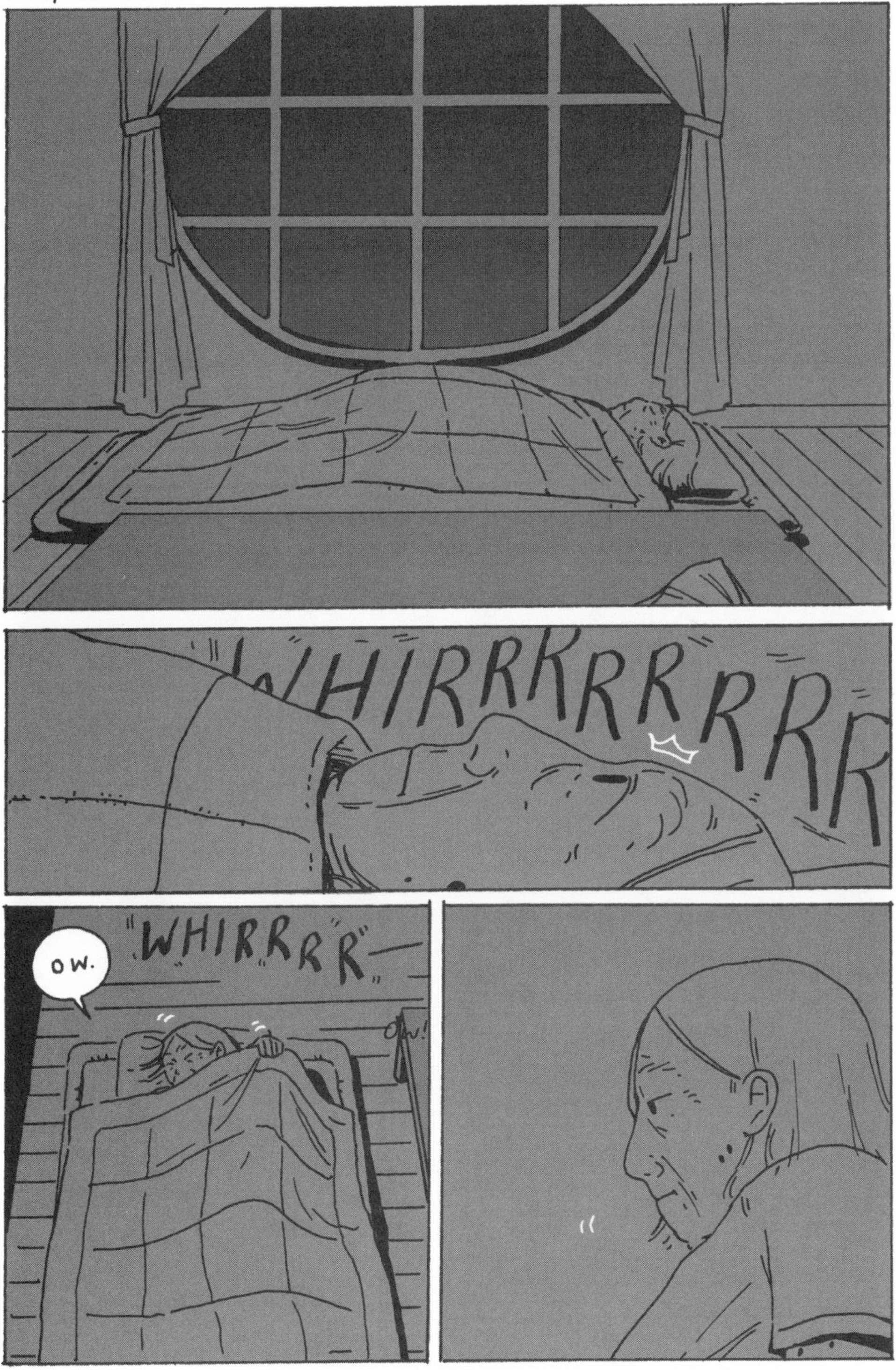
WHIRRRRRRRR
OW.
WHIRRRR
OW!

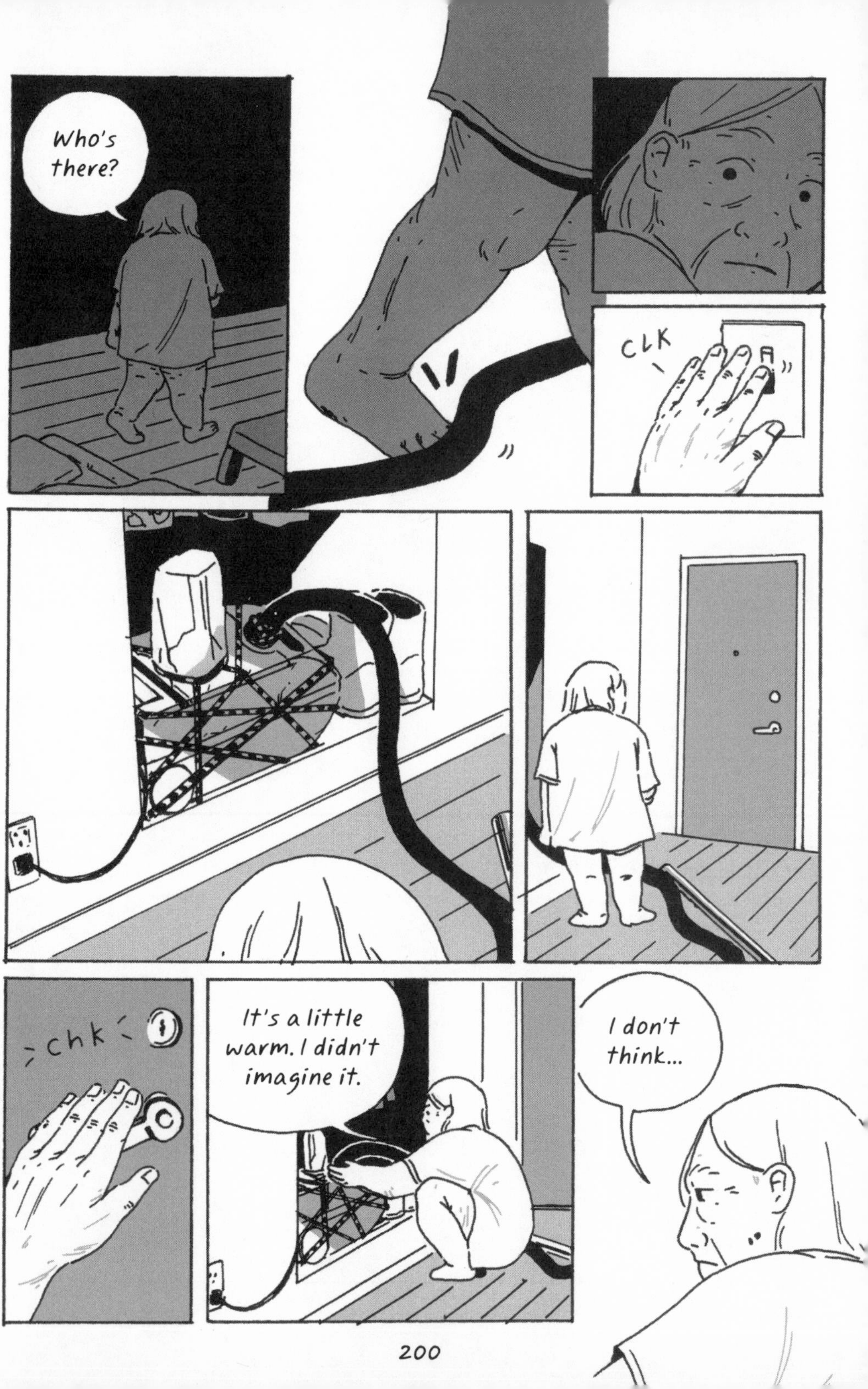
Who's there?
CLK
chk
It's a little warm. I didn't imagine it.
I don't think...

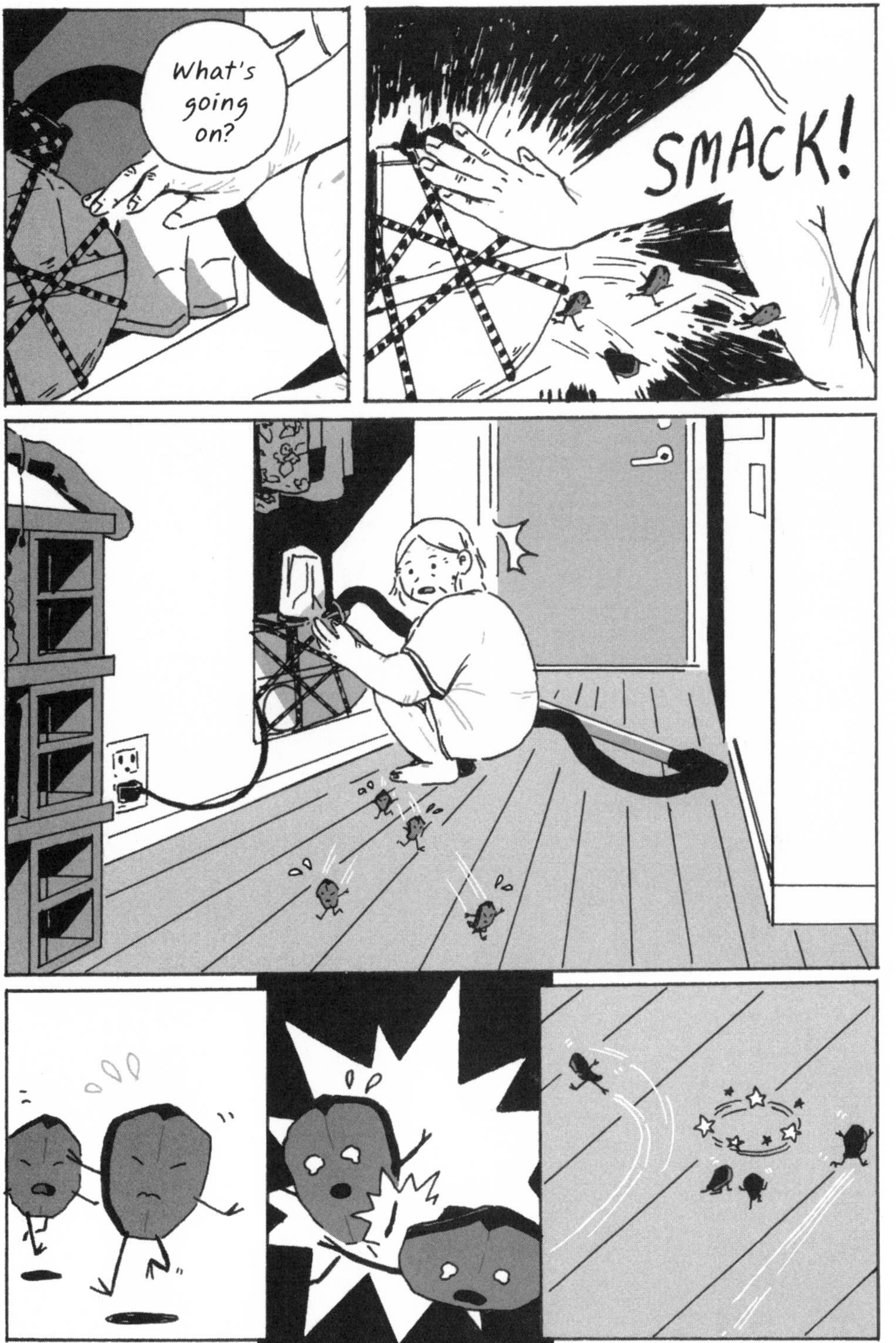
What's going on?
SMACK!

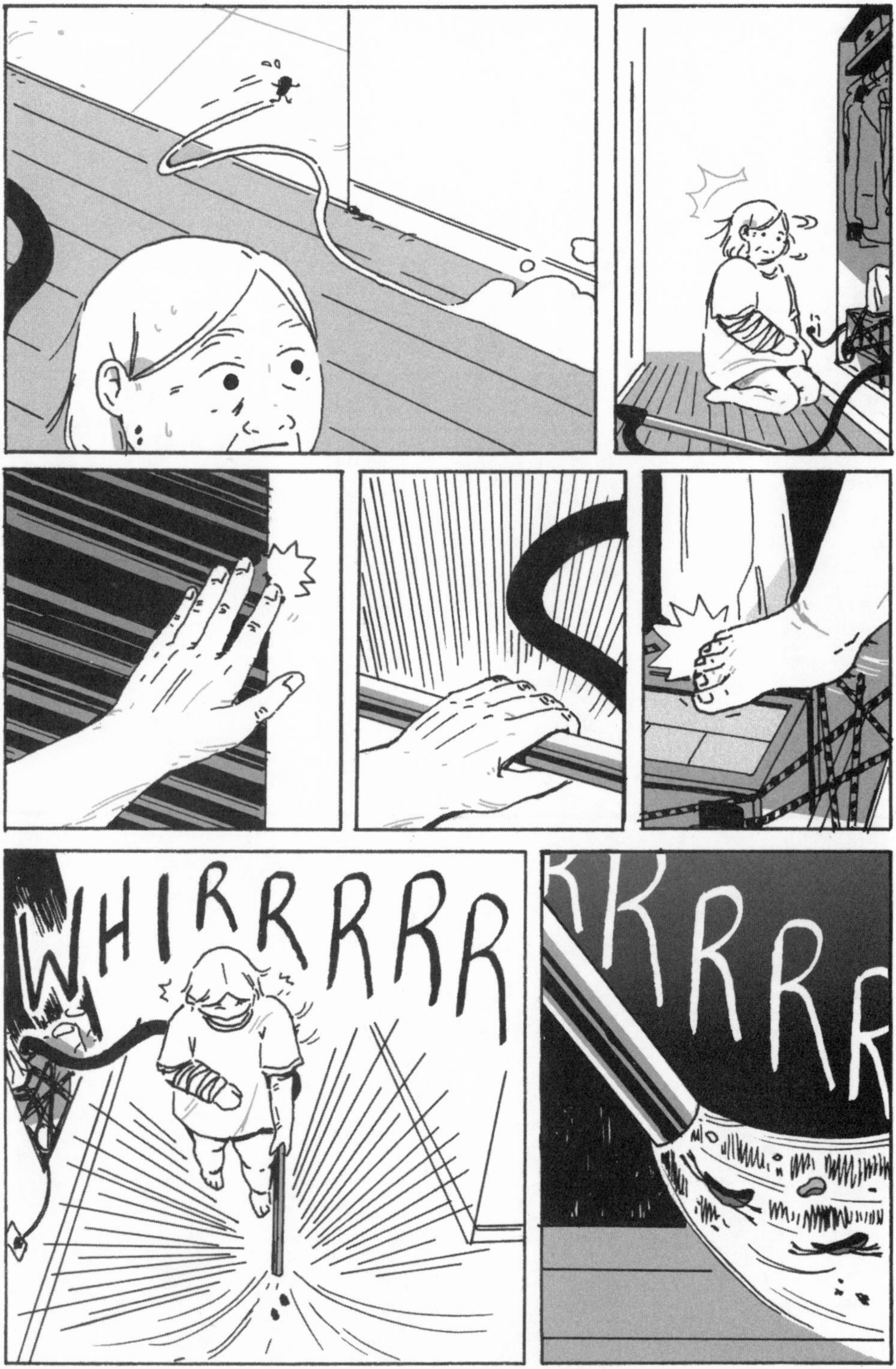
WHIRRRRRR
RRRRRR

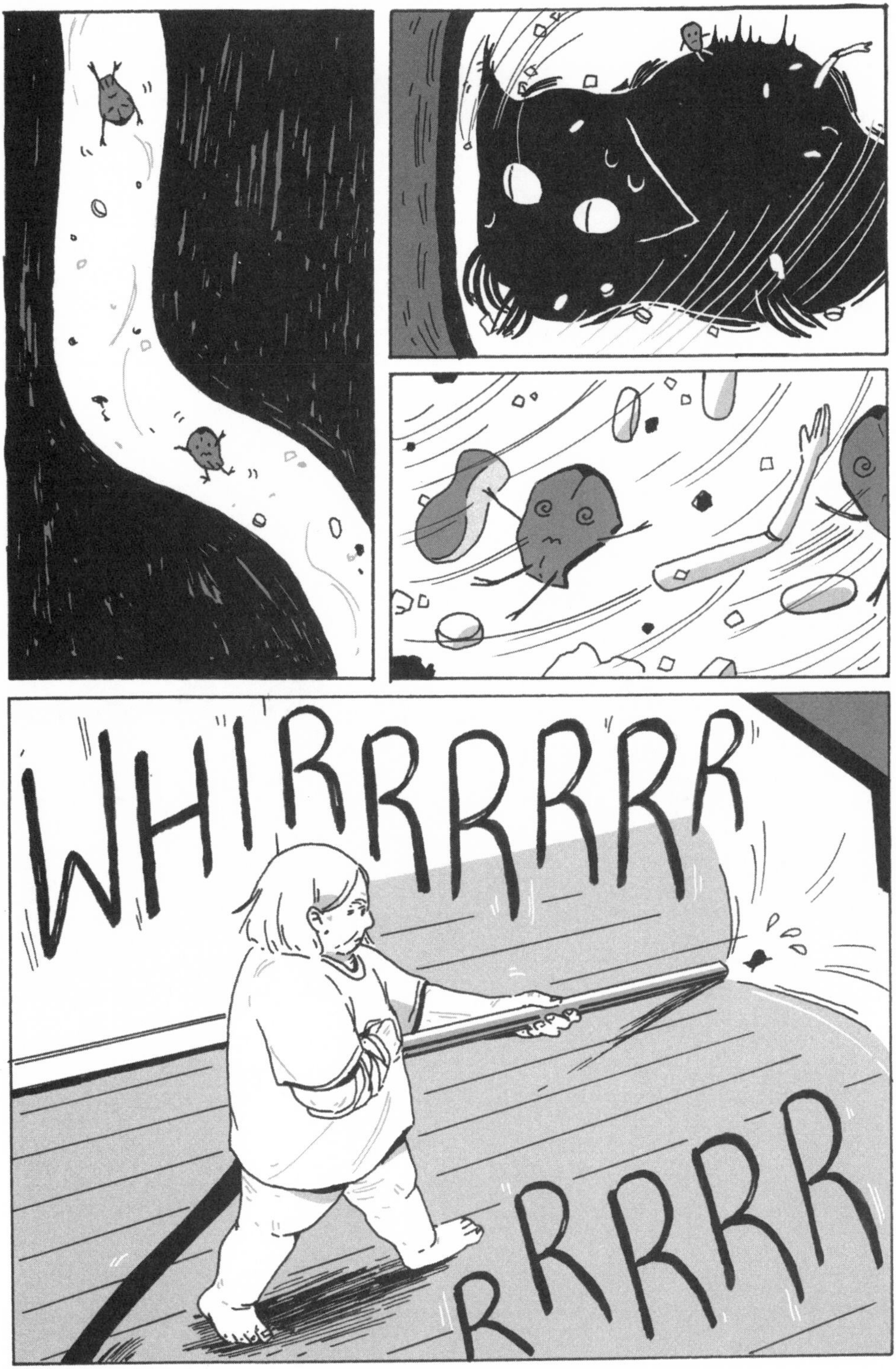
WHIRRRRRR
RRRRRR

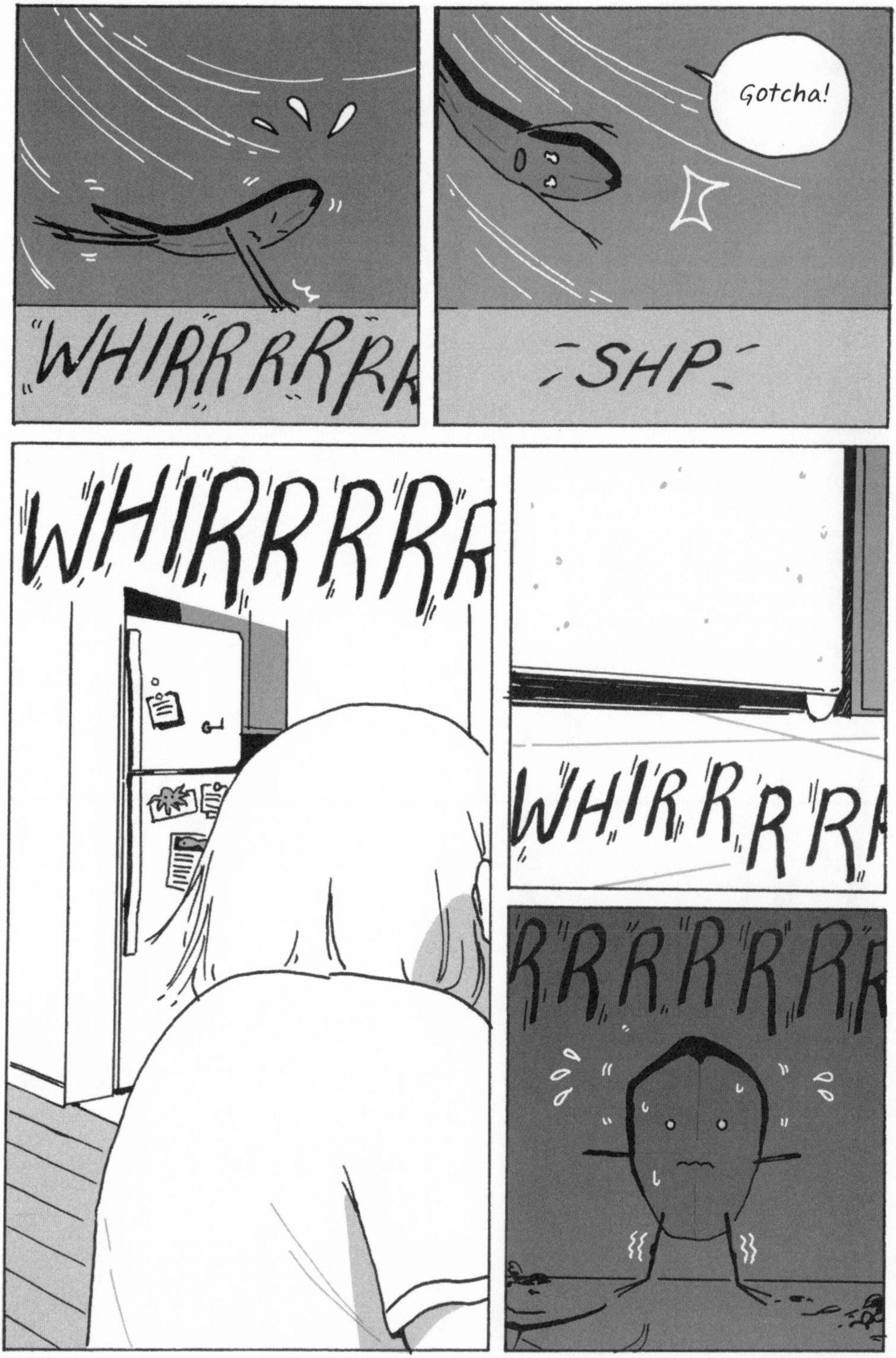
WHIRRRRR
Gotcha!
SHP
WHIRRRRRR
WHIRRRR
RRRRRRR

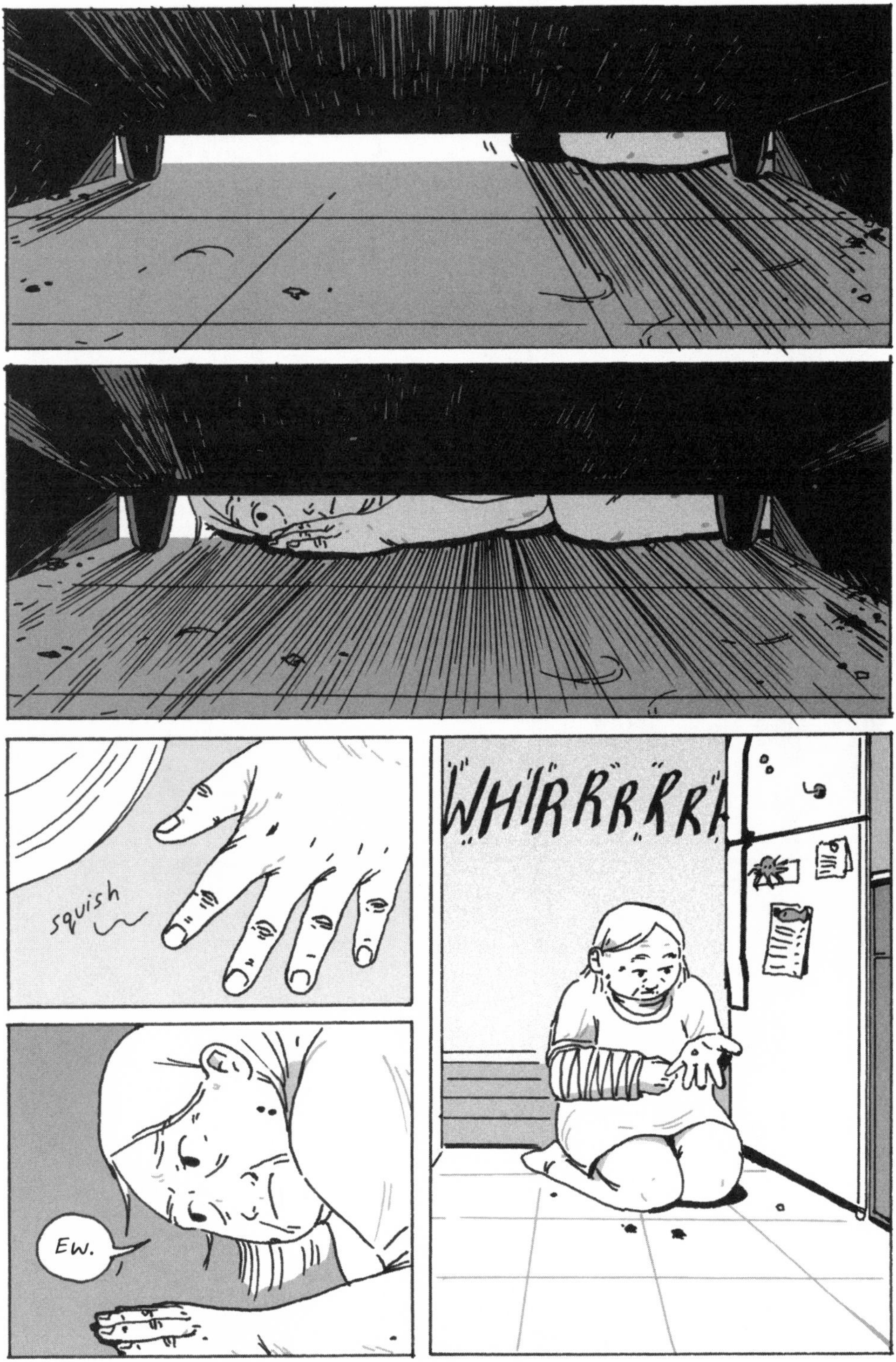
squish
WHIRRRRRA
Ew.

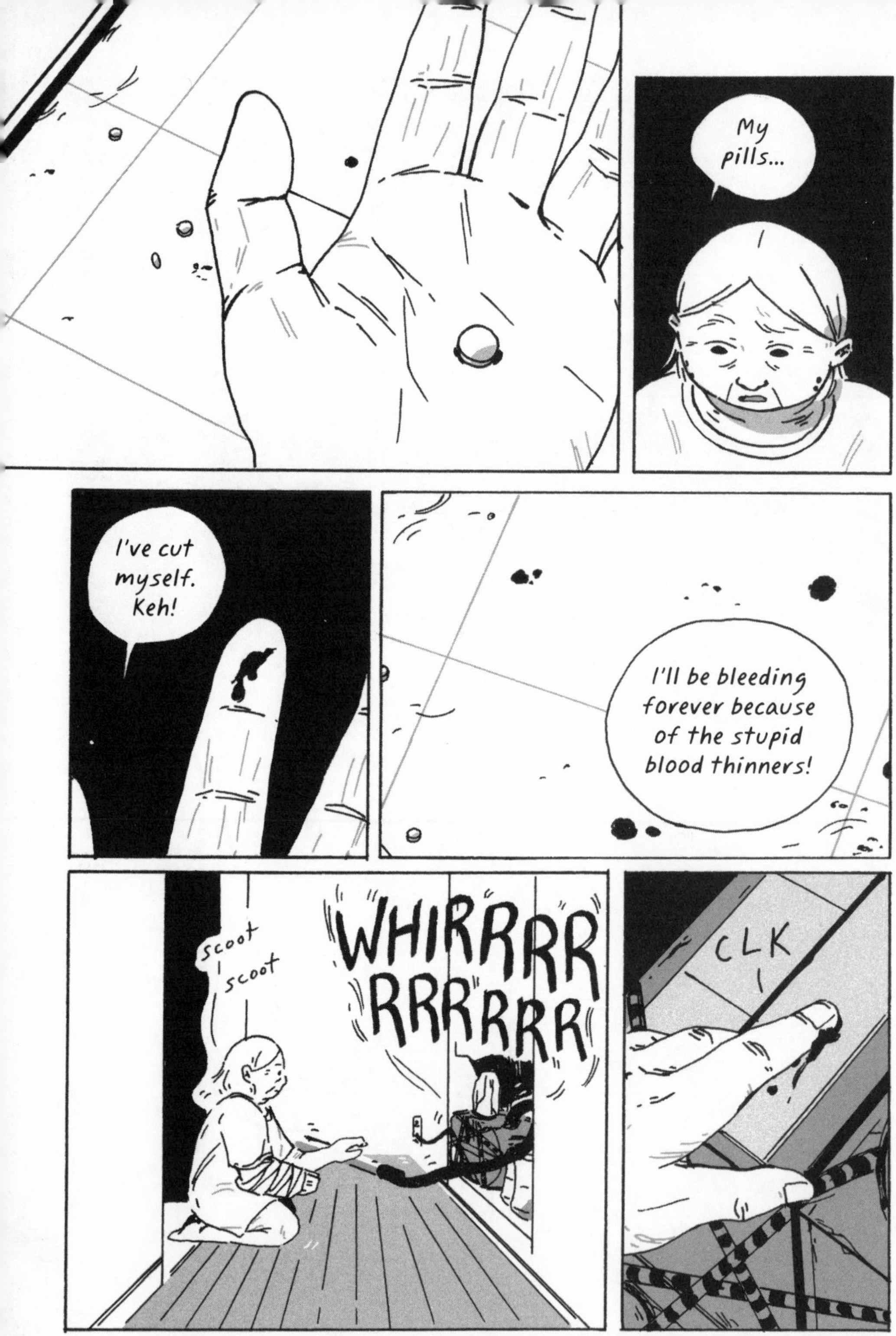
My pills...
I've cut myself. Keh!
I'll be bleeding forever because of the stupid blood thinners!
scoot scoot
WHIRRRRRRRRRRR
CLK

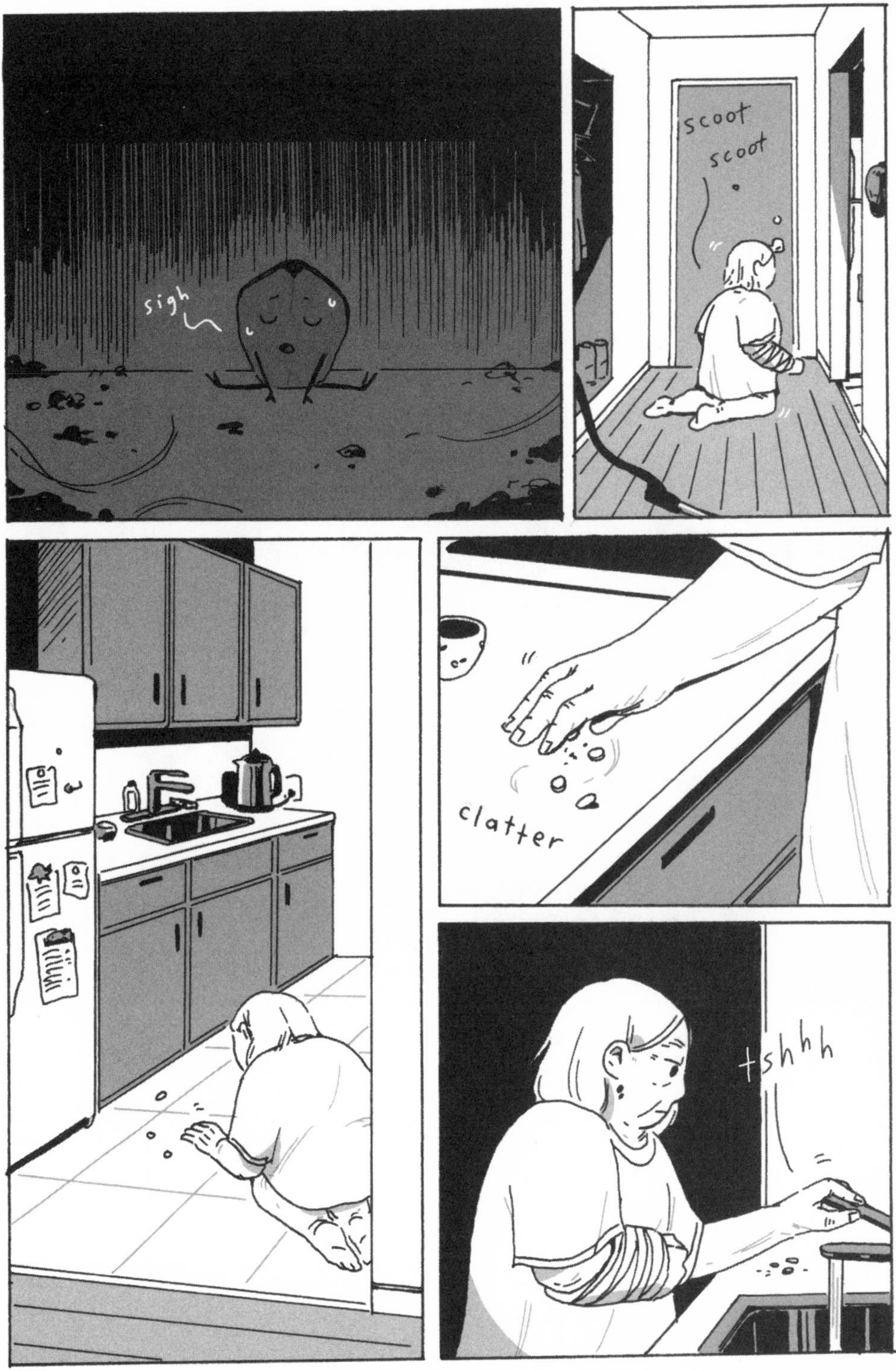
sigh
scoot
scoot
clatter
tshhh

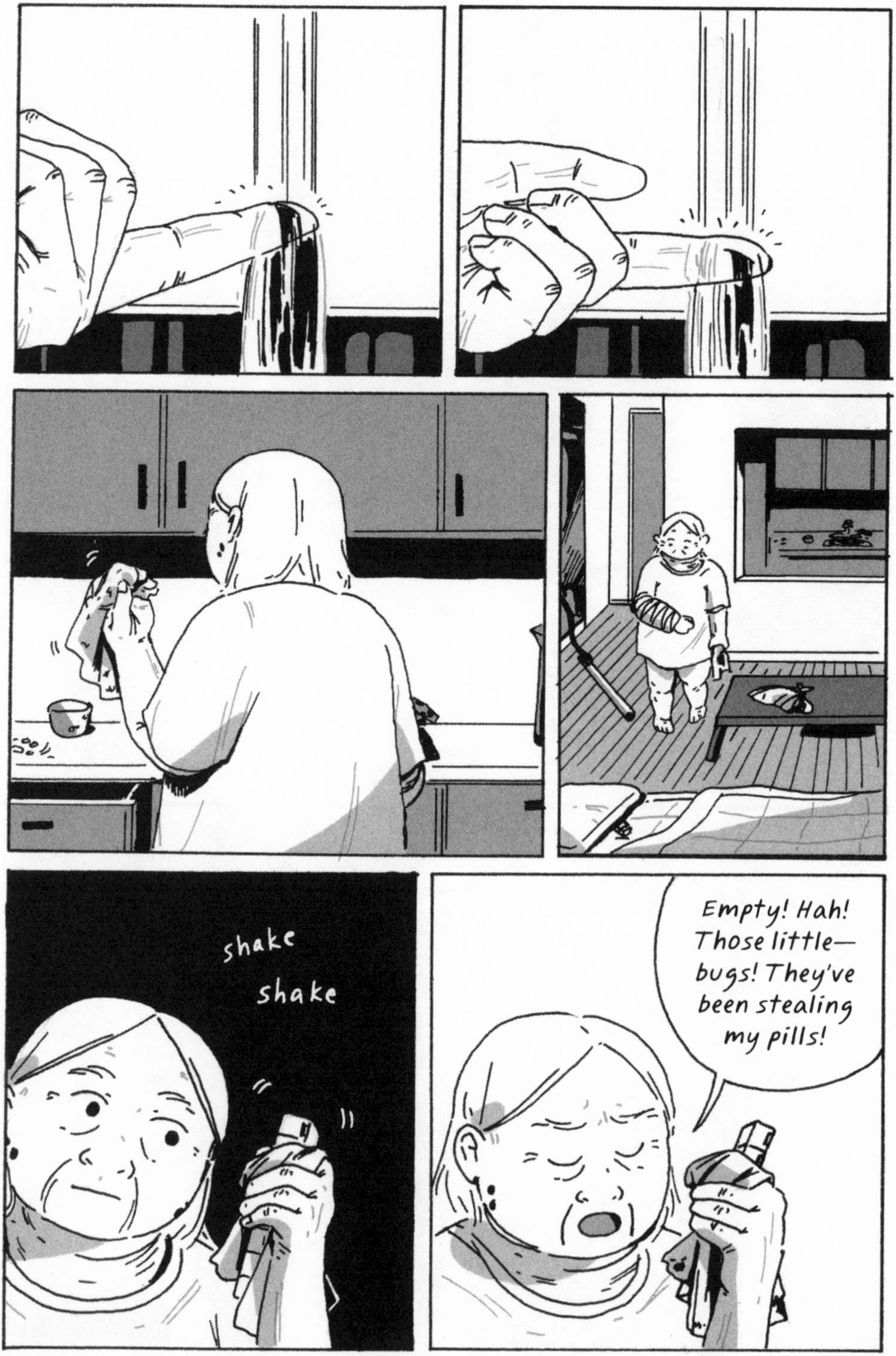
shake
shake
Empty! Hah! Those little— bugs! They've been stealing my pills!

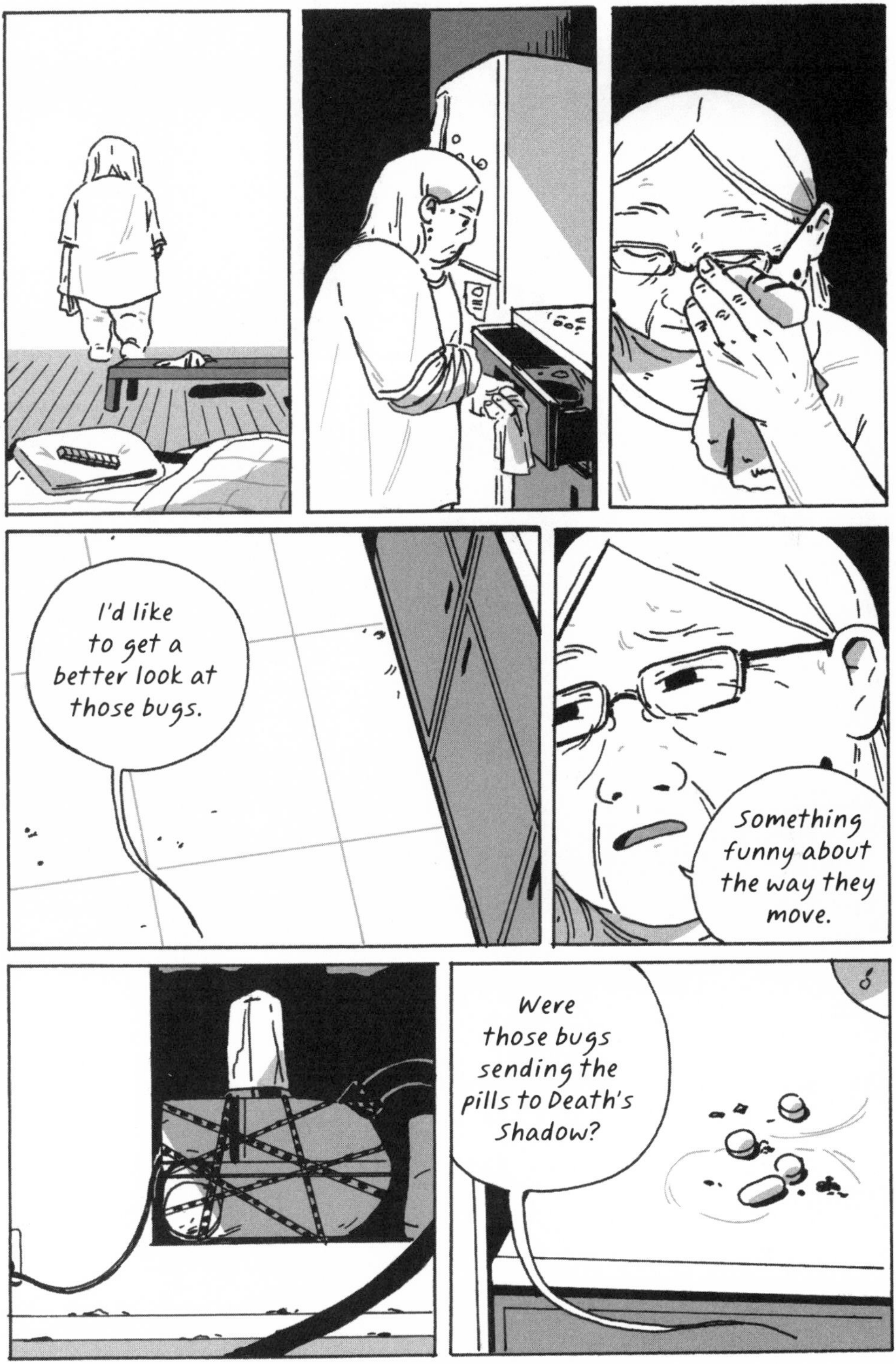
I'd like to get a better look at those bugs.
Something funny about the way they move.
Were those bugs sending the pills to Death's Shadow?

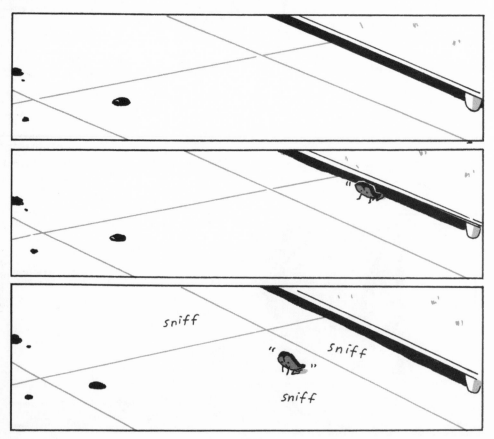

sniff

" sniff "

sniff

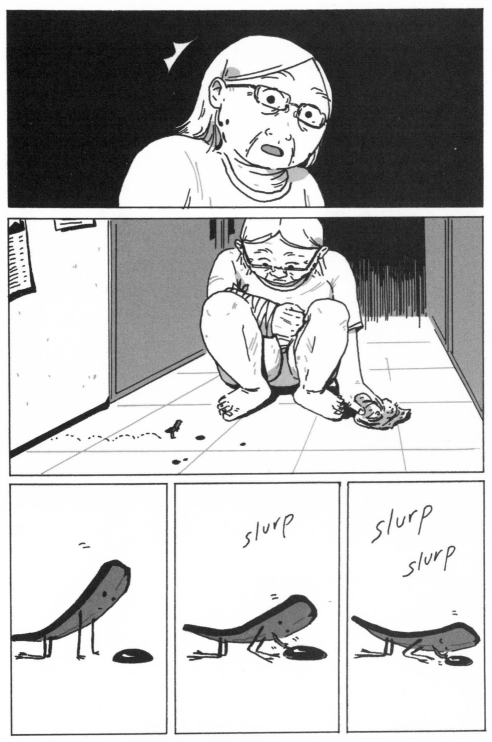

slurp

slurp
slurp

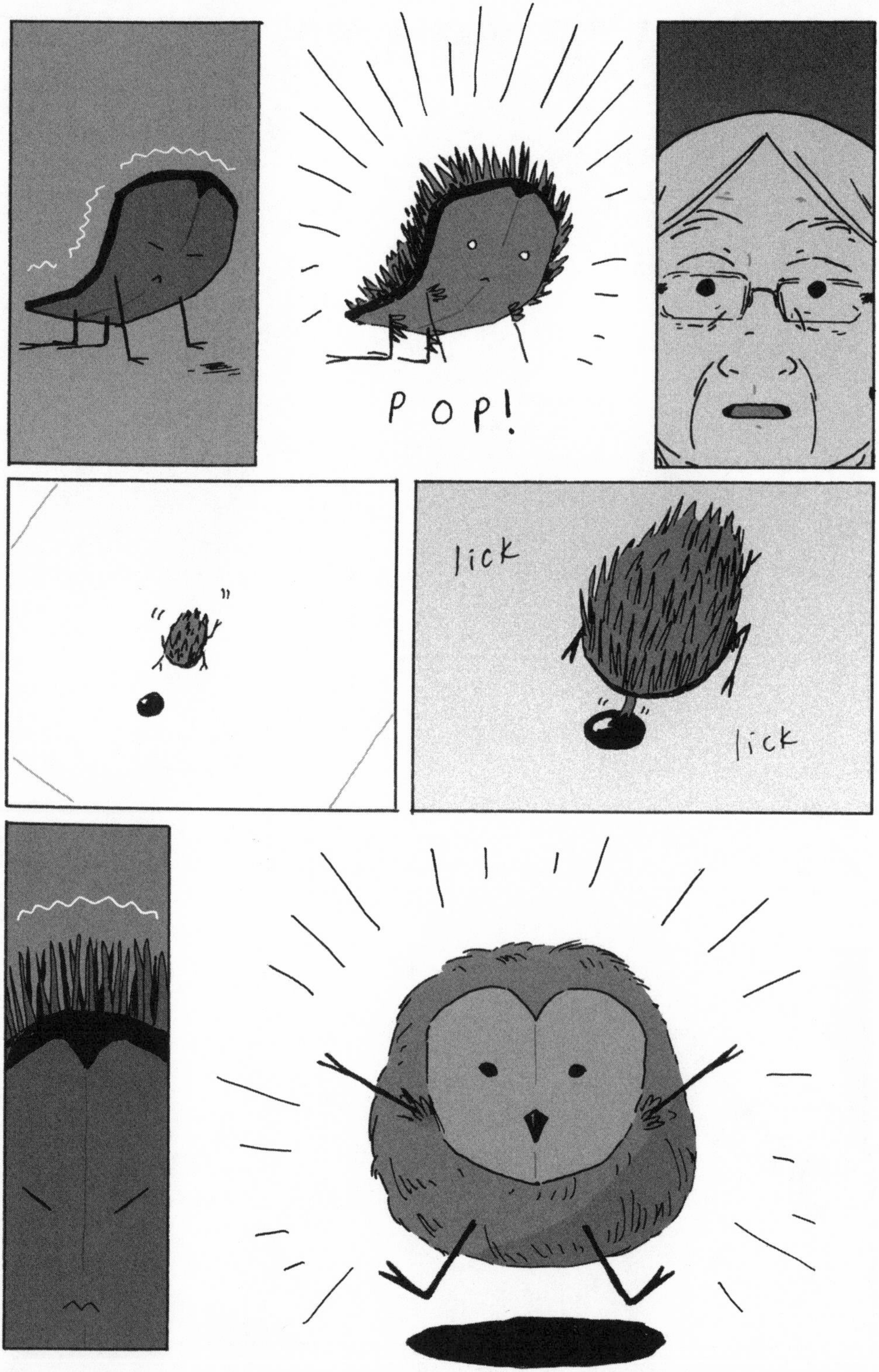
POP!
lick
lick

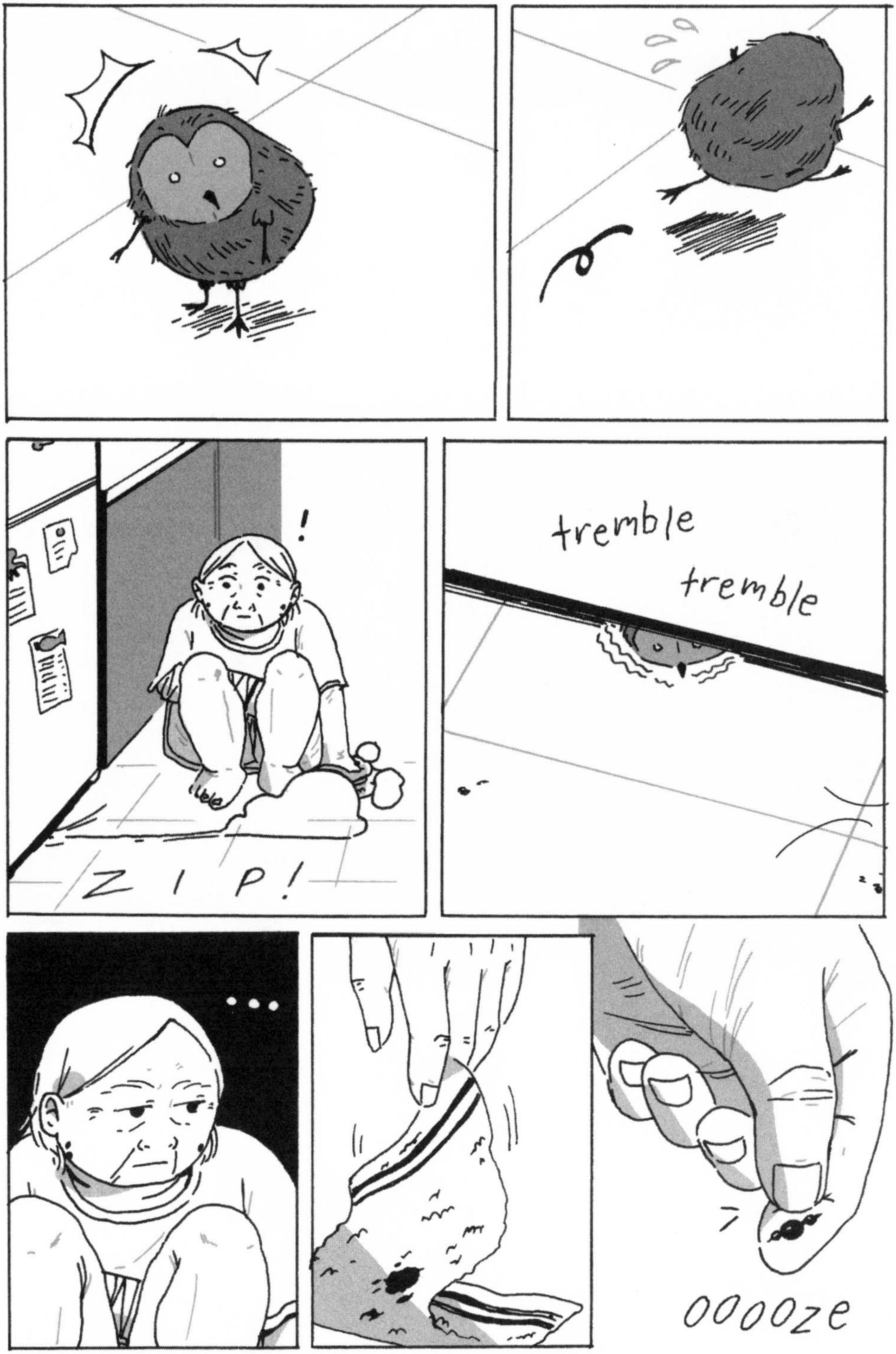
!
tremble
tremble
ZIP!
...
OOOOZE

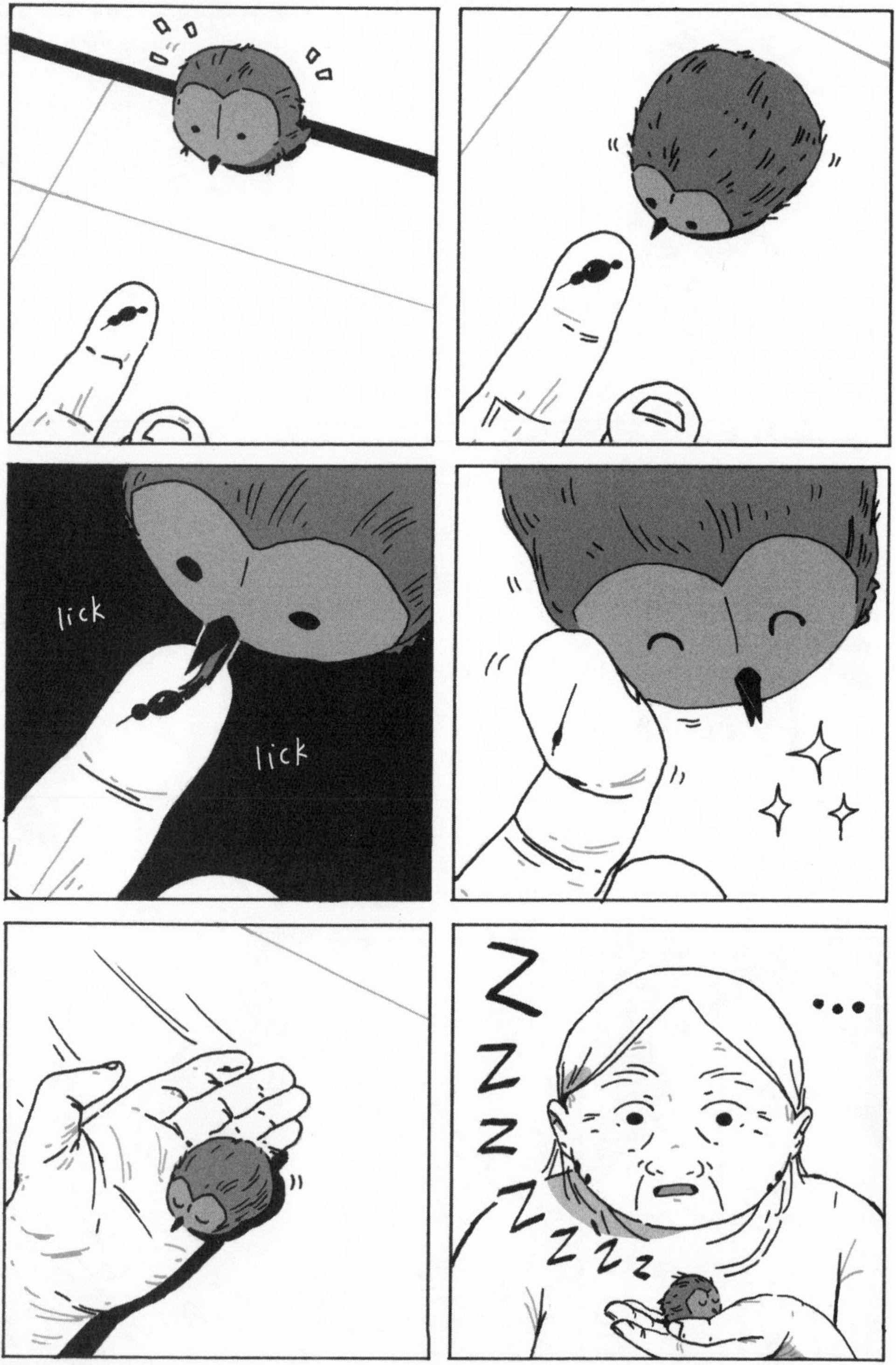
lick
lick
Z Z Z Z Z Z Z
...

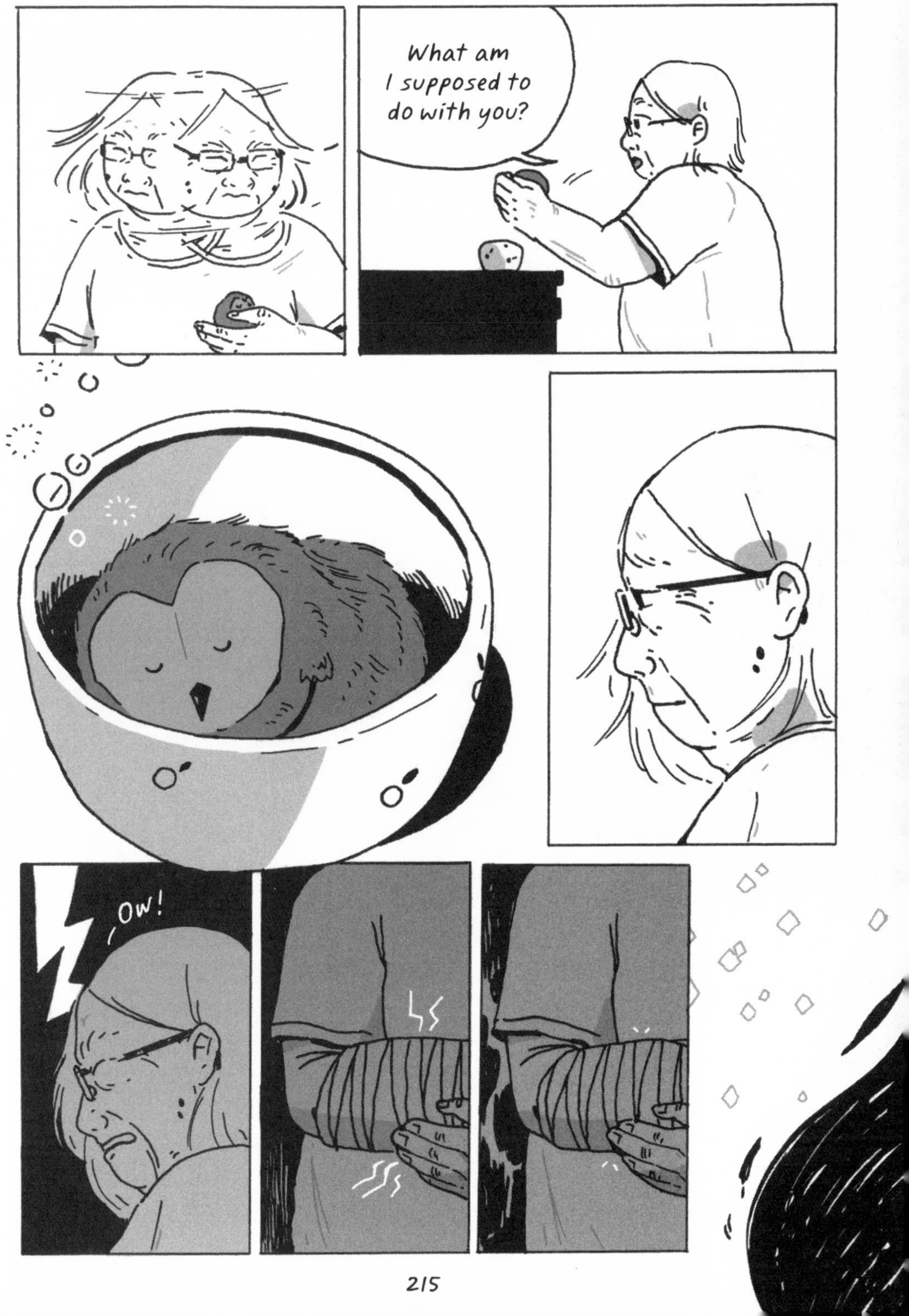
What am I supposed to do with you?
OW!

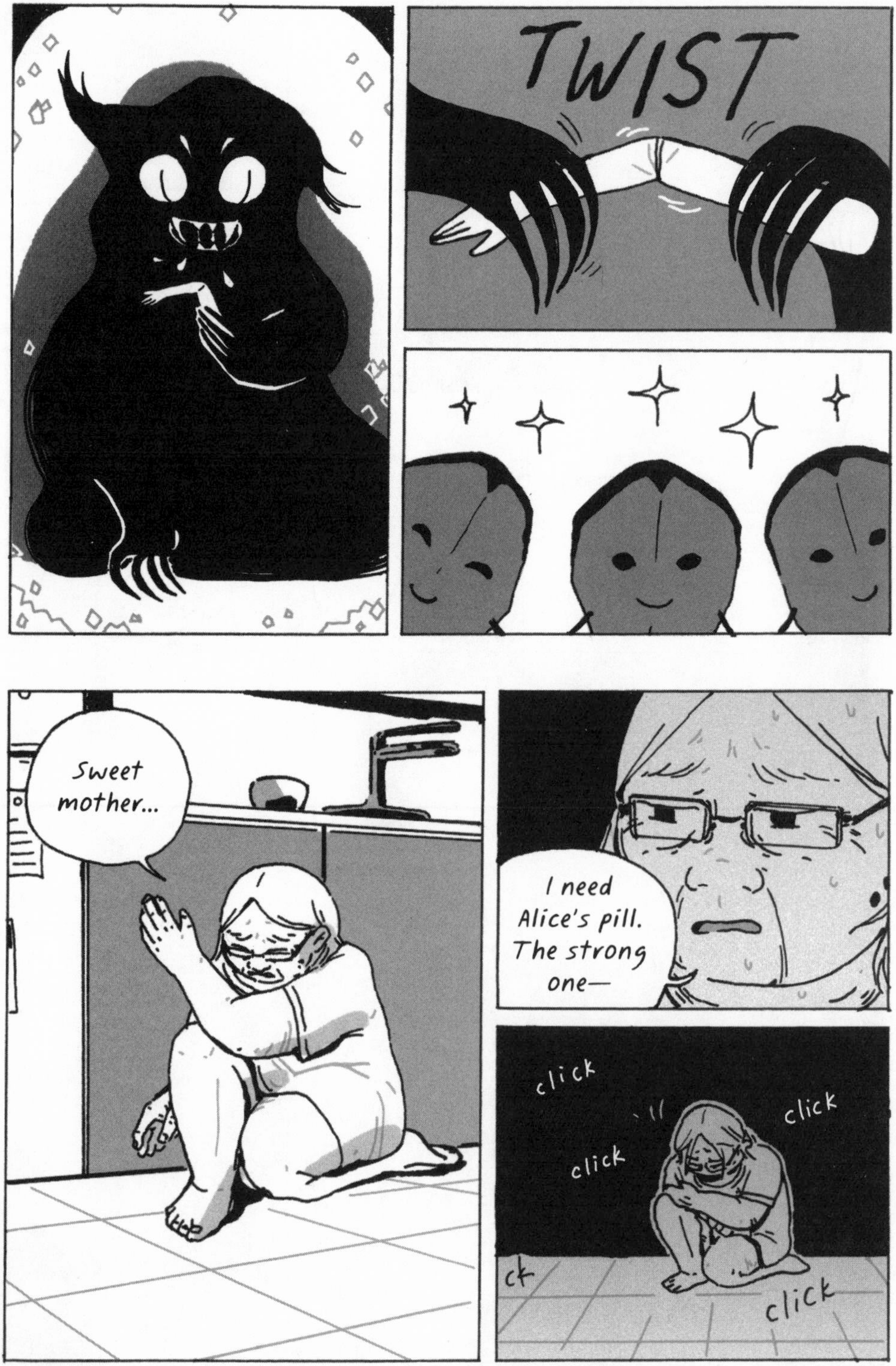
TWIST
Sweet mother...
I need Alice's pill. The strong one—
click
click
click
ck
click

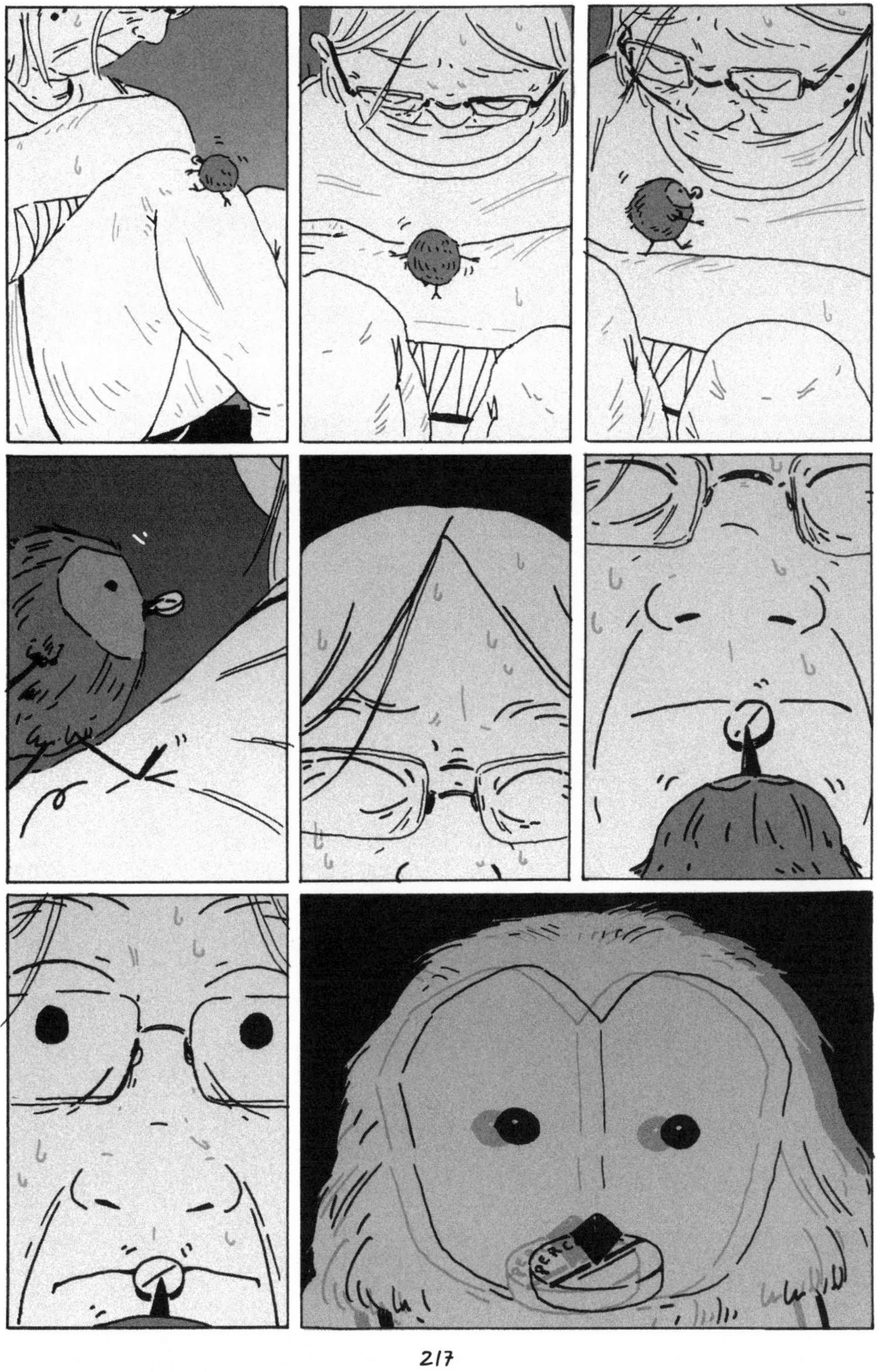
PERC

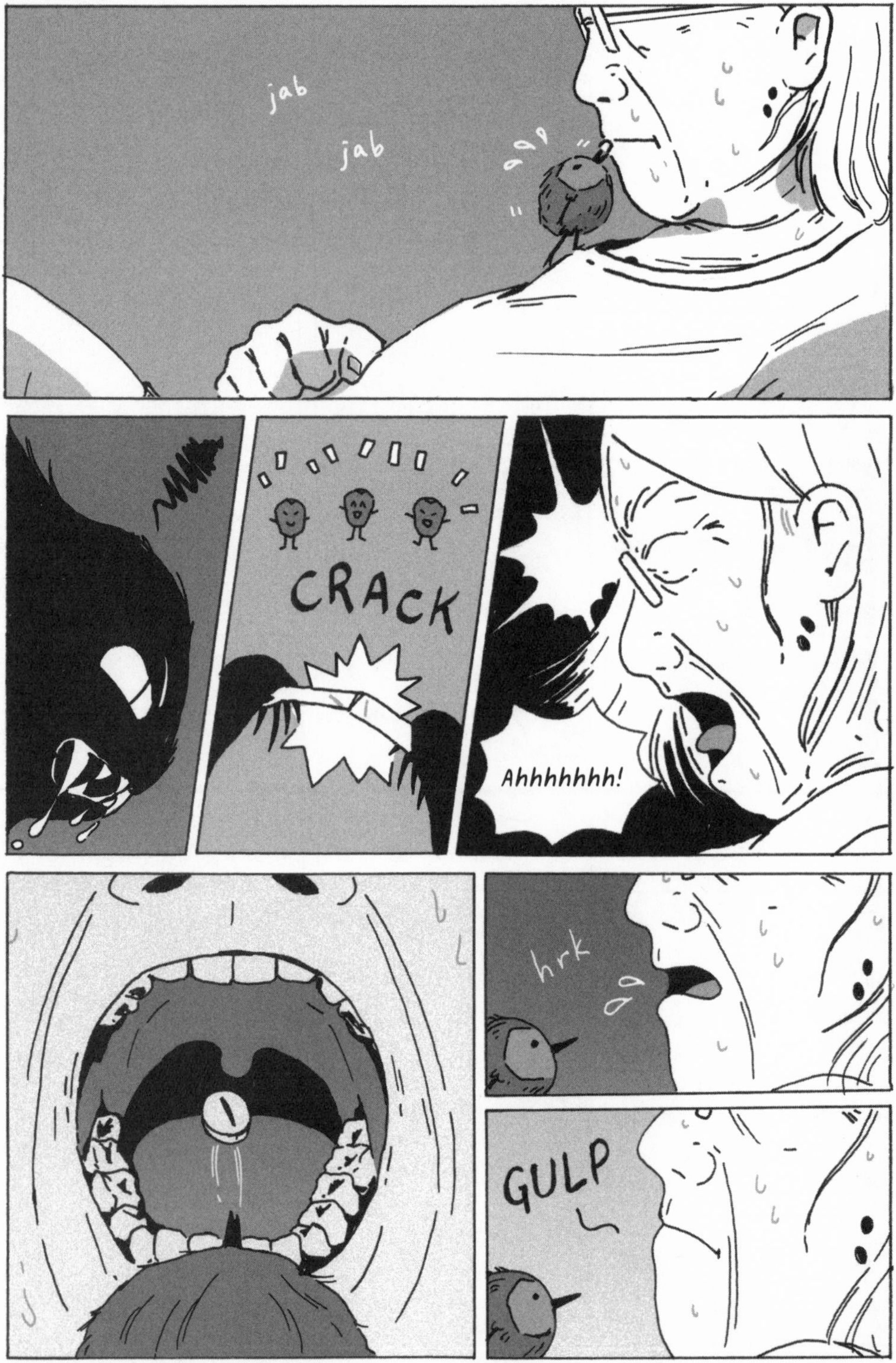
jab
jab
CRACK
Ahhhhhhh!
hrk
GULP

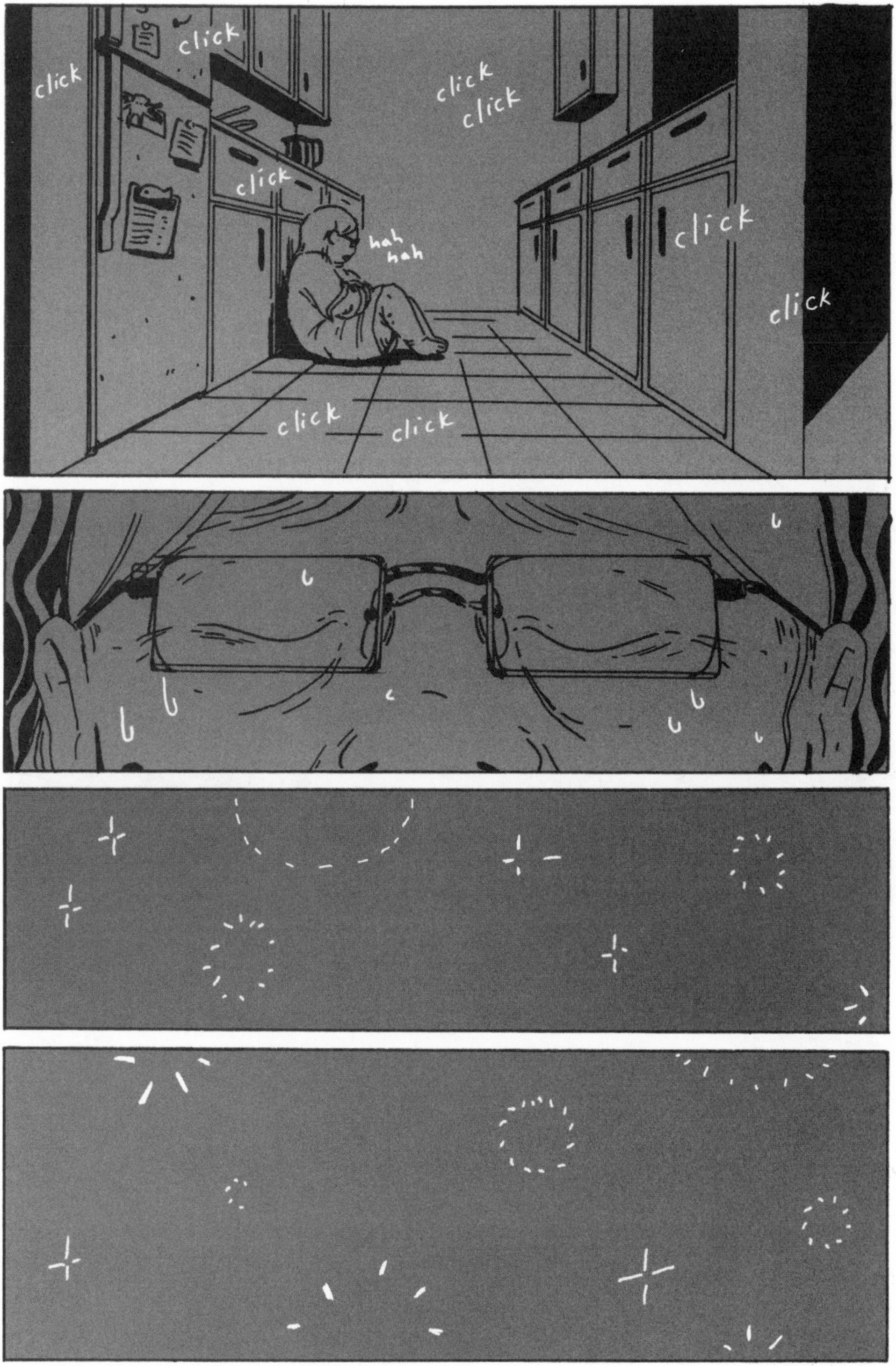
click
click
click
click
click
hah
hah
click
click
click
click

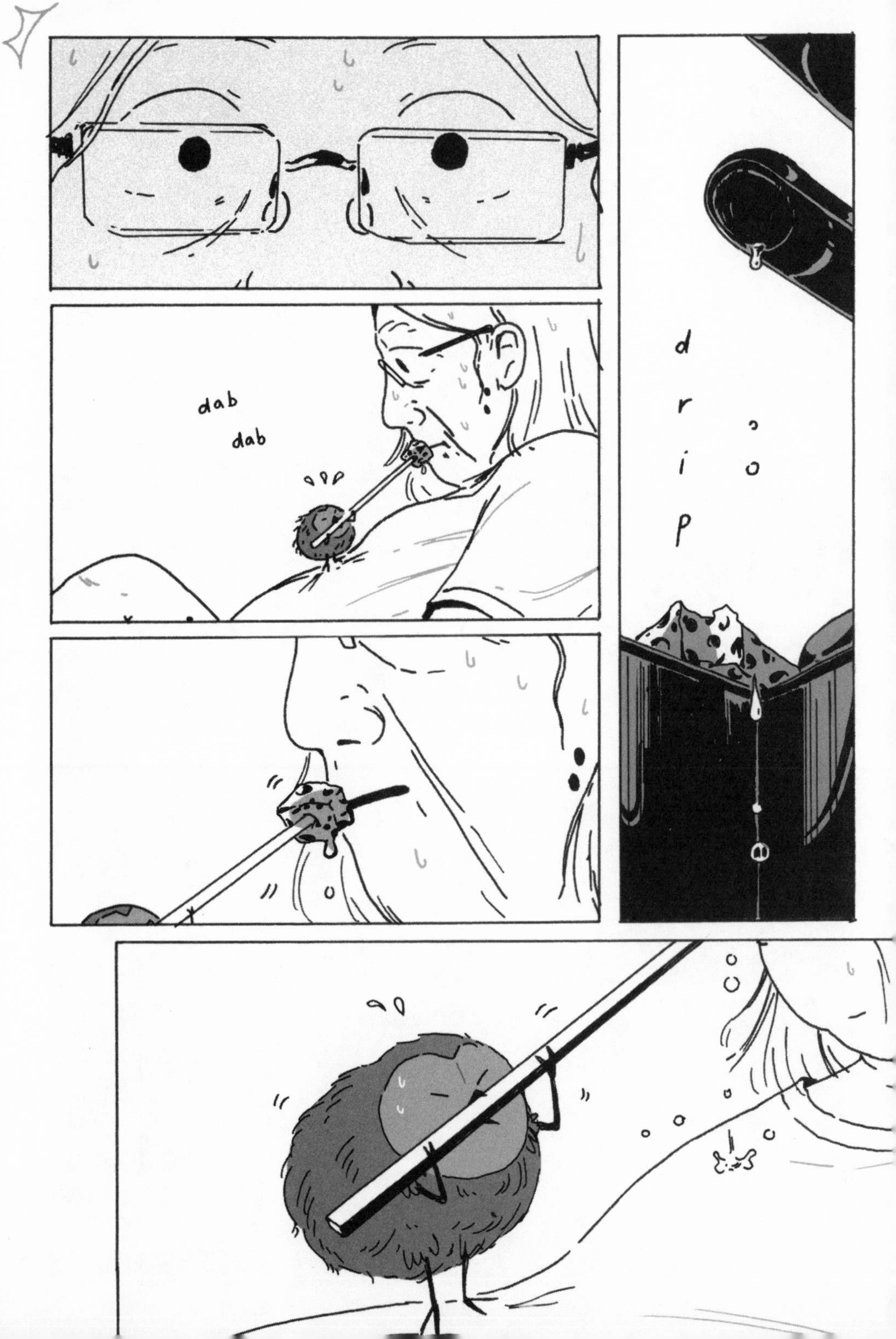
dab
dab
drip

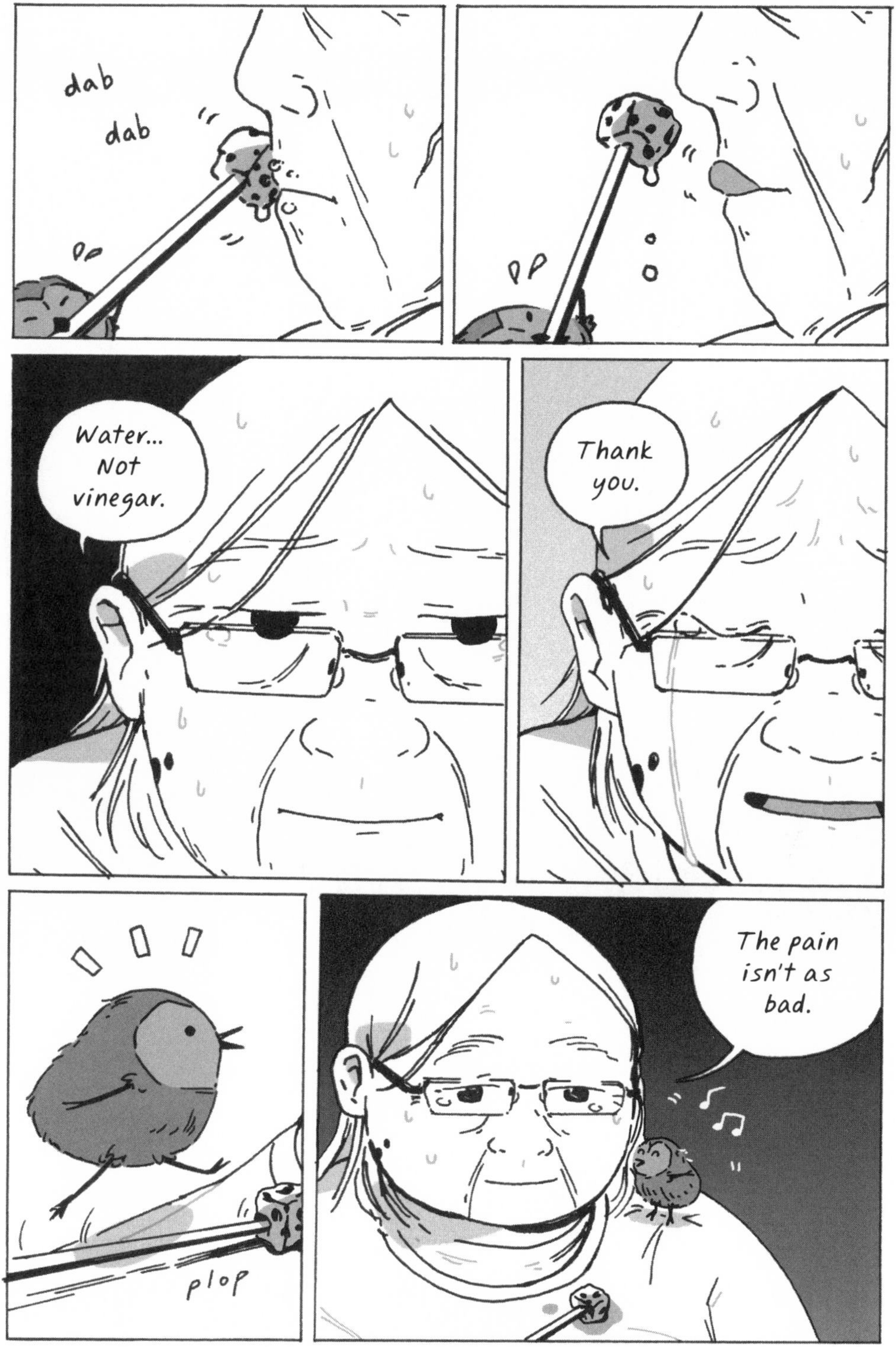
dab
dab
Water... Not vinegar.
Thank you.
The pain isn't as bad.
plop

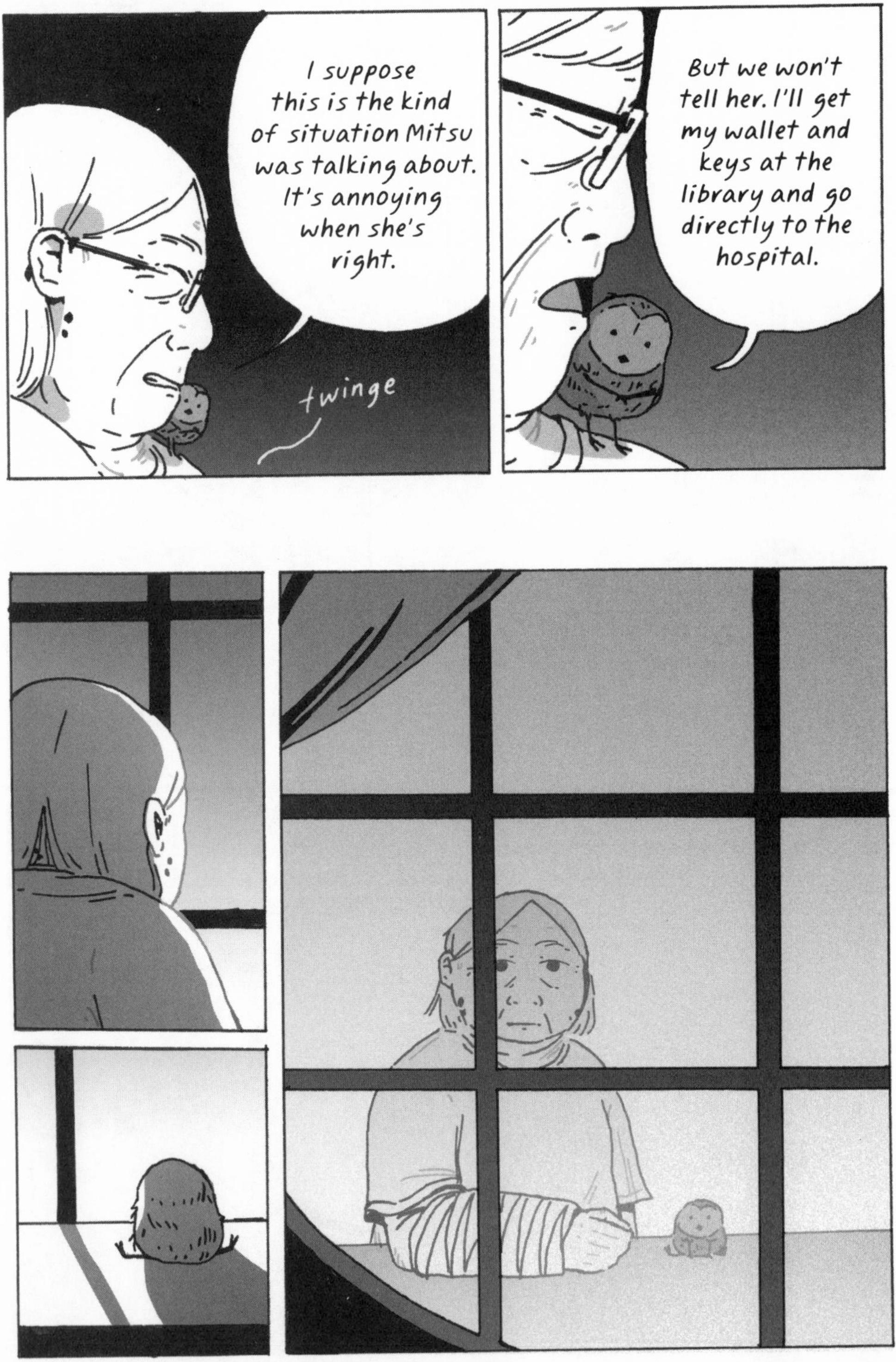
I suppose this is the kind of situation Mitsu was talking about. It's annoying when she's right.
twinge
But we won't tell her. I'll get my wallet and keys at the library and go directly to the hospital.

Chapter Twelve

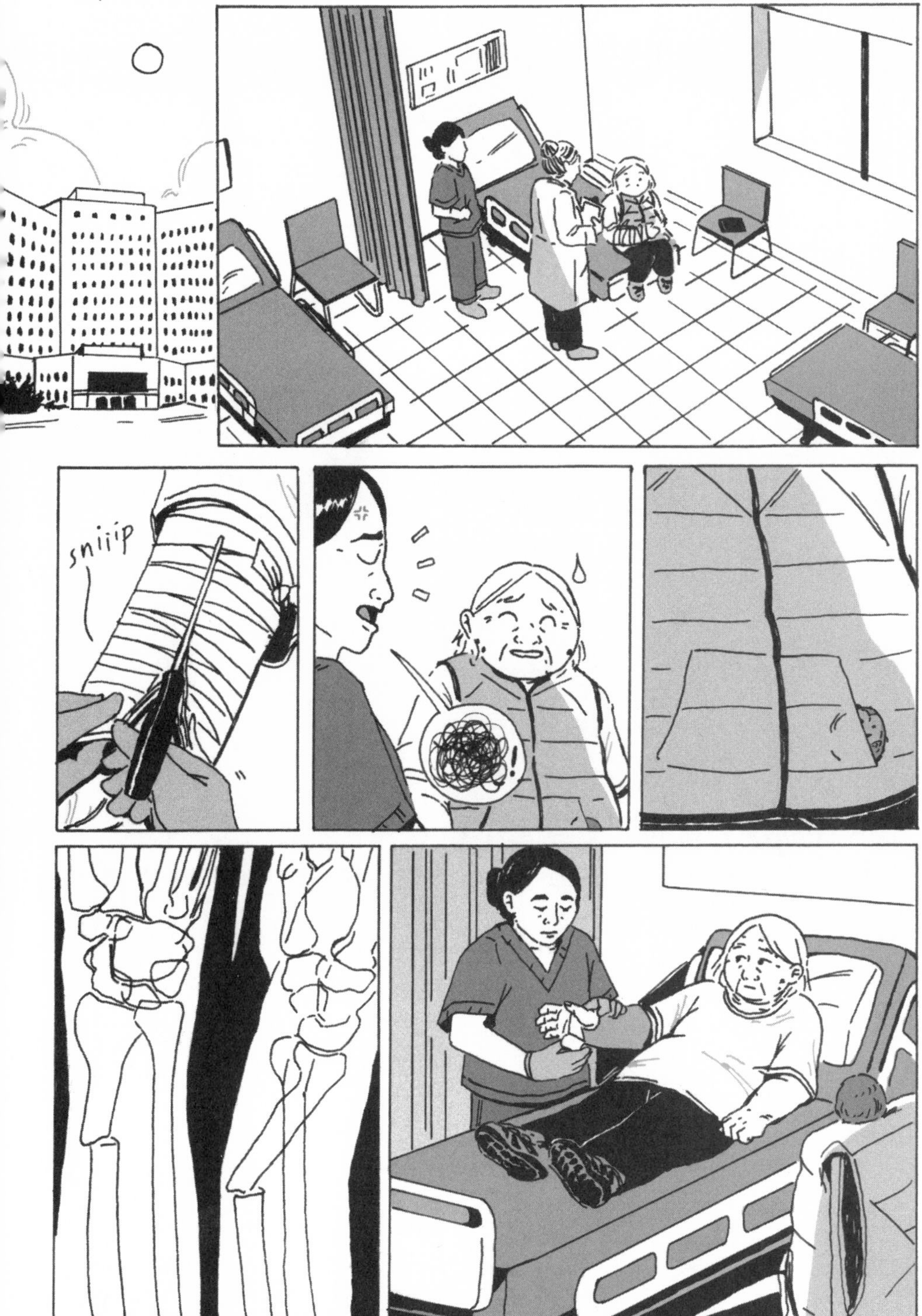
sniiip

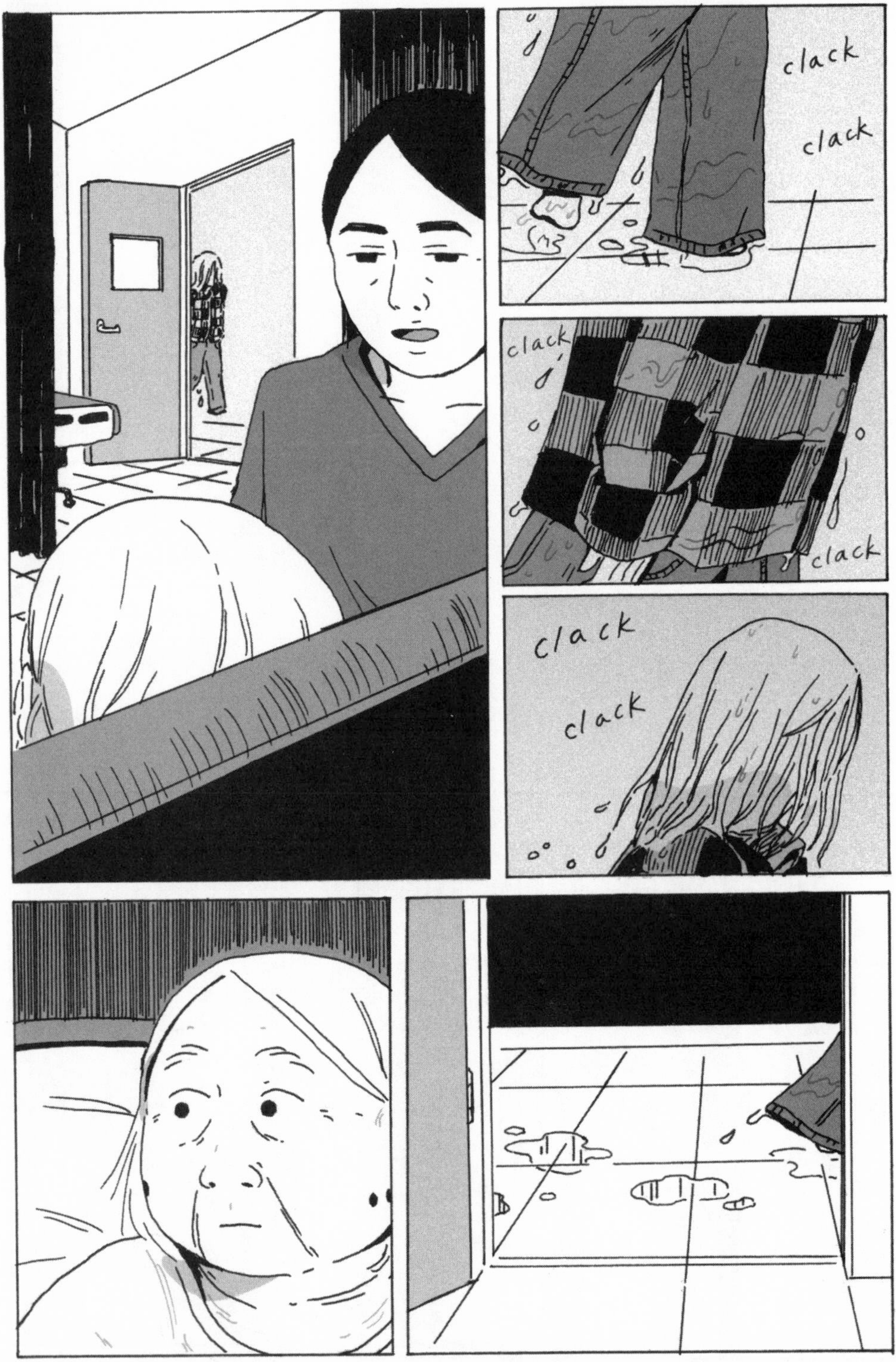
clack
clack
clack
clack
clack
clack

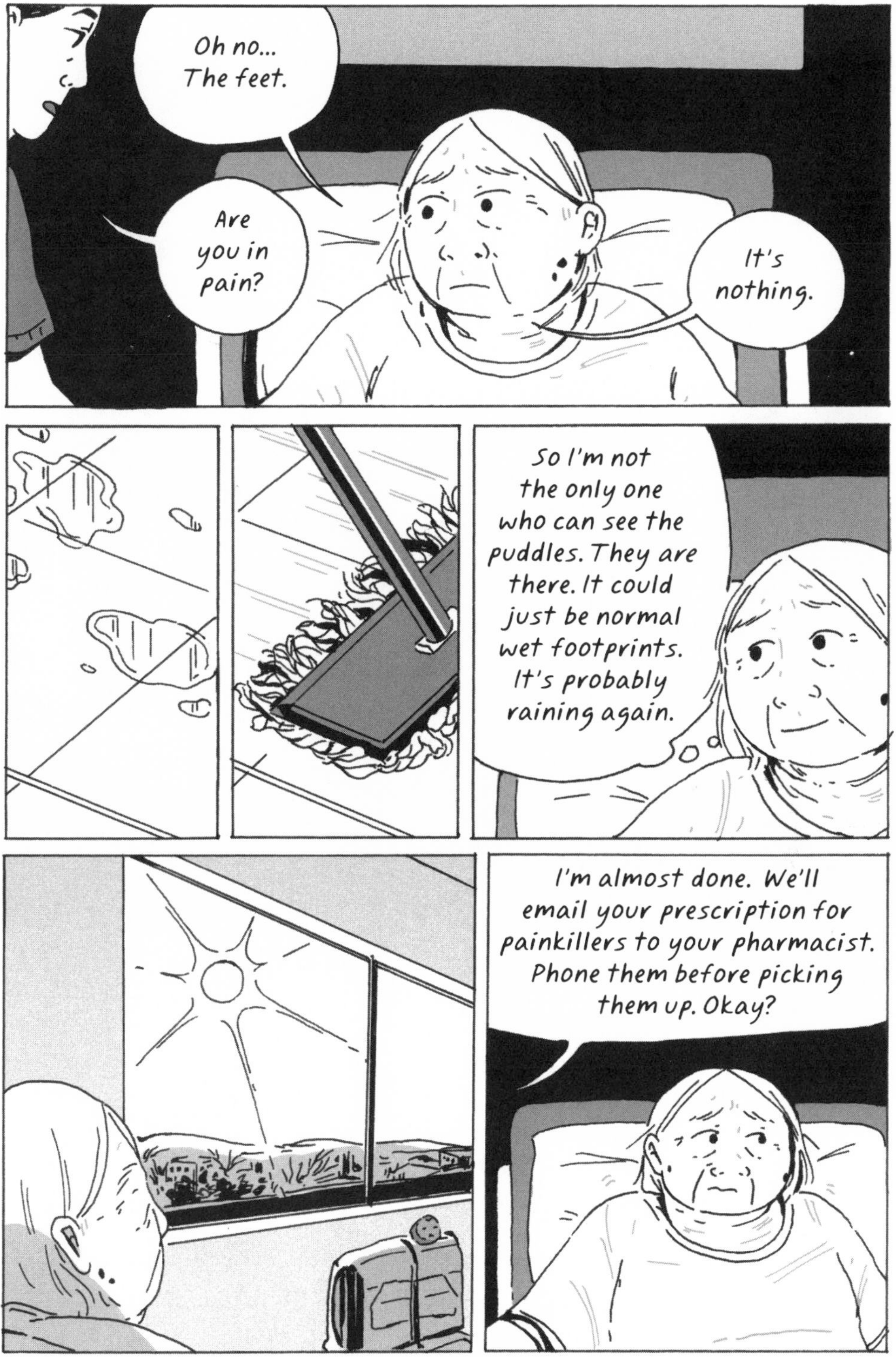
Oh no... The feet.
Are you in pain?
It's nothing.
So I'm not the only one who can see the puddles. They are there. It could just be normal wet footprints. It's probably raining again.
I'm almost done. We'll email your prescription for painkillers to your pharmacist. Phone them before picking them up. Okay?

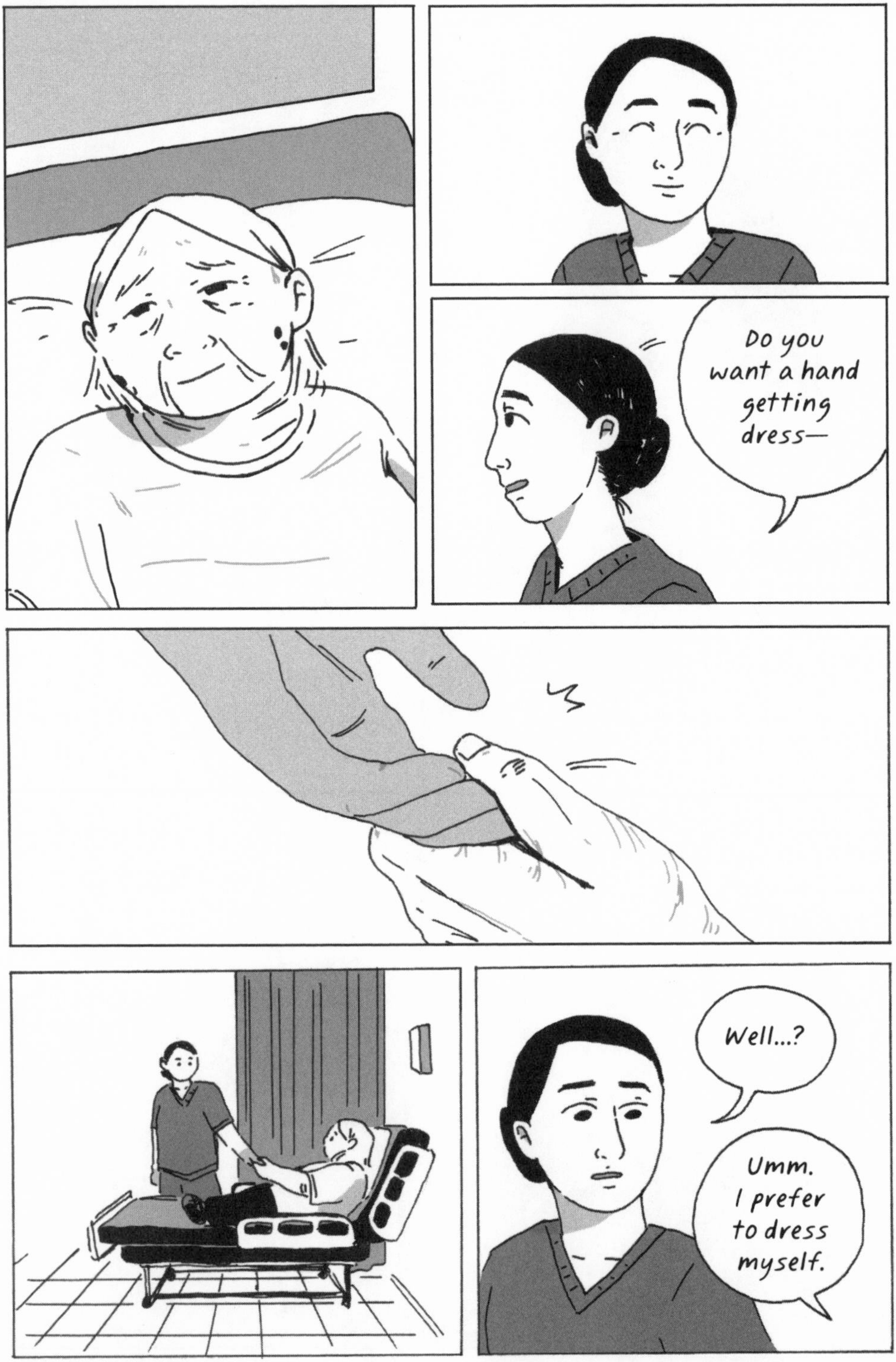
Do you want a hand getting dress—
Well...?
Umm. I prefer to dress myself.

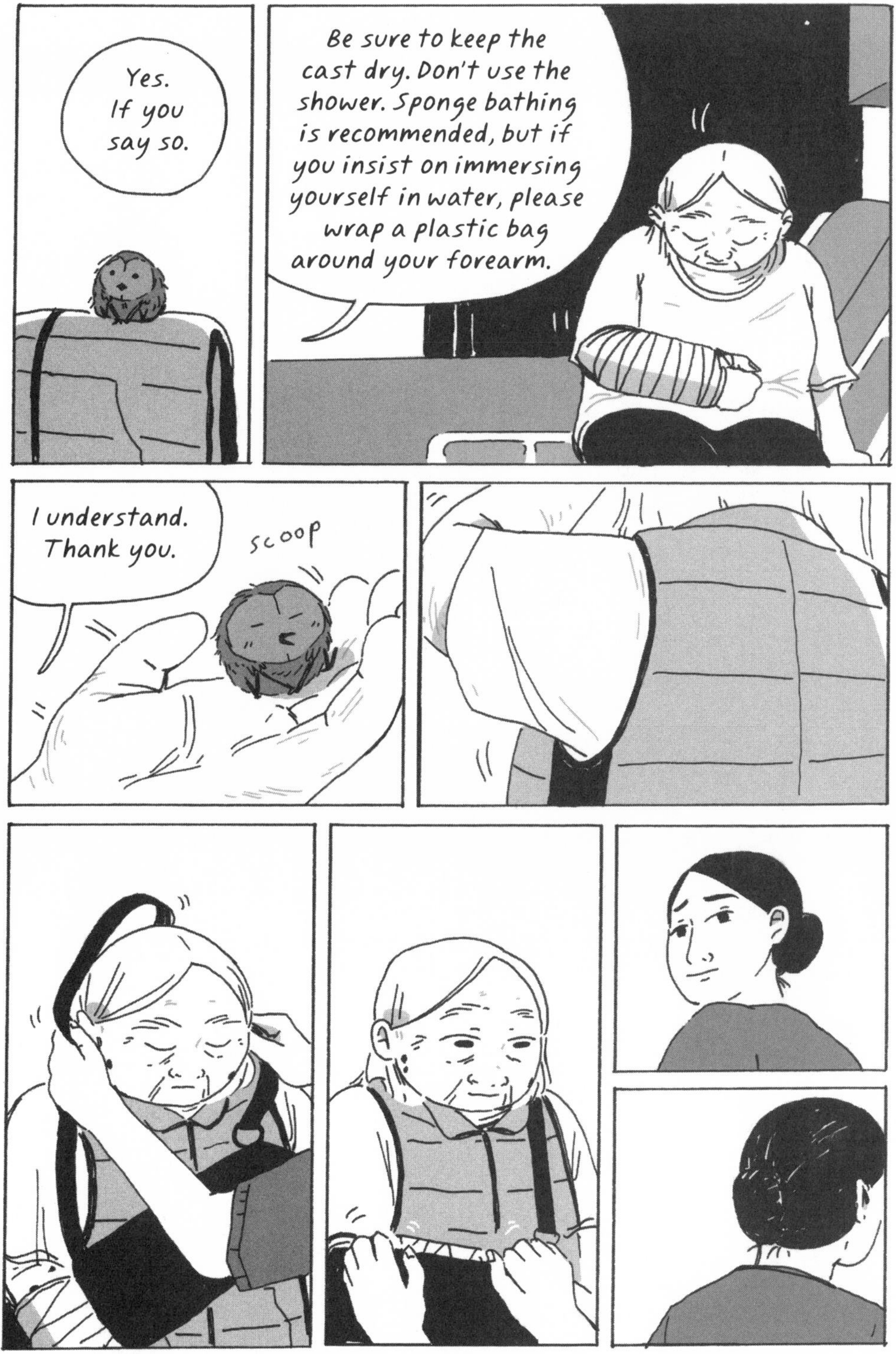
Yes. If you say so.
Be sure to keep the cast dry. Don't use the shower. Sponge bathing is recommended, but if you insist on immersing yourself in water, please wrap a plastic bag around your forearm.
I understand. Thank you.
scoop

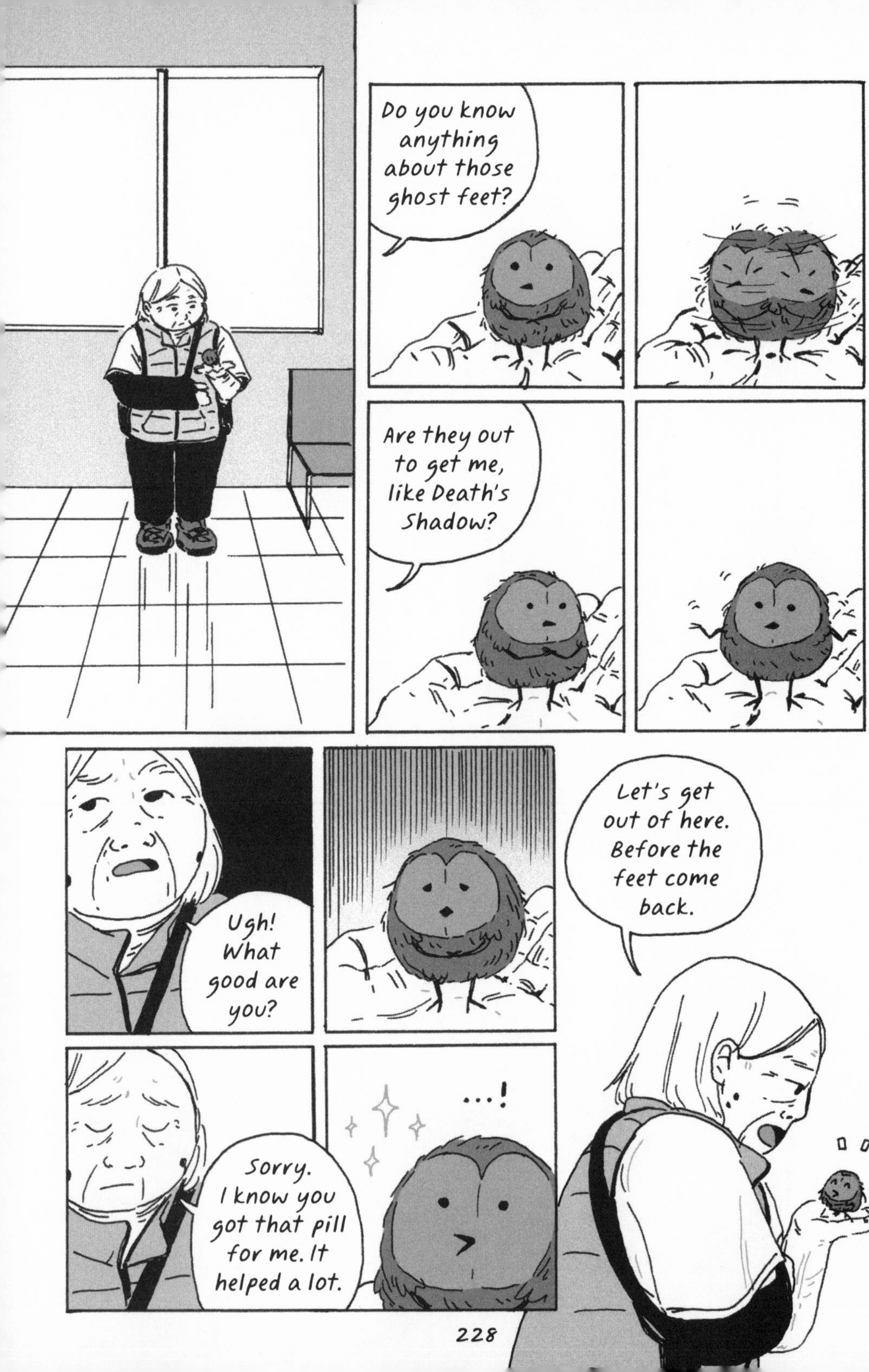
Do you know anything about those ghost feet?
Are they out to get me, like Death's Shadow?
Ugh! What good are you?
Let's get out of here. Before the feet come back.
Sorry. I know you got that pill for me. It helped a lot.
...!

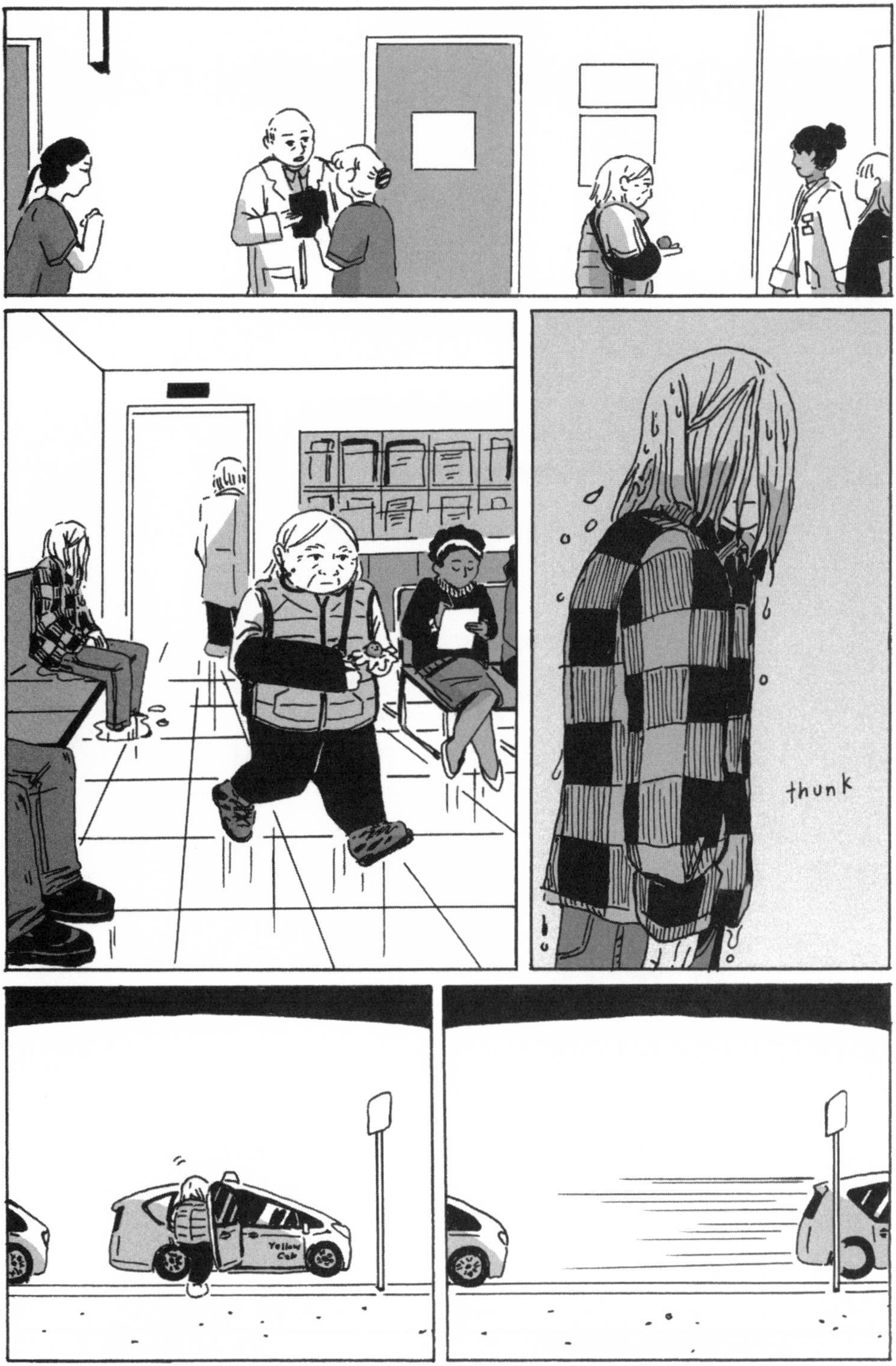
thunk
Yellow Cab

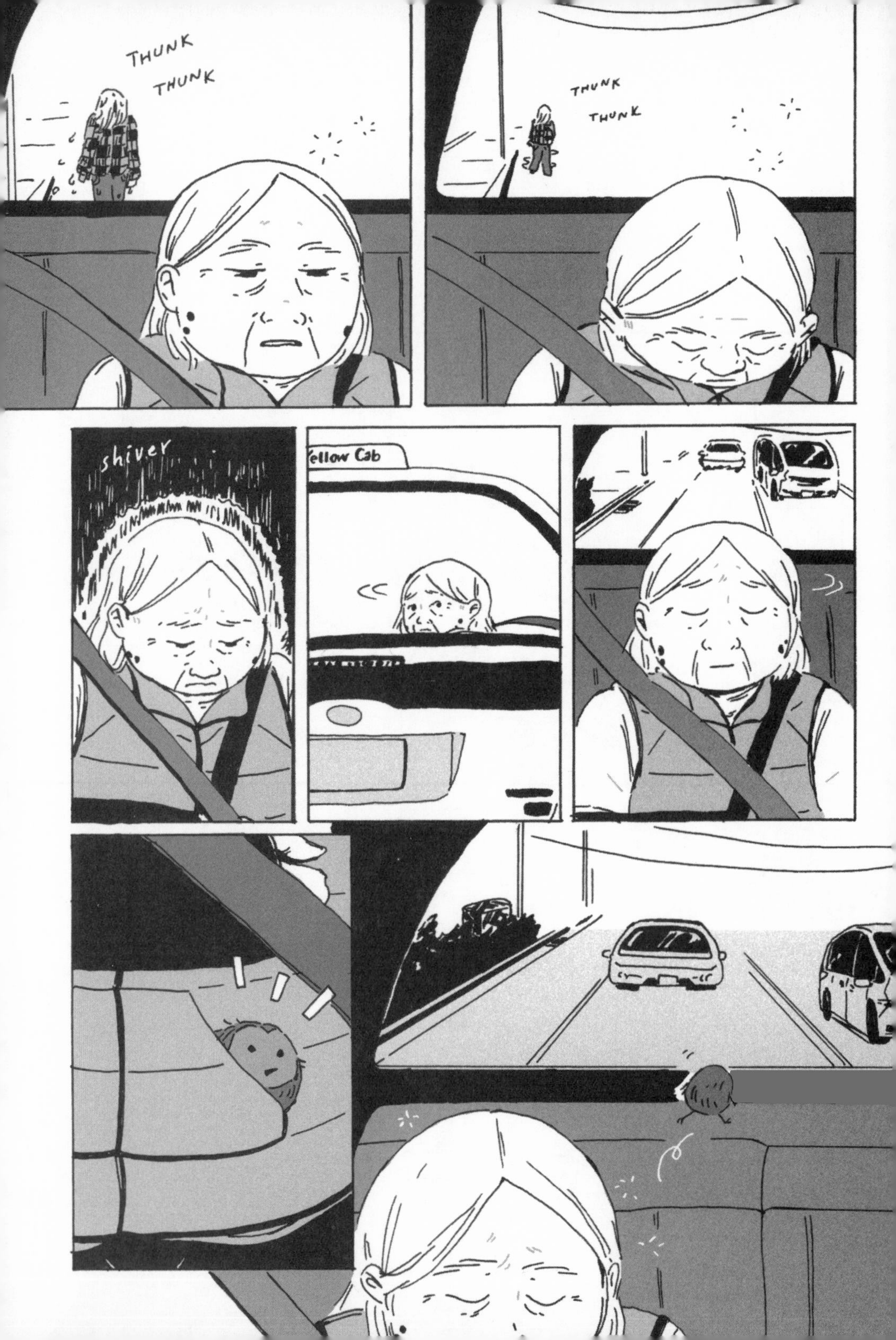
THUNK
THUNK
THUNK
THUNK
shiver
Yellow Cab

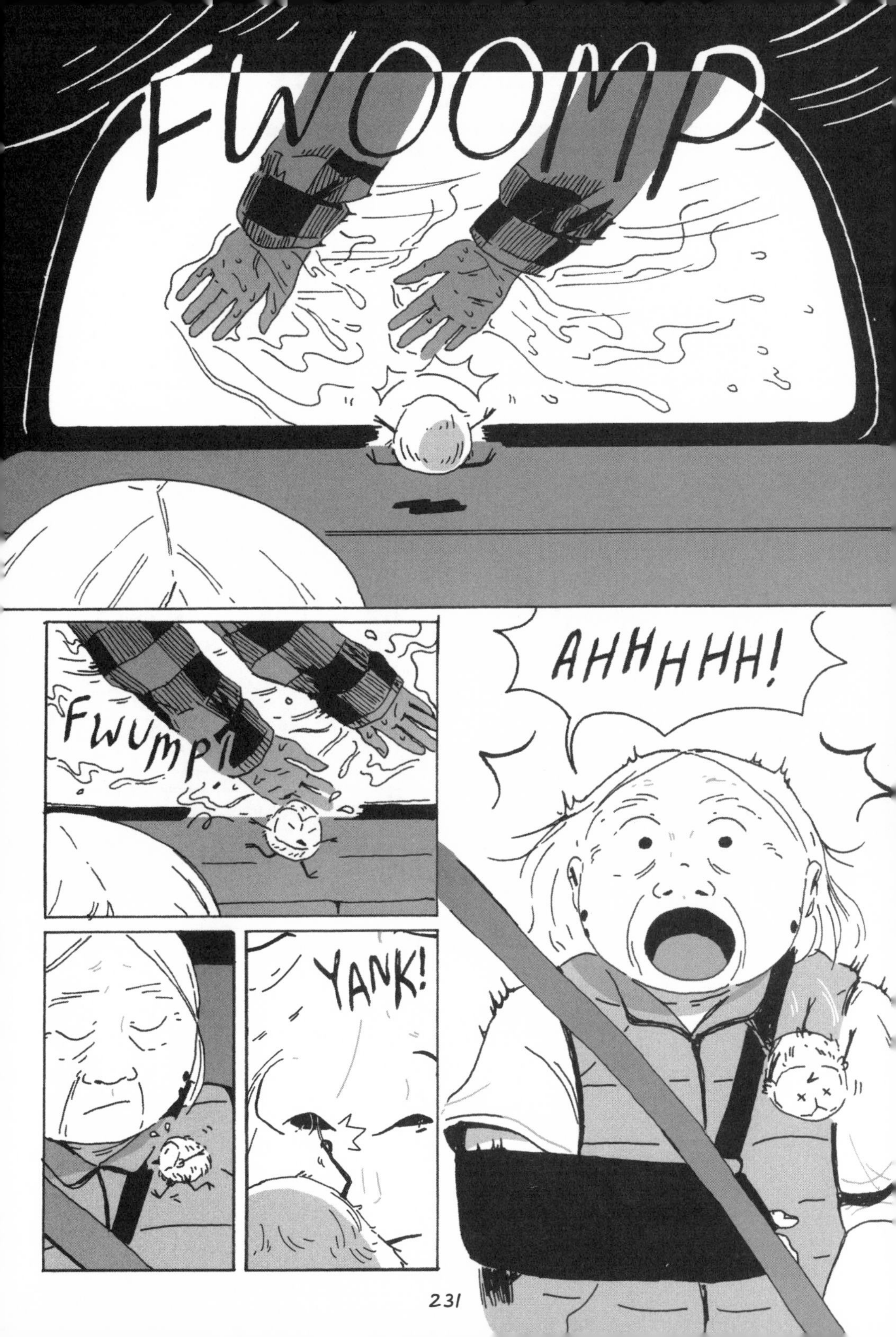
FWOOMP
FWUMP!
AHHHHHH!
YANK!

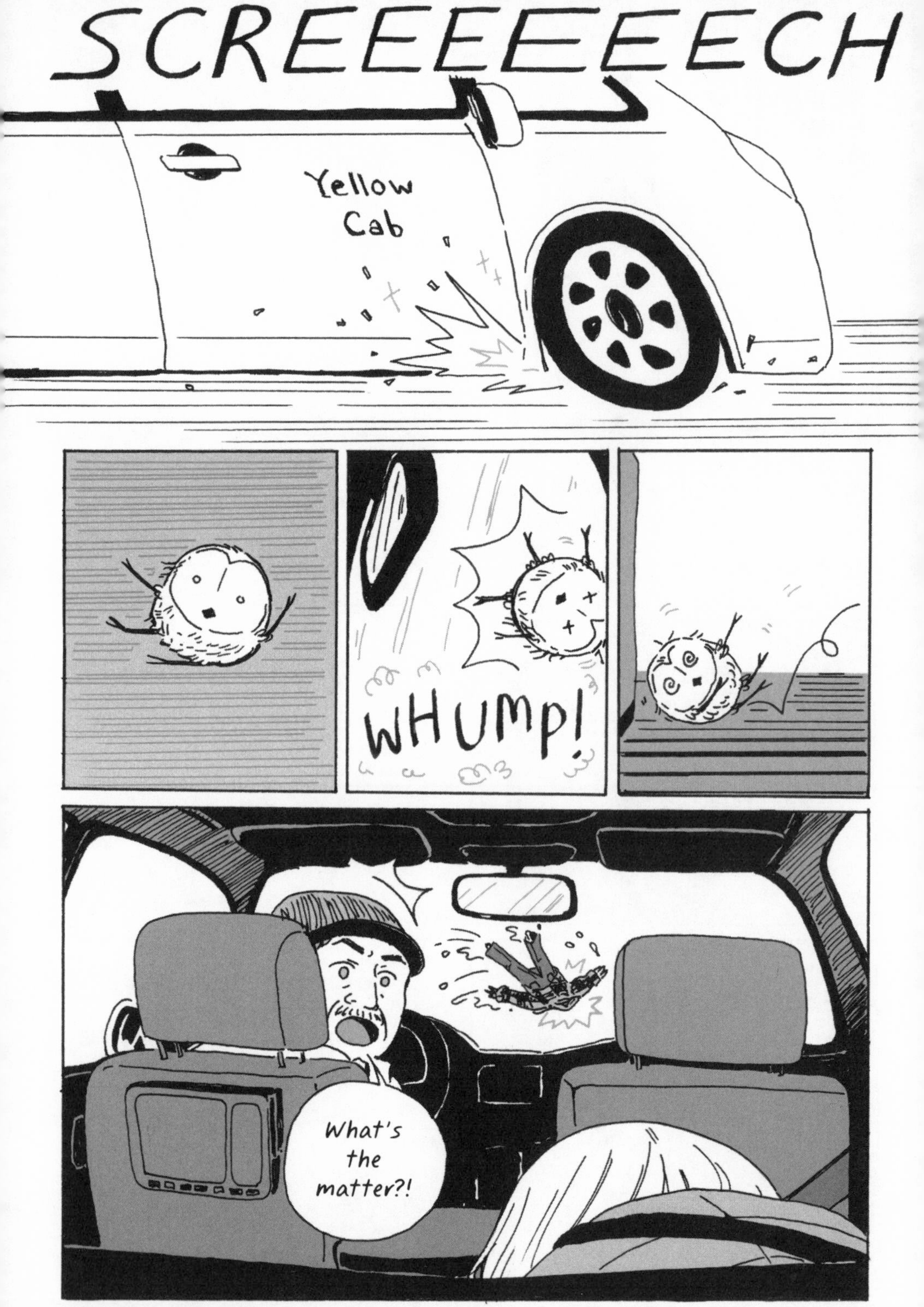
SCREEEEEEECH
Yellow Cab
WHUMP!
What's the matter?!

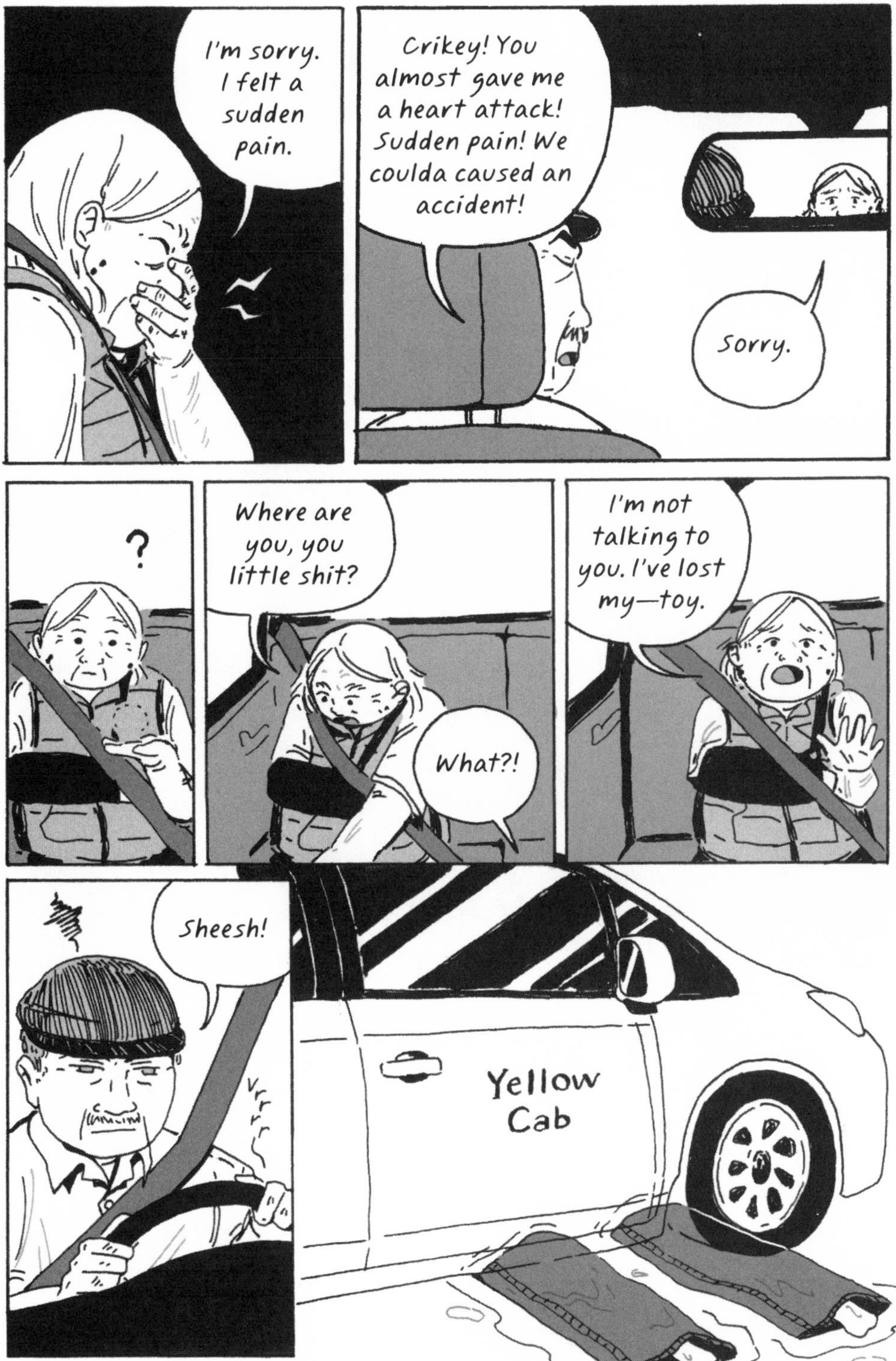
I'm sorry. I felt a sudden pain.
Crikey! You almost gave me a heart attack! Sudden pain! We coulda caused an accident!
Sorry.
?
Where are you, you little shit?
What?!
I'm not talking to you. I've lost my—toy.
Sheesh!
Vrrrr
Yellow Cab

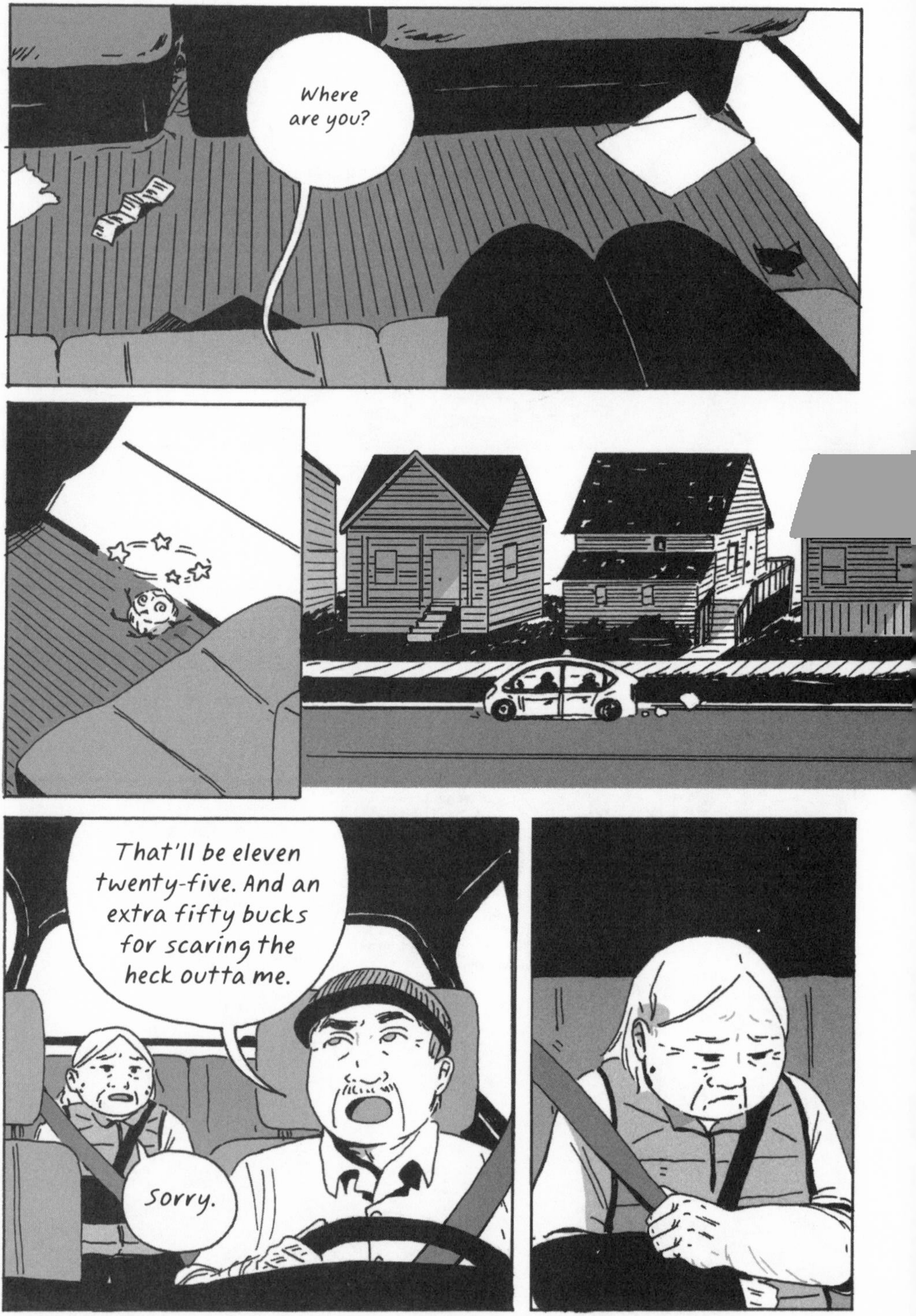
Where are you?
That'll be eleven twenty-five. And an extra fifty bucks for scaring the heck outta me.
Sorry.

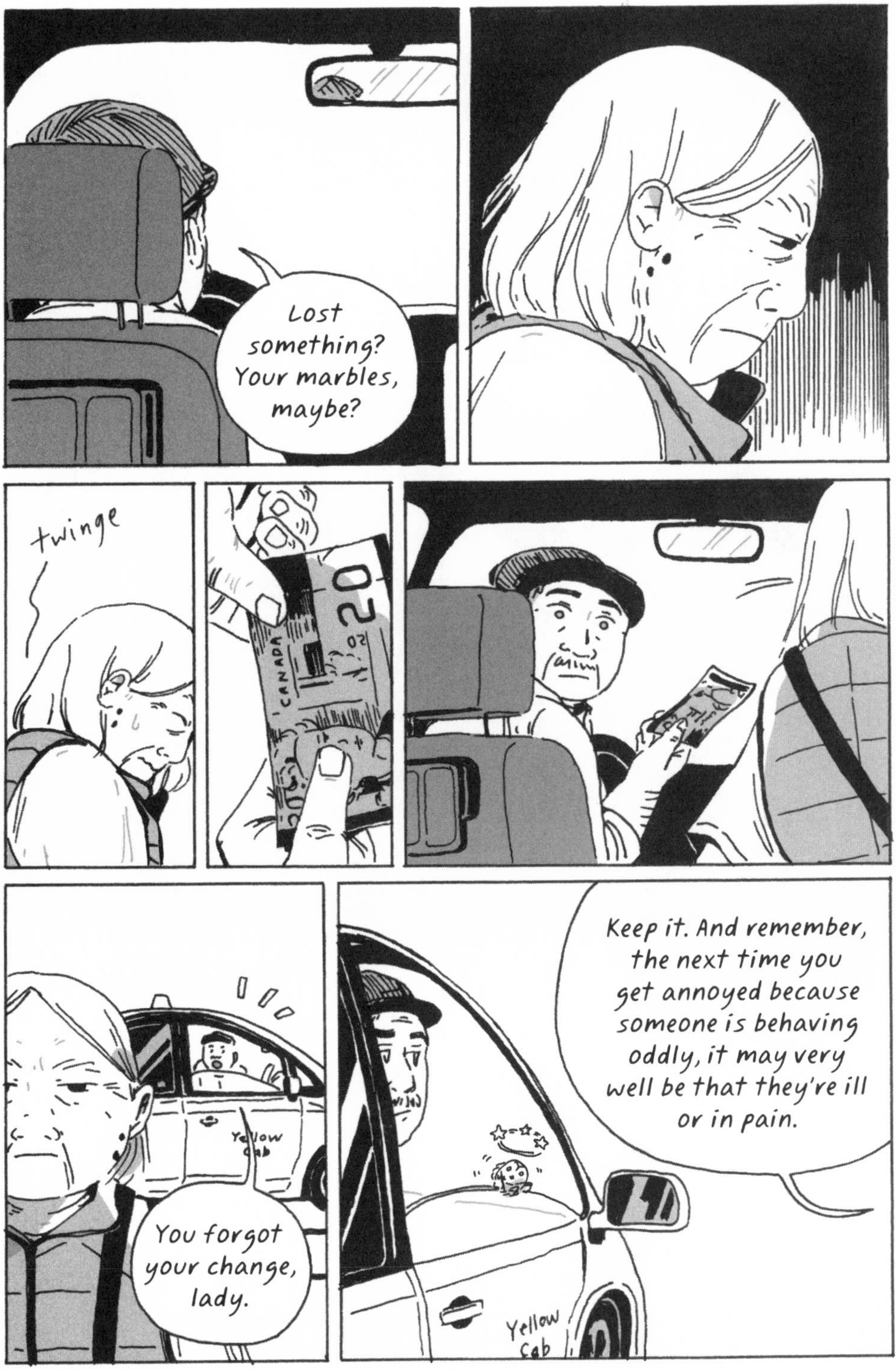
Lost something? Your marbles, maybe?
twinge
CANADA
20
Keep it. And remember, the next time you get annoyed because someone is behaving oddly, it may very well be that they're ill or in pain.
Yellow Cab
You forgot your change, lady.
Yellow Cab

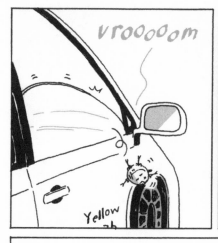

vrooooom

Yellow

FWOOMP!

lick   lick
lick

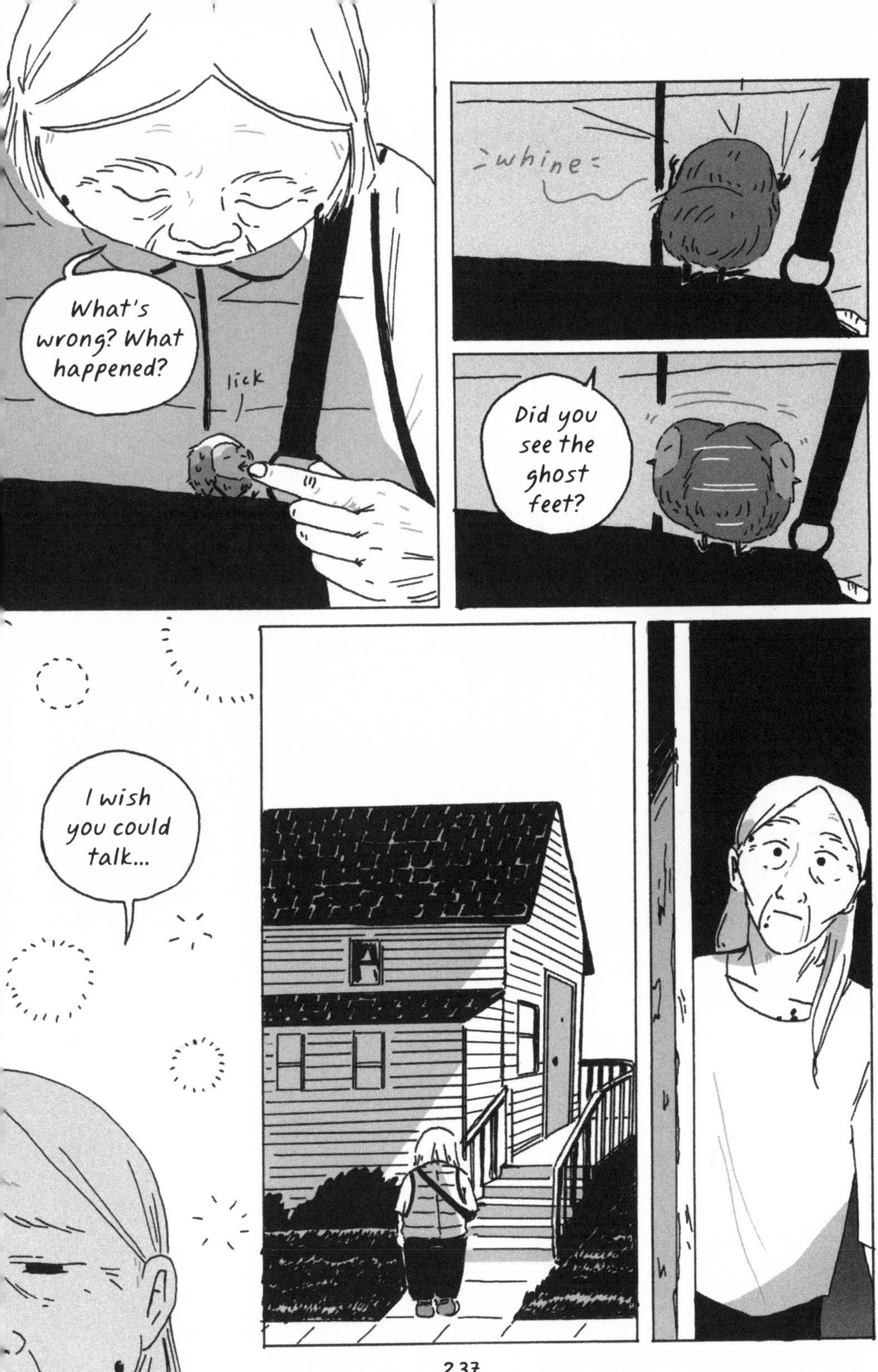
What's wrong? What happened?
lick
whine
Did you see the ghost feet?
I wish you could talk...

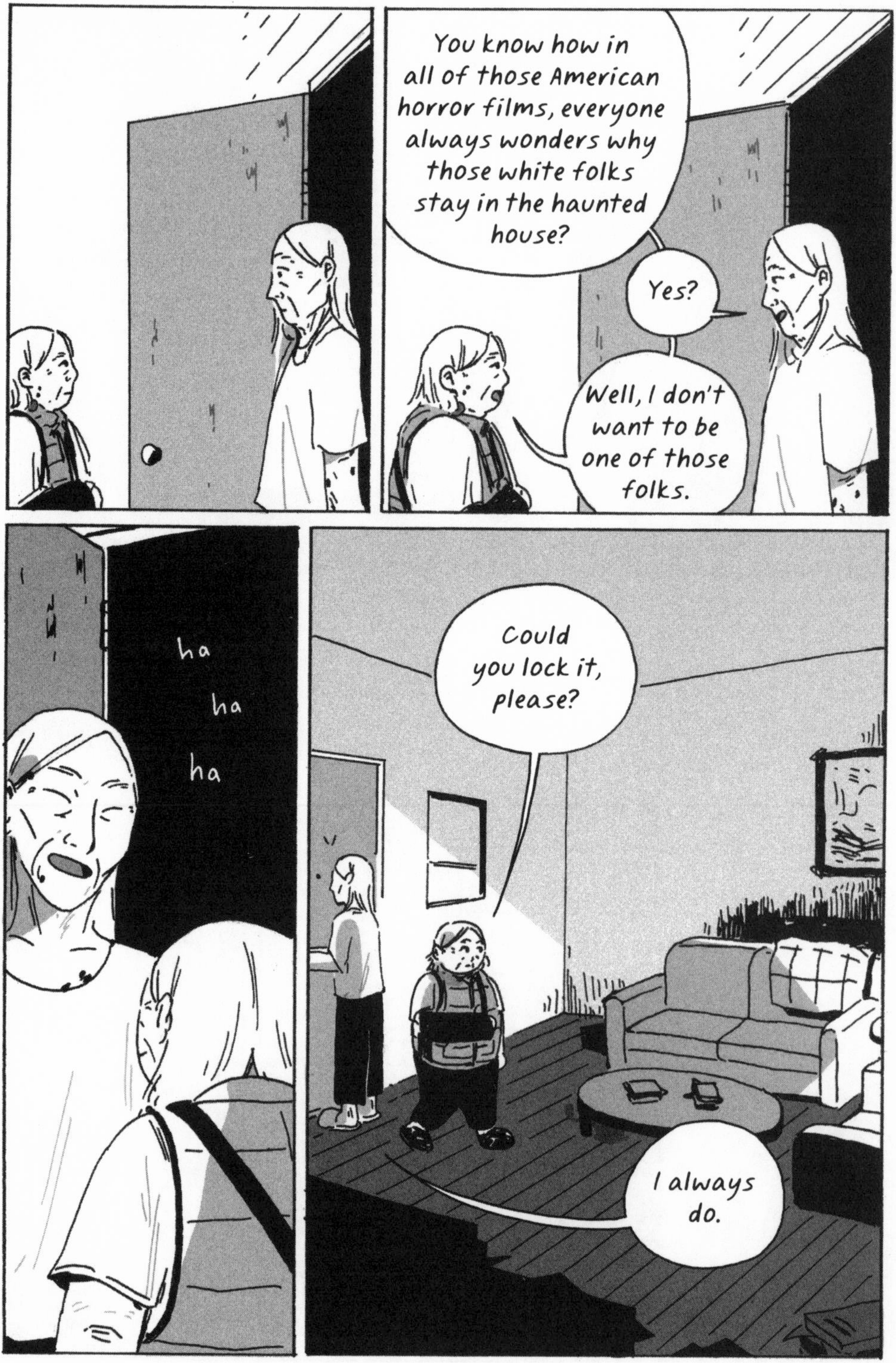
You know how in all of those American horror films, everyone always wonders why those white folks stay in the haunted house?
Yes?
Well, I don't want to be one of those folks.
ha
ha
ha
Could you lock it, please?
I always do.

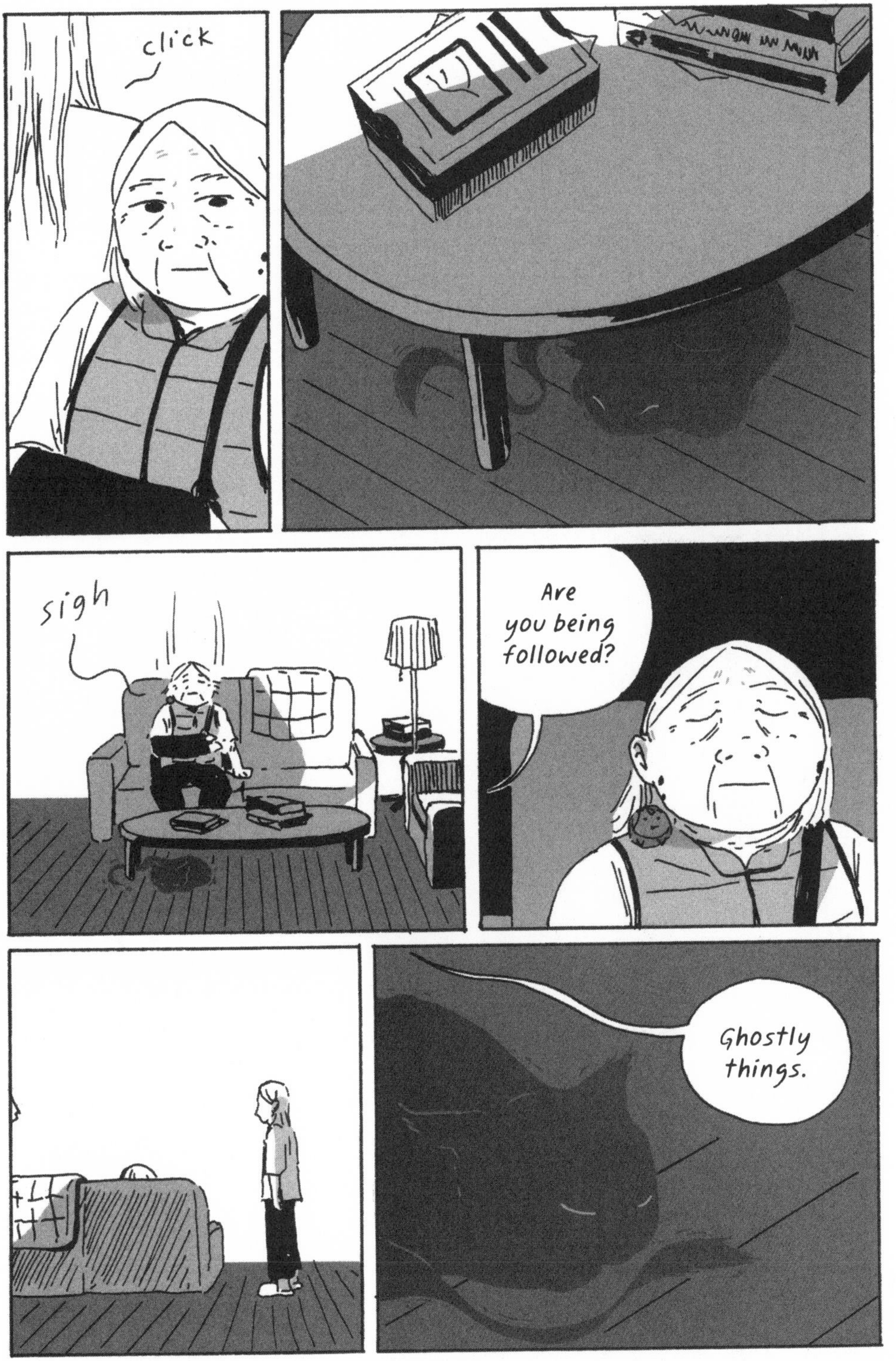
click
sigh
Are you being followed?
Ghostly things.

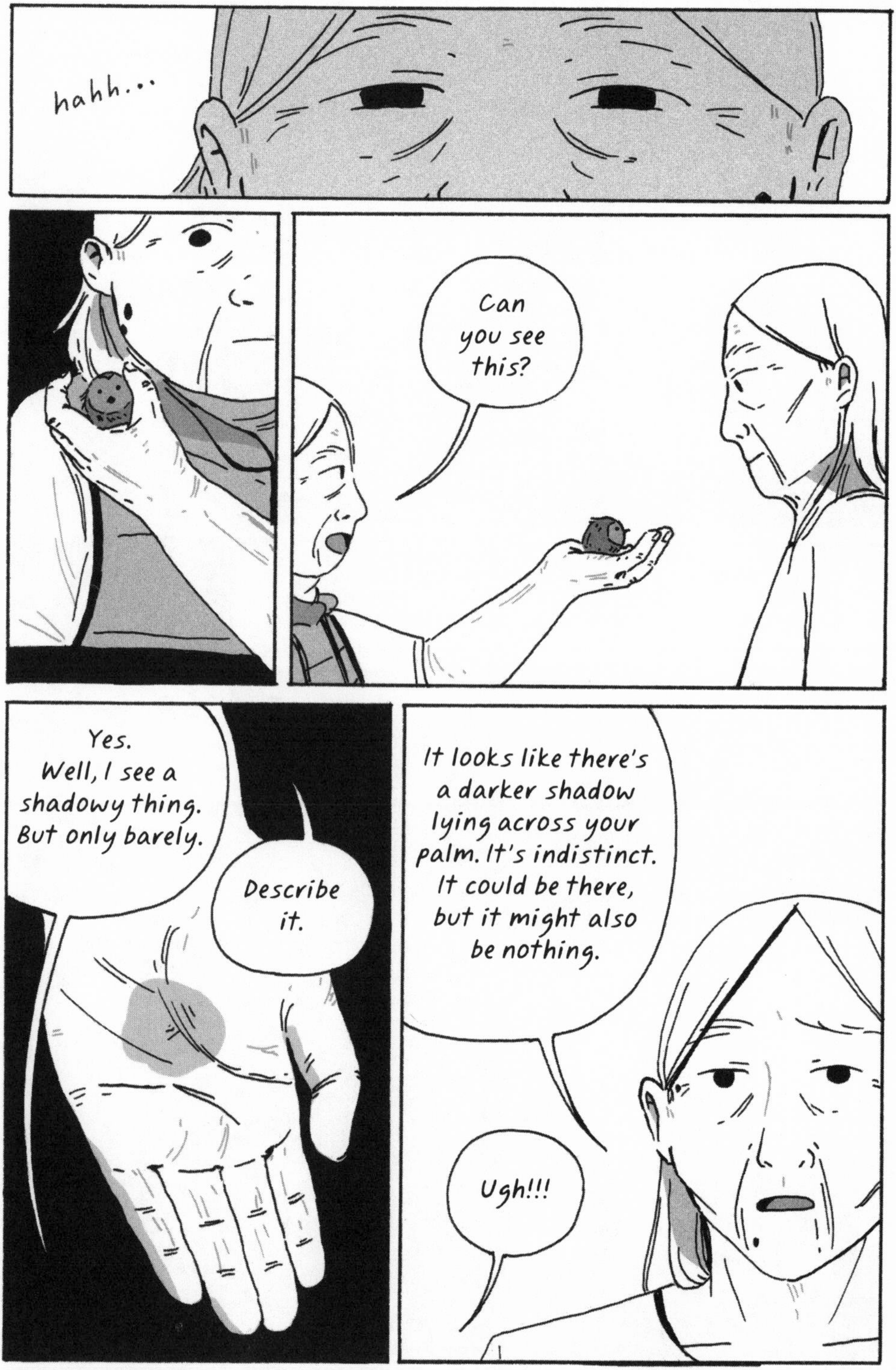
hahh...
Can you see this?
Yes. Well, I see a shadowy thing. But only barely.
Describe it.
It looks like there's a darker shadow lying across your palm. It's indistinct. It could be there, but it might also be nothing.
Ugh!!!

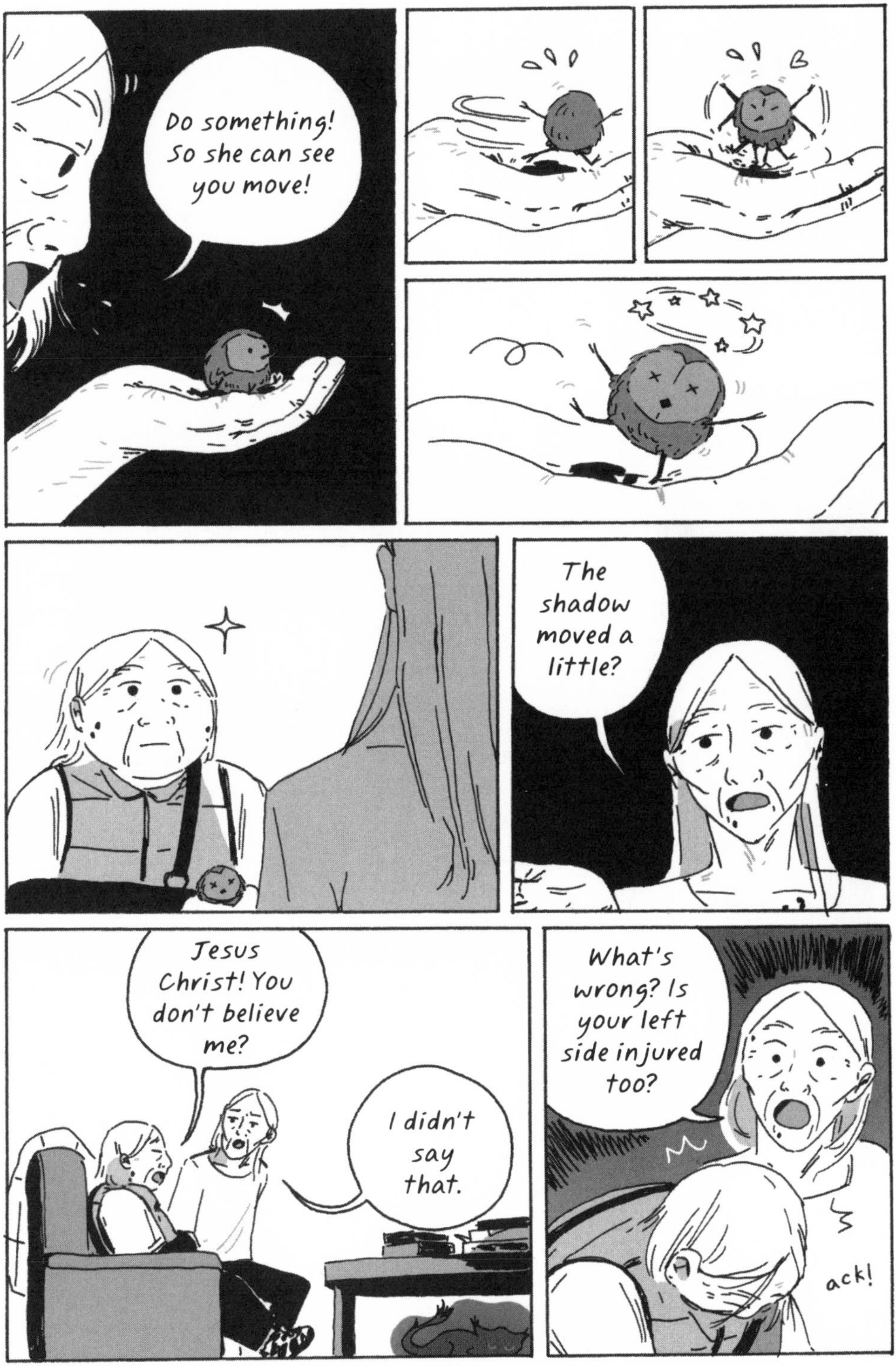
Do something! So she can see you move!
The shadow moved a little?
Jesus Christ! You don't believe me?
I didn't say that.
What's wrong? Is your left side injured too?
ack!

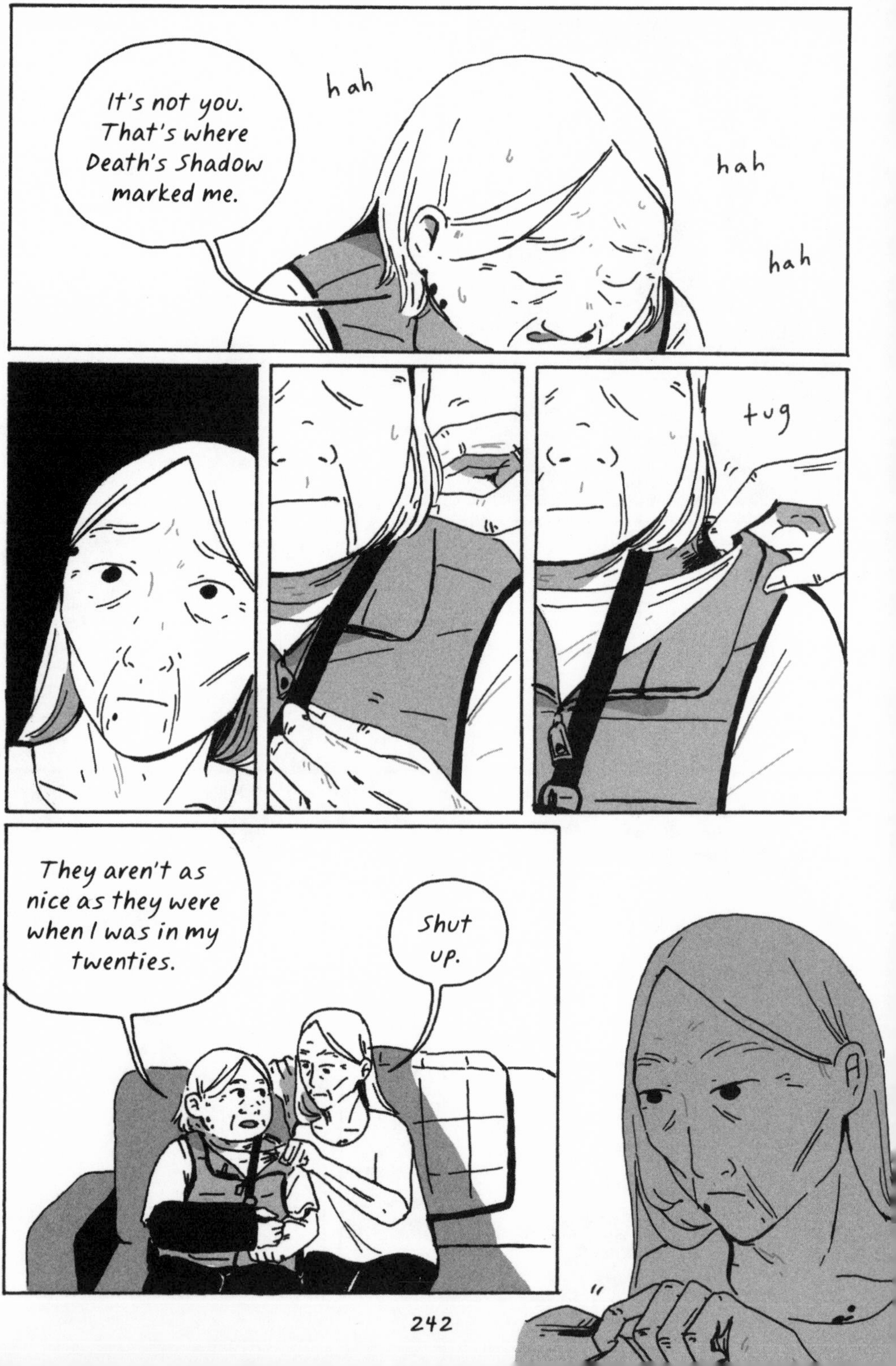
It's not you. That's where Death's Shadow marked me.
hah
hah
hah
tug
They aren't as nice as they were when I was in my twenties.
Shut up.

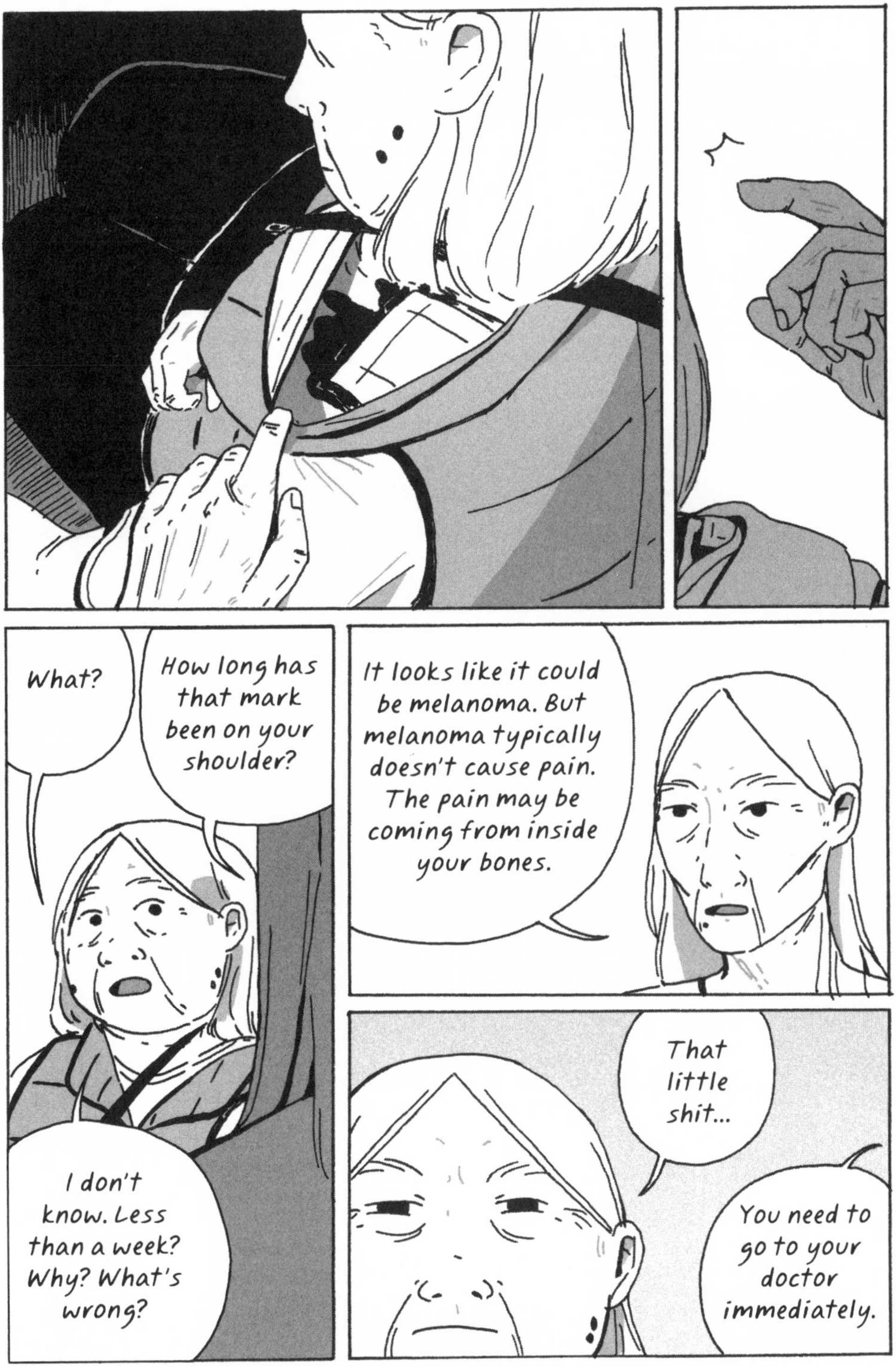
What?
How long has that mark been on your shoulder?
I don't know. Less than a week? Why? What's wrong?
It looks like it could be melanoma. But melanoma typically doesn't cause pain. The pain may be coming from inside your bones.
That little shit...
You need to go to your doctor immediately.

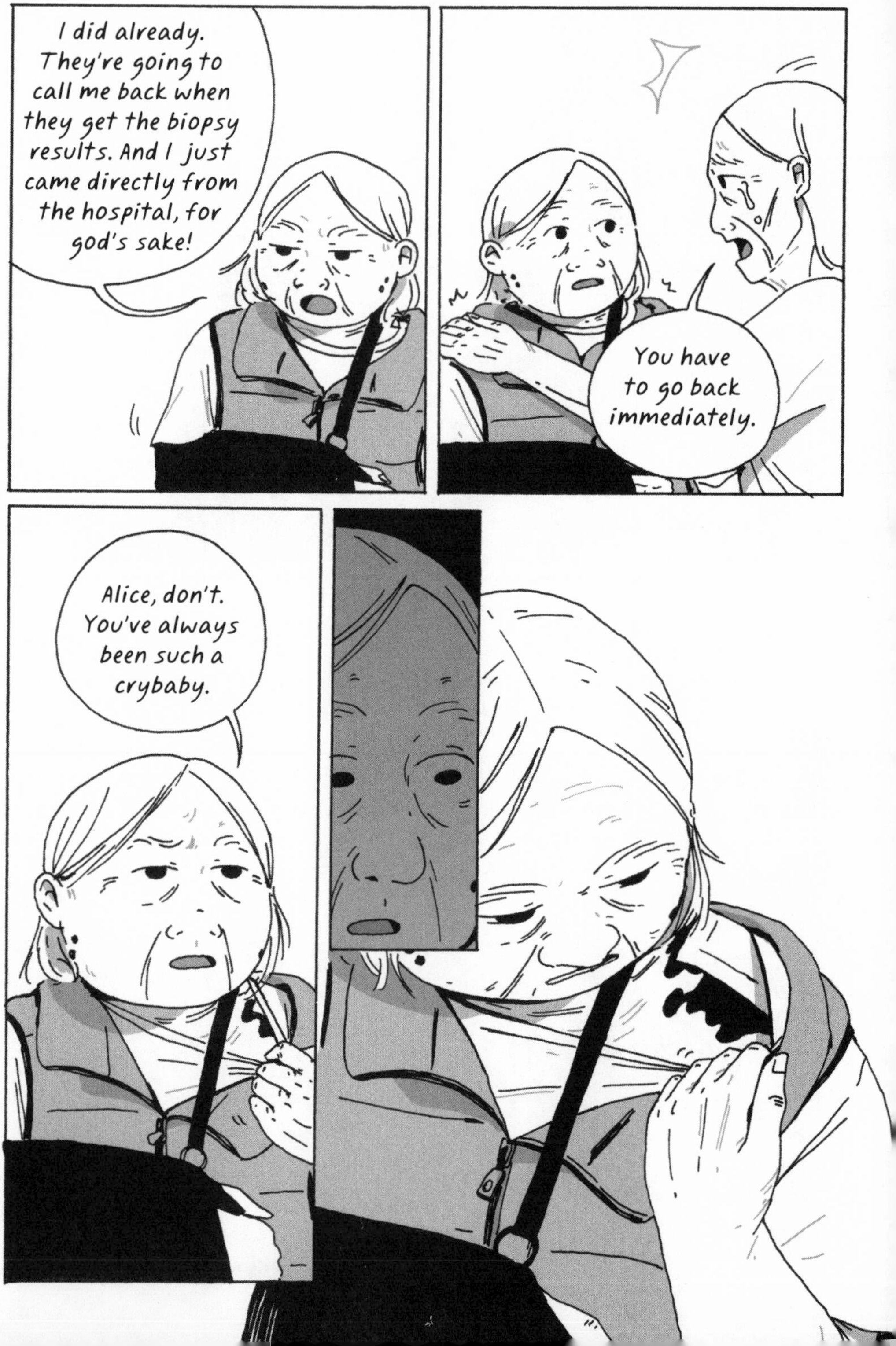
I did already. They're going to call me back when they get the biopsy results. And I just came directly from the hospital, for god's sake!
You have to go back immediately.
Alice, don't. You've always been such a crybaby.

Chapter Thirteen

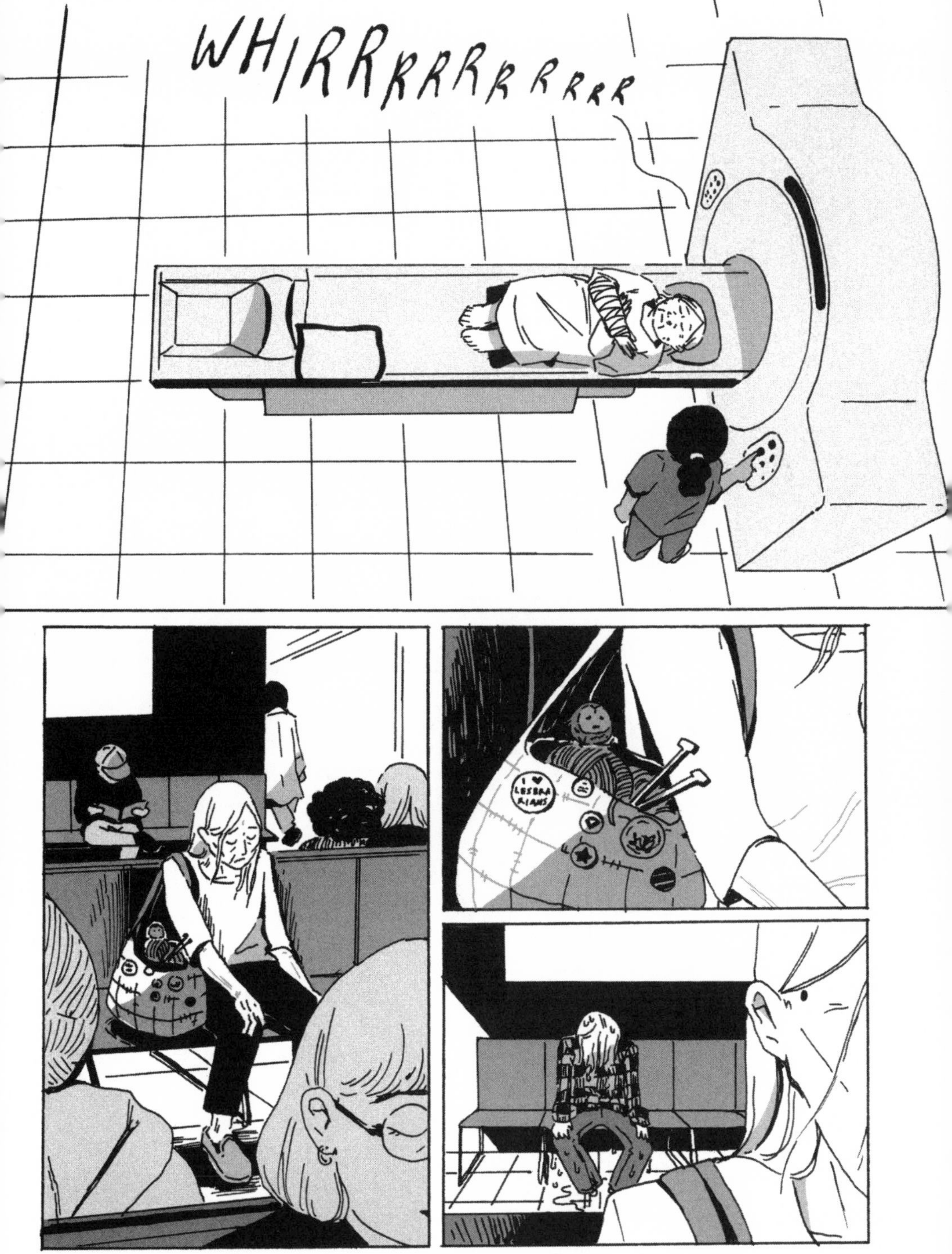
WHIRRRRRRRRRRR
I ♥ LESBRARIANS

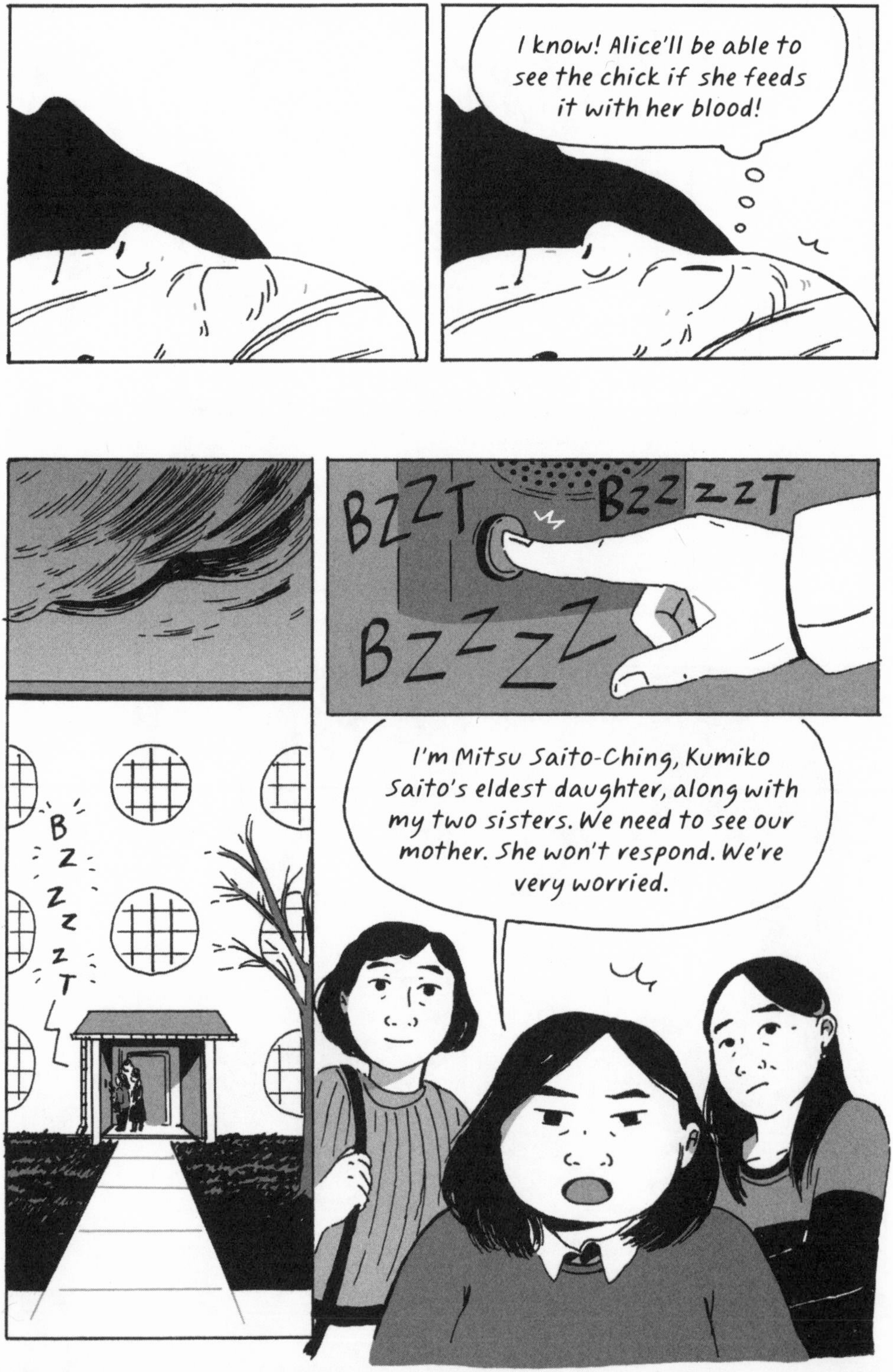
I know! Alice'll be able to see the chick if she feeds it with her blood!
BZZT
BzzzzzT
BZZZZ
B Z Z Z Z T
I'm Mitsu Saito-Ching, Kumiko Saito's eldest daughter, along with my two sisters. We need to see our mother. She won't respond. We're very worried.

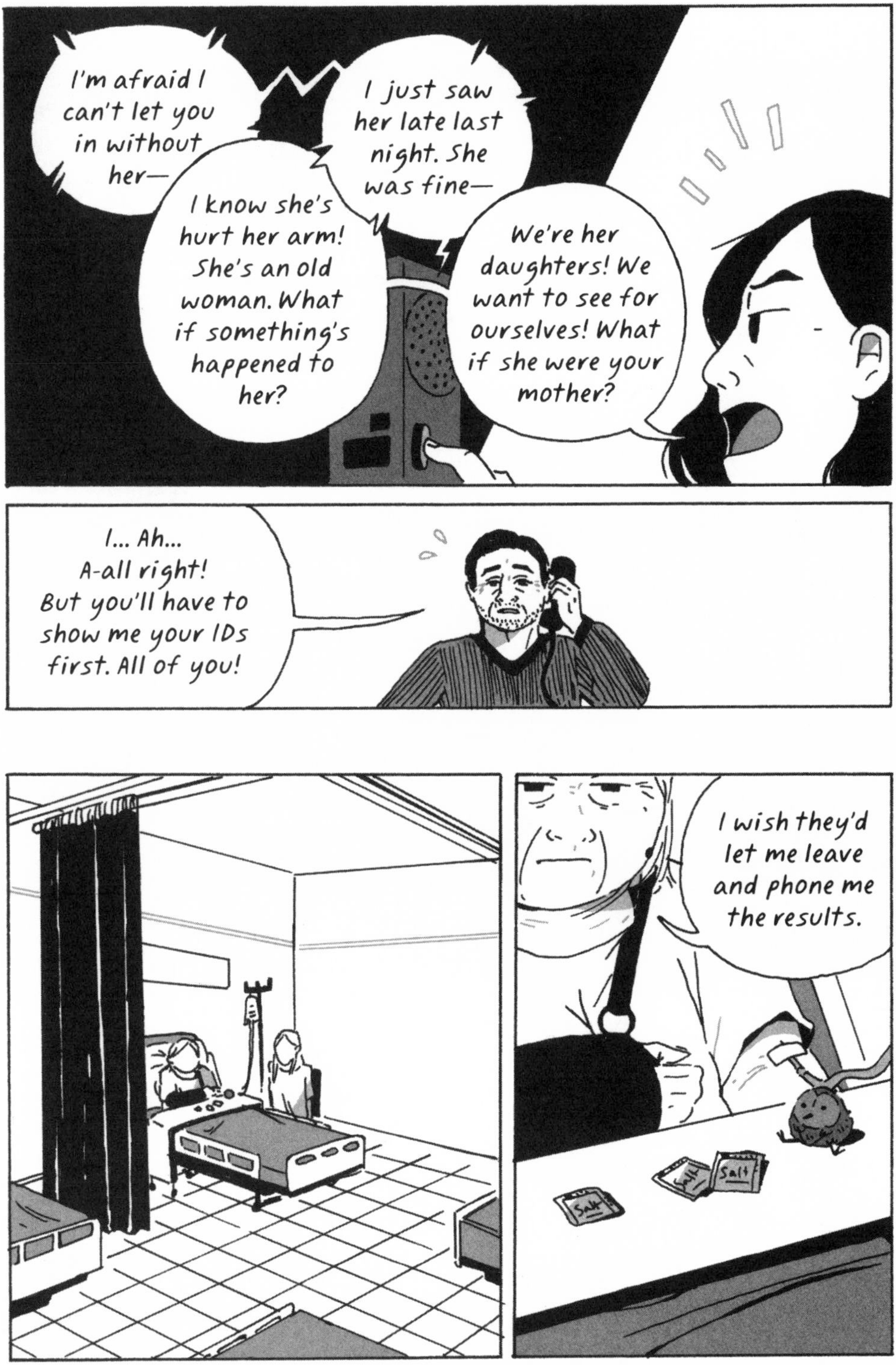
I'm afraid I can't let you in without her—
I just saw her late last night. She was fine—
I know she's hurt her arm! She's an old woman. What if something's happened to her?
We're her daughters! We want to see for ourselves! What if she were your mother?
I... Ah... A-all right! But you'll have to show me your IDs first. All of you!
I wish they'd let me leave and phone me the results.
Salt
Salt
Salt

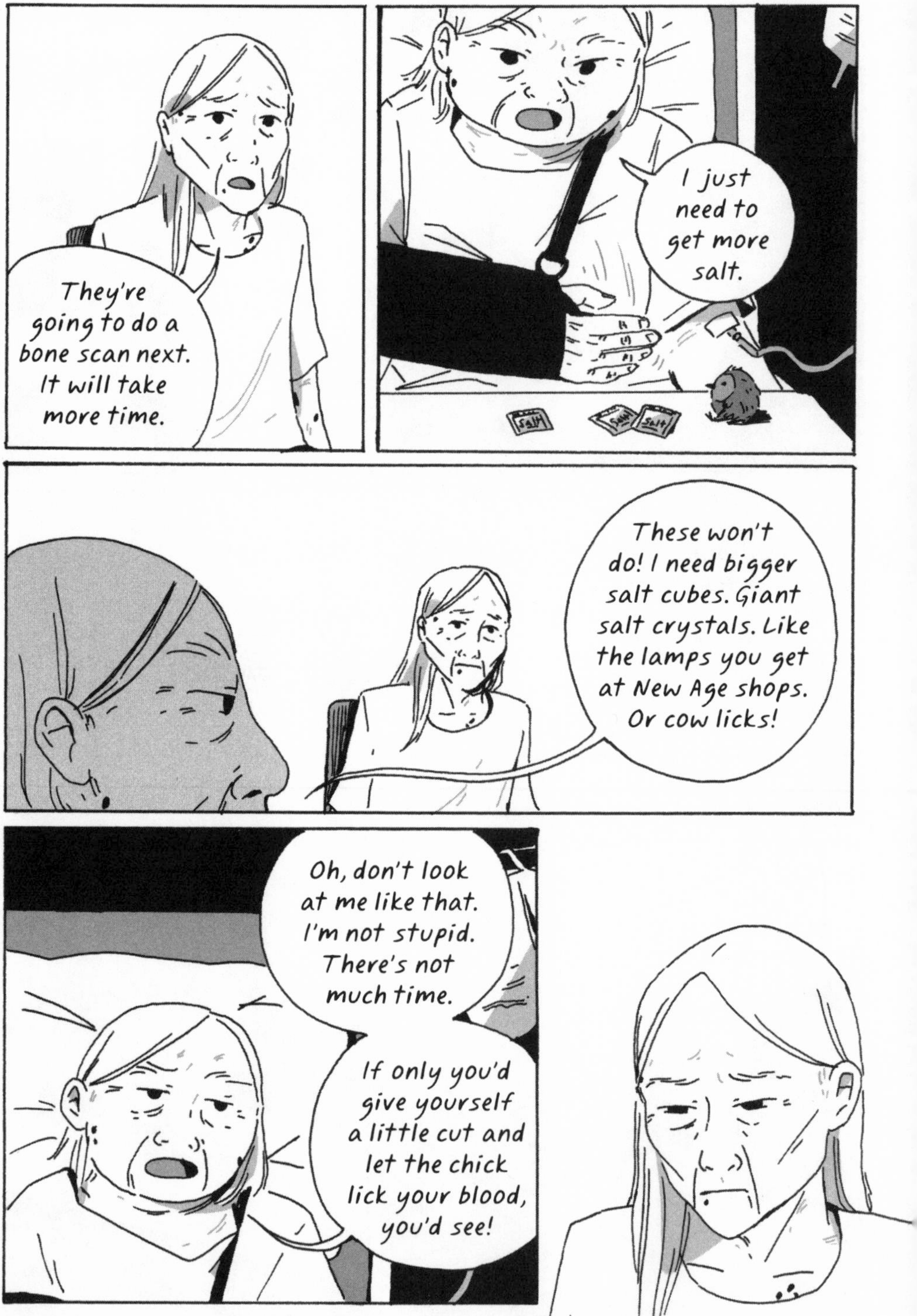
They're going to do a bone scan next. It will take more time.
I just need to get more salt.
These won't do! I need bigger salt cubes. Giant salt crystals. Like the lamps you get at New Age shops. Or cow licks!
Oh, don't look at me like that. I'm not stupid. There's not much time.
If only you'd give yourself a little cut and let the chick lick your blood, you'd see!

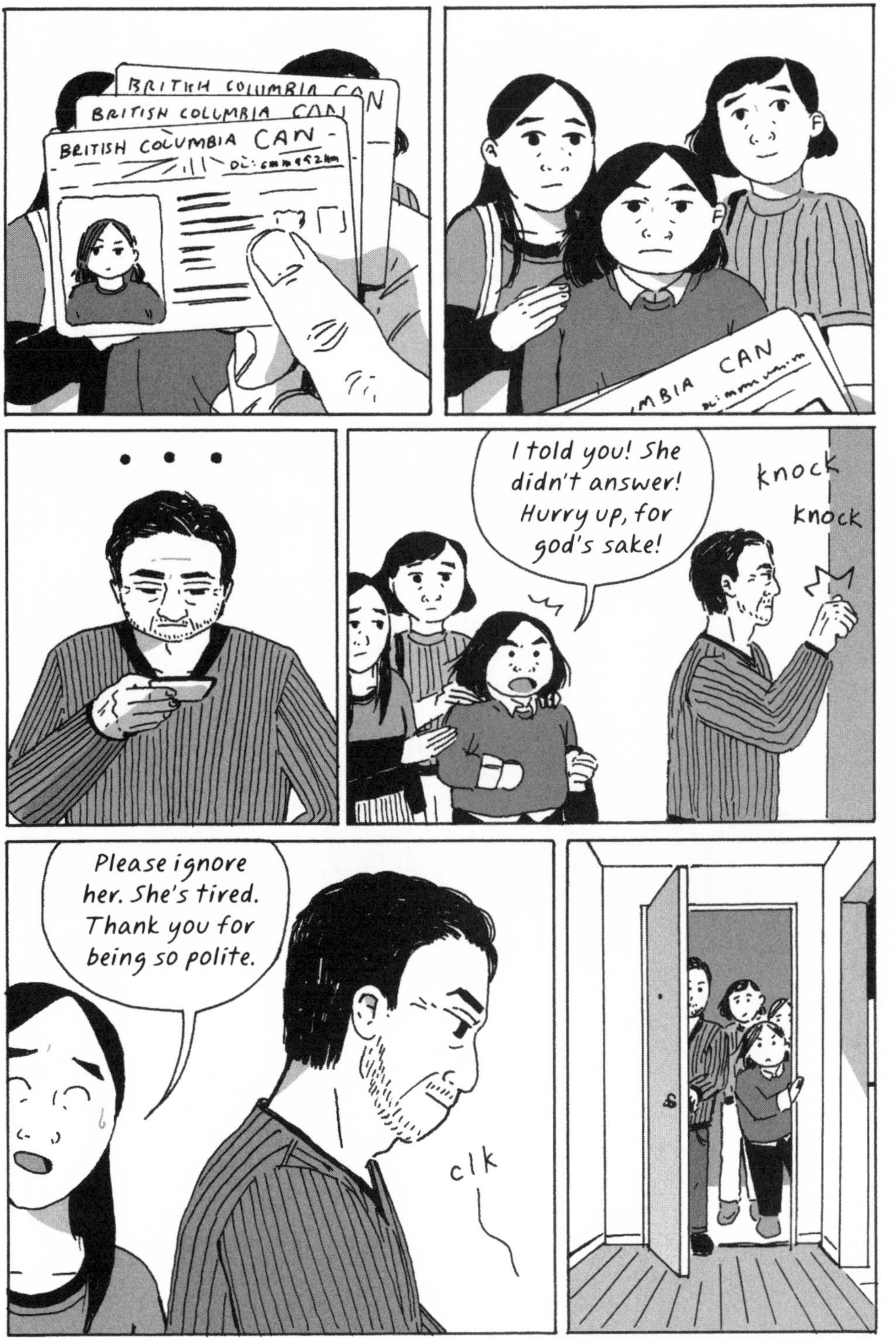
BRITISH COLUMBIA CAN
BRITISH COLUMBIA CAN
BRITISH COLUMBIA CAN
MBIA CAN
• • •
I told you! She didn't answer! Hurry up, for god's sake!
knock
knock
Please ignore her. She's tired. Thank you for being so polite.
clk

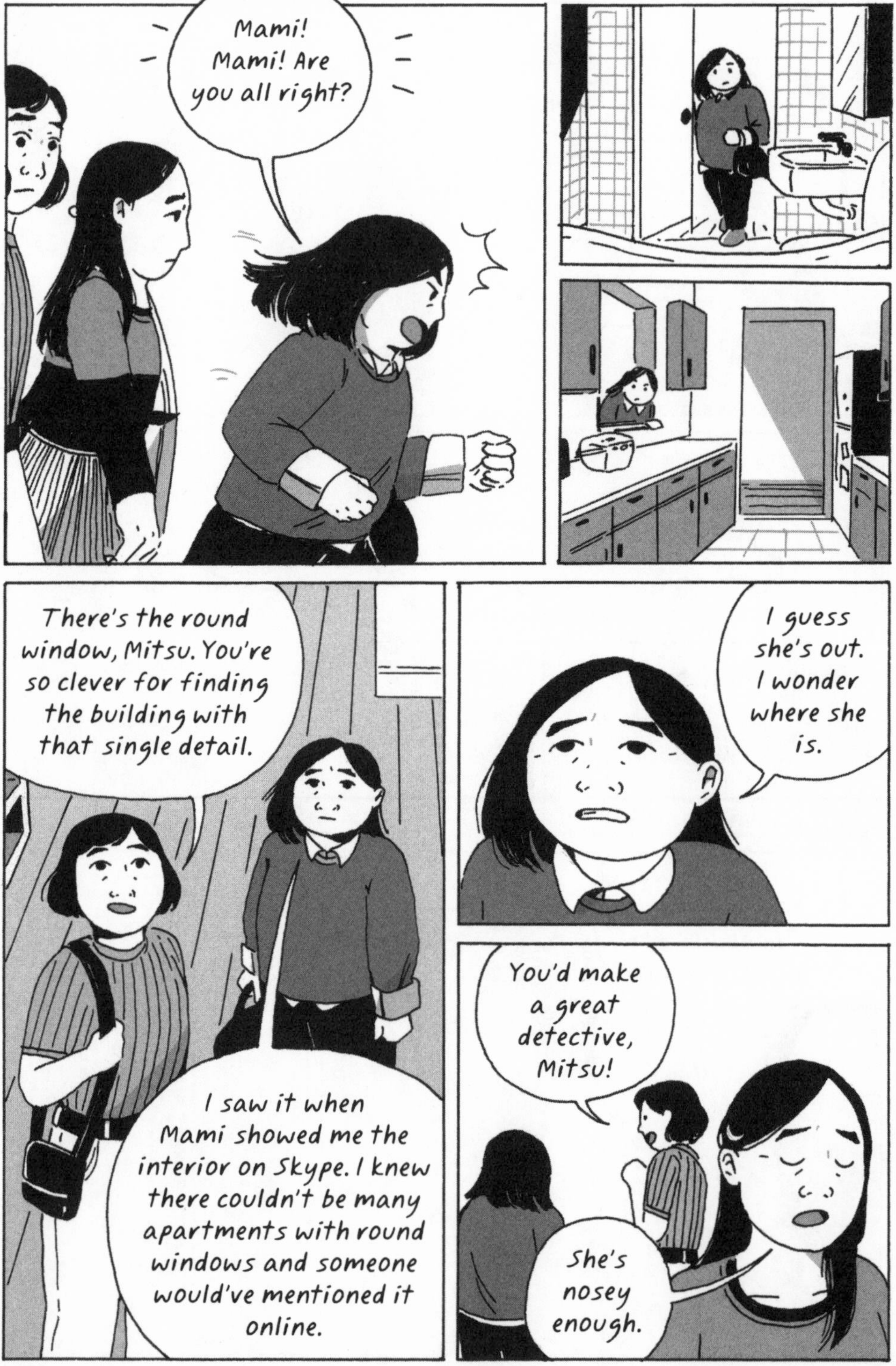
Mami!
Mami! Are you all right?
There's the round window, Mitsu. You're so clever for finding the building with that single detail.
I saw it when Mami showed me the interior on Skype. I knew there couldn't be many apartments with round windows and someone would've mentioned it online.
I guess she's out. I wonder where she is.
You'd make a great detective, Mitsu!
She's nosey enough.

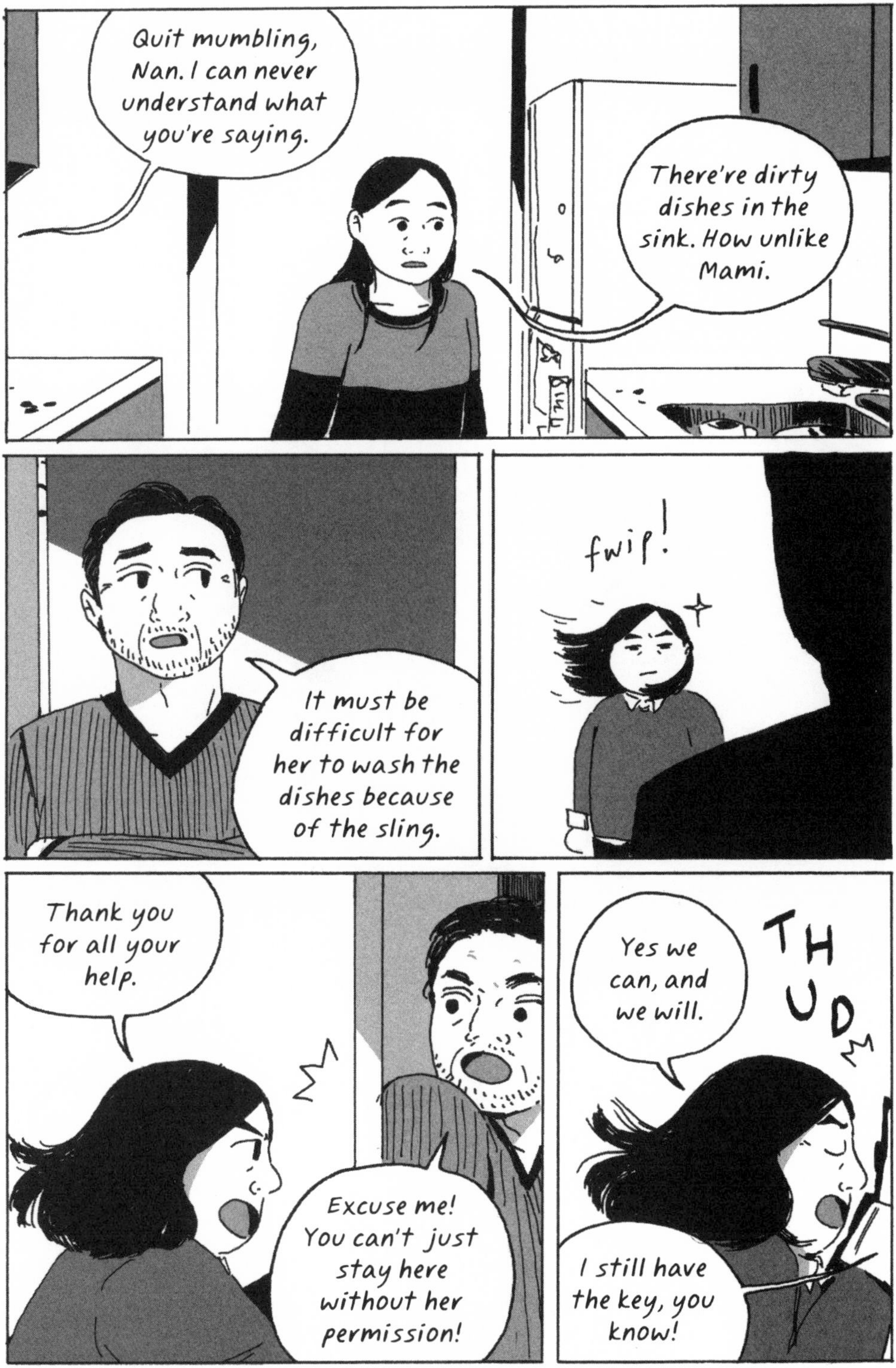
Quit mumbling, Nan. I can never understand what you're saying.
There're dirty dishes in the sink. How unlike Mami.
It must be difficult for her to wash the dishes because of the sling.
fwip!
Thank you for all your help.
Excuse me! You can't just stay here without her permission!
Yes we can, and we will.
THUD
I still have the key, you know!

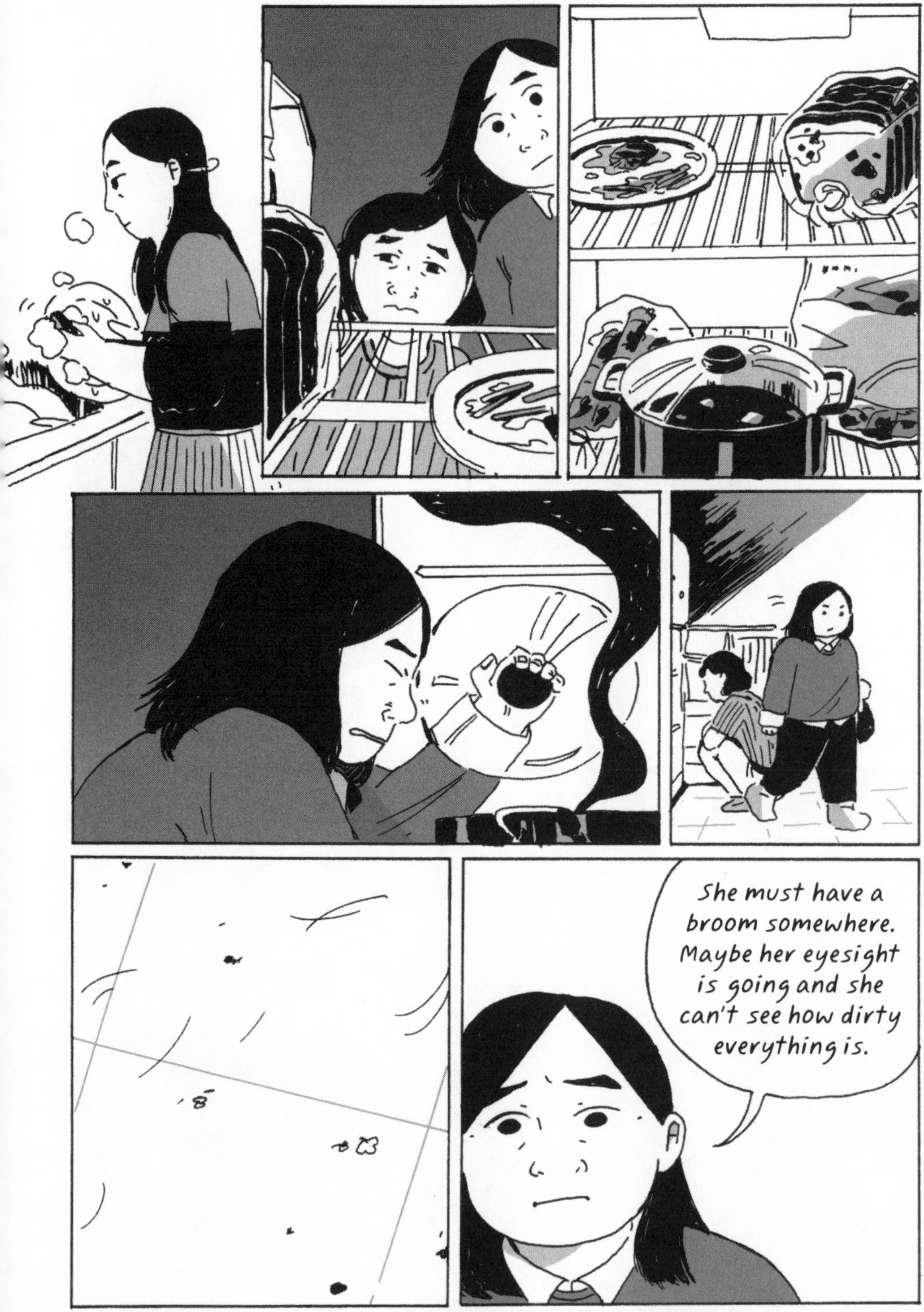
She must have a broom somewhere. Maybe her eyesight is going and she can't see how dirty everything is.

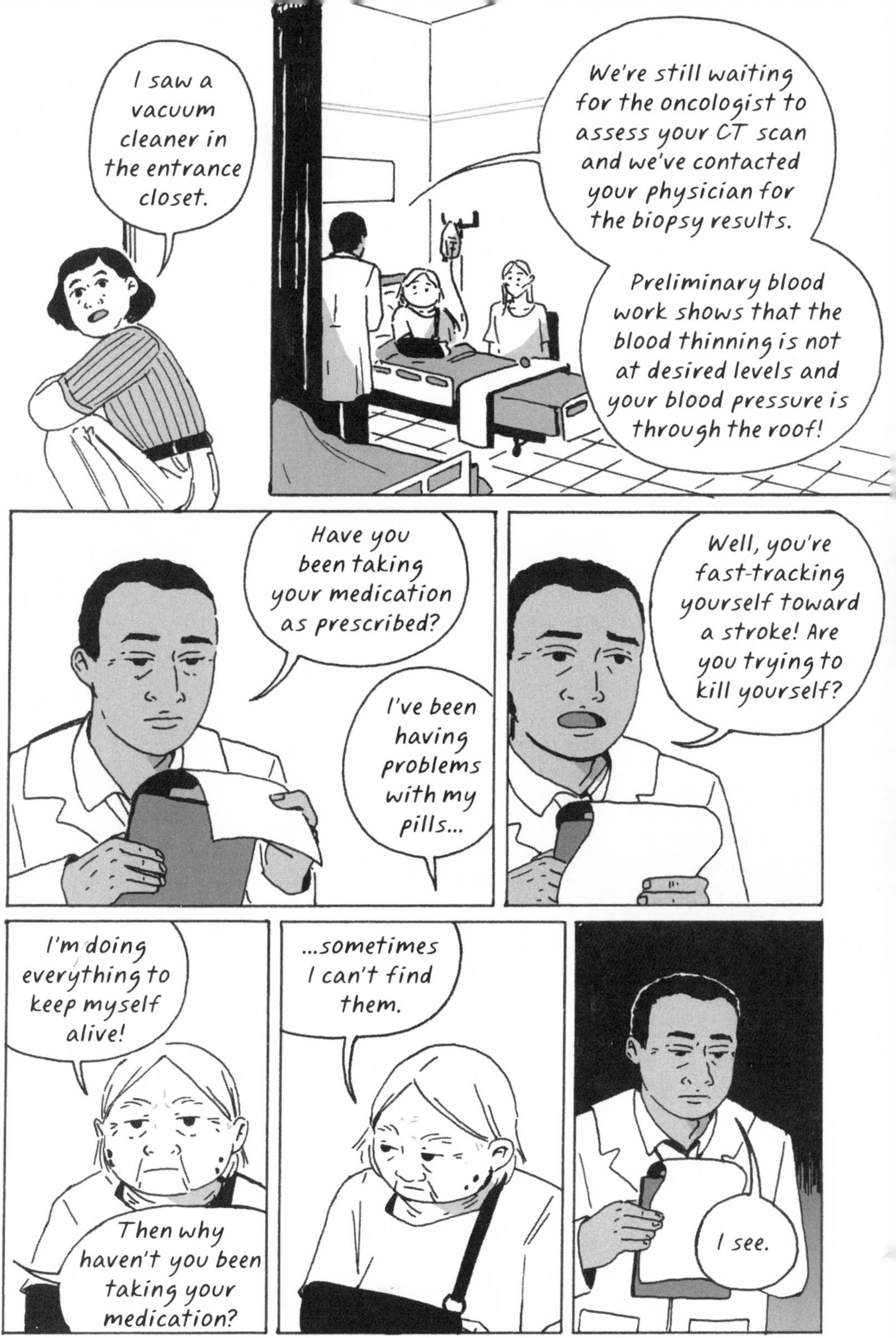
I saw a vacuum cleaner in the entrance closet.
We're still waiting for the oncologist to assess your CT scan and we've contacted your physician for the biopsy results.
Preliminary blood work shows that the blood thinning is not at desired levels and your blood pressure is through the roof!
Have you been taking your medication as prescribed?
I've been having problems with my pills...
Well, you're fast-tracking yourself toward a stroke! Are you trying to kill yourself?
I'm doing everything to keep myself alive!
Then why haven't you been taking your medication?
...sometimes I can't find them.
I see.

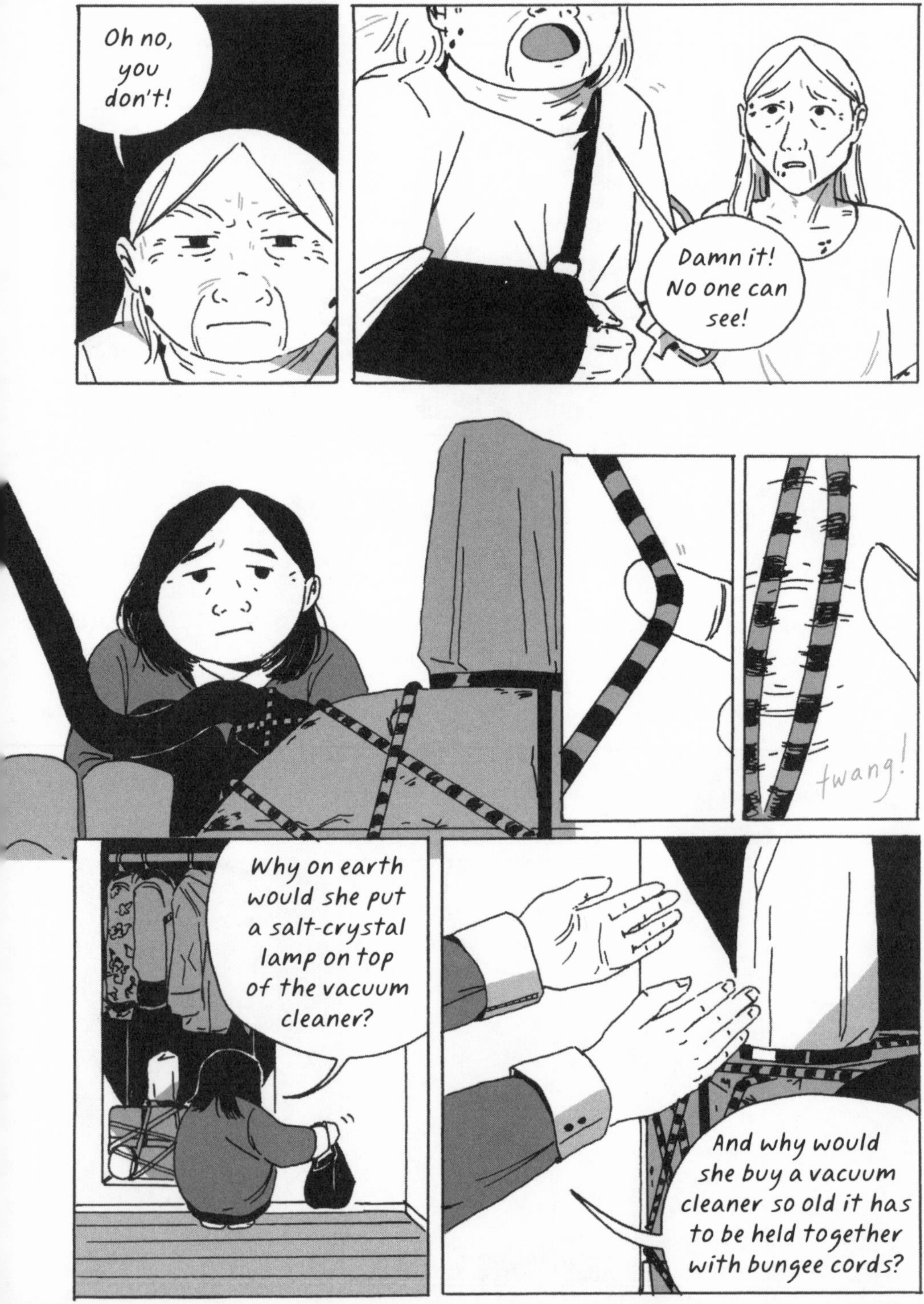
Oh no, you don't!
Damn it! No one can see!
twang!
Why on earth would she put a salt-crystal lamp on top of the vacuum cleaner?
And why would she buy a vacuum cleaner so old it has to be held together with bungee cords?

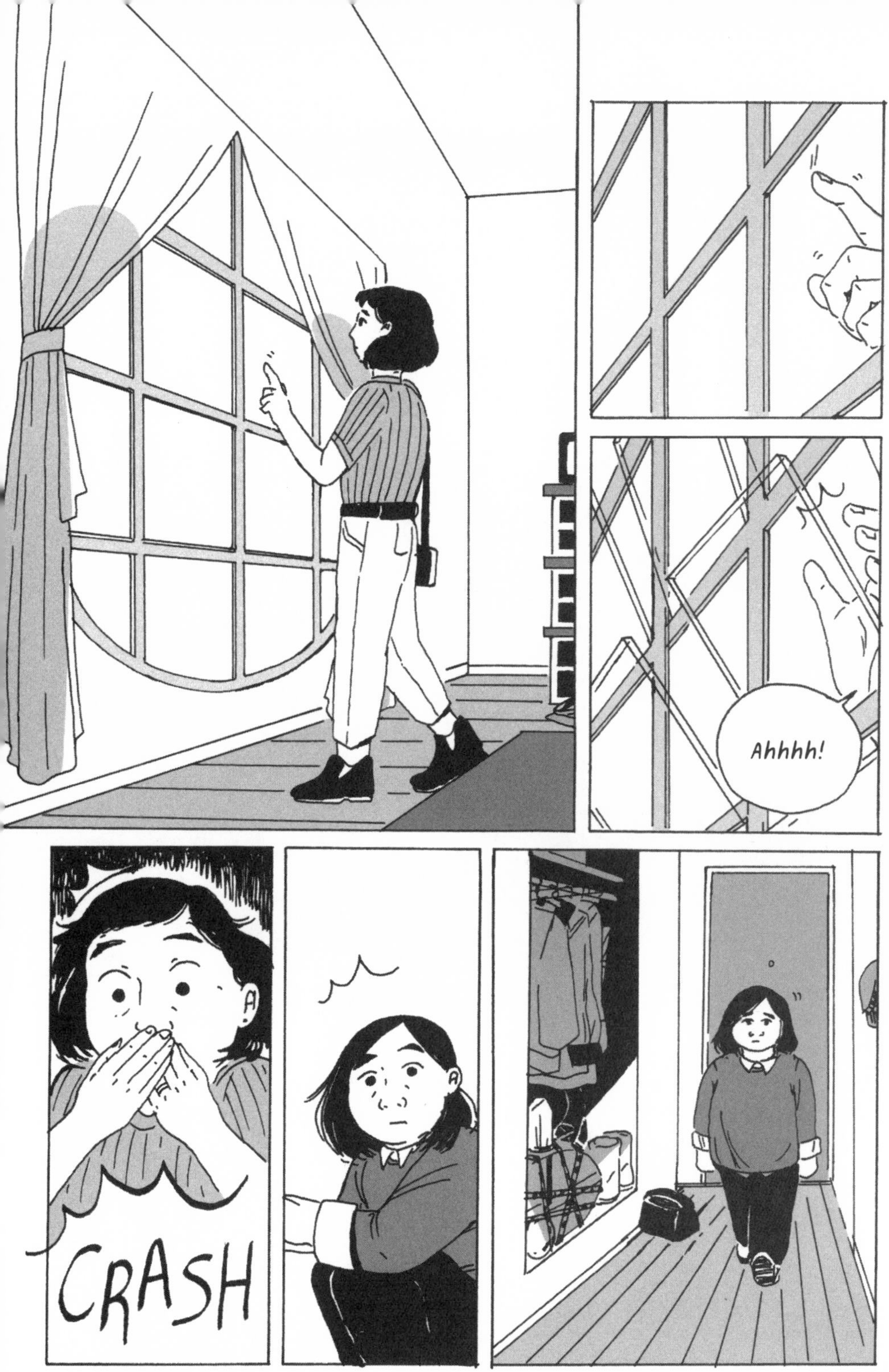
Ahhhh!
CRASH

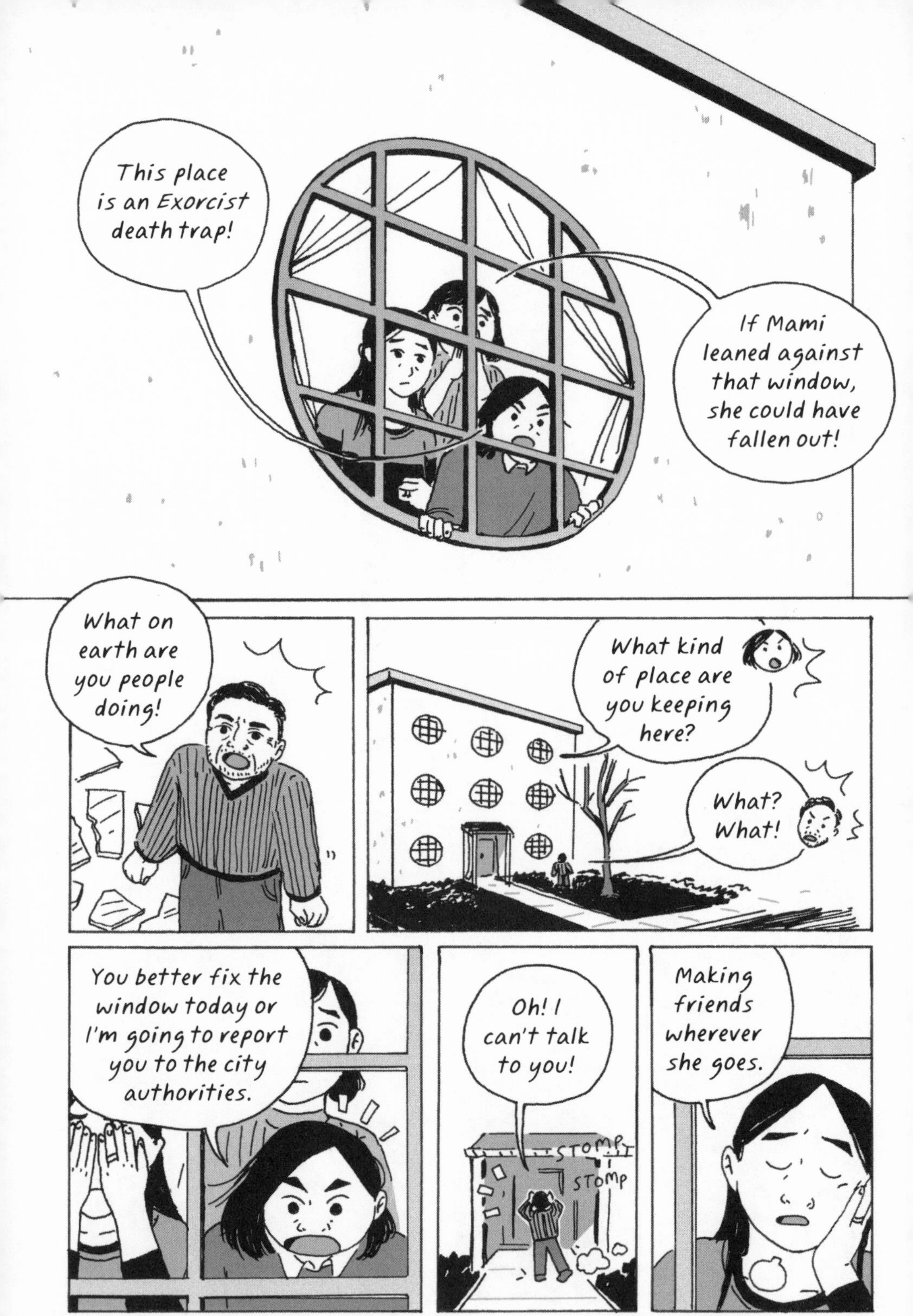
This place is an Exorcist death trap!
If Mami leaned against that window, she could have fallen out!
What on earth are you people doing!
What kind of place are you keeping here?
What? What!
You better fix the window today or I'm going to report you to the city authorities.
Oh! I can't talk to you!
STOMP
STOMP
Making friends wherever she goes.

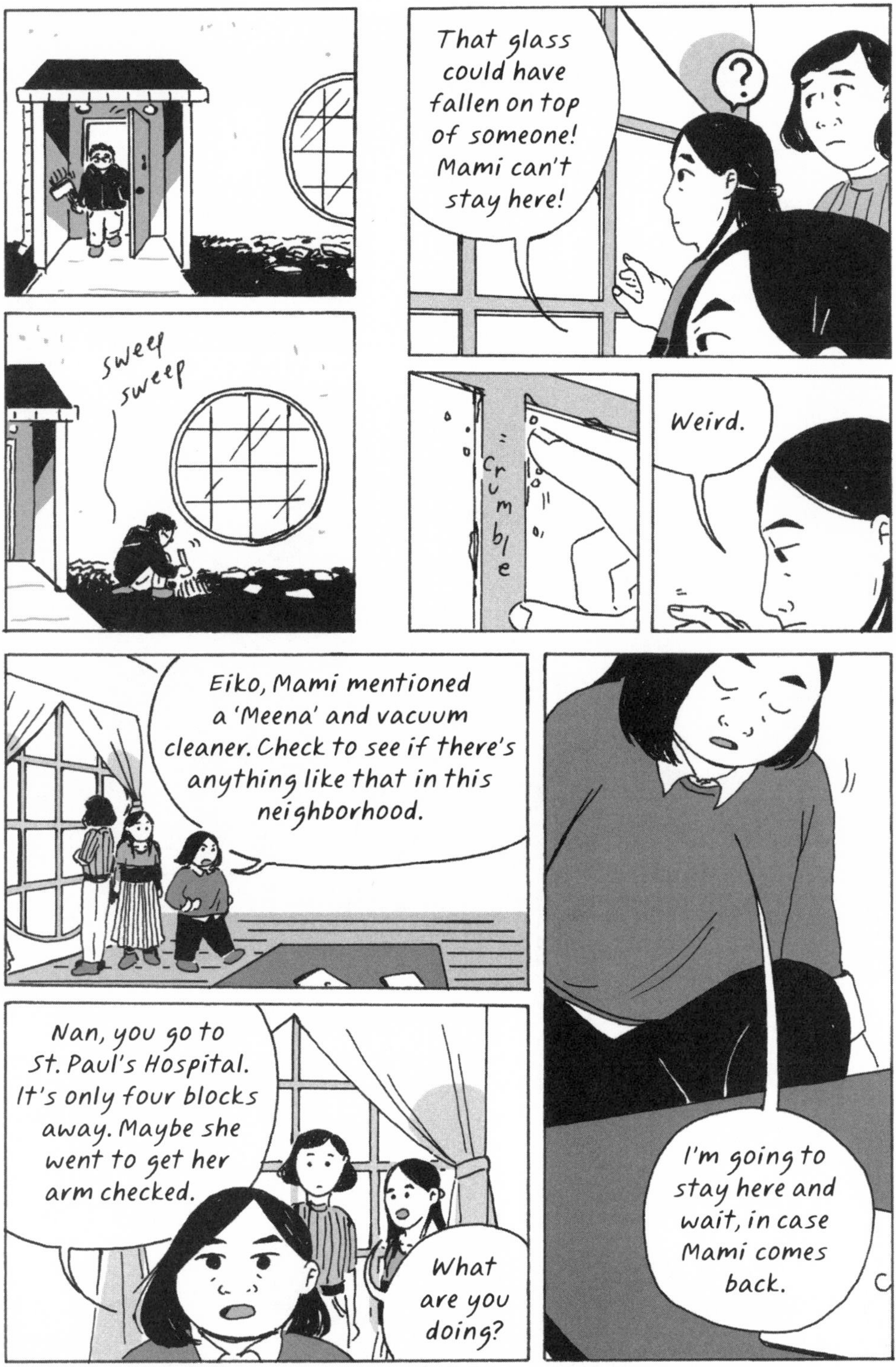
That glass could have fallen on top of someone! Mami can't stay here!
sweep sweep
crumble
Weird.
Eiko, Mami mentioned a 'Meena' and vacuum cleaner. Check to see if there's anything like that in this neighborhood.
Nan, you go to St. Paul's Hospital. It's only four blocks away. Maybe she went to get her arm checked.
What are you doing?
I'm going to stay here and wait, in case Mami comes back.

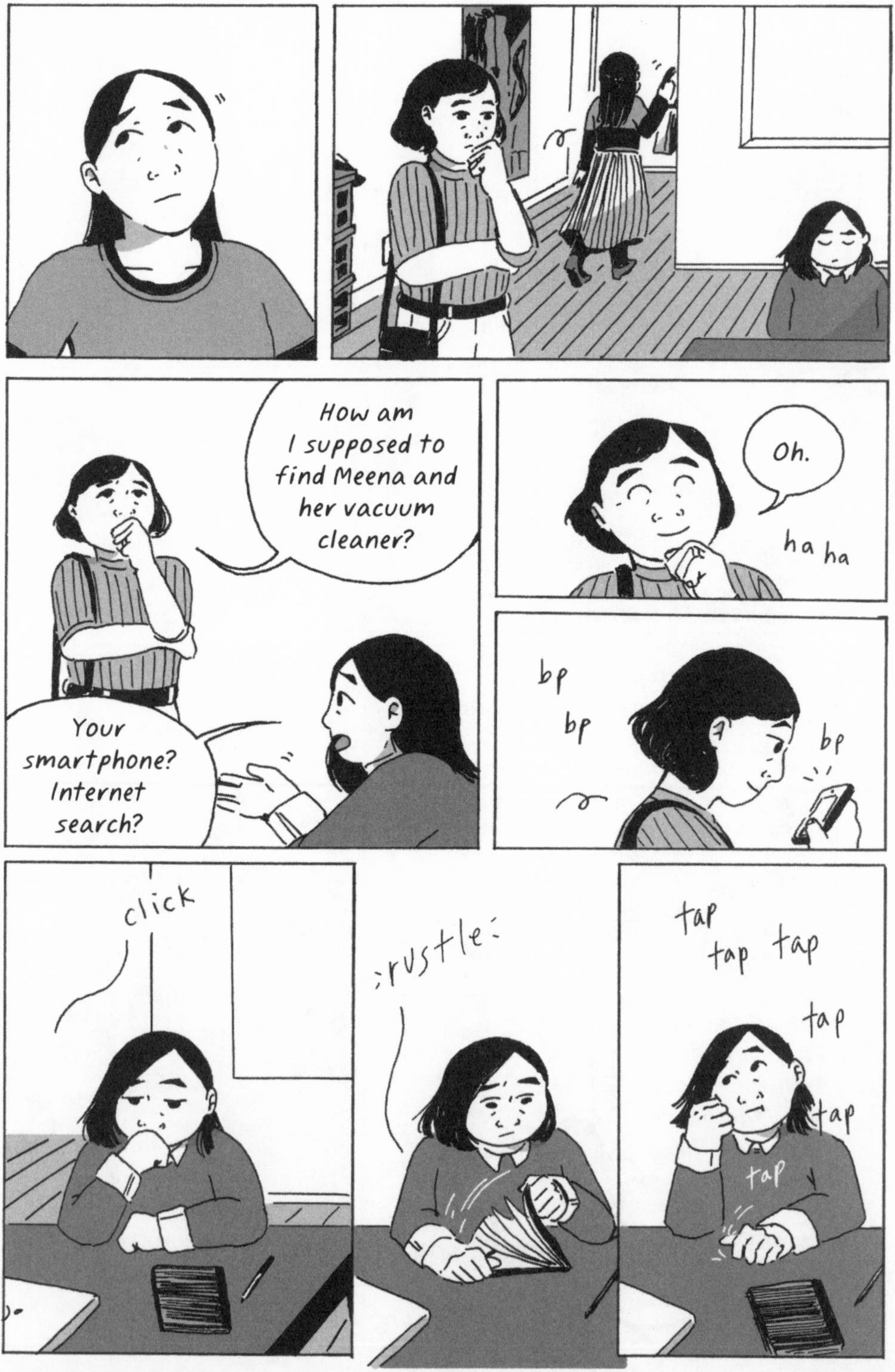
How am I supposed to find Meena and her vacuum cleaner?
Your smartphone? Internet search?
Oh.
ha ha
bp
bp
bp
click
rustle
tap
tap tap
tap
tap
tap

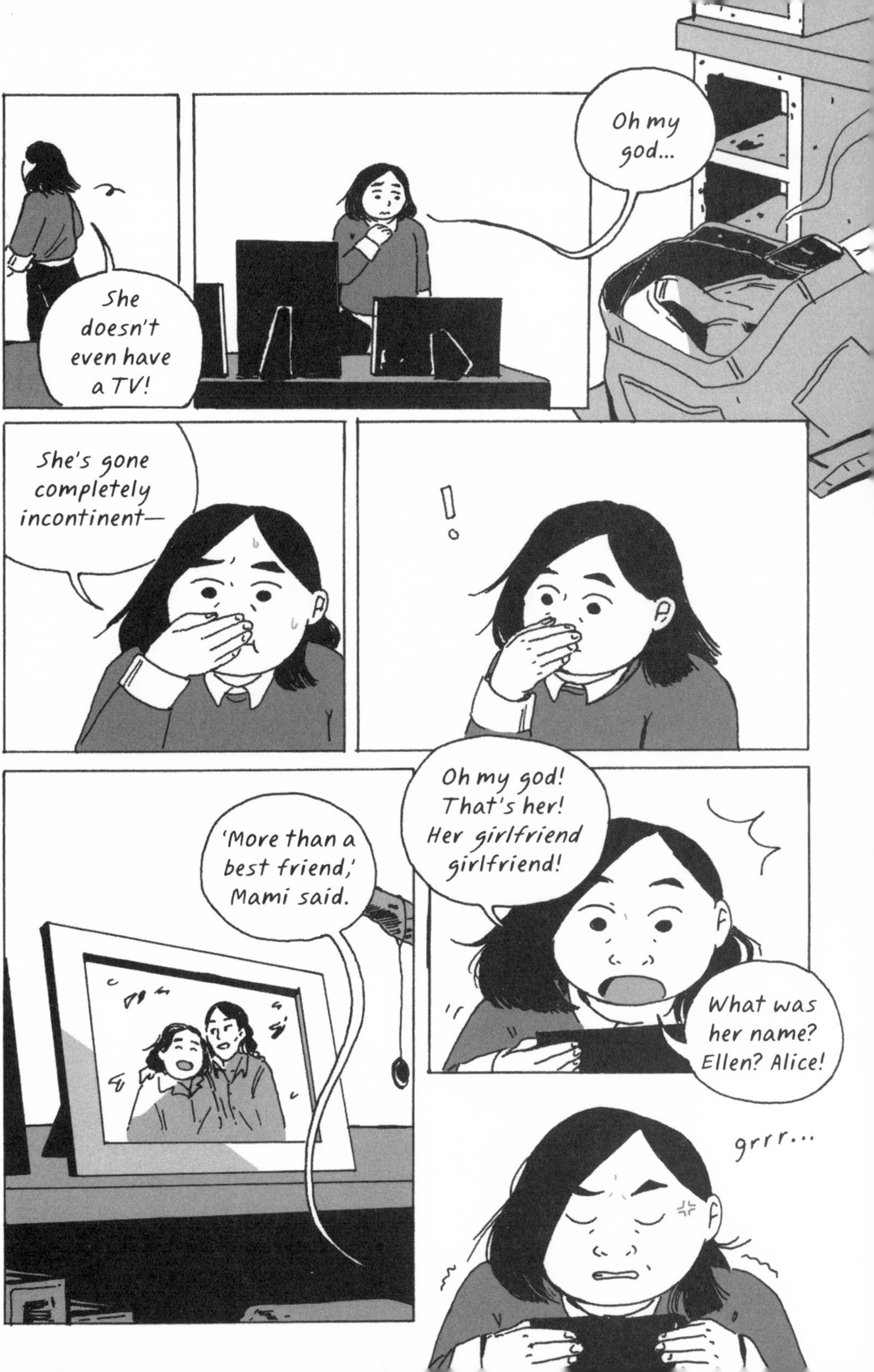
She doesn't even have a TV!
Oh my god...
She's gone completely incontinent—
!
'More than a best friend,' Mami said.
Oh my god! That's her! Her girlfriend girlfriend!
What was her name? Ellen? Alice!
grrr...

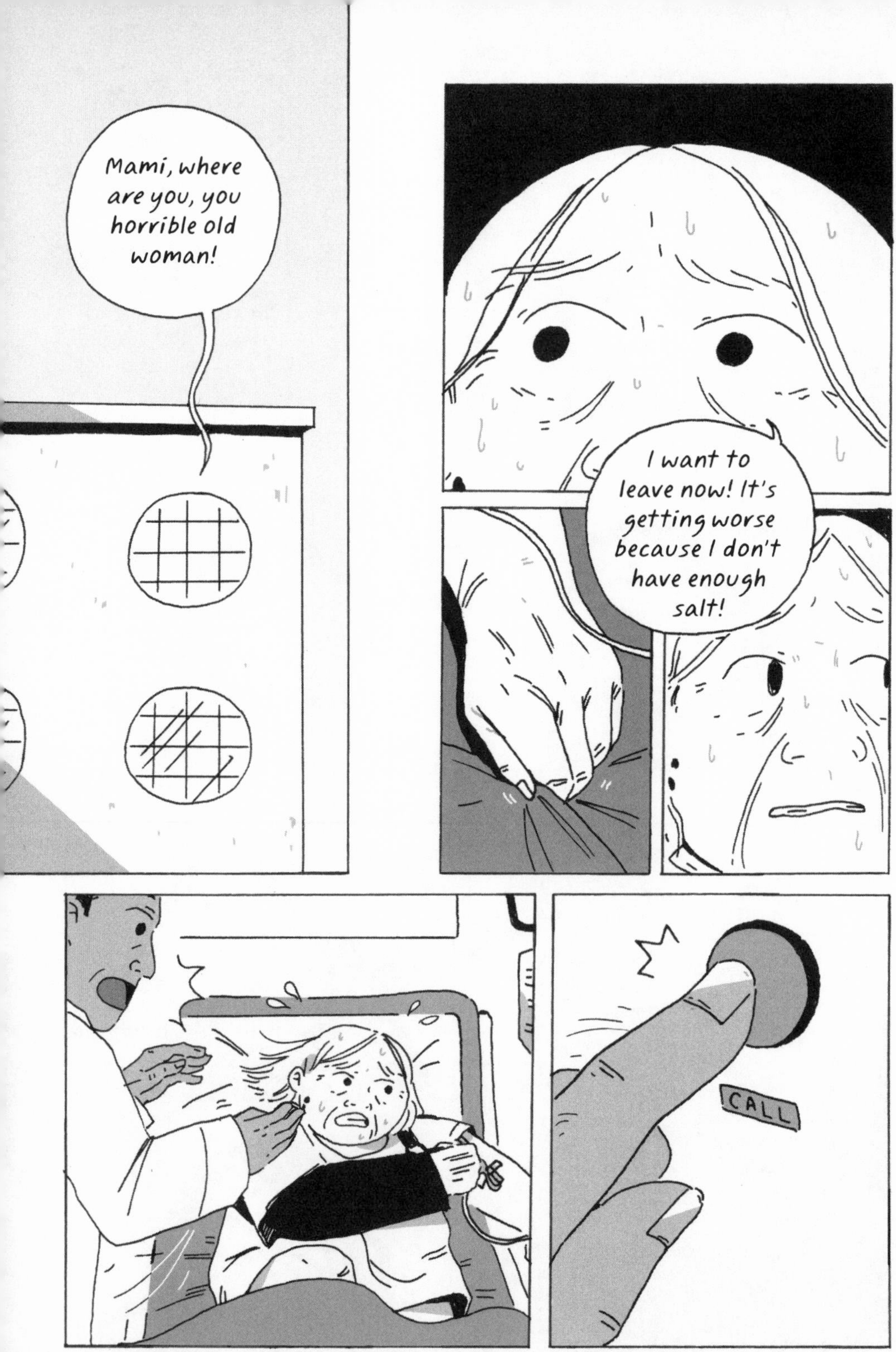
Mami, where are you, you horrible old woman!
I want to leave now! It's getting worse because I don't have enough salt!
CALL

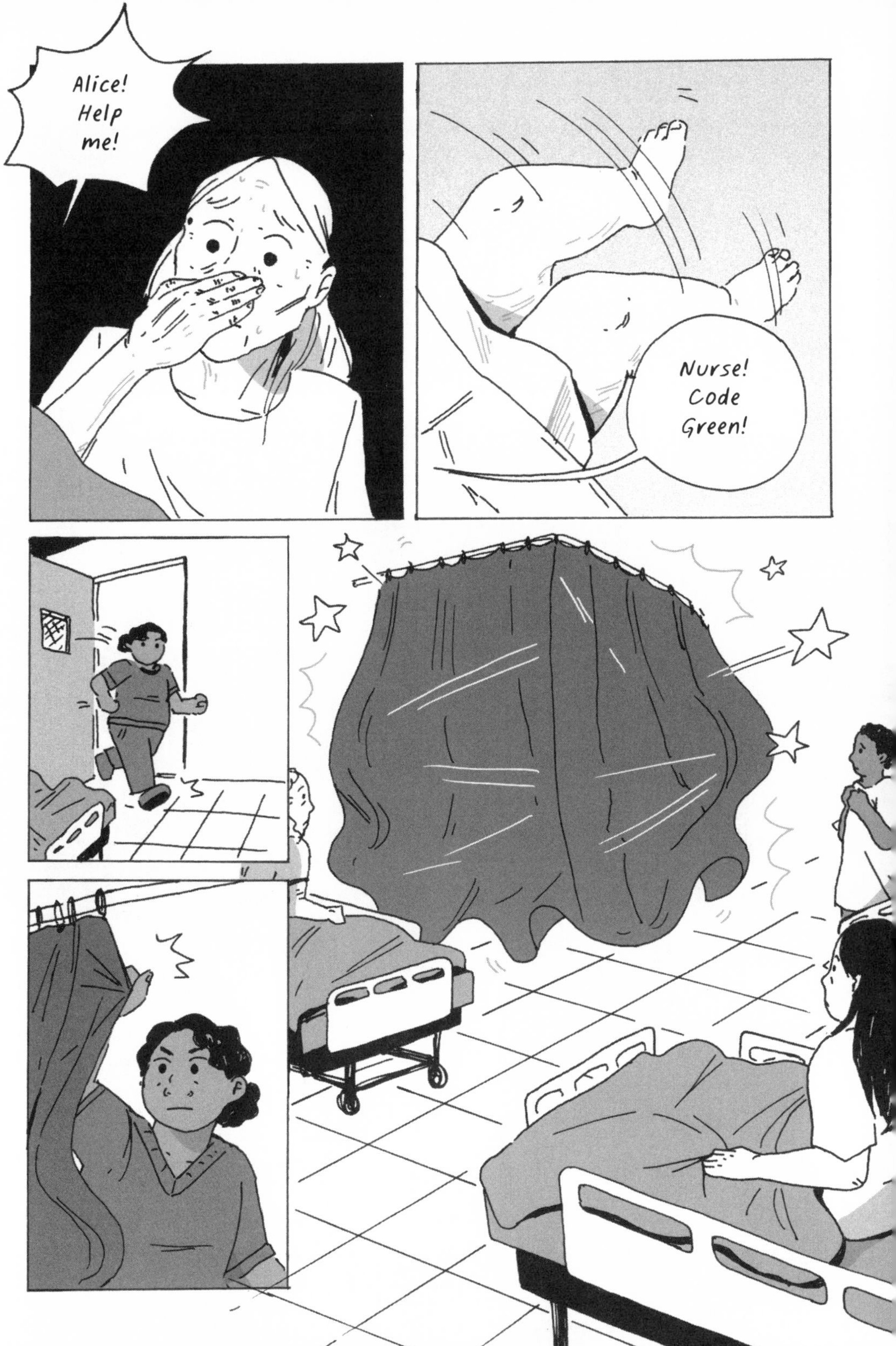

Alice! Help me!
Nurse! Code Green!

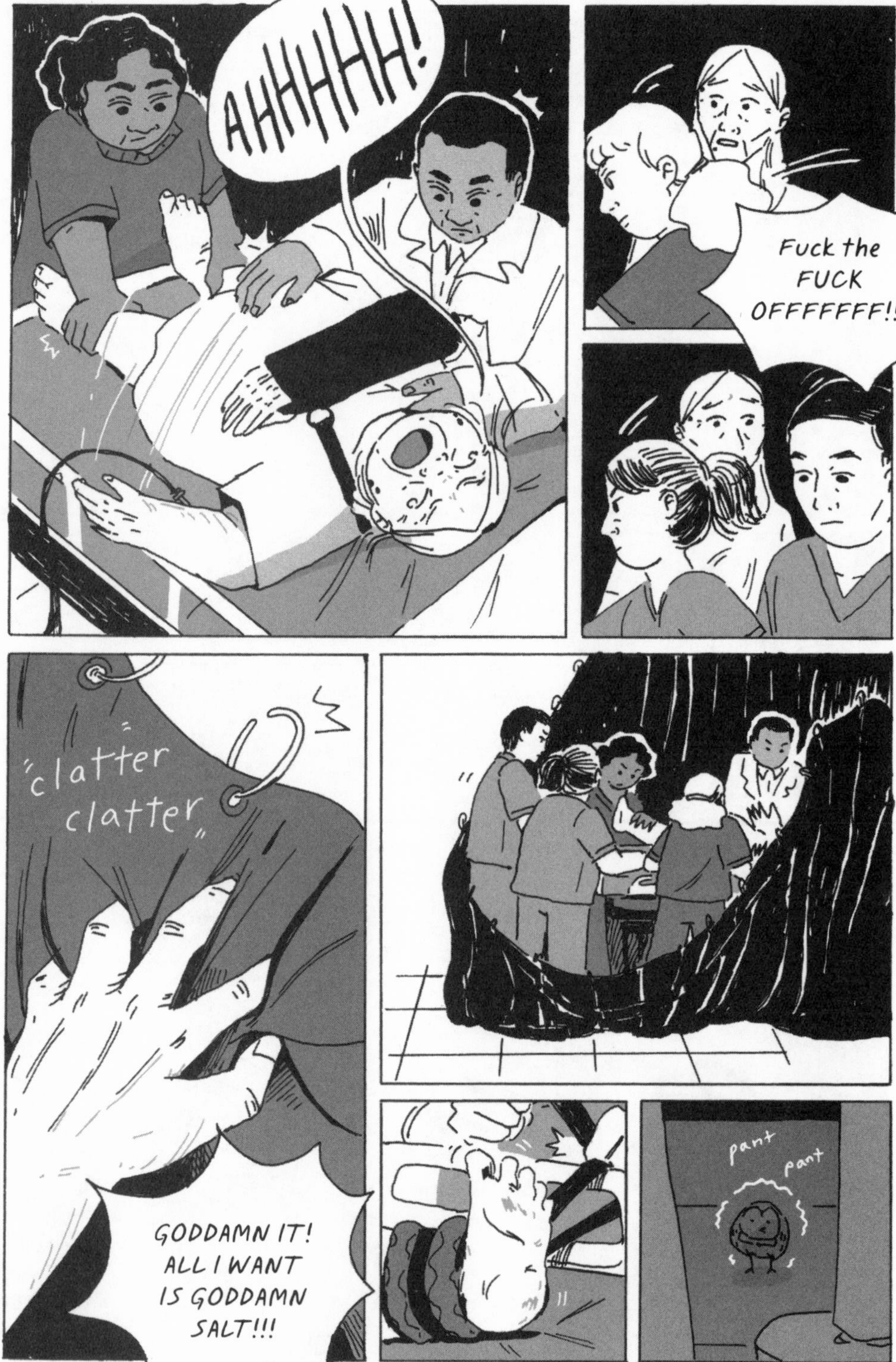
AHHHHHH!
Fuck the FUCK OFFFFFFF!!!
clatter clatter
GODDAMN IT! ALL I WANT IS GODDAMN SALT!!!
pant pant

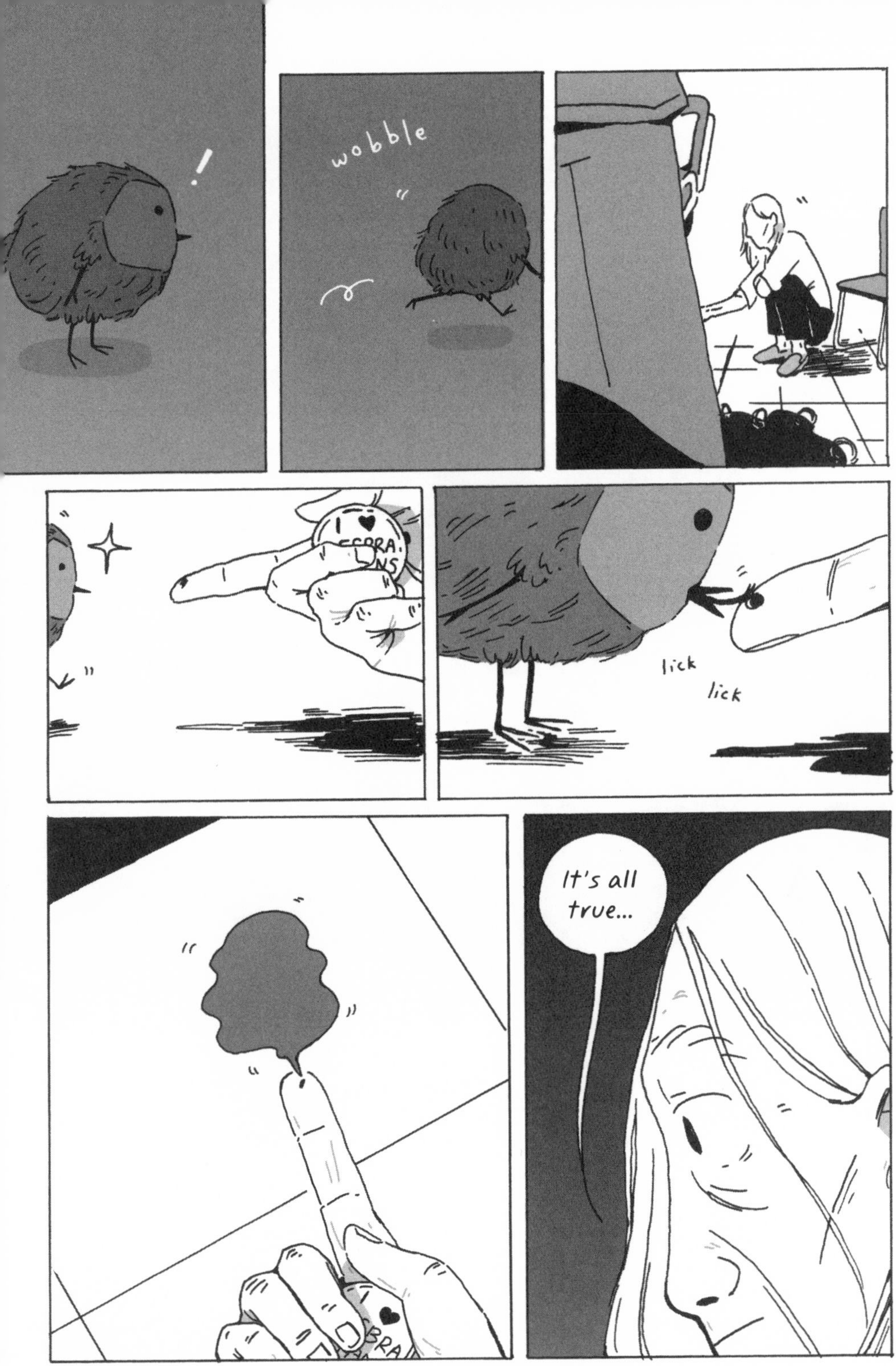
!
wobble
lick
lick
It's all true...

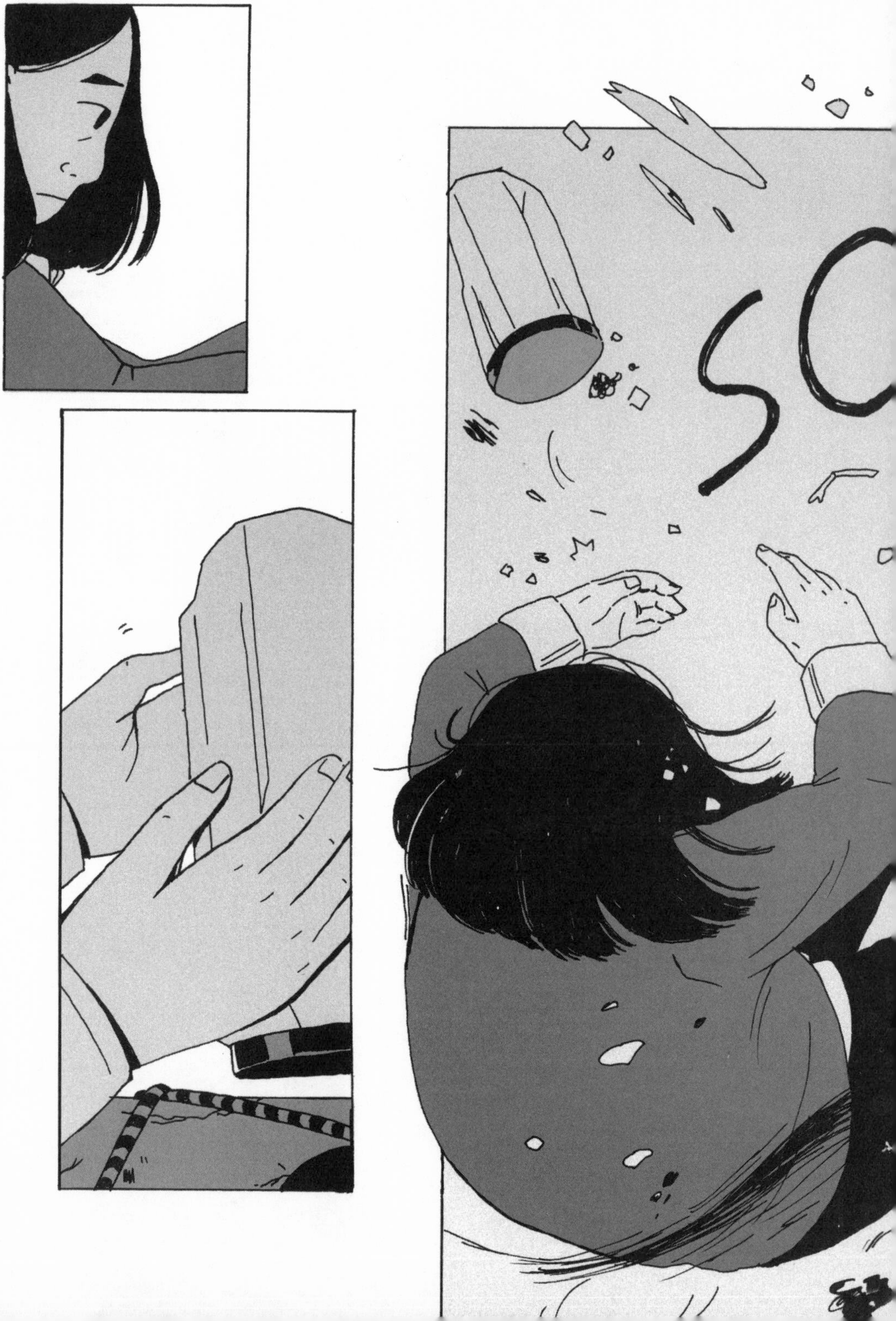
SO

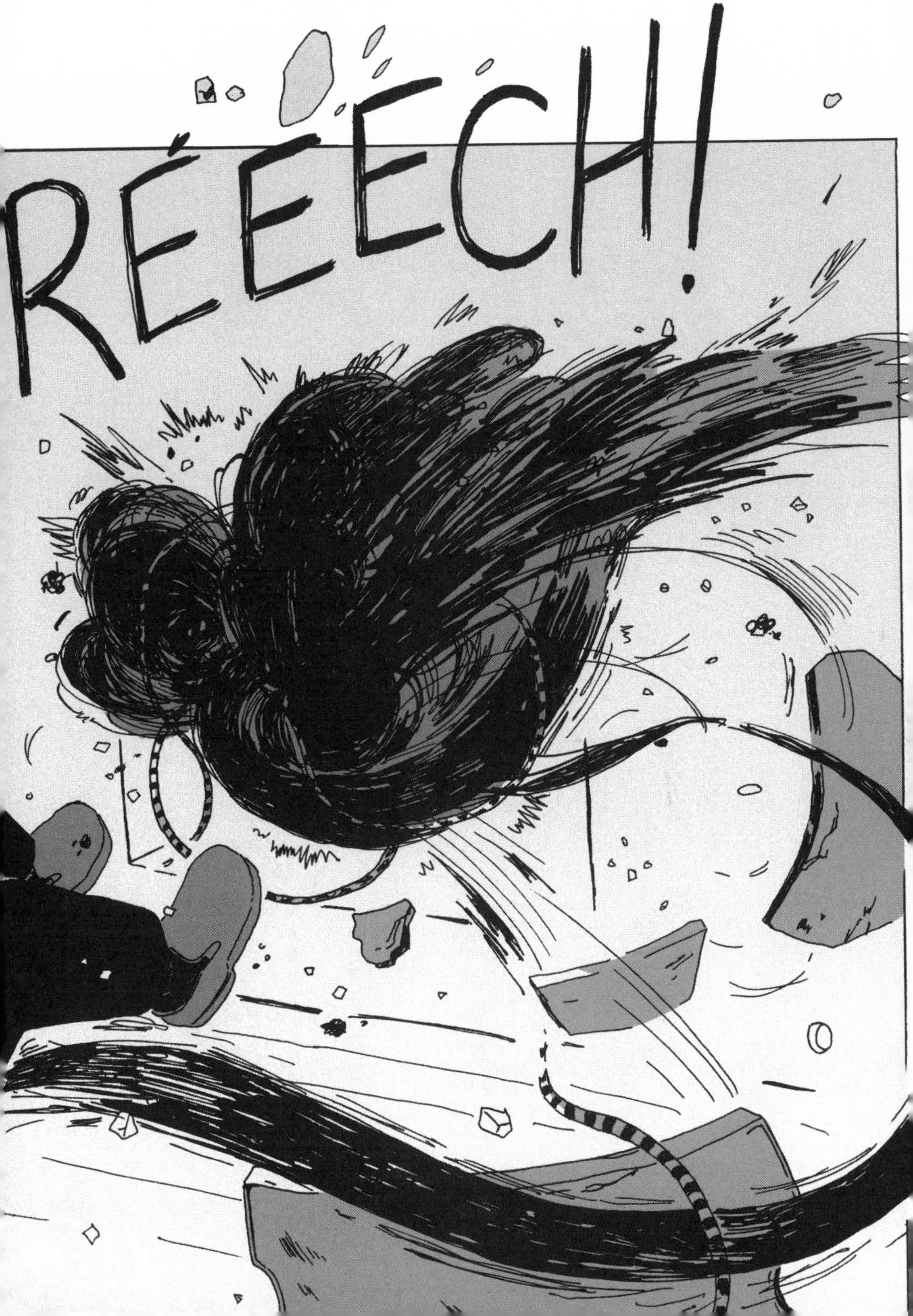
REEECH!

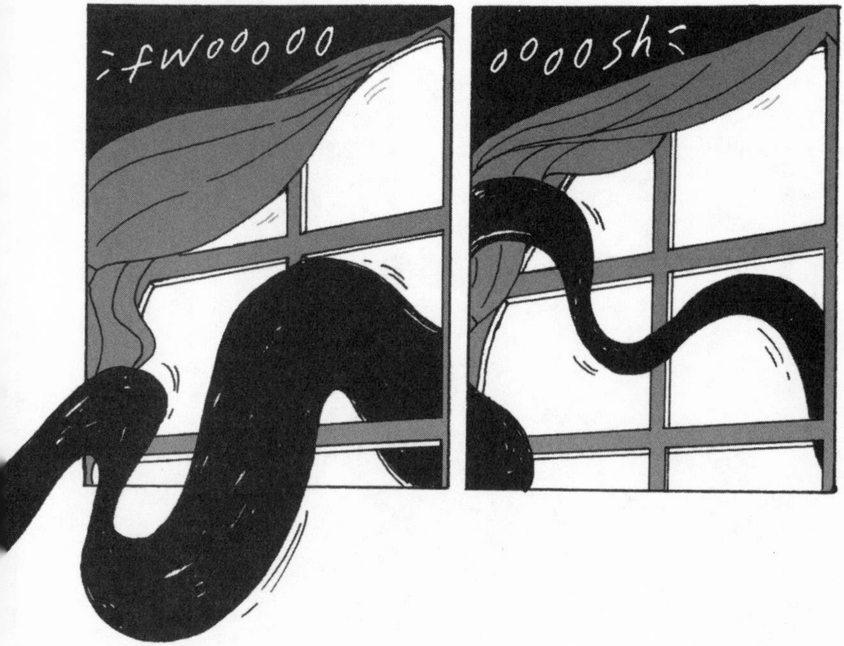
fwooooo
oooosh

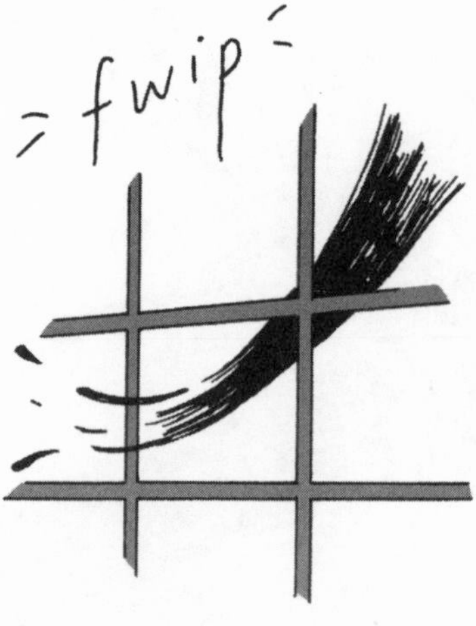
fwip

Chapter Fourteen

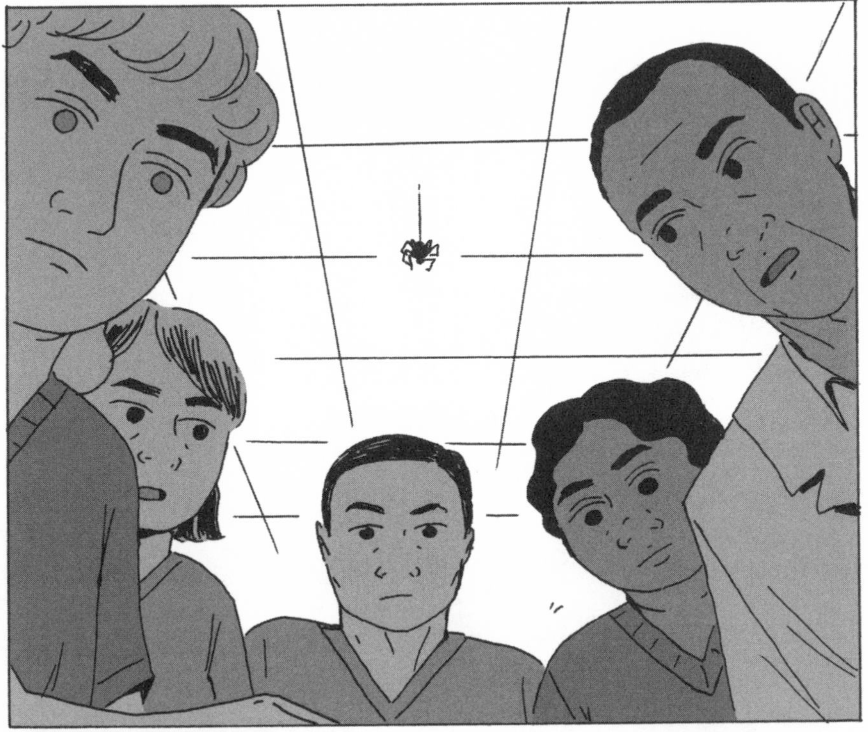

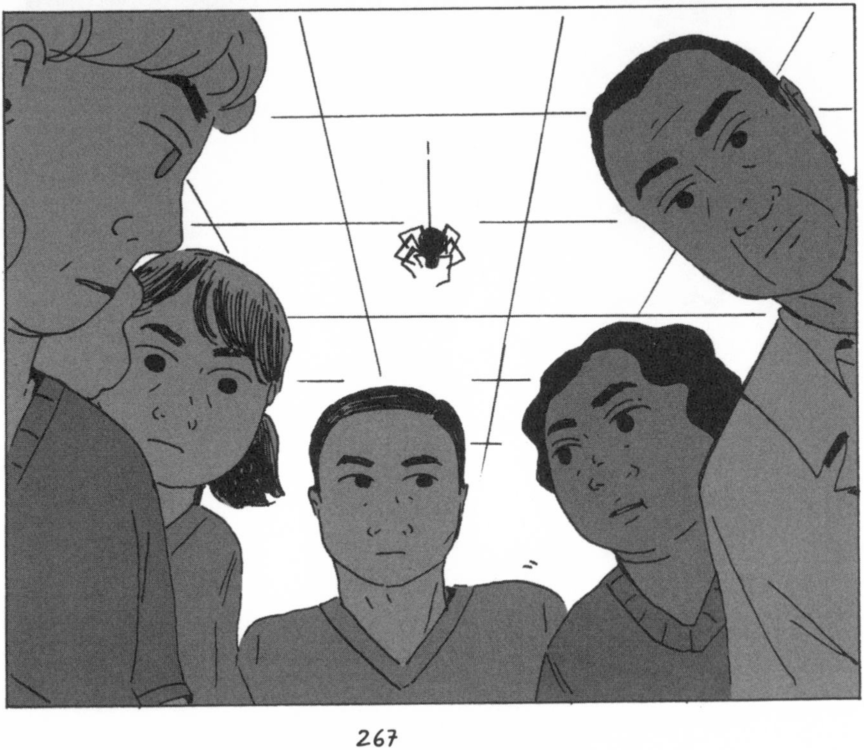

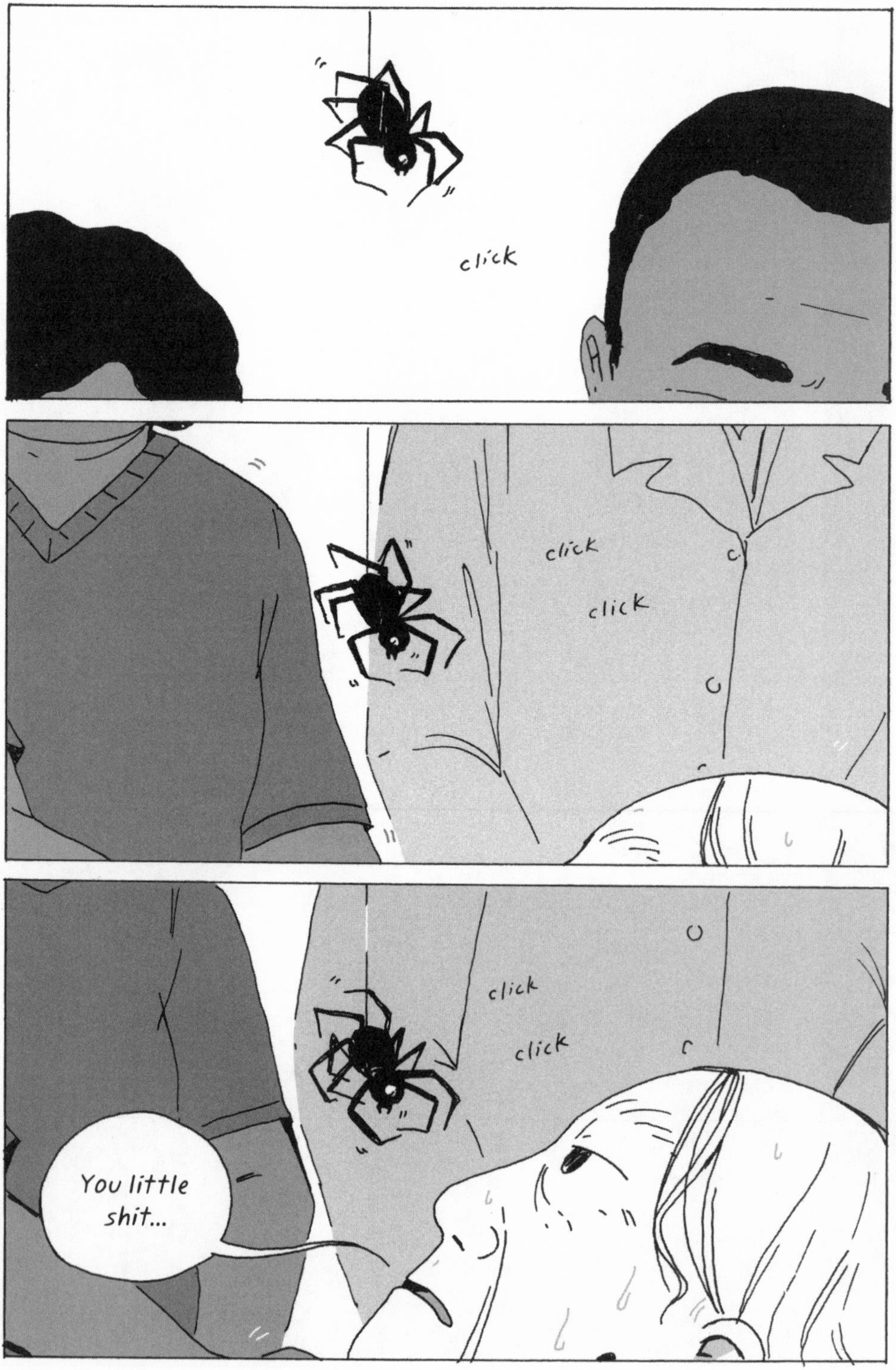
click
click
click
click
click
You little shit...

fwump

Don't go.

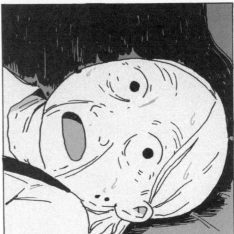

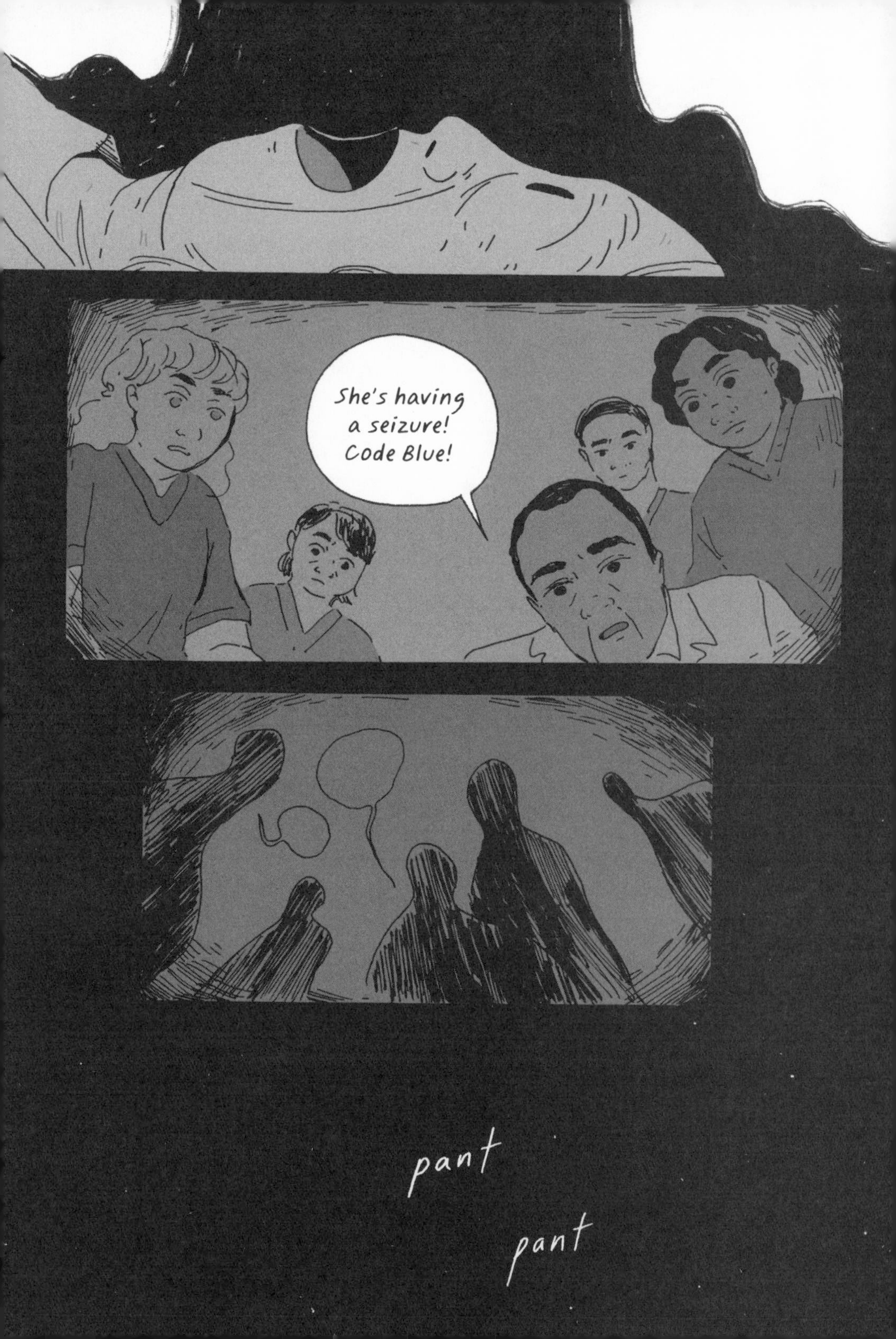
She's having a seizure! Code Blue!
pant
pant

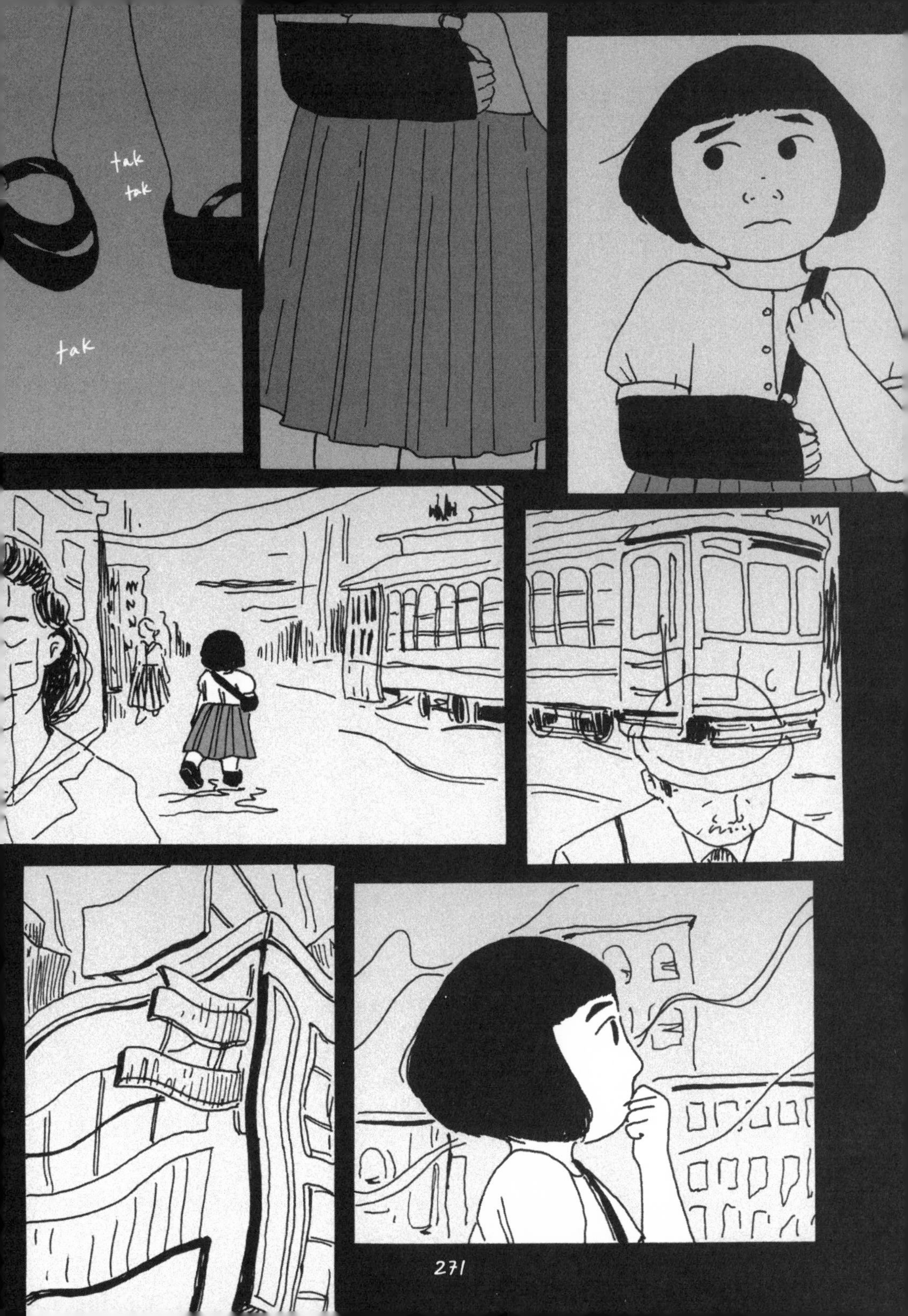
tak
tak
tak

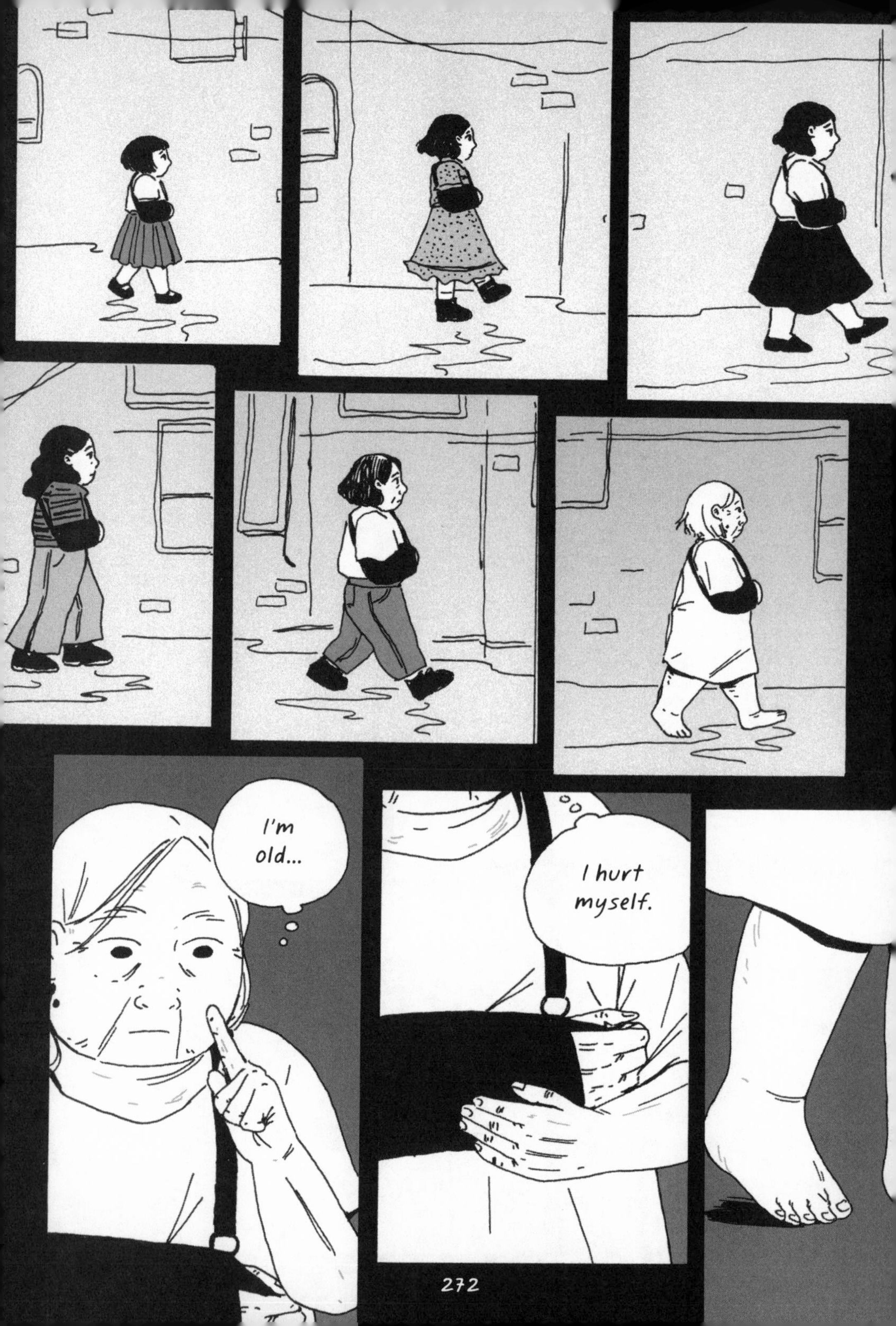
I'm old...
I hurt myself.

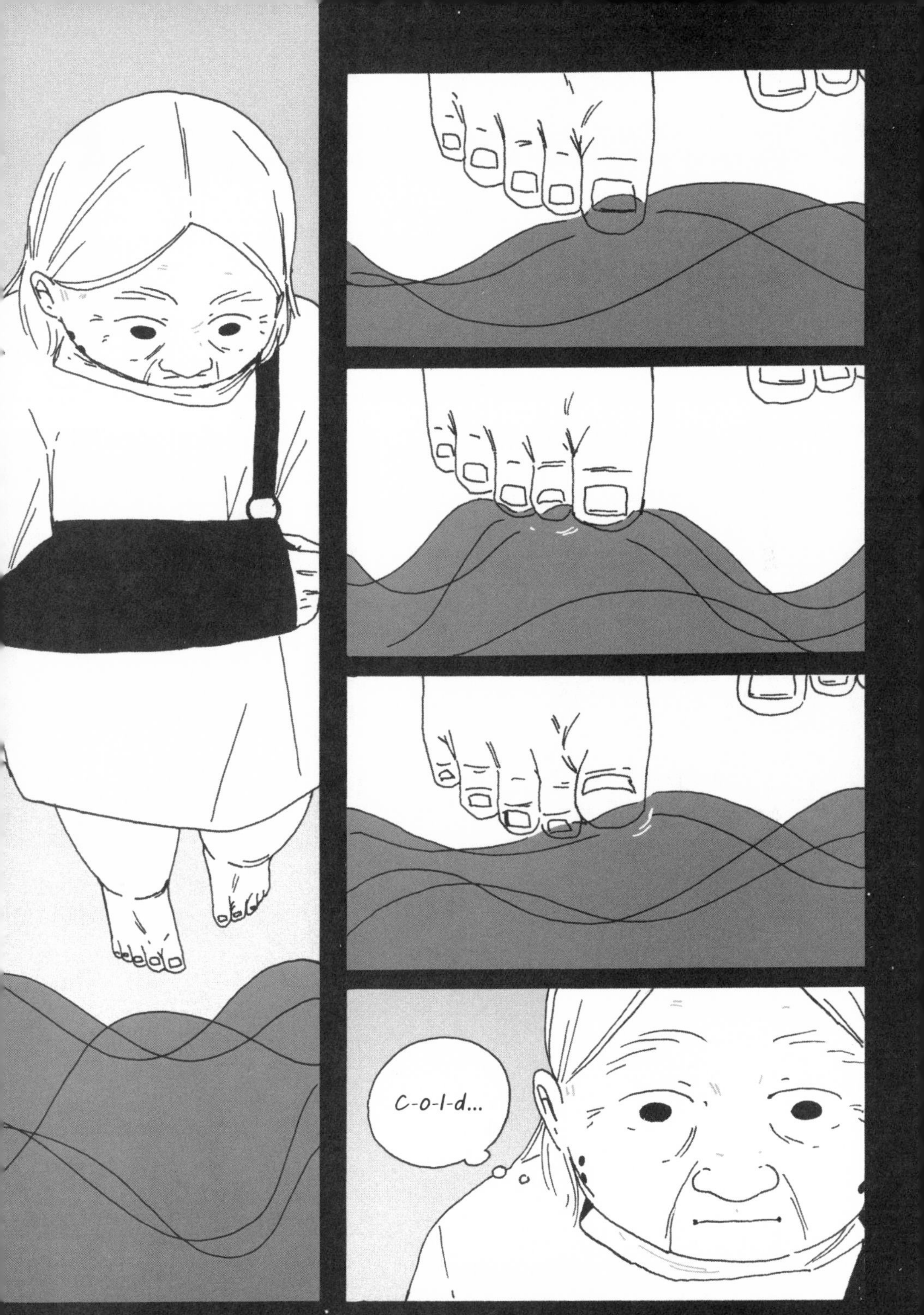
C-o-l-d...

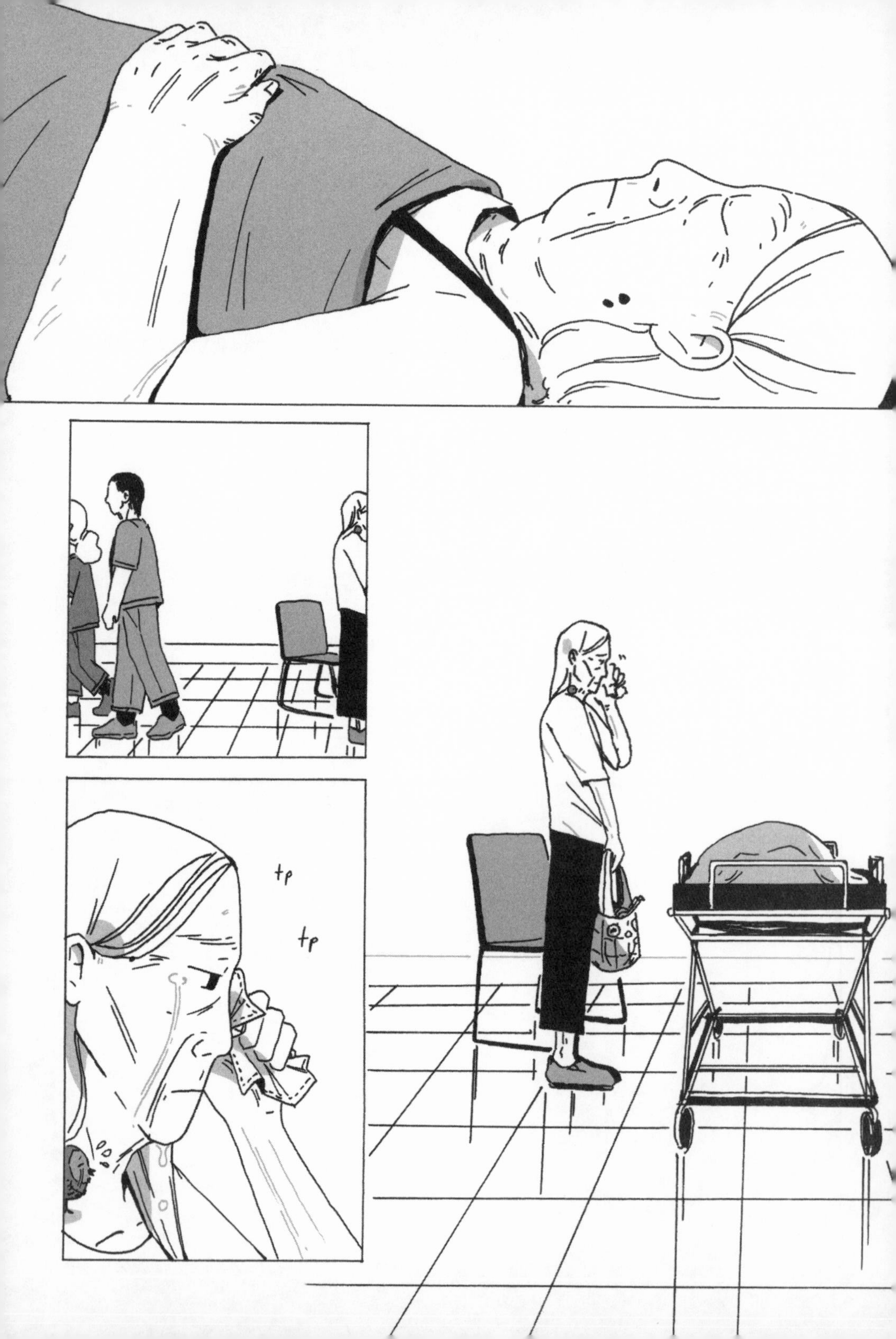
tp
tp

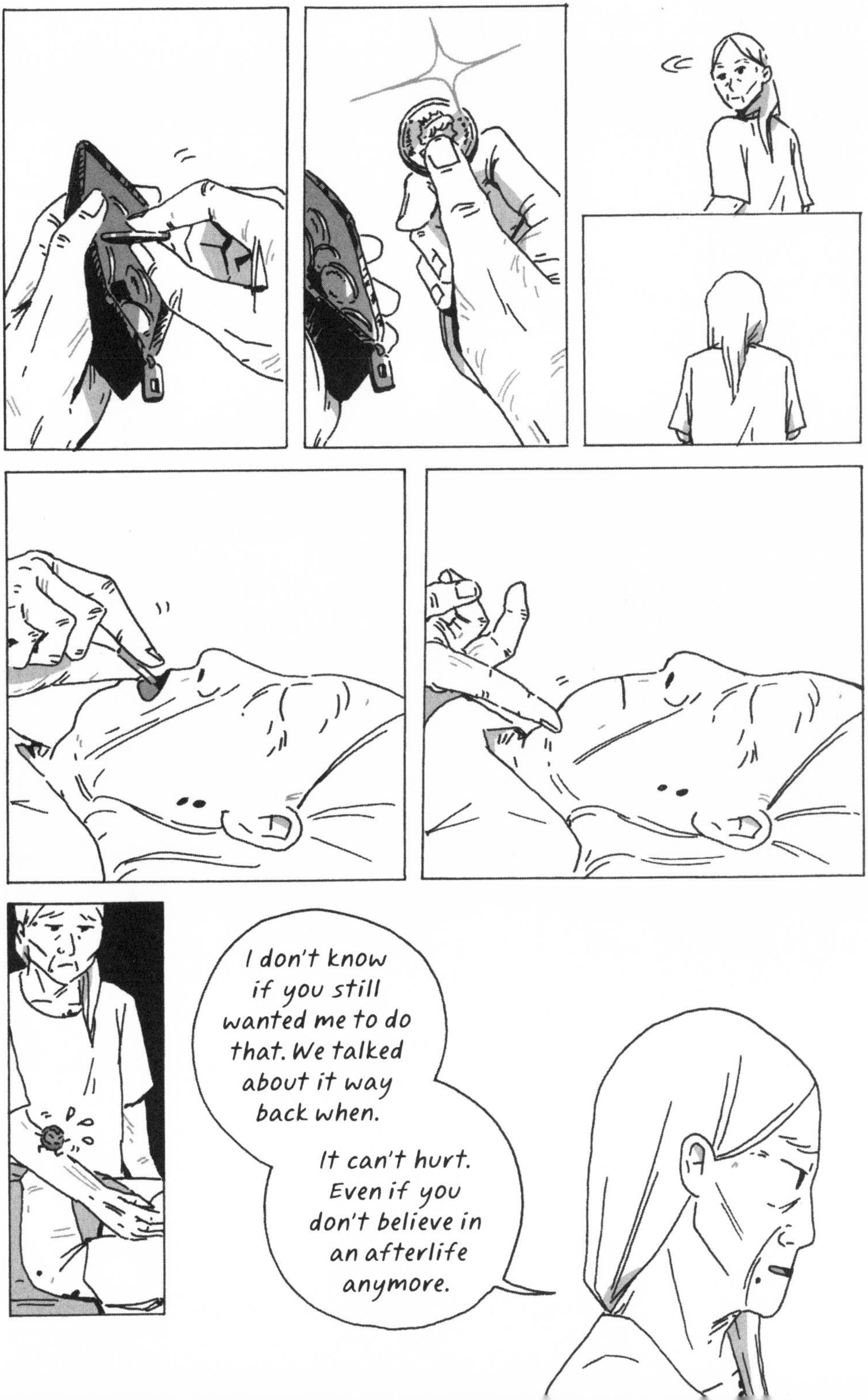
I don't know if you still wanted me to do that. We talked about it way back when.
It can't hurt. Even if you don't believe in an afterlife anymore.

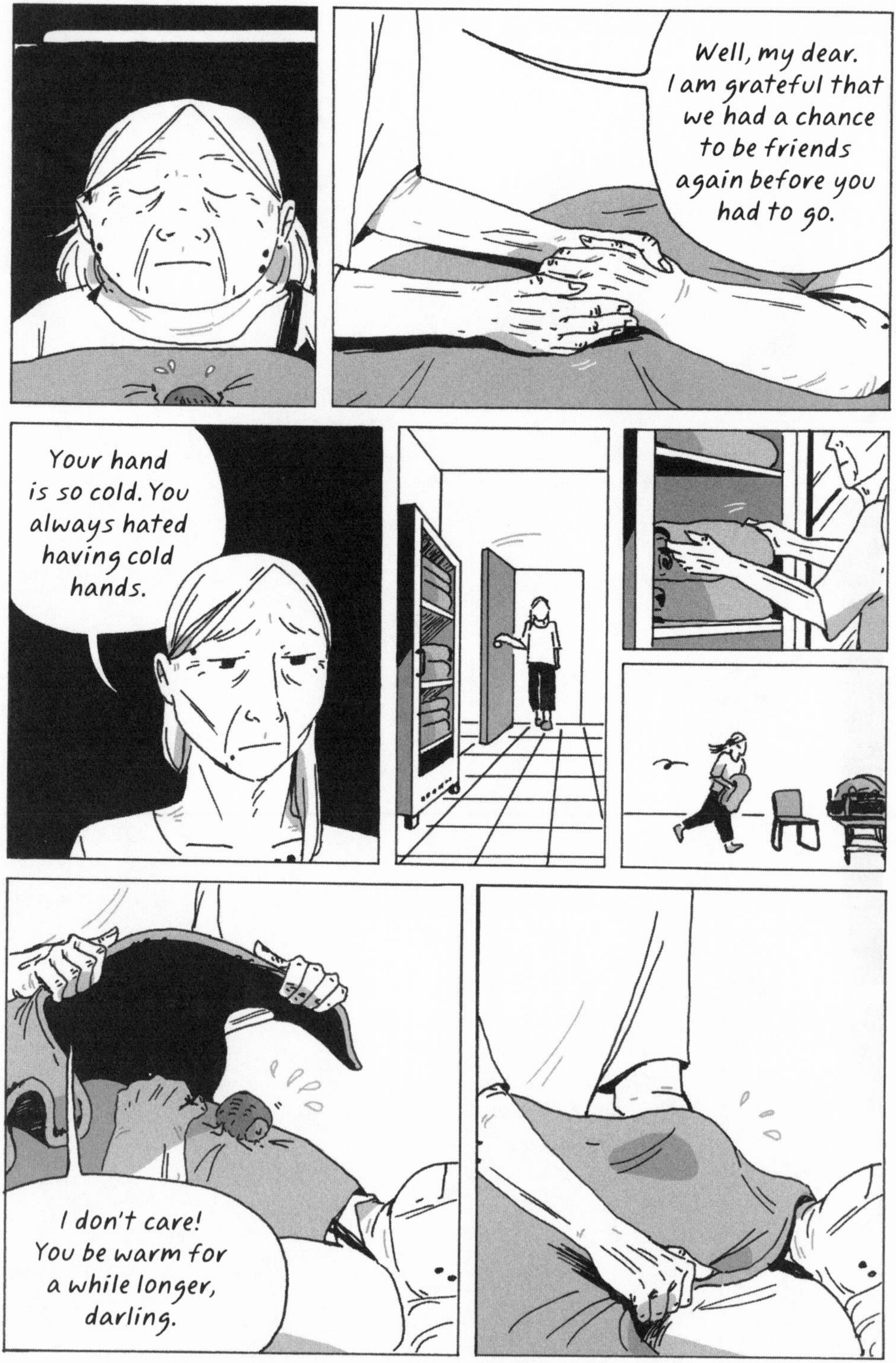
Well, my dear. I am grateful that we had a chance to be friends again before you had to go.
Your hand is so cold. You always hated having cold hands.
I don't care! You be warm for a while longer, darling.

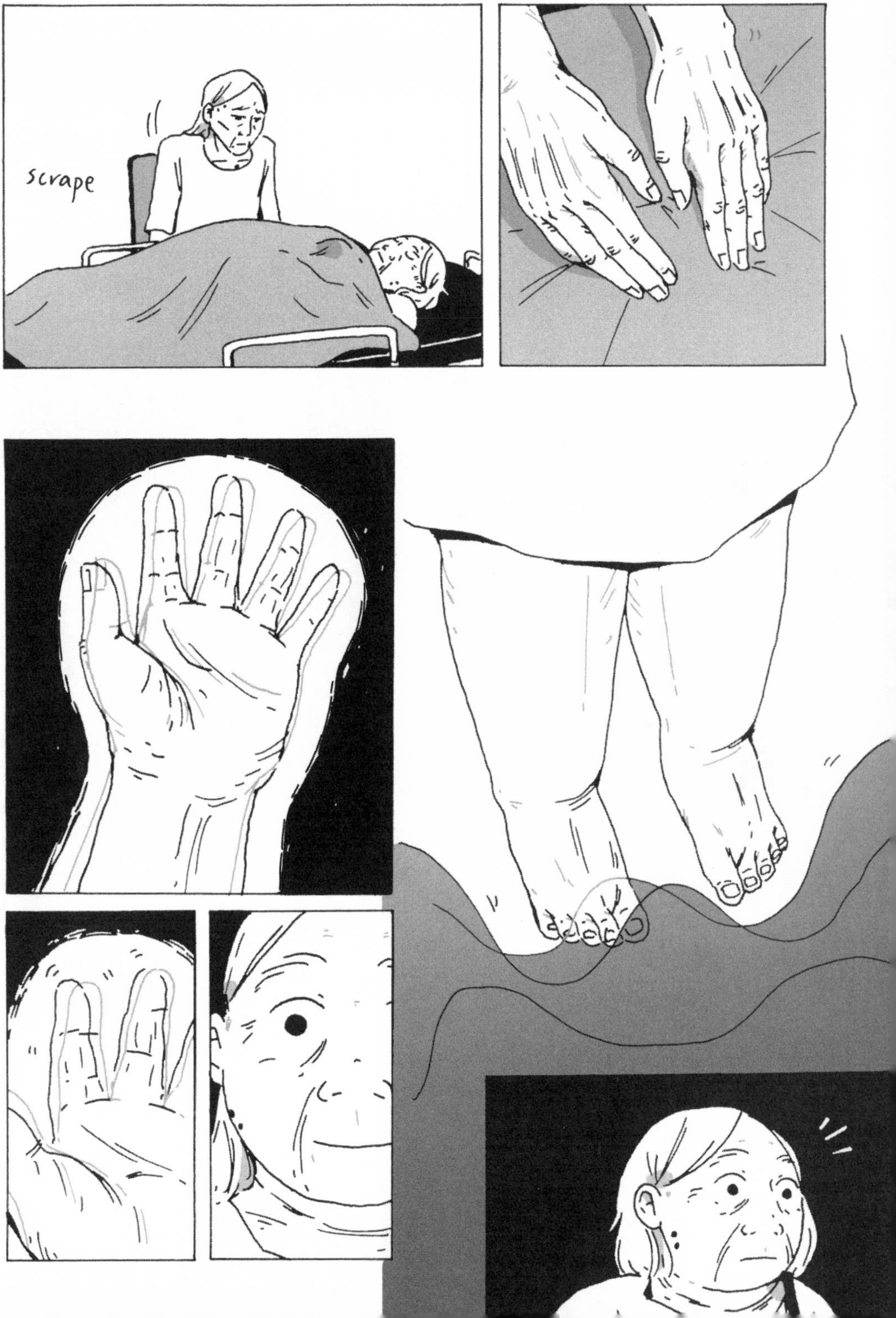
scrape

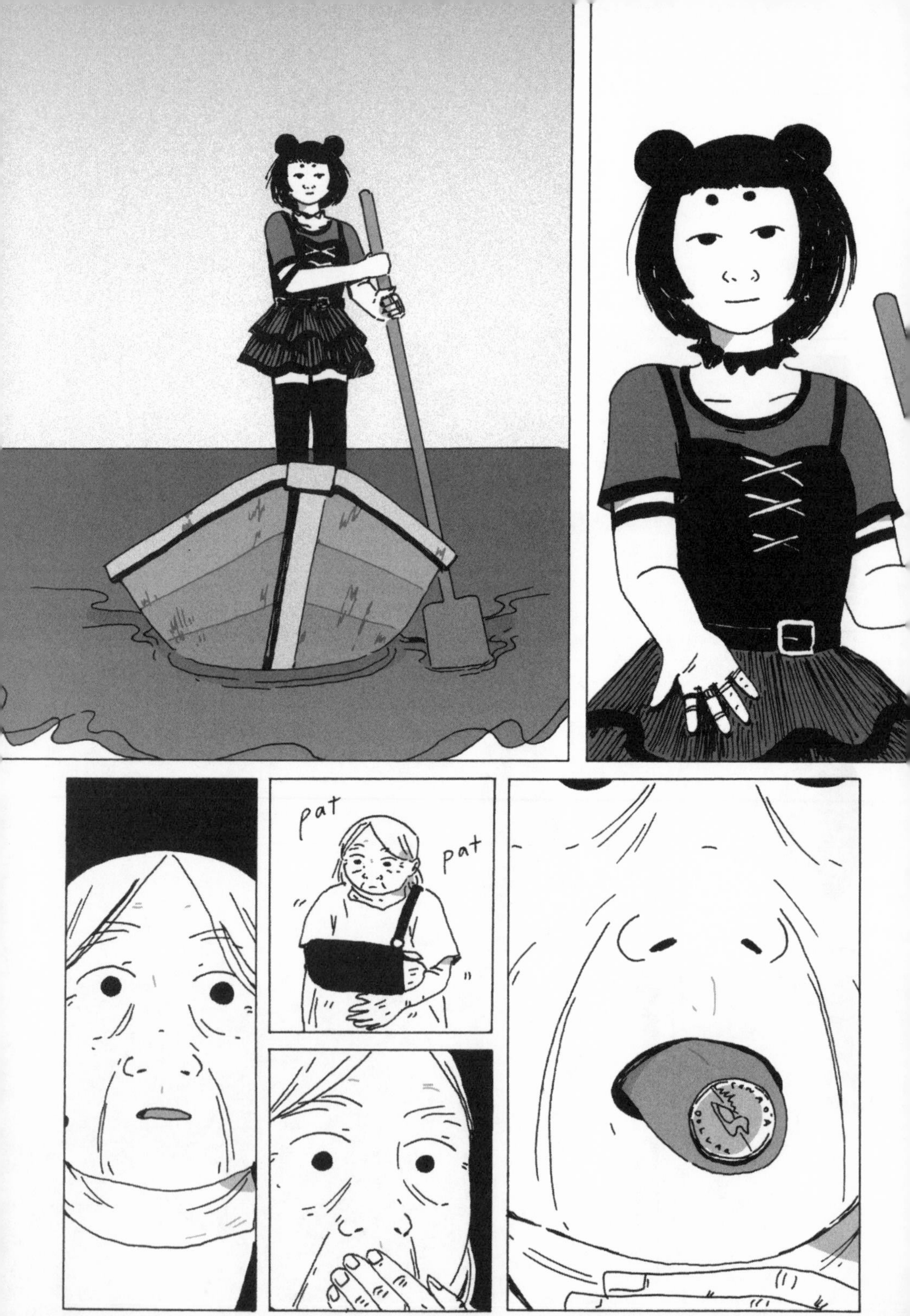
pat
pat

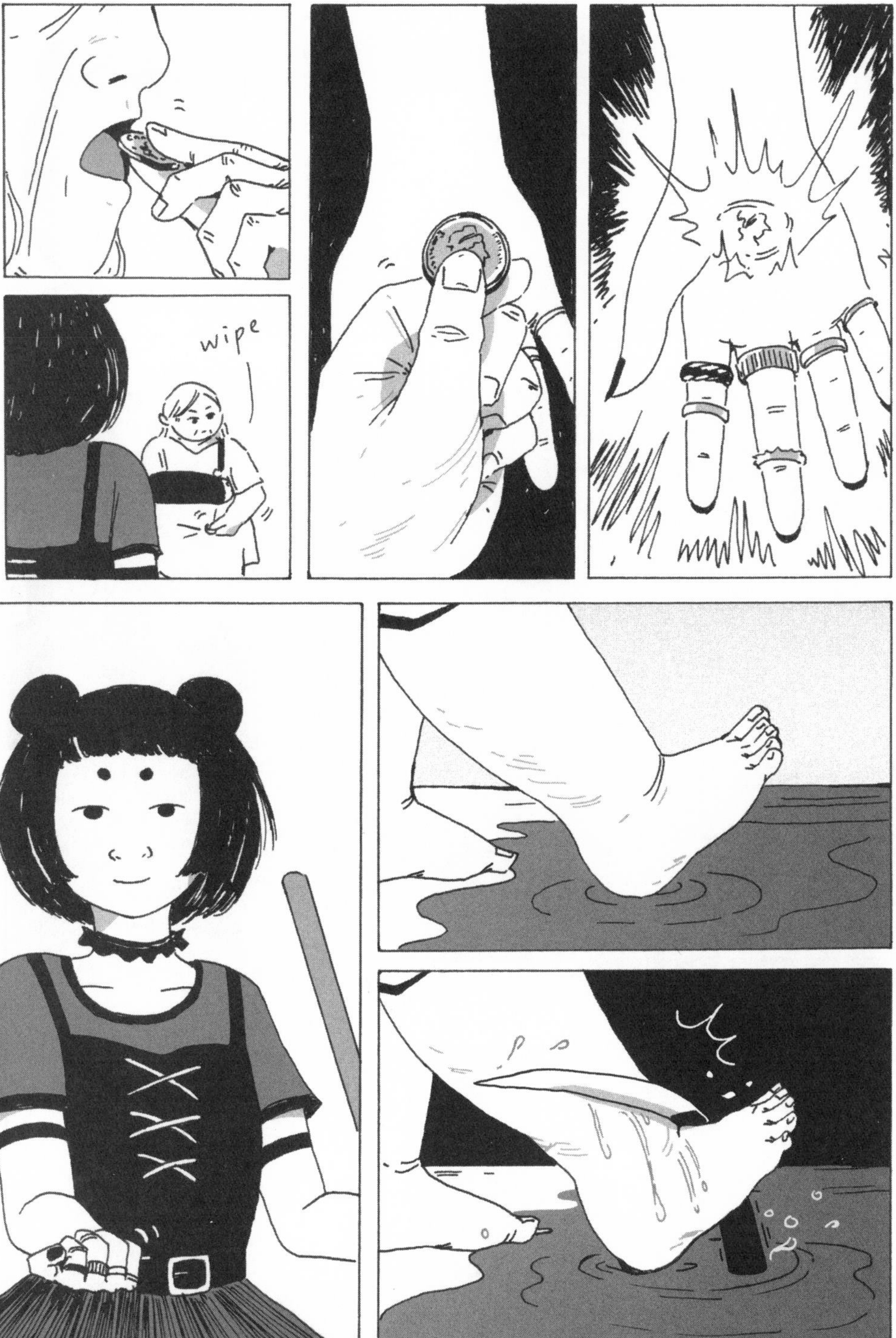
wipe

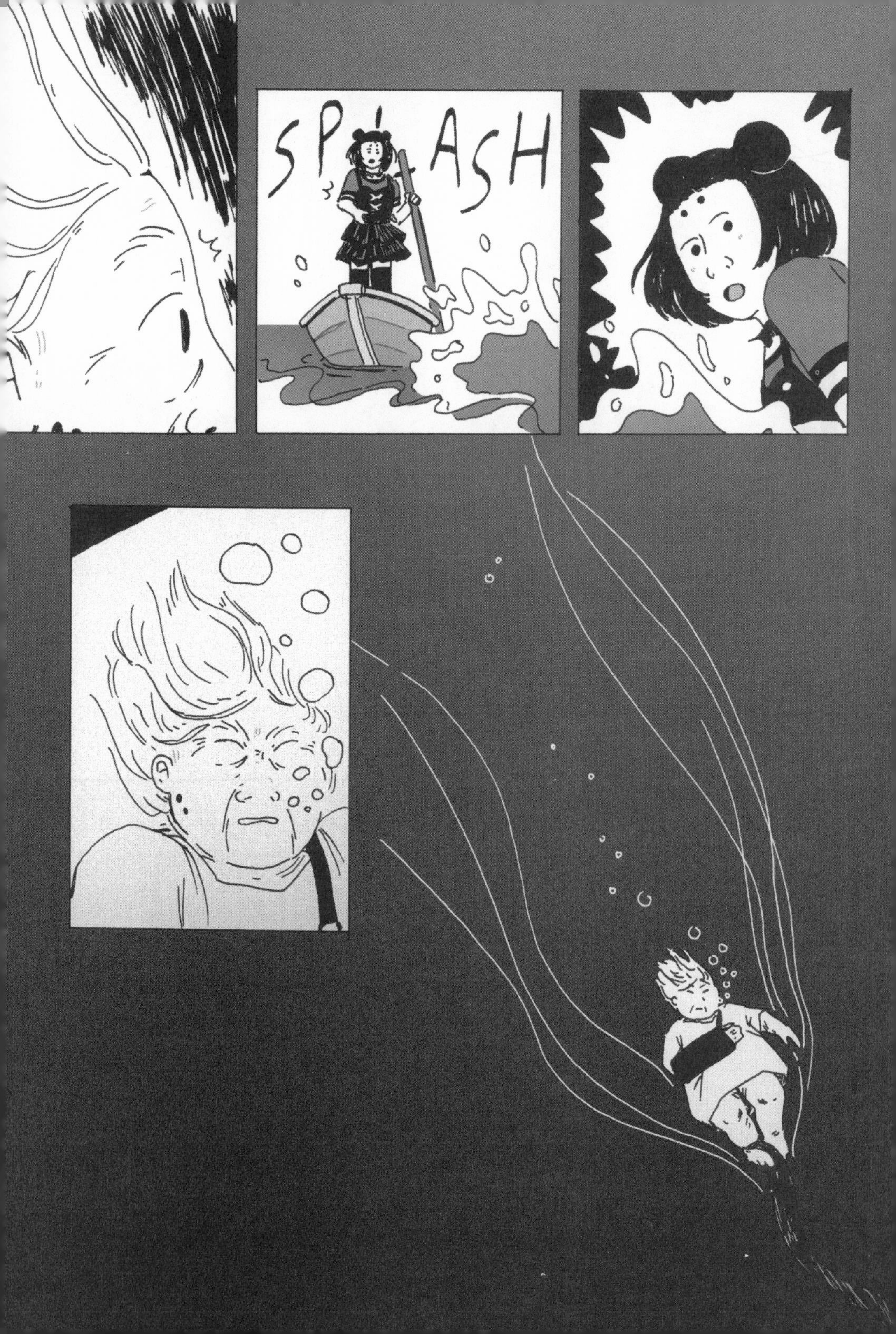
SPLASH

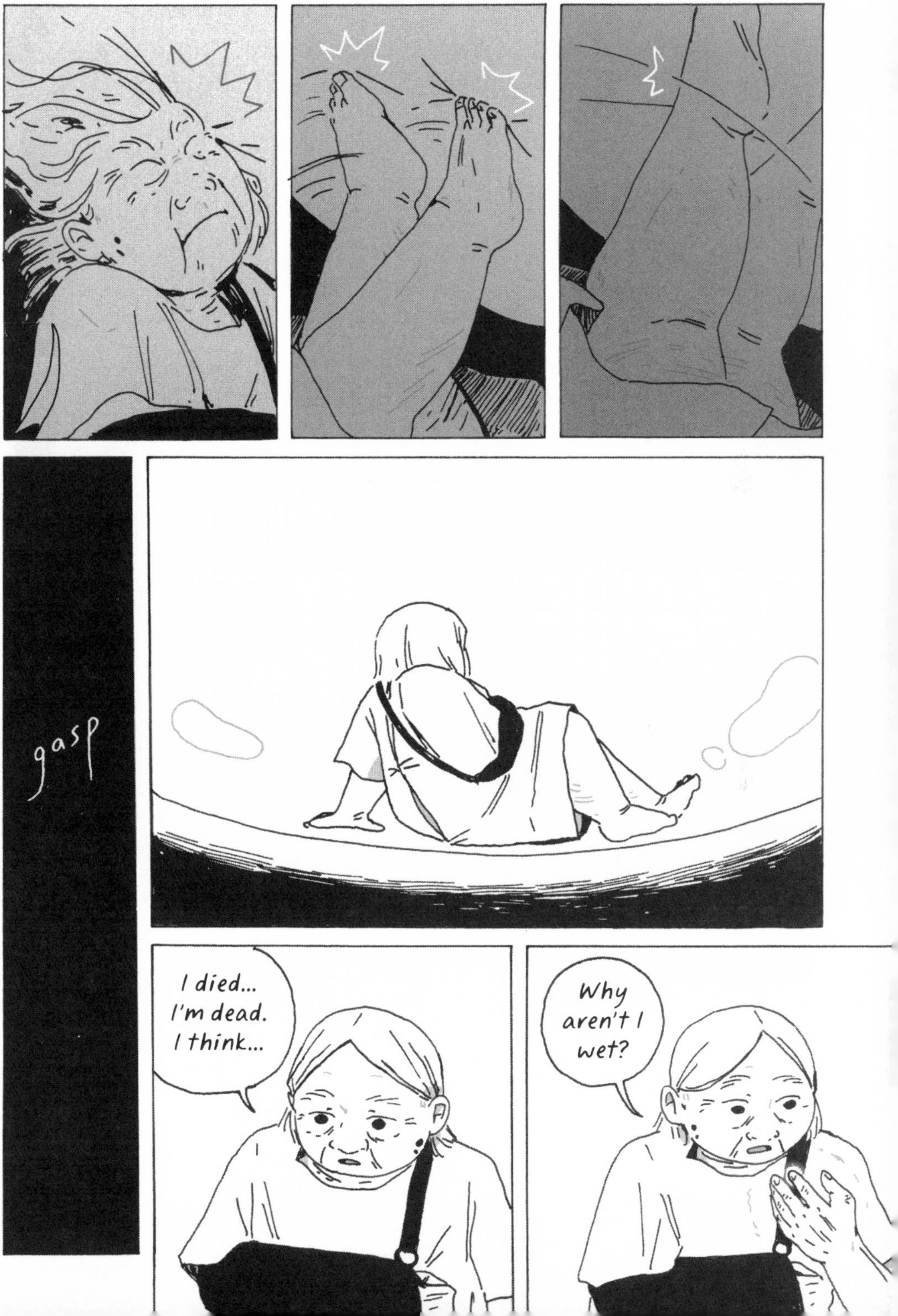
gasp
I died... I'm dead. I think...
Why aren't I wet?

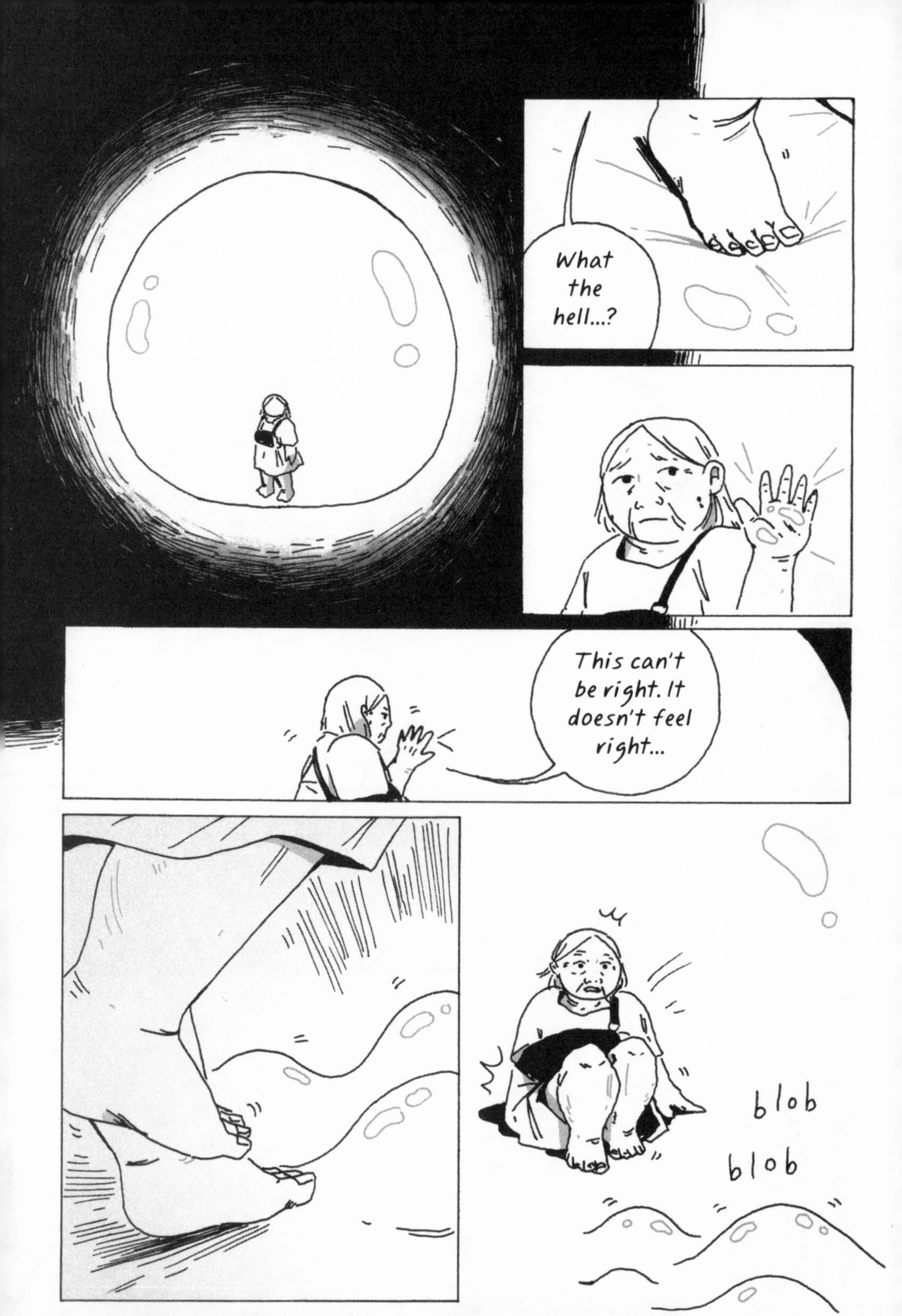
What the hell...?
This can't be right. It doesn't feel right...
blob
blob

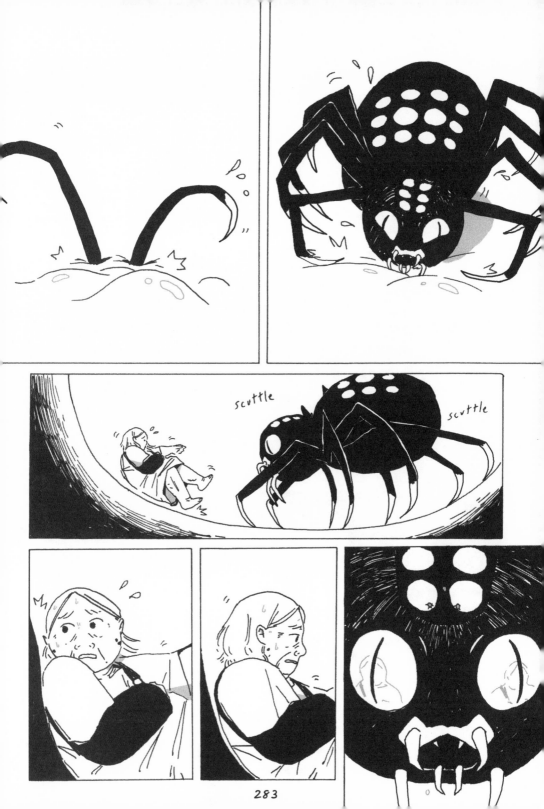

scuttle

scuttle

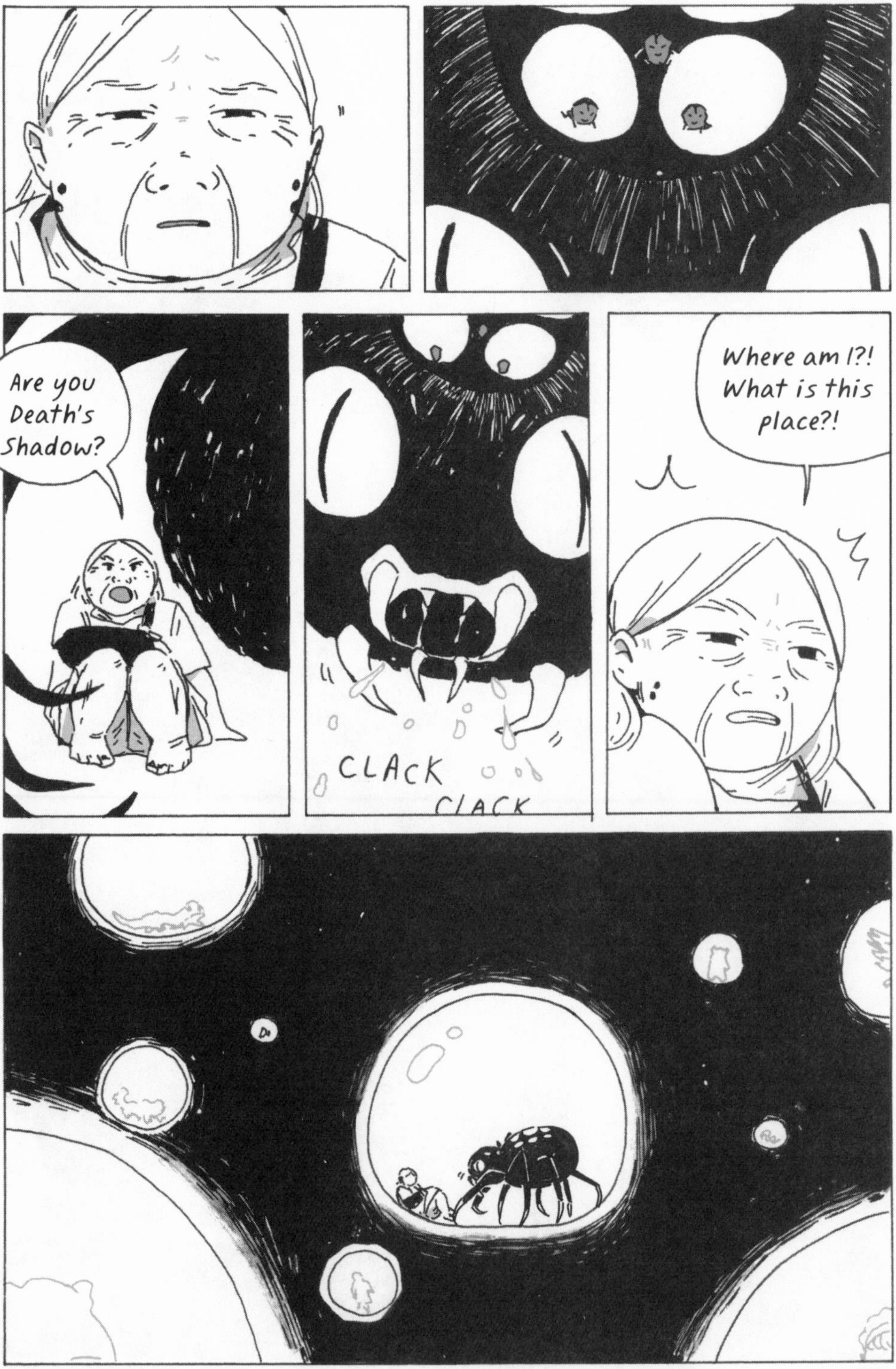
Are you Death's Shadow?
CLACK
CLACK
Where am I?! What is this place?!

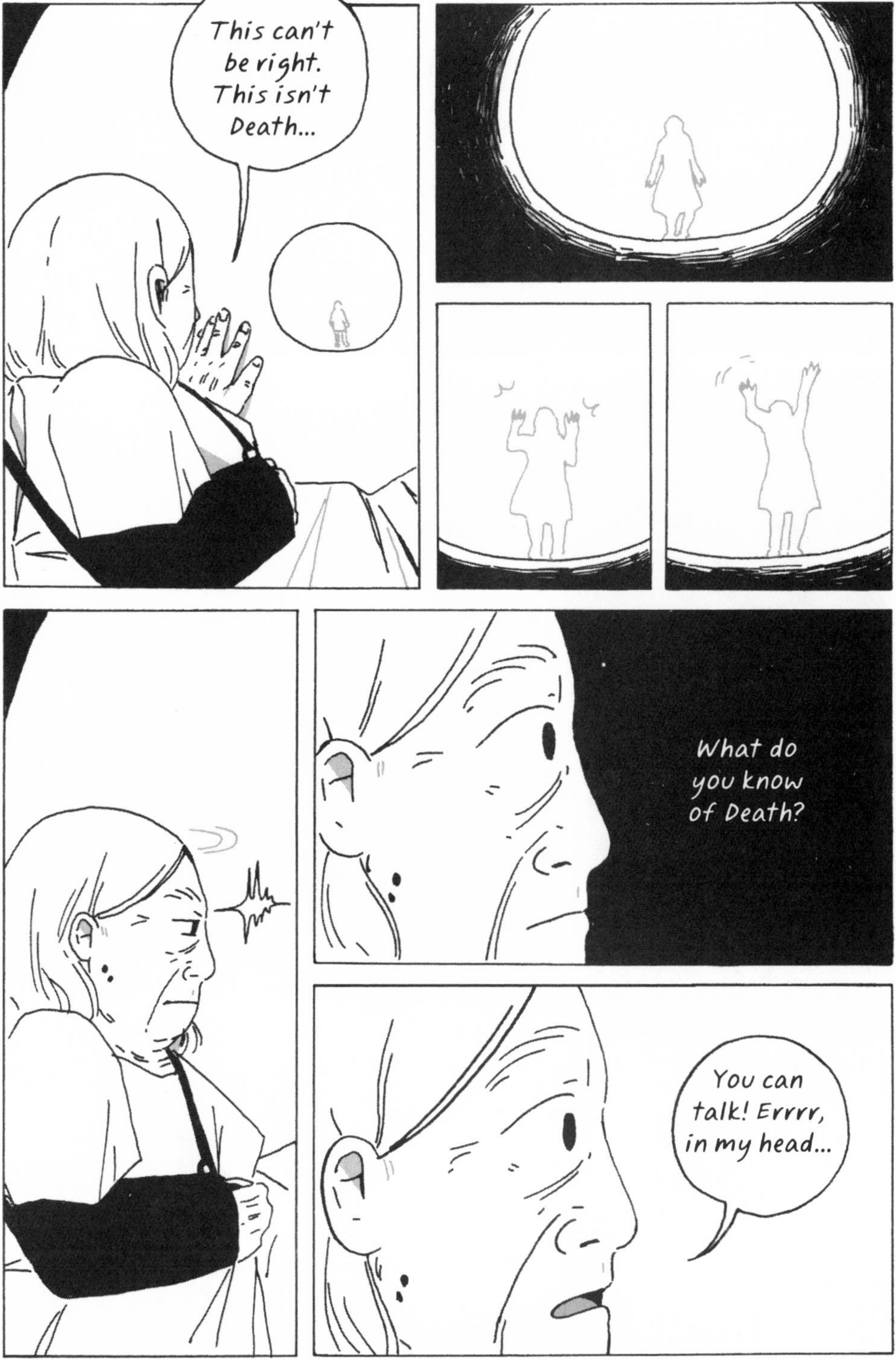
This can't be right. This isn't Death...
What do you know of Death?
You can talk! Errrr, in my head...

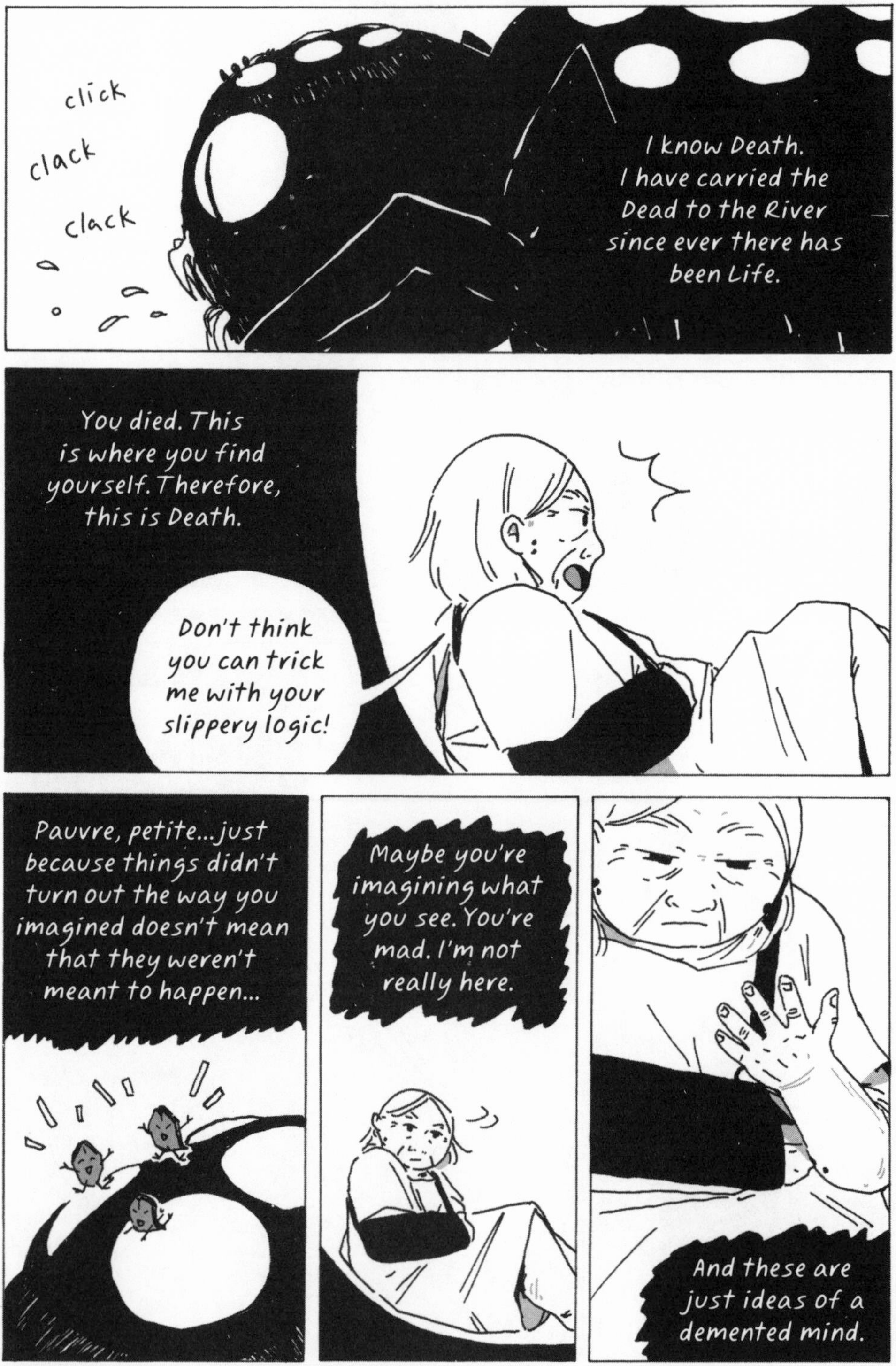
click
clack
clack
I know Death. I have carried the Dead to the River since ever there has been Life.
You died. This is where you find yourself. Therefore, this is Death.
Don't think you can trick me with your slippery logic!
Pauvre, petite... just because things didn't turn out the way you imagined doesn't mean that they weren't meant to happen...
Maybe you're imagining what you see. You're mad. I'm not really here.
And these are just ideas of a demented mind.

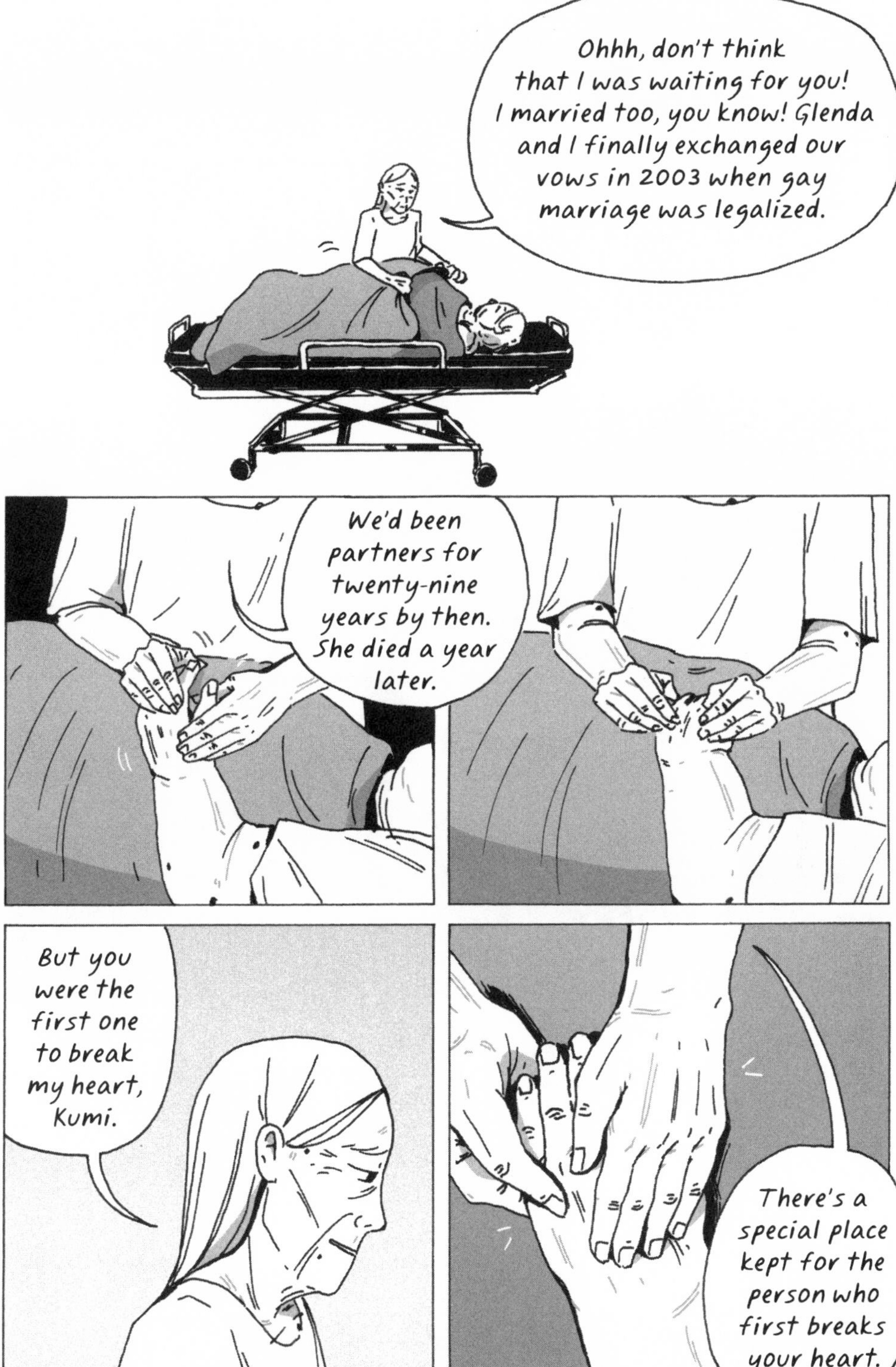
Ohhh, don't think that I was waiting for you! I married too, you know! Glenda and I finally exchanged our vows in 2003 when gay marriage was legalized.
We'd been partners for twenty-nine years by then. She died a year later.
But you were the first one to break my heart, Kumi.
There's a special place kept for the person who first breaks your heart.

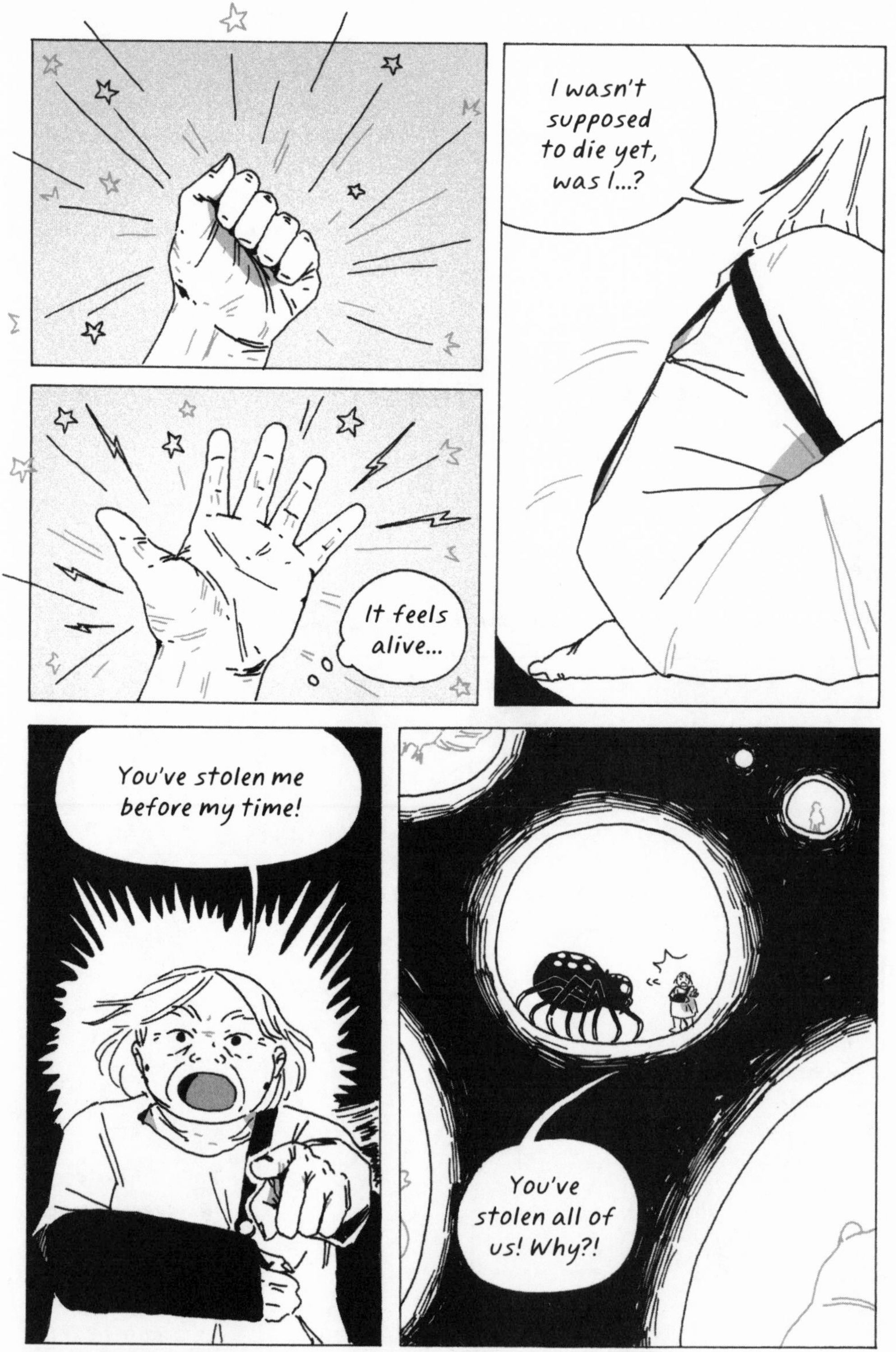
I wasn't supposed to die yet, was I...?
It feels alive...
You've stolen me before my time!
You've stolen all of us! Why?!

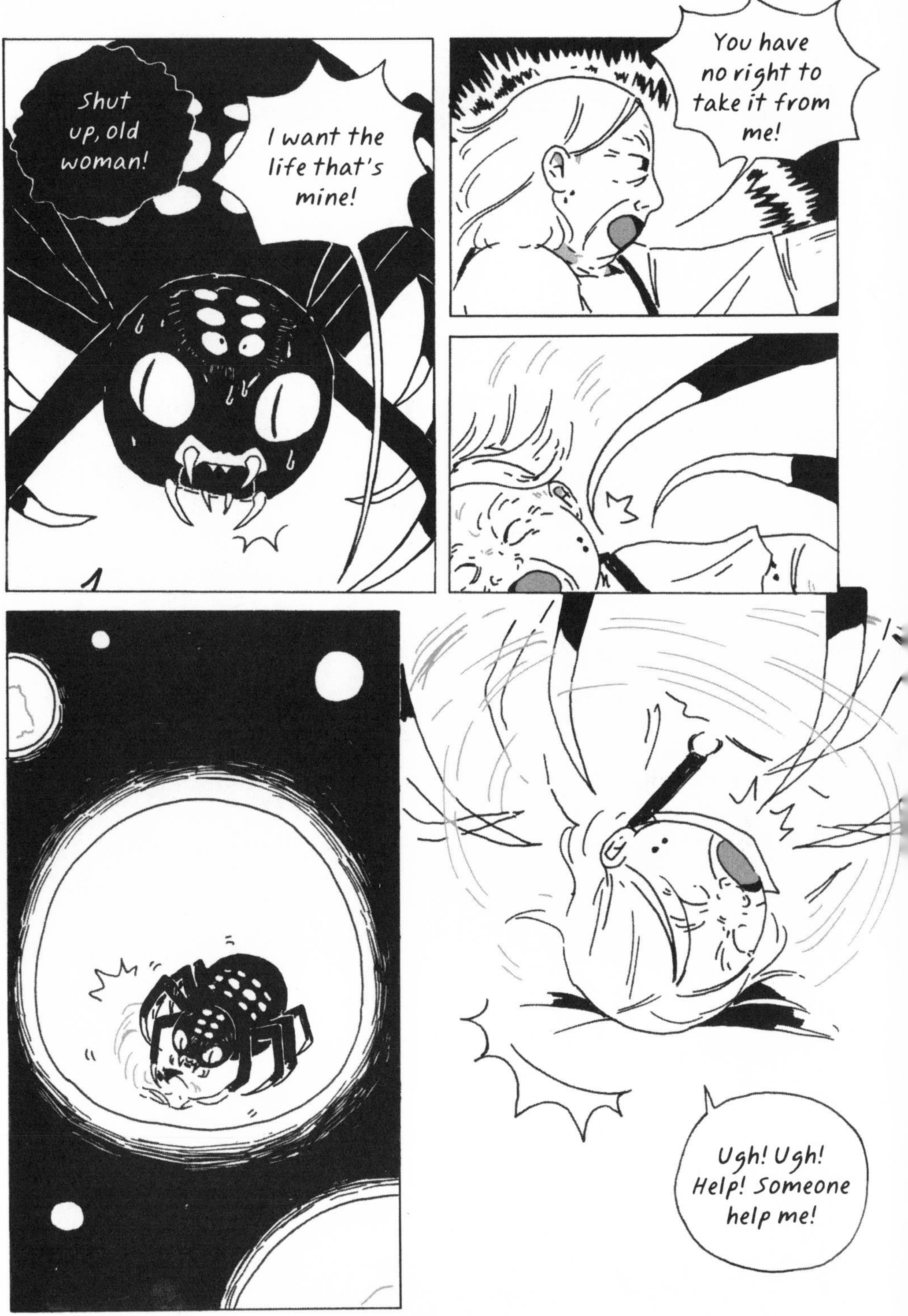
Shut up, old woman!
I want the life that's mine!
You have no right to take it from me!
Ugh! Ugh! Help! Someone help me!

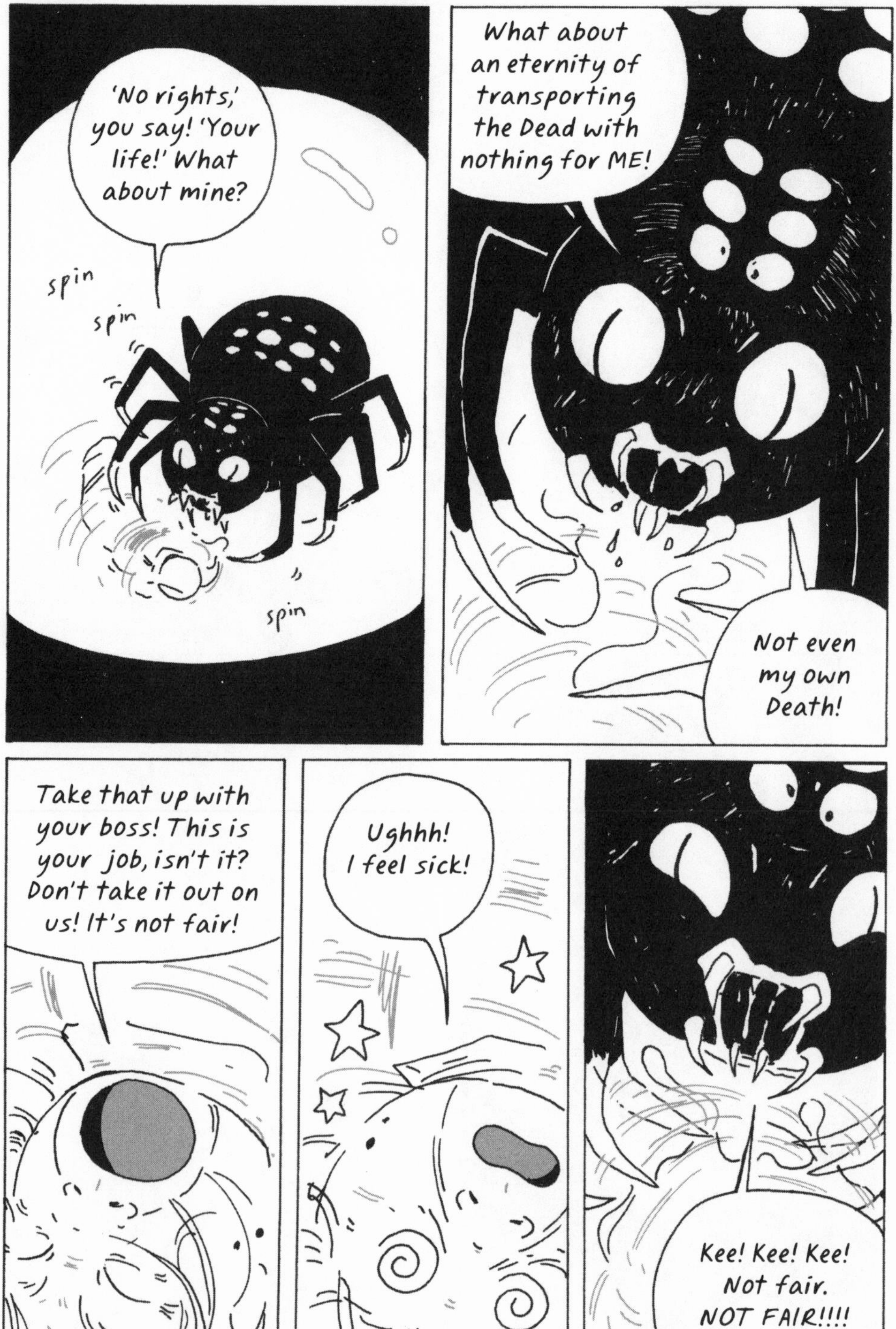
'No rights,' you say! 'Your life!' What about mine?
spin
spin
spin
What about an eternity of transporting the Dead with nothing for ME!
Not even my own Death!
Take that up with your boss! This is your job, isn't it? Don't take it out on us! It's not fair!
Ughhh! I feel sick!
Kee! Kee! Kee! Not fair. NOT FAIR!!!!

I borrow a little from Life. So very little. For minor home renovations... Who would begrudge me that?
gasp!
Twice you've stolen from me. Once, when I came for your daughter.

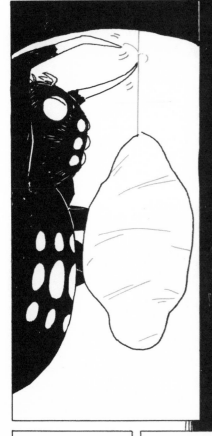

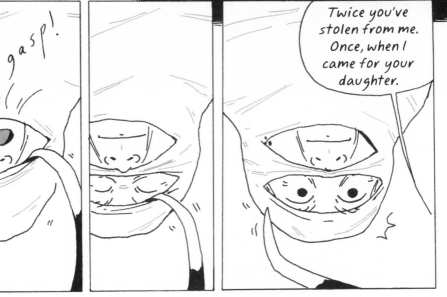

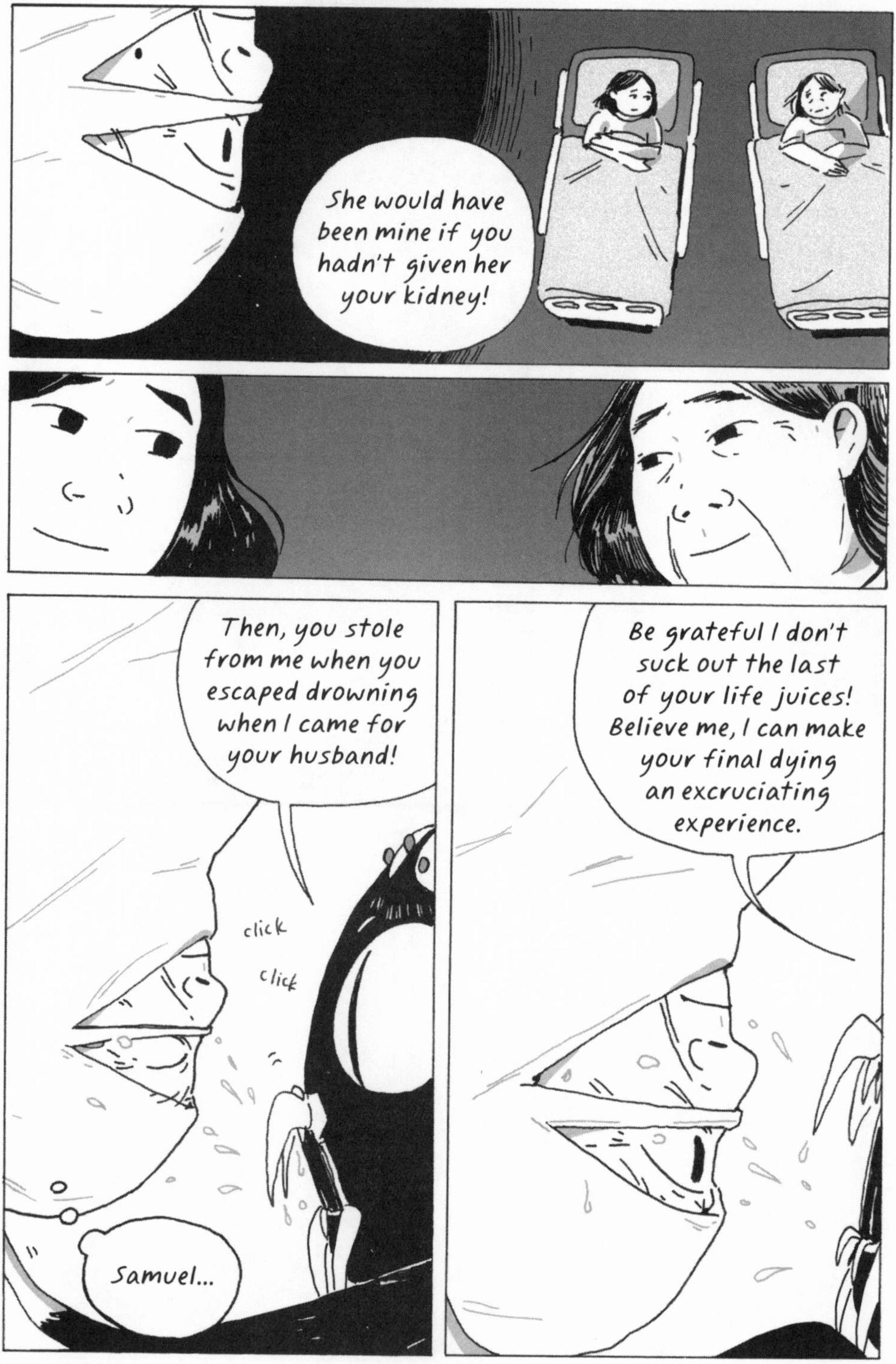
She would have been mine if you hadn't given her your kidney!
Then, you stole from me when you escaped drowning when I came for your husband!
click
click
Samuel...
Be grateful I don't suck out the last of your life juices! Believe me, I can make your final dying an excruciating experience.

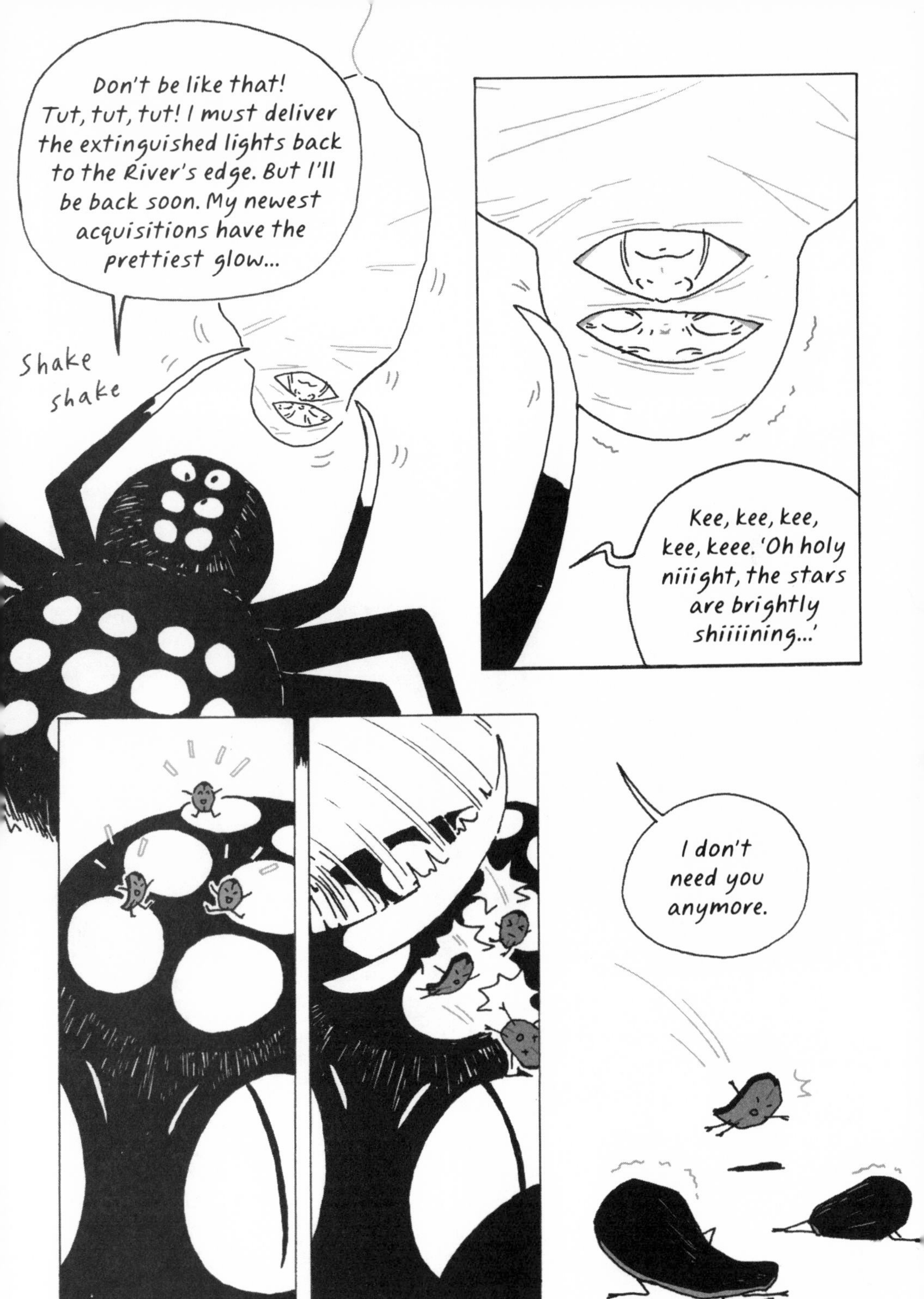
Don't be like that! Tut, tut, tut! I must deliver the extinguished lights back to the River's edge. But I'll be back soon. My newest acquisitions have the prettiest glow...
Shake shake
Kee, kee, kee, kee, keee. 'Oh holy niiight, the stars are brightly shiiiining...'
I don't need you anymore.

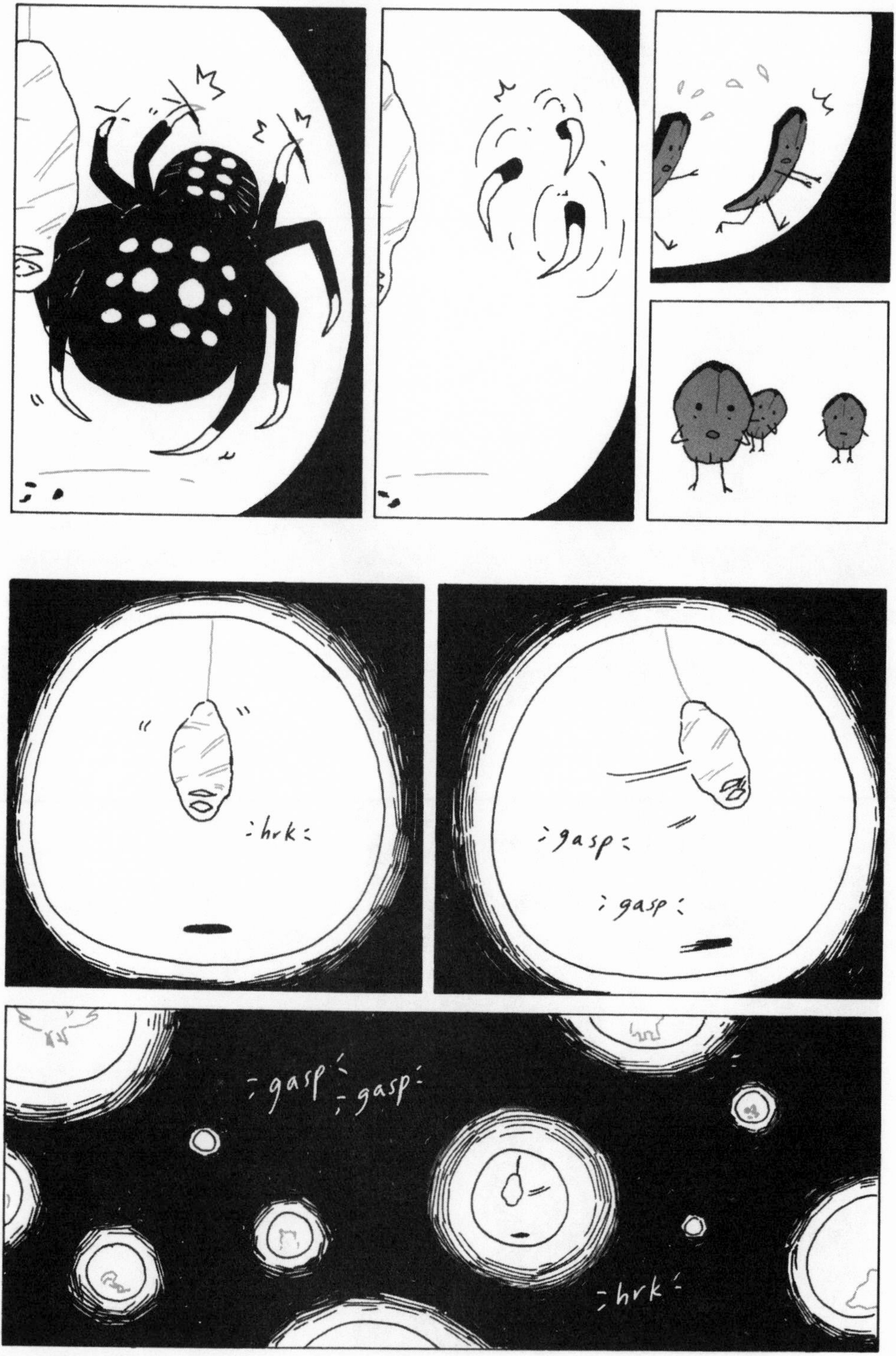
:hrk:
:gasp:
:gasp:
:gasp: :gasp:
:hrk:

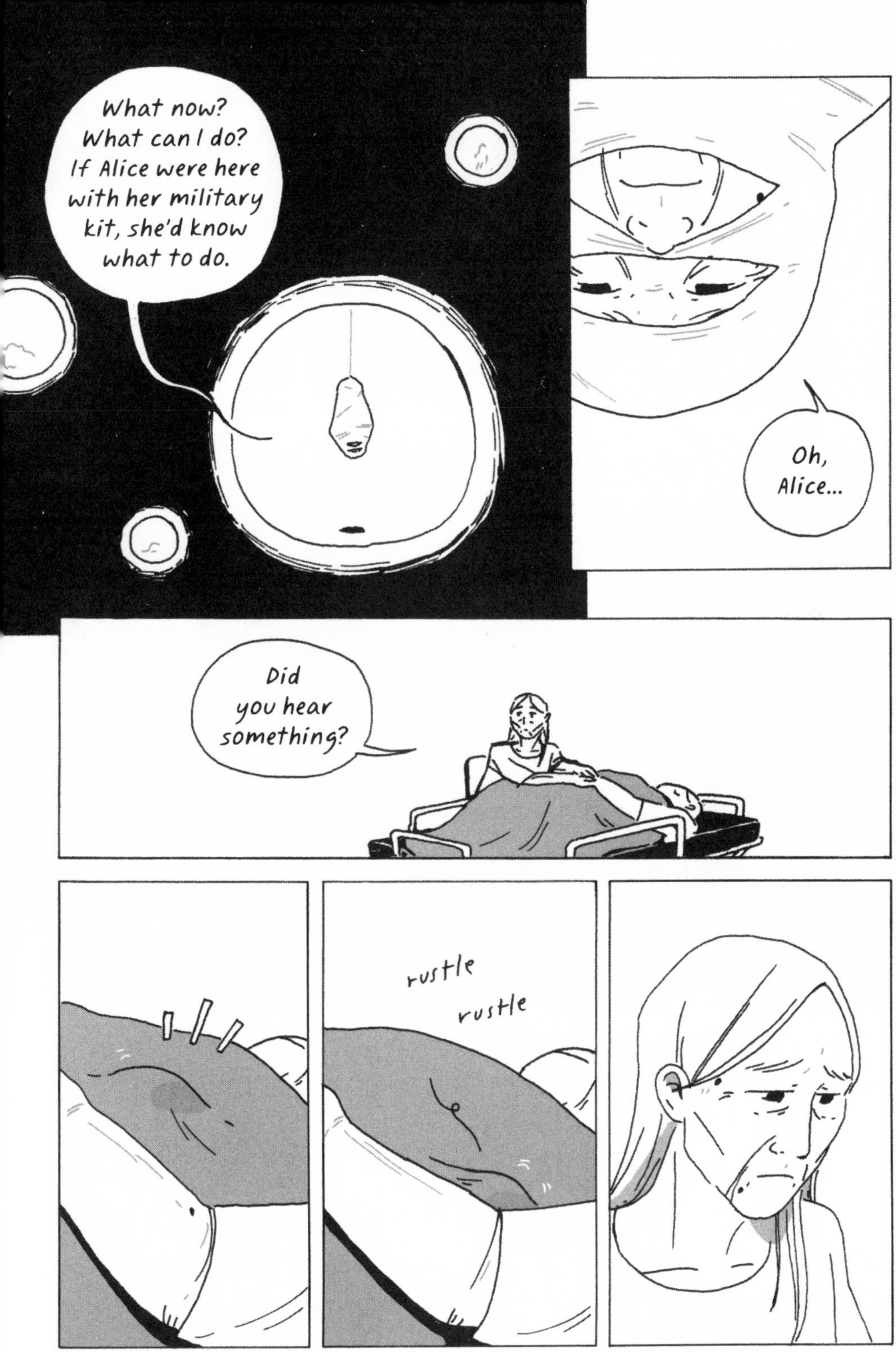
What now? What can I do? If Alice were here with her military kit, she'd know what to do.
Oh, Alice...
Did you hear something?
rustle
rustle

Don't be ridiculous.
gasp
It's not fair.
gasp
gasp
I'm supposed to have more time.
gasp
gasp
IT'S MY TIME!
splash!

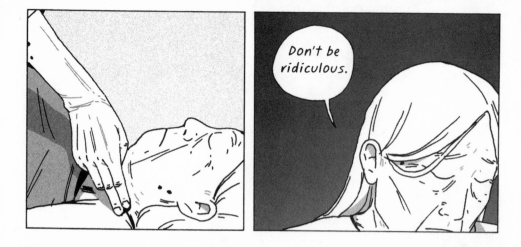

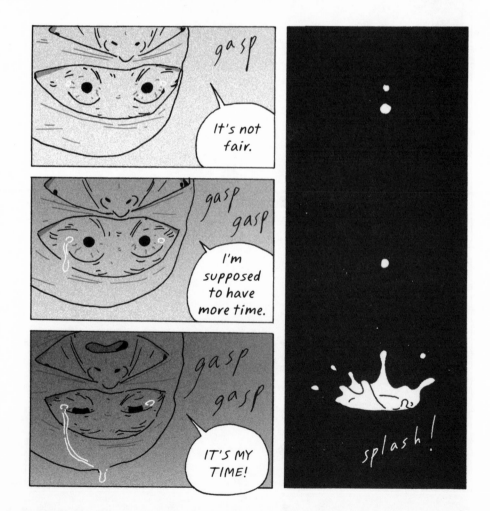

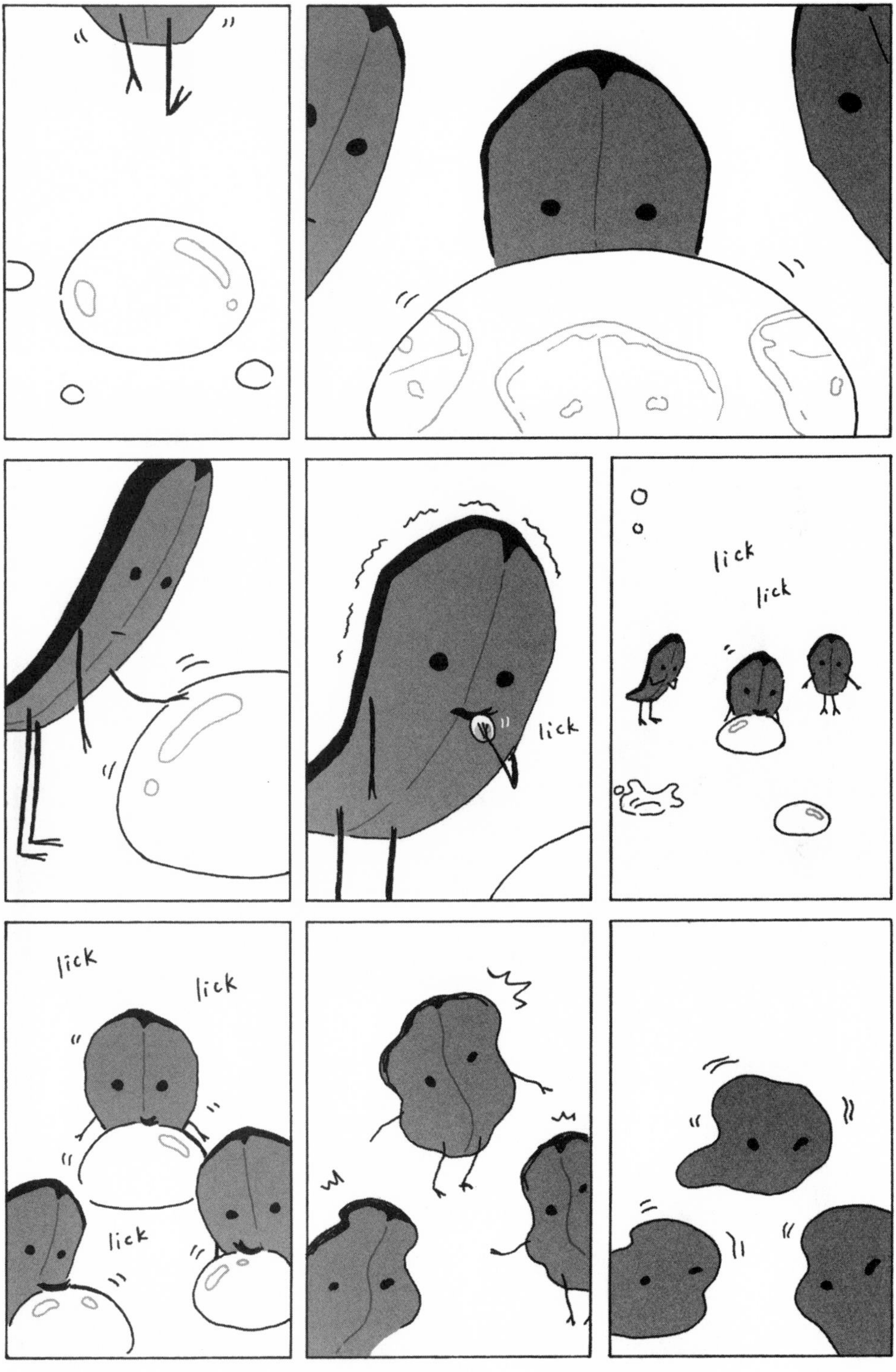
lick
lick
lick
lick
lick
lick
lick

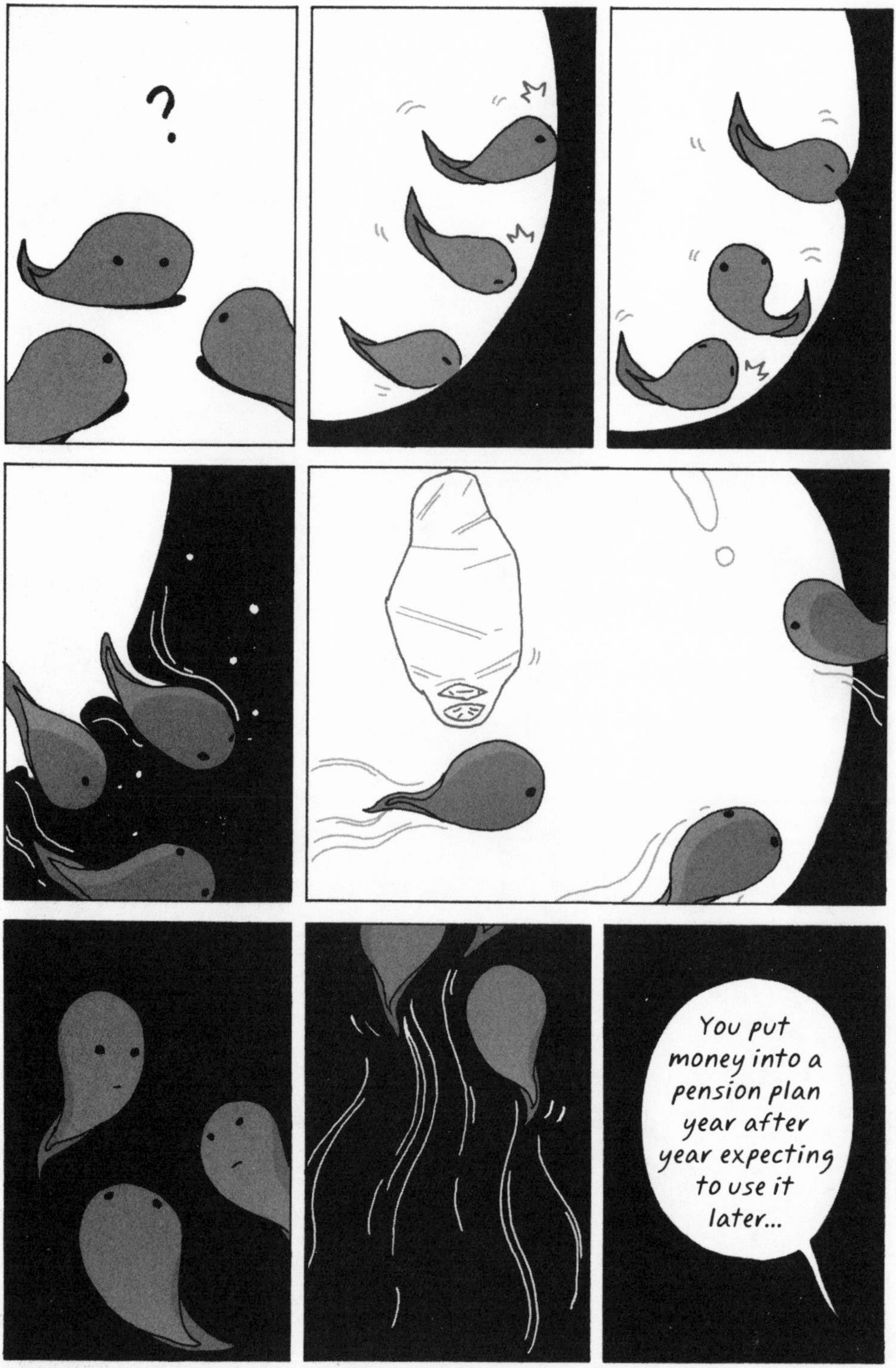
?
You put money into a pension plan year after year expecting to use it later...

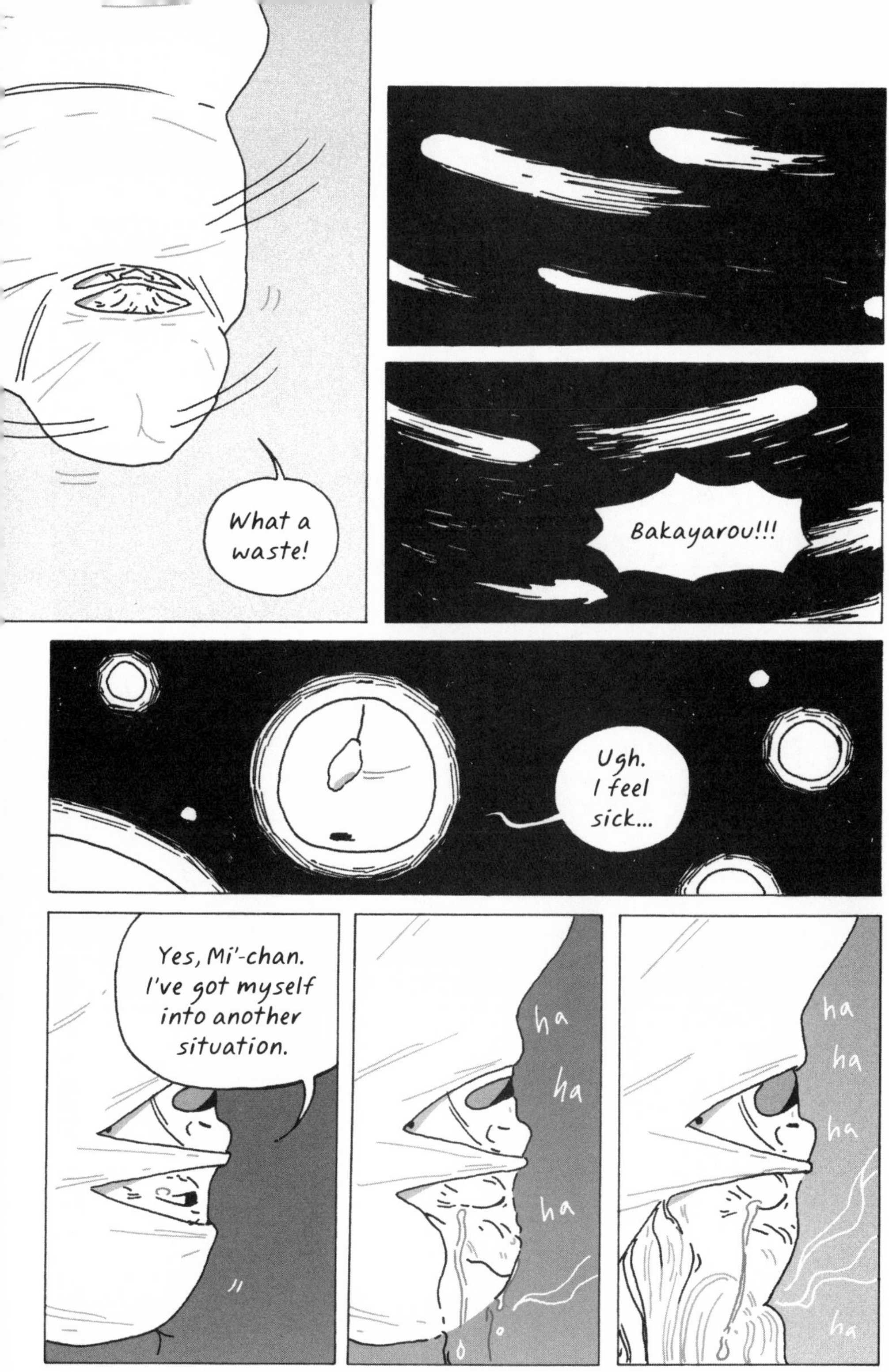
What a waste!
Bakayarou!!!
Ugh. I feel sick...
Yes, Mi'-chan. I've got myself into another situation.
ha ha ha
ha ha ha ha

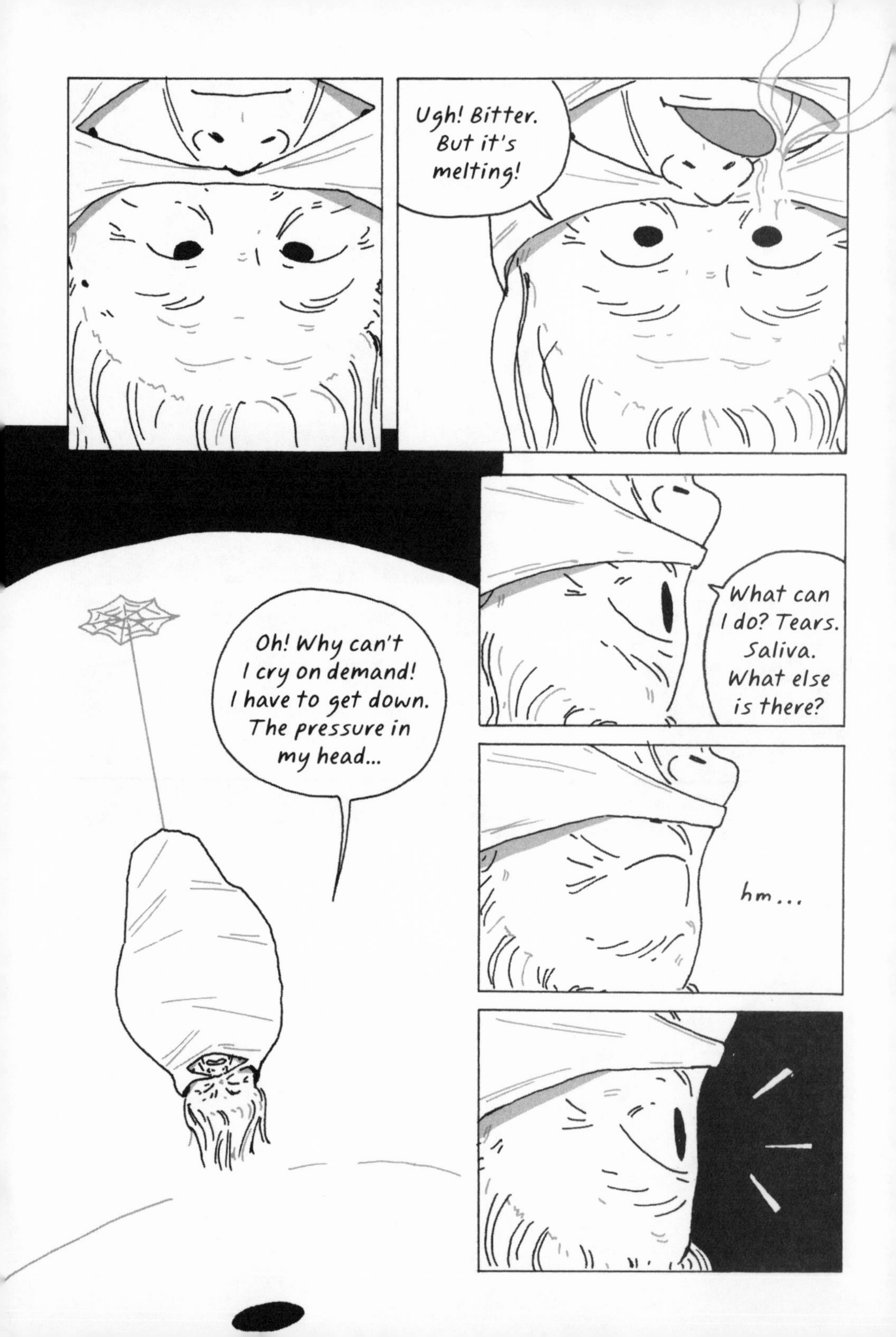
Ugh! Bitter. But it's melting!
What can I do? Tears. Saliva. What else is there?
Oh! Why can't I cry on demand! I have to get down. The pressure in my head...
hm...

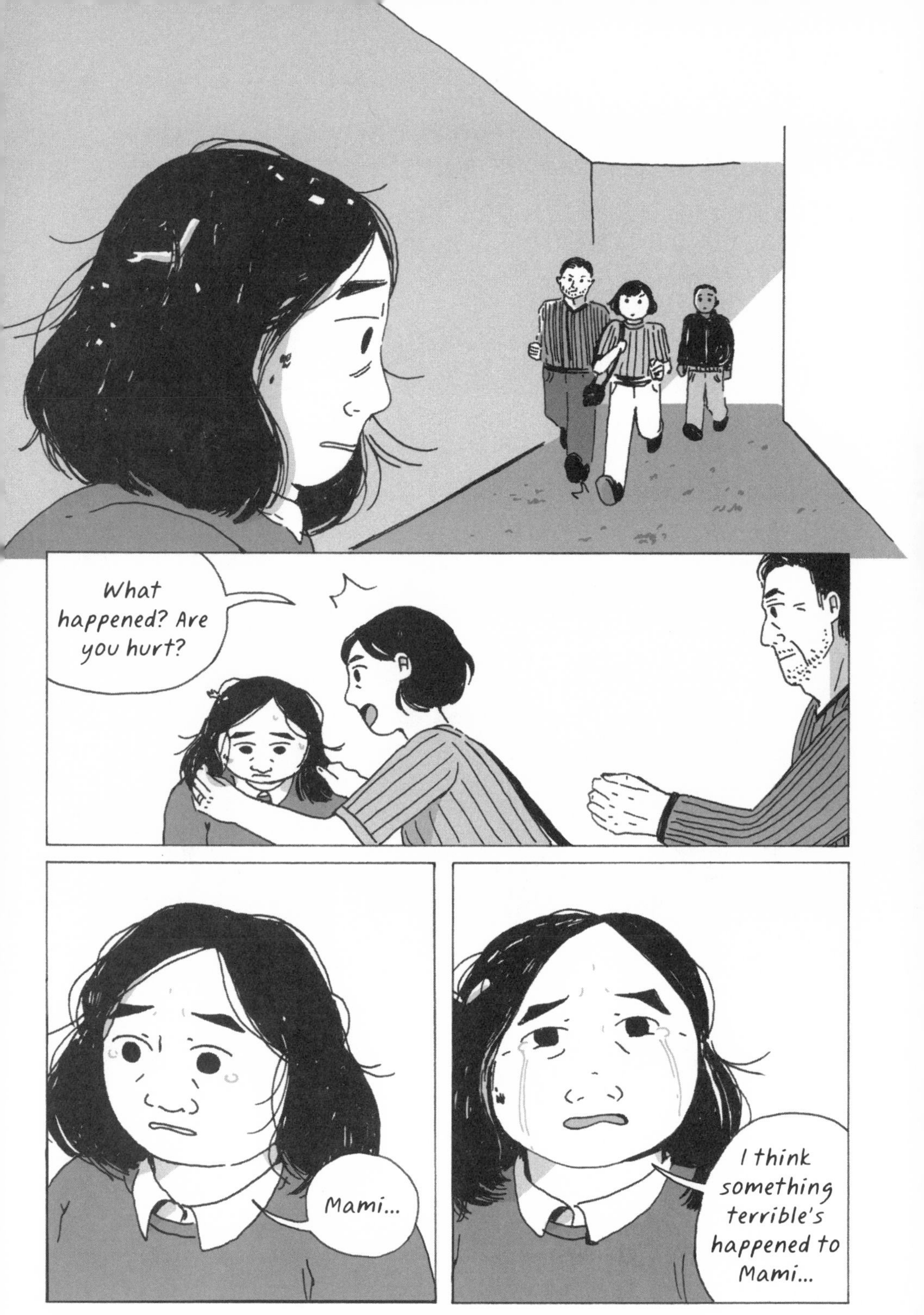
What happened? Are you hurt?
Mami...
I think something terrible's happened to Mami...

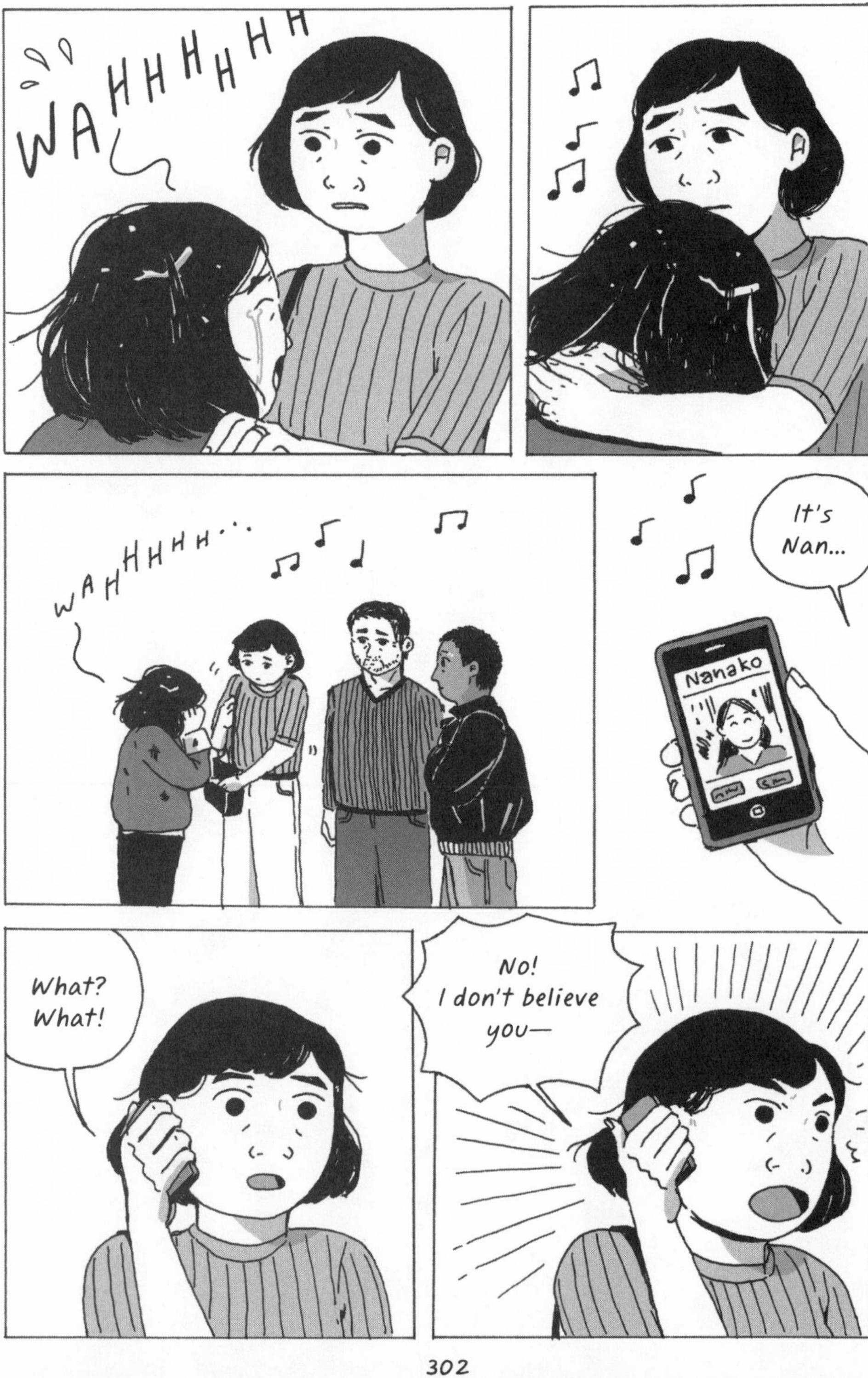
WAHHHHHHH
WAHHHHH...
It's Nan...
Nanako
What? What!
No! I don't believe you—

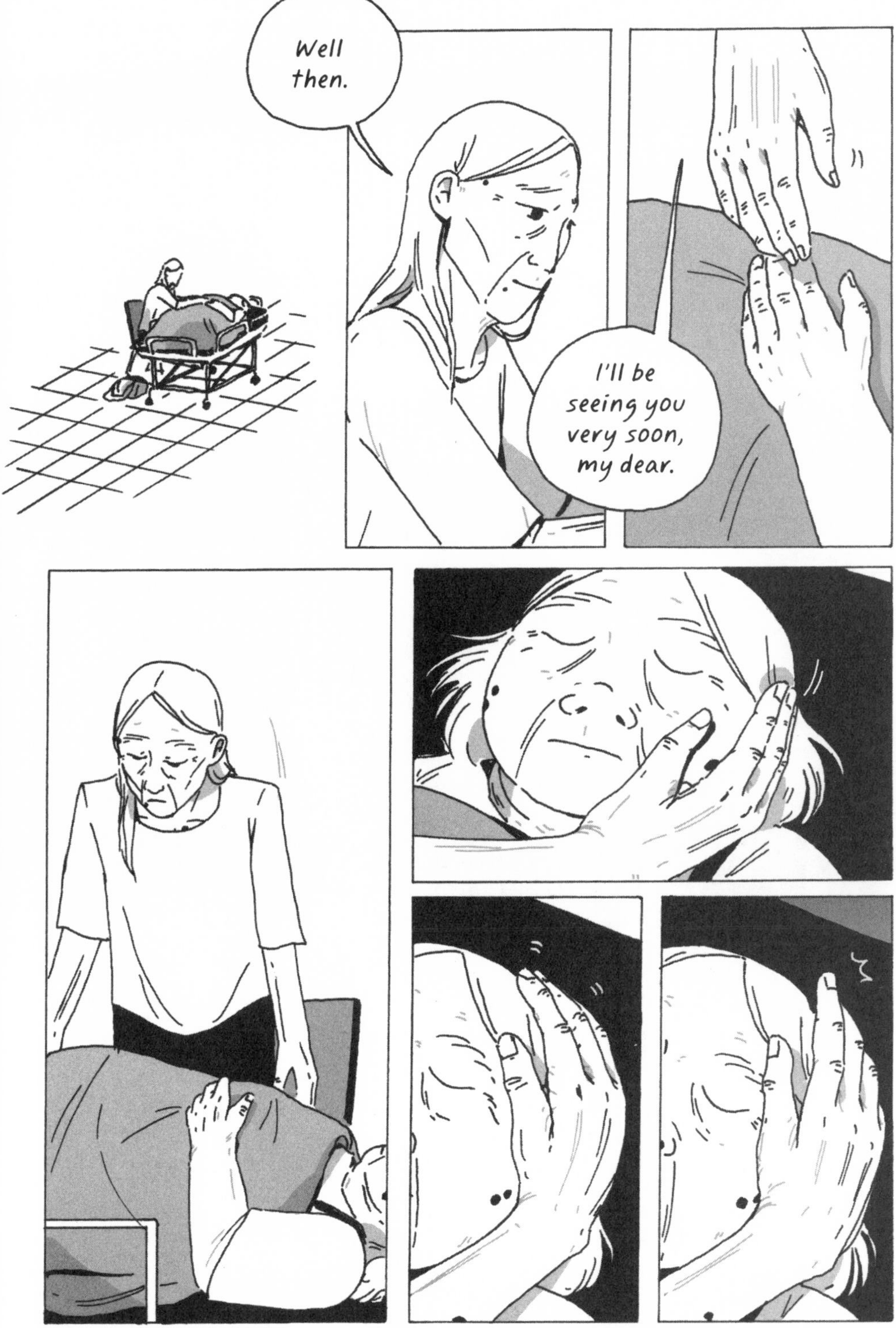
Well then.
I'll be seeing you very soon, my dear.

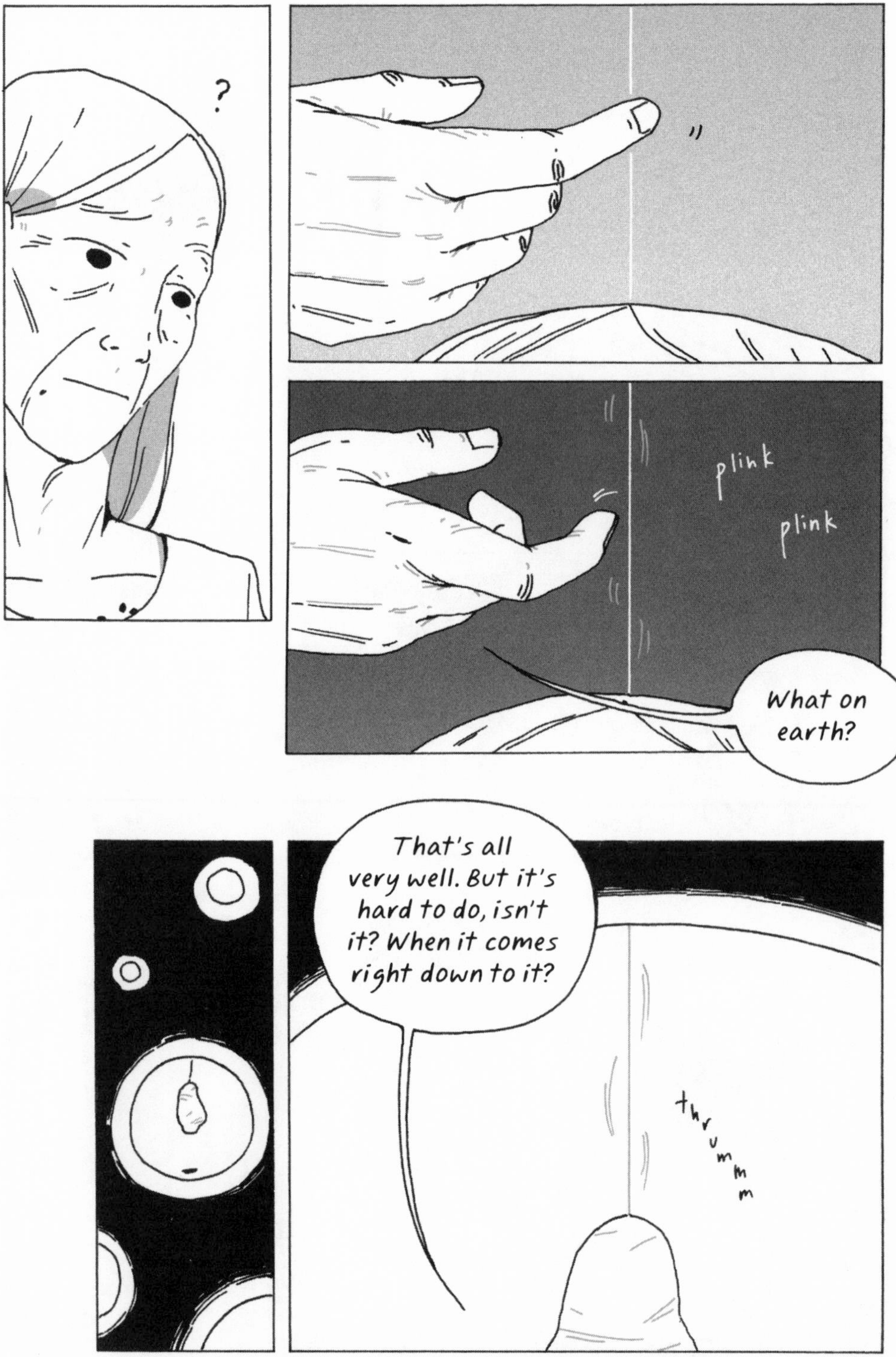
?
plink
plink
What on earth?
That's all very well. But it's hard to do, isn't it? When it comes right down to it?
thrummm

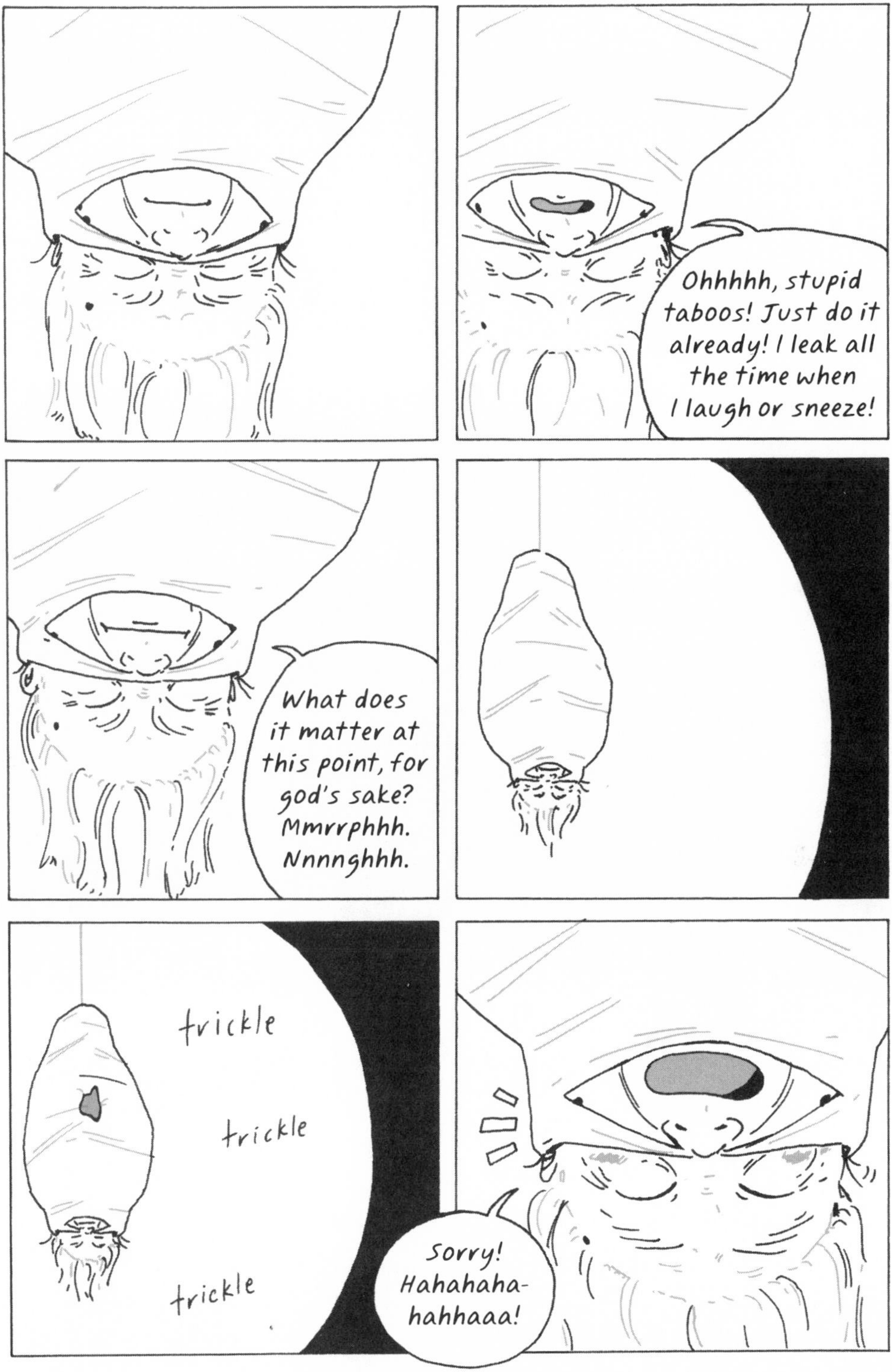
Ohhhhh, stupid taboos! Just do it already! I leak all the time when I laugh or sneeze!
What does it matter at this point, for god's sake? Mmrrphhh. Nnnnghhh.
trickle
trickle
trickle
Sorry! Hahahaha-hahhaaa!

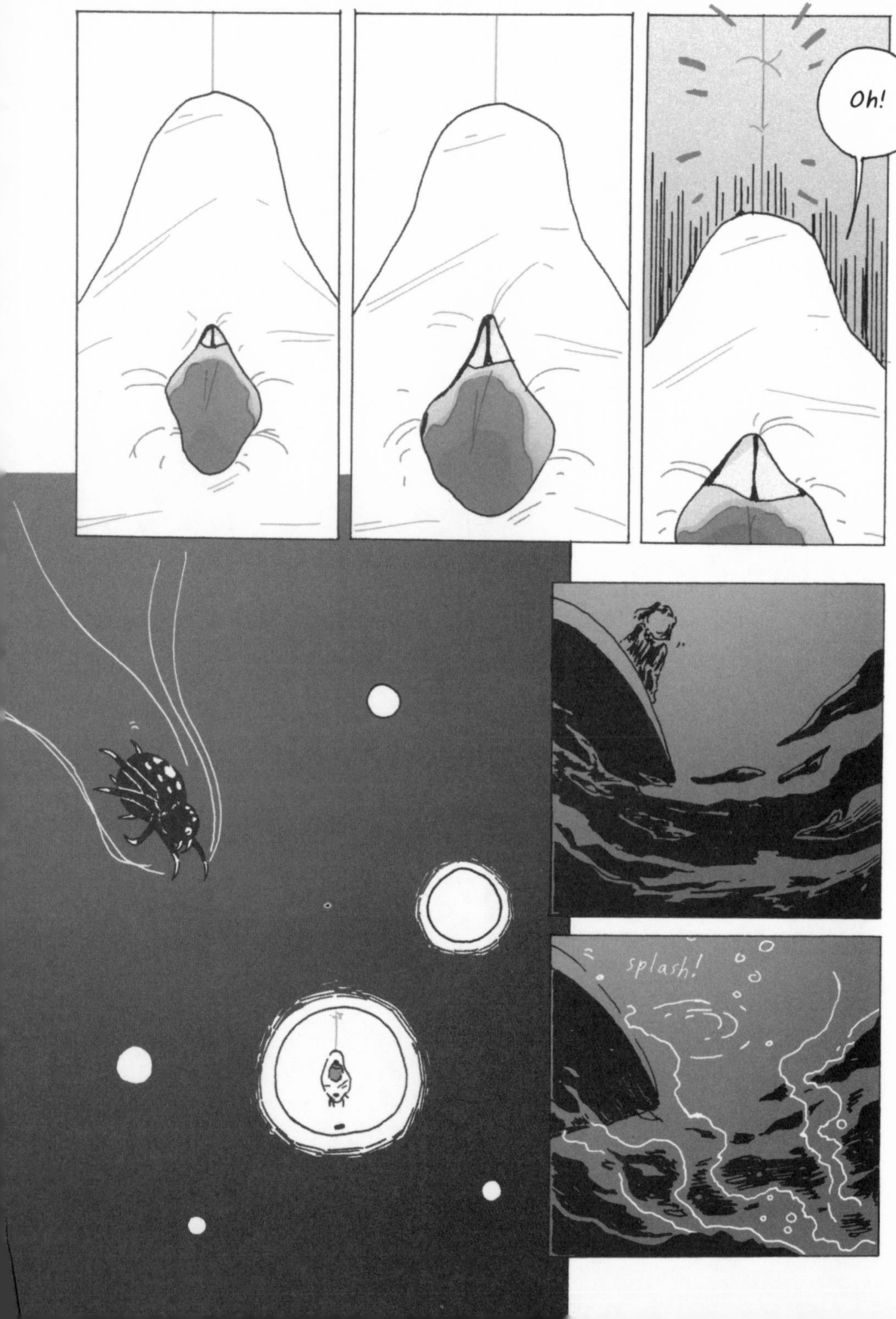
Oh!
splash!

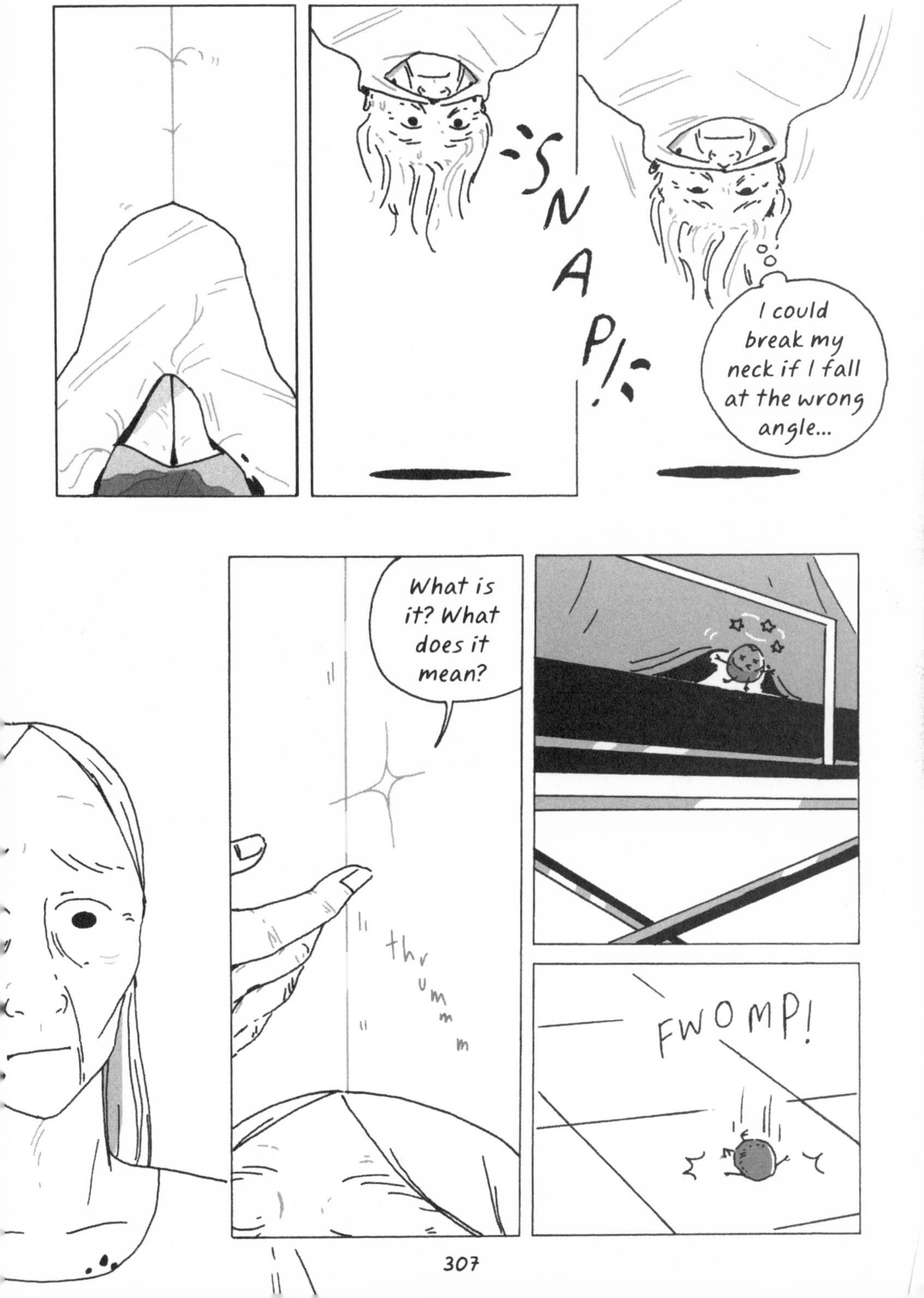
SNAP!
I could break my neck if I fall at the wrong angle...
What is it? What does it mean?
thrummmm
FWOMP!

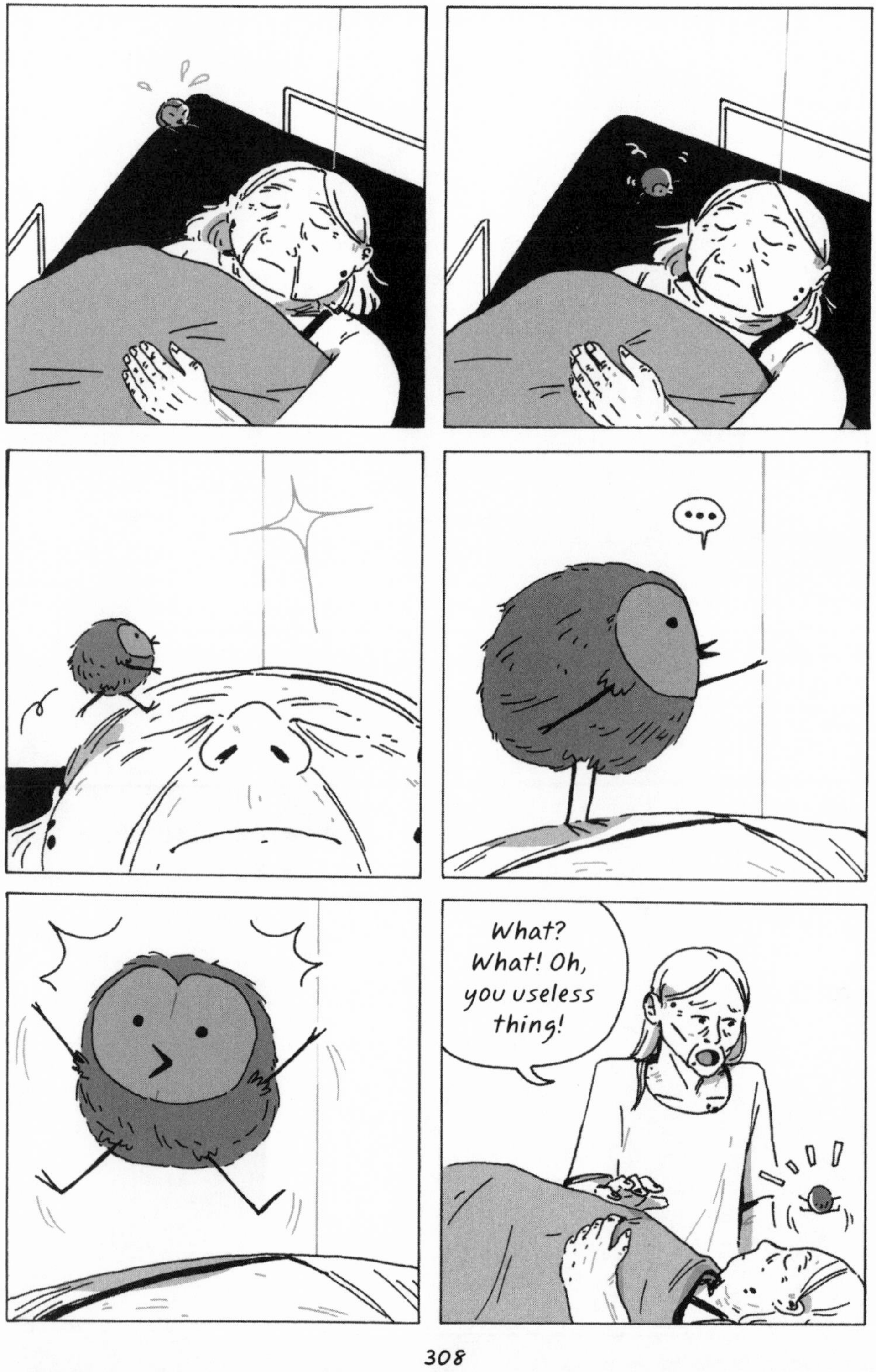
...
What?
What! Oh,
you useless
thing!

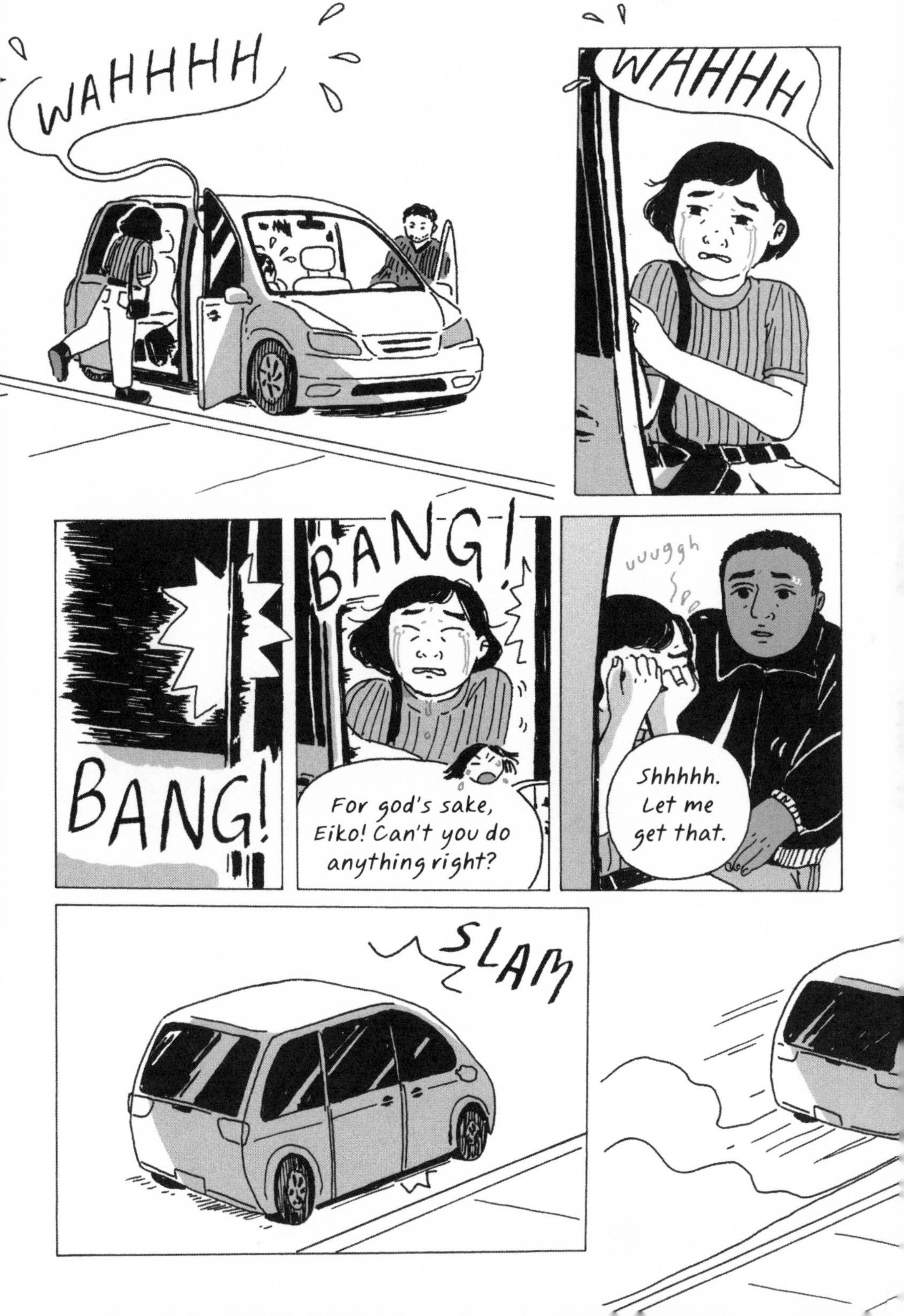
WAHHHH
WAHHHH
BANG!
BANG!
For god's sake, Eiko! Can't you do anything right?
uuuggh
Shhhhh. Let me get that.
SLAM

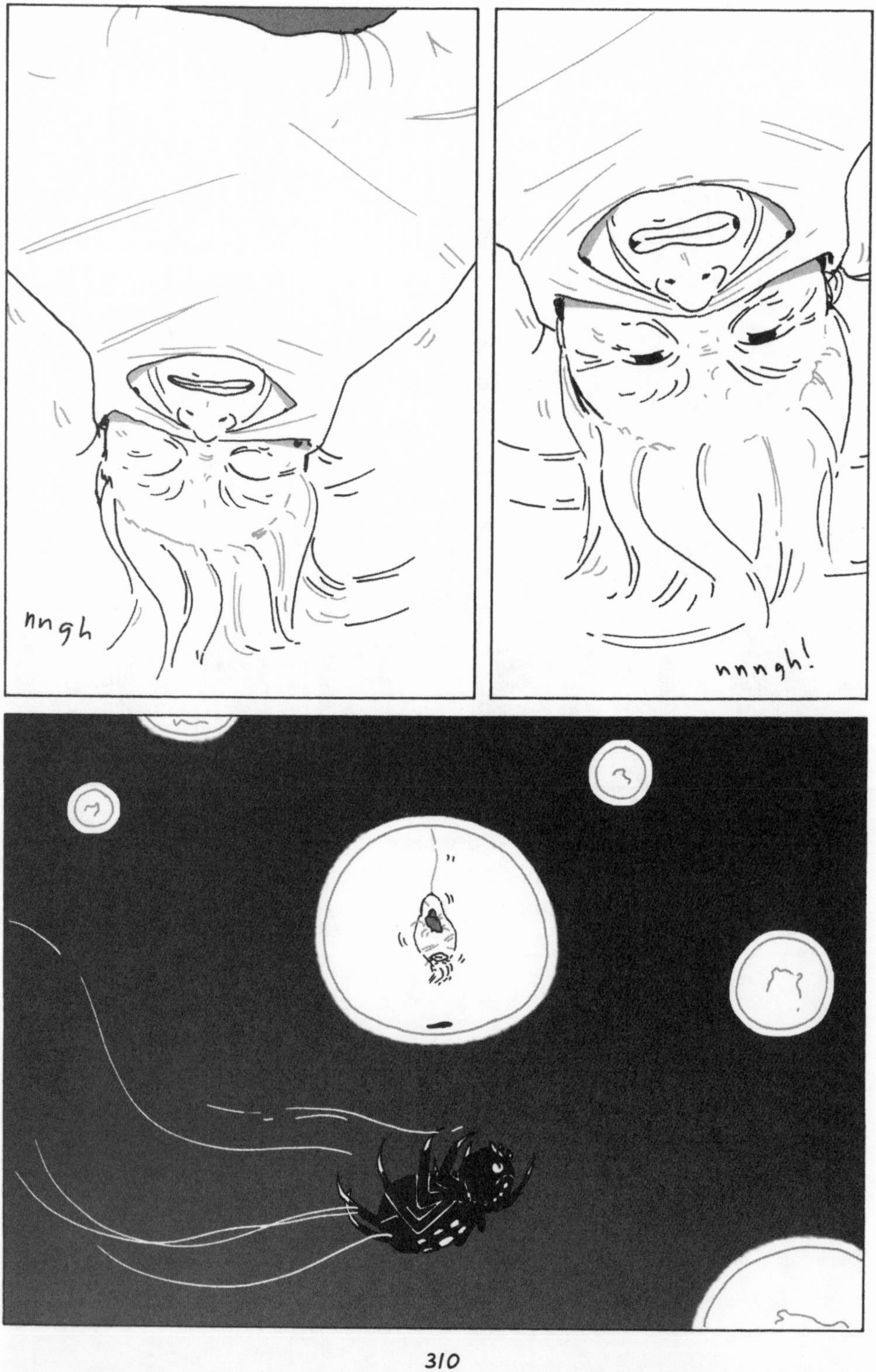
nngh
nnngh!

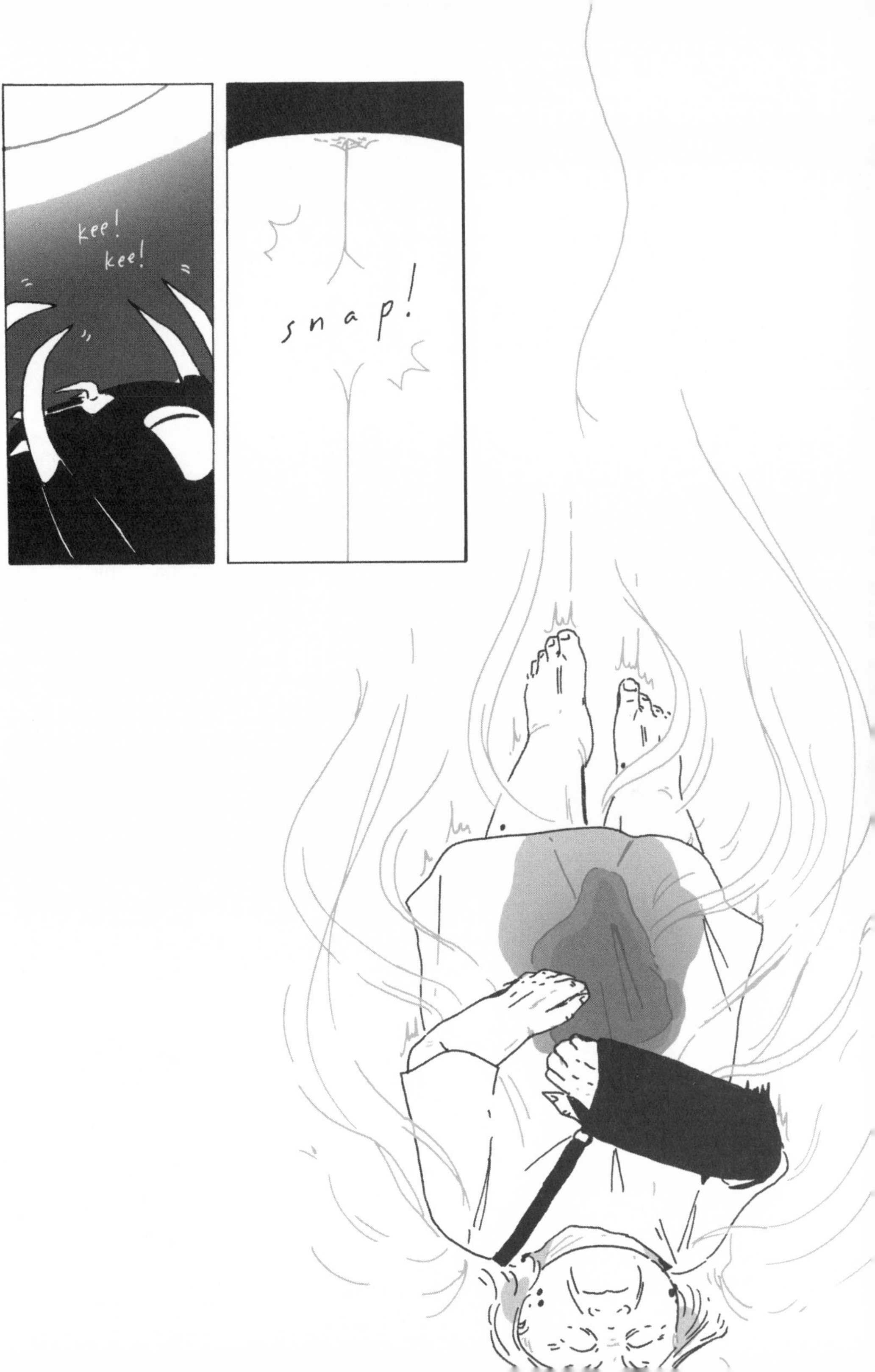
kee!
kee!
snap!

Chapter Sixteen

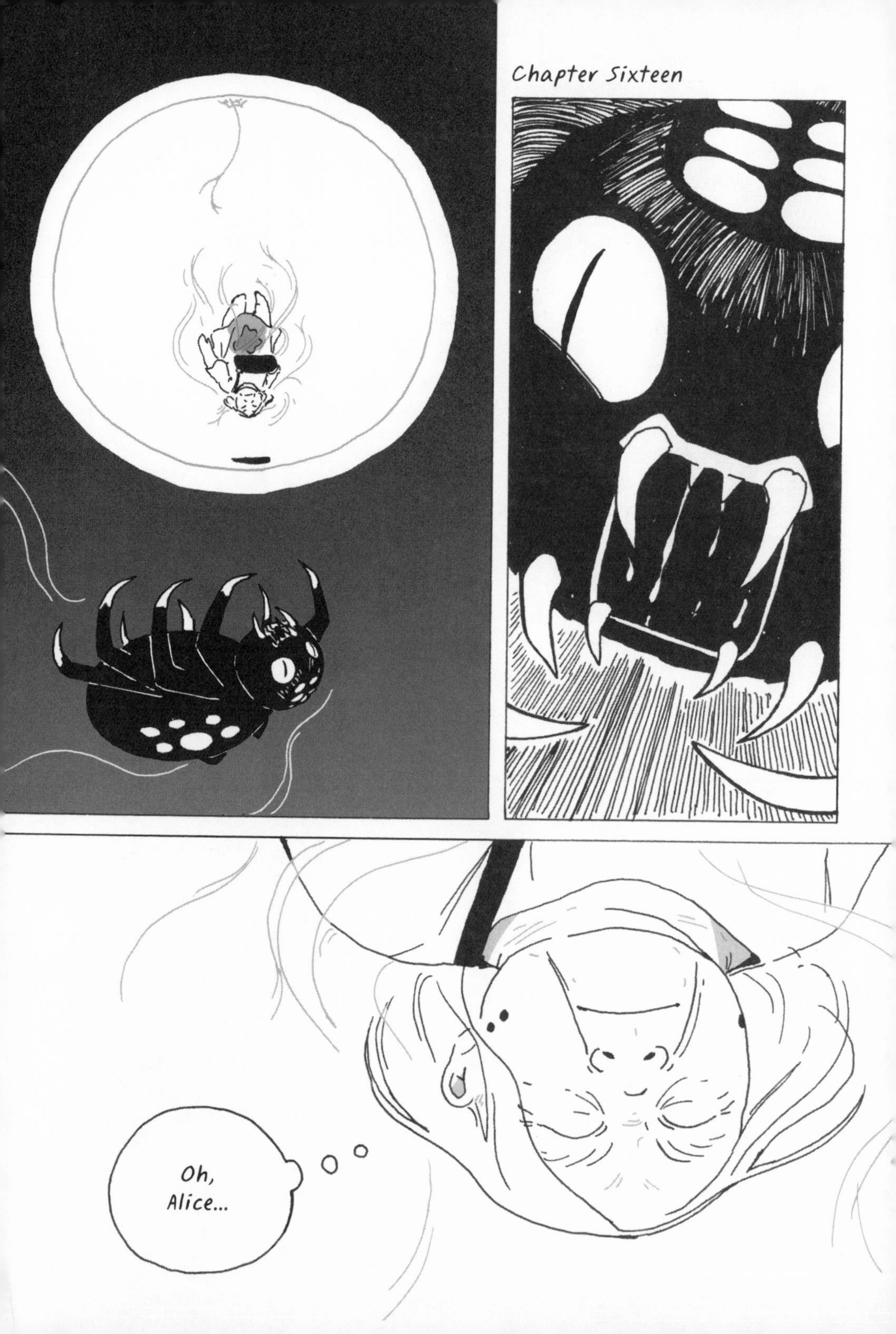
Oh, Alice...

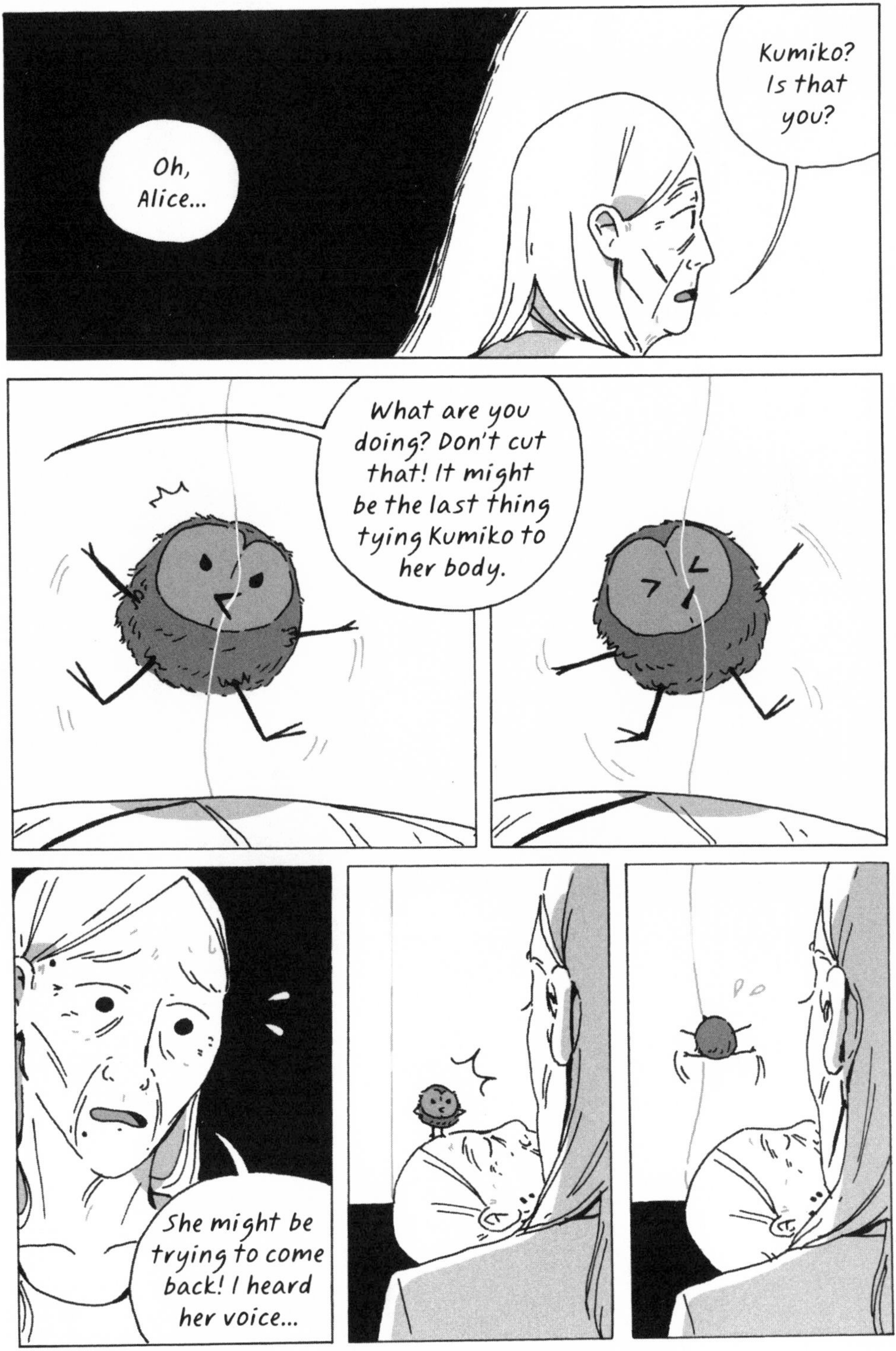
Kumiko? Is that you?
Oh, Alice...
What are you doing? Don't cut that! It might be the last thing tying Kumiko to her body.
She might be trying to come back! I heard her voice...

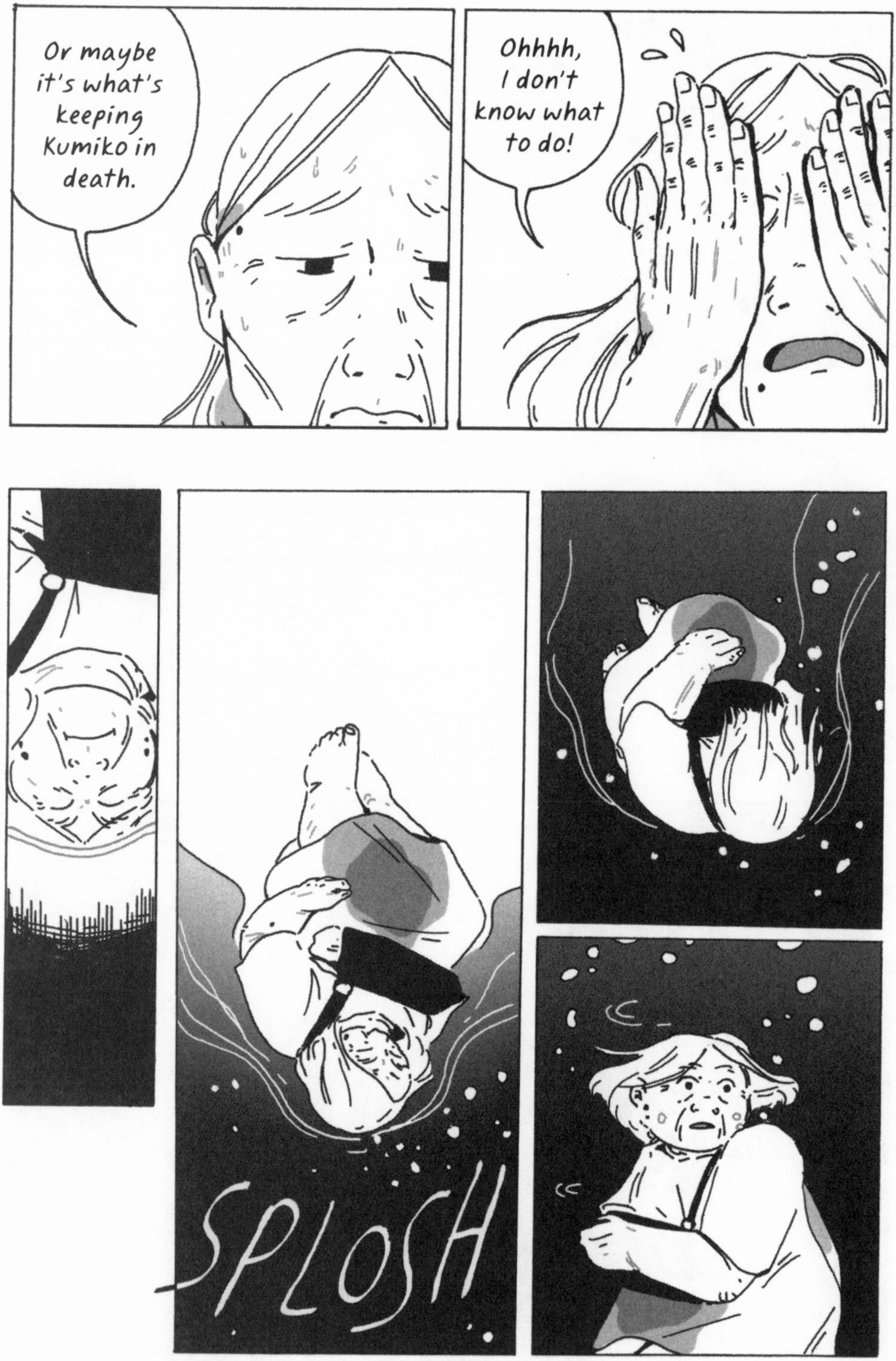
Or maybe it's what's keeping Kumiko in death.
Ohhhh, I don't know what to do!
SPLOSH

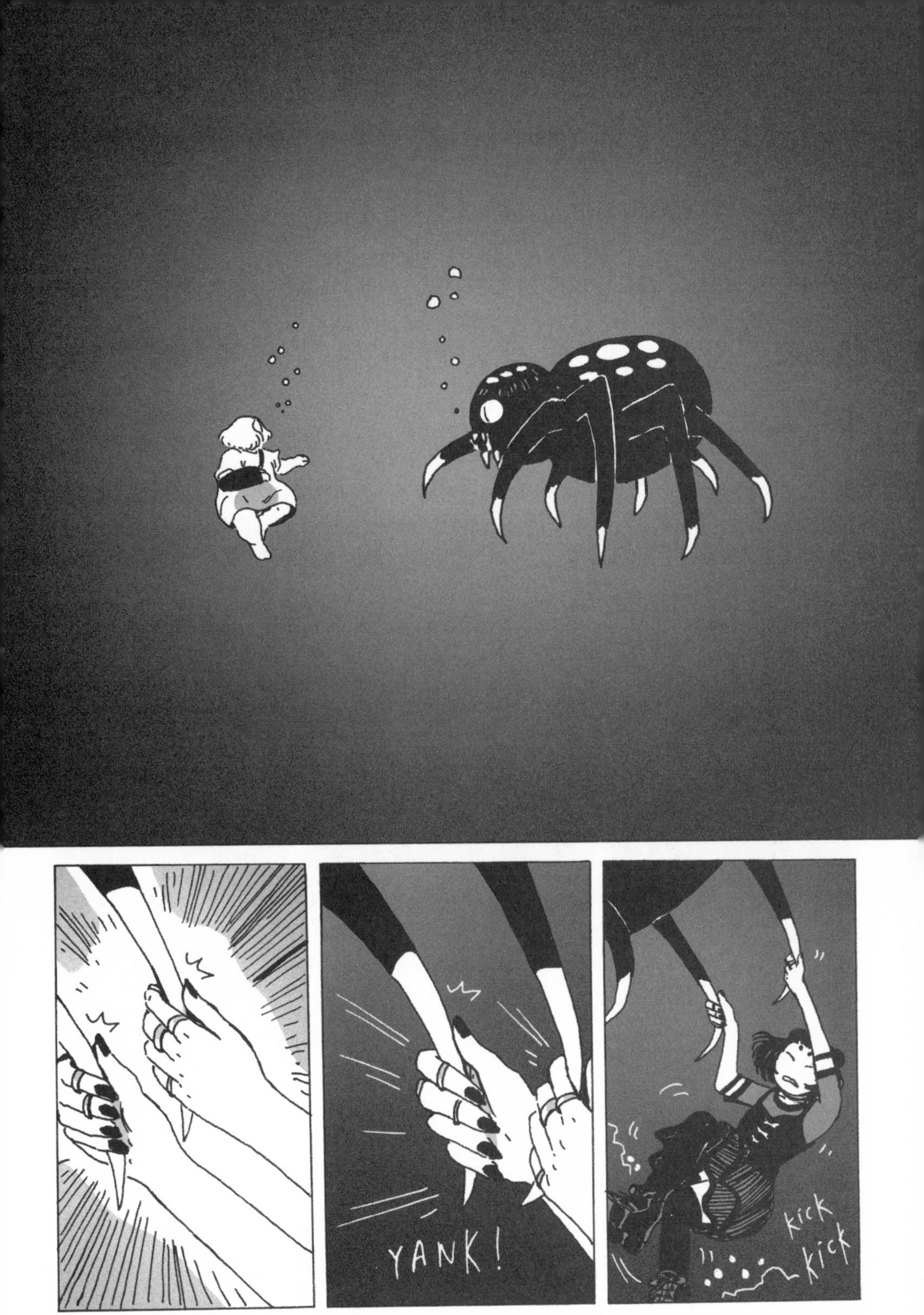
YANK!
kick
kick

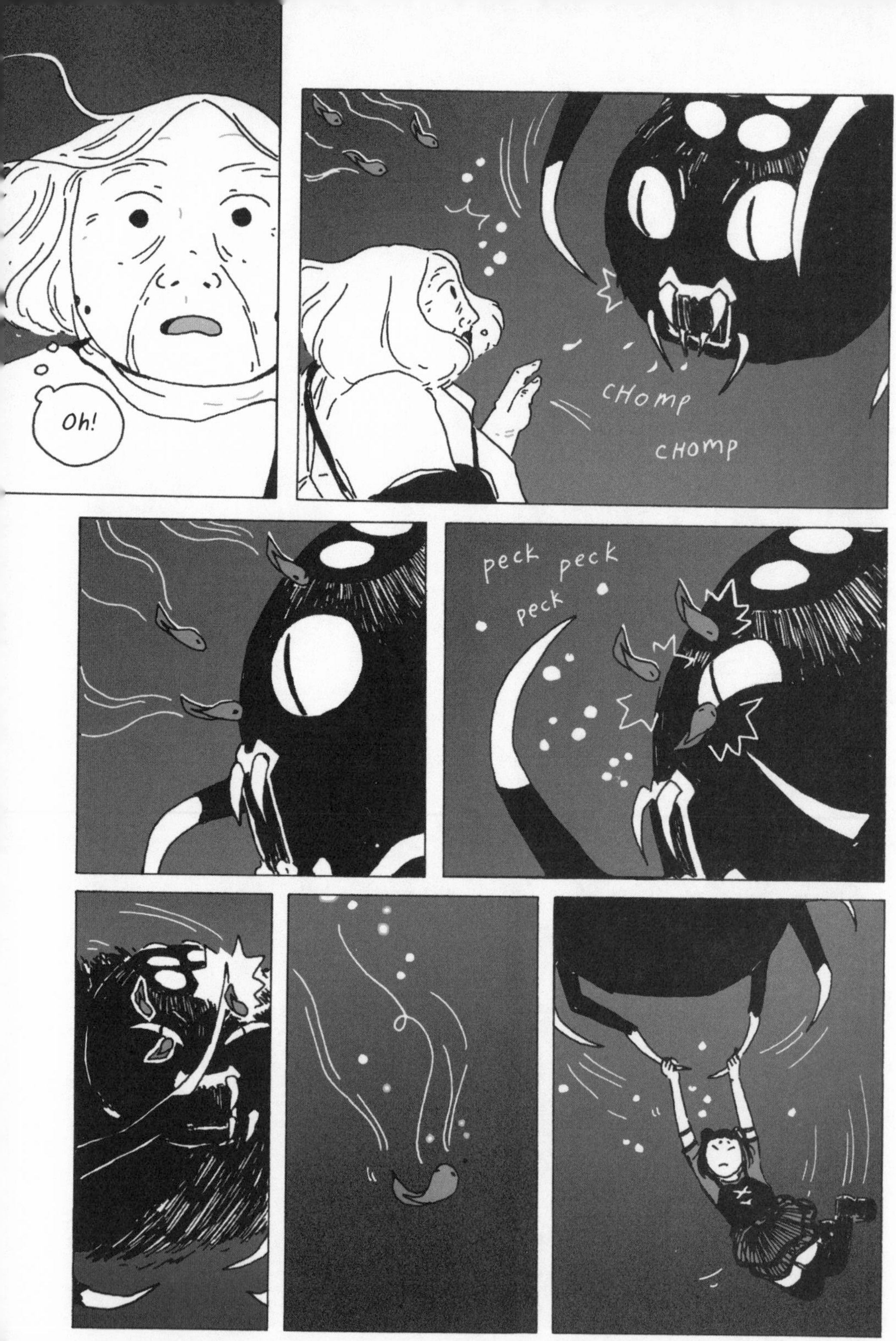
Oh!
CHOMP
CHOMP
peck
peck
peck

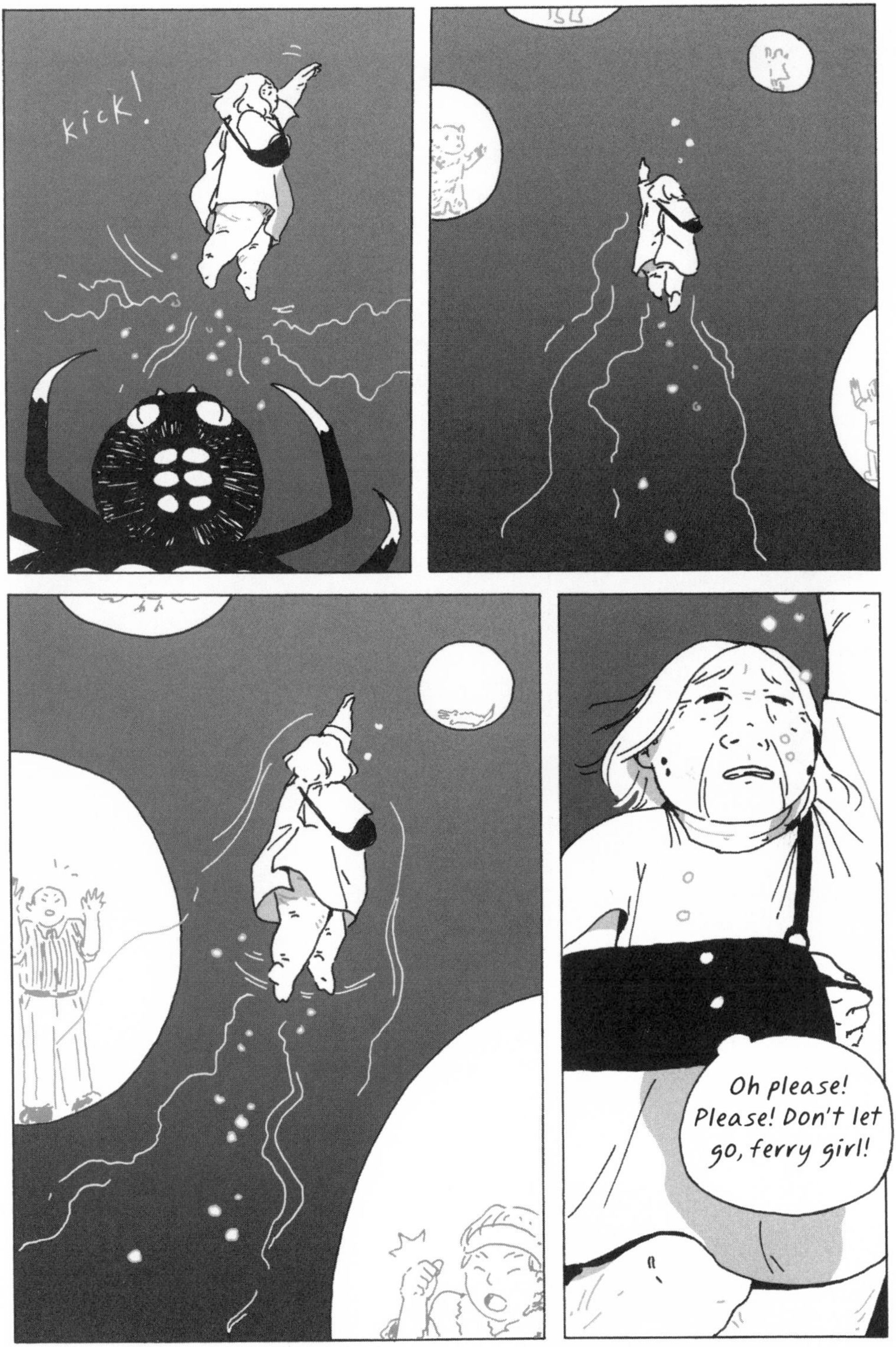
kick!
Oh please! Please! Don't let go, ferry girl!

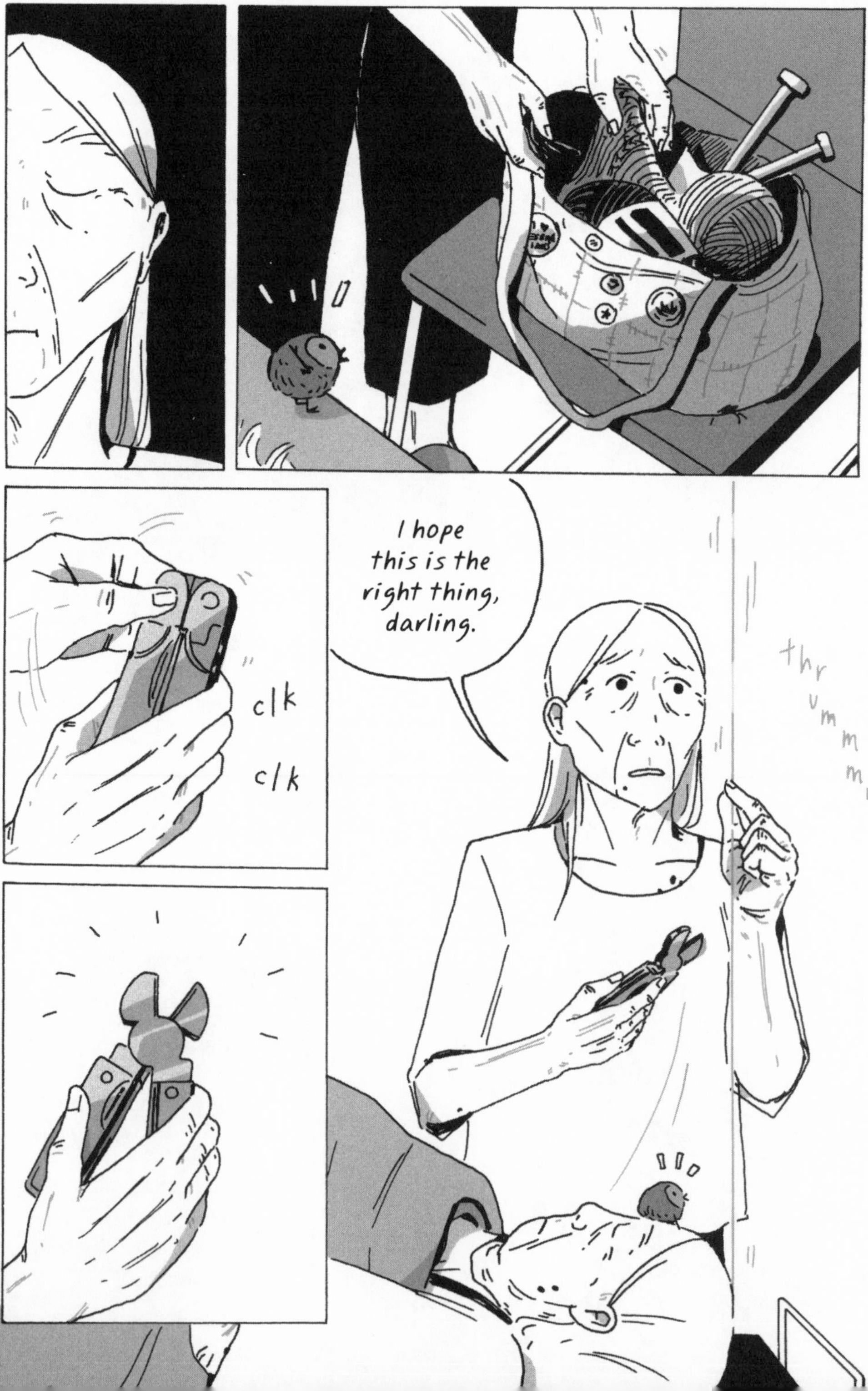

clk
clk
I hope this is the right thing, darling.
thrummmmm

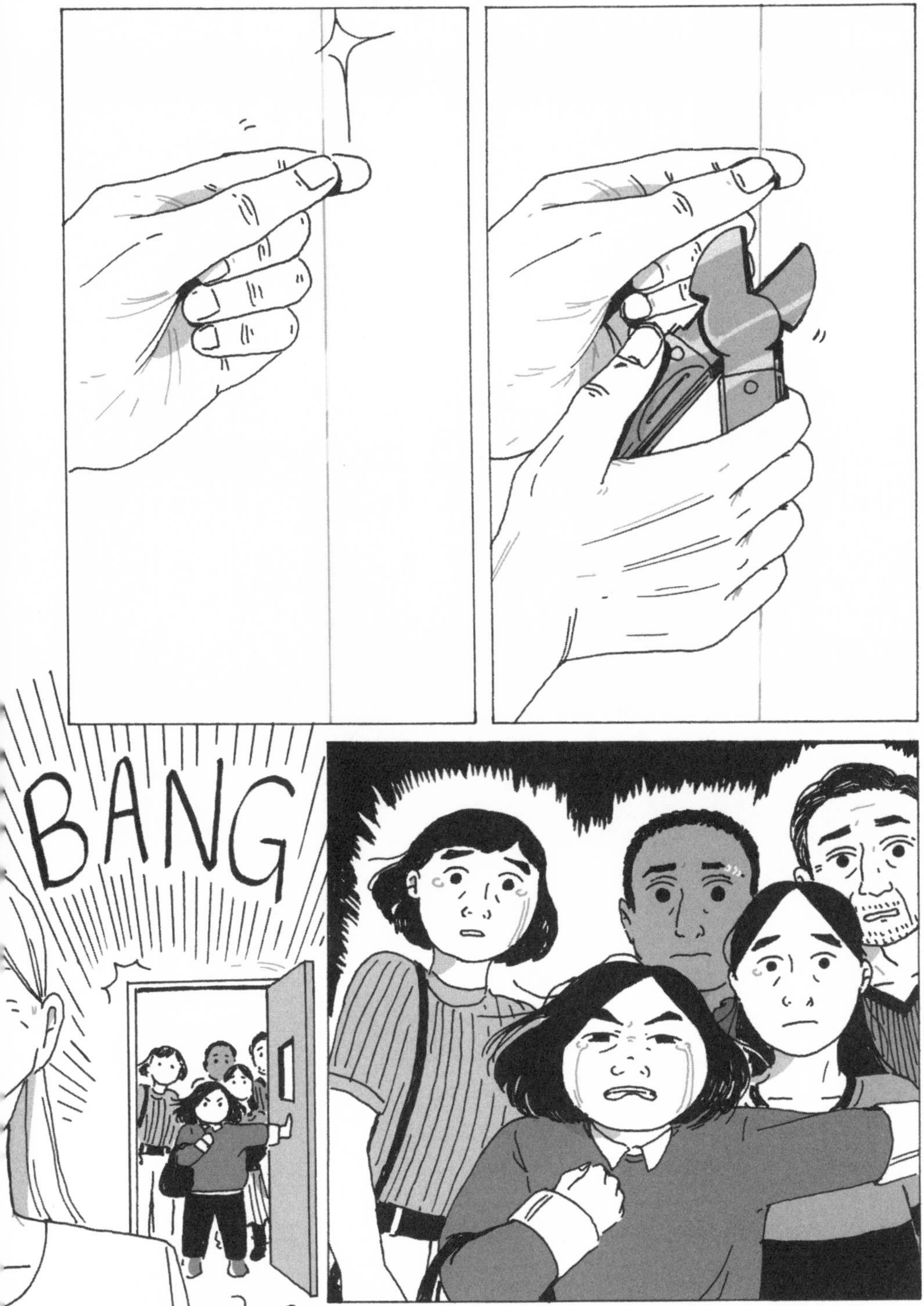
BANG

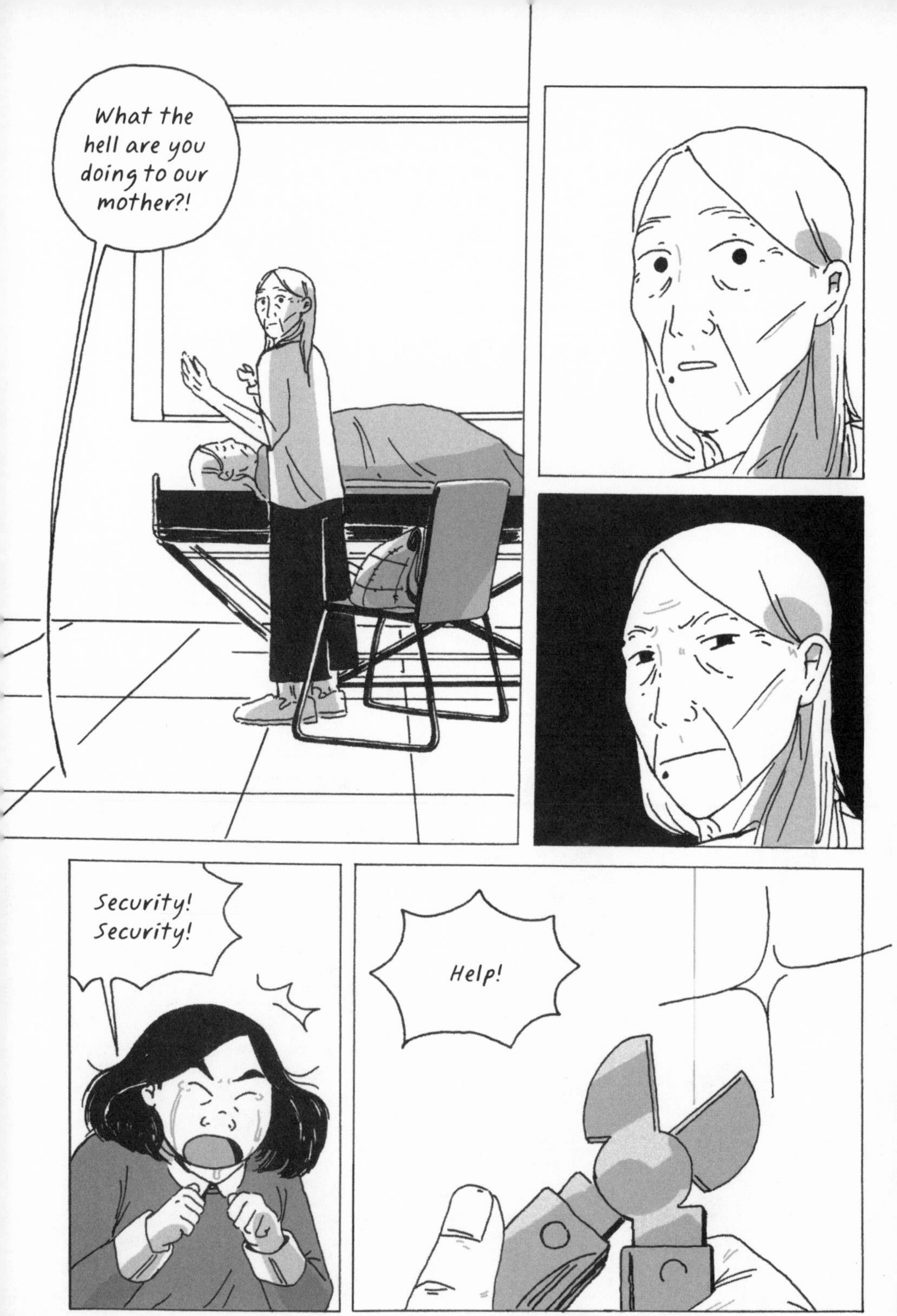
What the hell are you doing to our mother?!
Security! Security!
Help!

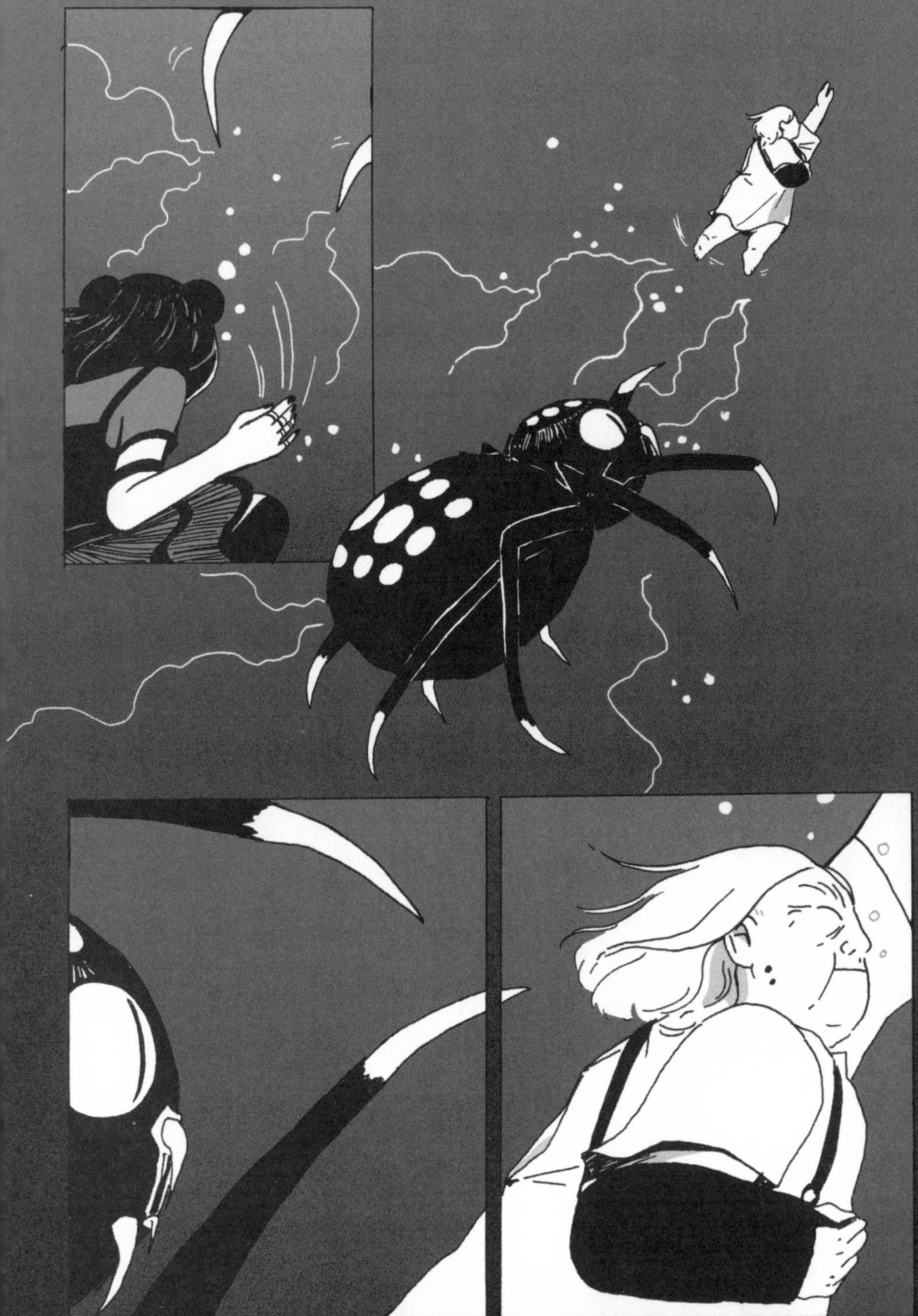

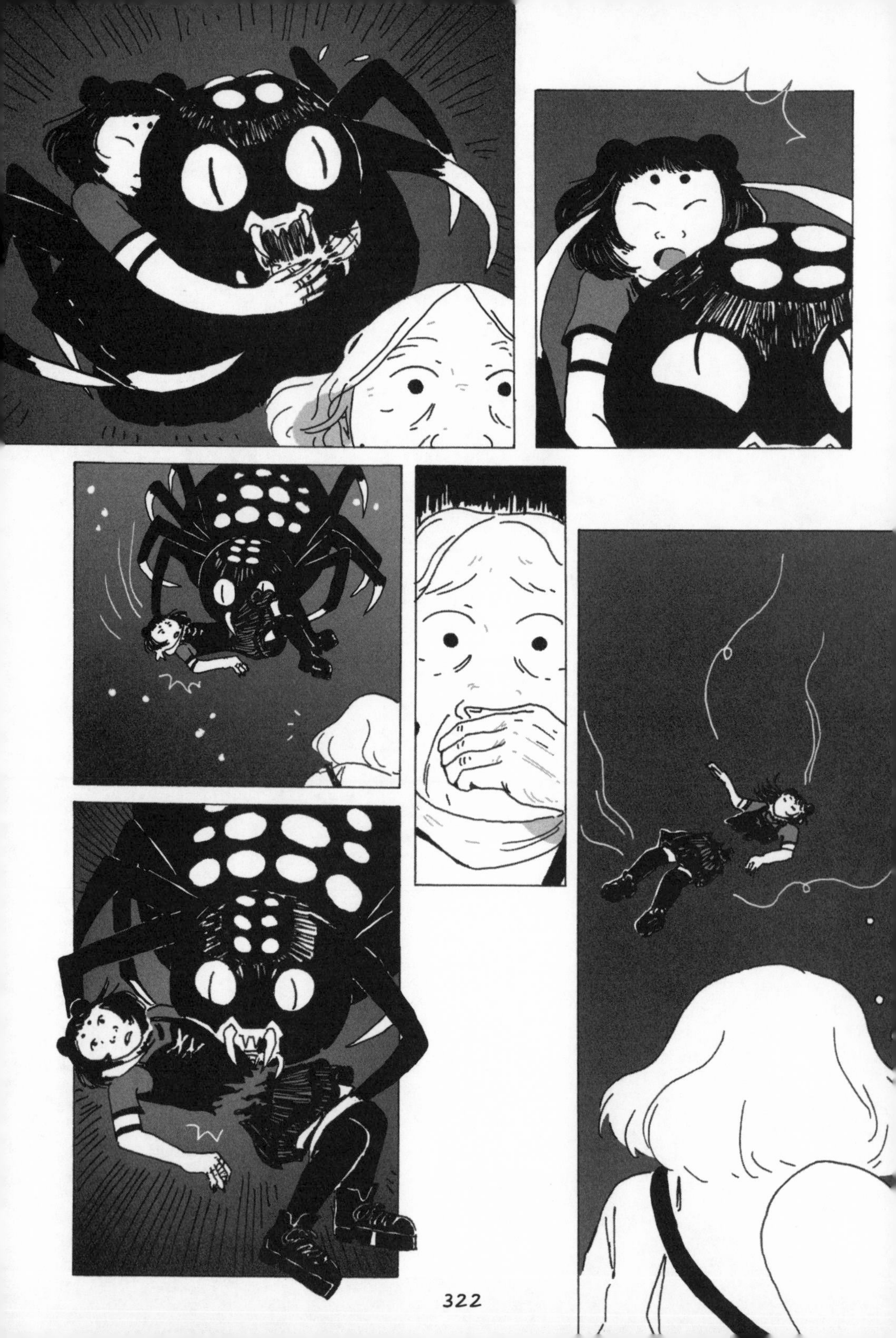

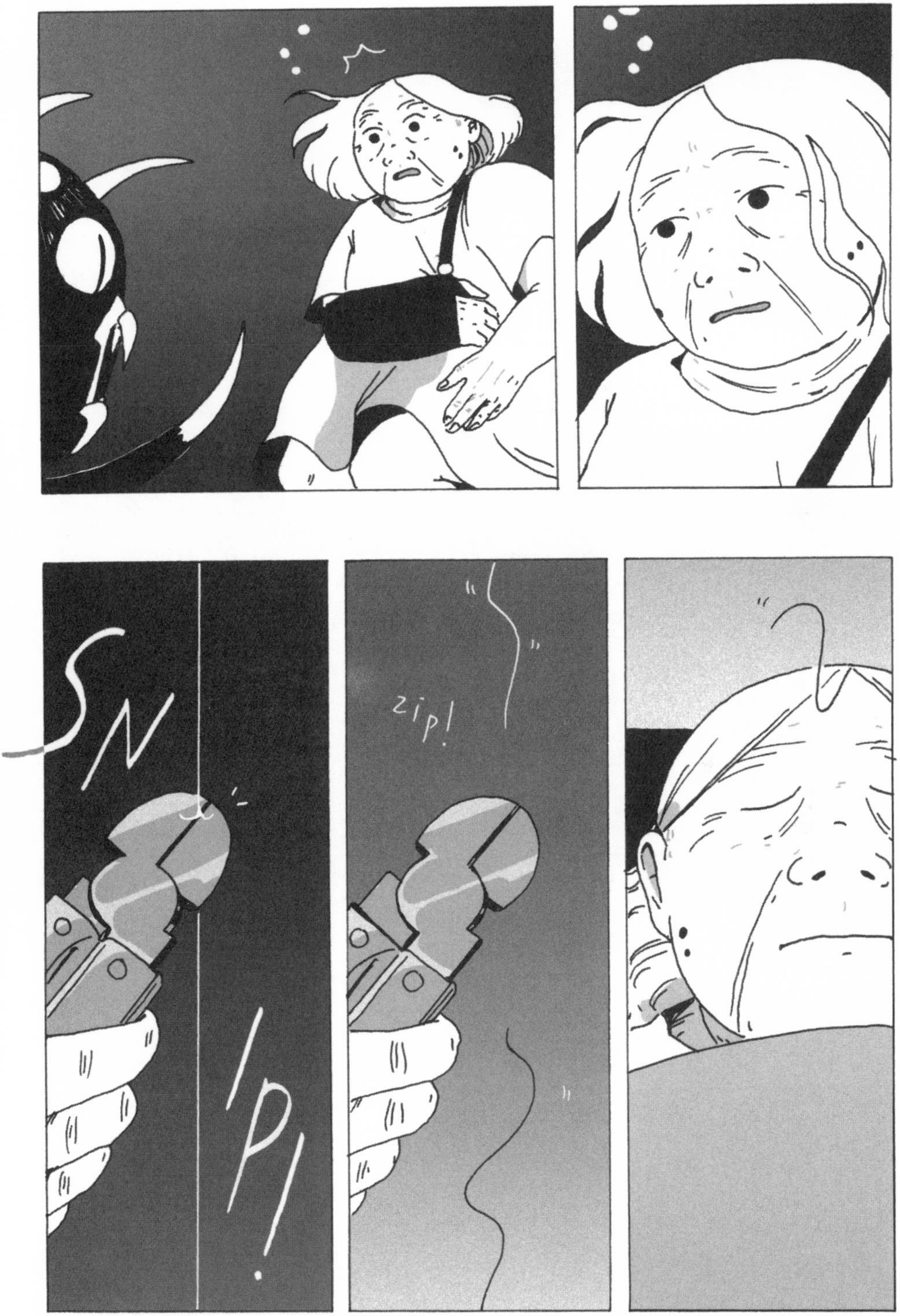
SNIP!
zip!

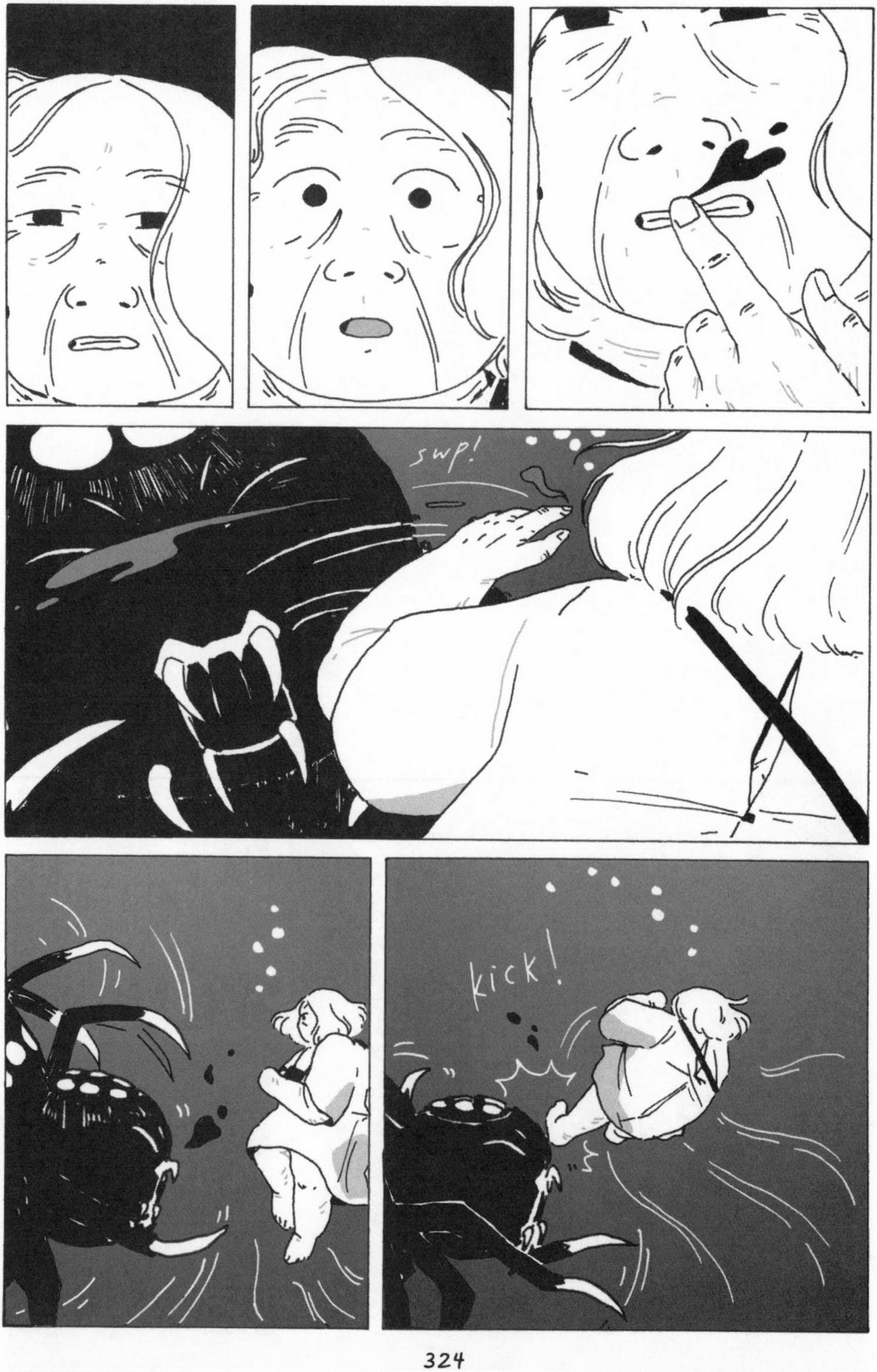
swp!
kick!

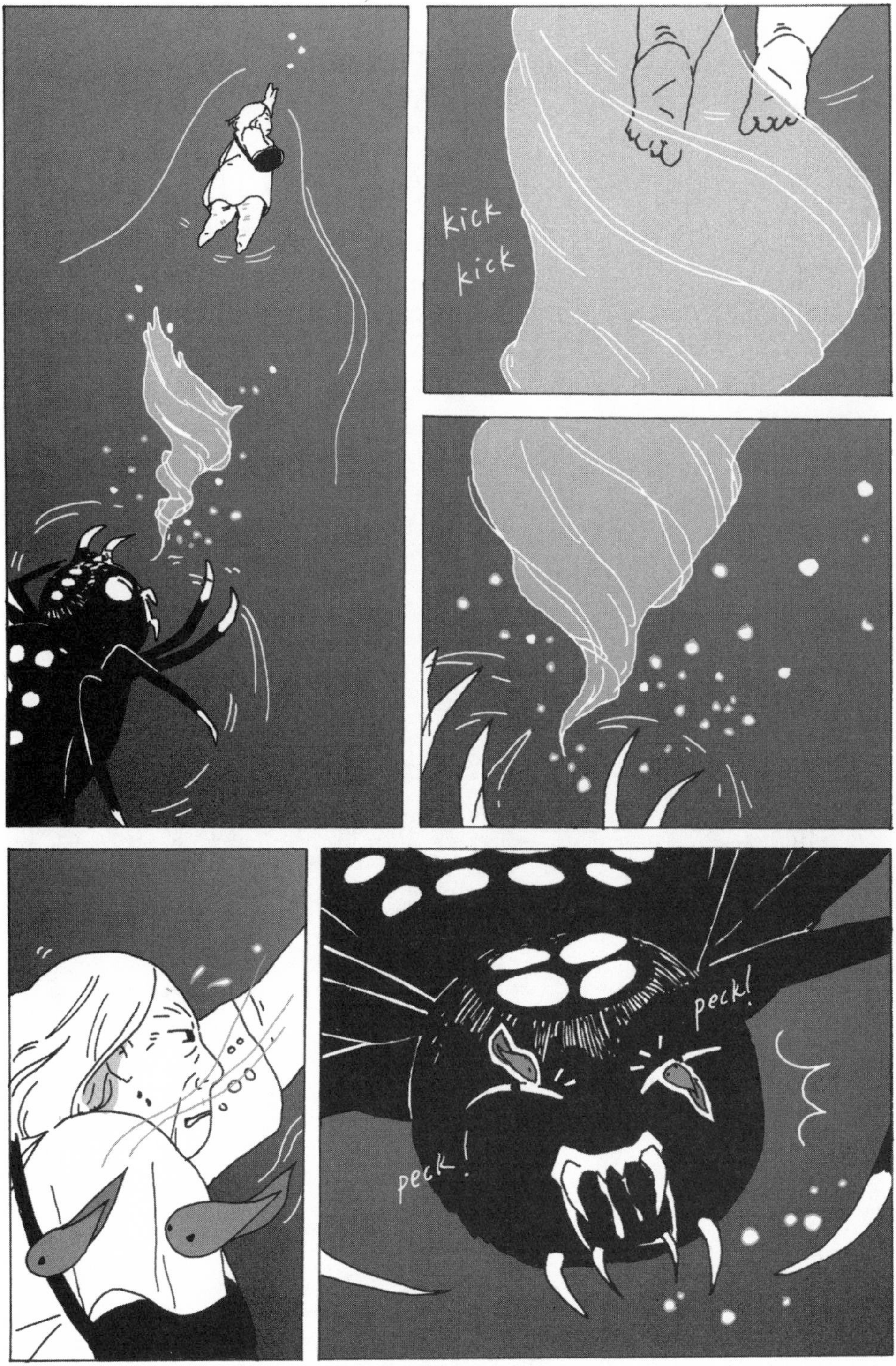
kick
kick
peck!
peck!

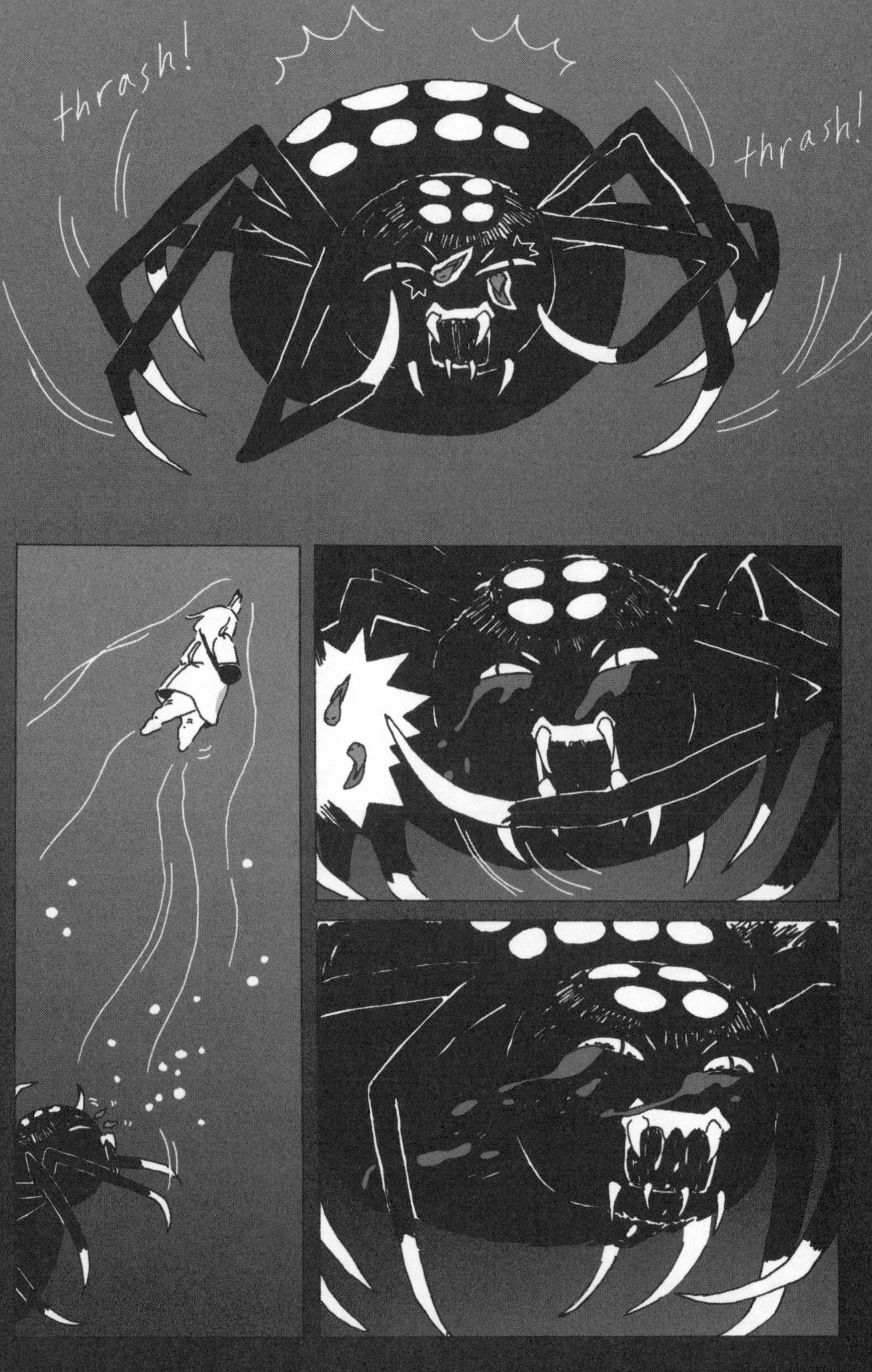
thrash!
thrash!

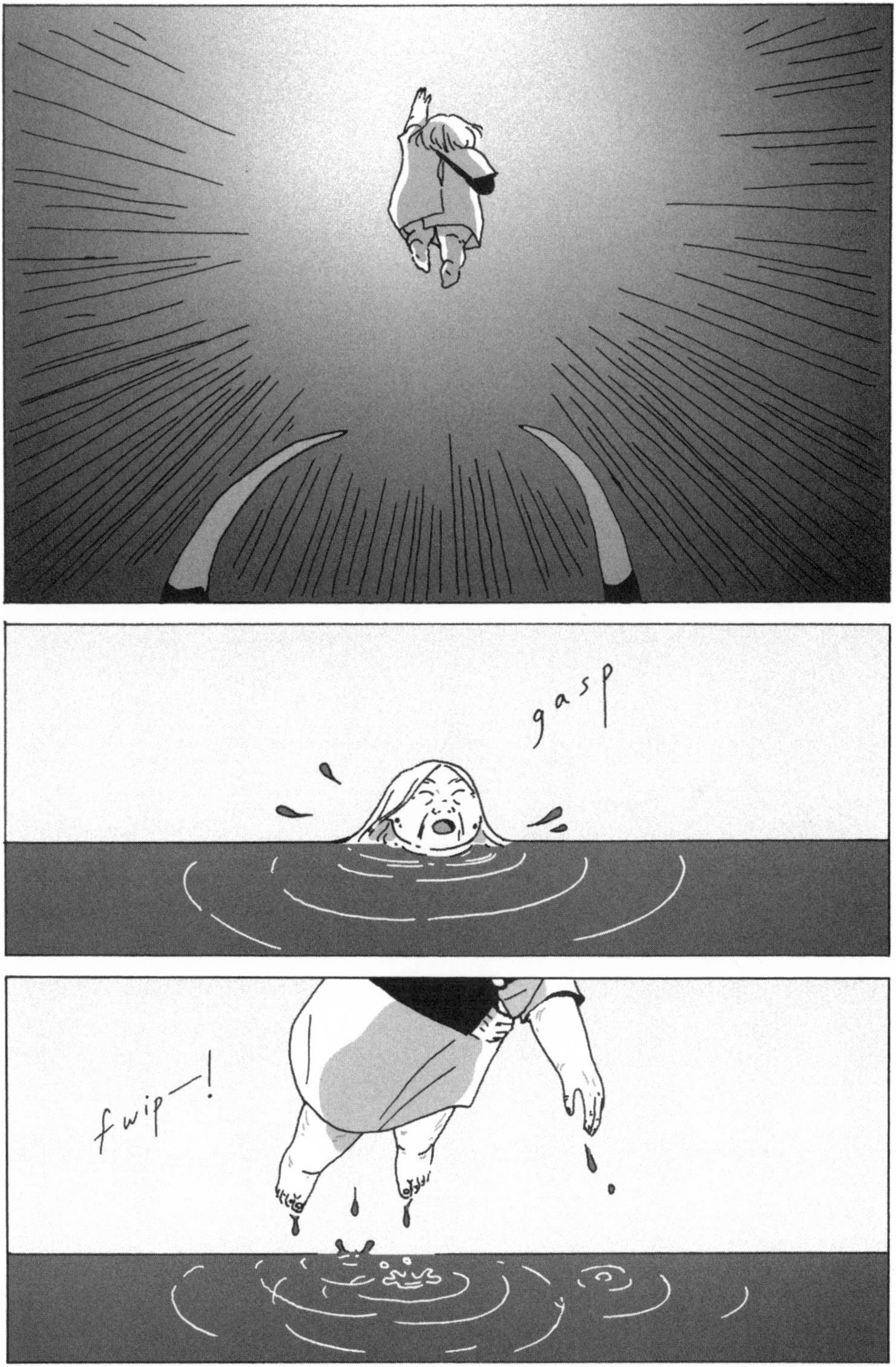
gasp
fwip—!

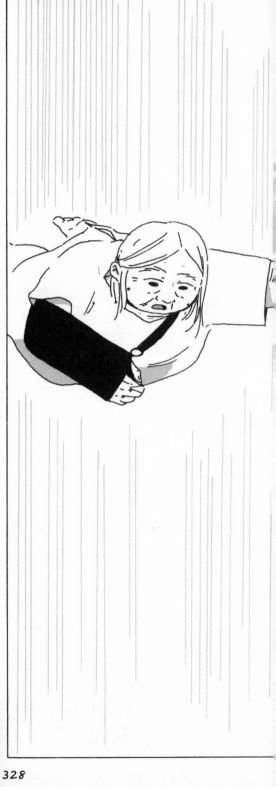

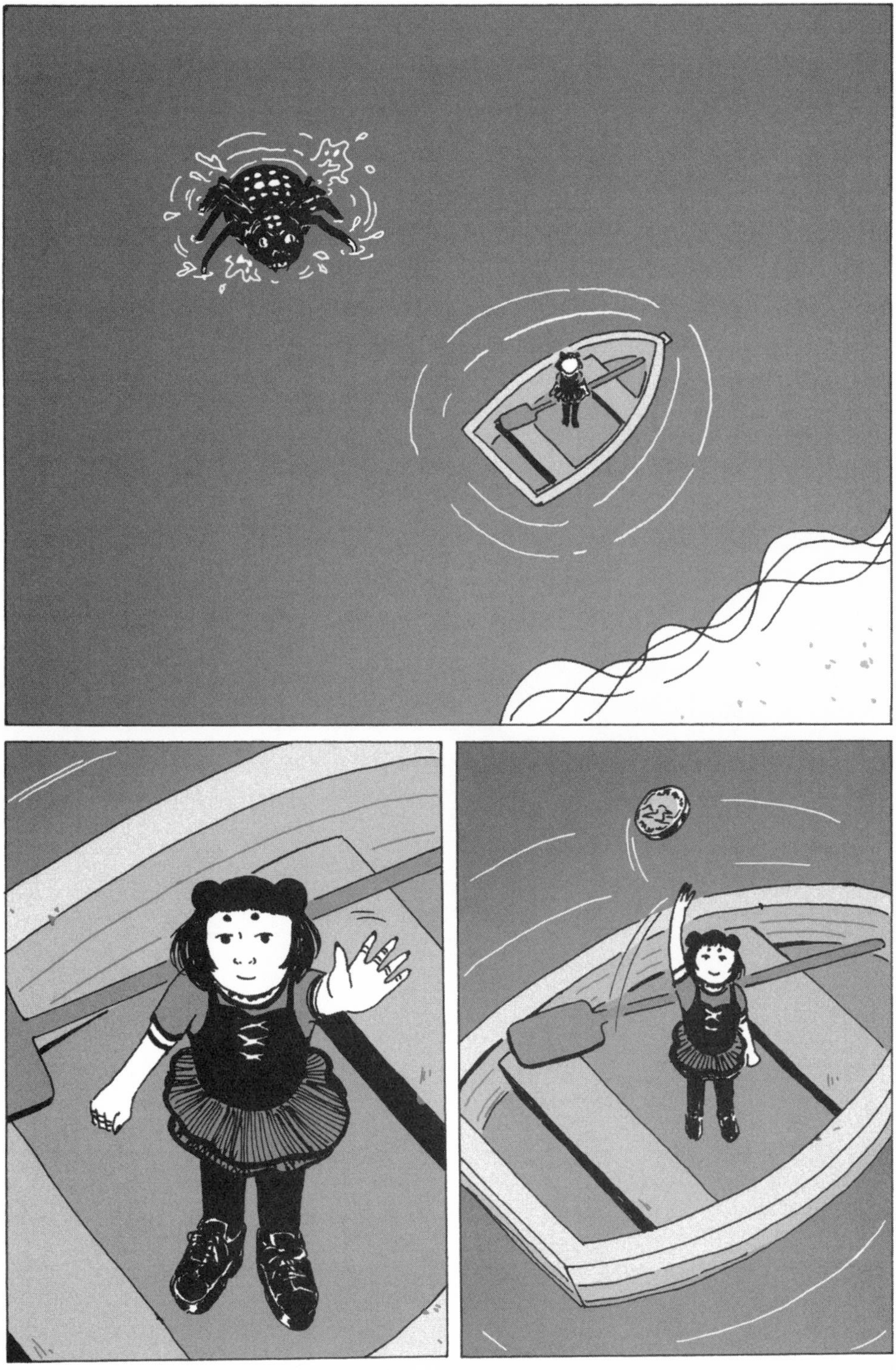

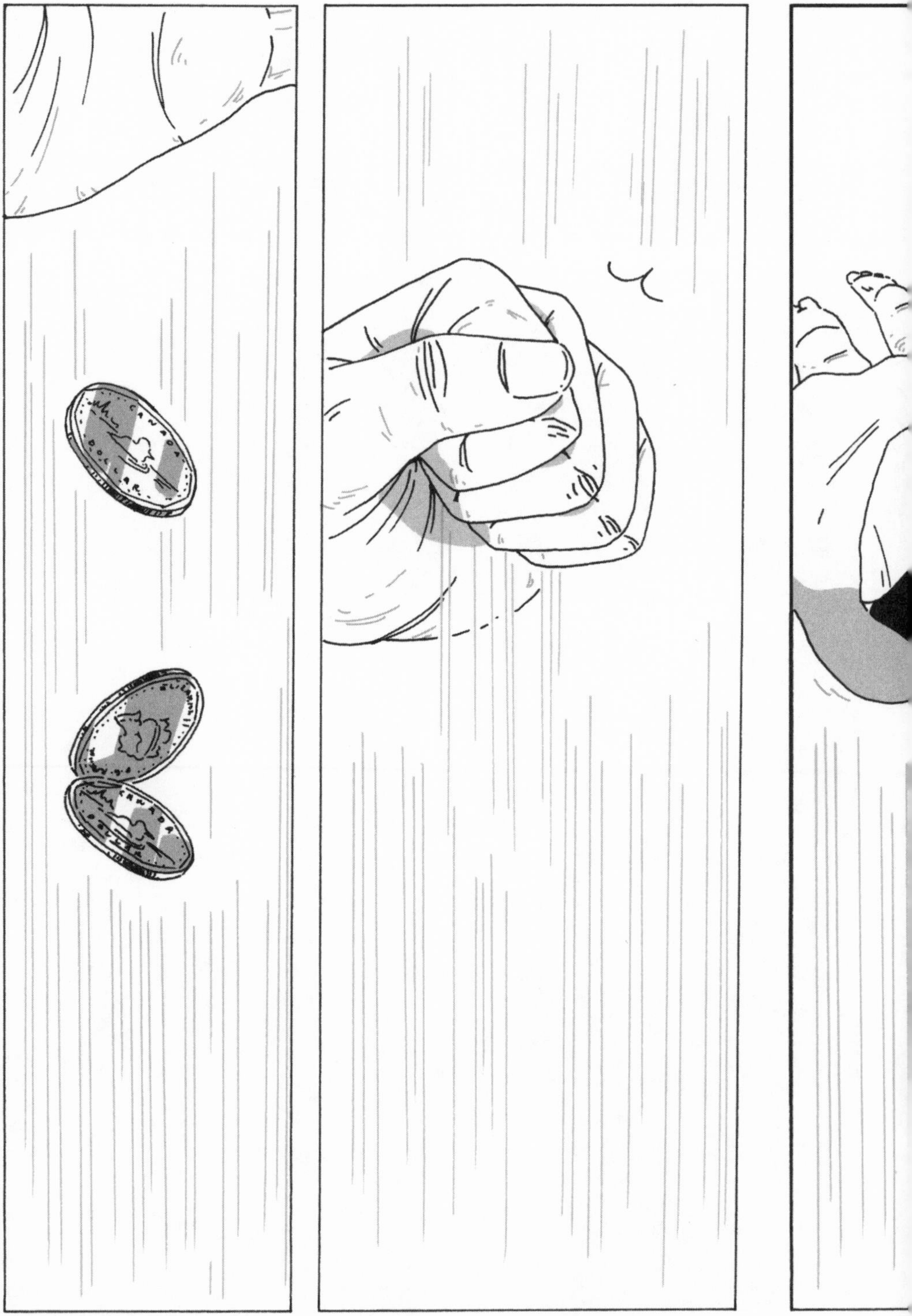

roarrrrr
roarrr

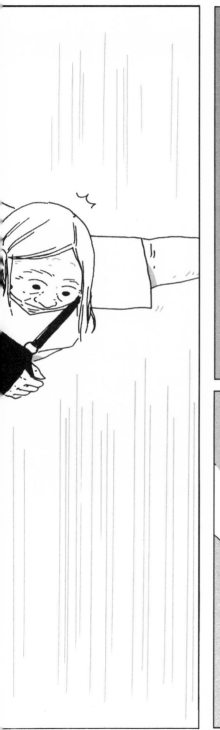

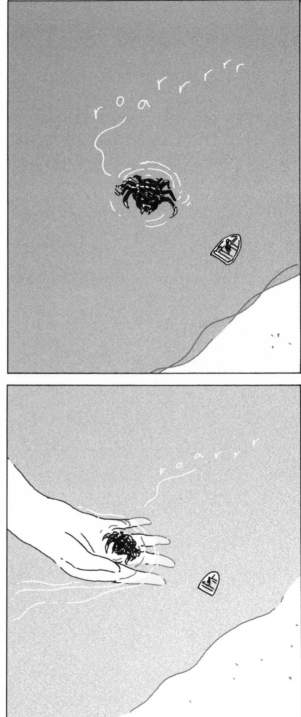

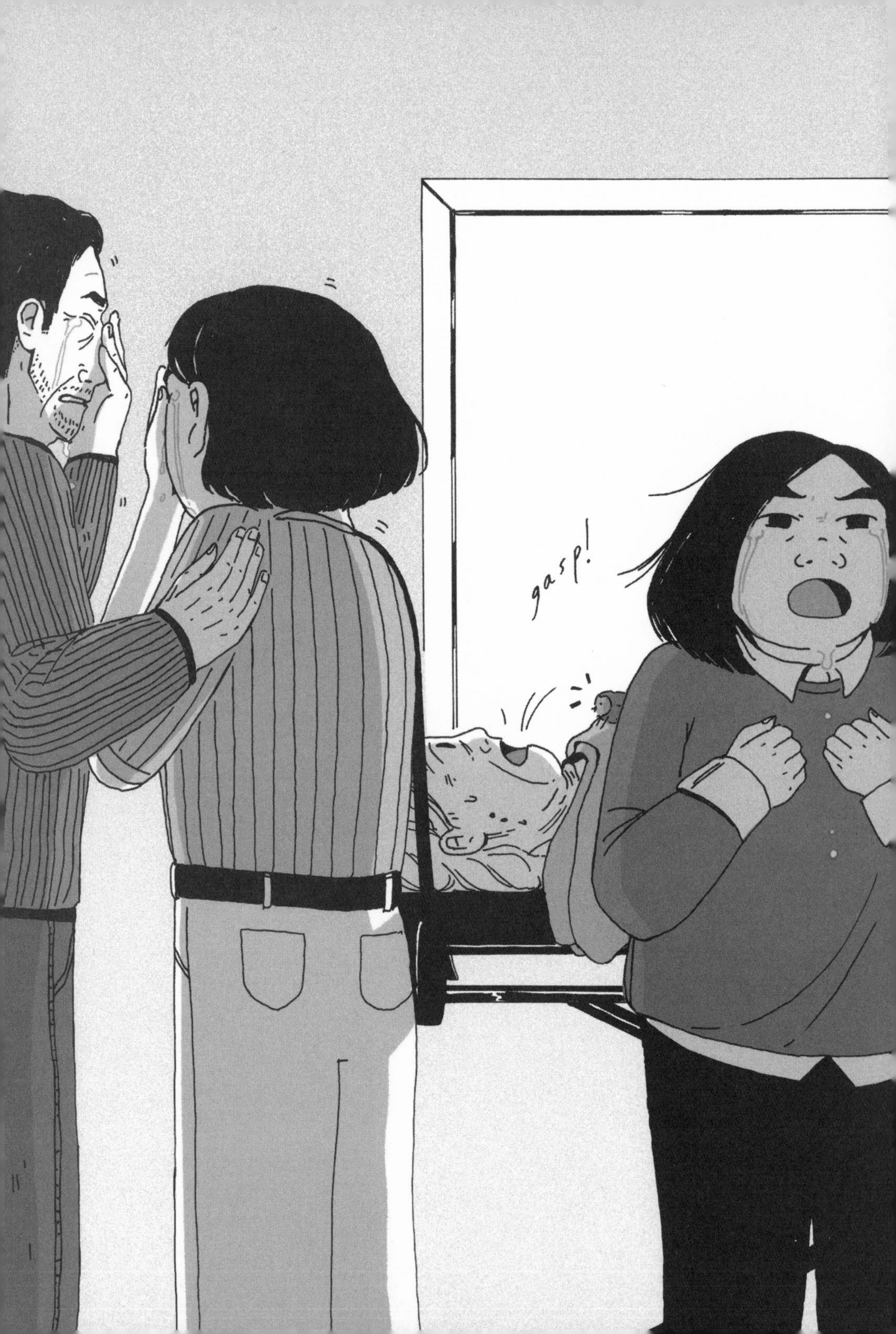
gasp!

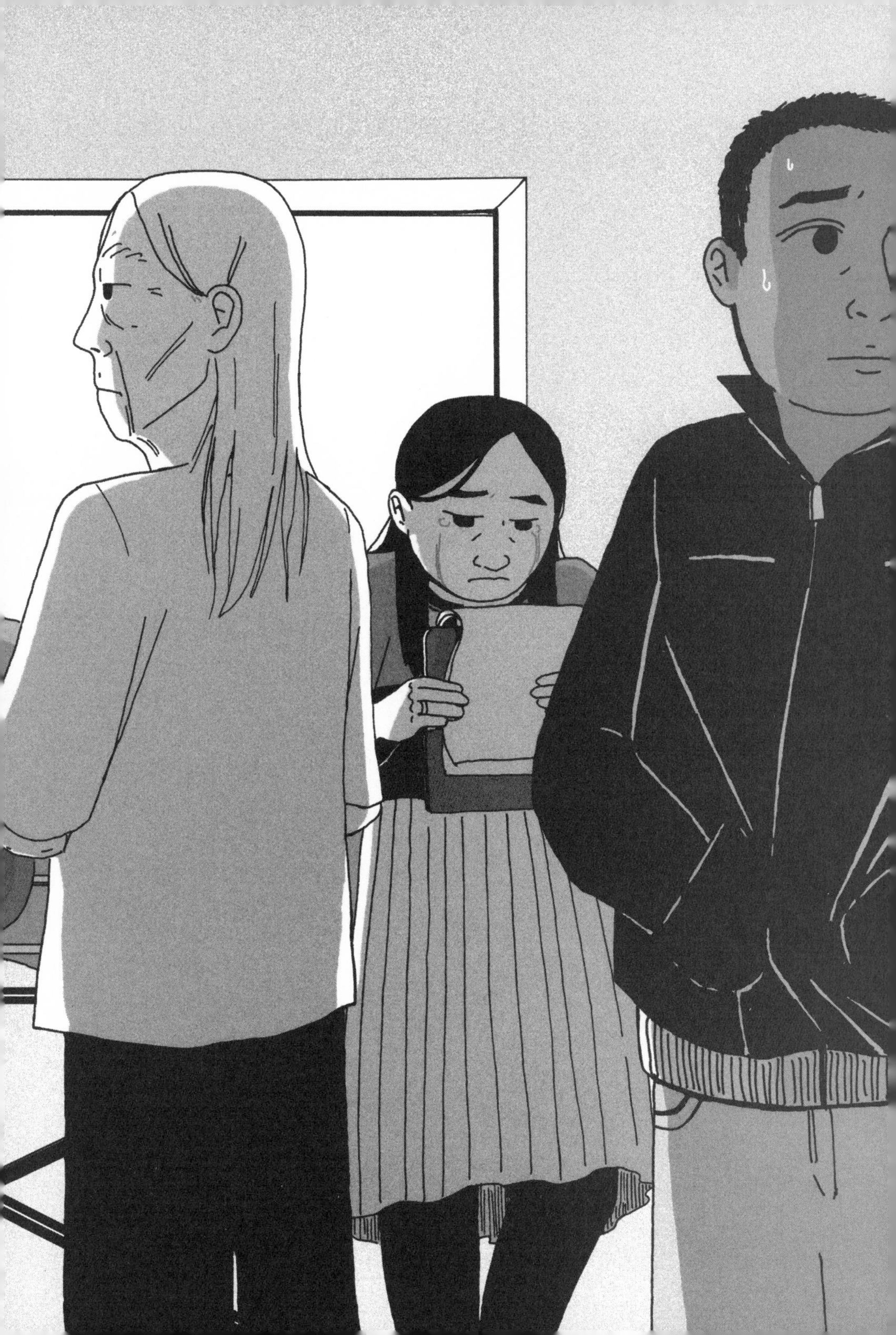

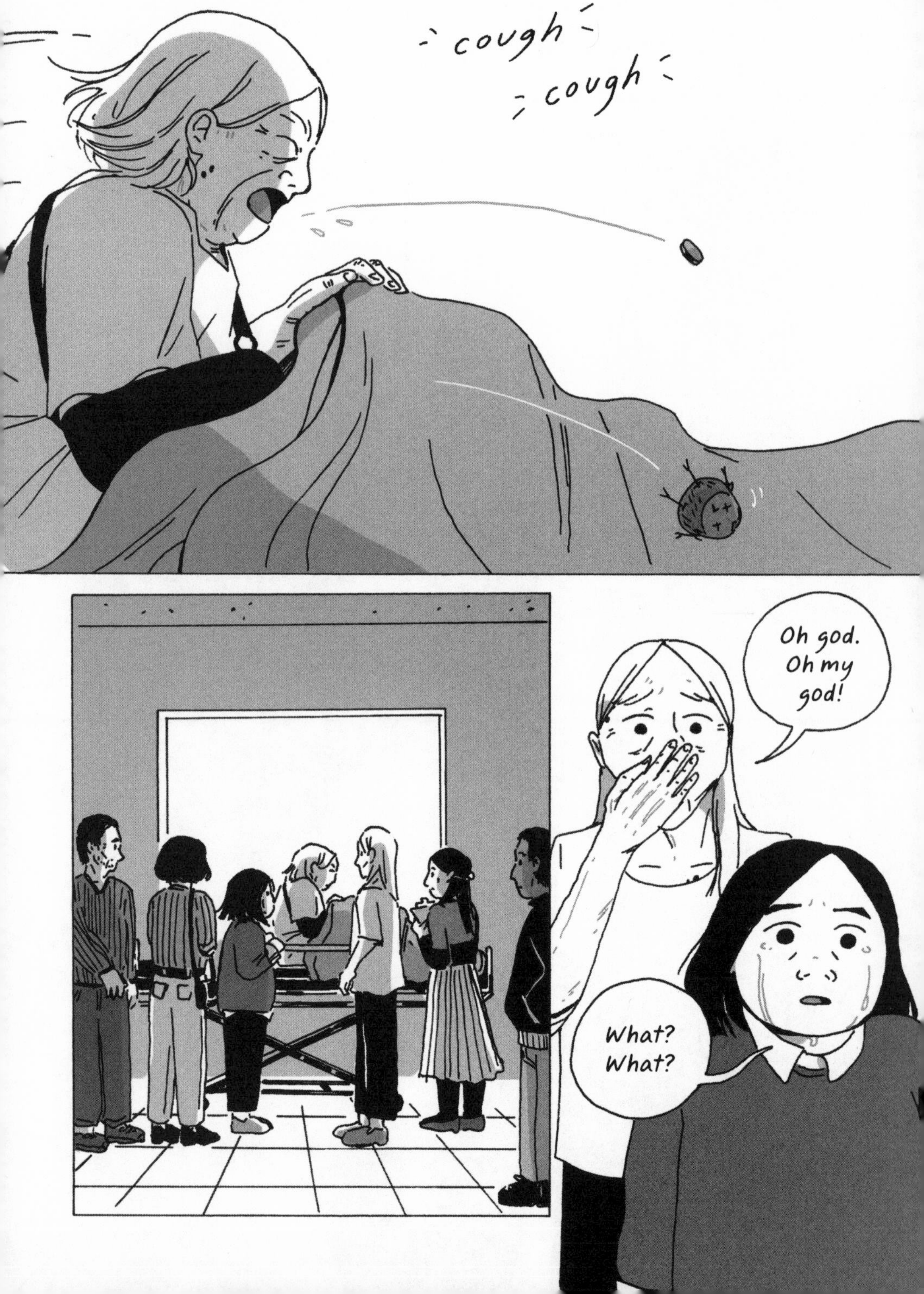
cough
cough
Oh god. Oh my god!
What? What?

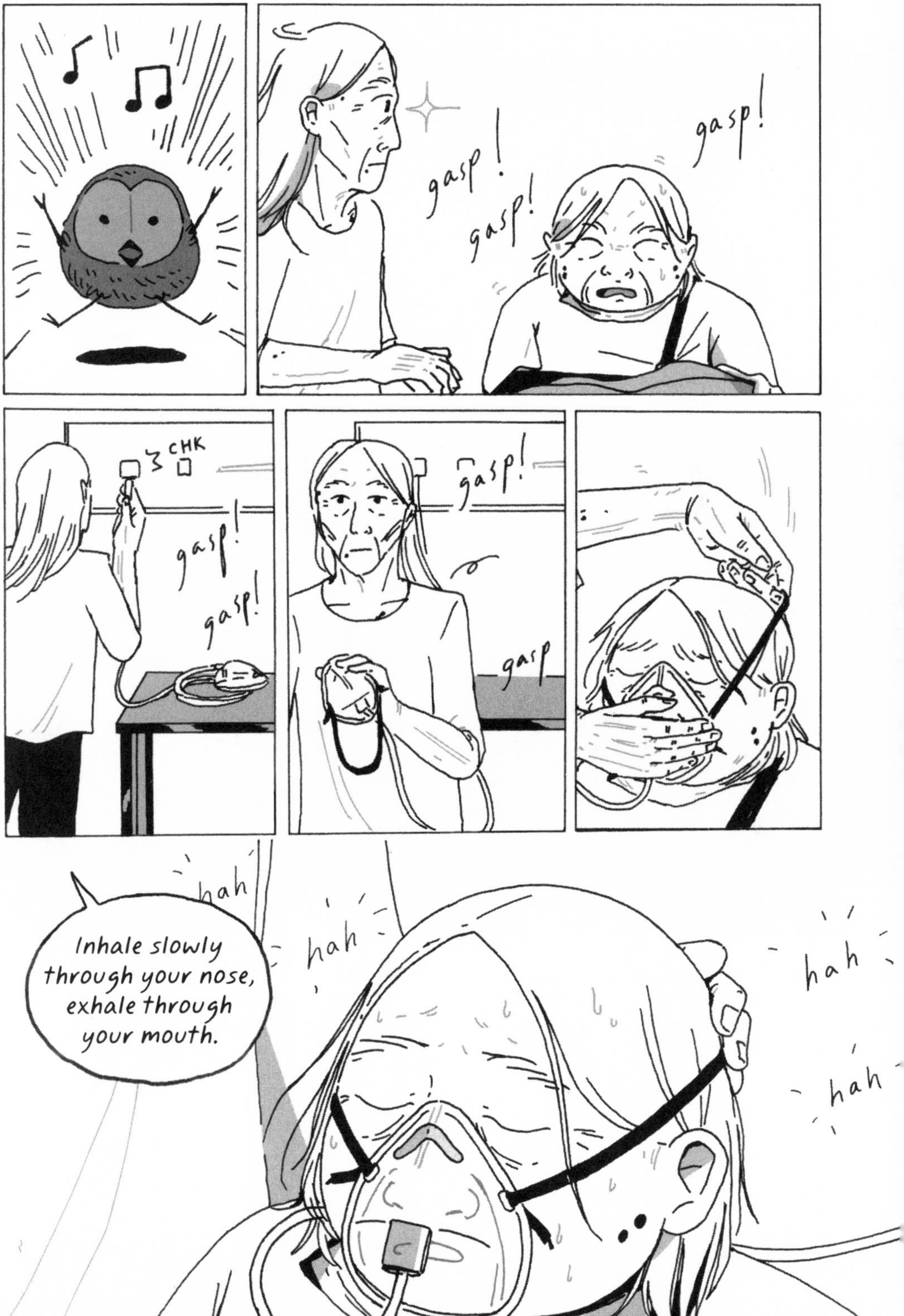
gasp!
gasp!
gasp!
CHK
gasp!
gasp!
gasp!
gasp
hah
hah
Inhale slowly through your nose, exhale through your mouth.
hah
hah

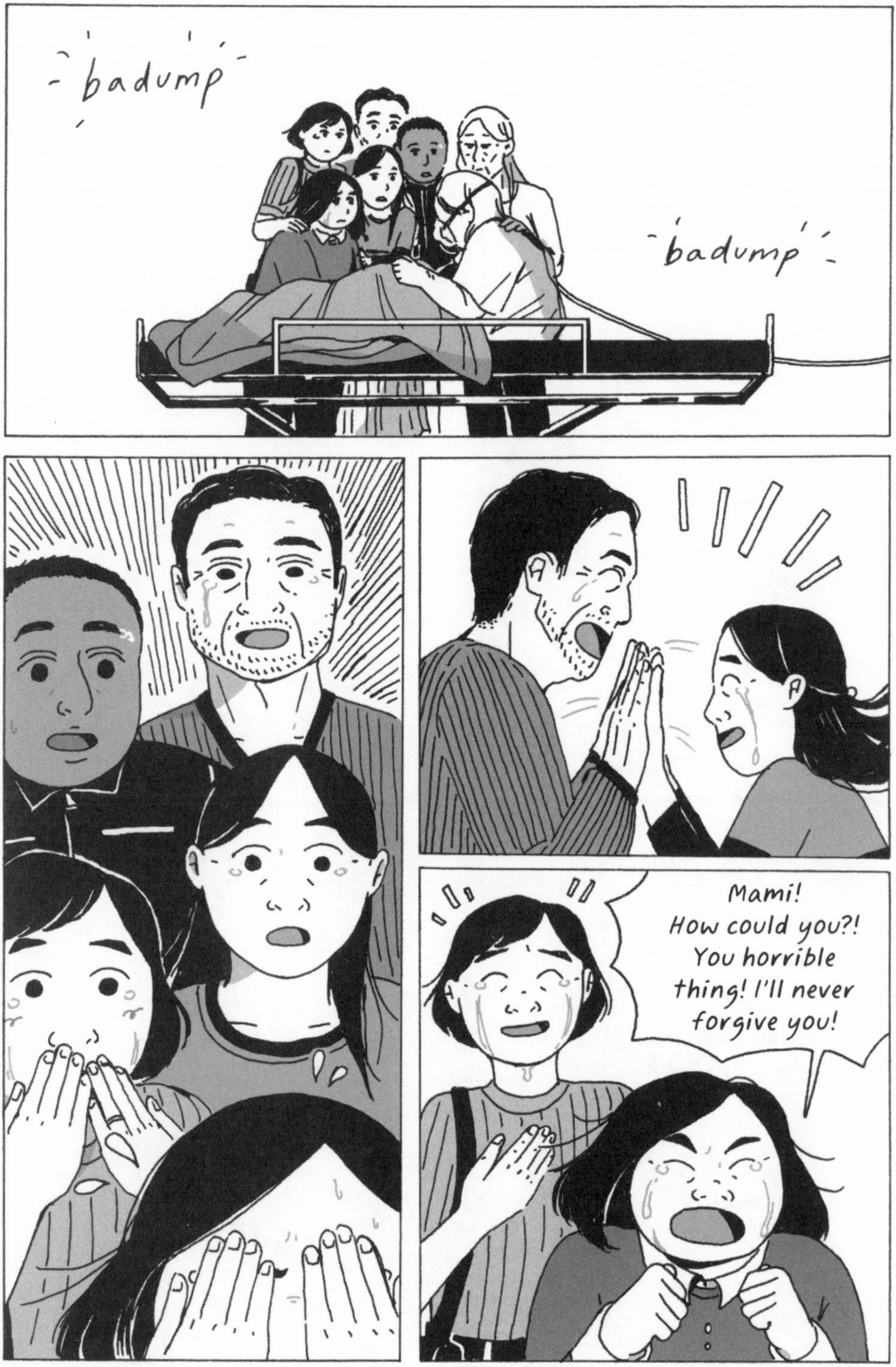
badump
badump
Mami!
How could you?!
You horrible
thing! I'll never
forgive you!

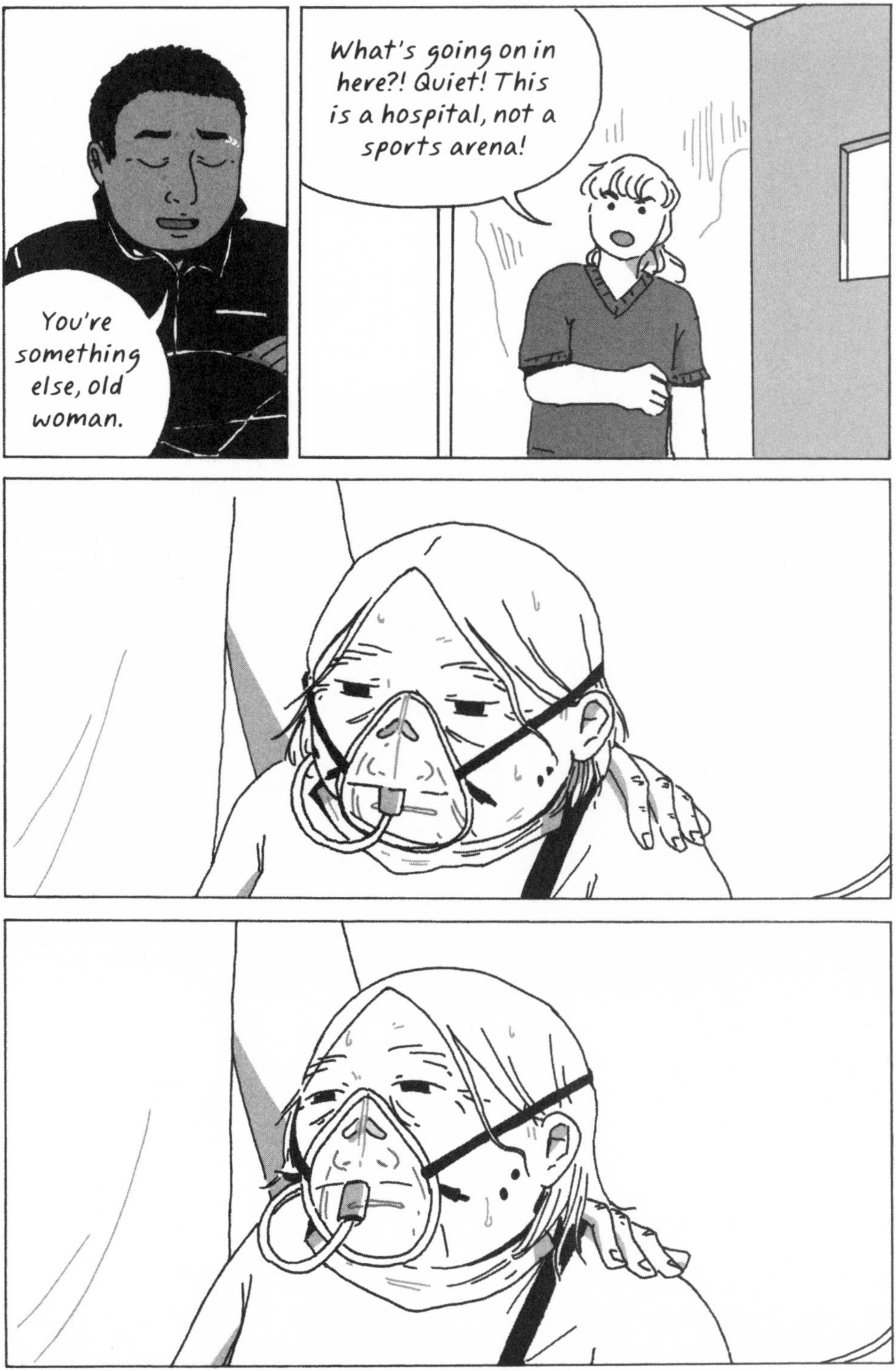
You're something else, old woman.
What's going on in here?! Quiet! This is a hospital, not a sports arena!

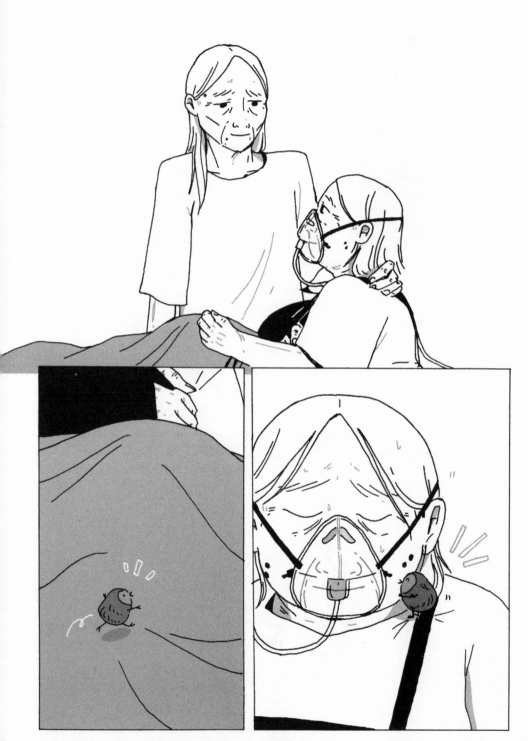

340

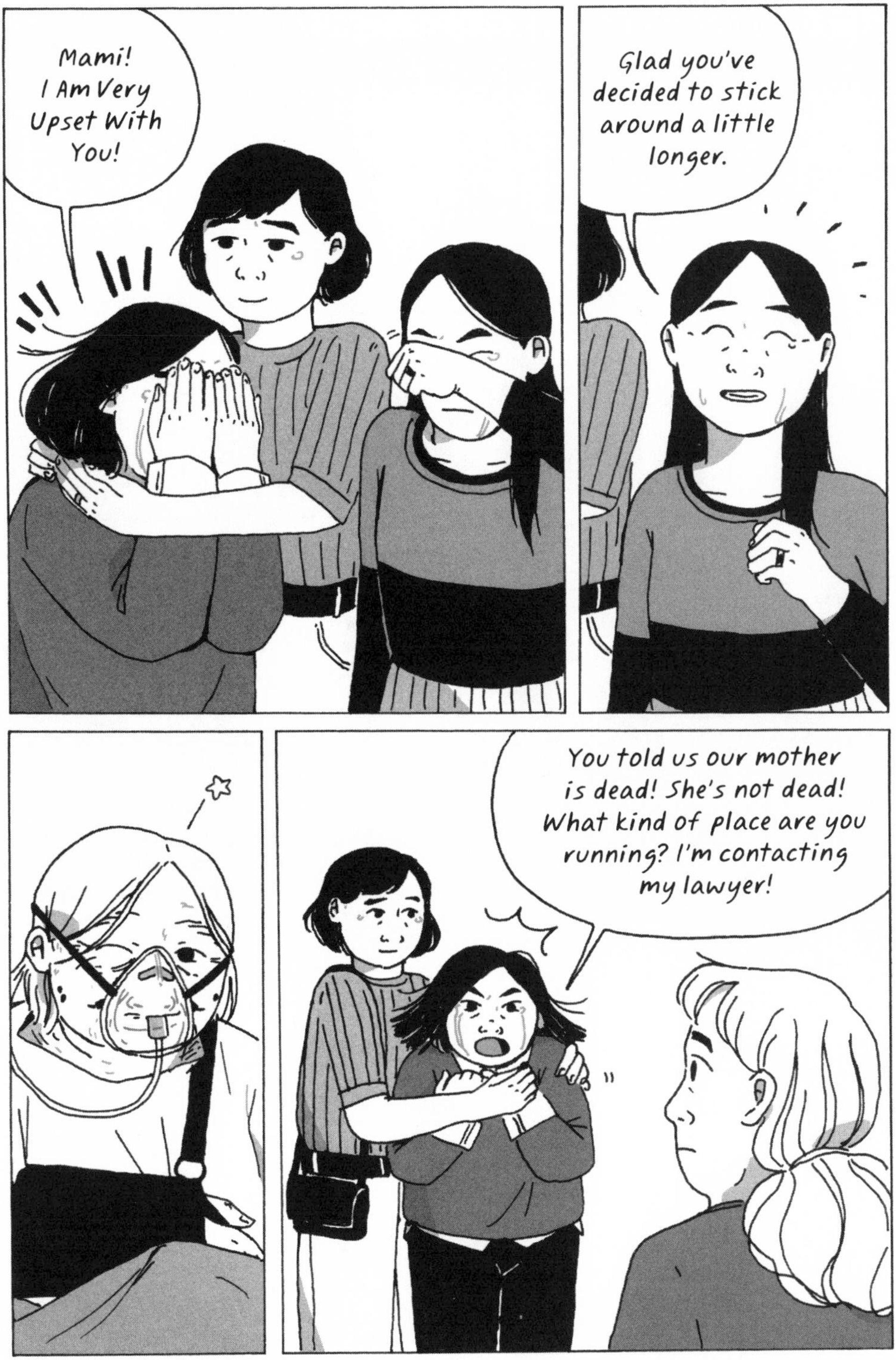
Mami! I Am Very Upset With You!
Glad you've decided to stick around a little longer.
You told us our mother is dead! She's not dead! What kind of place are you running? I'm contacting my lawyer!

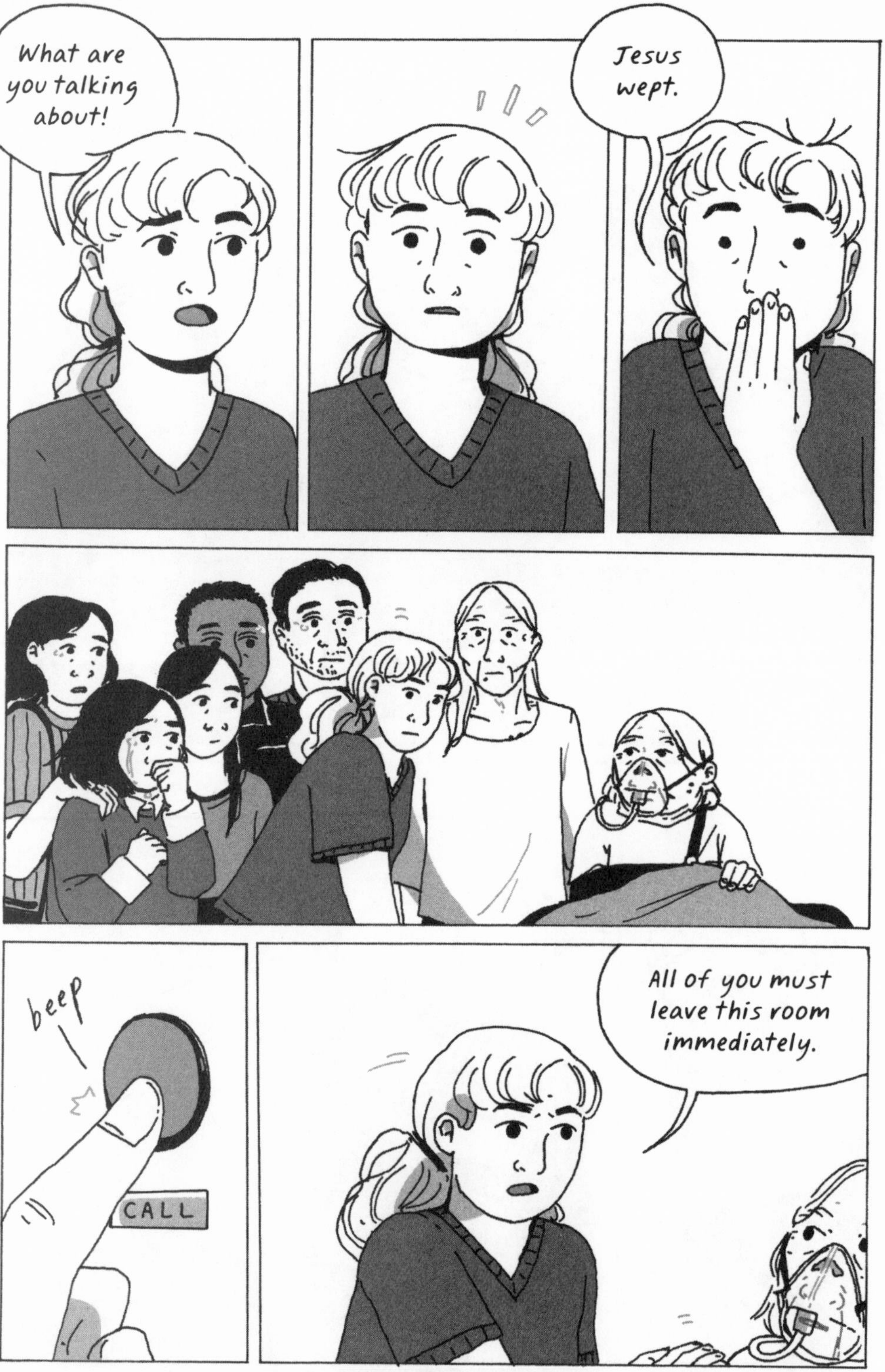
What are you talking about!
Jesus wept.
beep
CALL
All of you must leave this room immediately.

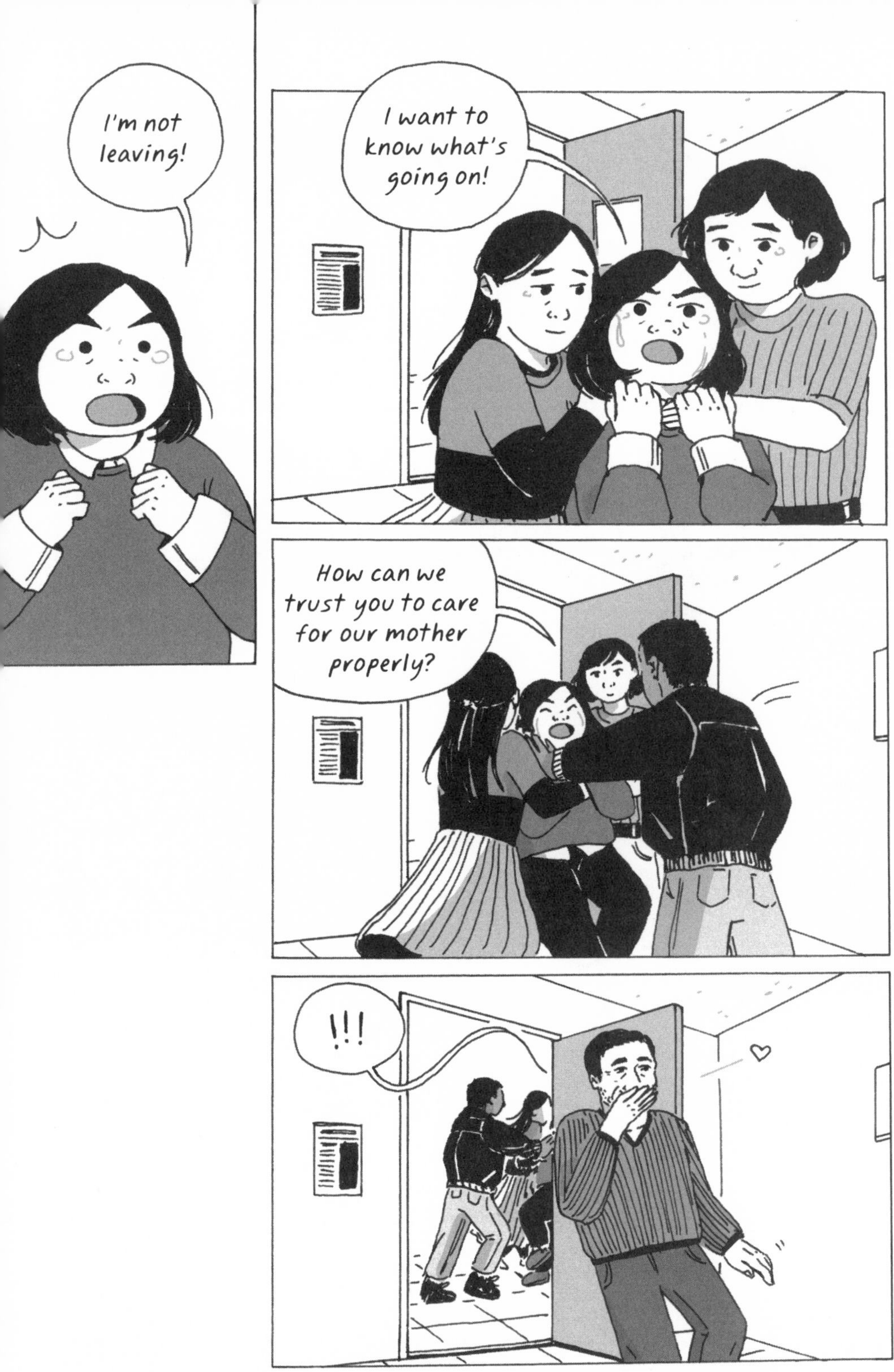
I'm not leaving!
I want to know what's going on!
How can we trust you to care for our mother properly?
!!!

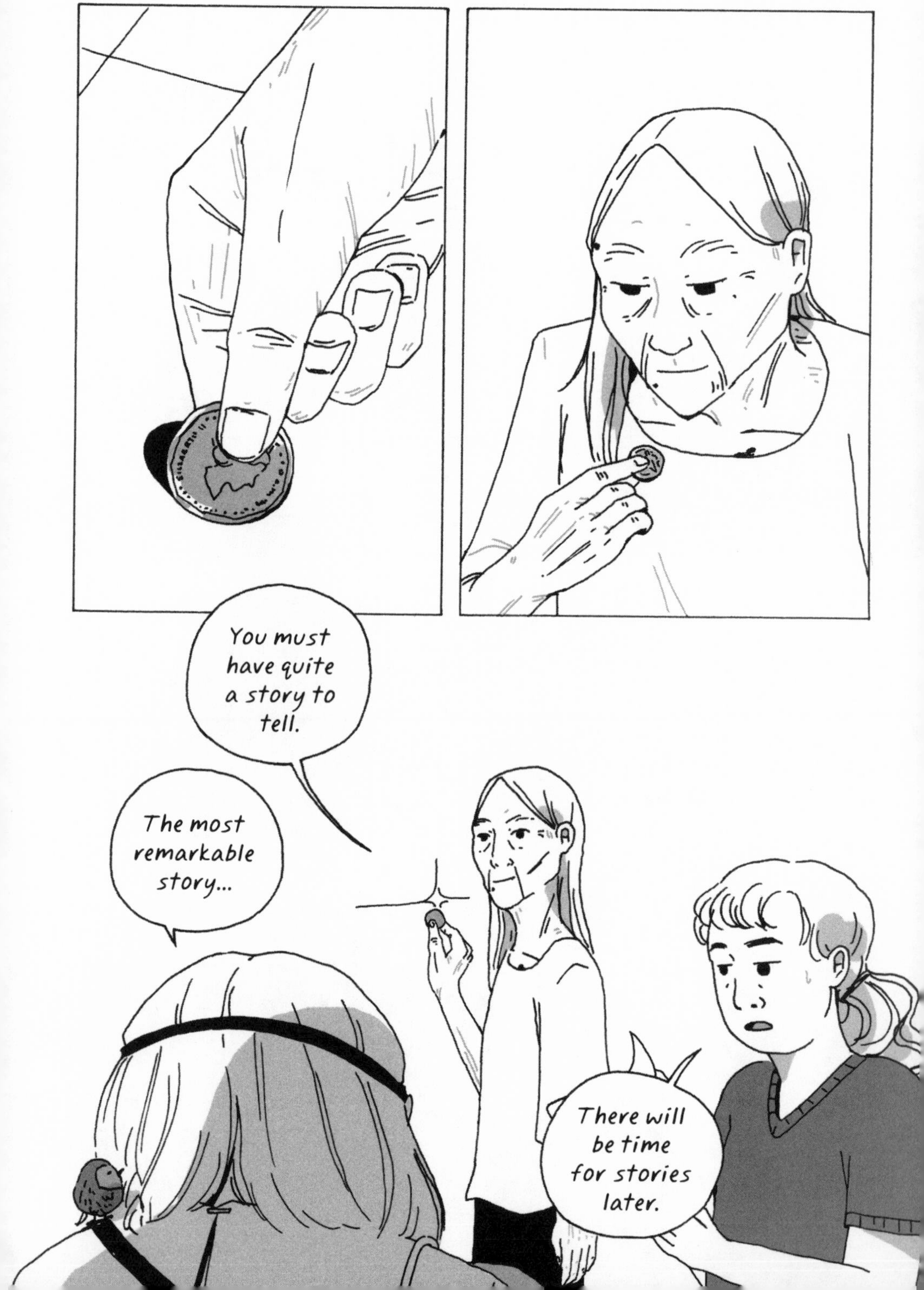
You must have quite a story to tell.
The most remarkable story...
There will be time for stories later.

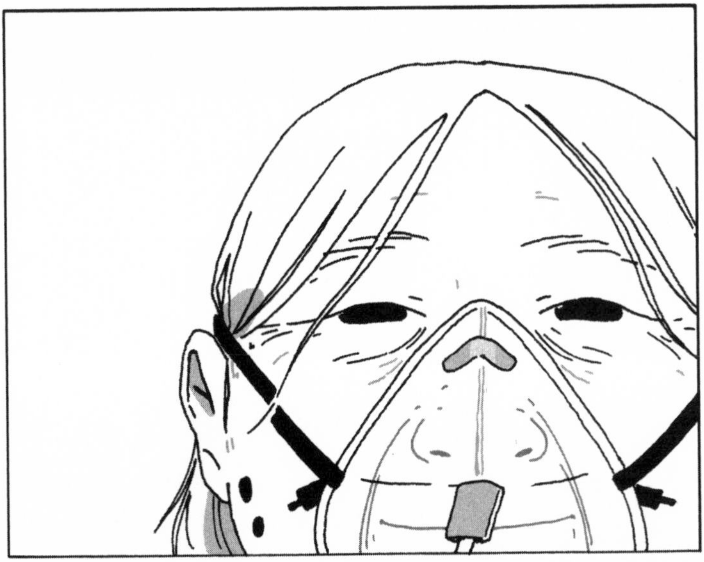

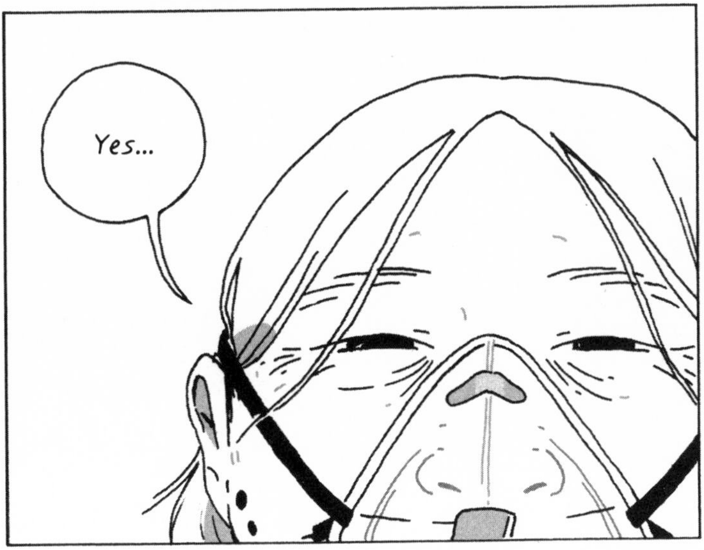
Yes...

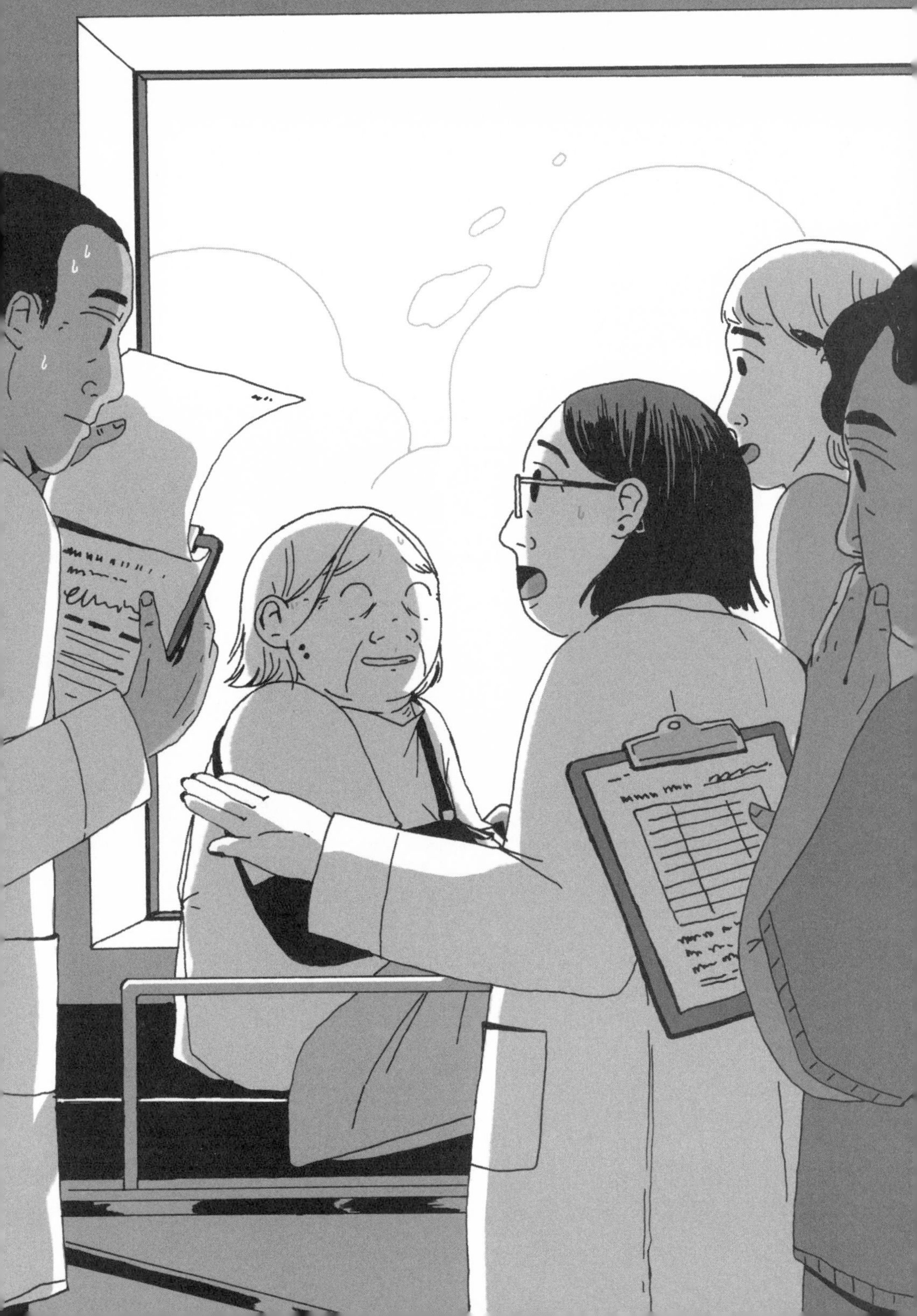

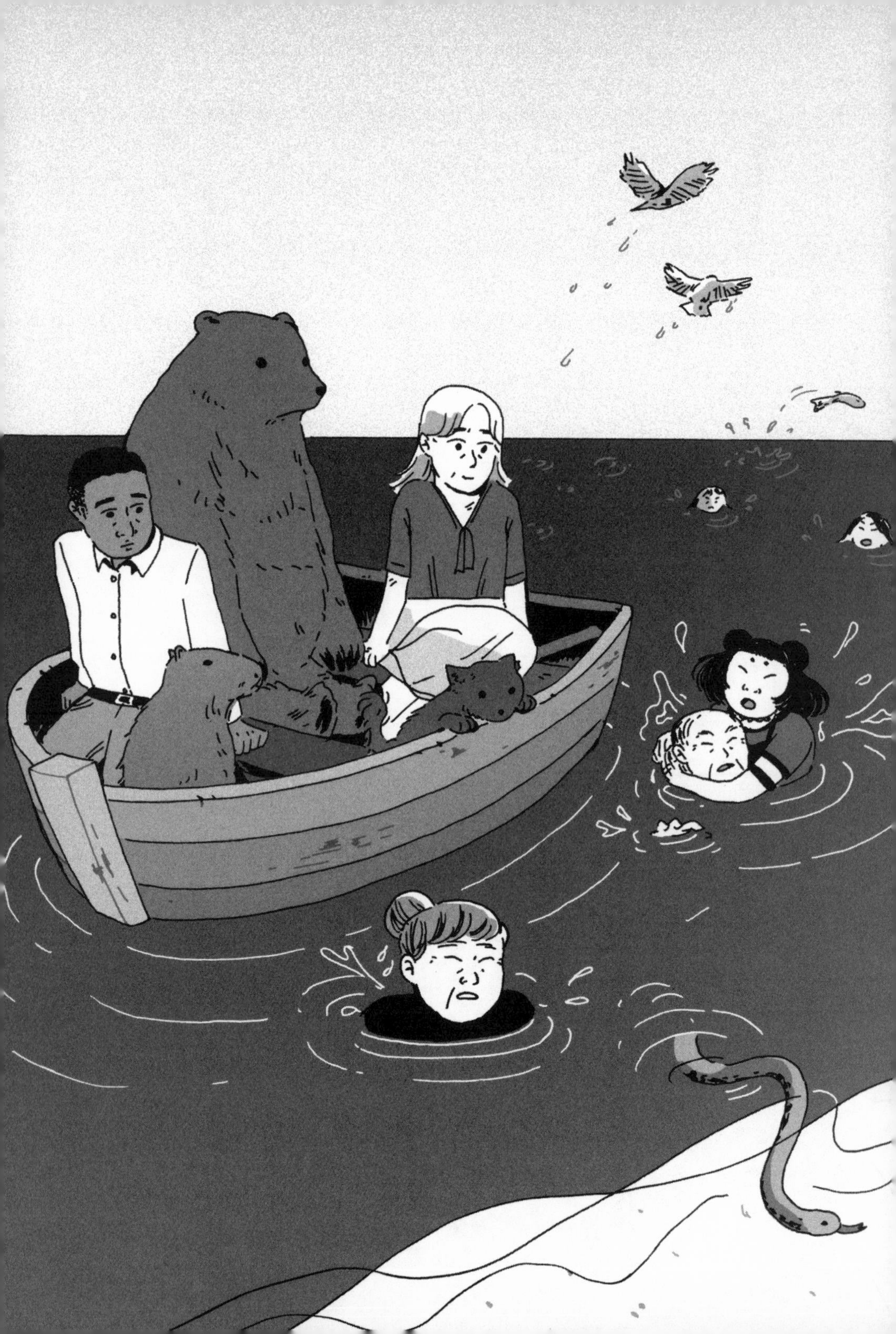

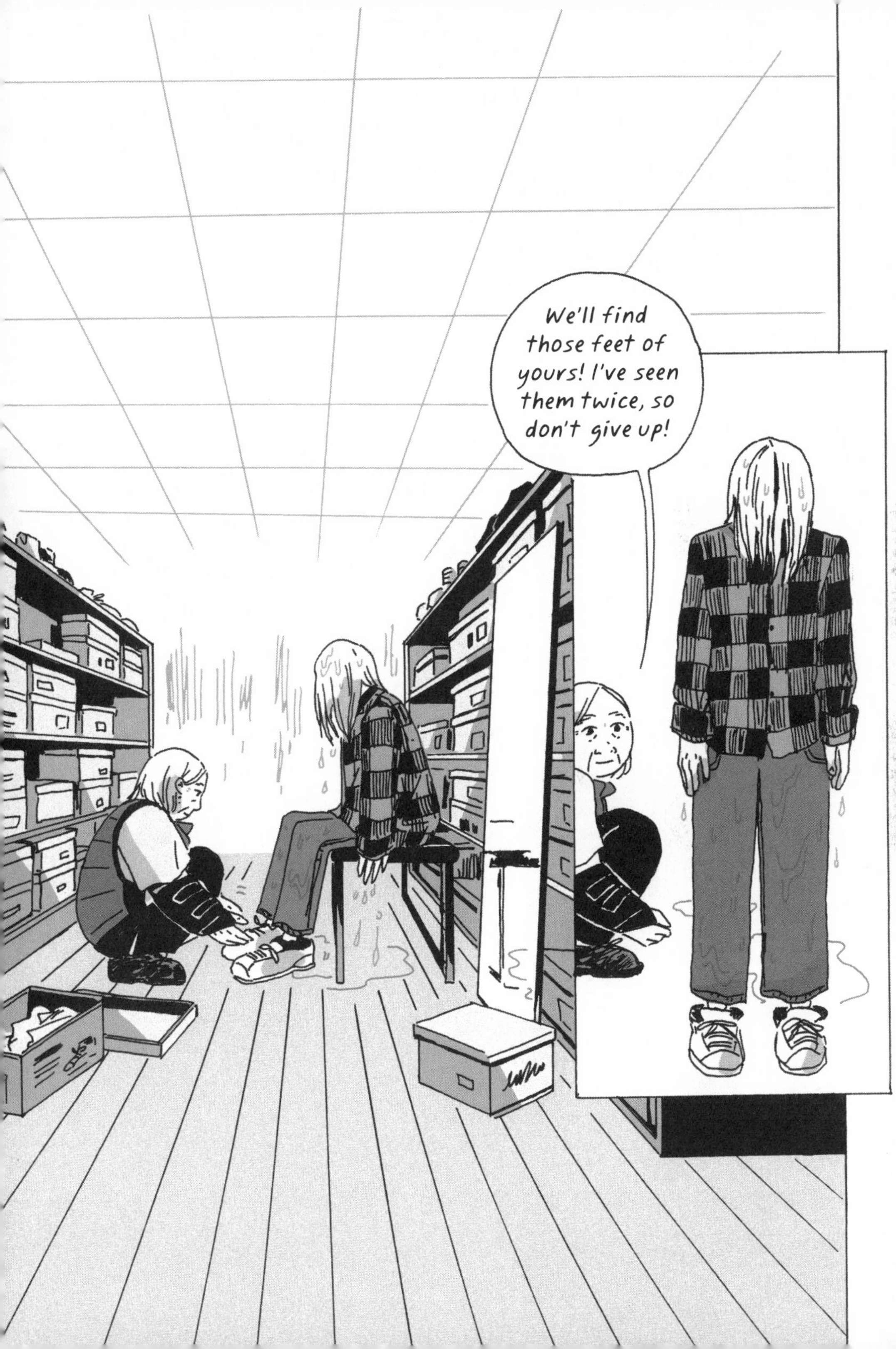
We'll find those feet of yours! I've seen them twice, so don't give up!

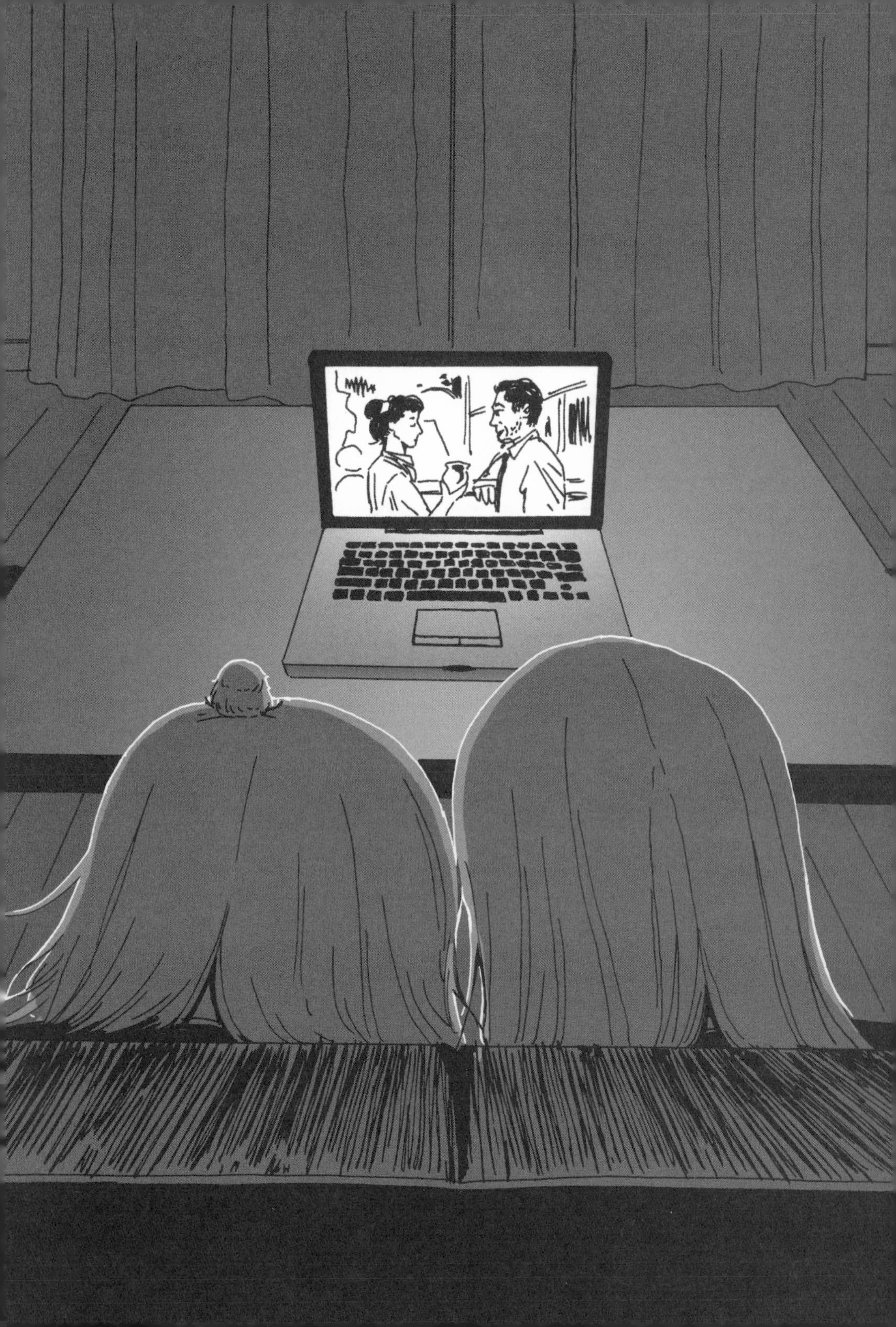

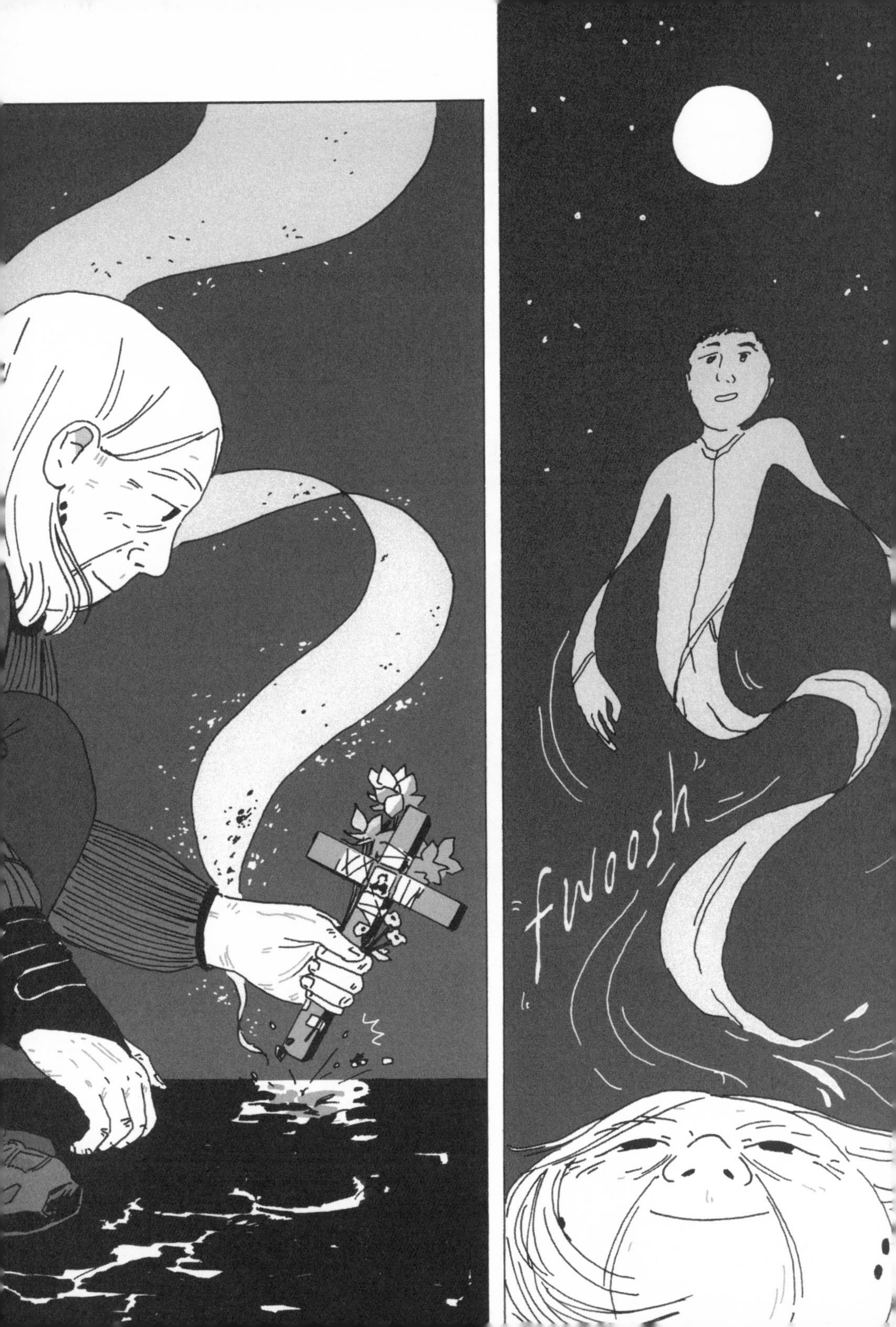
fwoosh

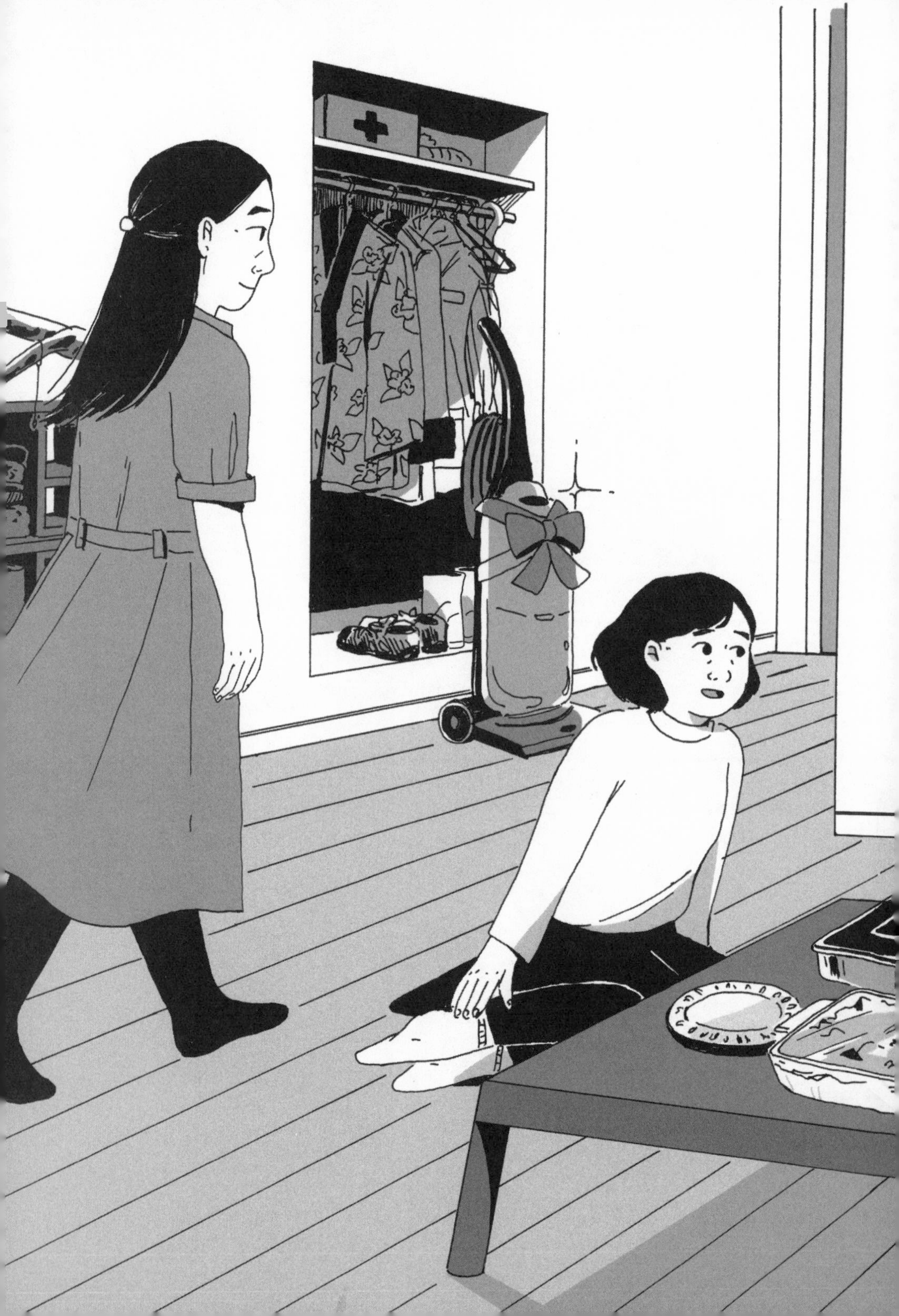

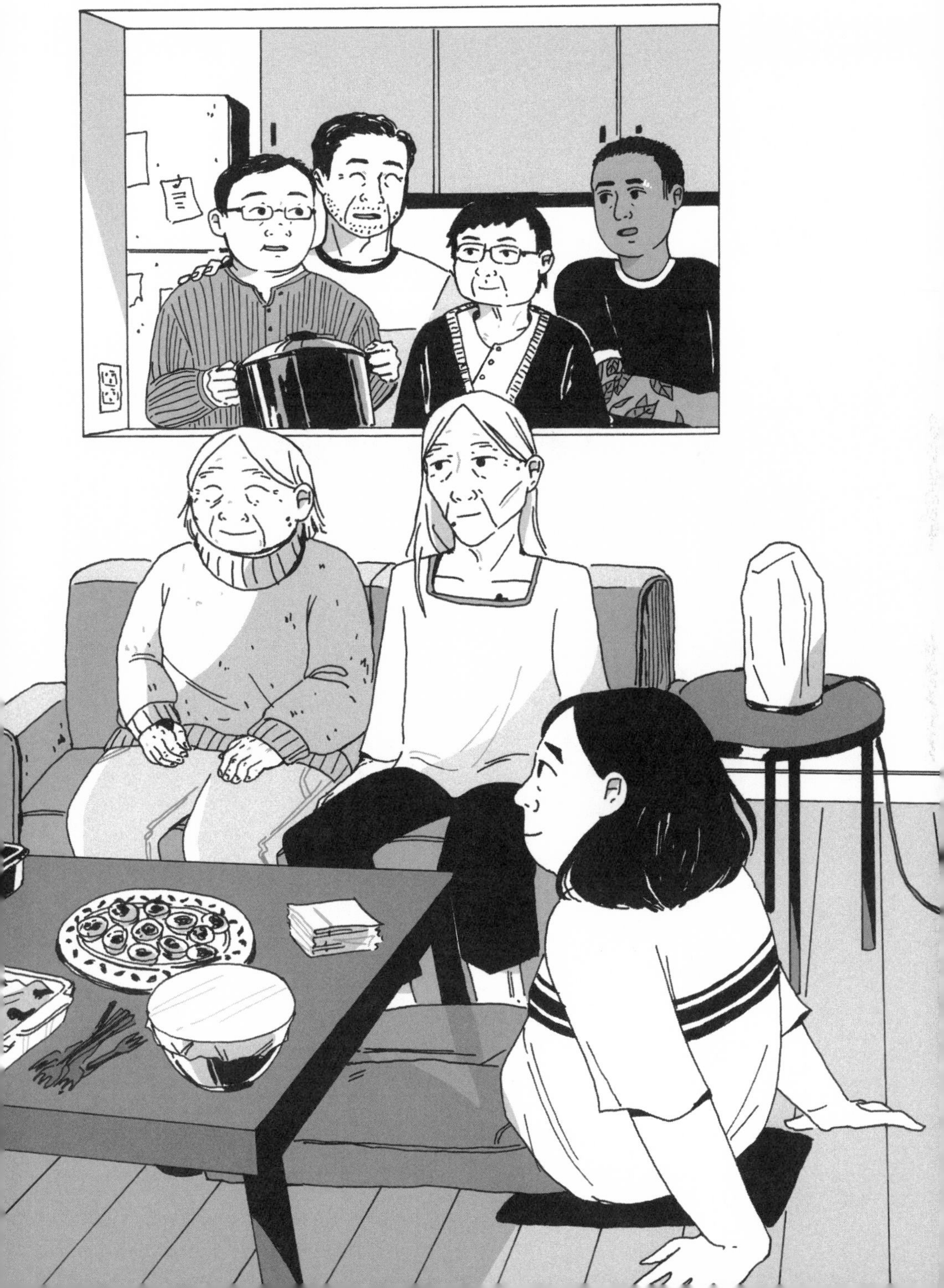

Sketches

CHAPTER ONE

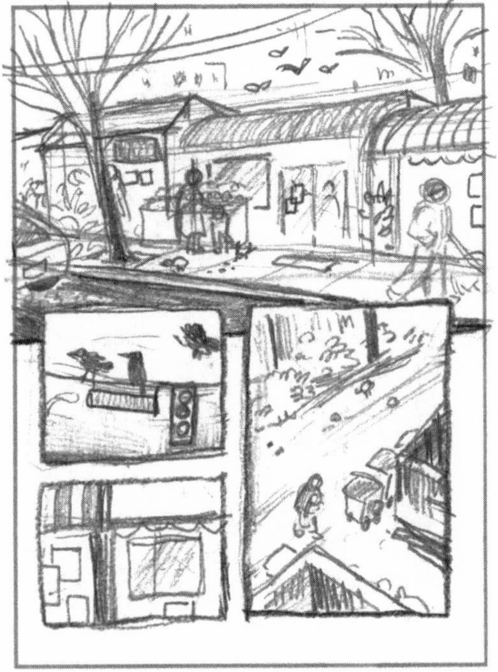

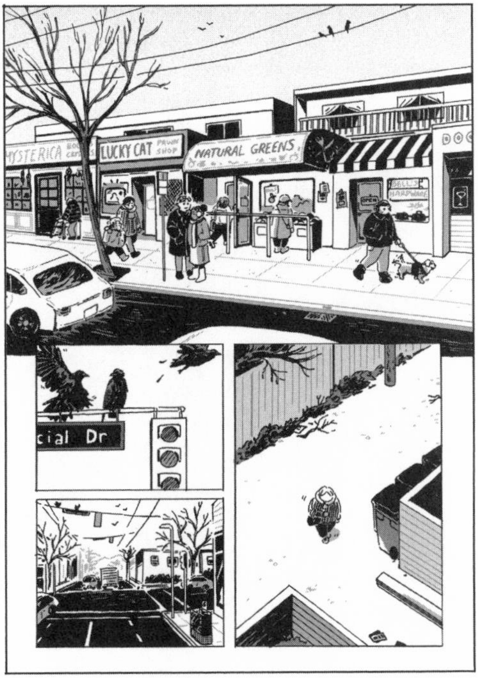
HYSTERICA
LUCKY CAT
PAWN SHOP
NATURAL GREENS
cial Dr

The end result used more zoomed-out compositions of panels 1 and 3 to establish the space in the setting, since this is our first view of Kumiko's neighborhood.

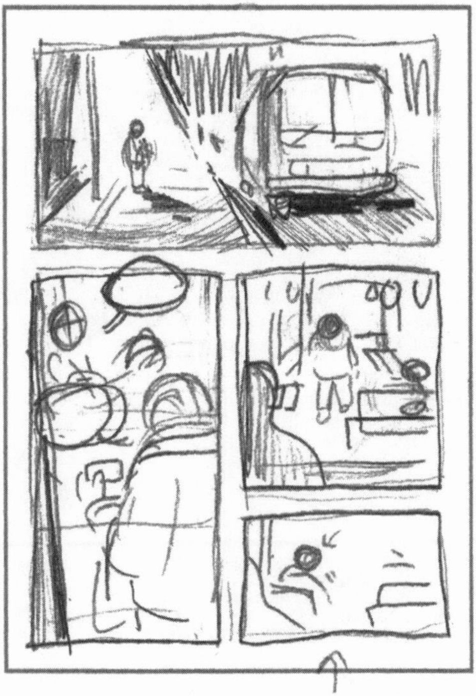

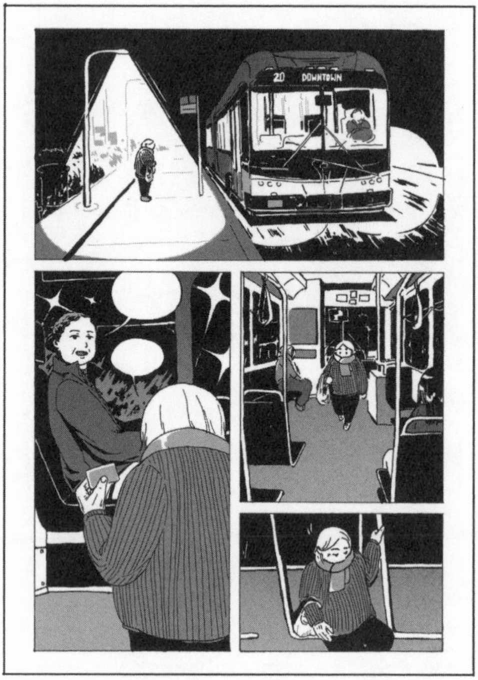
20 DOWNTOWN

I loved drawing these scenes where you could see the bright lights against the black sky.

Sketches for Kumiko's pose
on the cover.

I drew a few different variations, including some more zoomed-in poses cropped from the torso up. In the end, we went with a full-body view of Kumiko standing strong with her vacuum cleaner. The key trait to communicate was her groundedness and sense of determination.

Author's Note

My first novel, *Chorus of Mushrooms*, was published in 1994 when I was in my mid-twenties. One of the two main characters is eighty-five-year-old Naoe Kiyokawa—based on my grandmother who raised me and my sisters. Since that time there have been many characters in my books and stories who are older Asian women. The influence of my Oba-chan on my own life has been immeasurable. I think that this is likely a shared experience for many people—an elder has been a support and strength for you so that you could thrive...

Representations of older women as interesting, heroic, powerful, and complex are not common in popular culture. Mainstream media often figure older women in cliched roles, and ageism often frames them as the punchline of a joke. I've seen many films about grumpy old white men, but far fewer of old women. And no mainstream North American films that center on BIPOC queer elders. I bring up film because this is the most visual form of representation that hits the eyes and minds of broad cultural demographics. For the sighted, in many ways, seeing is believing.

Graphic novels are visual articulations of story that demonstrate material possibilities that novels cannot. They can reach different kinds of audiences, and they perform representation, literally. What a marvel to write something, and then to be able to see it. Artist Ann Xu's brilliance, creativity, and labor has brought this story to life in a way that I could never have imagined.

I'm fifty-three years old now, and I will continue to write stories about older women. Spirits willing, there will come a time when I'll reach the age of the characters I've been writing since my youth... Maybe one of the reasons I write about older women is because it helps me imagine who I will become. It is my dream to become more like my grandmother. As I continue to age I feel closer to her and this fills me with strength and direction.

The manuscript for this book was written nearly ten years ago. So I find myself writing this author's note long after Kumiko's story was completed; I am writing it in the midst of a global pandemic. Social isolation is keeping people physically apart. We are no longer in the libraries, gathering in bookstores, going to theaters and concerts. Schools, universities, community centers, and places of worship are closed. People have been laid off, shops shuttered—business is not as usual. Many of us who have the privilege of a home are weathering out the storm in a variety of ways. But anxiety and fear shadow our thoughts. It is an uneasy time. In times uncertain, there are stories that I return to that comfort me. There are some books that offer me a safe and familiar harbor. A place where my mind and spirit can abide, a kind of sanctuary. I hope that *Shadow Life* will transport you—offer laughter, hope, excitement, and solace. May Kumiko's story offer you some respite. Courage.

The future feels acutely uncertain in this moment. More of us feel closer to death than we have ever felt, but it is possible to live vibrantly, even near Death's shadow. Friendship, compassion, generosity, and caring cast the brightest light.

—Hiromi Goto

Acknowledgments

Hiromi Goto

I'd like to acknowledge how osewani nattemasu I am to the Coast Salish Peoples and their unceded lands—this is where I work, dream, write, live. I am deeply grateful for this privilege.

Thank you so very much, Ann Xu, for your beautiful and evocative art! It was a dream to work with you. Your professionalism and generosity were out of this world. Heartfelt thank-yous to my dear, gentle first reader, Dana Putnam. Your support and feedback are invaluable. How blessed I have been with family—my sisters, Naomi, Nozomi, and Ayumi, my mother, Kyoko, and my children and stepchild, Koji, Sae, and Sylvia. Thank you for all that you share with me. Oba-chan and my father, who have already flown to the farther shore...I feel your love, always. My dear friends who have seen me through so much—thank you Larissa Lai, Rita Wong, Chris Goto-Jones, Christine Stewart, Roy Miki, Kyo Maclear, Dorothy Christian, Eva T, Ivana Vukov, Anne Stone, Emily Pohl-Weary, Tamai Kobayashi, Edward Parker, Bridget MacKenzie, for being an inspiration, sharing a shoulder, and offering emergency feedback, love. Gratitude to Yuko Toda and Hidemi Kishino for your support. Thank you to Minah Lee for Korean translation, and to Dr. W. Lai for input on medical details. No one should use the health-related scenes found in this story to self-diagnose their conditions; this is a work of fiction. Thank you so much to everyone at The CookeMcDermid Agency; especially my stellar agent, Sally Harding, and Rachel Letofsky. A special thank-you to our editor, Mariah Huehner, who was so fabulous, First Second Books, Calista Brill, Kirk Benshoff, and Kiara Valdez for taking a chance on this first-time graphic novel writer. Thank you to the BC Arts Council, and the University of Athabasca WIR program for funding support during the writing of this project. Every single one of you made this work possible.

Ann Xu

Thank you to Hiromi Goto for writing this resonant story, and Mariah Huehner for your editing work. I'm endlessly grateful for the support you two gave me during this process. Thank you to my agent Susan Graham, Andrew Arnold who first reached out to me, and everyone at :01 who was indispensable in bringing this book to life. Thank you to Sunmi for your continuous encouragement, Angela Qiu for always being there to listen, and my friends both in person and online who gave me joy and support while I worked.

Supported by the Province of British Columbia

:01

First Second

Published by First Second
First Second is an imprint of Roaring Brook Press, a division
of Holtzbrinck Publishing Holdings Limited Partnership
120 Broadway, New York, NY 10271
firstsecondbooks.com

Library of Congress Control Number: 2019941111

Our books may be purchased in bulk for promotional, educational, or business use.
Please contact your local bookseller or the Macmillan Corporate and
Premium Sales Department at (800) 221-7945 ext. 5442 or by email at
MacmillanSpecialMarkets@macmillan.com.

FIRST

EDITION

First edition, 2021
Edited by Calista Brill, Mariah Huehner, and Kiara Valdez
Cover design by Kirk Benshoff
Interior book design by Sunny Lee
Printed in the United States of America

Sketched with a 2B and 4B pencil, inked with a 1.5mm Pilot Parallel Pen
and Pelikan Fount India ink. Toned and edited in Photoshop.

ISBN 978-1-62672-356-6
3 5 7 9 10 8 6 4

Don't miss your next favorite book from First Second!
For the latest updates go to firstsecondnewsletter.com
and sign up for our enewsletter.